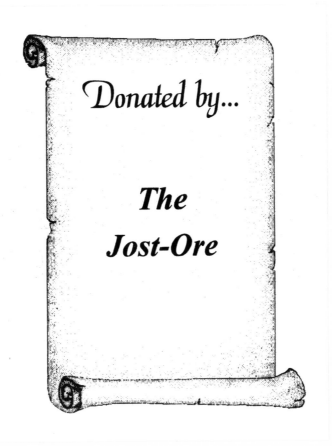

Donated by...

The

Jost-Ore

THE ——— GONNE–YEATS

LETTERS 1893–1938

*To the gone and
the not gone*

Always your friend

MaudGonne

f.

WBYeats

THE
GONNE–YEATS
LETTERS 1893–1938

Edited by
ANNA MacBRIDE WHITE
and
A. NORMAN JEFFARES

W•W Norton & Company
New York   London

Manufacturing by The Haddon Craftsmen, Inc

Library of Congress Cataloging-in-Publication Data

MacBride, Maud Gonne.
  [Correspondence—Selections]
  The Gonne-Yeats letters 1893–1938 / edited
by Anna MacBride White and A. Norman Jeffares.—1st American
ed.
     p. cm.
  Originally published : London : Hutchinson, 1992.
  Includes bibliographical references and index.
  1. MacBride, Maud Gonne—Correspondence.   2. Revolutionaries
—Ireland—Correspondence.   3. Politicians—Ireland—Corres-
pondence.   4. Feminists—Ireland—Correspondence.   5. Yeats,
W. B. (William Butler), 1865–1939—Correspondence.   6. Poets,
Irish—20th century—Correspondence.   7. Poets, Irish—19th
century—Correspondence. I. White, Anna MacBride. II. Jeffares,
A. Norman (Alexander Norman), 1920–   . III. Yeats, W. B.
(William Butler), 1865–1939. Correspondence. Selections. 1993. IV.
Title.
DA958.M25A4   1993
821'.8—dc20

[B]   92–1683
ISBN 0-393-03445-3

W. W. Norton & Company, Inc.
500 Fifth Avenue, New York, N. Y. 10110
W. W. Norton & Company Ltd.
10 Coptic Street, London WC1A 1PU

1 2 3 4 5 6 7 8 9 0

Contents

Acknowledgements

We wish to thank the following who have been most helpful in providing information and suggestions about the identification of people, places and various obscure references, and who have assisted in so many other different ways.

Beatrice Behan, Patricia Boylan, Katherine Bridgwater, Judith Chavasse, Jack Clarke, Brigid Clesham, Jacqueline and Conor Coghlan, Oisin Coghlan, Richard Cohen, Tim Pat Coogan, Arthur Dailey, Dr Peter Davidson, Frank Delaney, Terence Dixon, Col. Edward Doyle, Jarleth Duffey, Lady Judith Dunn, Sheila Durcan, David Forrister, Jean Francis Gabriac, Warwick Gould, Noel Guilfoyle, Seamus Haughey, the late Professor Barbara Hayley, Jacobus van Hespin, Professor R. F. V. Heuston, Tony Higgins, Noreen and Karl Johnston, Dr Miceal Ledwith, Liam McGonagle, Alasdair Macrae, Professor Augustine Martin, Didier Maus, Mark Mortimer, Pat Murphy, Loretta Murray, Louie O'Brien, Col. Eoghan O'Neill, Máire O'Sullivan, Elizabeth Paterson, Louis Raimbault, Jean François Robinet, Dick and Pam Roche, David Roche Kelly, Dr Jane Stevenson, Dr Bruce Stewart, Father Michael Sweetman, Deirdre Toomey, Mary MacBride Walsh, Professor Robert Welch, Anthony Whittome, Dr Kai Kim Yung.

The librarians and staff of the National Library of Ireland, of the National Library of Scotland, of St Andrew's University, of Seanad Eireann, of the University of Stirling, of the State Paper Office, Dublin, of Trinity College, Dublin, also Evêché de Laval Archives, Les Amis de Samois-sur-Seine, New York Public Library, Public Record Office, London, Representative Church Body, Dublin, Somerset House, London, South Mayo Family Research Society, Westport Historical Society.

Our particular thanks go to Linden Stafford for her patient and careful editing and to Margaret Fraser for her care in the designing of the book.

We would also like to thank our very patient partners, Jeanne and Declan, and Tiernan MacBride for all his practical assistance over the years as well as Maud Gonne's great-grandchildren, Iseult, Fiona, Clare, Christina, Conleth and Dara, who assisted in the putting together of this book in many different ways.

A. Norman Jeffares
Anna MacBride White
Fife Ness and Dublin, 1991

Illustrations

Editors' note

It is a harsh exercise to put into cold print and to bare all the faults of such subjective things as letters written 'in great haste' in the middle of a busy active life, and it requires the kindness and tolerance of the reader. Nuances in the handwriting, or insertion of omitted words and afterthoughts, or positioning of postscripts, are all lost in printing; while irregularities in spelling, punctuation, abbreviations and repetitive phrases are exaggerated.

Maud Gonne used her journalistic abilities to further her cause, correcting and rewriting her articles thoroughly, but never laid claim to be a writer. The immediacy and urgency of her letters did not allow for constructional considerations. She dashed them off frequently in telegraphic style on whatever paper was to hand, casually using line endings as intuitive pauses, with liberal use of dashes followed sometimes by capitals, sometimes not, and sometimes capitals with no punctuation or vice versa. They flow easily, providing the writing can be read, but interpreting squiggles is a combination of personal judgement and intuition, both open to error. On first meeting a person she was likely to spell their name incorrectly and in later letters rectify the error. In excitement or annoyance she would make hasty judgements and criticisms that were reconsidered later.

Mainly she wrote on her own headed notepaper with the family crest, used by her father on his notepaper, used by the family on their silver, and brought to America by Gonnes from Dublin in the late eighteenth century, the motto being *Ferendo et Sperando*, meaning 'Enduring and Hoping', which later she had translated into Irish. It was written around an open hand dexter erect, also brought to America by Gonnes and used by the Guns of Kerry, from whom the families claimed descent. When this paper was not available she used other kinds, frequently Irish-made with watermarks, such as Original Irish Vellum-Brown and Nolan, or with the round-tower motif of

Ancient Irish Vellum made in Saggart, County Dublin, or anything else which came to hand, including envelopes.

Afterthoughts and postcripts were fitted in wherever there was space, or across the main body of the letter in the fashion of her father. Finding personal matters difficult, she frequently squashed them in at the end, as if a supreme effort was needed actually to acknowledge their existence on paper.

Yeats was a professional and disciplined writer whose letters show his ease with and command of words, if not with spelling and punctuation. Being able to face and consider his reactions and emotions allowed him a greater ease of expression. The few of his letters to Maud Gonne that have survived were scattered through old bundles of correspondence. The only two kept particularly safe were together in an envelope, one marked 'last letter from W. B. Y.' which was written on 16 June 1938 from Steyning, Sussex, and the other a letter concerning the death of William Sharp which he had asked her to keep safely and which she must have put in a separate place, and so it survived. The letters he received from her before her marriage, of 10 and 24 February 1903, had been very crumpled as if carried around in his pocket and reread many times, then smoothed out to be put away with the others.

In preparing the letters we have regularised the position of address and date at the top right of the letter. The postmark and the address to which a letter was sent are given where known at the foot of each letter. The layout of the endings has also been standardised.

Most letters had no address or date, so estimated place, month and year are given in square brackets. Square brackets are also used to supply letters or words omitted where omission could be confusing, or for a word in error; and uncertain readings are preceded by a question mark in square brackets. Significant cancelled passages appear in angled brackets. Where the script presents particular difficulty we have inserted '[indecipherable]'.

Passages or words underlined once are in italics, twice in small capitals, and three times in large capitals.

Maud Gonne used old-fashioned abbreviations, and she frequently confused English and French spellings, with strange results. Most common abbreviations have been regularised here, as has the use of apostrophes, quotation marks and parentheses. Spellings of some common words have also been regularised, but obvious misspellings of names or alternative spellings have been retained. Maud Gonne was indiscriminate in relating full stops to new sentences, using line endings and gaps between words to act in their place, so we have used our judgement to clarify the meaning where necessary. Even capitals themselves are at times questionable, as are word endings. Both their ampersands are tiny and barely noticeable.

Postscripts and sentences or words written across the letter or all round the edges have been regularised.

In the case of Maud Gonne's letters the titles of books, poems and articles have been given as she wrote them. In Yeats's letters they have been regularised. If we know to what poem reference is made it is given in the notes.

As most of the letters were without date or address, placing and dating had to be determined by either internal or external evidence. Internal evidence was provided by the use of the term of address, such as 'Dear Mr Yeats' or 'My dear Willie', addresses when present, context and sequence or a particular run of notepaper. The most useful external evidence was Allan Wade's *The Letters of W. B. Yeats* combined with contemporary newspapers, in particular *Shan Van Vocht* and the *United Irishman*, which recorded Maud's activities faithfully and of which she had bound copies.

The notes attempt to identify individuals and subjects mentioned in the text, although in some cases identification of minor characters has proved impossible; they also offer some guidance to the background of political events and movements. Each note appears where the subject is first mentioned in a letter, even if previously mentioned in the editors' text, as in the case of Colonel Thomas Gonne and Lucien Millevoye, who had such an important bearing on Maud's life. Abbreviated source references are included in the notes with a key listed separately, as is a general bibliography. To avoid burdening the reader we have kept our references to contemporary people not mentioned in the letters to a basic minimum.

Chronology

1889 MG and WBY meet 30 January. Plan of Campaign active, many evictions.

1890 MG's son by Millevoye born. WBY initiated into Golden Dawn. Parnell cited in O'Shea divorce case.

1891 WBY proposes to MG. Her son dies 31 August. Boulanger commits suicide September. Parnell dies October. Irish Literary Society formed in London.

1892 Amnesty Associations formed. MG lectures in France. National Literary Society libraries scheme commenced.

1893 Gladstone's 2nd Home Rule Bill rejected by Lords. MG's account of Treason Felony prisoners in Portland Prison.

1894 Dreyfus arrested. WBY in Paris, sees MG February. Iseult Gonne, MG's daughter by Millevoye, born 6 August.

1895 WBY moves to Fountain Court, considers affair with Olivia Shakespear.

1896 *Shan Van Vocht* starts publication. James Connolly comes to Ireland. WBY moves to Woburn Buildings and starts affair with Olivia Shakespear February; meets Martyn, Lady Gregory and Moore; meets Synge in Paris December and helps MG to form Paris Young Ireland Society.

1897 MG starts *L'Irlande Libre*. Jubilee demonstrations. WBY's first long stay at Coole. '98 preparations commence. MG goes to USA.

1898 '98 celebrations under way. Famine in the west. United Ireland League founded. Local Government Act. Mystical marriage December. *Visions Notebook* commenced.

1899 WBY visits Paris, proposes to MG. First production of Irish Literary Theatre, *The Countess Cathleen*. MG in Mayo, evictions. *Shan Van Vocht* ceases and *United Irishman* commences publication March. Boer War October. Formation of Irish Brigade, Irish Transvaal Committee, anti-enlistment campaign. Visit of Chamberlain to Dublin.

1900 MG's 2nd tour in USA. Dr Leyds episode. Irish Parliamentary Party unites. 2nd season of Irish Literary Theatre February. Queen Victoria's visit. Suppression of *United Irishman*. MG's libel action.

Frank Hugh O'Donnell's pamphlets. WBY's trouble with Golden Dawn and Mathers April to May. Patriotic Children's Treat. Nationalist delegation to Paris in July. Founding of Inghínidhe na hÉireann and Cumann na nGaedheal October. John MacBride in Paris November.

1901   MG's 3rd tour in USA with MacBride; he proposes to her. Inghínidhe theatrical productions. 3rd Irish Literary Theatre season October. WBY sees Fays act and experiments with psaltery.

1902   MG's lectures in Paris. Her nurse dies. Inghínidhe na hÉireann and Fays perform *Cathleen ni Houlihan* and *Deirdre* April. Irish National Theatre Society formed. MG rents house in Coulson Ave, decides to marry John MacBride, visits de Freyne estate and Westport. Cumann na nGaedheal Samhain week. WBY meets John Quinn and later Joyce in London.

1903   MG in Dublin January. Received into Catholic Church and marries John MacBride February. Spain and Normandy. King Edward VII visits Dublin, Battle of Rotunda. MG and Hyde withdraw from National Theatre Society. WBY's tour of USA.

1904   MG's son Seán born. John MacBride visits USA. MG and children in Dublin for Seán's baptism May. First productions in the Abbey Theatre. MG decides to seek separation December.

1905   WBY hears of break-up of MG's marriage. Legal proceedings commence. Irish National Theatre becomes limited company. Cumann na nGaedheal Samhain convention does not re-elect MG vice-president. John MacBride takes libel action against the *Irish Independent*. MG starts painting. Death of William Sharp.

1906   John MacBride's libel action fixes his domicile in Ireland. Divorce verdict. MG and family go to Bourboule August, MG in Dublin October. WBY's *Poems 1899–1905*.

1907   *Playboy* riots. Death of John O'Leary. WBY in Italy. MG spends summer in Colleville and begins work on illustrations for Ella Young's books. Dungannon clubs, Cumann na nGaedheal and National Council are now Sinn Féin. WBY's father leaves for New York December.

1908   Fays resign from Abbey. MG's appeal refuses divorce. WBY begins affair with Mabel Dickinson, visits MG in Paris, mystical marriage June, meets Ezra Pound. WBY's *Collected Works* published. Mrs Campbell in *Deirdre*. WBY goes to Paris to work on *The Player Queen* December.

1909   Lady Gregory ill. Synge dies. Madame Avril ill. MG goes to Dublin. MG and family at Bernex; Colleville for the summer; episode of moving picture. WBY quarrels with John Quinn, considers buying Abbey from Miss Horniman.

1910   Paris floods. Dublin school feeding. Miss Horniman withdraws from Abbey. WBY visits Colleville May. MG and family visit Mayo in summer; Colleville and school feeding in the autumn. WBY granted Civil List pension. *Celtic Wonder Tales* published with MG's illustrations. Accession of George V.

1911   School meals campaign. United Arts Club. WBY visits Paris while

MG is in Italy April. MG and family at Colleville for summer. WBY accompanies Abbey Players to USA.

1912   MG moves from 13 Rue de Passy to 17 Rue de l'Annonciation. 3rd Home Rule Bill (Asquith). WBY meets Tagore, then stays in Colleville. MG goes to Brussels and Dublin on school meals campaign. MG and family go to Italy for Christmas.

1913   Seán has measles. MG very ill with congestion of the lungs. Home Rule Bill does not pass Lords. Ulster Volunteers organised. MG goes to Dax and with family spends summer in Pyrenees. WBY rents Stone Cottage with Pound as his secretary. MG in Dublin. Strike and lockout. Formation of Citizen Army and Irish Volunteers.

1914   WBY in USA, is reconciled with Quinn, with MG investigates miracle at Mirebeau. MG and family in Pyrenees for summer. Ulster Volunteer Force gun-running. Convention on amendment to Home Rule Bill for exclusion of Ulster. Irish Volunteers gunrunning at Howth. Home Rule Bill passed as Government of Ireland Act (1914) but suspended because of outbreak of First World War. Beginning of Irish Volunteer split. MG and Iseult nursing the wounded in Pyrenees. WBY begins his memoirs.

1915   WBY in Stone Cottage January–February. Hugh Lane drowned in *Lusitania*. WBY gets a grant for Joyce, refuses a knighthood. MG nurses in Paris-Plage and Paris; she hears strange prophetic music. Military Council of IRB formed in December by future signatories of Proclamation of the Irish Republic who are subsequently executed.

1916   WBY at Stone Cottage. MG nursing in Paris. Family spend Easter at Colleville where they hear of the Rising. Executions. WBY visits MG at Colleville, he proposes, she refuses. MG begins trying to get back to Ireland. Ulster Unionists agree to immediate implementation of Home Rule provided Ulster is temporarily excluded. Sinn Féin opts for a republic. Internees released for Christmas.

1917   Count Plunkett wins first Sinn Féin by-election February. WBY buys Ballylee; visits Colleville in summer, proposes to Iseult, is refused; accompanies MG and family to London, where they are not allowed to proceed to Dublin. WBY marries Georgie Hyde Lees. MG escapes to Ireland in disguise.

1918   MG buys house at 73 St Stephen's Green. Millevoye dies. Conscription threatened in Ireland. German Plot arrests May, MG in Holloway Prison, released end October. Sinn Féin wins general election. George (as Georgie now known) Yeats seriously ill in MG's house. First World War ends. MG escapes to Ireland in disguise.

1919   MG working for Sinn Féin government. Kathleen dies in Switzerland. WBY's daughter Anne born February. Iseult meets Harry Francis Stuart. Guerrilla warfare in Ireland. Seán joins IRA. Sinn Féin Dáil declared illegal. WBY gives up Woburn Buildings. First number of *Irish Bulletin* November.

1920   First Black and Tans arrive. WBY in USA. Iseult marries Stuart.

Sectarian riots in Belfast. WBY helps to resolve difficulties of Iseult's marriage. MG spends summer in her house in Glenmalure. Seán and Constance de Markiewicz arrested. MG begins relief work as war escalates.

1921 Desmond Fitzgerald arrested. Childers takes over the *Bulletin*. White Cross formed February. WBY speaks to the Oxford Union. Iseult's baby born 9 March, dies 24 July. Truce July. WBY's son born August. Treaty signed December.

1922 Provisional Government takes over January. Anti-treaty forces seize Four Courts April. General election. MG in Paris (16 June) for Provisional Government when it attacks Four Courts. Civil War. Collins shot and Griffith dies suddenly. Cosgrave's Free State Government. November–May 1923 77 prisoners shot as reprisals. MG forms Women's Prisoners' Defence League. MG and Mrs Despard move to Roebuck House. WBY's father dies and WBY becomes a senator.

1923 Civil War ends. Irish Free State enters League of Nations. MG and Mrs Despard form industries, continue protests against government's repressive measures. Seán on the run and active in IRA. WBY wins Nobel Prize.

1926 Seán marries while on the run. De Valera forms political party.

1927 Seán takes over Roebuck Jam. Kevin O'Higgins shot, Seán arrested for his murder, finally released.

1929 WBY dangerously ill in Rapallo.

1932 De Valera wins general election. WBY spends winter and spring at Coole. Lady Gregory dies.

1935 WBY has congestion of the lungs, goes to Majorca for winter.

1936 WBY seriously ill. IRA declared illegal.

1937 De Valera's new constitution approved.

1938 WBY's last public appearance at Abbey. MG visits him at Riversdale late summer. WBY leaves for South of France late November.

1939 WBY dies 28 January and is buried at Roquebrune in France. Second World War declared.

1946 Clann na Poblachta founded.

1948 De Valera loses general election, new inter-party government formed. Republic of Ireland leaves the Commonwealth. WBY's body reinterred in Drumcliffe churchyard, Sligo.

1953 MG dies.

Prologue

ANNA MACBRIDE WHITE

Character isolated by a deed
To engross the present and dominate the memory.

When I passed the door of my grandmother's room it had become such an automatic movement to turn the handle and go in that, after she died, the instinctive movement ended in a lost, aimless gesture. Visiting her in her room had always been part of my life, and those last months more so than ever. For a long time the empty room was a sad reminder of her absence.

She had loved the big dilapidated old house, with its large trees and a walled garden, only a short distance from Floraville, where she had lived, and the Donnybrook road, where she had walked as a child before her mother died. Her room was her sanctuary in a busy household; there she read, wrote, sewed and played patience amidst the jumble of her books, papers, knitting wools, embroidery silks, birds and plants. It was a place one could call into just to say hello, show off one's new purchases, borrow a book, be given a little job watering the plants, giving the birds some seed, finding her specs or emptying the always overflowing ashtray.

I was the second grandchild by six weeks, but the first one living in the same house, so from the start I was taken about – so much so that my poor mother was not quite sure whether she had a child or not. We went on trips into town shopping, with the occasional thrill of a taxi home; we went to the Horse Show, Spring Show and Christmas Aonachs in the Mansion House, where she sat behind her black-draped stall selling her shell flowers displayed like jewels on a gleaming mirror, while I roved round gathering leaflets and samples, returning to base occasionally for reassurance. I 'helped' her at home making the shell flowers, or in the garden 'weeding', or in the kitchen on those ceremonial occasions when Christmas puddings and cakes were being prepared. I was taken to the 'flicks' and to my first opera, Wagner's *Das Rheingold*, the only part of which I remember being the magical waving green underwater scene of the Rhine Maidens.

In those days I remember having a conversation with her about what I should call her instead of Granny, which she did not like. No easy solution was found, so like everyone else, except those who had known her in the early days, I naturally came to call her Madame – a name, not a formality, for there was little formality about her. To outsiders it may have seemed strange, as the sight of the tall old lady dressed in long black clothes and veil with the little girl must have seemed strange. I only became aware of this occasionally when she was stopped in the street by some poor person and I would catch other people staring. She always used to say, quoting her Great-Aunt Mary, that once one had found a perfume to suit one then one made it one's own and used it. I think that was her attitude towards her clothes. Having found a simple formula derived from another age and country, she adopted and used it all the time – which made life very simple, the same garments and the same veil lasting for years.

Gradually, as I grew busier with school and she less active, treats became fewer. She spent more time in bed reading and writing. Prisoners' defence, social credit, monetary reform, corporal punishment, repatriation of sterling assets and prison reform were all subjects dear to her heart, and we heard of them endlessly. But I was more likely to share an interest in the latest thrillers, with which my mother kept the household supplied in an endless flow from a selection of libraries. I was also free to browse through her bookcase, fascinated by the mythological stories, O'Curry's *Manners and Customs of the Ancient Irish* or the sad romantic nationalism of Pearse's writings.

Her other three grandchildren have their own special memories. All her geese were swans, all with their particular qualities and endearments. Anger I do not remember, occasional irritation, yes, when one made 'life unbearable'. One of my father's indelible memories was that once for some misbehaviour when he was a child she actually refused to take him to the circus even though the tickets had been bought. I do not think her grandchildren were ever visited with such dire punishment.

She never bored us with endless stories of the past, though hearing her talk to her visitors on her pet hobby-horses could become monotonous, but she did not expect us to partake, or even to follow in her footsteps. There were two stories she did love to tell. Recounting her first adventure travelling to Russia alone with secret papers, she laughed like a girl as she described how she had charmed the very man she was trying to outwit into helping her. Also, when worrying about her granddaughters' dearth of 'young men', she would tell of her first proposal of marriage in the Colosseum by moonlight at sixteen – aeons from the postwar stringency of the Ireland of bikes, 'hops' and hopeless shyness.

She would recall people of the past. Her father, Tommy, was

always the first. Willie Yeats was the long-time friend remembered with affection, tolerance and amusement, and Arthur Griffith was another who merited loyalty; both were her longest and most enduring friends. One name I used to puzzle over, someone who had a special place in her memory, and that was Willie Rooney. He is never mentioned in the letters to Yeats, perhaps because, as with Griffith, Yeats may not have had much to do with him. But I have discovered that Willie Rooney's charisma made an indelible impression on those who knew him, and his early death was considered a great tragedy for Ireland. To the end she had many good friends who came regularly to see her, and Sunday teas were open house for all who cared to call, when my mother made huge batches of scones.

She said of her marriage and honeymoon that she and MacBride were planning an adventure from which they did not expect to return; because of this, at the time of her separation she could have sought an annulment, but that would have meant that her son would have been illegitimate. I do not remember her talking of Millevoye or MacBride, but Iseult and she would have long talks of the past. Iseult was one of the very few she could share it with, and one who could be objective, clearsighted and understanding.

My mother, who used to drive her to Riversdale in Rathfarnham to see Willie, said that latterly she was disappointed in him and found his poetry difficult and his talk bawdy – which, in her, was understandable, since she thought that all life, and art which expresses life, should strive for beauty and harmony, and that sex should only be used for procreation. 'Conduct and work grow coarse and coarse the soul.'

By then she had gone far beyond personal ambition of any kind, though her mind was still preoccupied with the injustices of the day. She had always believed that the young should be allowed to take over from the old and forge ahead and was interested in that process, keeping abreast of everything that happened, feeling that Ireland was taking shape; but in reality she wished to be gone and said she hated the lingering process. Yet there was never any bitterness or apparent depression, only unobservable patience whereby the remoteness of our lives from her past did not prevent her being present with us, always interested and remembering to thank us for any little thing we did. This strength came from her inner spirituality, outwardly visible when she knelt to pray.

Mrs Yeats kindly returned the package of my grandmother's letters around the time that Joseph Hone was working on his biography of Yeats, published in 1942. Writing to thank Mrs Yeats, she said:

I have not the courage to open it today. You must know, I think, what a strain it is looking over old papers which bring back so many things but I will try and do so before Mr Hone comes to see me next Monday, he said you suggested his coming to see me to tell him about the early days of Willie, when I met him as a boy. He asked me if I had any letters of his. Alas in all the many raids in my house, most have been lost and destroyed and very many I did not keep, because I always feared keeping papers connected with material which might be got hold of by the enemy . . . I hope we may have a chance of meeting sometime but I am so old, I always fear I bore my friends. When you are a little freer from the worry of house moving perhaps you will spare me one afternoon and we can have tea together.

Your affectionate,

Maud Gonne MacBride.

The letters were undated, jumbled in large manila envelopes in approximate periods, and roughly sorted with her name and the period written on the flap in Yeats's writing, as, for instance, 'Gonne (Maude) 1913–1914–1917'. I have no idea whether she ever did read them. I think Yeats may have from time to time, as some of them he had kept originally in a loose-leaf folder, for they have punch-holes.

I found it hard to connect the young girl of her biography and the young woman of the 1890s with the grandmother I knew, but I realised the letters forged a connecting link between the two as I pieced the story together gradually, like parts of a gigantic puzzle, a detective story of clues and counter-clues, unfolding in ragged disjointed sections. It was fascinating, for the more I pored over the clues, struggled to fit the pieces, the closer I came to understanding and knowing the person who had grown to be the grandmother I loved. The letters put into perspective the person she actually was, revealing the tensions her personality, life and sex engendered, and showed how she dealt with them. They were like snapshots, immediate with instant reactions when judgement is suspended or again carefully evaluated, or episodic like dream sequences.

Maud Gonne became politically active over a hundred years ago. It was the era that followed the period of great material growth and expansion of the nineteenth century, with trains steaming in and out of their great iron-girdered cathedrals, the Eiffel Tower and flying machines proving that man could tackle any problem. At that time too the arts were restless, breaking boundaries, and inspired by symbolism and the occult. Over all hung the feeling of doom: the Armageddon was at hand.

Non-judgemental, she did not think the poor deserved to be poor, the imprisoned, regardless of their supposed crime, to be treated inhumanely or their dependants to starve; and she counted her enemies those she considered to be responsible for maintaining such conditions. Like all nationalists she felt that if the right to self-determination was granted these problems could be tackled and solved.

While her main theme was social justice achieved by gaining

national identity, Willie Yeats's was literature derived from and transcending national identity. Where their aims met was where their lives met, first on the mystical level, with the idea that the collective soul of the nation could be drawn out of the darkness of its unconscious and made a living thing. To this end they worked on Celtic mysticism, using the symbols of Ireland's ancient mythology rather than those of other ancient lores. Secondly, in practical terms poverty demands political activity, and building a national literature presupposes a nation. Both were practical people who worked grinding hours in committees, in correspondence, in travel, attending to the structures needed for bringing their ideals to reality.

Nowadays Maud Gonne is looked upon as an adjunct of Yeats and is marginalised in history. Because she was a woman she could not be considered part of the mainstream; she sued her husband for divorce, which a woman was never supposed to do – the responsibility of holding a marriage together or allowing its break-up usually being laid at the woman's door – and when it was all over she did not enter into recriminations or explanations. Consequently the rumours spread by the ranks of the IRB, which supported MacBride at the time of the separation, are what remain in many people's minds, as well as what is selectively gathered from Yeats's writing once his appreciation has been deducted; so she has been compartmentalised as a scarlet woman who betrayed the hero MacBride or a frigid goddess who led the famous poet by the nose unwillingly through politics, or some bizarre eccentric combination of the two, and not simply what she was, a remarkable person. Such people are usually out of step, since they incorporate greater diversities and tensions within them, more particularly if they have stepped out of the norm of the carefully delineated woman's role. As a woman she can be better appreciated today than in her own time because she was too advanced to be understood properly by her contemporaries, but she pursued her objectives not as a woman but as a person.

Maud Gonne was born in Aldershot on 21 December 1866. Her mother, Edith Frith Cook, was twenty-two when she was born and her father, Captain Thomas Gonne of the 17th Lancers, was thirty-one. Captain Gonne and his family came to Ireland in 1868 in the aftermath of the Fenian rising, when the army was being reinforced by British regiments for fear of Fenian infiltration. Since 1792 the strength of the army in Ireland had been doubled, because of the threat of the United Irishmen and the fear of a French invasion, which nearly became a reality in 1796 when Wolfe Tone and General Lazare Hoche with a large expeditionary force were prevented by storms from landing at Bantry Bay, and which actually occurred when a French force landed in Mayo in August 1798. Although defeated, the United Irishmen became a potent part of the national myth and Wolfe Tone became the father of Irish republicanism. It was these events that were used one hundred years later as a pivotal centre for unifying Irish national political life.

The authorities' fear of the Fenians was grounded on experience of the United Irishmen, a mainly middle-class dissenter radical republican movement that had first harnessed the restless endemic agrarian violence of the eighteenth century and turned it into a unified force. This violence – caused by a people denied their cultural independence and spiritual autonomy – was also harnessed and strictly disciplined by O'Connell in his popular movements for Catholic emancipation and repeal of the Union from the 1820s to the 1840s, to which the Young Ireland movement of the 1840s acted as a foil. Its paper, *The Nation*, became the voice of the repeal movement and was circulated widely through O'Connell's Repeal Association reading rooms, drawing together the mystical sense of nationality current in Europe with Ireland's ancient culture, the ideals of the independent Ascendancy Parliament of the late eighteenth century and the United Irishmen's concept of a new nation founded on a merging of the identities of Catholic, Protestant and Dissenter. These ideas were carried through in varying forms and degrees up to the foundation of the present state of Ireland.

Political activity came to an end with the genocidal disaster of the Famine when the population was halved by starvation and emigration; the people who suffered and died were those who lived at subsistence level on the margins of society. In some of the very poor areas of the country, vestiges of this poverty remained well into the present century, but as a whole the majority left were the more well-to-do Catholic small and middle farmers, and their mores altered to ones of puritanism, caution and consolidation.

When crushing an abortive Young Ireland rising in 1848, as the Famine abated, the government introduced a Treason Felony Bill with power to impose heavy penalties on instigators of rebellion, which was to catch many men in its net in the subsequent years. It was exiled Young Irelanders from this rising who founded the Fenian movement in 1858. In Ireland the organisation was oath-bound and called the Irish Republican Brotherhood (the IRB); it was allied to the Fenian Brotherhood in America, which was not oath-bound but was designed to support the IRB. The IRB's radical republican paper was edited by a young man instilled with the ideals of the Young Irelanders, John O'Leary. Though their abortive rising was effectively put down, the authorities knew the extent of the IRB network, the same as had existed in the days of the United Irishmen and of O'Connell, though it remained fairly dormant and the army was not called into action.

It was, however, a bleak period for army service in Ireland, the duties being to aid the civil powers in the maintenance of order, and to be on the alert for further disturbances with flying columns ready to move into action wherever trouble might break out.

Captain Gonne first lived in Athgarvin Lodge, overlooking the river Liffey near the Curragh Military Camp in County Kildare, where his second daughter, Kathleen, was born in September 1868. Later the family moved to Donnybrook outside Dublin until Edith Gonne, fatally ill with tuberculosis and expecting her third child, went back to England where she died shortly afterwards in 1871, her baby dying a few weeks later. Captain Gonne brought his two little girls and their nurse back to a military bungalow in the Curragh; Maud was four and a half years old and Kathleen not quite three. From then on, as far as his military career allowed, he raised the girls in as free and loving an atmosphere as possible, but in a life that, like his own, was frequently shifting. Maud's health gave him regular anxiety, and because of it he rented a little house, recently built by a local jarvey, near the Bailey lighthouse on Howth, the peninsula forming the north of Dublin Bay.

In her autobiography, written in her seventies, Maud's childhood memories centre on two periods in particular which seemed to have had the greatest influence on her life. The first was her happy memories of Howth, full of adventure around the sea cliffs or on the heather of the hill; where she and Kathleen joined in the play of the local children and were welcomed into their homes, meeting with great kindness, 'for the creatures, God help them, they have no mother'. The second was later when, also because of Maud's health, her father, now Colonel Gonne, on his way to join his regiment in India, settled the sisters in the south of France where for a short period they had a French governess. She influenced Maud greatly in many ways, being efficient, practical and able to instil a love of learning combined with a human understanding. One of the things Maud remembered was her comparison of the misfortunes of Poland and Ireland. And since early childhood she had a strange companion, an apparition she called her grey lady, 'a beautiful dark woman with sorrowful eyes . . . dressed in grey veils'.

All the time while he was away, in Austria, India or Russia, their father wrote to the girls every fortnight – charming letters full of anecdotes and irreverent accounts of generals, princes, sultans and emperors, and of his pets, particularly his beloved horses. Though he always kept unpleasantness from them, his anxiety showed through, particularly for Maud's health, writing to her: 'you must be packed up in Cotton Wool and never be undone'.

His last posting abroad was as military attaché to the court of St Petersburg. He appears to have brought the girls back to Dublin, for on 6 May 1882 they watched the state entry of Lord Spencer,

Gladstone's new Lord-Lieutenant of Ireland, accompanied by the new Chief Secretary, Lord Frederick Cavendish, and that evening witnessed the stunning effect of the assassination of Cavendish and his under-secretary in the Phoenix Park by the Invincibles.

Gladstone had come to power at the head of a Liberal government in England in 1868. He began to treat Ireland as a separate country, and parliamentary agitation again came to the fore. Parnell was elected MP in 1875 and in a few short years, as leader of a highly disciplined Irish Parliamentary Party, became a national leader as no one had been since the days of O'Connell. He joined forces with Michael Davitt, who had founded the Land League to protect the people against rack-renting and eviction. He also came to a tacit understanding with revolutionary Fenianism whereby it was agreed to allow parliamentary action to attempt to achieve radical reform. Gladstone introduced his Home Rule and Land Bills.

In 1867 Clann na Gael was founded in New York as an oath-bound organisation recognising the Supreme Council of the IRB as the legitimate 'government of Ireland'; it became widespread and powerful in Irish American politics. An extreme wing financed the dynamiting campaign in England in the 1880s.

From 1883 to 1885 Tommy Gonne had no particular posting, and it is possible at this time that he and the girls travelled around Europe accompanied as always by their nurse 'Bowie'. In Paris they met their Great-Aunt Mary, Comtesse de la Sizeranne, who later wished to launch Maud as a professional beauty after she had come to the attention of the notorious Edward, Prince of Wales. Maud received a proposal by moonlight in the Colosseum in Rome, not from an Italian as she said, but from a young family friend, Charles Eyre. Tommy, as the girls called him, guided his high-spirited young daughter gently around these hazards, but apparently made no objection when at a dinner attended by General Prince Saxe-Weimar in Kilmainham Royal Hospital for old soldiers in Dublin, she recited a ballad, 'Emmet's Death', about the romantic young United Irishman who led an abortive rising in Dublin in 1803:

> 'He dies to-day,' said the heartless judge,
>> Whilst he sate him down to the feast,
> And a smile was upon his ashy lip
>> As he uttered a ribald jest;
> For a demon dwelt where his heart should be,
>> That lived upon blood and sin,
> And oft as that vile judge gave him food
>> The demon throbbed within . . . .
>
> But the martyr's name, like a spell
>> That is murmured alone in prayer,

As long, in the land that he loved, shall dwell
    As a pure heart lingers there,
May wail him not with the harp's sad string,
    Let him sleep with the mournful past,
His spirit is here like an earth-pent spring
    And will sparkle to light at last.

By this time Tommy had taken up the post of Assistant Adjutant-General of the Dublin District, and Maud had been presented at a grand levee and was leading the life of a débutante and her father's hostess.

Protected though they were by their father, the girls could not have been completely unaware that the decade of the 1880s was one of intense political and agrarian activity, and Tommy had told Maud that, being of Irish descent and influenced by the Land War, he had decided to join the Home Rule movement. An incident Maud uses to highlight her coming to awareness was a callous and merciless remark by her host when she was staying in Cavan. Speaking of an evicted tenant whose family were lying in a ditch, he said, 'The woman will be dead before to-morrow.' She fled home to her father.

However, her father was not there much longer to protect her. He died suddenly of typhoid fever in the Royal Barracks, Dublin, on 30 November 1886, just before she was twenty. His body was carried with all ceremony and full military honours along the Dublin quays to the boat and taken to be buried beside his wife in England.

Shortly after the sisters' arrival in London, where they stayed with their guardian, their uncle William Gonne, a woman came to him for help, saying that Colonel Gonne was the father of her baby daughter. Maud, knowing this claim to be true, intervened against her uncle's wishes and promised Mrs Wilson assistance; she provided over and above what the family would have given. Later she procured her a post as governess to the family of a Russian, Ignatiy Platonovich Zakrevsky, whom she met in 1892. The little girl, Eileen, was given into the care of Maud and Kathleen's beloved nurse Bowie, who was now retired and living in Farnborough, where Kathleen's children also stayed from time to time.

What follows must be viewed in the light of their father's premature death. The girls had adored him. He had been educated on the Continent and spoke six languages, was charming, easy, popular, liberal and cosmopolitan. It is hard to say whether they ever recovered from his sudden death or how much they sought him throughout their lives. All through her life Maud was aware of his presence and love. She never forgot two things he had said: first, never to be afraid; secondly, that will was a force that could achieve anything.

Now they were taken over by their upper-middle-class English relatives at whose head was their disapproving bachelor uncle, William. Kathleen, younger by nearly two years and quieter by nature, accepted her fate docilely, but Maud, after she had recovered from the initial paralysing shock, seems to have ricocheted from one event to another until finally caught by circumstances.

In 1887, led by Uncle William to believe that she was poor, and determined to be independent, she took up acting as a career, and a horrified Uncle William received a poster of a touring company billing her as leading lady in *Adrienne Lecouvreur* (a play about the tragic actress by Eugène Scribe and Ernest Wilfrid Legouré). Falling ill, she was rescued by her Great-Aunt Mary and taken to Royat in the Auvergne, where she met Lucien Millevoye, the charming older man with whom she fell in love barely a year after her father's death. They made a pact to fight together against England, their joint hereditary enemy, she for Ireland and he for Alsace-Lorraine. He was involved with General Boulanger and brought her to meet the general at La Belle Meunière nearby in October 1887; the Boulangists were a strange mixture of republicans, royalists and socialists. She then went to Turkey to stay with an old schoolfriend, Lilla White (daughter of the British ambassador there), armed for her safety with a revolver that Millevoye had bought her. In December she came of age and acquired the means to live an independent life. She returned to France, where she was asked by the Boulangists to go to St Petersburg with secret proposals for a treaty with Russia – her first secret mission, which she accomplished with great pleasure. Early the previous year Boulanger had revealed that he had written a letter to the Tsar seeking a Russian alliance in case of war with Germany. As he was then closely watched by German spies, Maud's mission was probably a follow-up to this approach.

Having decided intellectually that she wanted to work for Ireland, she presented herself to Michael Davitt at Westminster, but he did not quite know what to make of her, suspecting her of being a spy. He was the first of many to have such suspicions.

In 1888 Maud was in Dublin while Kathleen was being presented at court, and she went out to visit the owners of the house in Howth where she had lived for about four years as a little girl. At night she would creep out to sleep on the heather of the hill, full of memories of her happy childhood and of Tommy, belonging more to this place – the earth protecting her as a mother – than any other place in her peripatetic life. She was ready to absorb mystical nationalism.

It was only later with Willie Yeats, whose childhood was also one of movement, that she could share this experience, for he felt the same sense of attachment to place and, like the country people, was aware of the past and the thin veil between the natural and supernatural with passage between. Aware of her psychic faculties (the vision of her grey lady was her regular companion), having identified herself with Ireland intellectually and experiencing this deep emotional bond with the earth as a life-yielding force, she went about her mission in a practical way.

Both she and Yeats became involved with Irish affairs about the same time; both became leading, outstanding and influential figures on the nationalist stage in the next decade, when parliamentary politics were moribund after the split in the Parliamentary Party over Parnell's private life and death. Yet it was the people working tirelessly in this period who laid the foundations and opened up the way for all that was to follow. It was a time when many strands came together to produce remarkable and lasting results.

The post-famine church, in line with the unifying policy of Rome, had made serious efforts to stamp out what it considered super-stitious practices, introducing such religious devotions as the rosary and novenas. With that and the gradual dying out of the language, the ancient lore was fading and Ireland was becoming more and more anglicised. A thread of scholarship had kept Gaelic antiquities alive through the centuries. Thomas Moore popularised them early in the century and the poets of the Young Ireland movement had continued and extended what he had started. In the 1830s and 1840s the work of the Ordnance Survey, O'Donovan and O'Curry brought together the old Irish tradition of learning with the scholarship of the Ascendancy. Celtic studies became respectable and of interest to international scholars. Standish O'Grady popularised the sagas rediscovered by O'Curry and O'Donovan in his *History of Ireland – Heroic Period* (1878, 1881) and subsequent works which inspired the young Yeats with his dream of a mystical Celtic literature. Yeats began writing his first long poem on an Irish subject, *The Wanderings of Oisin*, in 1886. The preceding year John O'Leary returned from imprisonment and an exile of thirteen years in Paris where he had kept in close contact with affairs in Ireland. With his patrician appearance, his integrity and erudite literary Fenianism he influenced the younger generation of radical nationalists.

Yeats's entry into Irish affairs followed a natural progression – from not enjoying his school in England before he went to the High School in Dublin, through endless discussions stimulated by his father's Home Rule attitudes and those he experienced in the Contemporary Club, reinforced by his reading of Irish material, often supplied by O'Leary.

Maud Gonne's entry was a little later. In 1888 a friend introduced her to Charles Oldham, who had founded the Protestant Home Rule Association and the Contemporary Club, stimulating and alive with literary and political nationalism and shades of unionism. Oldham in turn introduced her to John O'Leary and the other members of the

Contemporary Club, many of whom she was to know for the rest of her life.

Maud also sought out Timothy Harrington MP. He suggested that she should go to Donegal, where the Plan of Campaign was in confrontation with the landlord, Olpherts, and a policeman had been killed while trying to arrest the local priest, Father MacFadden. In 1886, after the suppression of the Land League, the MPs William O'Brien and Timothy Harrington of the Irish National League had started a rent strike policy and collective bargaining for reduced rents against selected landlords. This was called the Plan of Campaign. Tenants who were evicted for refusing to pay their rents were housed in 'Land League huts' and supported by the National League from a central fund. With the Parnell split and his death in 1891, the organisation broke down and many evicted tenants were left stranded.

In January 1889 Maud Gonne was in London. On the 30th she called on the Yeats family in Bedford Park with an introduction from John O'Leary's sister, Ellen, and Yeats wrote later that 'the troubling of my life began'. Several of his letters at that time mention her. In a letter to Ellen O'Leary he wrote: 'Did I tell you how much I admire Miss Gonne? She will make many converts to her political belief.' In March she had rooms in Dublin over Morrow's bookshop on the corner of South Frederick Street and Nassau Street, where she entertained her new friends and took Irish lessons from Douglas Hyde.

In April 1889 General Boulanger fled to Brussels and his whole movement collapsed. It was around this time that Maud conceived her first child by Millevoye. It is possible that their relationship only developed to this extent at this time perhaps through compassion at the tragic collapse of Millevoye's hopes. Millevoye was married and had told her at some stage that he would get a divorce and marry her. In her autobiography she says that later, when his political aspirations were in ruins, she struggled with his despair, encouraging him to take up the editorship of *La Patrie*.

From the time of her child's conception she was more or less committed to her life in France. Where else could she have gone? But she continued to be involved with her spiritual home, travelling back and forth through London, where she stayed with her family, mostly with her sister Kathleen or her cousins May and Chotie, and occasionally with an aunt. In Ireland she busied herself with evictions, and also Oldham's Protestant Home Rule Association and the Contemporary Club. In London she developed her interest in occultism and mysticism, encouraged by Yeats, who brought her to meet the theosophist, Madame Blavatsky. In France she and Millevoye may have met discreetly at Samois (their relationship was kept secret), and she probably had a loving environment around the child, Georges, who was born in January 1890. In his *Memoirs* Yeats wrote of what she told him years later of the time when she became Millevoye's mistress: 'She was often away from him for physical love soon began to repel her but for all that was very much in love.' She had gone on to say he had failed her in various ways, that he had asked her to become the mistress of someone else to further his political aims, that she had thought of leaving him, and that she believed that 'sexual love was only justified by children'.

Maud's biggest political preoccupations then were the evictions in Gweedore, where a legend grew that she was a woman of the Sídhe (the fairies) – such was the sense of the affinity between natural and supernatural in the minds of the people. She fell ill and went to the south of France to recover, with Millevoye and probably Georges. In July she was back in Ireland, and Yeats records that he was worried about her health. He proposed to her; she refused, saying there were reasons why she could not marry, and asked for his friendship. The next day they went walking around the cliffs of Howth and visited the house of her childhood. In August she attended a meeting of the Home Rule Association; then, according to Yeats, she was recalled to France and shortly after wrote to him that a child she had adopted had died, 'the death bird had pecked at the nursery window the day it had taken ill, and how at sight of the bird she had brought doctor after doctor.' The death bird, as she said later, 'often heralds the death of members of our family'.

According to his death certificate, Georges Silvère, aged nineteen and a half months, died at Avenue de la Grande Armée 66, 31 August 1891 at 5 pm, son of a father and mother whose names were not given. He was buried at Samois.

Samois is a pleasant little village on the edge of the forest of Fontainebleau by the banks of the Seine, a favourite haunt of the artistic and literary. In the graveyard at Samois in the largest tomb in the far corner near the trees lies the little body of Georges Silvère. Maud adored her child, who according to her had 'some great intangible quality of goodness'. Unable to express her grief in an open and natural way, she had a family tomb built for him, to be maintained in perpetuity. Above it was a little chamber with a window and a place for flowers where she could go to feel near him.

A month after Georges's death General Boulanger committed suicide on 30 September 1891 in Brussels, and Parnell died on 6 October; no wonder Maud was in a distraught condition when she arrived in Dublin on the same boat as Parnell's coffin. Yeats, aware of her grief but not of its full cause, helped her all he could. In his *Memoirs* he writes of this period: 'She went over the details of the death – speech was a relief to her. She was plainly very ill. . . . We spoke often of the state of death.' George Russell 'spoke of reincarnation and Maud Gonne asked him "How soon a child was reborn, and if where?" He said, "It may be reborn in the same family." ' Also she told Yeats and Russell of her vision of the grey lady, who later 'showed herself as evil and described herself as a murderess of children'. Yeats dedicated a little vellum manuscript book of poems to her, interested her in his practical efforts to spread Irish literature through a library scheme, and was responsible for her being initiated into the Golden Dawn.

Millevoye helped her to write her first article on the Donegal evictions, 'Un Peuple Opprimé', published in *La Nouvelle Revue Internationale*. She entered the journalistic world of Paris and counted among her friends many whom W. T. Stead described in 1892 as 'that new phenomenon, the woman journalist', including Ghénia de Sainte-Croix and Madame Séverine, described as the leading lady journalist of Europe. Maud observed that 'this period of my life was one of ceaseless activity and travelling, I rarely spent a month in the same place', and Yeats said she told him that her correspondence took up to eight hours a day. The ceaseless activity was concerned with evictions, the imprisoned tenants and those forgotten men of Irish politics, the dynamiters of the 1880s. Maud spoke at Amnesty meetings in England and Ireland, lectured in France on these subjects, wrote articles, gave interviews, in an endless stream of activity, punctuated by bouts of illness no doubt induced by exhaustion and stress due to both overwork and the strain of her double life.

As a woman Maud was excluded from the political organisations, so she worked alone. As she wrote in her autobiography, she 'was incapable of planning ahead, and therefore soon realised I could never be a leader'. Her non-judgemental capacity and her belief that everyone should work in their own way would not have been leadership qualities, but her glowing personality, her gentleness and kindness turning to dignified indignation in anger, allied to her invincible determination, were qualities to be reckoned with.

In those crowded years Maud Gonne's name was to the fore in all the nationalist activities; the only other woman approaching her in this type of work was the poet and co-founder of the *Shan Van Vocht*, Alice Milligan. While her outer life was busy, indeed at times frenetic, she had a recurring dream of wandering on and on in a desert and wrote years later of a constant sense of loneliness. She probably found it nearly impossible to speak of the succession of tragedies that tied her when young to a pattern of life and turned her energy increasingly outward, causing her to work with dedication and compassion for her ideal in a life of political activity and popular acclaim until that too fell apart. So the reserve of her earlier letters is due not only to the natural conventions of her time but also to her fear of facing her inner realities.

Neither her autobiography nor her letters are revealing. Most of what is known about her personal emotions derives from Yeats's writing, coloured and filtered by his intense infatuation and possibly telescoped and rounded by his well-known love of a good story. As he says, she did not seem to have any deep awareness of what he suffered through his love, looking on him more as a close friend or brother who shared many unusual common interests and on whom she could rely for help at times of great distress.

In her autobiography, *Flowering Dusk*, Ella Young leaves a vivid picture of them together:

I see her standing with W. B. Yeats, the poet, in front of Whistler's Miss Alexander in the Dublin gallery where some pictures by Whistler are astonishing a select few. These two people delight the bystanders more than the pictures. Everyone stops looking at canvas and manoeuvres himself or herself into a position to watch these two. They are almost of equal height. Yeats has a dark, romantic cloak about him; Maud Gonne has a dress that changes colour as she moves. They pay no attention to the stir they are creating; they stand there discussing the picture.

I catch sight of them again in the reading room of the National Library. They have a pile of books between them and are consulting the books and each other. No one else is consulting a book. Everyone is conscious of those two as the denizens of a woodland lake might be conscious of a flamingo, or of a Japanese heron, if it suddenly descended among them.

Later, in the narrow curve of Grafton Street, I notice people are stopping and turning their heads. It is Maud Gonne and the poet. She has a radiance as of sunlight. Yeats, that leopard of the moon, holds back in a leash a huge lion-coloured Great Dane – Maud Gonne's dog, Dagda.

Introduction

A. NORMAN JEFFARES

What is love? A question that Bacon's 'jesting Pilate' might have asked, and the answer he might have provoked, in Yeats's case, would embrace admiration of Maud Gonne's appearance, the excitement of attraction, idealised desire, poetic devotion, disagreements, close friendships, the spiritualised sharing of a mystic marriage, hatred, reconciliation, short-lived sex, affectionate amity, deep political differences, regrets, regard, memories – in short, obsession. At least we know when and where this complex, changing yet persistent experience, the troubling of his life as he called it, began. On 30 January 1889 a hansom cab brought Maud Gonne from Belgravia ostensibly to visit Yeats's father in Blenheim Road in Bedford Park, but also to meet the young poet.

Tall, mesmerically beautiful, graceful, she was at twenty-two poised, self-possessed and independent in mind and means. She seemed like a goddess to the twenty-three-year-old Irish poet, tall himself, thin, raven-haired, shy but incessantly talkative, insecure, penniless and ambitious. She wanted to work for Ireland and so did he.

Yeats had never thought to see in a woman such great beauty. He poured out his dreams to her that first heady evening when he dined with her in her Ebury Street rooms, and on the other eight evenings of her nine-day stay in London. In his *Memoirs* he records how he wished to become an Irish Victor Hugo. He wanted to write about the heroic people of Irish mythology and the places in Ireland associated with them. He wanted Irish people to become aware of their past, their unique identity that was to be discovered in legends and tales, oral as well as written; but he wanted to re-create this legacy in literature worthy of that past tradition. Maud had read his first major achievement in handling Gaelic legend and transmuting it into the inventions of his own idiom, *The Wanderings of Oisin*, published a few weeks before her visit to Bedford Park. Now he

17

promised to write a play for her, *The Countess Cathleen*.

Maud had histrionic gifts, but her first attempt at acting, two years earlier, had ended when she became ill and began her liaison with Millevoye at the spa at Royat. When she met Yeats she was already involved with Irish nationalism, despite the difficulty she found, as a woman, in being accepted among the nationalists' ranks. She was campaigning in support of evicted tenants, whose desolate, homeless plight stirred her deeply, and to whom she offered practical aid by renting rooms and arranging shelter. She wanted action, she had energy, and she enjoyed excitement.

Maud Gonne brought into Willie Yeats's life 'an overpowering tumult'. He realised they were seeking different ends: she thought almost any means justified if the end were successful; he thought only the means could justify the end. She spoke to him of her desire for power; he spoke to her of his spiritual philosophy. His father had not approved of Maud's praise of war; one of his sisters had hated her 'sort of royal smile', and the other recorded that for all her airs she was in her slippers when she called on them. The Yeats family never took to her. Though Willie was in love, he 'had not spoken of love and never meant to speak'. But he wrote with a certain bravura to Ellen O'Leary – who had written the letter of introduction to Yeats's father that had brought Maud to Bedford Park – that Maud Gonne would make many converts to her political belief: 'If she said the world was flat or the moon an old caubeen [a shapeless old hat] tossed up in the sky I would be proud to be of her party.' However, he made light of Katharine Tynan's suggestion that he was 'taken up with Miss Gonne'. He thought she was very good-looking, he replied, and that was all he thought about her. As the months passed, he recorded in his *Memoirs*, he grew master of himself again: ' "What wife could she make?" I thought. "What share could she have in the life of a student?" '

Both were busily pursuing their own lives. In 1889 Yeats began work on *The Countess Cathleen* and on the edition of Blake in which he and Edwin Ellis collaborated; his *Stories from Carleton* was published. In 1890 he and Ernest Rhys founded the Rhymers' Club. He was an active member of the Esoteric Section of the Theosophical Society (from which he was asked to resign in October) and was initiated into the Hermetic Order of the Golden Dawn in March, the month he finished work on *Representative Irish Tales*. In March 1891, when it was published, he sent a copy to Maud Gonne.

She too had been leading a full life. To be near Millevoye she lived in Paris, where she had an apartment, 61 Avenue Wagram. She became pregnant in the spring of 1889, then went to London to nurse her sister Kathleen, who was seriously ill. Having heard she was in London, Willie saw her briefly for a few minutes but did not realise she was pregnant. She was back in London again for her sister's wedding in December, and on 11 January 1890 her son Georges was born in Paris. Maud was determined to keep her affair with Millevoye secret; her political as well as her social life demanded it. In any case she was not by nature domestic. She returned to her campaigning in Donegal. Millevoye arrived unexpectedly in Ireland but fell ill with a fever in Dunfanaghy. She nursed him back to health so that he could return, without her, to France, where he thought she should concentrate her energies. When she was in Dublin, Dr George Sigerson, with whom she was working on a book of poems by Ellen O'Leary, thought that her consumptive condition might be cured by injections and advised her not to return to Donegal. She refused his advice, as she had Millevoye's, and went back to help in hut-building and other work for the evicted tenants. In June 1890 she spent some time campaigning in Barrow-in-Furness on behalf of Duncan, a Gladstonian Liberal, making her first highly emotional public speech there with great success. Eventually the news that a warrant was out for her arrest persuaded her to return from Donegal to France.

Both Maud and Willie drove themselves hard. In the autumn of 1890 he had a mild collapse, his heart affected; the doctor told him that he had been wearing himself out, that he must live 'more deliberately and leisurely'. He wanted to get out of London, to go to Dublin or Sligo, but didn't manage to do so. Maud, however, once back in France, was able to go to Saint-Raphaël with Millevoye to restore her health. She then returned to Paris before going to Ireland in the summer of 1891.

Yeats called on her on 22 July in her Dublin hotel, finding her no longer full of 'hard resonance' but 'gentle and indolent', hinting at some unhappiness, some disillusionment. He found himself in love once more 'and no longer wished to fight against it', no longer thinking 'what kind of wife would this woman make, but of her need for protection and peace'. None the less he went off to stay with Charles Johnson, an old schoolfriend, in County Down. There he got a letter from Maud, 'touching a little on her sadness and telling a dream of some past life' when they had been brother and sister and had been sold into slavery. He responded by returning to Dublin at once, on 3 August, and asking her to marry him. She replied in words she was to use later on similar occasions: 'No, she could not marry – there were reasons – she would never marry.' They should be friends; the world would thank her for not marrying him. A pattern in their friendship was established. She would draw upon his support as though he were the brother of her dream. Next day they visited Howth, where Maud had spent happy years as a child, and where Willie as an adolescent had climbed the cliffs, imagining himself to be some heroic figure like Alastor or Manfred, and thinking of women who 'accompanied their lovers through all manner of wild places, lawless women without homes and without children'.

They walked on the cliff paths and had dinner in a thatched cottage belonging to an old servant of Maud's. At the day's end Willie found that he 'had spent ten shillings', which seemed to him 'a very great sum' – a reminder, perhaps, of the Yeats family's severe financial stresses and certainly a warning of the costs of domesticity; a reminder that homes and children were not associated with those lawless women loved by his hero figures. Escape from the travails of human reality could be found in dreaming. As they sat in the heather and two seagulls flew over them, Maud asked him to write her a poem about them (a seagull was the bird she would most like to be). Three days later Willie sent her 'The White Birds', with its plangent wish that 'we were, my beloved, white birds on the foam of the sea'.

His declaration triggered off six of the seven lyrics, written between July and October 1891, that he inscribed in *The Flame of the Spirit*, a vellum notebook he presented to her on 20 October 1891. Four of these poems were included in *The Rosy Cross Lyrics*, a collection of six poems dated from August to November which he probably made in November 1891. *The Flame of the Spirit* had the titles of eleven other poems pencilled in on later pages. These poems had theosophical associations – Maud, too, had been a theosophist – though they also indicate that Yeats was hoping to involve her in the Order of the Golden Dawn. They also, of course, deal with her effect on him, as 'Cycles Ago', with its subtitle 'In Memory of Your Dream One July Night', makes clear:

> My world was fallen and over, for your dark soft eyes on it shone;
> A thousand years it had waited and now it is gone, it is gone.

He read her the as yet unfinished text of *The Countess Cathleen*; they 'saw each other continually'.

Suddenly Maud returned to Paris, saying she had been summoned by a secret society. In reality Millevoye (with whom she was disillusioned) had informed her that Georges was desperately ill; he died of meningitis on 31 August. To Willie, who knew nothing of her affair with Millevoye nor of the child's existence, she wrote 'a letter of wild sorrow', telling him a child she had adopted had died. On 11 October she arrived in black clothes on the mailboat that brought Parnell's body back to Ireland. She told Willie that she had built a memorial chapel for the child (whose body, he learned later, had been embalmed); she forgot her French, she became temporarily addicted to chloroform, which she took to make herself sleep; she was immersed in grief. She found Willie's spiritual philosophy a comfort, but was consoled even more by George Russell's view of reincarnation, his belief that a child could be reborn in the same family. Willie thought that her need of him would become love. He wrote her 'The Sorrow of Love' and 'When You Are Old' which recorded his love of 'the pilgrim soul' in her. He began to form plans for their devoting their lives to mystic truth. In London he persuaded her to join the Order of the Golden Dawn, and she was initiated into it on 2 November 1891. Basically no bohemian, Willie envisaged an eventual marriage, inspired by that of the fourteenth-century alchemist Nicholas Flamel and his wife Pernella.

Maud went back to Paris, and May Gonne, her cousin, suggested to Yeats that he should go there in the spring – as he told George Russell in a letter requesting him to go and see Maud when she was in Dublin and 'keep her from forgetting me and occultism'. He also asked John O'Leary to help her to urge on the work of the Young Ireland League. Although he had involved her in his pursuit of mystic truth, he realised that her energy would return, that 'a secret mystic propaganda' would not be sufficient to hold her attention. In any case, she did not think much of the other members of the Golden Dawn, finding them drab and mediocre, 'an awful set' who seemed to her 'the very essence of British middle-class dullness' (she was to leave the Order in December 1894). As for his going to Paris, the answer was simple: he had no money. Indeed, Yeats wrote to O'Leary on 25 November asking if he could borrow a pound because he did 'not want to be without the price of cabs, etc.' when Maud returned to London. Writing later to thank O'Leary for postal orders he had sent, he assured him that Maud 'does not let me pay the whole fare but stipulated a good while ago that she should pay her own share'. When he had asked for the loan he had 'just three-halfpence and no hope of more for a month'. Some of his optimism about eventually persuading her to marry him may have informed 'The Rose of the World' (written in January 1892), in which he links Maud with Helen of Troy and Deirdre, the third stanza being prompted by their walking on rough roads in the Dublin mountains.

Maud's refusal of Willie's proposal in 1891, however, at least relieved him of the worry that he did not earn enough money to get married. At all events, he had to content himself with what became a decidedly long-term courtship – what he later described, with reason, as a 'perplexed wooing'.

By late 1891, Yeats was entering into literary politics. Thinking that the death of Parnell had created a lull in the political movement towards Home Rule, he busied himself planning societies and movements to encourage Irish literature: the Irish Literary Society of London was set up in 1891 and the National Literary Society in Dublin in 1892. He saw a role for Maud Gonne here: she was to found country branches of the National Literary Society to which collections of books could be presented. He and she were appointed to the Libraries Sub-committee of the National Literary Society and for a time he envisaged her becoming 'the fiery hand of the literary movement'.

While Willie was steering her towards mysticism and the nascent literary movement, Maud found, as he put it, 'more exciting work' in the north-west of Ireland, where she continued to help the evicted tenants. She also spoke at large meetings in France, on their behalf and on behalf of the Amnesty Association, in support of the release of Irish political prisoners held in Portland Gaol. While she seemed to understand 'every subtlety of my own art, and especially all my spiritual philosophy', and said he had saved her from despair, she did not seem to realise how deeply he was disappointed in losing a battle for control of the new Library of Ireland to Sir Charles Gavan Duffy and T. W. Rolleston; nor indeed did she see it as more than 'a troublesome dispute among her friends', whereas he thought the intellectual future of Ireland was at stake. Willie's project for libraries, backed up by the speeches he arranged for Maud to make in Loughrea and New Ross, was heavily criticised for being badly administered.

Angry at this rebuff, tortured by sexual frustration and jealous of the influence on Maud of others – notably the barrister J. F. Taylor, who had supported Duffy – Willie had a violent quarrel with her in 1893. Maud became severely ill with congestion of the lungs and Dr Sigerson, with whom he had quarrelled over Gavan Duffy, refused Yeats admittance to see her. The story told in Yeats's *Memoirs* is melodramatic. A woman, apparently mentally deranged, took on the duty of a nurse. Yeats met her nightly in a public garden to get news of Maud, who, she reported, loved another, perhaps two others, for she intended, ill as she was, to return to Paris to prevent a duel between them. May Gonne came to Dublin, and, against Sigerson's wishes, arranged for her cousin to be carried to the train. After she left, Yeats learned of a rumour that he had been Maud's lover and been present at an illegal operation. In his *Memoirs* he recorded how he had 'heard much scandal about her but had dismissed the grosser scandal at once', and had put away one persistent story 'with the thought "She would have told me if it were true." ' Although it seemed that the intimacy of their minds could not have been greater, marriage had slipped further away. Yeats thought this was due to his own 'immaturity and lack of achievement'; he realised she was complete and he was not.

Maud returned to France to receive Millevoye's praise for the effects of her lecture tour there in 1892; this, he told her, had achieved far more than any of her efforts in Ireland – a place he regarded as obscure and unhealthy. Yeats retired briefly to Sligo to recoup his courage. 'Into the Twilight', written in June 1893, records his gloom, addressing his 'Out-worn heart, in a time out-worn':

> Though hope fall from you and love decay,
> Burning in fires of a slanderous tongue.

His literary politics apparently frustrated as well as his love, he returned to Bedford Park and involved himself in the work of the Second Order of the Golden Dawn (which he had entered in January) until mid-September 1893. Millevoye too was depressed, for he had had to resign as a deputy. Maud reached a rapprochement with him and a second child was conceived. Thinking of reincarnation, she hoped this had happened on an occasion in the vault of the memorial chapel which housed Georges's body.

Unable to understand why Maud Gonne had turned from him, Yeats channelled his despair into writing *The Land of Heart's Desire*. In February 1894 he went for the first time to Paris and stayed with the occultist MacGregor Mathers and his wife. There he saw Maud and thought their relations, though friendly enough, did not have their old intimacy; he does not seem to have seriously contemplated the possibility of her being in love with someone else; and he certainly did not realise that she was pregnant. In March *The Land of Heart's Desire* was staged in London. From October to May he was busy revising poems and plays and writing *The Shadowy Waters*, staying with his uncle George Pollexfen in Sligo. While he still considered himself in love with Maud and had 'but just' written her 'The Lover Tells of the Rose in his Heart', he toyed briefly with proposing to Eva Gore-Booth, whom he met in November 1894 on a brief visit to Lissadell, the family's 'big house' outside Sligo. However, he quickly realised that the Gore-Booths 'would never accept so penniless a suitor'.

Although his literary reputation was growing after the publication of *The Celtic Twilight* in December 1893, money, or rather the lack of it, continued to be a problem. In October 1895 Willie left home; the house in Blenheim Road was at that time a sad place, his father ill, inactive and deeply depressed, his mother withdrawn, 'her mind gone'. He went to stay in rooms that Arthur Symons sublet him in Fountain Court in the Middle Temple, and his sister Lollie reported him as saying he could live on ten shillings a week, to which she added: 'Let him try.' The reason for his move was his involvement with Olivia Shakespear, whom he first met in 1894. Yeats had been corresponding with her and he asked her to leave her husband to live with him. If he could not get the woman he loved, 'it would be a comfort even but for a little while' to devote himself to another. It wasn't easy: on one occasion Mrs Shakespear and a friend came to tea, and afterwards Yeats spent three hours talking to Symons about Maud Gonne, who a few days later wrote him what he called 'a wild letter' saying that, on the day of the tea party, he had appeared to her in a vision. The letter, however, did not disrupt the developing relationship; Olivia, who had decided it would be kinder to deceive than leave her husband, helped Yeats to furnish rooms very cheaply in 18 Woburn Buildings (then a very run-down place), which he took in February 1896. There she initiated him into sex and they 'had many days of happiness'.

Maud had moved too, to a large apartment on the Avenue d'Eylau: her life in France expanded as she entertained men of influence, and through Millevoye's editorship of *La Patrie* and Drumont's of *La Libre Parole* she continued her propaganda campaign against Britain's treatment of Ireland.

For Yeats, Maud remained 'the old lure'. Though enjoying Olivia's company and writing her several poems, he went back to Paris in December 1896 to see Maud and to involve her in the work of creating a Celtic Order of Mysteries. He had told her of seeing a castle in Lough Key, County Roscommon, when he was staying with Douglas Hyde in April 1895; this would make a Castle of Heroes, a place for meditation. He was trying to write a novel, *The Speckled Bird*, for which he had received his first advance. This largely autobiographical novel was about attempts to combine art with magic through the creation of a mystical brotherhood. He was convinced of the need for rituals which could reunite perception of the spirit with natural beauty. Both he and Maud felt Ireland possessed hidden forces, was invisibly peopled, and believed they could gain strength by getting in touch with these. They shared their visions and dreams.

While Willie was involving Maud in this work, she was responsible for his moving into more political activity. He helped her to found a Young Ireland Society in Paris. When celebrations of the centenary of the 1798 rebellion were being planned, he became president of the Executive Committee of the Centenary Association for Great Britain and France, seeing himself briefly in the role of a political leader who would unite the Irish parties; their members were to sit in Parliament 'as a deputation from us'. Yeats had become a member of the IRB in about 1886; now he was involved in helping the 'New Movement', the Irish National Brotherhood. He called a meeting at Woburn Buildings and got Maud authorisation to collect funds in America for a Wolfe Tone memorial when she had been refused by the Dublin body.

Yeats's turning to political activity was motivated partly by a desire to impress Maud. He had been helpful in opposing the slanders of Charles MacCarthy Teeling, who accused her of being a British spy; later they were both involved in countering the machinations of Frank Hugh O'Donnell, whom Yeats characterised, not inaccurately, as 'the mad rogue'. However, his desire to prove himself to her as a politician backfired on the occasion of the Jubilee riots in Dublin in June 1897. Maud had made an inflammatory speech, after which she and Yeats walked to the National Club in Rutland Square, preceded by a mock funeral she had devised. Its coffin, with 'The British Empire' written on it, was thrown into the Liffey, rioting began and windows were smashed. As they had tea in the National Club they were told of a police baton charge outside, whereupon Willie had the door locked and refused to let Maud go out. His account in his *Memoirs* is matched by Maud's letter reproaching him for making her do 'the most cowardly thing'. Her father's daughter, she says, 'Do you ask a soldier for explanations on the battlefield?', tells him there is a 'need for *immediate action*' and adds that for a long time she has felt she should not encourage him to mix himself up in 'the *outer* side of politics'; the riot and police charge have shown her that he should not get involved in what is really not his line of action: 'You have a higher work to do. With me it is different. I was born to be in the midst of a crowd.'

Yeats's life, however, was about to be changed by a new friendship. He had met Lady Gregory briefly at a party in London in 1894; then in 1896, when he was staying with Edward Martyn at Tillyra Castle in Galway, she came to call, and invited Yeats to Coole Park, her nearby house. It was a short, successful visit, and led to a longer one the following summer. Yeats was impressed by Lady Gregory's sense of security, the poise of her aristocratic code, and her paradoxical combination of pride and humility. She wanted to join the literary movement and appreciated his abilities; in turn she answered many of his needs. When she nearly died in 1909 he was to describe her as being to him 'mother, friend, sister and brother'. When Yeats arrived at Coole in late July 1897 Lady Gregory realised that he was in urgent need of care. He had lost his voice; his nerves were frayed; he was mentally and physically worn out. His affair with Olivia Shakespear had ended after a year when she realised he was still obsessed with Maud, with whom he had dined in London. Slowly he recovered his health during his two-month stay in Galway, though his emotional and sexual frustration was such that often when he walked in the woods of Coole 'it would have been a relief to have screamed aloud'. Lady Gregory whipped up his flagging energies when the possibility of an Irish theatre was discussed. Like Maud, she too had what he called a 'feeling for immediate action'. As he later described it, the curtain had fallen on the first act of his drama – his propaganda, his editing, his articles, his speeches, his setting up of societies, which had been directed to the creation of a new kind of Irish literature. He wrote: 'In 1897 a new scene was set, new actors appeared.'

In the autumn Yeats resumed his work for the '98 Centenary Association. Sometimes he accompanied Maud, who was making speeches in Paris, London, Glasgow, Manchester, York, Dublin and Cork. She was now in what he called her 'shining days':

> And the tongues of the crowd
> And of new friends are glad with your praise.

He wrote to Lady Gregory on 3 October from Manchester that Maud was 'very kind and friendly, but whether more than that I cannot tell'; ten days later Maud was to write that a letter of his had distressed her a good deal: 'I don't want you to give me so much place in your life. It is not well that you should.' She left for her American tour in October.

While their political interests separated, their mutal interest in mysticism continued. Maud joined Yeats in his work on Celtic mysticism with members of the Golden Dawn in London in early 1898 and in Paris that spring. Their personal relationship altered dramatically in November 1898 when they were in Dublin together – he never stayed in the same hotel, though she often laughed at his scruple. One night he dreamed she had kissed him, and when he met her after breakfast in the Nassau Hotel she asked if he had had a strange dream. He recounted his dream, and that evening she told him that after falling asleep the night before she had seen a great spirit who had put her hand in Yeats's and told her that they were married. Then for the first time 'with the bodily mouth she kissed me.' The next day she apologised to him; she could never be his wife. And out came the story of her secret life, some of which he had heard 'all twisted awry by scandal' and had disbelieved. So he heard of the pact Maud had made with the devil, a fortnight before her father's death in 1886: she believed the devil had obtained her soul in exchange for her freedom to live as she chose. He learned of her affair with Millevoye, the birth and death of Georges, the birth of Iseult in August 1894, and her dislike of sexual love – which, she told him, was only justified by children. Since Iseult's birth, Maud said, she and Millevoye had lived apart, though she felt her influence was necessary to keep him to his political ideals.

It was almost too much for Yeats. He accused himself later of acting from a dread of moral responsibility, for he resolved to touch her 'as one might a sister'; if she was to come to him it must be with the approval of her conscience. Days later she told him she heard a voice saying, 'You are about to receive the initiation of the spear.' They became silent. A double vision unfolded itself: 'She thought herself a great stone statue through which passed flame, and I felt myself becoming flame and mounting up through and looking out of the eyes of a great stone Minerva.'

Maud became 'always very emotional', and would kiss him, but said marriage seemed to her impossible, telling him she had a horror

26

of physical love. She returned to Paris. Despite Lady Gregory's offer of money to travel and advice not to leave Maud till he had her promise to marry him, he replied that he was too exhausted, he could do no more. Nevertheless he went to Paris in February 1899 and proposed again; she told him more about her past. Yeats renewed his pleas that she would leave the world of politics for that of mystic truth.

Thus the strange 'spiritual marriage' came into being, pursued in dreams and projections of personalities. Yeats's notebooks headed *Visions* recorded some of these experiences: the first book began on 11 July 1898, the second on 25 November 1899, continuing to March 1901.

Again, however, both of them were separately occupied in many diverse activities. Yeats was involved with the plays of the Irish Literary Theatre in 1899 and 1900, with the row in the Golden Dawn in 1900 and 1901 in which he played a leading part, with a difficult collaboration with George Moore during 1899 and 1900 in the writing of *Diarmuid and Grania*; and there were his letters to the papers and other protests against Queen Victoria's visit to Ireland in 1900. Apart from *The Wind Among the Reeds* (1899) with its many despairing poems to Maud, and a revised edition of *Poems* (1895), he was increasingly occupied with theatre business. Lady Gregory put into simple and dramatically effective language his idea for *Cathleen ni Houlihan*.

While he had spent the summers at Coole in ideal, orderly conditions which suited his methods of writing, Maud had been almost frantically busy in the world of politics. Opposition to Britain's Boer War reactivated her political alliance with Millevoye, but a friendship with Arthur Griffith gave her a better journalistic outlet than *La Patrie* and she wrote many pieces for Griffith's *United Irishman*. She was active in the Irish Transvaal Committee which supported the Irish Brigade, organised to fight on the side of the Boers. Her friendship with James Connolly, forged in the Jubilee riots of 1897, was strengthened on the occasion of the Beresford Place rally in Dublin when the police were successfully and spectacularly defied.

In January 1900 Maud went to the United States to lecture on behalf of the Boers and also collected funds for the *United Irishman*. Ill after this tour and so unable to be in Ireland to protest against Queen Victoria's visit, she hurled off an article for *L'Irlande Libre* which appeared in English as 'The Famine Queen' in the *United Irishman*. Back in Ireland she won a libel action against the editor of the Dublin *Figaro*; she organised a massive counter-demonstration to the free treat, given to 5000 schoolchildren in the Phoenix Park as a demonstration of loyalty, by assembling well over 20,000 children in the procession of the Patriotic Children's Treat to Clonturk Park where they were fed and heard inflammatory speeches. Out of this activity came the formation of Inghínidhe na hÉireann – the Daughters of Erin – of which Maud was elected president. This group of women was affiliated with Cumann na nGaedheal, a federation of various literary, athletic and political societies of which Maud became an honorary secretary. This gave Inghínidhe na hÉireann political standing and Maud an organisation which meant she could not now be ignored as a mere freelance, independent political activist. The group gave free classes in various Irish subjects to Dublin children, and through it Maud made many women friends who shared her interest in Irish legends and mythology, and who were also motivated by a desire to demonstrate their efficiency and their capacity to contribute to the nationalist revival.

Now, after thirteen years, Maud's political and personal relationship with Millevoye was coming to an end. In the summer of 1900 she realised that he had a new mistress, a singer from a *café-chantant*, whose views on Alsace-Lorraine appealed to him more than those of Maud's 'absurd' Irish revolutionaries. At what seemed a final meeting at Chamonix, at the foot of Mont Blanc, Maud felt her heart turn to stone. In late September she went to Ireland, and while she was there Millevoye requested another meeting as a matter of extreme urgency. She then discovered that her anti-British work in France had been undone, for Millevoye brought a Captain Robert to question her about her having introduced 'Colonel L' of French Military Intelligence to members of the IRB in London. The colonel had been betrayed by the IRB to the British authorities (it turned out to have been the work of Frank Hugh O'Donnell) and repatriated by the French embassy in London at the instigation of the British government. Maud told the two Frenchmen how she had earlier offered Dr Leyds, the Transvaal representative in Europe based in Brussels, a plan for the IRB to conceal bombs in the coal bunkers of British troopships. Although he had rejected her plan, next day she received a message from him promising that he would send her £2000 – she would 'know what it was for'. This money was intercepted by Frank Hugh O'Donnell, who called on Leyds saying that he was from the IRB and had been sent to collect it – which was untrue. (Some of the £2000 was diverted to the Irish Parliamentary Party by him but returned to the IRB after Yeats made representations to John Redmond.) Millevoye commented that she might at last realise that the Irish revolutionists were only a set of *farceurs*. The upshot was that she resigned from the IRB (as did Yeats), unwilling to waste time on 'an organisation which had successfully prevented Ireland making England's difficulty an opportunity'.

H. W. Nevinson, who greatly admired Yeats's work, had met

Maud in 1899 and realised 'her longing was for action in place of all theorising talk'. As though by some prophetic insight, he foresaw the kind of marriage she would make – 'the first man of resolute action whom she meets will have her at his mercy'. A year after Nevinson wrote this, there arrived in Paris, fresh from fighting the British forces in South Africa, Major John MacBride, of the Irish Brigade (which was about to be disbanded). He was met at the Gare du Nord by his friend Griffith and introduced to Maud Gonne, who was accompanied by Stephen McKenna and other members of the Paris Young Ireland Society. Obviously MacBride could not return to Ireland, so Maud and Griffith arranged an American lecture tour for him. Finding lecturing – which meant reading the script they had prepared for him – difficult, he asked Maud to join him there. She did so, and their joint appearances during the spring of 1901 were successful. In America he proposed to her, to be refused on the grounds that marriage was not in her thoughts while there was a war on.

Maud returned from America, saw Iseult (and gave her an alligator) at a convent in Laval where she had placed her, and went to London to visit Kathleen, who was seriously ill. Then in London again for her cousin May's wedding, she refused in the usual way yet another proposal from Willie for a more than mystic marriage. The poem that emerged from his first seeing her after her arrival in her sister's house, 'Adam's Curse', records a conversation there and refers to an inability to maintain the 'old high way of love'. Next day they paid a customary visit to Westminster Abbey to see the Lia Fáil, the Stone of Destiny. Yeats spoke of the four jewels brought by the Tuatha Dé Danann to Ireland, and their counterparts in the Grail legends, the symbols on the tarot cards and, in debased form, on playing cards; Maud contemplated the stone being brought to Ireland in triumph, ceremony and rejoicing.

In Ireland Maud now had a house in Dublin, in Coulson Avenue, and from there she travelled to Cork, Limerick and Ballina to establish branches of Inghínidhe na hÉireann. The Dublin group organised *tableaux vivants* and patriotic plays; its amateur actresses were coached by William and Frank Fay, and Maud told Willie that she would act Cathleen if he gave the Fay brothers his *Cathleen ni Houlihan* to produce. The electrifying effect of Maud's performance in April 1902 is well known. Ireland's Joan of Arc, the Woman of the Sídhe, now became Cathleen, a personification of Ireland. While Maud thought Willie's insistence upon refined literary standards less important than the popular emotive appeal he achieved in *Cathleen ni Houlihan*, he wondered whether the speeches at her Patriotic Children's Treat and the effect of *Cathleen ni Houlihan* would lead to the use of guns and bombs, although, ironically, his subsequent, more esoteric use of the Cúchulain myth was no less influential in its effect upon those who became leaders of the 1916 Rising.

The wheel had apparently completed a circle. In 1889, wanting to impress her by demonstrating that he had a very public talent, Willie had promised to write a play, *The Countess Cathleen*, for Maud, but she had refused to act in it; now, however, she had given public life to *Cathleen ni Houlihan*, a more politically effective drama, one that seemed a shared literary and political gesture made publicly by both of them. Then he had spoken much to her of his spiritual philosophy; now they were sharing visions, and her clairvoyant capacities were engaged in the co-operative creation of a Celtic Order of Mysteries. In 1891, when he first proposed to her, she had told him she could never marry; but now they were linked in a mystic marriage.

To make such comments is merely to reflect Yeats's reactions. Though he spoke freely of his spiritual marriage, it surprised others; H. W. Nevinson, for instance, described it as 'atrocious'. Yet a poem recording that his well-belovèd's hair had threads of grey still praised Maud's nobleness, and repeated a friend's comment that all he needed was patience. The friend was probably Lady Gregory, who when she first met Maud Gonne in 1898 had asked what her intentions were in regard to Willie, to be told that she and Willie had more important things to think about than marriage. The spiritual marriage, however, with all its physical strains and frustration, seems to have settled into habit on his part. It had suited the poetic strains of defeatism, the melancholia, the *fin de siècle* languor and the sheer weariness of many of the poems that appeared in *The Wind Among the Reeds* (1899). 'The Autumn of the Body', originally and significantly entitled 'The Autumn of the Flesh', an essay of 1898, had put Yeats's generalised view that man had 'wooed and won the world' and 'fallen weary . . . with a weariness that will not end until the last autumn'; poetry would result from 'an ever more arduous search for an almost disembodied ecstasy'. By 1902, however, he had found in Nietzsche sanction for a shifting away from what he considered his own Dionysiac phase to an Apollonian one; he no longer was in sympathy with 'The Autumn of the Body'. Like Yeats's earlier poetry, the Dionysiac enthusiasm of the Greeks had been 'sad and desirous'; the Apollonian was 'joyful and self-sufficient'.

He had need of self-sufficiency when he heard with surprise and shock that Maud was becoming a Catholic and intended to marry John MacBride, and his attitude was spelled out plainly and painfully (see letter WBY 3). MacBride's family and friends were opposed to a marriage; so were hers. Even her dead father, Maud thought, had said to her as she finished packing and tidying up a now empty apartment, 'Lambkin, don't do it. You must not get married.' Her sister suggested she would be happier with Willie but was told that, though she loved him dearly as a friend, she 'could not for one moment imagine marrying him'.

Maud's marriage on 21 February 1903 shattered Yeats; poems record how he gave his heart and lost, how he grew to be out of fashion, how dear words meant nothing. The pungent final phrase of four unpublished lines may have been founded upon Tennyson's 'Locksley Hall', where Locksley rebukes Amy for marrying another:

> As the husband is, the wife is; thou art mated with a clown,
> And the grossness of his nature will have weight to drag thee down.

Yeats's lines, however, record Maud's reactions to his pleas to her not to marry MacBride (his letter, WBY 3, expresses his fear that she intends to place her soul in a lower order of faith, to thrust herself down socially). They indicate her anger at him as well as his own rage at MacBride's presumption in marrying Maud, his own goddess, to whom he regarded himself as bound not only by the love expressed in his poetic devotion to her but by their spiritual marriage:

> My dear is angry that of late
> I cry all base blood down
> As if she had not taught me hate
> By kisses to a clown.

He sought consolation in an affair with Florence Farr, brief because she got bored, and later in a revival of his close friendship with the forgiving Olivia Shakespear. Maud spent the first part of her honeymoon in Spain; a plan for MacBride to assassinate Edward VII, who was to visit Gibraltar, fell through, probably because of MacBride's excessive drinking, which was to be one of the main causes of the alienation between husband and wife. Because of his activities in Africa he could not accompany her to Ireland, where in the summer of 1903 she organised what became known as the Battle of the Rotunda, which eventually resulted in Dublin Corporation refusing to welcome the King on his visit to Ireland. There followed the less violent 'Battle of Coulson Avenue', when, ostensibly in mourning for the death of Pope Leo VIII, Maud flew a black petticoat from a broom handle among the neighbouring Union Jacks celebrating the King's visit. Her walking out of the first-night performance of Synge's *In the Shadow of the Glen* led to the dissolution of the Irish National Theatre, of which she had been a director, and was on political grounds – she was doubtful that an Irish play was national if Irish people neither understood nor liked it. She supported the Cumann na nGaedheal Theatre Company, later thinking Yeats lost to nationalism when the Abbey Theatre, financed by Miss Horniman, at her behest provided no sixpenny seats.

In France she had used a legacy to buy Les Mouettes, an ugly house at Colleville in Normandy, with a garden running down to the sea. Her son Jean Seagan (later known as Seán) was born on 26 January 1904, but that year her marriage broke up and she filed for divorce on 25 February 1905 on the grounds of MacBride's debauchery, adultery and other matters. 'Dix faits' were cited: 'scènes précises de débauches, d'adultère et d'attentat aux moeurs et même de tentative de viol'. Drunkenness was an element: 'il apparait que cette ivresse devait conduire MacBride aux pires immoralités.' Yeats was deeply distressed and unloaded some of his anxieties on to Lady Gregory, observing that if Maud 'were the uttermost stranger, or one's bitterest enemy, one would have, even to the putting aside of all else, to help her'. Maud's letters in 1905 and 1906 deal mainly with the problems and strains of the divorce proceedings. After she was granted a separation (not a divorce because of legal complications about MacBride's domicile), she returned to Dublin in October 1906, and was hissed in the Abbey Theatre when she and Yeats attended the opening night of Lady Gregory's *The Gaol Gate*.

Because of the divorce and the unwelcome publicity stirred up partly by MacBride's friends, political activity in Ireland seemed impossible for Maud at the time. She did not, however, blame the people generally for this state of affairs in a letter of May 1907, but 'the frauds who I had exposed, the publicans & drunkards I had driven out, the cowards who I had made own their cowardice'; they had joined MacBride's party and were whispering calumny. But neither in Yeats's case (she was alluding to the row over the *Playboy* in January 1907) nor in her own should he or she grow indignant with the crowd. Yeats used her comments in this letter in 'The People', a poem written in 1915 and first published in 1916 which puts his complaint about 'the daily spite of this unmannerly town' and her reproof; she had never 'now nor any time,/Complained of the people'.

Maud did not want to bring Seán back to Ireland in case MacBride laid claim to him, so she lived in France – in summer at Colleville, in winter in Paris – where she studied, illustrated books and exhibited and sold paintings. Some of her letters in 1907 show a wish to return to the kind of friendship she and Willie had shared in the period of the mystic marriage. Maud appreciated his continuing concern for her; and, just as she had earlier argued that active political life did not suit his nature and could prevent his effectiveness as an author, now she frequently expressed her regret that the Abbey Theatre made such inroads upon his energy, and her anxiety that the theatre was consuming time that he should devote to his own writing. She asked if he remembered a particular vision and if he still had the book in which he used to note such things, reminded him of the beauty of Howth, told him she could see visions again. Willie sent her incense (which resulted mainly in drowsiness, though she did hear voices when using it); he arranged for her horoscope to be cast by J. R. Wallace. Their relationship was becoming closer again.

Maud had more visions about Willie in the spring of 1908. At that time he began an affair, predominantly physical, with Mabel Dickinson, a well-connected masseuse. In June he went to visit Maud in Paris, writing to Mabel from there to say that when he was in Paris ten years before he had wanted a twilight of religious mystery in everyone's eyes and would probably not have liked her then; but now he was tired by the modern mystery of Rossetti's romantic women and liked 'clear light, strong bodies' such as Mabel's. Maud, however, suggested that they renew the mystic marriage: it must have seemed more viable to him now that his sexual desire was being satisfied by Mabel. After he left, Maud wrote to tell him a most wonderful thing had happened – 'the most wonderful I have met in life. If we are only strong enough to hold the doors open I think we shall obtain knowledge and life we have never dreamed of.' Yeats noted, in the white calf-bound manuscript book Maud had given him for recording their astral unions and visions, that he had 'made evocation' on the 'night of 25th' and sought union with her. Her letter of 26 July told him of her having seen an Egyptian-like form floating over her, dressed in moth-like garments and with gold-edged wings, which she thought was herself, a body in which she could go out into the astral. She put on this body and desired to go to him. They went somewhere in space, he in the form of a serpent, and they kissed and melted into each other till they formed '*one being, a being greater than ourselves* who felt all & knew all with double intensity'. She had this experience three times, each time being brought back by a noise in the house. Afterwards she went to bed and dreamed they discussed this spiritual vision. In the dream he said it would increase physical desire, which she said 'troubles me a little – for there was nothing physical in that union – material union is but a pale shadow compared to it'.

Yeats made another visit to Paris in December 1908 and worked on *The Player Queen* there. Though he had begun a poem in the summer of 1908 with an accurate report – 'All things can tempt me from this craft of verse' – in December he seemed to have found a new genre of love poetry, looking back with an intense yet detached mood at the past. 'No Second Troy' is the supreme example, with its lofty rhetoric and perception of Maud as a Homeric character. The renewal of the mystic marriage was later expressed in the general title under which he grouped the first eight poems of *The Green Helmet*, 'Raymond Lully and his Wife Pernella' ('Raymond Lully' being altered to 'Nicholas Flamel' in an erratum slip after Maud had queried it).

It seems likely that they did sleep together, a view supported by Mrs Yeats in conversation with me (see also Richard Ellmann, *Golden Codgers* (1973), p. 108). This probably happened in December 1908. There is a change in the tone of Maud's letters at this point; after a letter of 5 October addressing him as 'Dear Willie', her next letter begins 'Dearest' and continues in a way that suggests a change in their relationship:

It was hard leaving you yesterday. . . . Life is so good when we are together. . . . dear one. . . . It is hard being away from each other so much there are moments when I . . . long to be with you . . . beloved I am glad & proud beyond measure of your love. . . . I have prayed so hard to have all earthly desire taken from my love for you & dearest, loving you as I do, I have prayed . . . that the bodily desire is gone. . . . Write to me soon.

The words 'earthly desire' suggest an apparent alteration in her attitude to Yeats. 'Bodily desire' had not seemed to affect her before; nor had there been 'a terrible struggle' to pray that such desire be taken from her love for him. Whatever happened between her and Yeats in December 1908 remains obscure. The tone of her letter implies that they have reached a new intimacy, a spiritual closeness. However, although the language of endearment she employs for the first time in this letter suggests that the lovers have been sexually united, the letter's message emphasises the spiritual. Certainly she seems to have been affected by physical desire in some way; but she is none the less rejecting all thoughts of any sexual union with him in the future. This can perhaps be explained as being a perception on her part that spiritual union with her would seem more significant to Yeats than any physical – or spiritual – congress he might subsequently have with any other woman, and that their love could now continue without the intrusion of sex (she wrote that the struggle was over and she had found peace: 'I think today I could let you marry another without losing it – for I know the spiritual union between us will outlive this life, even if we never see each other in this world again'). Sex with him had perhaps confirmed her lack of enthusiasm for its actuality, once their desires had been satisfied, however unsatisfactorily. (Does the strange phrase put in the mouth of 'The first of all the tribe' in 'His Memories' of 1926–7, 'Strike me if I shriek', indicate this?)

On 13 January 1909 she wrote, apropos of one of Yeats's dreams, asserting that Raphael 'bowed down to sex till it killed him when he was only 30', that Michelangelo 'denied the power of sex *for a year*' when painting the Sistine Chapel, that Leonardo probably held 'always the balance and centre in himself' and that Gustave Moreau 'cared little for love or that side of life'. Eight days later, Yeats wrote in a journal that they were divided by her religious ideas, by her Catholicism:

she will not divorce her husband and marry because of her church. Since she said this, she has not been further from me but is always very near. She too seems to love more than of old. In addition to this the old dread of physical love has awakened in her.

This dread has probably spoiled all her life, checking natural and instinctive selection, and leaving fantastic duties free to take its place. It is what philosophy is to me, a daily rooter out of instinct and guiding joy – and all the while she grows nobler under the touch of sorrow and denial. What end will it all have? I fear for her and for myself. She has all myself. I was never more deeply in love, but my desires must go elsewhere if I would escape their poison. I am in constant terror of some entanglement parting us, and all the while I know that she made me and I her. She is my innocence and I her wisdom. Of old she was a phoenix and I feared her, but now she is my child more than my sweetheart.

The increase in intimacy indicated in Maud's letter of December 1908 did, however, continue in some subsequent letters. She addresses Willie as 'Dearest' and 'Dearest Friend', reverts once to 'My dear Willie' when he hasn't written, then uses 'Dearest', 'Dear Friend' and 'My dear Friend', before the letter of 27 May 1909, which begins 'Beloved'. That letter may be a final firm renunciation of sex, perhaps in response to renewed requests on his part. She tells him her decision that sexual union was not desirable had not been made

without struggle & without suffering though once that decision come to, in answer to my prayers, the suffering & the struggle ceased in a way I surely do not deserve. Beloved I will pray with my whole strength that suffering & temptation may be taken from you as they have from me & that we may gain spiritual union stronger than earthly union could ever be.

She wondered if she would ever bring him happiness and peace to compensate for the suffering she had caused him: 'I pray to God that by holding our love pure it may be so.' She blamed herself 'for the forgetfulness of that spiritual marriage long ago, which if we had obeyed would have saved us both from the long weariness of separation'. The letter ends with an explanation of her marriage to MacBride, saying she had earned all the crushing sorrow that came on her: 'My loved one I belong to you more in this renunciation than if I came to you in sin. Did you not say yourself that our love must be holy?' The emotional intensity of her regard for him is rarely if ever so strongly expressed again.

For Yeats, 1909 had not been an easy year. He had had some kind of breakdown in January; in February Lady Gregory had nearly died, and Synge died in March; in August John Quinn quarrelled with him over indiscreet remarks made by the poet to and about John Quinn's mistress Dorothy Coates (it was a quarrel that Maud tried to resolve); and Miss Horniman wanted the directors to buy her out of the Abbey, which meant raising money.

By November 1909 Maud was thinking that there had been some barrier between them at the end of the summer and told him:

It is hard to be so much apart & yet perhaps it is better for both of us until we grow very strong – When I know things are going well with you I am fairly content, but when I know you are sad, the temptation to write to you to come to me, or to go to you is terrible – Yet Willie I know we are doing the right thing. The love whose physical realisation we deny here will unite us in another life – If we did the easy thing and yielded to it now, very likely it would *part us here* & after.

She reflected on the short time they had had to see each other in Dublin, thought he was right in saying that they had never been nearer, praised his love – 'so wonderful, so pure, so unselfish' – and went on to say, 'Dearest in Art, in life in everything the easy thing is never the interesting thing. Only those who make an effort to surpass themselves are interesting.' She attributed the charm of his poetry to 'the terrible though unseen effort of its creation'.

As usual, Maud was driving herself hard. Having worked with the Paris relief committee to alleviate the effects of the disastrous floods of early 1910, she turned her attention to the needs of poor children in Dublin who did not get school meals. After a holiday in the west she set up a pilot scheme, a canteen in St Audeon's parish, and was in Ireland again in 1911. In 1912 she presided over a meeting in the Mansion House which recommended that Dublin Corporation should finance the feeding of the children. She was back in 1913 helping to feed poor children suffering from the effects of the Lockout. Her letters at times convey frustration: she has not been able to do much occult work; she has been unable to remember the work she dreamed that Willie and she were engaged upon. She thinks her work will not remain because she has been possessed by demons of hate, while what has been written for her will live.

Yeats's life was changing. The death in September 1910 of his uncle George Pollexfen marked the end of Yeats's close family connection with Sligo; that year he gave up managing the Abbey and was granted a Civil List pension. Though he stayed with Maud in Colleville in May 1910, they were becoming less close – her letters show some signs of their drifting apart. She complained in February 1911 that it was ages since she had heard from him: 'Where are you? Are you in love? I think there must be something very interesting which keeps you from writing to me for so long. I hope you are not going to get married!'

In May 1911 he came to Paris when she was in Italy. She continued to resent his commitment to theatre management and wrote perspicaciously to him when he was on a brief visit to America with the Abbey players:

Our children were your poems of which I was the Father sowing the unrest & storm which made them possible & you the mother who brought them forth in suffering & in the highest beauty & our children had wings –

You & Lady Gregory have a child also the theatre company & Lady Gregory is the Father who hold[s] you to your duty of motherhood in true marriage style. That child requires much feeding & looking after. I am sometimes jealous for my children.

In August 1912 Yeats again stayed at Colleville, but in the ensuing months he missed a number of opportunities to meet her. Maud was seriously ill in February 1913, and there is a sad note in a letter she wrote in April:

Now that you do so little occult work I never know at a distance as I used to what you are thinking or what will interest or bore you – You did not even know when I was almost dying, & for three days nearly unconscious & when I wrote to you the words didn't convey anything to you. I think you were astonished yourself they did not.

It is not I think that you had ceased to like me but because a mood you were in wrapped you round completely.

You were perhaps trying to write a poem that was hard to find.

In a letter in May she wrote, perhaps not altogether teasingly, that she would like to see his rooms in Woburn Buildings, because she was sure he must have made them beautiful:

for you have the art of making beauty, but you are thinking dangerously much about a wife, think how she would disarrange your things! Matrimony I think requires great space either a castle & vast rooms or a cottage where one only enters to sleep & all the wide world outside.

Mabel Dickinson may have thought of marriage to Yeats, but their affair ended with a stormy meeting in June 1913 at the Victoria and Albert Museum. Mabel had sent him a telegram when he was at Coole to say she was pregnant. It turned out that she wasn't, but he was deeply upset, and a letter to Maud records how he had been given 'a piece of false information' that had 'an overwhelming effect on him'. Though he told her that his 'period of trouble' was over – he had thought, apparently erroneously, that he was being trapped into marriage – he went on to deny her view, expressed in an earlier letter to him, that physical love was the one thing he required of a woman. His gloom, he explained, was due to loneliness. Florence Farr was in Ceylon; he had quarrelled with Annie Horniman; his eyesight prevented his reading or going to the theatre; he found dining out upset his nerves. He remarked gloomily that 'a mistress cannot give one a home, and a home I shall never have'. This is the dark mood expressed in the 'Introductory Rhymes' to *Responsibilities*, probably written in 1913. In this poem he sees his 'barren passion' for Maud as the reason why, close to forty-nine, he has no child to carry on the Yeats and Pollexfen lines. Lady Gregory obviously thought his age no hindrance to marriage – had she not married, at twenty-seven, a man thirty years older than herself? – and thought that Yeats should marry now. She introduced him to various attractive and well-to-do young women.

Two years before, in May 1911, he had met Georgie Hyde Lees. Her mother, Nelly, had recently married Olivia Shakespear's brother Harry Tucker, and Yeats met Georgie in Olivia's house. He started to visit the Tuckers for one or two weeks at a time, and Nelly Tucker began to fear that he might propose to Georgie (who told a cousin of hers as a secret that she planned to marry the poet). Georgie was a friend of Olivia's daughter Dorothy, who was to marry Ezra Pound (whom Yeats also met through Olivia). Olivia too thought that Willie should marry. He seems neither to have told Maud about Mabel Dickinson, judging by Maud's friendly reference to her in a letter written to him in November 1913 (see letter 283), nor to have indicated his growing friendship with Georgie Hyde Lees, who attended seances with him – 'a very flirtatious business' – and whom he was to sponsor as a member of the Golden Dawn in 1914.

Yeats's interest in spiritualism brought him in touch with Everard Feilding, with whom he and Maud visited Mirebeau in May 1914 to investigate an apparent miracle of a bleeding oleograph. *Responsibilities* (1914) – though mainly a collection of angry disillusioned poems, political, sceptical, sardonic – contains poems about Maud: 'Fallen Majesty' (of 1912) praises her by recording 'What's gone'; 'Friends' (1911) observes that it is impossible to praise her, 'Remembering what she had / What eagle look still shows'; 'That the Night Come' (c. 1912) describes her living 'in storm and strife'; while 'The Grey Rock' (before 1913) relates how she

> *when her blood ran wild,*
> *Had ravelled her own story out,*
> *And said, 'In two or in three years*
> *I needs must marry some poor lout,'*
> *And having said it, burst in tears.*

'A Memory of Youth' (of 1912) records an occasion on which, despite his praise of her and her pleasure in it, they sat 'as silent as a stone':

> We knew, though she'd not said a word,
> That even the best of love must die,
> And had been savagely undone

> Were it not that Love upon the cry
> Of a most ridiculous little bird
> Tore from the clouds his marvellous moon.

In 1915 came more exalted tributes to her (possibly because his memory had been ranging over the past when he began writing his autobiographies at the end of 1914) in 'Her Praise', 'His Phoenix', 'A Thought from Propertius', 'Broken Dreams', 'A Deep-Sworn Love' and 'Presences'. 'Vague memories,' he wrote, 'nothing but memories', as he went over the past in these poems about her, which were published in *The Wild Swans at Coole* (1919).

Yeats was, however, obviously thinking of marriage in 1915. Georgie Hyde Lees seems to have thought he proposed to her in November 1915, and she was certainly in love with him then, but exigencies of her war work may have caused the matter to be put aside.

'A Song', a poem of 1915, had the refrain '*O Who could have foretold / That the heart grows old?*' Yeats was beginning to think adversely of his age. This may have been because he was conscious of Maud's daughter Iseult's attractiveness. In 1910 she had suggested their marrying, but apart from her being only fifteen he thought there was too much Mars in her horoscope. His attitude to her was somewhat fatherly at first. He had written poems to her, 'To a Child Dancing in the Wind' and 'Two Years Later' (December 1912 or 1913), and now in 1915 came 'To a Young Girl' in which he knows what makes her 'heart beat so', linking her to a memory of Maud's wild thought

> That she denies
> And has forgot,
> Set all her blood astir
> And glittered in her eyes.

In 'Presences' (November 1915) Iseult, however, is a child 'That never looked upon man with desire'.

The Easter Rising took place in Dublin in April 1916, and John MacBride was shot as one of its leaders. Maud first wrote to Willie that MacBride had died for Ireland, and then that by his death he had left Seán a name to be proud of. She sent Iseult to stay with her cousin May in London, and Yeats introduced the young girl to many of his friends. As he told Lady Gregory, she looked very distinguished and self-possessed; he felt sad because if his life had been normal he might have had a daughter of her age. 'That means, I suppose,' he added, 'that I am beginning to get old.' He went to France with Iseult in June, and then at Colleville, on 1 July, proposed again to Maud. She refused him in the usual words. It was almost as if they were by now enacting a well-established ritual. Maud was surprised when a week later he asked her whether she would object if he proposed to Iseult; she replied that Iseult would not take him seriously. The effect on him of Iseult's youth was to accentuate his awareness of his age, as 'Men improve with the Years', a poem of July 1916, indicates:

> O would that we had met
> When I had my burning youth!
> But I grow old among dreams,
> A weather-worn, marble triton
> Among the streams.

Lady Gregory was in favour of his marrying Iseult; but Yeats, writing from Colleville to Coole in August, stated: 'as father, but as father only, I have been a great success.' Iseult enjoyed the summer flirtation with Willie, while Maud fretted at not being able to get permission to return to Ireland.

Maud thought the Easter Rising had brought tragic dignity to Ireland. Yeats recorded his more complex attitudes in 'Easter 1916', a poem begun in May in London, read to Maud on the seashore at Colleville and finished in September. In it he alluded to the bitter wrong MacBride had done to 'some that are near my heart' and he saw Maud's single-mindedness as a stone troubling a stream. This, ironically, was the image she had used earlier of her own heart when she realised her relationship with Millevoye was over. She wrote to Willie in November criticising 'Easter 1916' as unworthy of him (he had probably sent her a revised copy of the poem, later privately printed in a limited edition of twenty-five copies). Thinking he might be angry that she was writing so frankly, she said, 'but I am always frank with my friends & though our ideals are wide apart we are still friends.' He doesn't seem to have replied to this letter; a month later she was asking why he had not written.

Yeats was working hard on the essays of *Per Amica Silentia Lunae* (the prologue was addressed to Iseult) and a play, *The Dreaming of the Bones*, in which a revolutionary of 1916, on the run, refuses to forgive the ghosts of Dermot and Dervorgilla for being the cause of the Anglo-Normans coming to Ireland in 1189. While he was busy with this work, he was excited at the prospect of buying Ballylee Castle, a medieval building near Coole, once owned by the Norman-descended de Burgo family; he acquired it for £35 in April 1917. During this time it is likely that he was also pondering the problems of marriage. A poem written in July 1916, 'The Collar Bone of a Hare', had expressed a desire to laugh at the 'old bitter world where they marry in churches', but in March 1917 he discussed marriage with Georgie Hyde Lees. Her mother, feeling a little unkind at her long neglect of him (she had not considered him free to propose to Georgie in 1915), had invited him to visit her, believing there was no longer any question of his marrying her daughter. Olivia Shakespear thought he should, since it would keep him within her circle of friends and relatives. However, Yeats went to France again in August and again proposed to Iseult, though he wrote to Lady Gregory that he didn't think she'd accept. It is possible that 'The Living Beauty', written in 1917, reflects some of his frustration:

> O heart, we are old;
> The living beauty is for younger men;
> We cannot pay its tribute of wild tears.

He found Maud no longer bitter; he went for long walks with Iseult, who had 'always been something like a daughter'. His relationship with Iseult in some ways echoed his early brotherly attitude to Maud, in that at times he seems to have devised defensive, masochistic barriers to prevent over-closeness in the case of both mother and daughter, so that he was less upset than he might have been. Maud was now in 'a joyous and self-forgetting condition of political hate'. He accompanied the family to England and gave Iseult an ultimatum: she must give him an answer in a week's time; if she did not marry him there was someone who would. Iseult said no, and he was, he wrote to Lady Gregory, on 19 September, 'rather in a whirlpool', but had decided to go to Mrs Tucker's and ask Georgie to marry him: 'Perhaps she is tired of the idea. I shall however make it clear that I will still be friend and guardian to Iseult.'

Iseult and Maud found his marriage plans decidedly prosaic. Arthur Symons (who adored Iseult) reported Maud as laughing at it: 'a good woman of 25 – rich of course – who has to look after him; she might either become his slave or run away from him after a certain length of time.' Yeats married Georgie on 20 October 1917, and for the first few days he was in a state of misery. 'The Lover Speaks', a poem written four days after his marriage, presents a somewhat mythologised version of his summer courting of Iseult in Normandy:

> But O! my Heart could bear no more when the upland caught the wind;
> I ran, I ran, from my love's side because my Heart went mad.

'The Heart Replies', written three days later, discusses both Iseult and his wife:

> I did not find in any cage the woman at my side
> O but her heart would break to learn my thoughts are far away.
>
>   . . . who cares,
> Now that your tongue cannot persuade the child till she mistake
> Her childish gratitude for love and match your fifty years?
> O let her choose a young man now and all for his wild sake.

His young wife's automatic writing saved the day, or rather the marriage. She had first attempted this to distract him from his unhappiness, and he grew excited when she wrote down that all was well 'with the bird' (Iseult). In the ensuing sessions of automatic writing Yeats asked questions about his relationships with Maud, Olivia, Mabel, Iseult and his wife – now called George. The answers communicated through George, often elliptical, often plainly commonsensical, lessened his feelings of guilt. His play, *The Only Jealousy of Emer*, used Irish mythology to deal with issues raised in his own life – the goddess Fand (Maud), the wife Emer (George Yeats), and the mistress Eithne Inguba (Iseult) all affecting Cuchulain (Yeats) emotionally. George became friendly with Iseult, who stayed with the Yeatses at Christmas 1917.

Willie and George Yeats went to Ireland in spring 1918 and busied themselves with Ballylee Castle, where Maud – who had disguised herself and defied the ban on her going to Ireland – visited them in February. When the Yeatses were out of London, Maud and her family (who had first stayed at 265 King's Road, Chelsea, on their arrival from France in 1917) lived at 18 Woburn Buildings (where Ezra Pound, 'a wild young man' no doubt, seduced Iseult), but Maud wished to establish her home in Ireland and bought 73 St Stephen's Green in Dublin. In May she was arrested in Dublin, and saw from the police van the fourteen-year-old Seán vainly running after it. She was deported to Holloway Gaol, where she was confined in the VD wing until protests were made about this. Her letter of 14 June to Willie describes her captivity. Her health deteriorated, and Willie wrote to influential friends about her condition. In September he and George left Galway for Dublin so that their child could be born there; furnished accommodation couldn't be found, so they rented 73 St Stephen's Green from Maud. A Harley Street specialist's report finally led to Maud's being sent to a nursing home. After five days, Seán had noticed that the CID did not shadow the nursing home between 7 and 8 am, so she went in early November to Woburn Buildings; Iseult and Seán were there. Maud wrote to Willie asking him to try to get her permission to return to Dublin with her children, but she went to the home of 'a rich Englishman whose housekeeper was an Irishwoman and disguised herself as the woman's grandmother', then crossed to Dublin and went to St Stephen's Green. Worried about George, who had had pneumonia and was seven months pregnant, Yeats – without consulting George – refused to let her in, fearing the effect on his wife's health of possible police or military raids. A violent quarrel ensued; Maud accused him of cowardice and lack of patriotic feeling, but friendship was soon restored. The Yeatses found various lodgings in Dublin, and by Christmas Maud and her family had returned to 73 St Stephen's

Green where Yeats was soon attending Maud's 'at homes'. He had continued to be anxious about Iseult after his marriage, and 'Two Songs of a Fool', written between July and September 1918, capture the sense of responsibility he felt for her. While his wife is a 'speckled cat', Iseult is a 'tame hare'; both look up to him for 'learning and defence', but he fears that

> The hare may run till it's found
> The horn's sweet note and the tooth of the hound.

By October he had written 'To a Young Beauty', rebuking Iseult for keeping bohemian company:

> Dear fellow-artist, why so free
> With every sort of company,
> With every Jack and Jill?

Concern for his infant daughter, Anne Butler Yeats, who was born in Dublin in February 1919, led to 'A Prayer for my Daughter', written between her birth and the following June. The poem praises his wife's 'glad kindness' but contemplates how fine women – Helen and the goddess Aphrodite – were (like Maud) not good at choosing men. He sees the destructive force of hatred, particularly intellectual hatred, and contemplates Maud, 'the loveliest woman born', who because of her opinionated mind has bartered the Horn of Plenty 'For an old bellows full of angry wind'. He prays that his daughter may escape the arrogance and hatred 'Peddled in the thoroughfares'. This is a wish perhaps caused by his unease at Iseult's bohemian friendships as well as by his dislike of the increasing bitterness of Irish nationalism.

The Yeatses spent the summer at Ballylee, the winter at Oxford. Then followed an American lecture tour until May 1920. This meant that Yeats did not see much of Maud and Iseult, but when he and George returned from America Maud wrote him letter after letter about Iseult, who had just married Francis Stuart.

The previous November Yeats had suggested that Iseult should marry Lennox Robinson, who was in love with her. She, however, then twenty-five, was attracted by the seventeen-year-old Francis Stuart, and married him in April 1920. After spending some time in London, the couple moved to 'the last house in the valley' at Glenmalure, a remote part of County Wicklow. Their relationship was stormy, full of unresolved quarrels. Maud, not unnaturally extremely worried about the situation (and the fact that Stuart's father had 'died in a lunatic asylum and his mother's father died of drink'), sent Willie a telegram and he came to Ireland in August to help. His letters to his wife record this period as 'a rambling empty life'; he felt lost without her; there was 'no order in the day' or peace in his thought. However, while he and Maud were 'very good friends now', he admired Iseult's 'subtle thought' but had no contact with her mind. She was in a Dublin nursing home; in a letter to Dr Solomons, the gynaecologist, Yeats drew up a seven-point plan for creating 'a situation calculated to impress the conscience of Francis Stuart' and characterised as 'pure drama'. There was an irredeemable antipathy between Maud and Francis Stuart, but in July Maud realised that Iseult, who was pregnant, did not want to break with her husband. In October Yeats stayed with Maud and Iseult at Glenmalure and was not to meet Stuart until 1923.

By then the treaty between Great Britain and Ireland had been signed and the Irish Free State established. Maud's son Seán, a member of the Fianna, the republican organisation for boys set up by Countess Markiewicz, had joined the IRA (probably late in 1918), but Maud did not learn this until 1920, and then accidentally. Maud and Seán became opposed to the treaty (though Seán had gone to the negotiations as Michael Collins's aide-de-camp). Initially it had seemed an improvement on the pre-war Home Rule Bill (which Yeats and Maud had thought acceptable) and Maud had first regarded it as a stepping stone to total freedom. Seán MacBride, however, was violently opposed to the treaty. When the civil war broke out he was taken prisoner by Free State government forces on the surrender of the Four Courts in June 1922. (Francis Stuart was to be interned in August.) One half of a peace delegation, a group of women organised by Maud, went with the Lord Mayor to the government, which was headed by her friend Arthur Griffith, and the other half went to the republican forces to propose a ceasefire. Their plan failed, and Maud's previous relatively neutral attitude to the treaty gave way to an angry and continuous dislike of the Free State government. It was no longer run by Griffith, who died in August, nor by Collins, killed in an ambush ten days later, but by William Cosgrave, Richard Mulcahy and Kevin O'Higgins, with none of whom she had any rapport, since she disliked their ruthless suppression of republican opposition.

When Free State soldiers raided her house in St Stephen's Green, Dublin, she told me – in answer to an enquiry about whether she had kept Yeats's very many letters to her – that the great loss was that most of her papers were burnt in the street and among them her letters from him. Very few indeed have survived, those before 1923 having been among papers that somehow escaped the search and subsequent burning by the troops because she had kept them particularly carefully.

Always distressed by the fate of those incarcerated – an instinctive feeling reinforced by her own experience of imprisonment – Maud was appalled by the new Irish government's treatment of prisoners, and became secretary of the Women's Prisoners' Defence League, an organisation banned early in 1923. She was herself imprisoned in Mountjoy Gaol, but released next morning.

Yeats had heard of her arrest in January 1923 and offered 'to help with the authorities in the matter of warm blankets'. He told Olivia Shakespear that she had written the day before her arrest to say that if he did not denounce the government she would renounce his society for ever. He feared that his help in the matter of blankets, 'instead of her release (where I could do nothing), will not make her less resentful. She had to choose (perhaps all women must) between broomstick and distaff and she has chosen the broomstick.' The previous December he had become a senator of the Irish Free State, something Maud did not forgive him. She was arrested again on 10 April; she had been organising support for the women prisoners who were hunger-striking. She went on hunger-strike herself while her friend Charlotte Despard sat outside Kilmainham Gaol for the twenty days Maud was inside. Yeats wrote to Cosgrave, now President, and reminded him Maud was fifty-seven and could not be 'expected to stand the strain as a younger woman'. Cosgrave had no sympathy with women who took to politics, but it would have been decidedly impolitic to allow the group of prominent women arrested in April to die. Maud left prison in an ambulance. When Yeats came to see Francis Stuart at Roebuck House, Maud's house in Clonskeagh a few miles south of Dublin, to tell him he had been awarded a prize for his poems, *We have Kept the Faith*, by the Royal Irish Academy in August 1924, he thought it unwise to meet Maud. She had attended Sunday meetings in O'Connell Street for five years, first to 'prevent the civil war and when that failed for the political prisoners. As Redmond told Asquith years ago, about the Treason Felony prisoners & my campaign for them, you might tell the Staters today – "The only way to stop the meetings is to release the prisoners." '

Yeats had been deeply disappointed when Maud walked out of Synge's *In the Shadow of the Glen* in 1903; in 1926 O'Casey's *The Plough and the Stars* met angry demonstrations in the Abbey – it was regarded by extreme republicans as a vilification of those who had been involved in the 1916 Rising. Yeats, having called in the police, told the audience it had disgraced itself again: 'Is this to be an ever-recurring celebration of Irish genius? Synge first and then O'Casey.' This time Maud sat through the performance in silence, but later joined Hannah Skeffington in a public debate with O'Casey on the play at the Universities' Republican Club. Maud's reactions to the plays of Synge and O'Casey may well have been caused by the same attitude of mind that shaped her view of Joyce: she had a distaste for the element of vulgarity, the bawdy tone, and the portrayal of mean or contemptible characters, particularly by Irish writers.

Her relationship with Yeats was similarly coloured by such

basically political (as well as aesthetic and moral) views, the more so when Kevin O'Higgins was murdered in July 1927, for on 24 August Seán MacBride was arrested, among others, and charged with the killing. He had an alibi but was then held under the Public Safety Act. Maud wrote several outraged letters to Willie about Seán's situation (and Yeats tried unsuccessfully to get him released temporarily). She blended into her denunciations of the Free State authorities her philosophical views, founded on St John, and her description of her instinctive nationalism. These comments were partly in reply to Yeats's letters explaining his attitude: 'One does not vote for "treason bills" and the like out of hatred of anyone,' he said, 'but because one believes they are necessary to protect many harmless people against anxiety, danger, poverty & perhaps death.' Somewhat detachedly he told her he had not answered one of her letters because 'we will never change each other's politics. They are too deeply rooted in our characters.'

The gulf between them widened. Yeats realised, writing to Maud from Algeciras in November 1927, that they had been arguing the same old problem ever since they were in their mid-twenties, and reminded her that she had told him in 1909 or 1910 that she had taken part in movements which had hate for their motive power. He greatly disliked Mrs Despard, who had shared in the purchase of Roebuck House; her bitterness seemed to him destructive, and so he did not visit Maud there. In any case they had too deep a difference in their political views, her republicanism diametrically opposed to his conservatism and his support of the Free State government.

In 1928, thanking Yeats for sending her *The Tower*, Maud remarked on his hatred of old age, saying that she did so too, but pointing out that she, who was more 'a rebel against man' than he, rebelled less against nature and accepted the inevitable. He was to describe her as 'almost the sole surviving friend of his early manhood, protesting in sybilline old age, as once in youth and beauty, against what seems to her a tyranny'.

The tyranny of time intensified Yeats's memories and perceptions of Maud. His poem sequence *A Man Young and Old*, written between 1926 and 1927, records 'the wild regrets for youth and love of an old man'. The final stanza of the sixth poem makes its strange allusion, through the Helen image he associated with her, to their brief sexual union:

> The first of all the tribe lay there
> And did such pleasure take –
> She who had brought great Hector down
> And put all Troy to wreck –
> That she cried into this ear,
> 'Strike me if I shriek.'

'Quarrel in Old Age' (November 1931) recalls Maud's rage at what he thought some 'Fantasy or incident / Not worth thinking of' – Mrs Yeats thought the poem probably reflects an argument over the treatment of women prisoners. Here he reverts to the old imagery of her as goddess:

> Somewhere beyond the curtain
> Of distorting days
> Lives that lovely thing
> That shone before these eyes
> Targeted, trod like Spring.

There were occasional moments of contact – more of them after he had resigned from the Senate in 1928. When she decided to sell her copy of the three-volume Blake that he and Edwin Ellis had edited, he signed it so as to enhance its value; when she was writing her autobiography, he told her she could say anything she liked about him and quote his poems. Even to the end, the insecure young man seeking to impress her was within the successful poet and man of the world. Did she realise when in 1933 he asked her to meet him in the Kildare Street Club, the stronghold of the Anglo-Irish aristocracy, that his having become a member was an enormous achievement? Did she realise the immense pleasure it must have given him in the mid-1930s to invite her to lunch with him at Jammet's, the most expensive restaurant in Dublin? Did she realise in his penultimate letter to her, in June 1938, the pride of telling her that he was still attractive to women, was staying with a friend, someone 'once the best-paid woman journalist in the world', and was then going on to stay with Lady Dorothy Wellesley? And did he realise that she would not have realised how much such things meant to him? Or, if she had, that she wouldn't have thought them worthy of consideration?

What did matter to them both now was that, sometimes in different ways, the other remembered things they once had shared. These memories still had pulsating power. Some of them, as in 'Long-Legged Fly', were simply appreciative of the child-like qualities he loved in her:

> She thinks, part woman, three parts a child,
> That nobody looks; her feet
> Practise a tinker shuffle
> Picked up on a street.
> *Like a long-legged fly upon the stream*
> *Her mind moves upon silence.*

In other late poems, however, he remembered her vulnerability. 'The Circus Animals' Desertion' refers to his writing *The Countess Cathleen*, when

> I thought my dear must her own soul destroy,
> So did fanaticism and hatred enslave it.

'A Bronze Head', inspired by a bronze-painted plaster cast of Maud in the Municipal Gallery in Dublin, contemplates her complex nature. Although she was 'a most gentle woman', he had seen the wildness in her soul, shattered by a vision of the terror that it must live through, and he too

> had grown wild
> And wandered murmuring everywhere, 'My child, my child!'

He ends this poem, however, by recording that he had thought her supernatural, harking back to his first vision of her in 1889 as resembling a goddess. When over seventy, he remembers, in 'Beautiful Lofty Things', clearly and with an exalted, dignified simplicity, how he had seen her at twenty-six:

> Maud Gonne at Howth station waiting a train,
> Pallas Athene in that straight back and arrogant head.

In 1938, when he was seventy-three and she seventy-two, in response to a warm invitation she went to see him at Riversdale, a small old house, leased in 1932, at the foot of the Dublin mountains outside Rathfarnham. When she arrived he was able to rise from his armchair only with great effort, and said to her: 'Maud, we should have gone on with our Castle of the Heroes, we might still do it.' She was so surprised he had remembered that she could not reply. It was their last meeting.

Shining Days
1893–1899

Though you are in your shining days,
Voices among the crowd
And new friends busy with your praise,
Be not unkind or proud,
But think about old friends the most:
Time's bitter flood will rise,
Your beauty perish and be lost
For all eyes but these eyes.

W. B. Yeats, 'The Lover Pleads with his
Friend for Old Friends' (first published July 1897)

 *1893*

Only a few letters are available as early as 1893, including one from Yeats in January and a couple shortly after from Maud Gonne, in connection with the new Irish libraries' scheme in which they were involved with Count Plunkett, C. H. Oldham and others. Maud was not able to fulfil all the engagements made for her as she was ill in Paris in January, but in February she lectured in Loughrea and New Ross. Her first letter also indicates their common interest in mysticism and visions.

WBY 1 (fragment)   [London]
[January 1893]

My dear 'Scotia'[1]

I am trying to arrange the following set of lectures for you and am writing to all the places except Omagh which Plunkett undertakes and Cork for which a certain John O'Mahony[2] will be responsible. The[re] will I think be no difficulty as we have been already applied to by all the places mentioned. At Cork between 20 & 27th of January, at Westport (Co Mayo) between 27th & 2nd Feb at Castlerea (Roscommon) between 4th & 8th of Feb, Loughrea between 12th & 15th Feb. There is a meeting in Dublin on 17th February at which we hope you will speak & report progress. You

will then go to New Ross & lecture between 20th Feb & Feb 25 &
then go on to Listowel &
[End of letter missing]

1   66 Avenue de la Grande Armée
                                 Paris
                                 Tuesday [January or February 1893]

My dear Mr Yeats
     I have sent the cheque for £10 to Count Plunket[1] 26 Upper
Fitzwilliam St as you told me £5 collected, £5 from myself.
     I have also written to Mr Oldham[2] to ask him to give books to
any one sent by the library society to fetch them. I have asked Count
Plunkett that the £10 should be exclusively spent in buying books.
The money I collected was given me for that purpose & I am in a
certain measure responsible for it –
     I hope Library accounts are going to be kept separate from general
accounts of the Society.[3]
     I have lecture engagements in France all through March.[4] I am
much better but still very weak & have not been out of the house
yet – I will let you know as soon as I can the date when I will be in
Ireland.
     I am so glad the work is going on so well.
     Thank you so much for paper with the accounts of Blake[5] it must
be very interesting I am so happy that it is such a success.
     I have amused myself painting one or two of my visions which I
will show you when we meet, the painting is extremely rough &
bad but somehow it gives the idea. I have painted the grey woman[6]
in the dancing glory of life. I sent you an article which I wrote
in bed on Amnesty[7] which was produced in the form of an interview.
     Thank you so much for going on with the library work. I am so
much interested in it & feel so wretched to think how little I am able
to do towards it – You are working very hard.
     With very kind regards
     I remain dear Mr Yeats
     Very sincerely your friend
          Maud Gonne

Undated fragment   [1893]

if you have any articles about it will you send it to me. If you care
about the foreign press I can speak of your work in a revue which is
very well known La Société Nouvelle[1] which is published in Brussels
& for which I am asked to write some articles on Ireland.

I read the criticism of your work in United Ireland[2] with great interest.

2   56 Rue de la Tour
                                           Passy
                                           Paris
                                           13th [?October 1893]

Dear Mr Yeats

I am not very well & have had to give up the meeting in Limerick as the *journey* would be too tiring as I must be with my sister[1] in London 20th of this month. I shall therefore stay quietly in Paris till 20th when I come to my sister's 10 Park Street. I fear you will not be in London then, but if not I hope to see you in Dublin.

Tell Miss Horniman[2] I shall be in London from the 20th to the 29th & will be delighted to meet her.

I have lots more things very interesting about my grey woman but I have not time to write it to-day.

I have decided not to accept the journalistic proposition of which I spoke to you.[3] It would tie my hands too much, as you know, I appreciate *Liberty* before all things.

If you are not in London perhaps Mrs Emery[4] would kindly examine me for my 3°–8°[5]

With kind regards

Dear Mr Yeats I remain

very sincerely yours

Maud Gonne

Thank you for the poem but I must ask you most earnestly not to publish it.

It may have been the birth of her sister Kathleen's son Tommy on 30th October 1893 that brought Maud Gonne to London for the 20th, as a similar event did at a later date. The house in Park Street belonged to Cook relatives, and their Great-Aunt Augusta, Mrs Tarlton, lived there.

She is also referring to a stage in her initiation into the Hermetic Order of the Golden Dawn in which Yeats had interested her and of which Annie Horniman and Florence Farr were members.

—— *1895* ——

Around November 1893 Maud Gonne conceived her second child by Millevoye. Yeats visited Paris in February 1894 and wrote of her in his Memoirs: *'She had not left France for a long time now and was, I was told, ill again. I saw her, and our relations, which were friendly enough, had not our old intimacy.' He noted that she 'mounted the stairs slowly and with difficulty' and that she 'had not gone on with her work in the Order, and was soon to withdraw altogether.' However, they went to see the symbolic play* Axel, *which had a profound effect on his work. The only personal details of this period come from Yeats's* Memoirs *recounting what he learned years later. Presuming that she was still very unhappy and with George Russell's words on reincarnation spoken two years previously still in her mind, he notes: 'The idea came to her that the lost child might be reborn, and she had gone back to Millevoye, in the vault under the memorial chapel' in Samois. He also says that she told him she had lived apart from Millevoye since the birth of her daughter Iseult on 6 August 1894. In April 1895 she moved into an apartment at 7 Avenue d'Eylau.*

It was from early October 1895, when Yeats left the family home at Blenheim Road and moved into rooms with Arthur Symons at Fountain Court in the Temple, that the bulk of her letters to him have survived. One of his reasons for moving from home was probably that he was contemplating an affair with Mrs Olivia Shakespear, whom he had met the year before. He was honest about it in his Memoirs, *writing: 'if I could not get the woman I loved, it would be a comfort even but for a little while to devote myself to another.' Maud Gonne had a strong intuitive feeling about this relationship.*

3

Maples Hotel
Kildare Street
Dublin
3rd Nov [1895]

My dear Mr Yeats

Have you been having any occult work or visions in which I have been in any way mixed within the last week?

I have a particular reason for asking this which I will tell you another time.[1]

I have been here in Dublin for a fortnight & shall very likely be in London for a day or two in about a week, if so I hope I shall have the pleasure of seeing you.

I have been reading your new book of poems[2] & like them even better than I did the first time I read them. They are so wild and fasinatingly Irish.

I have met your friend Mr Hughes the Sculptor[3] & like him very much he has real genius.

I hope you are well, & that your eyes are stronger[4]

Always

Very sincerely your friend

    Maud Gonne

4
                                      Maples Hotel
                                      Kildare Street
                                      Dublin
                                      [November 1895]

Dear Mr Yeats

Your letter has just arrived as I was writing to you *again*, to ask if all was well with you, or if you were doing any occult work into which I came, for yesterday I again had the most curious occult interview with you.

When I wrote to you before I had only a *vague*, but very *persistent* feeling that I was connected with some work you were doing. The feeling was so strong & persistent that I wrote to you, but it was all rather vaguely defined.

Yesterday evening however somewhere about 9 o'clock I was sitting in the drawing room of this hotel with several persons when suddenly I became conscious that you were there, standing near a table on which your book which I had been reading lay. Those in the room knew nothing of occultism & would not have understood. So mentally I gave you rendezvous for midnight when I knew they would be gone & said when sleep had set my soul free I would go with you where you liked.

At a little before 12 I got into half-waking half-sleeping state then I saw you again and together we went down to the cliffs at Howth, but the sea birds were all asleep & it was dark & so cold, & the wind blew so horribly.

I came back & quite woke up, but I knew you were still not far off. I then sent myself to sleep by IMAGINING I am taking chloroform[1] or some strong narcotic which is a way I often send myself to sleep when I want to get free from my body. Before me I saw the prithiti [Prithivi] & Akasa tatura [tatwas] meeting the teiyus [Tejas] tatura[2] then I can remember no more distinctly only floating in the air but I know I got free. I do not know what we talked about the second time, but today I had several new ideas, as to the direction of my work which may have been the result though I can't remember.

I will tell you more of this when we meet. Please *burn* this letter at once as it sounds slightly mad. If you understand it at all write and tell me. I will be here till Monday when I go to *Belfast Central Hotel*[3] then I shall be in London on the 13th, Charing Cross Hotel. You might come and dine with me at 7.30 if you are disengaged.

I shall very likely be going to Irish National League[4] about 10 o'clock but that is not certain.

In haste
I remain
Very sincerely yours
        Maud Gonne

Yeats was expecting Mrs Shakespear and a friend to tea. They had previously decided to postpone living together 'until her mother, a very old woman, had died', as he wrote in his Memoirs. *Coming home with a cake for the tea he started 'to think of Maud Gonne till my thought was interrupted by my finding the door locked, I had forgotten the key'. That night he talked to Symons of his love for her for half the night. 'A couple of days later I got a wild letter from Maud Gonne, who was in Dublin. Was I ill? Had some accident happened? On a day that was, I found, the day I had those guests and lost the key, I had walked into the room in her hotel where she was sitting with friends. At first she thought I was really there, but presently on finding that no one else saw me knew that it was my ghost. She told me to return at twelve that night and I vanished. At twelve I had stood, dressed in some strange, priest-like costume, at her bedside and brought her soul away, and we wandered round the cliffs [of] Howth where we had been together years before. I remember one phrase very clearly, "It was very sad, and all the seagulls were asleep." All my old love had returned and began to struggle with the new.'*

For Maud to feel that Howth was cold and dark, and the seagulls asleep, shows how strong her intuition was about his distancing himself from her – in contrast to the warmth of his feeling when they had walked around the cliffs that day in August 1891 after he had proposed to her when she had been ill. A few days later he had written his poem 'The White Birds' to her:

*Soon far from the rose and the lily and fret of the flames would we be,
Were we only white birds, my beloved, buoyed out on the foam of the sea.*

Her letters encourage him to let nothing interfere with his literary work. With her being in London in November, his distress must have increased, but his relationship with Mrs Shakespear continued.

5
Charing Cross Hotel
London
One o'clock morning
14th Nov 1895

My dear Mr Yeats

I was very glad to see you, but very sorry to see that you were still troubled & worried.

All I would say is go on with the great work you are doing for Ireland by raising our literature. For the honour of our country, the world must recognise you one of the Great Poets of the century.

Be true to yourself & let nothing interfere with your literary work. That is surely your first duty. Do not let your life be *tied* down by other lesser ones.

With that pure & noble ambition before you things will seem simpler & duties less puzzling.

I remain
Dear Mr Yeats
Very Sincerely your friend
    Maud Gonne

6
Charing Cross Hotel
London
Thursday morning [15 November 1895]

Dear Mr Yeats

I have read the Chronicle article[1] (which I return) with the greatest interest. It is far far the best criticism or rather statement of your work which has appeared yet.

Mr Johnston[2] can write of your work, because he has seen and recognized the Divine and Eternal Rose[3] which so many are incapable of discovering in this world where they are drearily groping.

I have opened the letter I wrote last night to add this one & on re-reading it I fear it seems like uncalled for advice (which is a thing I have in horror!) Last night when I wrote it, it did not seem like that. I thought you were *hesitating* about *writing* me of the trouble about which you said it would perhaps not be right to tell me & I seemed to answer your unspoken unwritten communication.

I feel inclined almost to tear this letter & not send it, only 1st impulses are generally the right ones & it may be that it is an example of materialised form [?of mine] astral message or conversation. Anyhow I send it & I know you understand these things too well to misunderstand me or to be vexed.

I am returning to France Saturday my address there is 7 Avenue d'Eylau
Very sincerely yours
    Maud Gonne

On an envelope to W. B. Yeats Esqre, Fountain Court, Temple, London, is a postscript written across the address.

The housemaid has tidied away Miss Gile's[4] address so I can't go & see her, I am so sorry please send me her address I will write to her I also don't know your exact address so send this to be forwarded to you from Blenheim Rd.

7
                                      7 Avenue d'Eylau
                                      Paris
                                      Christmas [1895]

My dear Mr Yeats
    I am sending you a copy of the Magazine International which has just been started by some young literary men who are friends of mine here. I think it is going to be a success it has for object as you will see to make known foreign literature in France & to be a sort of International Art Centre.

    I thought perhaps you might like to have one or two of your poems given & a short sketch of your work & the Literary movement in Ireland.

    I have spoken of you a great deal to Mr Bazalgette & Mr Ackerman, the editors, they will be very happy to publish anything I send them about your work.

    If you like it let me know & say also what poems or extracts you would prefer to have given.

    Thank you very much for your letters & the papers. I hardly think the war with America will come just yet:[1] I *wish* it would, I had a dream a short while ago which I did not like at all, but I never trust dreams. I feel the Anglo-Saxon race is such a fearfully strong force. If the fight comes with America it means the breaking of this force into two which may well be the destruction of England for with the American side will be the Celtic & many other forces.

    I would like to do some occultism with you. We should I believe get some very interesting things. Next week I shall be working a little at occultism and will let you know if I have anything which will interest you only unfortunately I have forgotten so much. Lately, I have been taken up by outside things that I have not been able to do much.

I am having my portrait painted[2] it promises rather well The middle & the end of Jany I shall be very busy lecturing.

The Irish Literary Society London Sec Graves[3] have sent me a most rude letter because my subscription was unpaid – threatening to post my name up in their rooms for a year – the threat amuses me greatly – I have never been to their rooms since the once I went with you three years ago. I have always paid my subscription & I don't know how I forgot this year. I am sending it to them, but I leave their Society as I am not used to receiving impertinent letters also I really don't care to belong to a Society who lectures in favour of Oliver Cromwell.

New Year
I was interrupted & put my letter on one side, & only take it up again to-day to wish you a very happy & fortunate New Year.
  With very kind regards
  I remain
  Very sincerely your friend
    Maud Gonne

Tell me what is the best and shortest account of the new literary movement in Ireland

—— 1896 ——

8
7 Avenue d'Eylau
Paris
14th Jany [1896]

My dear Mr Yeats
  a few words in great haste to thank you for your letter, which I received safely but *no papers*.

There is a short account of you in the Bookman[1] which I have.

I saw Messrs Bazalgette and Ackerman (the editors of the *Magazine International*) & hear from them that they are in correspondence with Mr Davidson[2] & that he has offered to write an article on your work. I am sure he will do it far better than I can, so I told them to let him do it.

I have begun my lectures & am very busy.[3] I think Miss Horniman is probably right in her idea that the great crisis will not come for another year or two yet.

Your idea of working in France is very good for an Irish Poet it

would not be good to live always in London.
I must end now as I have no more time.
Very sincerely your friend
Maud Gonne

9   7 Avenue d'Eylau
                                                          Paris
                                                          14 Feby [1896]
My dear Mr Yeats
The Editor of the Magazine International came to see me yesterday
to ask me after all to do the article on Irish literature & on your work
– there was some mistake about Davidson. I have begun & hope I
shall be able to make something interesting with the help of the
newspaper cuttings you have sent me but I am not much use as a
writer. However I will do my best.
Your poems are very difficult to translate it is hard to give in
French their weird mystic fascination & of course one loses the
musical charm & melody of the verses which is so characteristic of
your poems.
I am scribbling in great haste. I will send you the article when it
appears.
I am so glad to hear you are getting on so splendidly.
Ever
Your very Sincere friend
Maud Gonne

Addressed to Fountain Court, Temple, London, Angleterre.
Postmark: Place Victor Hugo 14 Fevr 96.

10   7 Avenue d'Eylau
                                                          Paris
                                                          [February or early March 1896]
My dear Mr Yeats
Will you send me as soon as you can one or two little biographical
notes for the article on your work in the Magazine International as
soon as you can. Date & place of your birth, a little about your
childhood & at what age you wrote & at what age you published
your first poems & anything else you like to give us.
I may be in London about the 10th March & if so hope to see you.
I remain in great haste
Very sincerely your friend
Maud Gonne

11   7 Avenue d'Eylau
                                                   Paris
                                                   21 March [1896]

My dear Mr Yeats

One little word in great haste to send you the address of the Mathers cousins.[1]

I saw the Mathers at the St Patrick's banquet.[2] I said you would probably be writing to him about organising lectures but I had no opportunity for more than a few words on the subject.

Keep to the idea of *lectures*[3] & nothing else. You were very clever to think of this way of finding out the truth.

I am starting for another lecture tour in a day or so.

In gt haste very sincerely
      yours Maud Gonne

12   Norfolk Hotel
                                                   Harrington Road
                                                   opposite South Kensington Station
                                                   [London]
                                                   Friday [March or April 1896]

My dear Mr Yeats

Many thanks for your letter which followed me here [?where] I arrived Wednesday.

I would like so much to see you but I fear I shall not have time this visit to London as every hour of my time is taken up & I have to leave London tomorrow to be at an amnesty meeting in Glasgow on Sunday.

I think article on your poetry will appear in Magazine International this month but I am very angry and disappointed about it. I had written a long article on your work naming your principal works etc but all my French articles require considerable corrections & as I was leaving Paris, I gave it to Mlle de Ste Croix[1] & Mr Ackerman one of the Editors of the review with permission to correct & alter if necessary.

They sent me the proofs on my return to Paris which were almost unrecognisable, they had cut out more than half & all the best parts of it leaving only a short biographical notice of you. I was very angry but it was too late to change, however to make up they promised to give a good many translations from your works which perhaps is the more useful thing after all. It will appear this month & will be sent to you at once. It is far from what I had hoped & would not have happened like this if I had been in Paris.

Your idea is very good about meeting with the highlanders &

discussing things with them without any way engaging ourselves with them.

I shall see Dr Ryan[2] this morning. I am so sorry not to see you. If you have time by any chance can you come & breakfast with me to-morrow at 9 o'clock? it is an unholy uncivilised hour to propose it but it is the *only* moment I have.

From Glasgow I go to Belfast[3] & then to Dublin Maples Hotel where I shall be on and off for the next month.

With kindest regards
Dear Mr Yeats
I remain
Very Sincerely Yours
    Maud Gonne

13
                               Maples Hotel
                               Kildare Street
                               Dublin
                               May 23rd [1896]

Dear Mr Yeats

there is an interesting piece of news going about Dublin, taken I believe from some London papers, & that is, that you have lately married a widow!

At first I thought this could not be as having seen you in London I thought we were sufficiently friends for you to have told me, but on reflection this is absurd as marriage after all is only a little detail in life (a foolish one generally I think, as one would have to spend so much energy & time in loosening a chain one had forged) So it is quite possible you are married & didn't think it important enough to talk to me about.

Well if you are, I won't congratulate you, or even condole, as I hope it will make no difference in your life or work or character.

I am just starting for the west of Ireland I shall be wandering about different places every day!

I shall be in London I think 1st or 2nd of June until the 6th so if you can arrange for me to meet the friends you spoke of in London I shall be very glad. I will let you know later where I will be staying.

I shall be in Dublin at this address on the 28th of May.

Always
Very sincerely your friend
    Maud Gonne

On 26 May Yeats said in a letter to John O'Leary: 'I hear that there is a rumour in Dublin that I have recently married a widow. I am charmed and longing for particulars.' In 1899 to his sister Lily he wrote: 'I have a namesake who gets married and votes and does all kinds of embarrassing things. I forget how many letters of congratulation I had when the unnecessary man got married.'

Kathleen's husband, David Pilcher, was Deputy Assistant Adjutant-General of the Dublin District, with offices in Dublin Castle. The family lived at 14 Ely Place during this time. Toby, the eldest child, was ill with typhoid fever, and Kathleen's youngest child, Pat, was due. Yeats passed through Dublin with Arthur Symons on his way to the west, where he stayed with Edward Martyn at Tillyra Castle and afterwards briefly with Lady Gregory at Coole Park for the first time.

14
14 Ely Place
Dublin
Saturday Aug 15th [1896]

My dear Mr Yeats

I got your letter just before leaving France it was most interesting. I am staying with my sister for a month she is not well.[1]

If you are passing through Dublin soon let me know & come & see me. I should be glad to meet Mr Symons[2] again if he is still in Ireland. What an interesting time you must be having in the West. I envy you & would like very much to join you. I *ought* to go to Westport & Castlebar lecturing this month, but I don't think I shall be able to leave my sister.

I hope to be in Paris the end of Oct & I shall be very glad to see you there. I wish Irishmen would come oftener to Paris. There is lots of interesting work to be done there. We want to have Ireland better known & her struggles for independence brought more prominently before the world.

I won't write more now as I hope to see you soon.

With kindest regards

I remain

Dear Mr Yeats

Very sincerely your friend

Maud Gonne

I went to Beyreuth[3] this year, it was wonderful!

15   14 Ely Place
                                                      Dublin
                                                      [late August 1896]

My dear Mr Yeats

Thank you so much for the nos of the Savoy. The articles on Blake
are most fascinating.[1] I read them to my sister who was very much
interested.

Did you get my letter?

Let me know when you are likely to be in Dublin. I should like
to have a talk with you – Madame Rowley[2] was in Dublin for three
days she left yesterday. She sent you the manuscripts of Miss
Delaney.[3] It is so kind of you taking trouble about them. Thank you
so much. It would be such a great thing for the girl if she could get
something published. I had a letter from her a few days ago she was
in gt despair but consoled by the idea of a vision she had a long while
ago which told her that this year she would succeed & some great
good would happen to her. She is getting very anxious and nervous
as the first half of the year has passed and nothing has come.

With kindest regards
Dear Mr Yeats
I remain
Very sincerely yours
    Maud Gonne

Madame Rowley's address is Tyrone Lodge Bundoran Co Donegal.

16   14 Ely Place
                                                      Dublin
                                                      [late August or September 1896]

My dear Mr Yeats

I was very interested in hearing of your work, and look forward
greatly to reading your wild dreamy stories.[1] I would like [so] much
to see you & have some long talks on many subjects, but I cannot
come to the west, or indeed leave Dublin at all just now on account
of my sister's health & I am sure you are right to stay in that beautiful
sad mysterious Western coast until your present work is finished.

I shall hope to see you in Paris in the winter, when your story[2]
takes you there.

I would have loved to have spent a week in Sligo while you were
there we would have tried if the fairies would have been good to us
& shown us some glimpses of that lovely world which we so seldom
see but that must be for some future time –

Of course I shall be glad to do anything for the *Young Ireland
Society* & will arrange a date for a lecture later on.

I have been doing a good deal of Amnesty work lately –

Thank you for taking so much trouble for Miss Delaney. If it does not bother you too much speak to anyone in London who you think might take her things. I know well what you mean about the difficulty in placing them. They are not artistic but the sensational weirdness of some of them might suit a certain class of not very cultivated people & it would be doing such a charity to the poor girl. She has written to me to know what you think of them, I must tell her some part of what you said.

I met Miss Mabel Gore Booth[3] one day at Miss Purser's[4] & thought her very beautiful & very charming.

With kindest regards

Dear Mr Yeats

Always your friend

    Maud Gonne

I could not read the *name* of the French review which you said has an article on your work.[5] Please send it.

1897

Before Christmas 1896 Yeats went to Paris. In April 1895, while visiting Douglas Hyde at Frenchpark, he had gone to Lough Key where he saw an uninhabited island called Castle Rock. He thought it was a place which could be made holy in the Celtic rites on which he and Maud Gonne had been working, 'which would unite the radical truths of Christianity to those of a more ancient world'. There people would go for spiritual inspiration and teaching, and to draw strength for their work of reuniting 'the perception of the spirit of the divine, with natural beauty' using Celtic symbols 'to bring again into imaginative life the old sacred places'. Maud Gonne felt that if they could 'make contact with the hidden forces of the land it would give us strength for the freeing of Ireland'. This, exemplified by their feeling for Howth, was one of the strongest links between them. They worked closely on ancient mythologies, particularly those of Ireland, enlisting the help of MacGregor Mathers, who had worked out the rituals for the Golden Dawn, all of which were germane to Yeats's novel The Speckled Bird. *It was for the purpose of this work that he went to Paris (which at that time was full of cults), and it is what the letters mainly refer to when they touch on visions and Celtic mythology.*

Yeats helped Maud Gonne to form a Paris Young Ireland Society among the Irish living there, such as Miss Delaney, who acted as its secretary, Stephen McKenna, Arthur Lynch and J. M. Synge, whom Yeats first met at this time. Synge was a member of the society for a while but according to Yeats he disapproved of the 'Fenian turn' Maud Gonne gave it, saying that 'England would only do Ireland right when she felt herself to be safe.'

For some time plans had been formulated for commemorating the United Irishmen and the rising of 1798 in order to revive the national spirit and to endeavour to bring some unity into political life. The Young Ireland League called a public meeting of nationalists in the City Hall, Dublin, on 4 March, to draw up plans. Even at that stage it was apparent that unity was going to be difficult to achieve, and the splits and subdivisions preoccupy much of the letters at this time.

Maud Gonne spoke at a Young Ireland Society meeting in Glasgow on 28 February and in Paris was busy preparing the issue of her little paper L'Irlande Libre, *which first appeared on 1 May 1897 as part of the build-up to the '98 centenary celebrations of the next year. She also busied herself with the Paris Young Ireland Society's plans for honouring General Hoche, who in 1796 had led one of the French expeditions to Ireland.*

In his Memoirs *Yeats wrote that he had thought: 'Perhaps if I allowed myself to be elected President of the English committee, I could keep the movement from dividing up into its elements. I was elected and found the task heavy. . . . Presently I formed a grandiose plan without considering the men I had to work with, exactly as if [I] were writing something in a story. . . . Why could we not turn this council into an Irish Parliament?'*

The following letters reveal the trouble caused by Charles MacCarthy Teeling, a bitter eccentric, formerly a vice-president of the Young Ireland Society from which he had been expelled for refusing to accept a decision of the chairman, John O'Leary, and for throwing a chair at him. Yeats, in a letter of 31 March, reminded O'Leary of Teeling's insolence to him, and remarked that Teeling had 'for years been slandering Miss Gonne in the most ignoble and infamous way'.

These slanders had made her out to be a spy. Jones, the Dublin police commissioner, in a report on this affair the following year, held that she was distrusted by Frank Hugh O'Donnell, John O'Leary and others, while Major Gosselin of the Home Office, in a memo to the under-secretary on this report, noted that he thought it was the 'exact opposite'.

17 [Paris]
[early March 1897]

My dear Mr Yeats

Many thanks for your letter. I am rather disappointed about the result of the meeting to arrange about 98 committee.[1]

From newspaper reports I thought it might have been possible to secure a fairly representative committee but of course one can't well judge at [a] distance. It looks so bad to have a split about honoring the United Irishmen's movement[2] that I should have been inclined to be very conciliatory, however if YOU did not succeed in this no one else would have been able, for you have so much tact and diplomacy in these matters.

I still hope you may succeed.

My journey to America has been put off till the Autumn[3] as everyone told me it was too late in the year to make a lecture tour a real success & owing to the difficulties this side I did not persist as by Sept I hope things in Ireland will be definitely and peaceably arranged. It is possible I may go to American *not* to lecture but merely to meet people in about a month's time. What do you think of the idea. Then I would go again in Sept to lecture. Of course I don't particularly care about the idea of a double journey but if necessary I will do it. First however I want to bring out our paper here. '*L'Irlande Libre*'[4] is to be the title.

Our Society[5] is doing very good work.

Who are the people who are attacking me in Dublin? I don't think they will be believed in America. Is it Teeling?[6] or others please tell me, also I would like to hear what they say. You know such things never trouble me at all.

I am so busy just now I don't quite know when I can come to London but will do so if really necessary to consult about committee but I hardly think it will be.

With kindest regards
dear Mr Yeats
Very sincerely yours
     Maud Gonne

18 7 Avenue d'Eylau
Paris
Wednesday [early March 1897]

My dear Mr Yeats

Thank you so much for your letter. I enclose article for United Ireland[1] let me know when it appears and send me a copy as I don't always see it. I am very busy with the paper '*L'Irlande Libre*'. For the 1st no Jean Richepin[2] has promised me an article, for the 2nd

Francois Coppée.[3] Redmond[4] and Davitt[5] have both promised articles. Party questions & quarrels are to be kept entirely out of the paper as being no concern for foreigners. I hope you will give us a short article some time though I hesitate to ask you knowing how busy you are.

I was much amused by the account you gave of the awful accusations & slanders brought against me. They are certainly not worth contradicting or bothering about. I will be in London for Easter, & hope to go to America the week after.

The Young Ireland Society here is a great success and doing very good work.

With kindest regards & hoping the friction of the Centenary committee will subside.

I remain
Very sincerely your friend,
    Maud Gonne

Tell me what you think of my article. The Independent also asked me for an interview which I have sent.

19   7 Avenue d'Eylau
                                                        Paris
                                                        Thursday [late March 1897]

My dear Mr Yeats
    The Secretary of the St Patrick's Association the Comte de Crémont[1] called on me yesterday to tell me of an incident which occurred before the St Patrick's Banquet.[2]

He was calling on Mr Némour Godré[2] one of the St Patrick's Committee the afternoon before the banquet there he found Mr Teeling, who told him he had been sent by the nationalists of Ireland to attend the St Patrick's banquet & there to denounce Miss Gonne as an adventuress & a spy who had no right what ever to speak in the name of Ireland. She being English the daughter of an English Colonel he went on to say that she was left very poor at her father's death, & had become the spy of the English government against the Irish, later she had come to Paris engaged by the German govt to spy on France.[3]

Crémont told him that if he dared to say one word against me at the banquet he would immediately as president for that evening declare the high esteem he had for Miss Gonne and have Mr Teeling put out by the servants. This must have cooled the valiant Mr Teeling's ardour for he came to the banquet & made a very good speech about England but did not dare to say one word of attack against me though as you will see from enclosed paragraph the principal orator of the evening Mr Albert Monniott[4] specially addressed his toast to me.

Crémont said that Teeling had been trying while in Paris to integrate himself with the members of the committee of the St Patrick's Association by posing as a very pious Catholic & disapproving loudly the action taken of the Young Ireland Society in placing a wreath on Hoche's statue because Hoche was a Republican![5]

This delighted some of the old legitimates like Nemour Godré.

Teeling wishes to have himself elected Correspondent d'honneur pour L'Irlande à la Société de St Patrice in place of Alderman Hall of Limerick who has just resigned.

Crémont does not want this of course he asked me if I could get any of the presidents of the nationalist committees or societies in Ireland to write to him telling him what position Teeling has in Ireland & if he is authorised to speak in the name of Irish Nationalists.

Would you, as president of a branch of the Young Ireland Society, write to Crémont & say that hearing there was some talk of Mr Teeling being elected to the St Patrick's Society you thought it well to mention that he had been expelled some years ago from the Young Ireland Society (I think it was you who told me he had been) If it bothers you in the least to do this perhaps the Secy of the Young Ireland Society might be able to do so. Will you see Dr Ryan about it & hear what he says. You can show him my letter, also to any one else you think fit.

It would be a pity if Teeling were named Correspondent d'honneur à la Société de St Patrice because though the St Patrick's Association has no weight in France now, people in Ireland do not know this & Teeling would be able to make capital for himself out of the fact.

Still it doesn't very much matter, & if it bothers you in the least don't take any trouble about the affair.

The person who of course would be best to write to Crémont would be Mr O'Leary[6] as he was actually president of the Society at the time Teeling was turned out of it & probably he knows more of Teeling than we do.

Last year when I heard Teeling's attacks against myself in Dublin I did not think that necessarily he was in the pay of the English Govt. I thought more probably that he was some narrow minded idiot who was scandalised at a woman leading an independent life & perhaps was jealous of me into the bargain never having himself succeeded in anything but now I begin to think worse of him than that. He evidently *lied* when he said he had been sent by the Nationalists of Ireland to denounce me as a spy of the English & German Govts & I would like some authorised person to write to the secretary of the

St Patrick's Association to say that Mr Teeling is certainly not authorised to speak for the nationalists of Ireland, and that he was turned out of their committee[s]

Perhaps I'm making too much of what really is very little consequence. The work here is going splendidly. Our paper will be a great success I have had 300 press notices about the Young Ireland Society here since it started without having taken any trouble which shows how popular the Irish Cause is in France.

Hoping to hear from you soon.

I remain

Very sincerely yours

    Maud Gonne

WBY 2   [March 1897]

Sir[1]

I have heard that a man called MacCarthy Tealing is a candidate for the post of Honorary Correspondent for Ireland of the Society of St Patrick & that he has stated he was deputed by the Nationalists of Ireland to denounce Miss Maud Gonne at the banquet of that society. I think it only right to inform you that Mr MacCarthy Tealing has the confidence of no body of Irishmen whatever & that he was expelled from the Young Ireland Society of Dublin some years ago for insolence towards its President Mr John O'Leary, a man greatly respected in Ireland and known, I believe, to your society. In conclusion I can only repeat that Mr MacCarthy Tealing is not a member of 'The Young Ireland Society of London' of which I am President, as it would give me much pleasure to preside at his unanimous expulsion. You are at liberty to show this letter to your committee.

I remain yours sncry

    W. B. Yeats

To the Hon Sec of the Society of St Patrick.

20   7 Avenue d'Eylau
                                                                        Paris
                                                                        28th March [1897]

Dear Mr Yeats

Thank you so much for at once taking so much trouble on my behalf – you are a true friend –

Yes I will be very glad if you will go & see Mr Redmond, you or Dr Ryan. It is an excellent idea.

I enclose a letter from M de Crémont. After seeing him the other day I wrote and asked him if he would kindly *write* what he had told me, as I wanted to send it to nationalists in Ireland.

Make what use of the letter you think fit, but I would like to have it back some time, it might be useful to me. Very few of the French papers mentioned Teeling's presence at the St Patrick's banquet one or two did however & said that he was representative of the Irish National Party. I sent these cuttings away but I will get others, as they are useful to prove that he gave himself out as representing the nationalist party.

I am writing in gt haste so please excuse more
Once again thanking you for all the trouble you are taking
I remain
Very sincerely your friend
 Maud Gonne

I had to write to Mr O'Leary yesterday about the paper so I mentioned the Teeling incident.

Did you get my article for United Ireland?

21   [Paris]
                [April 1897]

Dear Mr Yeats
 Miss Holmes[1] address is 4 Rue Juliette Lamber Paris.

Thank you so much for all the trouble you have taken about the Teeling affair. I got another letter this morning from the Comte de Crémont saying that he had put off the council meeting of the St Patrick Society so as to wait the letters from Ireland exposing Teeling's lies when he says he represents the Irish national Party. Crémont writes that Teeling visited several other members of the association before leaving Paris, among others Monsignor Lescailles[2] & repeated his slanders against me.

I sent this letter to Mr Harrington[3] whose name as former president of the National League is well know there & he had already written me a very nice letter & offered to write to Crémont if necessary.

I haven't received the Secret Rose[4] yet but no doubt it will arrive this evening.

Once again thanking you for all the trouble you have taken.
I remain very sincerely your friend
 Maud Gonne

I suppose I may put your name as one of our collaborators for Irlande Libre.

Harrington and Davitt, on opposite sides of the parliamentary divide at this time, both supported Maud Gonne in the Teeling affair, and she wrote in her autobiography: 'I was really touched by those generous letters of praise from Harrington and Michael Davitt for I had at that time openly opposed them on several occasions.'
  The following letter mentions Yeats's elaborate stories in The Secret Rose *which deal with an invented character founded partially on MacGregor Mathers and George Russell, called Michael Robartes, and his preoccupation with magic and mysticism. There is a reference to a dream drug. Both Maud Gonne and Yeats had taken hashish in Paris in 1894 to enhance their capacity for vision; later they experimented with mescal given to Yeats by Havelock Ellis.*

22   Grosvenor Hotel
                                                London
                                                Sunday [April or May 1897]

My dear Mr Yeats
    Thank you so much for your letters. I have been meaning to write very often lately, but have been so busy. I wanted often to write & tell you how much I love your book The Secret Rose, it is what I like best of all your work. I have it by my bed & I read a little every night. I have read it all through & go back & read some of it many times, especially Rosa Alchemica.[1] That is what I think I like the best. The language is so lovely, it is like some wonderful eastern jewel. One never tires of it – it must be heavenly to be able to express one's thoughts like that –
    Then, I wanted to write about the 98 affairs, but that we will talk of I hope, for I am coming to Ireland next week. My address in Dublin is *14 Ely Place*.
    I hear that you are going to be in Dublin for the 98 meeting 22nd June
    Then I wanted to write when I got your letter about Teeling & tell you how kind I think it of you to take so much interest in such a dull affair. The President of the St Patricks Assn has written another & this time a most crushing letter to the *Nation* & *United Ireland* which I hope will effectively terminate the affair.[2] Teeling is still in Paris. Perhaps he feels rather nervous about returning to Dublin where I hear some people probably make it rather unpleasant for him if he ventures into any of the national meetings.

Then I have to thank you for the dream drug[3] which I have not tried as yet being very busy & having need of all my energy & activity for the moment but I mean to try it soon.

I saw Dr Ryan yesterday. He told me you were again suffering from your eyes,[4] have you been working too much? or trying too much vision work? Do take care. Let me know how you are.

With kindest regards

Always your very sincere friend

Maud Gonne

23   14 Ely Place
                                                          Dublin
                                                          Sunday night [June 1897]

My dear Mr Yeats

I hope you will be in Dublin for the meeting on the 22nd we have fixed it for the 22nd as a protest against the Jubilee. Do come for it as you & I will be the only delegates from London & I must have someone to support me.

I think both the 2 committees here & in London are really anxious for united action for the 98 movement so our task will I hope be easy. Do come to Dublin for the meeting – it is necessary!

Hoping to see you soon. I will write no more to-day, as I am very busy getting the material for *Irlande Libre* off.

With very kind regards

I remain in haste

Very sincerely yours

Maud Gonne

Yeats had been staying with his uncle George Pollexfen in Sligo for a few months. The meeting of the 22nd was the '98 Convention meeting in the City Hall, Dublin. Maud Gonne was very busy in the days leading up to it, in preparation for the counter-demonstrations for Queen Victoria's Diamond Jubilee. As Wolfe Tone's anniversary on 20 June was the national day for the decoration of the patriot graves, she sent a wreath to Tone's grave in Bodenstown, County Kildare, and went herself to St Michan's Church in Dublin to lay a wreath on Robert Emmet's, only to find the gate barred and chained. The following evening at a socialist meeting organised by James Connolly she made her first public open-air speech in Dublin. She sent the crowd wild by asking in low tones that carried, 'Must the graves of our dead go undecorated because Victoria has her Jubilee?'

The first of her big public demonstrations was the next day, after the '98 Convention, when the delegates and a crowd went in procession – led by a mock funeral with a coffin with 'British Empire' written on it and the names of those hanged for treason written on black flags – to the National Club in Rutland (now Parnell) Square. There a magic lantern show was in progress showing the portraits of the '98 dead, with a large crowd already watching. In his Memoirs *Yeats says: 'Maud Gonne was walking with a joyous face; she had taken all those people into her heart.' The police reported that 'The Orange Hall and the National Club were alongside each other both full of the most ardent adherents of each party'; caught between the two crowds, they 'charged to clear the street'. The police charge angered the crowd and resulted in hundreds of injuries and the smashing of shop windows decorated for the Jubilee. Maud Gonne and Yeats were having tea in the club at this stage. Yeats wrote that, on hearing of the trouble, 'Maud Gonne got [up] and said she was going out and somebody else said she would be hurt. I told them to lock the door and keep her in. . . . I refused to let her out unless she explained what she meant to do.'*

24
[Letterhead]
The Grosvenor Hotel
Victoria Station
Belgravia
London S.W.
Wednesday [1897]

My dear Mr Yeats

Many thanks for your very charming letter. Yes we are friends, we will always remain so I hope. You have often been of great help to me when I was very unhappy.

Our friendship must indeed be strong for me not to hate you, for you made me do the most cowardly thing I have ever done in my life. It is quite absurd to say I should have reasoned & given explanations.

Do you ask a soldier for explanations on the battlefield of course it is only a very small thing a riot & a police charge but the same need for *immediate action* is there – there is no time to give explanations. I don't ask for obedience from others, I only am answerable for my own acts. I less than any others, would be capable of giving lengthy explanations of what I want and I intend to do, as my rule in life is to obey inspirations which come to me & which always guide me right.

For a long time, I had a feeling that I should not encourage you to mix yourself up in the *outer* side of politics & you know I have never asked you to do so. I see now that I was wrong in not obeying this feeling more completely & probably you were allowed to hinder me on that comparatively unimportant occasion to show me that it is necessary you should not mix in what is really not in your line of action. You have a higher work to do – With me it is different I was born to be in the midst of a crowd.

To return to the unfortunate event in Rutland Square everyone who remained in the club & did not go out to the rescue of the people who were batoned by the police ought to feel ashamed of themselves, owing to their action, or rather their *inaction*, that poor old woman Mrs Fitzsimon was taken to hospital on a car & allowed to fall from that car by a half-drunken, wholly mad policeman.[1] This would not have happened if I had been able to do my duty.

Do you know that to be a coward for those we love, is only a degree less bad than to be a coward for oneself. The latter I know well you are not, the former you know well you are.

It is therefore impossible for us ever to do any work together where there is likely to be excitement or physical danger & now let us never allude to this stupid subject again.

Your speech at the 98 Centenary convention[2] was quite the best I have ever heard you make, it was magnificent. You have done splendid work in this '98 movement. I trust that things will go on smoothly I believe they will. I havn't see Dr Ryan yet as I only arrived this morning. There is a meeting in the Arbitration Hall tonight.

I think I shall go to Paris tomorrow anyhow my address is 7 Avenue d'Eylau Paris & letters will always follow me from there.

With kindest regards dear Mr Yeats & hoping that you will [not] be very vexed or hurt at anything I have said in this letter

I remain
Very sincerely yours
Maud Gonne

Addressed to W.B. Yeats Esq, Tillyra Castle, Ardrahan, Co Galway, Ireland.
Postmark: Ardrahan Jy 3 97.

In his Memoirs *Yeats wrote: 'That night I went to all the newspaper offices and took responsibility for my action. My memory is that two hundred people were taken to hospital and that one old woman was killed.' At Maud Gonne's suggestion a defence fund for those arrested was set up.*

Yeats also remembered the 'meeting of the council [of the '98 Convention] at which she succeeded in winning so much support among our opponents – we had only a handful among the two

*hundred or three hundred delegates – . . . Passions had been very
high, those secret societies undermining all, and yet so gracious had
she been, her voice always low and sweet, that she was applauded by
friend and enemy alike.'*

*After speaking at a meeting in Glasgow on 2 July, tired and
suffering from rheumatism, Maud Gonne went with her cousin May
to Aix-les-Bains. At the casino she won more money than she needed
for the defence of the Jubilee prisoners and won 400 francs for an
impoverished French countess. She then went to her house at Samois,
a little village outside Paris.*

*Yeats went first to Edward Martyn at Tillyra Castle and then on
to make his first long stay with Lady Gregory at Coole. He had been
suffering ill health and eyestrain for some time as a result of the
tension of the '98 politics culminating in the Jubilee demonstrations,
his unrequited love for Maud Gonne, and loneliness at the end of his
affair with Olivia Shakespear, and he badly needed the quiet
restfulness of Coole. There, he said in his* Memoirs, *he found what he
had been seeking – 'a life of order and of labour, where all outward
things were the image of an inward life'. It was at Coole in
conversations with Lady Gregory and Edward Martyn that his dream
of an Irish Theatre began to become a practical reality.*

25
Samois[1]
Seine et Marne
24th July [1897]

My dear Mr Yeats

Thank you so much for your letter & the play[2] which I have read
with the greatest interest. I like it immensely & feel sure it will be a
great success. It makes me anxious to meet its author.

You will not be one little bit surprised however if I tell you at once
that nothing would induce me to act in it, or in any play whatever.

You would have been surprised on the contrary, had I accepted as
you must feel that it is not my role – It was very well when I was a
child – It was admirable in the days when I thought we were ruined
& that I would have to gain my independence of my family by work
but now that I have undertaken a great mission I have to act
accordingly & many of the small & in themselves quite harmless
things in my life I have to give up because they would be out of
harmony with the great end in view – one's life I think should be like
a picture, to be beautiful it must be harmonious. It is this aesthetic
sense of beauty & dignity in life which takes the place of morals with
me.

It is a theory which allows one to be very indulgent to others for
as there can be harmony in all colors so there can be beauty in all

lives – only they must be harmonious & you know as well as I do that it would be altogether wrong for Maud Gonne to act in a play in Dublin – even in a Celtic Drama.

That said – I most fully approve & sympathise with your plans, & will gladly give all the assistance in my power, apart from acting –

I believe the Celtic literary movement[3] is most important in fact, absolutely essential for the carrying out of our scheme for the liberation of Ireland.

I am not at all well & am going to Aix les Bains for a month. I start next Sunday my address will be Hotel Thermal Aix les Bains, Savoie. The doctor says I must keep quiet for a little & I have lots of work on hand for the paper & I hope in a few weeks' time I shall be quite well again & able to return to my active work.

With kindest regards
Dear Mr Yeats
alwys very sincerely your friend
Maud Gonne

How are your eyes? Do you take care of yourself.
I am returning manuscript.

26   Samois
                                                             Seine et Marne
                                                             [August 1897]

My dear Mr Yeats
Yes I have been waiting all this while to know just when I would be able to come to Ireland. I expect to start this next week. I MUST be in the west at Foxford[1] by the 17th as I am announced to speak at a tenants' meeting on that day. I am quite well again and have been home about a week. Aix les Bains did me a lot of good as far as health goes though the life there is so frivolous & mondaine that work is impossible & even one's thoughts begin to stagnate. I am making up for lost time now by working hard. I hope I shall meet you when I am in Ireland & we can have a long talk over all the things which interest us both so much.

Will you kindly send my subscription to Standish O'Grady for his new enterprise[2] it will be most interesting. On second thoughts I don't see why I should trouble you with this, so I will write him directly on the subject – You must have thought it strange of me not writing to you for so long, I can hardly explain it myself except at times it seems when I have no work on hand, my mind goes to sleep & I am capable of nothing until the inspiration comes again. I think it is what I told you. I am galvanised by the great spiritual forces of Ireland for a certain work, & when they, for any reason, withdraw from me I can do nothing – luckily these periods do not last long & when I come out of them it is with renewed energy & a clear vision of the special work to do –

Please give my kindest regards to Lady Gregory.[3]

Hoping to see you when I am in Ireland.

I remain

my dear friend Very sincerely yours,

    Maud Gonne

I leave Paris on the 12th I think & will be in Dublin Nassau Hotel on the 15th

With Maud's French contacts, her specific area in the commemoration plans was in the west, covering the ground followed by Humbert's army which landed at Killala, County Mayo, on 22 August 1798 and went to Ballina, won a battle at Castlebar, went through Foxford and Swinford, into Sligo at Tubercurry and Collooney and on to Lough Gill until they were halted and defeated at Ballinamuck on 8 September.

27   Paris

                                            Sunday [August 1897]

My dear Friend

I shall be in Dublin the 15th but will have to leave the 16th for Foxford & Ballina.

After my meeting the 17th it will be easier to fix a meeting as in Dublin I shall have very little time. Write to me Nassau Hotel Just starting for London.

In haste

Very sincerely your friend

    Maud Gonne

28   [Letterhead]

                                       L'Irlande Libre

                                     6 Rue des Martyrs, 6

                                     Paris

                                     6th Sept. 1897

My dear Mr Yeats

I have been meaning to write & thank you so much for your letter but I have been busy & lazy at the same time which is against letter writing, as I don't care for writing you a short hand note. Your vision is quite right, my letters are formal perhaps – as my manner is generally, but they are not unkind.

Your visions are very interesting. I don't know if the initiation you spoke of refers to me or not. Possibly it does though I am not conscious of any actual ceremony such as you describe but lately I seem to have made a step in advance on the spiritual plane. I seem now to be able to put my soul in communication with the souls of those great & strong heroes who lived only for their ideal & to whom the material things of life count for naught. I get strength therefrom to go on with my work.

At times I have a horror of all the little things & the materialities of life, they all take away from the concentration of one's will. One would be much stronger if one had no ties, no belongings, no possessions even. Every now & then I have a feeling that I should get rid of every thing & live as though I were quite poor. This idea grows stronger & stronger.

I had a talk with Jules Bois[1] the other day about your idea of reviving the Celtique mysticism[2] he thought it would be most important & assist the National movement in Ireland.

I am quite well again & ready for work. I shall be at the '98 Convention in Manchester[3] on the 3rd October & after spend a week in Ireland & probably go to America for a month or two.

Sometime, when you have time, if that time ever comes, will you give me an article for Irlande Libre. Something on the Celtique Renaissance would be very interesting & no one could do it as well as you, for it is you who have made it in the 1st part.

I hope your eyes are better. Where are you now? When are you coming to London or Dublin?

With kindest regards dear Mr Yeats

I remain always your friend,

   Maud Gonne

Thank you so much for the beautiful little poem. I am not the least inclined to forget old friends.[4]

29   Samois
                                          par Fontainbleau
                                          Seine et Marne
                                          22nd October[1] [1897]

My dear Friend

Thank you so much for your most interesting letter. I write a word now in gt haste to tell you that I will be at the Manchester Convention 3rd Oct & shall go from there to Dublin where I shall remain probably for something less than a week then I intend going to the west. I have several plans & I want to visit the worst parts of the congested districts[2] where the people are the poorest & also several places where there are large nos of Evicted Tenants. I expect to leave for America about the end of Oct. All these plans however are a little vague. But one thing is certain I must arrange to meet with you somewhere & have a long talk with you about various subjects in which we are interested. If you come to Manchester I dare say we can arrange to travel to Ireland together if not we will arrange to meet either in Dublin or in the West.

As I shall see you shortly I write no more now.

I remain in haste

Very sincerely your friend

    Maud Gonne

I leave France for England 28th my address will be 28 Hyde Park Gate[3]

On 3 October Yeats wrote to Lady Gregory from Manchester, where Maud Gonne and he were attending the London and Paris '98 Convention and where the split over the affiliation of the '98 clubs was to the fore. 'We had a long and exhausting political meeting this morning and will have another to-night. After the meeting this morning Miss Gonne and myself went to the picture gallery to see a Rossetti that is there. She is very kind and friendly, but whether more than that I cannot tell. I have been explaining the Celtic movement and she is enthusiastic over it in its more mystical development.'

30   [Ireland][1]
                                                    13th October [1897]

My dear Friend

Thank you so much for your letters, I will write you at length from the ship for I am terribly busy before starting for America. I would have written before, for I guessed you had not got my note sent to Moran's Hotel[2] but I have been so bothered & worried & overworked, – such complications owing to party political differences[3] about my going to America!! Then great differences in the '98 Committee, always about that unfortunate North of England Seagrave affair.[4] I hope they won't send delegates to the meeting in the north. They ought to try and let matters there do & not mix the Central executive in these quarrels & London should not enquire too closely as to whether Seagrave & his branches are affiliated over here or not. It is absurd making an open quarrel – which will harm the '98 Movement. I have done what I can for now things must take their chance.

Good bye my dear Friend I envy you in the quiet of the country in the beautiful & fairy West.

Always most sincerely your friend
Maud Gonne

Your letter distressed me a good deal – I don't want you to give me so much place in your life. It is not well that you should as to what you told me, please don't think for a moment that I blamed you in the very least quite the contrary. I will write you a better letter soon, I only say these few words in answer at once

Maud Gonne left for the USA in the autumn of 1897. Her first meeting was on 24 October, when she asked for funds for a Wolfe Tone monument and for the Irish Amnesty Association. Yeats wrote to Lady Gregory on 1 November 1897: 'I am afraid Miss Gonne will have a bad time in America. O'Leary has heard from there that the Irish parties, opposed to hers, have been busy circulating the spy story. They have made it most detailed, including machinations against Ireland by an imaginary brother.' In spite of an unfavourable start, she claimed that her tour in America was successful.

Her balance sheet, signed by Craig Gardiner & Co, in September 1898, shows $4476 collected during November and December at twenty-one venues; some of it was still coming in during August 1898. Half was used for receiving and entertaining the foreign delegates invited by the Executive Committee of the Centenary Association for Great Britain and France, and the rest went to James Egan for the Amnesty Association.

Michael Lambert of the Amnesty Association, and Patrick Tobin, an INB member on the '98 Executive, joined with Tim Harrington MP, and others disillusioned by or excluded from the '98 Centenary Executive, in forming the United Irishmen Centennial Association. This was made public early in January 1898 as an association 'in which all Irish Nationalists may be proud to take part'. Now there were two bodies working throughout the country forming branches, and lecturing, with the secret society men recruiting hard as well, in direct opposition to each other.

While this squabbling continued there was severe famine in parts of the West, including Mayo, where Maud Gonne went on her arrival in Ireland.

31   Narragansett Hotel
                                                Providence, Rhode Island
                                                Xmas Day [1897]

My dear Friend

I leave America for Ireland on the 29th of this month arriving
Queenstown on the 3rd or 4th of Jany. [If I have time] I shall go
directly to Castlebar, c/o James Daly[1] will find me, after meeting on
the 6th of Jan[2] I will go to Dublin to see Mr O'Leary & arrange
matters about the money I have <collected> made by lectures in
America. I have *not collected* anywhere, it is all *gate money*. I have
not all the returns in yet, but I fancy it must be about £1000, half of
this is for the Amnesty Association. I was obliged to make this
arrangement for reasons I will explain when we meet. £500 therefore
is for '98. I want your advice before deciding what to do with it, for
I don't know exactly how things have been going on in the '98
Committee since my absence. I see that the treasurers have been
changed! Why? I see also that delegates were sent to the North of
England, which I think was a gt mistake.

I hear that Mr Tobin[3] has formed a reception committee, if this is
done in a *broad* way & not in direct hostility to the General executive
perhaps it would be best to give them part of the money, one half of
it is for the London 98 Committee[4] who have helped me so much in
my work here, the Dublin Committee did nothing to support me
<here>, except Mr O'Leary who in a private capacity not as president
of the 98 Committee has done all he could for me. My mission has,
on the whole, been a *great success*.

Please write to Castlebar your views on these matters. In Dublin
I shall stay at the Shelbourne Hotel, Stephen's Green.

I will have lots to tell you about my work here when we meet
which I hope will be in London about the 10th Jany. I am very tired
& worn out & anxious to get home for a complete rest as soon as
possible.

With kindest wishes for the New Year
Affecly your friend.
Maud Gonne.

Letter addressed to 10 or 3 Woburn Buildings.
Postmark: London Ja 5 98.

———— *1898* ————

Writing to AE from London on 22 January 1898, Yeats says he is 'deep in Celtic Mysticism' and that 'Maud Gonne has seen a vision of a little temple of heroes which she proposes to build somewhere in Ireland when '98 is over and to make the centre of our mystical and literary movement.' He also wondered how much it would cost to live in the country as he and Maud Gonne thought of going to 'some country place' to get 'the forms and shapes of the gods' as Russell did, and wondered if they could join him where he was then working in Mayo. He added that he was going to Dublin 'arranging '98 work' in February and could arrange to join Russell, but later wrote that Maud Gonne had changed the dates because of work.

On 22 January the Executive Committee of the '98 Centenary Association for Great Britain and France issued a manifesto regretting the interference of party politics into what was intended as a united nationalist effort because the National League had set up a rival organisation in London.

32   [Paris]
                                                               1st Feby [1898]
My dear Friend

Thank you so much for your letters.

1st about banquet[1] I am sorry it is to be a banquet in my honor; '98 would be better. 2nd it is QUITE impossible for me to be in London 1st March. The Convention on the 20th Feb is the very latest date I can be in England, from Manchester[2] I will go directly to Ireland & remain there a month or six weeks.

I would like to have got over our Dublin negotiations *before* the 20th but I suppose this would be inconvenient to you. In case it were not I would come over about the 12th & we could go to Dublin together, settle matters there, then go to Manchester, & after the convention I would go to Ballina & the west.

However if this does not suit you I will come over in time for convention, then spend a day or two in Dublin & go to Ballina by about the 25th. Send me a line by return of post about this.

I have just written to Mr Lavelle[3] about date of banquet in answer to his letter I said I could come any day before the 20th, (but I don't think they will be able to arrange that) if not, I said, I could not attend banquet as I shall certainly not be in England again until the *end* of March.

Thank you so much for the articles you promise for *l'Irlande*

Libre.[4] The idea is excellent we shall be very grateful, & *if necessary* can easily mention where they were taken from.

I am very busy today so won't write more. I have had influenza like every one else but am almost well again & going out.

Thank you so much for the lovely photo. Almost all the beautiful photos I have been given me by you.

I am sending you my photo
In haste
very sincerely your friend
    Maud Gonne

Addressed to 18 Woburn Buildings.
Postmark: Pl. Victor Hugo/London Fe 2 98.

33   [Dublin]
[February 1898]

Private

My dear Mr Yeats

I have just seen Dixon[1] & have got no satisfaction at all from him. He is as proud as the proverbial peacock, of his policy of *shelving* difficulties & has adopted an oracular & somewhat ridiculous manner.

There is no convention on the 4th of March. Dixon says it was never decided on & that there is materially no time to get their business into shape & call it by the 4th. Of course this only means that Dixon foresees complications & doesn't mean to have the convention before he is *absolutely* obliged when the shortness of time before celebrations will make every one anxious to work harmoniously & the power having nominally been in their hands so long it will look factional & destructive to oppose them.

Probably from his point of view it is a wise policy, but how will our people take it? I tried to extract a promise that he would use his influence to prevent the recognition in any way of the Seagrave faction but did not succeed. 'Thank heaven' said Dixon complacently, 'we have peace on that subject, I wrote a very fair proposal suggesting a meeting of the three bodies at Chester or some given point. I got some sort of a reply from London requesting a statement in writing of Seagrave's grievances, since then I have heard no more thank goodness from either party & there is a sub-committee appointed to enquire into the matter, but as neither side has supplied us with the facts the sub-committee can do nothing & so the matter rests.'

I told him it would mean trouble at the first convention held if they admitted Seagrave, he refused to say anything at all on that subject.

They have no funds but still Dixon says he doesn't want the money I have, & proposed that it should all go to Wolf Tone Statue. I declined saying the matter was very simple, if they didn't need the money in Dublin then Great Britain & France Exec. does – that I had got the money for organising & receiving & intend to use it for that purpose. Dixon hastily added that his committee had not refused, but many on it thought like himself.

According to Dixon they have scored a victory over the United Irishmen Centennial committee last Sunday at Nenagh where these last had arranged a public meeting.[2] Cork hill exec.[3] sent two delegates uninvited who were not allowed to speak. Dixon says meeting was a failure and couldn't start [a] branch & that Cork Hill delegates held an improvised meeting & started a branch & will hold a public meeting next Sunday. This probably means a row. Lambert[4] who I saw last night at Amnesty meeting says Nenagh meeting was a success for them so one doesn't know what to believe. Lambert is coming here this evening to talk things over with me.

I fancy they are somewhat conciliatory, but I don't think Dixon is.

Dixon's main object is to keep out M.P.s & also I think to 'boss' the thing himself.

I think he intends having a public meeting in Phoenix Park on the 6th March at which he has asked me to attend & at which he hopes you will also speak, the date of central meeting still is 21st Aug but there is talk of changing it.

One strange thing Dixon said was, he wished the Irish Central Committee had nothing at all to do with either North of England or London executive. Only trouble their heads about Ireland and ignore all outside. I pointed out that the exec. of Gt Britain & France would have been quite willing to work independently & it was only as a concession to Dublin that our members had been induced to accept a subordinate position. I feel negotiations with Dixon as far as I am concerned would be hopeless.

I will see O'Leary tomorrow but I am inclined not to trouble about negotiations & to trust to chance & luck to keep things fairly peaceable.

I think it will be wiser not to <write to> acquaint our committee in London with what Dixon says, they would grow fierce and as the one essential thing is there should be no open quarrel we must try & calm things down.

Of course it will be necessary for you to tell them that the Convention on the 4th of March is postponed.

What we have to do is to organise as many new branches in Gt Britain as possible, get them to Ireland at the same time. Bring the French delegates there and have monster meetings in the West where we are very strong & if possible get central demonstration on some date at which some if not all our men can be present. I am writing to France to know if the 1st week in August will suit them, immediately I get a reply, I will try & induce James Daly to alter his date for Castlebar meeting from the 27th Aug to 1st week. Dixon would not hear of this, but if Connaught committee say a date Dixon is powerless in the matter.

Now about the medal & this is *important*.

The medals can be made in Dublin & at about the same price as those shown us. Therefore O'Donnell[5] lied when he said he had tried everywhere in Dublin & Belfast. I saw the very English name of a jeweller on the box containing wax medal which we were given, & I didn't like it. I also heard that Cork Hill committee have been getting into trouble for having had some of their printing done on *English made paper*. The question of Irish manufacture is a hot one in Dublin just now, & rightly so.

This morning I took my wax medal to Johnston Jeweller Grafton St who made all the Parnell medals and *Trinity College medals* & asked him if the work was done in Dublin & what the prices would be etc, he says that the *die* is made in England but that the medals are all struck in Dublin & can be done as cheaply if not cheaper than in England, he would give exact estimate if required. I think this should be brought before the committee & matter enquired into & O'Donnell written to, he might be allowed to make arrangements directly with Johnston & could probably get the same terms as mentioned & it might save our committee a row.

Now a few words on quite a different subject. In Liverpool & London I talked to you far more freely than is my wont about myself persons & things in general. I did so because you complained of a certain want of confidence on my part. I must ask you & *very seriously* to be very careful not to mention even the seemingly *unimportant* things to any one. Once a long time ago I found you had repeated a great deal of conversations I had with you. Of course I did not tell you not to do so & it really did not matter but still I *hate* it – I am very reserved always & talk of myself to VERY few people. While I do not mind in the least what wild lies & calumnies people tell of me it is very painful to me to find that the one or two people I speak freely to repeat my conversation – for instance – if the palmists in Dublin speak to you of my sister's fortune I would not like you to confirm their predictions by telling them what you know from me about her – this is only an unimportant instance.

I hope you will not be vexed at my writing to you like this, but if our friendship is to be solid & permanent & trustful as I hope it is to be we should understand one another thoroughly at least in certain things for no one ever thoroughly understands any one else – we hardly understand ourselves.

It was very pleasant seeing you in London & Liverpool. But you must think very well, what is best for your genius, that *should* be your 1st consideration. If you find that an absolutely *platonic friendship* which is all I can or ever will be able to give, unsettles you & spoils your work then you must have the strength & courage at once to give up meeting me. You *owe* your genius to Ireland, it belongs to Ireland, you have no right to allow anything to injure it –

I go to the West on Thursday letters sent to James Daly Castlebar Co Mayo will find me.

In haste

Very sincerely your friend

   Maud Gonne

Addressed to 18 Woburn Buildings.
Postmark: Dublin Fe 22 98; London Fe 23 98.

34   Belmullet[1]
                                               Co Mayo
                                               [late February 1898]

                                               Private

My dear Mr Yeats

   This written as usual in haste I am terribly busy.

   Saw O'Leary. He is most anxious to hurry on Convention says Dixon is trying to keep things altogether in his own hands. He listened to me when I pointed out the danger of Seagrave North of England affair & will back us up on the matter he said he intended to force on Convention. Personally I think he would be glad if United Irishmen Centennial would unite, it would of course mean admitting M.P.s & I think he would make things as easy as he could in this direction.

   Dixon *I think* would be against it –

   One of the most vigorous opponents of admitting M.P.s is Mr Doran of Queenstown.[2]

   I saw Lambert, Gregan, & Bermingham.[3] Allen is their only objection I think to Cork Hill. 'If Allen were not there we would unite at once.' & they do not like being considered Harrington's men.

   I saw Harrington. He is for unity with the executive by admitting M.P.s & priests on their own terms – there is all I know on this very complicated situation.

   Personally I remain on good terms with all parties though I refused to attend a meeting of the United Irishmen Centennial.

   I will be in Dublin for Phoenix Park meeting on the 6th but return west in a few days after as I lecture in Ballina[4] on the 12th & address a public meeting there on the 13th.

　In gt haste,
　I remain
　Your affecate friend
　　Maud Gonne

The poverty here is AWFUL

Startling conditions of poverty and over-population persisted along the western seaboard, and because of the potato failure of the preceding autumn there was famine again in 1898. On her return from America in January Maud Gonne had gone directly to Mayo where she became acutely concerned with the growing famine and the inadequate measures being taken to alleviate it or prevent its recurrence. Haunted by the memory of the Great Famine fifty years previously, and worried at the prospect of continued widespread starvation as all the seed potatoes in Mayo had been eaten, she prepared a leaflet with James Connolly, who had been to the famine areas of Kerry. She organised nursing of those sick from famine fever, organised school feeding and generally put heart into the people. She confronted the Belmullet Board of Guardians with a set of minimum demands backed by the threat of a patient but starving throng outside in the street. Then she used her influence with the Congested Districts Board to erect a fish-curing plant on the north Mayo coast at Belderrig to provide a permanent source of alternative food to the potato.

35　　　　　　　　　　　　　　　　　　　　Ballina
　　　　　　　　　　　　　　　　　　Sunday [early March 1898]
My dear Mr Yeats
　I have just returned from Erris.[1] Poverty more awful than anything I had imagined. I have written some articles on it which I will send to you as soon as they appear so won't write more on the subject except to say I have preached the doctrine I told you[2] under the auspices of the priests, who are desperate at the condition of misery of the people. I am now going to Dublin to try & get some help for them there & probably return to Erris after the Ballina meetings on the 12th & 13th –
　Dublin committee have done a strange & very foolish thing in changing the date of their meeting of the 6th to the 13th so as to clash with Ballina – The people of Connaught are very fierce about it. They had done everything to please the Dublin committee. I enclose resolutions which show that. They had invited several members of

the executive, they had sent their posters to them last week & yet Dublin *changes* its announced date as to clash with Ballina. This means that they will practically have no Connaught platform in the Phoenix Park meeting as in their present state of feeling I don't think many Connaught men will go.

I cannot possibly throw over Ballina. I promised them to speak at a meeting & to lecture for them at the French Hill meeting in Jany. They wrote & consulted me in Paris before fixing date.

They have been working under a good deal of difficulties owing to a certain amount of opposition from the priests & indirectly from William O'Brien's United League,[3] they say they would be ruined now if they put off their meeting.

I believe the action of the Dublin committee is owing to two causes. 1st Allen knows North of England affair will be brought up & does not want me at convention as I always carry a large number of neutral country delegates' votes, he is also glad to snub Connaught where he has been able to get no foot hold. 2nd a number of the Dublin committee outside Allen's party have been much aggravated by Dixon's attempt to keep things in his own hands & not consult them by shelving things & putting off the convention. They wanted convention at all price. You will see that O'Byrne (Allen's man)[4] proposed to fix convention for the 12th & postpone public meeting from the 6th to 13th. Dixon opposed this & suggested holding both a week later. I believe he did so in order not to clash with Connaught, but I dare say many thought he wanted to put off convention altogether & follow his usual policy of shelving.

Now the position is this.

Convention coming off on the 12th. Very few if any Connaught delegates will attend & these Western men are all strong supporters of the London Executive.

I can't attend & I carry a lot of neutral votes when there, which Allen may capture in my absence. Great Britain & France Executive will surely not get fair play under the circumstances.

Doctor Ryan was sent last week an invitation to the <Connaught> Ballina meeting asking him to attend, but it was sent I believe to a wrong address in Drury Lane. No answer has been received.[5] People here are very anxious to see him. Would it be well for him to write & tell Dublin that having accepted Ballina invitation he can't throw <them> it over & suggest changing date of convention as so many delegates cannot attend –

Think well over this & what effect it would have. Ballina is a great Western Centre for the '98 movement – If Dr Ryan came it would have a tremendous effect.

James Daly, Connaught President, will I believe come to Ballina. It would of course weaken if not altogether destroy Dublin

Convention. On the other hand if London delegates attend and are in the minority, it will mean Allen getting his own way & a certainty of eventual split between London & Dublin Executive. I have decided to follow London Exec if it comes to a fight & to resign as Treasurer of Dublin Committee. I told John O'Leary so, possibly it is as well not to tell the London men that, it might make them more untransacting than they are.

I have been asked by the Committee here to write & urge your Dr Ryan to come to Ballina meeting, I have told them I can only lay the matter before you without the slightest advice one way or the other. I am rather angry with Dublin, they never even telegraphed me change of date only sent me printed circular which I got only on my road to Dublin to attend meeting which put out all my plans.

I feel Allen's intrigues are succeeding & am consequently cross & not in good frame of mind for impartial judgment, so I merely state facts & ask you all to consider them, I shall approve & back up London in its decision whatever that may be. The men here accuse Dublin Committee of not sending invitations to all delegates & say Allen is manipulating but I have no actual proof of this.

Please see Dr Ryan.

[End of letter missing]

36   Ballina
                                                              Monday March [1898]

My dear Friend

Thank you so much for your letter, I am much relieved to hear of the very peaceable convention,[1] & congratulate you greatly on your tact & cleverness in managing things so well.

We had an enormous meeting here yesterday market square quite full twelve thousand persons at least enthusiasm tremendous.

Write to me here if you have time.

I go to Gurteen Co Sligo[2] for 98 Meeting on St Patrick's Day and *probably* after that to Erris.

In gt haste & once more thanking you for your letter & for all you are doing for the 98 Movement.

Your affecate friend
   Maud Gonne

I know it is not fair nor right to ask you to do so much tiresome & fatiguing work in the committees.

I hope you will not have much more of it to do.

Your first & most important work must always be your literature. It belongs to Ireland, to take you from that for other things is in a way robbing Ireland of one of her most valuable treasures.

I have had some rather lovely ideas of which I want to talk to you & hope we will meet soon.

In gt haste
   Maud G.

Addressed to Crown Hotel, Dublin.
Blurred postmark: Ballina Mr 14.

37   Tubbercurry[1]
                                                         16th March [1898]

My dear Friend
   This evening at about quarter to 7 o'clock I was driving across the Gap by Glen Ersk lake into your beautiful county of Sligo. I thought I would get you to come & show it to me, so I *went* to you & putting my hands on your shoulder asked you to come with me. We stood by that beautiful lake amid the twilight shadows, then you were on the car beside me driving among the mountains. Here we were interrupted for my travelling companion James Daly had been talking to me of matters which acquired my attention. Some half hour or so later it had grown almost dark, I looked for you but you were gone so I went again to *fetch you* but this time you were eating your dinner with friends so I did not even try to attract your attention.

   All this sounds slightly mad, but you will not think it so, & it is not at all – now please tell me exactly and truthfully were you conscious of any of this or not? Also what you were doing at 7 o'clock this evening, or at 7.30 or 8 o'clock. Write to me at Ballina. I return there after my meeting at Gurteen tomorrow or Friday. As usual I am *very* busy so will not write more now except to thank you for your letter & to congratulate you on the result of convention.

   I remain
   Alwys your friend
      Maud Gonne

try at any price to get the United Irishmen Centennial to unite with Exec. It is very important. Tell Lambert & Bermingham & the advanced men on U.I.C. that the Federation[2] are ruining *their association* (U.I.C.) entirely in places where they have branches they are working *against* the advanced party openly.

Maud Gonne returned to Paris where she fell ill. The American tour, '98 politics and famine relief had taken their toll. Some time after the dinner organised by the '98 Executive of Great Britain in London on 13 April, Yeats went to stay with MacGregor Mathers in Paris to work on the Celtic mysteries. He wrote to Lady Gregory on 25 April: 'I have been out on a bicycle in the Bois de Boulogne and it was like a summer ride. I am buried in Celtic mythology and shall be for a couple of weeks or so. Miss Gonne has been ill with bronchitis. One of her lungs is affected a little so that she has to rest She is unable to do any politics for the time and looks ill and tired. She comes here to-morrow to see visions.'

38
7 Avenue d'Eylau
Paris
Saturday [May 1898]

My dear Friend
Will you bring your tarot cards[1] on Sunday. There is some thing I want so much to find out for my sister. I know you don't generally like doing these things but for my sister, I am sure you will make an exception.
Au revoir donc
till Sunday 7.30
Yours alwys
Maud Gonne

[In Yeats's handwriting] received 8 o'clock – 7 May 98

While Maud Gonne and Yeats were in Paris, both '98 executives had joined forces and held a torchlight procession through the streets of Dublin on 23 May. Back in Dublin, Yeats and Maud Gonne were still hoping 'to get the forms of gods and spirits and to get sacred earth for evocation' by going to the prehistoric site of Newgrange.

39
Nassau Hotel
[Dublin]
Wednesday [June 1898]

My dear Mr Yeats
I am so sorry I find it will be impossible for me to go to New Grange just now.[1] I have an overwhelming amount of work which MUST be done.
I am so disappointed – We will go together some other time.
In great haste
I remain
Always your friend
Maud Gonne

Bon voyage & a very pleasant time in the West, if I should not see you before you start.

In June, Maud Gonne had an accident in Dublin on her way to the unveiling of a memorial tablet at the house where Lord Edward Fitzgerald was arrested in 1798. A very agitated Yeats wrote to Lady Gregory on 14 June: 'Miss Gonne was thrown from a car yesterday by a horse falling. Her arm is broken and her face scratched and bruised. . . . She is so self-reliant that she would probably ask no one to nurse her, if she could get on at all without – I cannot leave now . . . I am most anxious about the shock for she has been very ill this spring with her old trouble in her lungs, and was looking pale and ill as it was.' Later he added that she was not as bad as he had first feared and that she was going to stay with the Pursers. He delayed his journey to Coole 'for two or three days to see if I can be of any use about political correspondence and the like'.

40   [London]
                                                    [late June 1898]

My dear Friend

A few little words to tell you I arrived last night in London none the worse for the journey & to thank you for all your kindness to me in Dublin. It was so good of you giving up your journey & spending all those days in a horrid hotel doing uncongenial work in order to help me. I did not half thank you in Dublin.

I went & thanked you last evening but I don't know if you understood.

I read the Dome on the journey. I read over & over again your poem[1] until I didn't need the book to read it, it is so beautiful.

I lent the Dome to my sister who will send it to you in a few days.

On the boat leaving Ireland I had a curious half waking, half sleeping dream. I seemed to get a distinct order to go to New Grange & to take earth from the House of Dagda & water from the sacred Boyne[2] & give some of each to you & to keep some myself. To look on this earth & water as something infinitely sacred, to carry them with us whenever we left Ireland & they would become to us most powerful talismen for the invoking of our Gods.

I will do this next time I am in Ireland.

Now I must end dear friend as my arm is too tired to write more

Alwys your friend

Maud Gonne

Write to 7 Avenue d'Eylau, Paris. I am not sure of your address.

41

Hotel Thermal
Aix les Bains
Savoie
7th July [1898]

My dear Friend

Thank you so much for your two letters. I did not consciously go to see you on Monday but I probably did so *unconsciously* as I was thinking of you, & I find one's *thoughts* often *really* carry one to places & people.[1]

Monday morning I arrived at Aix-les-Bains at six o'clock. I did not go to bed & began arranging my papers which took me some time, it must have been somewhere about 8 o'clock that I had your last letter in my hand & I thought of answering it at once, & then felt too tired & lazy to do so & put it away & sat doing nothing – It must have been *then* that I went to you.

I have not used your article on Russell[2] in *L'Irlande Libre*, it is fearfully hard to translate & I doubt it being understood very well by our readers. Thank you so much for sending it. It is so good of you always being ready to help me.

I am glad you are working well & easily now – You wanted badly the rest & quiet of the country.

I am having a very quiet time here with my cousin.[3] Gambling is my only distraction. The whole morning till 12 o'clock is taken up with baths, douches, massage, drinking waters etc the afternoon I write & work steadily, the evening I go to the Casino – for three weeks this life is possible, it wouldn't be for longer.

When I got to Paris I found that the committee had not sold any tickets or done any serious work, though they had taken the largest hall in Paris. There was only 5 days before the meeting & I was not feeling strong enough to rush round the press & work things up so I wrote to Willie Redmond & others who had promised to speak & prevented them coming & refused to let the thing have any political significance at all or any speeches it was just a concert with a good deal of Irish music and as such I believe was a fair success, but I was not in Paris for it.

An Irish meeting in Paris not absolutely crowded would do us more harm than good, we will have a meeting later.

I have a lot of writing to do so goodbye.

I remain

Affecy your friend
Maud Gonne

On L'Irlande Libre *notepaper.*

Yeats returned to London from Coole for the '98 centenary celebrations. On 9 August there was a banquet at Frascati's and the following day a meeting at St Martin's Hall, with Yeats in the chair and Maud Gonne as principal speaker.

On Monday, 15 August, the Dublin celebrations took place. In spite of police cynicism and early internal strife, the event was a great success. Huge crowds attended, and the wagonette decorated with the French tricolour which carried Maud Gonne and the French visitors 'was the signal for outbursts of applause and enthusiasm'. According to Yeats in his Autobiographies, *the procession was 'the greatest in living memory', with Maud Gonne 'cheered everywhere'.*

After the laying of the foundation stone for the Wolfe Tone monument on the corner of St Stephen's Green, opposite Grafton Street, Maud Gonne and the French delegation went to Ballina and Castlebar, where she received a tumultuous welcome. Millevoye wrote in La Patrie: *'In the name of the patriots of France I address to the patriots of Ireland the most ardent expression of friendship and admiration of France.' However, a letter from 'a Mr Teeling of Paris' to the people in the west said that Miss Gonne was 'a vile abandoned woman who has had more than one illegitimate child and that she is suspected by the French of giving information to the English'. Her work in Erris outweighed these rumours. As Yeats put it in 'Her Praise':*

> *Though she had young men's praise and old men's blame,*
> *Among the poor both old and young gave her praise.*

42
Castlebar
28th August [1898]

My dear Friend

I have received your two letters. The one contained the doctor's[1] letter & returned statement but NOT YOUR REPLY. Could this have been taken out in post or did you forget to send it?[2]

It ought to be attended to at once. I am writing very strongly on the subject to the Dr – Please do so also. I have taken copy of statement & return you the original, I have corrected the signature of the Dublin organisation from pamphlets. I enclose Frank Hugh's last production.[3] Please return it to me to Dublin Nassau Hotel Nassau Street. I shall want it in London.

I have been awfully hard worked lately & alas I have still a lot of hard work & worry before me.

Meetings have been very successful. French friends[4] are very pleased & have written splendid articles. The French press is splendid Ireland has never been so much to the fore in France before.

We return to Dublin tomorrow. I shall probably remain there a few days to settle accounts with 98 committee etc.[5] then I must have a few days in London to talk over affairs with friends there. Teeling has again begun his ignoble campaign against me, I feel sure now that he is in the English pay. He has been writing letters to people in all the towns in the West with villainous things against me.[6] I want to get hold of one of those letters if possible.

I will write more interesting letters when I have a little time. Au revoir my dear friend. Thank you so much for your letters. Your friendship is such a charming restful thing & I am sure so sure of it.

I remain
Yours always
    Maud Gonne

Addressed to Coole Park, Gort.
Postmark: Castlebar Au 28 98; Gort Au 29 98.

43   [Dublin]
                                                                     [September 1898]

My dear Friend
I am sending you a parcel containing 1st a little box of earth from *New Grange* from the very centre of that wonderful Irish pyramid

2nd a white bottle (it ought to be white & gold) containing water from the golden Boyne I got it in the morning sunlight & the river shone like gold

3rd the bottle you [?saw] containing water from a wonderful holy well at Ballina where I *saw* the FISH. By it was buried the wife of King Dathai,[1] they have just destroyed her grave to put her in the graveyard it was so wicked & the man who did it got an attack after & has lost all his strength.

That grey water seems to me to symbolise the *West*, & the cloudy hosts of the Sidhe,[2] while the Boyne water will tell you I think of more material things of Ireland. Try some experiments with them. I am doing so & I will write & tell you more when I have time. Touch your lips your eyes & ears & breast before sleeping & I think they will give you dreams.

I cross to <Ireland> England tonight. Write to me 7 Avenue d'Eylau Paris

The poem[3] is most beautiful.
Always your friend
    Maud Gonne.

Nassau Hotel envelope addressed to Coole Castle, Gort.
Blurred postmark: Se 6 [1898].

44   Samois
                                                                27th September [1898]

My dear Friend

I have been a long while answering your letters but I have not been
in a letter writing mood the reaction after all the noise & fatigue of
the Centenary made me very lazy –

1st about the protest. I saw the Doctor[1] he again affirms in such a
way that [I] believe him that he PERSONALLY did not know of the
disgraceful pamphlet. He says he taking any action on it would seem
to infer that he was responsible for it. I told him you & I were very
serious over the matter & considered it absolutely necessary that both
pamphlets should be repudiated.[2] He again made the offer he made
in the letter. I said that wouldn't do, he then offered to put me in
communication with someone in the Society who would get the
repudiation published, but as I was leaving town that day it wasn't
possible. He promised me that he would bring the matter again
before the Committee & urge on them publishing the thing. I have
heard no more since. It is getting so long after the publication of the
abominable pamphlets that I fear they have gained their points. No
repudiation will be made. I think however that the stand we have
made has done good & that in future no more such things will be
permitted. I almost feel *now* that it will be as well for us to let the
matter slide –

My plans are still a little vague I think I shall be in France till about
the 15th Oct when I shall probably come to Ireland for a week or
a fortnight before going to America but even my American trip
is not quite certain yet.[3] I should like very much to meet you & hear
about your visions & talk over the occult work together.

I believe more than ever in some terrible upheaval in Europe in the
near future. The other night here I saw the most extraordinary sight
I ever witnessed. I was lying on the grass in the garden in the evening
when all of a sudden I saw curious lines of light across the sky, at
first I thought it must be some huge fire somewhere, & I got up &
went out on the hill to see it. It was about 9.30 in the evening & the
sky was wonderfully clear but there was no moon [indecipherable].
Across the Northern & Western half of the heavens rose great rays
of light at first faint & then gradually brighter & brighter, several
times they faded & brightened, then in the middle of one of the
largest rays for a moment there flashed a spear of light, then the ray
gradually turned from white into a dull blood red & faded –

It was so wonderful I felt a sort of awe I am sure it presaged terrible
events.

The peasants saw the rays too, they said that in Paris people were
making experiments with electric light projections, but of course this
was nonsense. The papers say it was an Aurora Borealis.

I had a strange dream the first night of my return to France. It seemed as if I was awakened by a loud deafening cry, 'The Lion of the West is rising', 'The Lion is awake', I do not know what it means.

Goodbye my dear Friend I haven't time to write more now.

I remain ALWAYS your friend.

    Maud Gonne

I reopen letter to forward enclosed just received I am very glad it is most satisfactory.

Written on L'Irlande Libre *notepaper.*

In his Visions Notebook *Yeats recorded that while working on Celtic symbolism, feeling depressed and unwell, he dreamed he saw a lunar talisman and decided they were being attacked by a lunar power and needed to evoke the sun. Around the same time he sent Maud Gonne an account of a vision of Maeve experienced by his uncle's old servant Mary Battle.*

45
                               7 Avenue d'Eylau
                                     Paris
                            Friday [November 1898]

My dear Friend

How nice you are writing to me when I have been so lazy about answering, that is what I like so much about you, I am always sure of finding you the same – no matter what happens! I have been going through a state of mind I don't quite understand, for the last month I have been incapable of any sort of work, each time I tried something seemed to stop me. It was not that I had my mind full of other things, quite the contrary, my mind was blank and stupid. I thought it must be some of the forces that work for England that were paralysing my will so I have been imagining Celtic things with the water of the west & the earth from New Grange & suddenly feel as if the stupefying weight has disappeared & I can be active & useful again. Just when I got your letter about *Maeve* I had been invoking Maeve,[1] I shall send you very soon a drawing I have made of her which I think you will like, (though of course as you know I can't draw) Possibly the stupid state I have been in during the last month may be the reaction after the work & strain of the Centenary work.

I am dining with the McGregors tonight & Mrs McGregor has promised to try & see for me what forces have been at work – The translation of Fiona McCloud's poem[2] I think is very beautiful the painting on the cover is wonderful. The music is very *strange* &

difficult to understand. Certain phrases of it are beautiful. It is very plaintive, & not fierce & strong enough for Ulad[3] also it is *not* very CELTIC, it is simple enough, & it is not written in the *Celtic scale*. Still it is interesting.

McGregor & Jules Bois are working together just now to restore the Egyptian Mysteries in Paris, this will be very, very interesting I think.

Tonight they want to talk to me about Celtic things. I will let you know soon the result.

I cross to London on the 24th Nov. & go to Manchester for a meeting[4] on the 27th & shall be in Ireland by the end of this month write & let me know *where* you will be & where we can see each other & talk over the things which interest us.

In haste
I remain
Alwys your friend
    Maud Gonne

Yeats and Maud Gonne met in Dublin in December. He dreamed he had kissed her on the lips for the first time. When he told her of this she informed him that the same night she had gone out of her body and was taken away by the god Lugh, who put her hand in his and said they were married; she kissed him and all went dark. Having told him this, he wrote in his Memoirs, *'Then and there for the first time with the bodily mouth, she kissed me.' But the next day she apologised and said she could not marry him. Then she told him the story of her life and said that though she did not live with Millevoye she was necessary to him. Yeats felt she was held by a sense of duty. She was very emotional but still insisted that marriage was impossible for her: 'I have a horror and terror of physical love.'*

Preoccupied by her, Yeats noted in his Visions Notebook *that PIAL[5] had to give up her plans because of the disturbed state of France and had started on her journey on 19 December. He worked out her fortune until her return. He found that she would be depressed and wearied by tiresome hindrances.*

46   28 Hyde Park Gate
                                                      [London]
                                                      Wednesday [December 1898]
My dear Friend
    A few words in haste to say I got over quite safely – I do not think there is any particular cause to worry about the letter which I showed you from Kathleen. I saw the doctor yesterday & asked him his

candid opinion about [indecipherable] except that we already know, he says he has nothing against him, so there is nothing more to be done in the matter. If my little friend will make a fool of herself I can't help it, as I have nothing definite enough to bring forward & vague suspicions are of course useless.[1] Don't take any more trouble in the matter.

I hope you will go to the country as soon as you can – You ought really to take care of yourself & get rid of your cold, & in Dublin you don't take care at all. Write to me in Paris & tell me how you are.

My sister and cousin[2] are both much interested in our Celtic work. I expect both will join us in it. I am writing this in great haste. I do hope your cold is better. *Do* take care of yourself.
    Always Your friend
        Maud Gonne

Addressed to 6 Castlewood Ave, Rathmines, Dublin.
Postmark: South Kensington De 21 98.

In his Visions Notebook *Yeats recorded receiving the following letter on 2 January 1899. Probably disappointed in its tone after what had passed between them, he described her as busily at work and the letter as dealing with external matters.*

47   [Paris]
                                                [late December 1898]
My dear Friend
    These last three days I have been meaning to write to you, but I found so much work waiting me here that I have not had much time since my return.

This morning I received your nice letter – Monday or Tuesday night, I can't quite remember which, but I think it was Monday I dreamed of you. We were walking together & things referring to our work were going well – I only had general impressions but they were very good & next day I was able to work well at our occult things – I am sending you a copy of what I got about the spear initiation –

I am sorry you find the figure[1] about my work in Paris so bad, I trust you may have been in some way mistaken. How did you decide the time, etc? When I arrived in Paris I saw a very big shield held over me & I also saw the spear, it seemed protecting & encouraging.

I have seen a good many people but have not done anything of much importance. Willie Redmond was here I got several French députés to meet him & I think they were mutually pleased. we are going to arrange for a big Irish banquet in February. I fear with your work about the Celtic theatre you will hardly be able to come here for it. I have been working at Celtic things but have not got much that is new. Certainly we seem to get more actual teaching when we are together. But I am getting my ideas clearer as to the attributions colors etc. I enclose McGregor's document[2] which please return to me when you have done with [it] & also tell me what you think of it & if corrections should be made. I am in no hurry to enter into the matter with McGregor. He is busy for the time with other things which I consider fortunate. I believe for the present we are better working with such teaching as we can get ourselves directly.

I have such a lot of writing to get through today that I can't write more now –

I hope your cold is better, you say nothing of your health in your letter. You should take a little care of yourself it is so bad getting these constant colds.

Goodbye my friend write to me soon

Yours alwys

Maud Gonne

48

Initiation of the Spear[1]

Having been promised the initiation of the spear before going to sleep I went through the ceremonies of the cauldron, the stone.[2] Semias & Estras accompanied me, stood on each side of the bed when I lay down. I was just beginning to see Lug[3] when a crowd of dark thoughts came over my mind. I had to get up & go through the ceremonies again. When I came to the place of the sword I invoked Brighid[4] and saw her dimly, the black haired Usces, I asked their help, but this druid would not accompany me as the others did. I again lay down & this time fell into a deep sleep. I woke feeling very very tired & knew something had happened. I invoked Lug & asked to go through it again so as to remember. Then half waking, half sleeping, I saw Lug in his chariot. He touched me on the chest with the spear & I fell down on the ground & the fountain of fire played over me. Then he held out the spear over me & I grasped it & was raised to my feet through the fire fountain. I then got into the chariot & knelt there under Lug's great shield. The chariot rose to a great height & stopped at last on what seemed to be a sort of dazzling white platform on which stood a white altar & on it was inscribed a golden sun & a red rose lay on it, I was told that rose incense should be used for Lug's ceremonies. I found myself dressed in a long white shining garment.

Behind the altar stood Lug, he is so dazzling it is hard to describe him. I think he wears a shining gold helmet & shield & carries a long spear. I think he wears also a white tunic, but the light was so great & seemed to come from him that it is hard to see details. His face, which I could only distinguish when he turned it a little aside, was wonderfully beautiful & very pure, very strong & very proud. By my side stood Mo[?r]fessi, the red haired druid. He took both my hands & gazed into my eyes. (I was told this was the way we should be able to know who were fit to take the initiation of the spear) After a few moments Mo[?r]fessi said, 'She is not pure enough, is not strong enough, she is not silent enough.'

Then I saw two dark shadow forms standing behind me. A voice on the right hand of the altar cried out, 'We need her, purify her, strengthen her and seal her lips for the work.'

After a few moments I felt the fire fountain rising within me.

It seemed to come through my chest like a flame and rose high above & played over me.

Then Lug, from the other side of the altar, held his great spear over mine & said 'She is purified, she is strengthened and her lips are sealed for our service and woe to whoever turn back from the service of the Gods.'

The spear & shield were put into my hands & a voice said 'The spear is to fight the forces of Darkness, the spear is to fight the enemies of Eire, the shield is to protect from the attack of adversaries.'

Then all faded & grew dim & I fell sinking down, down to earth.

[Taken from *Visions Notebook*]

1899

Yeats's lobbying of MPs to get the obsolete licensing laws changed to enable the Irish Literary Theatre to perform in Dublin had been successful. The project was ready to be launched with the publication of Edward Martyn's Heather Field *and* Maeve, *so Yeats was busy publicly outlining and defending his plans for it. With the encouragement of his uncle George Pollexfen and Lady Gregory, he resolved to follow up the ground he seemed to have gained with Maud Gonne before Christmas 1898 by going to Paris.*

49

My dear Friend

Thank you for your most interesting & charming letter. I will answer it more fully in a few days & send you some Celtic symbolism which I have got which I think will interest you.

I write today in haste on a matter which I consider very serious –

Yesterday a French man (who once before gave me a correct warning about a person who came to my house & who has since been *publicly* proved to be a spy)[1] called on me for the purpose of warning me against McGregor who he says is undoubtedly in the English service. He doesn't know McGregor personally & can have no possible personal reason for speaking against him. I believe he saw him once at a soirée at my house –

I hate being suspicious & listening to bad things about people but yet there are warnings which it is foolish not to heed. I think this one sufficiently serious to make it quite impossible for me even in occultism to associate with McGregor. He doesn't know I am back yet & I shall avoid meeting him, though I shall not openly quarrel unless I can have absolute tangible proofs, which in cases like these are very difficult to obtain.

Please if you write to him be very guarded in what you say, as in case of any public scandal about him, he must not be able to say that he has the confidence of Irish men or belongs even to an Irish order of occultism. It would damage the cause very much. I am sorry to have to write like this but I think it is necessary to let you know.

In haste

I remain very sincerely your friend

Maud Gonne

50

My dear Willie

I have been so busy these last days that it is only now I find time to write to you & send you the Celtic things I spoke of in my last letter which by the way I sent to Sligo. I hope you got it safely. Thank you so much for your last letter & the papers about theatre & literary Society. The movement is going on well

I went to a Celtic banquet last night which was most successful. I am sending the account to all the Irish papers – I hope they will publish it. If you see Gill ask him to.[1] I enclose you a copy. Will you be so kind as to send me several copies of the papers with account so as I can send them to the Bretons[2] who will be very pleased. I hope to be able to get them to take the initiative in organising the Irish banquet as it would be more representative of all parties in France than if it were organised by any particular group of French Députés. They are more *bitterly* divided here[3] just now than we are in Ireland. The banquet to have weight must be organised by FRENCH not by our Irish Societies. This makes me uncertain yet about the date, as soon as I know I will write to you.

I had found out that Elathan[4] represents the Formore.[5] I have not invoked it as yet, we will try together some day but I don't think it NEED be bad any more than Akasa[6] is bad.

I have had a partial initiation of the sword[7] but feel it is not complete. This too we must try together.

I am amused at thinking of the dismay it may cause in the conservative Pan Celtic Society, the fact that the people at the head of the movement here invite me, in fact as far as Ireland is concerned I don't think they would do anything without me. They have invited me to their big festival in Brittany this August. If I can I shall go. They have a somewhat exaggerated idea of the *importance* of the *Pan Celts*. Fournier d'Albe[8] must be a wonderful man & Celtic imagination is strong.

I have in no way undeceived them for I *hope* it will grow into what they think it is & what we all would like it to be.

Goodbye my dear friend. I will write again soon.

Yours alwys
    Maud Gonne

51   [Paris]
                                               [late January 1899]

My dear Friend

A word in great haste to ask you to send your letter re *Irish Theatre* to M. Legras, Redacteur au Debate[1] 133 Boulevard St Germain & any other article on the subject you may have. Unfortunately I sent away the copy you sent me. He reads English perfectly, so can get the information from the Irish papers if you will mark your letter & articles. He is doing an article on Irish literature for the Debate I think & wants to refer to the theatre.

I congratulate you in your firmness in putting down Dublin snobbery in regard to Vice Regal visit to literary society.[2] It would have been scandalous if they treated the viceroy any differently to the ordinary public. I should at once have publicly severed my connection with them & I hope most nationalists would have done likewise. It would have been deplorable from any point of view. How fortunate you happened to be in Dublin!

I have just received your note saying you are in London & the

volume of Martyn's Plays[3] thank you so much.
      In great haste
      Very sincerely your friend
            Maud Gonne

52   Paris
                                                      [January 1899]
My dear Willie
      a word in gt haste to say I forgot to send enclosed yesterday, &
also that I think the *Elder from the canny North*[1] will want all the
documents we have well marshalled together shortly. He wrote to
me to have them ready, I have replied they are in your hands, so if
he wants them he will write to you. Of course don't give them up
except under the understanding they are to be returned to us. I am
sure there will be no difficulty about this.
      In gt haste
      Alwys your friend
            Maud Gonne

Yeats went to Paris on 31 January and stayed there over two weeks,
delaying his return in the hope of travelling back with Maud Gonne,
but he had to leave for rehearsals. Writing to Lady Gregory, he says
she has told him all except some things which 'are too painful for her
to talk of and about which I do not ask her. I do not wonder that she
shrinks from life. Hers has been in part the war of phantasy and of a
blinded idealism against eternal law.' He also said that he had 'a cold
of an astonishing violence' and that Maud 'is quite convinced that it
is the work of a certain rival mystic, or of one of his attendant spirits'.
(This may refer to the now questionable MacGregor Mathers.) At the
end of the letter he added: 'MG is going to Ireland to the evicted
tenants.'

53   [Paris]
                                                       March 4 99
My dear friend
      Thank you so much for your lovely books Iseult[1] is so pleased
with them
      I cross to England Saturday night come & see me 28 Hyde Park
Gate at *3 o'clock on Monday.*
      In gt haste
      Very sincerely yours
            Maud Gonne

54
Ballina
13th March [1899]

My dear Willie

A few words only for as usual I am overwhelmed with work –

I got this far with my letter but was called down to receive delegation from Ballycastle[1] –

– here are my plans for the present. I go to Colooney[2] tomorrow then to Belfast where I distribute prizes at the Gaelic Feis[3] on the 16th, I speak at an amnesty meeting on the 20th, return to Dublin 21st & hope to be able to remain there more or less till the end of the 1st week in April. So I expect to see you there sometime but I will have a great deal of work to do, work which won't I am afraid interest you at all, but which is very necessary. 14th I was again interrupted, you see how hard it is for me to find time to write when I am at work –

The west is looking so lovely & the weather is so beautiful I am so sorry to be leaving & going North. However it is useful & necessary to go to Belfast.

Our meetings here have been *very good indeed.*[4]

In haste

I remain

Yours always most sincerely

Maud Gonne

The following mad production from Delaney, this following on the letter [in] which she said I had always been a brute to her that she never wished to see me again. Do you think it is an artful attempt at peace making or real sincere madness

55
[Letterhead]
Nassau Hotel
Dublin
22nd March [1899]

My dear Willie

Just arrived in Dublin & find your letter. I am so glad you are coming over soon – I have had a very successful time both in West & in Belfast & now expect to be in Dublin for a fortnight at least.

I am so sorry what you say about Fiona.[1] Curiously I was thinking of her a great deal lately & I knew she was ill – I am so sorry for her – I believe she COULD be cured, but I don't think she *would* – I wish I knew her, I might be of use to her.

No I do not think I wear a mask, & I do not think I am lonely though I am a little *outside* of life – & I do not *want* to get back *into* life again. I never think whether I am lonely or not, I only think of my work, *that* interests me, so do my friends & *you know* I am always so glad to see you & talk with you over the many many things we both believe in. I have lots to talk over with you now but will keep it all till we meet for as you know I am no good at letter writing.

Alwys most sincerely your friend
Maud Gonne

The course of the Literary Theatre was not running smoothly. Edward Martyn had threatened to withdraw his backing from the Literary Theatre because he was worried about the orthodoxy of The Countess Cathleen *– the Countess sells her soul for gold to save her starving peasants. Yeats, with theological support, appeased him. On 9 April Yeats wrote to Lady Gregory from London:*

The last time we saw Martyn and [he] was in excellent spirits but said that if any person 'in authority' was to speak he would withdraw again. . . .

You will be interested to hear that Miss Gonne is probably coming with me to see Plunkett about a project to settle the evicted tenant question. Russell has been acting as an intermediary between them. The scheme is his. To-night she and Russell have another talk and then she sees Gill. She is anxious to prevent the MPs exploiting the tenants for the benefit of the parliamentary fund. The thing is private as yet.

Sir Horace Plunkett MP was president of the Irish Agricultural Organisation Society for which both Russell and Gill worked. The MPs referred to were probably the general body of nationalist MPs who had been operating an evicted tenants' fund over the years. Russell worked to get 'a good provisional Committee together to take the question of the tenants up' as he wrote to Yeats, and in late October the Evicted Tenants Restoration Fund made 'an appeal to friends of peace and good will irrespective of party distinction' to endeavour to restore or find alternative homes for the evicted tenants.

56   Nassau Hotel
                                                                [Dublin]
                                                                28 March [1899]

My dear Friend

I am so sorry to hear of all the bother you are having. It is too horrid for words on Martyn's part[1] what a contemptible creature. You must go on with Countess Kathleen[2] all the same. I really believe it will have much greater success alone without Martyn's very heavy & rather indigestible *Heather Field*.

You must get a short Gaelic piece[3] acted with it – which will answer the support of all the Gaelic people who are growing in influence & numbers daily. I believe the Parnellites will support you.

Of course I will do what I can. Let me know how things go on.

Enclosed is a letter from *I think* Miss Miligan[4] by the writing which is exactly like one I have just received from her. I would have forwarded it before, but expected seeing you every day.

With kindest regards dear Willie

Very sincerely your friend

Maud Gonne

Of course I won't mention the Martyn difficulty to anyone. As you know, I don't often speak of other people's affairs or my own for that matter.

I have a terrible lot of work in connection with evicted tenants convention[5] on the 30th

Addressed to 18 Woburn Buildings.
Postmark: 6.30 pm Dublin Mr 28 99; 6.45 am London Mr 29 99.

57   [Paris]
                                                                            [1899]

My dear Friend

Thank you so much for your letters & for the lovely book of verse[1] – how beautiful those poems are. In spite of the whirl of work in which I am engaged just now, I have read them many times, I read them at night.

Frank Hugh O'Donnell's pamphlet[2] is a scandal mean disgusting thing. I hope that this time Dr R.[3] will really have done with him for good.

I cross to Ireland with Mlle de Ste Croix on Sunday night & I shall stay at Nassau Hotel.

I have had influenza but am quite well again.

In Gt haste

Always most sincerely your friend

Maud Gonne

Addressed to 18 Woburn Buildings: To be forwarded.
Torn postmark: London My 5.

After attending the opening performance of the Irish Literary Theatre in the Antient Concert Rooms, Maud Gonne, Mlle de Ste Croix and other French friends went to Ballina for the unveiling of the Humbert Memorial. Bands played, flags flew, and at her speech 'a wild defiant cheer rang through the Mayo town' (Western People, 27 May 1899). The visitors were also taken to places associated with the French landing, accompanied by crowds of people while 'the Ballina Band played to the echo'. A number of eviction meetings were also held, and some tenants were reinstated; this was looked upon by the local people as a great victory. Maud Gonne was present in Ballyhaunus when it was brilliantly lit with barrels as a celebration. Yeats went to Coole.

58   Dublin
                                                                          29th May [1899]
My dear Willie

Forgive me for not having answered your letter sooner, but I have been half killed with work lately. Meetings every day; denouncing grabbers[1] advocating the merits of political prisoners etc. My headquarters have been Dublin ever since you left which means that my spirits are low, & as near discouragement as I ever get but that won't last long – To get courage again I went to Howth & walked all around those lovely cliffs amid the sea birds, it rained all the time but I didn't mind that – I don't think there is any place nicer than the cliff walk at Howth – Isn't it dreadful they are going to make a tram-way run all around Howth![2] On democratic socialist principles we ought to rejoice – But I don't a bit.

Wednesday next after the election, for which I am working for Clarke (one of the political prisoners)[3] I cross to England & in a few days after will return to Paris. I shall be glad to get a rest – I envy you down in the West. Are you writing much? Here everyone continues to talk about the success of the theatre & new literary movement – you have done a wonderful work in waking people up to the Irish ideals.

I must end now as I have to go to Amnesty meeting.[4]

Remember me very kindly to Lady Gregory. I will write from Paris about one or two occult things but I want to work a little quietly first.

In haste
Yours alwys
Maud Gonne

Postmark: Dublin 5.30am My 30 99; Gort 11.30 am My 30 99.

59   7 Avenue d'Eylau
                                                    Paris
                                                    24th Juin [1899]

My dear Willie

I am so sorry you have been ill[1] & was very glad to hear today from Lady Gregory that you are quite well again.

I have also been ill, on arriving in Paris I got a slight attack of fever. I think it was the hot weather & being over tired so I went at once to Samois, where Madame de Bourbonne[2] & Iseult were already – This was why I did not write to your brother[3] though Lady Gregory kindly sent me his address. I only came to Paris yesterday – For the last three weeks I have been perfectly stupid & unable to do any interesting work whatever. I seemed to have lost the power of getting into communion with the Forces of our country – all seemed dull & uninteresting & material – I think this is passing, for during the last day or two I have recovered my lost energy & belief – I believe soon I shall obtain some new knowledge I am waiting in a sort of strange expectancy.

Thank you so much for Fiona's book.[4] I wonder is she right to even thus far give to the world the sacred symbols.

Here the political atmosphere is thick & heavy.[5] It seems like a boiling cauldron & one does not know what will emerge from all the seething bubbles and vapour – I hope it will be the pure bright light of a shining sword which will guide France once more to glory but at present all is dark & troubled & England may well look on with satisfaction.

Lanessan[6] the president of the Entente Cordiale is Minister of the Navy! Waldeck Rousseau[7] *opportuniste* the lawyer of the jews and financiers has chosen Millerand socialist collectiviste[8] as minister of commerce & General Galifet the murderer of 30,000 french men, women & children – defenceless prisoners after the Commune, as Minister of War![9] & half of the revolutionists today descendants of those murdered communards of '71 applaud.

But not so the great mass of the French people, who look on in sullen disapproval, & on all sides one hears 'It cannot last' – But the power of the Golden Calf[10] is so great, that the end may not be yet & the struggle will be terrible –

But why am I writing you all of this you are far away <from all this> in green cloudy Ireland, but there also there can be no peace & rest for the people suffer too much, the English triumph too insolently.

I feel our cause is bound up with the cause of France – we have the same deadly enemy to fight the horrible plutocracy of which the English Empire is the symbol –

Goodbye dear friend I hope you are quite well again
Write to me soon.
Always very sincerely your friend
   Maud Gonne

Miss Purser lunched with me today she leaves Paris to-night for London –

60   7 Avenue d'Eylau
                                                      Paris
                                                      [July 1899]

My dear Willie
   I have had an attack of bronchitis. It is quite gone now & I came up to Paris yesterday to see my doctor. By his advice I have written to put off my meetings in Mayo as he says I ought not to do any public speaking for at least six weeks, so I shall go to Aix les Bains first before coming to Ireland, instead of later as I intended. Don't be anxious about me as I am really not ill now at all, only my voice and throat are weak –
   Many thanks for your letters. No I did not at all misunderstand what you said about not seeing enough of each other to be quite able to share all our interests – I know what you mean.
   Our work at first sight seems very far apart & different & yet it is curiously the same only on different plains – I go back to Samois today & will try & invoke Lir[1] & will write for the translations. I have again got into contact with the forces. It happened one night out on the hill at Samois during a curious night of Summer storm lit with bright flashes of lightning. I went through the four invocations & got a promise of help. The very next day I found the realisation of this promise in my work – I will tell you more of all this when we meet.
   What a lovely place it must be that you are in in the hills in Galway. I am making a talisman for evoking the Tuatha de Danaan & will do one for you as soon as I have got it right. The colors as yet are not quite right for though each separately seems the right color taken together they do not harmonise as they should which means that something is wrong –
   I have no time to write more today –
   I remain
   always very sincerely your friend
      Maud Gonne

Addressed c/o Lady Gregory, Coole Park, Co. Galway.
Postmark: Paris Place du Trocadéro 15 Juil 99; [Gort] 11.30 Jy 17 99.

Yeats spent the summer at Coole and Tillyra trying to complete The
Shadowy Waters *and collaborating with Martyn and Moore on* The
Bending of the Bough *and* Diarmuid and Grania *for the Literary
Theatre. At the end of August he wrote in his* Visions Notebook *that
he had not heard from PIAL for a long time and was worried about
her.*

61   Paris
                                                Sunday [September 1899]

My dear Friend
    I shall be in Dublin 15th but will have to leave 16th for Foxford
& Ballina.
    After my meeting 17th it will be easier to fix a meeting as in Dublin
I shall have very litle time
    Write to me Nassau Hotel
    Just starting for London
    In haste
    Very sincerely your friend
        Maud Gonne

62   [Letterhead]
                                                Nassau Hotel
                                                Dublin
                                                16th September [1899]

My dear Friend
    I go to Ballina tonight & then on to Belfast I expect to be in Dublin
on Friday next. It will be very nice seeing you if you can be in town
then. You might write to me c/o Robert Johnston Eqre Lisnaveane
Antrim Road Belfast.
    I too have a lot of rather interesting things to tell you about our
work but haven't time to write them.
    In haste
    Very sincerely your friend
        Maud Gonne

*War finally broke out in South Africa in September. Maud Gonne,
busy in Ballina with eviction and anti-war meetings, had come to
believe that in the west it was impossible for nationalists to ignore the
agrarian question. On the platforms with her was T. B. Kelly, who
said: 'We have to pay our share of ten millions voted by Parliament
to prosecute war. We protest against this war.'*
    On 19 September Yeats was trying to see what the four symbols

would show of his meeting with PIAL.

*From Ballina Maud Gonne went to Belfast. There she met Yeats
and they climbed Cave Hill, where Tone and his friends founded the
United Irishmen. It overlooks Belfast Lough, and there is an ancient
ring fort on it. She went back to Ballina for court hearings resulting
from her meetings in September.*

63   Nassau Hotel
                                                                  Dublin
                                                                  Monday [October 1899]

My dear Willie

Are you going to Sligo & when? If you are will you try and do
something for me not at all in your line. It may be quite impossible
and if so never mind. There is a poor old man called Durkan who
Lord Arran evicted under very hard circumstances.[1] A grabber took
his land but did not live on it & one day poor old Durkan took his
courage in both hands & went back to his house <& took forcible
possession> & lighted his hearth fire. The grabber came & tried to
put him out & a case of assault was brought against Durkan at the
petty assizes in Ballina but he was let off. He went straight back &
again took possession of his old home – he was again brought up at
petty sessions & this time returned for trial at Castlebar from there
he has been sent to the Winter Assizes in Sligo. The poor old man is
a most deserving case & he has a remarkably fine character. Every
effort was made to get him to swear that it was Miss Gonne's words
that made him go in, & though I certainly think they may have had
something to do with it he declared over & over again they had not.
So fearful was he of getting me into trouble over his case that he
never came to see me or asked my help while I was in Ballina. Sligo
by all accounts is a bad place to be tried in & a certain Malachy Kelly
crown prosecutor who prosecutes in this case can they say get a jury
there always to convict any man he likes.

If I openly interfered in this case I would I know only make things
worse for him, but I am particularly anxious to get him off. Cannot
you get your uncle or some unionist friends in Sligo to say a word
in his favour – Lord Arran I believe is bitter against the old man – I
am willing to pay to have him defended, but there again my name
had not better appear & his advocate should not be one of the usual
nationalist ones such as Harrington

Forgive me for bothering you about this. I know it cannot interest
you at all, only old Durkan has strange pathetic blue eyes with an
odd faithful expression in them, which though I have only seen him
once makes me want to help him –

I have been working desperately hard & am feeling rather worn out. I have one or two more meetings announced & then I must take a rest. I only go to Dublin today from Ballina. I read Evicted Tenants Restoration Scheme & must see Russell[2] about it, on the whole I approve & will help if I can.

I saw Lady Gregory's letter on the theatre. Write & tell me what plays have been decided on.[3] I must arrange to be in Dublin for all of them this year –

Are you writing much? I was in the room with George Moore[4] for a few moments at Oldham's the other day, but there were many people & I did not know it till after, so did not really see him. Is his play beautiful?

I am disappointed that *Shadowy Waters*[5] is not been given this year. When will it come out?

I wish I was out in the Transvaal the Boer victories are wonderful,[6] how I admire those people. What a ghastly horror war is, even while I am denouncing those poor fools of Irish soldiers who are out there in England's service, a miserable feeling of pity comes which makes me sad in spite of England's defeats but as for Chamberlain & the English Cabinet & financiers responsible for this war, all the Chinese tortures invented by Mirbeau's diseased brain in his *Jardin des Supplices*[7] would not be bad enough for them, from which very common place remarks you will see that I must be very tired & overworked & had better end this long dull letter.

Goodbye my friend, don't give yourself too much trouble about my old evicted tenant, only if you see the way to saying a good word for him to some likely unionist juror please do so. It is useless speaking to any nationalist they will be all told to stand aside. One voice in the jury would be enough I hear to save him.

Write to me soon

Very sincerely your friend

Maud Gonne

Yeats wrote to his sister Lily on 1 November from Coole: 'The spectacle of John Bull amassing 70 or 100 thousand men to fight 20 thousand and slapping his chest the while and calling on the heavens to witness his heroism has not been exhilarating. Ireland seems to be really excited and I am not at all sure that Maud Gonne may not be able to seriously check enlisting. She is working with extraordinary energy.'

64
Nassau Hotel
Nassau Street
Dublin
October 11th [1899]

My dear Willie

Many thanks for your letter. I am in such a whirl of work I don't know how to get through it all.

We have got a Transvaal Committee[1] for the purpose 1st of sending a beautiful Irish flag to the Irish regiment[2] who are going to fight against the English, 2nd to organise meeting[s] all over the country against recruiting.

I don't know when I shall be able to get away. You must have found me very cross in Dublin the last few days you were there, but I was so taken up with work that I could think of nothing else –

This Transvaal idea has taken hold in Dublin as nothing else has for a long while. I hope it will be the same in the provinces. The English papers are rampant at the idea of a campaign against enlisting, it only shows what a necessary & useful thing it will be to combat it.

I am glad to hear the Countess Kathleen is likely to be acted in New York. It is sure to be done well there as far as *staging* is concerned. I don't know much about American actors –

I hope you are getting on well with your writing & that you are feeling happy & contented in the beautiful dreamy West.

Parnell Demonstration[3] Sunday was a failure. Freeman report was absolutely correct. Lord Mayor hissed & booed all along the line for not having attended Boer meeting,[4] even Redmond hardly got a hearing –

I can't write more to-day. Remember me to Lady Gregory
Alwys my dear Willie
Very sincerely your friend
　Maud Gonne

65
Belfast
Friday [December 1899]

My dear Willie

As usual I am in such a whirl of work that I have had no time to write & even now you must not expect an interesting letter, for I have had no time for occult work & you do not care for the active political battle in which I am forever engaged. I can understand that so well, for the details of it are dull enough & sordid enough too at times, though I come across so much devotion & sacrifice & idealism among many of our people that it encourages me to go on & I am hopeful –

It is most provoking about the difficulty & uncertainty of getting the money for the literary theatre, I have heard nothing since on the subject.

I did try a little with the symbol you sent, but got nothing. I fancy it is too complex a method of working for me & also seems to me to belong to INDIVIDUAL rather than to GENERAL symbolism. But I am not in a good mood for occult work of that sort at present.

Did you read Horace Plunket's[1] most dishonest speech on the war delivered at the meeting of the Kingstown primrose league? He talked about it being a war to bring freedom & equality to South Africa & also referred to the GENEROSITY of England to Ireland at the present time. I am disappointed I thought Horace Plunket was honest & sincere. I think so no longer. I am sure Russell must be sad about it – He has certainly by that speech limited his power of usefulness to Ireland. No nationalist can support him now.

I return to Dublin tomorrow. There will be lively times in Dublin Corporation over the Boer resolution on Monday.[2]

Thank you so much for saying you will make a strong declaration against the war. But I do not want you to do so if you think it will harm you, as it is not in the direct line of your work. I must say I regret you did not follow your first idea of a poem against the war. First thoughts are always good, second always bad, third *sometimes* good if your reasoning power is strong.

I wonder if you would write something for the *United Irishman* some day.[3] They are very anxious to have a poem of yours. It is doing a wonderful work & the men who are running it deserve all support they are making such personal sacrifice for it – Its circulation has *doubled* during the last month & it is really *very* good, but I don't suppose you ever see it – They are going to give John O'Leary's portrait for the Xmas No – Couldn't you send a tiny poem – on anything you like –

There it is a shame of me worrying you for this, but you must forgive me.

In great haste

With many thanks for your charming letter.

Always

Most sincerely your friend

Maud Gonne

Postmark: Belfast 7.30 pm De 8 99

Maud Gonne refers to three people who were of great significance: the two men who founded and ran the United Irishman, *Willie Rooney and Arthur Griffith; and James Connolly. As well as pursuing their own lines, the three worked successfully with her, and were the most active publicists for the separatist ideal over those half-dozen years at the turn of the century. In the next few months the* United Irishman *(which she refers to as 'U.I.') covered all her extensive anti-war activities.*

The following letter refers to a meeting held in protest at the presentation of an honorary degree to the Colonial Secretary, Joseph Chamberlain.

66

[Nassau Hotel
Dublin]
[December 1899]

PRIVATE

My dear Willie

Many thanks for your letter. The one for publication was not read at the meeting as owing to the arrest of our friend Connolly[1] I was not at the beginning of the meeting held by O'Leary & the parliamentarians in the safety of the rooms of the Celtic Literary Society. I however gave it to the reporters & wrote a note to Brayden asking him to publish it in full.[2] The Freeman is the only paper in which I see it & they have only published the last paragraph. I am very sorry.

I arrived on Saturday night at 9.30 in Dublin after a fearfully rough crossing. I at once went to Committee meeting & found a crowded room & great enthusiasm on account of the proclamation forbidding <the> meeting which a detective had just come & delivered. Willie Redmond said instead of one we would have a dozen meetings & if necessary he was prepared to address the people from the top of a lamp post!!! It was decided that all the speakers should meet at Mr O'Leary's at 12.30 & a brake should drive in from there to Beresford Place. Next day W. Redmond called for me at 12. He seemed nervous & talked about arrests & also said he had been told the Govt would not only baton, but shoot down the people & we must be careful to prevent such needless sacrifice. Arrests I thought possible but the shooting idea quite absurd, England does not want to proclaim to the world that she is at war in Ireland.

Davitt was with O'Leary when we arrived, & after a few moments' awkward pause explained that he & Mr O'Leary considered it would be foolish & senseless going to Beresford Place, all our purpose was served by the proclamation of the meeting. Mr Redmond only half agreed & said some meeting ought to be held in a hall. I entirely disagreed & said I should go to Beresford Place whatever happened as when a meeting was announced it must be held or attempted at any cost so as not to set an example of cowardice to the crowd. Mr Davitt said his wife was only confined a week & it might kill her if anything happened to him, & rather in contradiction a few moments later said of course WE would risk nothing by going to Beresford Place, but he would not risk the crowd getting batonned. O'Leary agreed with Mr Davitt. Mr Redmond appealed to me for the sake of unity & appearance to first join with them in a meeting in the Celtic Literary Society rooms & then I was free to do what I liked after. The brake & committee arrived & great was their consternation when matters were explained to them. The M.P.s and Mr O'Leary decided it would be foolish & risky to drive down to the Celtic rooms in the brake, – they would each go separately.

I went in the brake & we drove to Beresford Place which was very strongly guarded. We forced an entrance & the crowd broke in on every side but the police were too strong they charged & succeeded in surrounding the brake & arrested our driver & marched the brake & all of us to the Police station an enormous crowd followed & cheering wildly. The police must have had orders not to arrest me, for they suddenly let go of our horses & Connolly took the reins & we drove all around the town, halting for passing our resolution in front of Trinity College & the Castle & waving Transvaal flag. The crowd was as numerous & as enthusiastic as at the Jubilee. The cheering for the Boers was deafening. They got out the mounted police & charged our brake, but didn't venture to arrest anyone. Finally we returned to the Celtic rooms & found Mr O'Leary presiding a meeting composed of 5 reporters & the M.P. orators. The moment I left the brake & got inside the Celtic rooms the police seized it & arrested Connolly so I went out again to try & bail him out. I returned in time for end of meeting, a few people possibly 80 had assembled. To appease & please me Davitt told me he had arranged to have several effigies of Chamberlain[3] burned in the town.

I had arranged for one to be burned, but hearing Davitt's friends had undertaken this work I at once counter ordered ours, as it was useless to risk my friends, if the thing was already arranged for, & I had no money in my hand to pay for defenses & fines in the case of more arrests. I regret to say that as far as I have heard No effigy of Chamberlain was burned. Moral – never trust to others to do what one can do oneself.

Goodbye my friend my plans are a little vague but probably I shall return to Paris for Xmas, & will let you know how long I shall be in London & when.

In gt haste for friends have just come in

I remain

Very sincerely Your Friend,

 Maud Gonne

Postmark: Dublin 5pm De 20 99; London 11.30 am De 21 99.

Of a Hero I had Made
1900–1904

> I had a thought for no one's but your ears:
> That you were beautiful, and that I strove
> To love you in the old high way of love;
> That it had all seemed happy, and yet we'd grown
> As weary-hearted as that hollow moon.

W. B. Yeats, 'Adam's Curse' (first published 1902)

1900

In spite of tensions and wrangles the national spirit had been raised by the '98 Centenary. The IRB resolved their difficulties with the INB. The '98 clubs in existence all over the country, run wholly or partly by the IRB, were active when the Local Government Act came into force in January 1899, giving all shades of nationalism a political voice in the new county councils. The United Irish League spread with amazing rapidity, and with its support the Parliamentary Party, after a decade of dissension, was united in January 1900 under the leadership of John Redmond. With these developments the IRB lost ground to the United Irish League and Parliamentary Party over the next ten years. Arthur Griffith developed his pacific separatist ideal of Sinn Féin. Intellectual and literary nationalism had by now laid solid foundations with a sense of a national identity growing among the people, and a national theatre was on the way to being realised. Yeats was working towards the Literary Theatre's second season in February and as the political pace slowed down he moved more towards the theatre and literature. Maud Gonne continued to work on the theme which was uniting many shades of opinion in Ireland: opposition to the war in Africa.

Some time before setting out on her second American tour she went to Brussels to see Dr Willem Leyds, the Transvaal representative in Europe, concerning the sending of a volunteer ambulance corps to the Transvaal. She also proposed a startling Fenian scheme to place bombs, disguised as lumps of coal, in the holds of troopships going to South Africa in order to deter recruiting. The IRB had the organisation to do it with the aid of the French but they would need the money to execute it. Dr Leyds decided to give her the necessary money. However, before she received it, someone else went to Leyds saying that he was collecting it for her. The money was not received. It was decided that the person who collected it was Frank Hugh O'Donnell, who had been told of the transaction by Dr Ryan. A donation made by him to the Parliamentary Party was all the money that was recovered, given to Yeats by John Dillon. Around the same time Maud Gonne had given a French intelligence officer a letter of introduction to Dr Ryan, and he asked Dr Ryan for a secretary. Dr Ryan gave him Frank Hugh O'Donnell. The intelligence officer was betrayed and sent back to France. Dr Ryan was not prepared to take action against O'Donnell. On hearing of these betrayals, some of the IRB wanted to shoot O'Donnell but Yeats and Maud Gonne prevented this. What they and Griffith did was to inform all the IRB in London and Dublin of the events so as to neutralise any further damage. Then Yeats and Maud Gonne left the IRB. O'Donnell continued to write his invective.

These events, which form the background to the following letters in 1900, seriously damaged Maud Gonne's credibility with the French intelligence. Because of the French government's gradual rapprochement with England over the next few years her influence in French establishment circles waned.

67   7 Avenue d'Eylau
                                               Paris
                                               Sunday 7th [January 1900]

My dear Willie
    How often I have meant to write to you these last few weeks & I have been so busy & worried about a lot of things that I have not had time, & my plans were so uncertain.
    Today they are quite decided I start next Saturday for America & shall only stay about a month –
    I liked your article so much in the North American Review.[1] It is all so true what you say about the hol<y>ness of places & in the power of tradition. I love your article because of its revolt against the hideous bourgeoisie, which you describe as the good citizen type, which would set a limit to every emotion and enthusiasm. I think possibly you might have made it a little clearer that you did not include the Young Irelanders & Fenians in this category for they were inspired by the ideals of the heroes of 98, & it seems to me that these men are after all pale reflections of the old Celtic heroes who communed with the Gods. We need this communion with the Gods increased & strengthened & then we shall have new Cuchulains and Dermotts[2] who will free us [from] the hideous tyranny of English materialism.

Your article is beautiful. I would like it reproduced everywhere in Ireland. I sent it to Mr Griffith & asked for it to be fully noticed in the U.I.[3]

I am not looking forward much to my American tour. I *hate* the *journey* & I want to be here & in Ireland. Still I think it will be successful.

With every good wish for the new year I remain my dear friend yours alwys
  Maud Gonne

Addressed to 18 Woburn Buildings.
Postmark: Ja 9 00.

68   [Paris]
            Monday [January 1900]
My dear Willie

I was so sorry to hear of the trouble & anxiety which you have been in.[1] I am so glad your Father[2] is keeping well & has plenty to occupy his mind. There is nothing like work when one is unhappy. It is always terrible to see one one loves go through the door of death & mystery before one but yet life is such a short short thing in eternity that we shall soon meet them again, & perhaps under happier conditions.

I have been in a terrible whirl of work lately worse than in Dublin. I start Friday for America & haven't even begun writing my lectures yet – my 1st lecture was put off till the 4th of Feb. so I changed my ticket & only start Friday next –

I hope my tour will be successful, I get various accounts from New York as to what my committee are capable of doing however I shall take the blue flag of Lug[3] with me & trust all will be well.

Forgive this hurried note people are waiting for me so I must end. I trust the plays[4] will be a great success. I *know* they will. I wish I could see them.

  Alwys
  Very sincerely your friend
    Maud Gonne

69   [France]
             [January 1900]
My dear Willie

Just a line to say I am starting tonight for America & to thank you for your letter. I wish I was home again before I start. Yes I think with you political events are hopeful and interesting. I have just got the fashionable influenza, but am starting all the same, I will have lots of time to stay in bed & get well on board. I hope to arrive in New York next Sunday week & stay at the Waldorf Astoria hotel. Write to me there & send me any papers of interest.

Will you see the doctor[1] & beg him to write to all his friends in America to help me for I am not at all sure things will go smoothly. I received two days ago an enthusiastic wire from Rocky Mountain O'Brien[2] saying '*Success insured Central Music Hall engaged 4th February great enthusiasm.*' Yesterday I got a cable from another Mick O'Brien[3] saying 'Best Friends advise against coming just now cable decision.' I have cabled *arrangements made am starting*.

Of the two O'Briens I should think Rocky Mountain has by far the most influence still I need all the support from my friends at home.

How sorry I am to miss the plays it is too disappointing. *Goodbye*. I hope to be home in six weeks.

Alwys Dear Willie your friend
Maud Gonne.

70   Boston[1]
                                                                     14th Feby [1900]

My dear Willie
So many thanks for your letter –
I am indeed sorry to hear of all the trouble & worry you are having about the theatre[2] & that you have been ill.[3] – I trust things are well again with you. I had endless worry here at first but all is going right now & my tour is a great success.[4] I hope to return home on the 8th by French line & shall be in Ireland middle of March.

New York is the only place to write to me, *5th Av Hotel*. I am lecturing nearly every night so you can imagine I have not much time & am very tired.

In gt haste.
I remain
Very sincerely your friend
Maud Gonne

I do hope you are well again – Write me a few words in New York.

71   7 Avenue d'Eylau
                                                     Thursday 22 [March 1900]

My dear Willie
Your letter is splendid & your suggestion of meeting in Rotunda to protest against Act of Union is most appropriate.[1]

I should have been in London ere this but on my return last Saturday I found little Iseult had been very ill with influenza & the Doctor said her lung was affected. I was worried over it & took her to a specialist yesterday who happily has reassured me about her – but she will want a lot of care & watching & as soon as I have fulfilled my present engagements in Ireland I shall return & take a rest with her at Samois.

I will probably cross to England next Monday & unless I write or telegraph you the contrary will arrive Victoria about 7 o'clock – (am not quite sure exact hour). You might see Dr Ryan & find out if he can see me that evening or Tuesday morning at 12 o'clock. I am lecturing in Cork on the 30th March.

My lecture tour was most successful but I will keep all news till we meet

Alwys your friend

Maud Gonne

The controversy over Queen Victoria's visit to Ireland was gathering momentum. Ostensibly she was coming for the centenary of the Act of Union, but it was regarded by nationalists as a recruiting manoeuvre. The Irish daily papers advertised arrangements for the Queen's breakfast for children to be held in the Phoenix Park, and it was announced that there would be special excursion trains from all over the country to the city.

72   [Paris]

[late March 1900]

My dear Willie

for several days I haven't been feeling well. I thought it was only the fatigue of the journey, but yesterday afternoon I got suddenly very ill & had to send for the doctor he says I have got enteritis from influenza & says I will have to stay in bed for *at least* a week.[1] It is too aggravating just now when there is so much to be done –

I have had to telegraph to Cork to put off my lecture there. Please tell Doctor Ryan. Dont worry about me, the doctor says if I keep in bed & take nothing but milk for a few days there is no danger at all & today I am better than yesterday. I am more annoyed than I can tell to be ill just now, when there is so much to do.

Excuse more as my head aches & writing tires me.

Alwys your friend

Maud Gonne

73   7 Avenue d'Eylau
                                                         29 Mars [1900]

My dear Willie

I am much better I am sitting up today. I am desperately hard at work & have been even while in bed for I am bringing out a special Queen's no of *l'Irlande Libre*,[1] for it will be necessary to do something to counteract the poisonous lies which the English press agencies will spread abroad about the Queen's visit.

The Harrington MacBride idea[2] is excellent. Harrington will be a fool not to accept for his popularity is at very low ebb in Dublin just now.

I hope to be well enough to travel in a week or 10 days. Send me any papers you think will be useful for reproduction here. Delaney & McKenna[3] & several others are good enough to help me distribute the news in the press.

I have been writing till I am tired out so goodbye. Thank you so much for your kind letter. Your letter to the papers on the Queen's visit is splendid.[4] I hope the suggestion will be carried out. Martyn's letter is very good, bravo![5]

I will write & congratulate him one of these days –
Always dear Willie
Your friend
     Maud Gonne

74   Nassau Hotel
                                                         [Dublin]
                                                         Good Friday [13 April 1900]

My dear Willie

Lug the Ioldana has delivered the enemy into our hands. He tempted him to write verse & that has been his undoing. Not even our gentle & conciliatory friend[1] will be able to get over this last effusion, he had heard of <them> it but had not seen <them> it, he ought to see <them> it, as soon as possible – That poetic effort is enough, *apart* from the personalities it contains, to give the reason needed for having nothing more to do with the author.

No one here, where the literature has been well discussed, can understand London[2] having any toleration. I will send you a copy of the publication shortly which please show & explain to your gentle friend who cannot fail I think to be struck by its gravity.

Collis in the *Figaro*[3] had called me a *liar* & expressed doubts as to the possibility of a liar being a lady & all this in defence of the loyal Dublin Fusiliers & their bravery. The editor of the U.I. seems to have exceptionally decided views on the responsibilities of an Editor, he said that no lady on the staff of the U.I. should be insulted so he called on Collis in his office & horse whipped him, Collis didn't defend himself but sprang to the window & yelled for help & finally got a policeman – Griffith is in jail for a fortnight because he refused to give bail not to beat Collis again for six months.

Every body I have seen even some unionists say Griffith was quite right & Collis only got what he deserved. I called on Griffith in Mountjoy[4] & found him in very good spirits not with standing wearing prison dress of an extraordinarily ugly description.

I am being taken great care of by Mr Mallon's brigade.[5] One stands opposite my Hotel all day & I think night too, another follows me around even into the shops, I have never seen such open & impudent shadowing before, however if it amuses them it doesn't hurt me. I unveil the Napper Tandy tablet[6] on Sunday & go to Cork on the 18th. I shall probably not be in London quite so early as I expected, but will let you know beforehand the exact date.

Goodbye dear Willie

Always your friend

Maud Gonne

On Easter Sunday, Maud Gonne unveiled the Napper Tandy memorial plaque, after she and O'Leary, travelling in a brake, had led a procession through Dublin. On the same day a group of women met in the Celtic Literary Society Rooms to organise the presentation to Arthur Griffith of 'a nice strong blackthorn stick with a silver ring' to replace the South African sjambok he had broken over Colles. They decided to follow Willie Rooney's suggestion in the United Irishman *of organising a treat for those children who had not attended the Queen's breakfast in the Phoenix Park.*

75   [Dublin]
                                            Thursday [19 April 1900]

My dear Willie

My case against Collis[1] has unexpectedly been fixed for hearing before the Recorder on Saturday & *may* drag on till Monday or Tuesday. This is not sure – but in any case I will not be able to leave before Saturday night & very possibly not till Tuesday, this is trying, but perhaps it is as well to get the thing over at once –

I shall be staying with my sister in London, so don't trouble to come & meet me. I will come & have tea with you & we might try & get some visions but I will not be in London more than a day or two as I *ought* to have been in Paris 10 days ago –

I will telegraph you as soon as I know decidedly the day I can start.

I hope you will arrange for me to meet Dr McBride.[2] Yes I would like to meet him at your house.

It is very late & I am so tired so Goodnight.

Alwys your friend

Maud Gonne

76   [Dublin]
                                        Monday [23 April 1900]

My dear Willie

You will see from enclosed that I am obliged to remain over here longer than I anticipated, the trial will be on Thursday. Of course I have no expectation of getting justice from the English law in Ireland when I believe it has already a ruling of the Bench that to call a man an informer is no libel, it being an *honor* to serve the English Govt. It is also against my principles to apply for help to that law which I repudiate & defy but I have to do so on this occasion for the sake of my friends the crowd who would not understand that Miss Gonne allows Dublin to be placarded with 'Miss Gonne in receipt of Governt pension'[1] without 'taking the law on the man <who says> responsible for it'.

I have *appalling documentary proof*[2] against the gentleman of whom we have spoken much lately. Proof such that none of his friends even the blindest can have anything more to do with him. Happily the consequences of this last affair though *mischievous* are not so *disastrous* as the one I referred to in London but MORALLY they are quite as bad.

Please see your gentle friend[3] & urge suspending all acquaintance until my arrival at the end of the week. It is urgently important or I wouldn't write even this much. If I had not a complete confidence & trust in the spear & the shield of Lug I would be very much worried, as it is I feel quite calm. I have had no more visions lately.

I like your article so much in the U.I.[4]

Anna Johnston has a poem in the same number[5] which is strong & dramatic & makes me want to recite again –

Au revoir –

Alwys your friend

Maud Gonne

77   [Dublin]
                                   Tuesday 24th [April 1900]

My dear Willie

Many thanks for your letter, how strange all you tell me about your legal affairs.[1] I am a good deal battered & not very well just now. I hope we are nearly through the bad influences, tell me when you write how long they are likely to last.[2]

You will not be surprised to hear that [?] Nally & Co[3] are repeating Collis' lie, *possibly* they suggested it to him.

Thank you so much for offering to come over but I don't think there is anything you can do for me. All my friends are as kind & eager to help me as possible & I hope to be soon in London when we can talk things over –

F. H.[4] is a really much more worrying & annoying affair – & all on the account of our friend's foolishness & LEGERETE.[5]

Once more thanking you for your letter.

I remain Alwys
your friend
        Maud Gonne

Addressed to 18 Woburn Buildings.
Postmark: Dublin AP 24 00.

78   [Dublin]
                              [after Thursday 26 April 1900]

My Dear Willie

I have just received your letter you will see by paper I sent that the libel case has been adjourned till Friday next[1] so I can't possibly go with you to hear Fiona's play[2] much as I would have liked it –

Oh what a bore & what a waste of time & energy this process[3] is & yet – it was necessary –

I am just starting for Belfast I return Monday
In haste
Alwys Your friend
        Maud Gonne

I am so sorry all the worries you are having with the G.D.[4] – legal matters are always horrid. I hope the bad influences are nearly over –

79   Nassau Hotel
                                          [Dublin]
                                          5th [May 1900]

My dear Willie

As you will see by papers all went well yesterday & Collis is returned for trial.

I am very tired & exhausted today for that cross-examination was a terrible nervous strain though everyone said I was wonderfully cool & collected & gained the approval of Mr O'Leary!

I have got to go to Limerick on Thursday & will cross to London on Friday night –

The spirit warnings you sent me are rather unquieting but I believe I am protected though at times I feel hostile forces around me.[1] All my work is going on very well.

I am so glad all went well with the G.D.[2]

In haste

Alwys your friend

    Maud Gonne

I want to see Doctor McBride will you make a rendezvous for me on SUNDAY in the day time.

80   [Dublin]

                            Saturday Evening [May 1900]

My dear Willie

Such strange things happened last night that I open my letter to add this & to ask you were you trying any occult experiments last night?

I had had a very hard day's work writing yesterday, after dinner I took a book of Lady Wilde's Irish legends[1] to read a while to rest before going out – it must have been about eight o'clock – suddenly I felt I was going to sleep – I who *never* can sleep in a chair, I felt it *was* not natural & hesitated whether to fight against it or to let myself go – I thought possibly I was wanted for some spiritual [?combat] somewhere. So invoking the protection of Lug & the spear & shield I *went* to sleep or into a trance I don't know which. It lasted about an hour & a half. I can remember nothing but when I woke I was tired & exhausted. I could do nothing. I gave up the idea of <going> out. I was *too tired*, I went to bed. I was very restless & lay awhile going to sleep. Suddenly I was awakened by a loud knock at my door, I called who is there, getting no answer I lighted the candle. The room was full of moving shadows & a distinctly hostile feeling pervaded. I don't know the time – perhaps between 12 & 1 o'clock –

Suddenly, my candle *was put out*, it did not flicker as though blown out, but the flame grew low & went out. This made me angry so I at once rose & lighted two candles. For some time they burned unevenly, sometimes flaring up very brightly sometimes sinking quite low. The flame was always quite straight there was no draught or flickering. I sat up & put a barrier between myself & who ever was there beyond the shapeless shadows I saw nothing. I did not try to see, for I felt it was [indecipherable] & to see them I would have to increase their force – after about an hour things got alright & I went to sleep.

Let me know if you had any strange experience or were trying occult experiments.[2]

In haste
Your friend
    Maud Gonne

81   Dublin
                                                        Sunday [13 May 1900]

My dear Willie

Collis apologised so case ended.[1] I am finishing off my work & will start for London tomorrow *Monday* evening. I shall be in town Tuesday & Wednesday & shall stay with my sister 12 St George's Terrace Gloucester Road.

Will you make an appointment for me to see Barry O'Brien[2] I dare say it will suit him best if we go to his house. Write to 12 St George's Terrace to tell me engagements you have made for me – I have so much to write so will add no more, will keep all news till we meet.

Yours alwys
    Maud Gonne

In Visions Notebook *Yeats wrote that PIAL had come from Ireland on 21 May. He thought the prophecies had in part been fulfilled; she had given him letters of O'Donnell which were quite dangerous and scandalous, and he was trying to deal with the matter without her having any part in it.*

Some of the next few letters are concerned with the suppression of the United Irishman. *It was regularly intercepted in the mail by order of Dublin Castle. The issue of 7 April containing Maud Gonne's article 'The Famine Queen' was seized by the police; the* United Irishman *offices were raided, copies were confiscated from newsagents around the country, and mail was intercepted.*

82   7 Avenue d'Eylau
                                                            Paris
                                                            24th [May 1900]

My dear Willie

Many thanks for your letter. The long suffering toleration of our gentle friend[1] is most exasperating & disheartening – We can do no more for the present I think – Of course I will be delighted if he will help with 'the politics of the feeding bottle and perambulator' I don't think there is any danger of the fraudulent purse in that[2] –

I am very tired & somewhat low-spirited & looking forward to

Saturday when I am going down to Samois for a week's rest & idleness with Iseult & the dogs cats & birds.

The exhibition[3] I hear is wonderful but I have hardly seen any of it yet. Please send me the papers with account of question about U.I.[4] on the estimates if you happen to notice it.

Once more thank you for all the trouble you are taking for me but don't worry too much over it, I have done what I can, & now trust to chance, & I think all will be well –

I have been writing such a lot today that my hand & brain are both tired, so Goodnight & forgive dull stupid letter

 Alwys your friend
  Maud Gonne

83   Samois
                   Seine et Marne
                   [May 1900]

My dear Willie

You will of course have heard of the 2nd suppression of the U.I.[1] It is probably on account of Dixon's <article> letter to the Lord Lieutenant of the illegality of the first seizure & of the villainous habit of detaining & stealing a certain nos of copies each week in the post & the publication of correspondence about which I tried to get question asked in house. It is doubly necessary to get that question asked now – & also to ask <why> the reason of this 2nd suppression.

Will you try & see some one of our 'representatives'. I hate giving you this trouble but the affair is really important. I am going to Paris tomorrow to get it properly written up in the French Press.

Will you also send your book[2] with autograph to *Joseph Smith Esqre* Board of Police *Lowell Mass.* He helped me more than anyone on my lecture tour in the Eastern States, he writes for the principal Boston papers & is I think vice president of the American Historical Society. He would be of great use to you if you decide in going to America he has the greatest admiration for your work.

I intended doing a little occultism here, but once more I find I am just as hard at work as I can be writing to America & France about the U.I.

I have been writing steadily since one o'clock today & it is now six & I am so tired I can hardly hold a pen therefore once again I must ask you to forgive a stupid business letter.

I will write a better one soon. I hope to be in London about 12 *June*.

 Alwys your friend
  Maud Gonne

84
                                                          Paris
                                          Tuesday [early June 1900]

My dear Willie

Herewith my copy of the U.I. the suppressed no.

If Griffith agrees to an English radical asking the question I think it will be a good lesson to the M.P.s but we should have to explain our *reasons* for asking an Englishman. It will always be a good thing for Reynold Newspaper to take up the matter.[1] Your idea of placarding is very good.

In haste

Alwys Your friend
        Maud Gonne.

Having spent about a month in Paris, Maud Gonne was back in Dublin for the final preparations for the Patriotic Children's Treat which took place on 1 July. The United Irishman *reported that 30,000 children took part in a procession that took an hour and a half to pass any point; on arriving at Clonturk Park, two miles from the city centre, the children were given refreshments. Twelve lorries and drays brought to the park three tons of sweets and biscuits, 50,000 buns, 300 dozen bottles of mineral waters, 80 casks of ginger beer, as well as cakes, fruit and sandwiches. Maud Gonne then addressed the crowd of children.*

85
                                                       [Dublin]
                                          Wednesday [4 July 1900]

My dear Willie

Here are the pictures. The treat was a wild success[1] I am still very busy. I hope you have received your watch safely. I forgot to put *Gort* on the address I gave jeweller if you haven't received it write to Johnston jeweller Grafton Street.

Many thanks for document about O'Donnell.

In greatest haste

Alwys your friend
        Maud Gonne

86
                                                  Nassau Hotel
                                                       [Dublin]
                                              7 July [1900]

My dear Willie

The bill for the watch can only be a few pence & will have probably been put on my account anyway it is no matter.

129

I haven't seen Davitt,[1] but have written him & find he cannot go to Paris just now. As I am leaving Ireland tomorrow I fear I shall not have time to see him before I go, but I think he is safe to be against F. H.[2] on account of personal attacks – As usual I am over-worked.

Thank you so much for your letter & for all the kind sweet things you say in it – but my dear Friend I do not want you to make up your mind to sacrifice yourself for me. I know that just now, perhaps, it is useless my saying to you 'love some other woman'. All I want of you is not to make up your mind *not* to, to put it before you as a duty, that would be wrong the gods do not want that, & it makes me very sad. As for me you are right in saying I will be always to you as a sister. I have chosen a life which to some might be hard, but which to me is the only one possible. I am not unhappy only supremely indifferent to all that is not my work or my friends. One cannot go through what I went through & have any personal human life left, what is quite natural & right for me is not natural or right for one[3] who has still his natural life to live – All I want of you is not to build up an imaginary wall of duty or effort between you and life – for the rest the gods will arrange, for you are one of those they have chosen to do their work.

As for the possible changes or dangers which you speak of for me, I am under the great shield of Lug, the day I am no longer protected, if that day comes, my work for Ireland will be over – I should not need, *I could not accept* protection from anyone, though I fully realise & understand the generous & unselfish thoughts that are in your heart & I love you for them.

I am glad you are in the country with lady Gregory, I am sure it is good for you to be with her & you will do beautiful work. There is a peace & restful ease you need, I am in my whirlwind but in the midst of that whirlwind is dead quiet calm which is peace too.

Goodbye my friend. I cross tomorrow to England. I will be with my cousins, 28 Hyde Park Gate, S.W. till Wednesday the 11th when I go to France.
　Always your friend
　Maud Gonne

In Visions Notebook *around this time Yeats set down an old secret Celtic rite for divine marriage and discipleship obtained from a Hebridean woman, adding that there was only one person to whom he might ever show it. In July he recorded the thought that Maud had come to him in his sleep, he having written to her recently relinquishing all love but the spiritual. He assumed that she had not understood him and thought he had become weary. However, practical matters seem to dominate Maud Gonne's mind with the preparations for the Irish nationalist delegates' visit to Paris and the continuing Boer War preoccupations.*

87
7 Avenue d'Eylau
Paris
Sunday [July 1900]

My dear Willie
Why haven't I heard from you all this long while? I hope you are not ill, write to me at once. I am more busy than I can tell you. Domestic worries, Irish delegation,[1] Transvaal volunteer returns[2] etc etc.

Will you please get Frank Hugh's[3] documents all together in an envelope & have them ready – a friend will call & bring them to me, either *Griffith* or Dr *Walsh*.[4] They are needed over here – Hoping to hear from you soon & to hear that you are well.

Alwys your friend
Maud Gonne

88
Samois
30th July [1900]

My dear Willie
Yes it is very very bad of me never having written you all this time, I know it very well & have no good excuse, except that after the strain & effort & work of conducting the Irish delegation in Paris, smoothing down quarrels among delegates, looking after press work, seeing visits were returned duly, cards left etc & bringing the delegation to the proper places at the proper times & offending nobody, I was so tired & exhausted that I have not gone outside the wall of my little garden since I came here or written any letters except the most strictly business ones –

It all went off splendidly & was a wild success. You will probably have seen accounts in the Irish papers the *U.I., Independent* & *Nation.* I am not sure about the *Freeman.* We were met at Dieppe great crowd at St Lazare Station Paris, lots of French M.P.s & Municipal Councillors at Banquet, receptions nearly every evening, seats in the official tribune of the Chambre at the review and escorted by French M.P.s reception of Irish delegates by the Municipal Council in the Hotel de Ville & all the delegates thoroughly pleased & glad of having taken part in such an important demonstration.

Of course you will have received Frank Hugh's last. It is as lying as all he writes. I am answering it you will be surprised I am giving him that much importance, but I think it is best to do so. He is still the friend & confidant of the confiding & gentle one[1] in London who defends him in spite of the indignation of all his friends. It almost passes belief, but it is so.

I go to Aix-les-Bains on the 6th & shall be there all through August. My sister & cousin are going to Brittany & are taking Iseult with them, I shall go & pick her up when I leave Aix. I shall be in Ireland about middle September – I hope I may be able to work a little occultism at Aix. I have not done anything up till now I was too weary – I return the G. D. paper[2] & think the characters very good as far as they go –

Are you working much? I am alwys so glad when you are in Galway. I know it is so good for your work & I feel you are happier there than anywhere else.

Your article in the Speaker[3] is reproduced in this week's U.I. it would have been before but Mr Griffith was in Paris & owing to the many engagements made for their entertainment the Delegates had to stay several days longer than anticipated – Mr Johnston,[4] Lisnaveana, Antrim Road is absolutely in agreement with us about F. Hugh O'Donnell. I am sending my pamphlet[5] to the U.I. office to get it printed & will tell Mr Griffith to send a proof to you in case there is anything you dislike very much in it – in which case let me know, & I may alter it. I don't think there will be however, it is simply an exact account of the reception in France with translations of speeches by prominent Frenchmen & a few translations from French press, my references to Frank Hugh are very short & to the point.

My address in Aix will be *Hôtel Thermal*
     Aix les Bains Savoie.
I go there on the 6th. On the 3rd I go to Paris.

Au revoir my friend thank you so much for your letters, do not think I do not write because I do not think of you, it is not so – only I hate writing letters. They say so little [of] what one means at least mine do, yours are always interesting & beautiful though sometimes they make me very sad.

I remain
Always your friend
 Maud Gonne

89   Hotel Thermal
                                                     Aix les Bains
                                                     Savoie
                                                     15th August [1900]

My dear Willie

I think you are quite right about not replying to Frank Hugh & though I had written really rather a good page about him [with] which I intended to preface my pamphlet which was a simple account of the Irish visit, with the translation of the speeches of the French M.P.s from manuscripts I had got from them, I have decided not to publish.

I have not been getting any visions lately, but I have been reading studying and thinking a good deal lately with the result that I have a good deal of interesting things to tell you. I will write them to you, probably tomorrow, today I have just finished an article for the U.I. & don't just like writing at length. I got all the colors like Russell's, the only one that puzzles me is the light blue. I get that as deep repose quiet which in a way corresponds to Russell's fixity & stability. It occurs to me the color of passivity but not with the color of the earth which I get now as green, now as yellow, but I am uncertain as to this & certainly I would rather trust Russell's vision than my own.

I have also got the three worlds as he got them & this symbol for them [rest unclear; with diagram][1]

I will try the symbols you send & let you know what I get but I am not very good at *seeing* just now though my mind is a good deal on those things. I am working a good deal at them.

Larmenie's Moytura[2] is very wonderful. I dare say the poetry is bad & that of course would disturb you in a way that it does not me, but the *ideas* in it are beautiful. Either he must have *studied* old Irish manuscripts very well or he was inspired. Do you know it?

Give my kindest regards to Lady Gregory if you think of it – Little Iseult is staying with my sister & her children & my cousin May at Port Aven in Brittany, where I am going to join them as soon as I have done my cure here at the end of this month. Iseult is enjoying herself wildly among the other children & I fear won't like returning to her solitary life.

Will you, when you write send me the name of the four cities[3] & the four Druids of the Tuatha de Danaan. I haven't the book with me & don't remember, but I want them for some work I am trying to do –

Au revoir dear Willie
Alwys your friend
    Maud Gonne

90   [France]
                                             [August 1900]
My dear Willie
    I am sending a résumé of things that I have learned lately partly
by vision, mostly by reading & meditation. Of course I am not sure
of their correctness, write & tell me what [you] think. I have much
more but to me it is such an effort to formulate things in words they
take meanings I do not intend to convey. These things are so subtle
that unless like you, one has complete mastery over words,
formulating them in words even to oneself leads to error –
    Nothing I have written is in *contradiction* with Jubainville's
[?book][1] though I have attributed [?meanings] which he would of
course reject. I rejected most of his explanations.
    I cannot write more today as I am very busy.
    Alwys your friend
        Maud Gonne

*After nearly three months in France Maud Gonne was back in
Dublin. Her letters do not give any indication of the amount of work
she was doing. It was in October that a provisional committee was
set up to form a federation of all nationalist societies, to be called
Cumann na nGaedheal, from which grew Sinn Féin, and the women
who organised the Patriotic Children's Treat formed an association
called Inghínidhe na hÉireann (Daughters of Ireland) with Maud
Gonne as their first president.*

91   Nassau Hotel
                                             Dublin
                                             Sunday [September 1900]
My dear Willie
    I have just arrived in Dublin. I haven't written to you for some
time for I have been going through a time of stupid little worries
which got on my nerves & made my temper bad. I think I am nearly
through them now & anyhow I have got <quite> back to my usual
serenity –
    I will be in Dublin I expect for the next three weeks & am not very
busy so if you can spare a week we may be able to do some occult
work together & get the Celtic rite a little defined my cousin is most
anxious to join it. She is not altogether satisfied by the G.D.[1] She,
like myself, was rather repelled by the Semitic tendency of the
teaching. I believe she would get much more strength & help from
the Celtic mysticism & I *know* she would be valuable to us. She is
most anxious we should send her some symbols to begin work with,

I promised to talk with you about it & if possible to send her some
    Let me know when you are likely to be in Dublin so I may be able
to keep a week free from work –
    Alwys your friend
        Maud Gonne

Addressed c/o Lady Gregory, Coole Park, nr Gort, Galway.
Postmark: Se 30 00.

92   73 Lower Mount Street
                                                Dublin
                                                [October 1900]

My dear Willie
    My only definite engagements are I lecture 14th for the Oliver
Bond Club[1] Dublin & there is a Davis Celebration[2] in Dublin I want
to attend on the 18th. Then I am to receive the Freedom of the City
of Limerick[3] sometime date not yet fixed probably after the 18th.
Miss Johnston wants me to go to Belfast,[4] but there also no date is
settled. So you see, I am pretty free of engagements just at present,
& shall be in Ireland till end of month so come any time that suits
you to come to Dublin we shall be able to do some work.
    If however you are busy with your writing & your work is in such
a condition that a *break* in your surroundings will interfere with it
& hinder it for sometime then don't come to Dublin yet – We shall
have other opportunities for the Celtic work. And your writing is far
too important to let ANYTHING interfere with it – I am employing
the comparatively idle time afforded me by the general election[5] in
SERIOUSLY taking lessons in Irish. I have a most CHARMING teacher
in Miss Killeen[6] with a wonderful Irish face & the most beautiful
black hair I have ever seen. She has a wild admiration for your poems
& says she has never read anything which moves her so much.
    Always dear Willie
    Your friend
        Maud Gonne

Do you think Moore[7] could be induced someday to give an article
to the U.I.?

135

93
32 Lower Mount Street
Dublin
Sunday [October 1900]

My dear Willie

I will expect to see you on Tuesday & I hope you will dine with me that evening. I am in an apartment which I have furnished. The rest of the house is a Hotel kept by Mr and Mrs O'Beirne (you know Mr O'Beirne who used to be in the *Independent*)[1] Mrs O'Beirne has asked me to recommend her hotel to my friends & I think you would be comfortable here, the prices I know are moderate –

I only write this because you say you are going to leave the Nassau Hotel & look for lodgings else where – Keep Friday evening disengaged as Sarah Purser & a few of our friends who want to see you very much are coming to spend the evening with me.

In haste & looking forward to seeing you
I remain alwys
your friend
Maud Gonne

Returning to Paris, Maud Gonne was there for the arrival of Major John MacBride from the Transvaal. Later in the month there was a delegation from Ireland which included John O'Leary, who joined in the general welcome given to President Kruger, who received him privately in his hotel.

After going to Liverpool for her lecture on 12 December, she travelled non-stop to Limerick in time to give a lecture in the Athenaeum before a crowded audience which gave her a standing ovation. Both lectures were on the Irish Brigade and Major MacBride as well as on Cumann na nGaedheal policy. The following day the Mayor of Limerick, John Daly, presented her with the Freedom of the City.

Police suspected her, John MacBride and the IRB of America and Great Britain of endeavouring to form an Irish Brigade for France.

94
73 Lower Mount Street
[Dublin]
Wednesday 12th [December 1900]

My dear Willie

I have just got back from Liverpool where I have had a rather exciting time. The police prohibited my lecture on 'Irishmen in the English army' which I had delivered in Glasgow without any opposition on the 29th of last month.

The Rev. Kennedy Vicar of Plumpton was to preside.[1] We

outwitted the police who with horse & foot to the number of two or three hundred & any amount of detectives guarded the hall where the lecture was to be given. We had a meeting in the open air in the Irish quarter of the town much larger than the one in the hall would have been. This was half through before the police came up in great force & dispersed the crowd. Next night they prohibited our banquet. For a country which boasts of the Liberty of speech this is not bad. I am delighted! I go today to Limerick where I lecture this evening & receive Freedom of the City tomorrow –

In the train from Holyhead to Chester in the same carriage with me was a most beautiful girl, quite young about 18, something about her attracted me & I began talking to her. I found she is Irish, & engaged for the first time to play in an *English* theatrical Company, some such horror as the *Geisha* or the *Greek Slave* & of course quite small parts. There was something so innocent & childlike in her face & yet she looks as if she could act – I don't think she has had much education except in music & from what she says all her family are musicians, her brother is 1st violin at the theatre, her sister a music teacher & she had taught dancing. Here is her address, if it wouldn't bore you too much, write her to come & see you. Possibly she might – if she has any dramatic talent in her, which of course I don't know – be useful sometime to act in some of the Irish plays. She is certainly beautiful enough for an Irish heroine. If you think well you might introduce her to Mrs Emery, she is certainly too good for a hideous English comedy troop.

What a horrible thing it is that so much that is beautiful in Ireland has to go & get destroyed in England for the sake of money.

I will be in London about the 30th for a day & will come & dine with you if you will have me – I will let you know exact day later on –

Alwys dear Willie

Your affecate friend

Maud Gonne

95   73 Lower Mount Street
                                          Dublin
                                          Sunday [December 1900]

My dear Willie

Anna Johnston, Seamus McManus[1] & myself have almost decided on forming a Club to be composed say of people, all carefully selected not to jar on one another if possible, literary people or closely connected with the Irish movement & to take a house in a gaelic speaking part of the country with a peasant woman as Caretaker & servant, to which *any* one, or all could go, any time they felt inclined or wanted to get away from the world either to write or work or learn gaelic.

I think the expense ought not exceed about £4 a month that divided into 12 would not be more than about 7 shillings a month each – McManus knows of a house which he says would just suit on Inniscoo off the Donegal coast.

I send you his letter on the subject as it will tell you all details & avoid time of writing. Will you join us? & can you suggest any suitable people to ask to join. Mr Piper[2] says he will, if he remains in Ireland which is not quite certain. Miss Sheila Maher a friend of Anna Johnston has also joined.

Tell me what you think & make suggestions. I am very pleased with the idea – it is a modification of what I have been dreaming of for a long while.

I am so sorry to hear of the trouble you are having with <your publ> the *Dome*.[3] Couldn't you get the article taken anywhere else & publish a short note of explanation as to *the reason for doing so*, so that those who hadn't read the 1st essays could get the back nos of Dome & read if they wanted – It would be a lovely way of punishing the *Dome*

Is anything settled yet as to date of Literary theatre?[4] My last fixed date here is the 28th Dec. *my children's treat*,[5] I may cross on the 30th but will let you know quite for certain.

I have so much writing to do today that I can't add more now.
Always your affcate friend
    Maud Gonne

96   [Dublin]
                                                   [December 1900]
My dear Willie

I have received Shadowy Waters[1] Oh it is beautiful, more beautiful even than I remembered it – When I come to London you must read it to me again.

I read it last night, I read it this morning, when instead I ought to have been working. It is perhaps the most beautiful thing you have ever written, & yet while I write this I feel that is treason to the Secret Rose & to the other poems.

I will probably cross on the 30th & will spend last evening of the year with you if you will have me – If you have arrangements made for that evening do not change them. If Lady Gregory has asked you for that evening *I do not want you to refuse* or alter any plans you have made, I will come then either on the 30th or the 1st but you can let me know.

In haste dear Willie I remain
Alwys your friend
    Maud Gonne

*John MacBride had gone to America in December with an introduc-
tion from John O'Leary to John Devoy. He wrote asking Maud
Gonne to accept the invitation from Clann na Gael to join his lecture
tour, since he felt he needed help.*

─────── *1901* ───────

97

[Letterhead]
Paquebot
Champagne
A Bord, le Havre
2nd Feb [1901]

My dear Willie

Just starting for America for a two months' tour.[1] I caught
influenza in London & was laid up with it most of Jany & then was
fearfully busy preparing for this tour, which is why I haven't written
you all this while.

I am well again but *hate* going away so far from all my friends –
I am going to lecture with McBride. 1st lecture New York 17th

I hope you are quite well again now & that arrangements about
play[2] are going smoothly

I have no time to write more as we are starting

Alwys your affecate friend

Maud Gonne

98

[Letterhead]
The Arlington Hotel
Calumet
Michigan
25th March [1901]

My dear Willie

Oh the weariness of an American lecture tour! The constant being
on show! the receptions, meetings, banquets etc – no you don't know
the weariness of it all & to have to go through all this for money I
who despise money but have realised that money is necessary to carry
on the work in Ireland. MacBride is going around with me, & is very
good & saves me all the worry & fatigue he can, he is becoming quite
a fine speaker – We are having good success everywhere & are making
a good deal of money though as I don't take up subscriptions & we
only get half the proceeds it takes a long time to get the sum I want

for the work at home, I prefer staying longer this year so as not to have to return next year or for many years I hope.

There is three foot of snow over everything here & we go about in sledges which is rather fun though I prefer a warmer climate. We are in the copper mining country – I had taken my passage back to Europe on the 18th April but they are trying to persuade me to remain a fortnight or a month longer & my love of FILTHY LUCRE may induce me to do so –

The *Irish World* organ of the United Irish League devoted a whole number to abuse of me – It appears my lecture tour just interferes with the tour Redmond had planned for the purpose of asking for funds, & as I am preaching that freedom will never be won by words & that parliamentary agitation is a waste of time & money I am hardly contributing, as I should according to the *Irish World*, to the success of the appeal for funds of the United Irish Parliamentary Party.

These gentlemen have had to postpone their intended visit to America till August when some of them will come out under Michael Davitt's wing & owing to a personal quarrel between Finerty of Chicago[1] & some of the leaders of the American tea party, or as Pat Ford of the *Irish World*[2] has christened <them> it 'The Standing Army' because <they> it never does anything but stand still. They will be received by Finerty & one or two advanced men as well as by all the constitutional politicians – I don't think the success of their tour will be very great – If any of the Irish papers have taken up Pat Ford's attack on me, or originated some for themselves, I would like to know – all my friends seem to have forgotten to send me the Irish papers.

In St Louis I met Mr Reidy the editor of a paper there who is wonderful well read on all the Irish literary movement & a great admirer of yours. He told me to tell you he reads everything of yours which appears – He also has read all Mr Russell has published, & was most enthusiastic over the Irish literary movement.

How is Grania[3] going? How I wish I were home. I have succeeded in stirring things up a little here but the real work is at home or at all events in Europe –

Why didn't the prediction that I was to get a great fortune come true! Alas alas –

I hope you are well & happy, write to me to 5th Avenue Hotel, New York City

I remain
Alwys your friend
Maud Gonne

Described by reporters as wearing a 'red dress with silver belt and broad picture hat' and at another time a 'blue velvet dress', Maud Gonne was said to speak effectively; 'she does not rouse her hearers by any oratorial outbursts'. Her speeches covered England, famine, the Boer War and Cumann na nGaedheal. She was quoted as saying 'why should we not succeed in our fight for independence as you Americans did, as the Boers will surely do' and that 'the Irish race owed a deep debt of gratitude to Major MacBride'. It was reported that Major MacBride was 'extremely modest and unassuming'; he related his experience in the Boer War and sought 'moral and financial assistance for a revolution in Ireland'.

Maud Gonne left John MacBride in Chicago to continue the tour on his own and he did not return to France until July. He proposed marriage to her while they were in America. On 24 May the Dublin Metropolitan Police noted that Maud Gonne had arrived in Great Britain from America and they were expecting her to suggest something in the nature of a crime 'as she was in funds'.

99
[Letterhead]
45 Hill Street
Knightsbridge
[London]
Monday [? June 1901]

My dear Willie
Many thanks for your letter – I succeeded very well in America but will tell you all about this when we meet – I got back very well but caught a bad cold & sore throat on arrival in France, I am well of that now – and am engaged nursing my poor little sister who has been *very* ill indeed. She is better & has been allowed to get up to-day. On Wednesday we are going to Norwood where the Doctor has ordered her to spend a week or 10 days to get up her strength enough to enable her to take a longer journey to some mountain place – I shall stay about a week longer with Kathleen. My address will be Queen's Hotel, Norwood. Than I am going to Ireland *73 Lower Mount Street*, but will only be there till the 1st week in July as I have to return to Paris for a meeting.

I would like very much to see you & do a little occult work – I have not done much, but on the boat I did a little, writing down some of my visions which may possibly be of use in the rite. I quite agree with your divisions of the ceremonies.

I have a lot of writing to do for my sister, so can't add more now – With great pleasure at the thought of seeing you shortly.
I remain
Alwys your friend
Maud Gonne[1]

100

Salvan
Suisse[1]
[July 1901]

My dear Willie

The heat in Paris tired little Iseult very much – without *seeming* to work hard she passed first in nearly every subject at her school, this may have been too much for her – she was looking very ill so I took her up to the top of a Swiss mountain to live the life of a little savage. Three days after her arrival she was taken very ill indeed, intense fever & one lung affected, for a day or two we feared meningitis, luckily a French doctor was taking his holidays & he was very good & helped me nurse her & now she is well again but he says she is frightfully delicate & for the future will be a great anxiety. She is much too tall & much too clever for her age –

This will explain to you why I have been so lazy about writing. I had tickets for Beyreuth & my cousin May was to go with me & didn't care to go alone so as Iseult was really well by that time & my friend Madame Avril (de St Croix) here I felt I could safely leave – so the 11th & 12th I spent in Beyreuth. I heard Parsifal, which is worth travelling round the whole world to hear. It did me more good than I can tell. I got back yesterday & found your letter.

About plans. I will be in Dublin, *if possible*, the 26th but as it is horse show week I would advise you to get put up by friends for Mrs O'Beirne lets every room in her hotel & generally puts three or four beds in each, of course she wouldn't do that to you, but as for getting waited on or fed that you will find most uncomfortable probably two or three people sleep on the dining room table.

I think the scenario for the play you have made for Hyde[2] very beautiful. I am so glad you are going to write it in English as well as the Irish. It ought to [be] very much appreciated by the public in Ireland & I believe it will be. It is just the sort of play wanted for the Daughters of Erin.[3] Don't let it be stolen this time in America. I should think it would be taken & make a great success. The idea is very beautiful.

I have so much to do so end this in haste
     Alwys your friend
          Maud Gonne

I leave for Paris in 2 days

At this time Inghínidhe na hÉireann, with the help of Alice Milligan, were adding to the theatrical life of Dublin with historical tableaux vivants and plays, including the original idea of presenting song and dance in the traditional atmosphere of a ceilidh or gathering in a homely kitchen.

101   [Dublin]
                                                            [September 1901]
My dear Willie

I read your article on *Magic*[1] last night in bed, I like it very very much.

I have been so busy or I would have written you before. Our entertainment at Ancient [Antient] Concert rooms went on improving both as to performance & audience till Saturday night house was packed & the Red Hugh play[2] was really admirably played. <I think Miss Milligan & I wrote the Brian thing between us but I wrote most of it> now I come to think of it she wrote it nearly all but it was done in a hurry & I don't think it was particularly well written –

I enclose a poem of Catherine Tynan's.[3] Did you ever read such drivel?

The meeting at Castlerea was a great success for the Nationalists, the whole crowd was with us! I felt sorry for Mr Hayden[4] the solitary M.P. invited & who is really a nice & patriotic man –

Frank Hugh[5] is busy again – an advertisement appeared in Reynold newspaper, in the paid advertisement column, running something this way 'Sword of honor to be presented to an Irish literary warrior in Paris, to avoid him any alarms the presentation to be performed by a complaisant English *woman*, signed – Mary Jane Griffith & Anarchino' It was longer than this but I don't remember it –

On the 11th a long article in the *Pall Mall Gazette* undoubtedly written by Frank Hugh, announcing the presentation of the sword of honor & of course written as if from an English man, but this breaks down in places & shows a more intimate knowledge of our alas not over secret affairs, than would be likely for any one outside the immediate circle of the tea party.[6] The article accuses MacBride of cowardice & says I am English & an adventuress, but that I have great influence over a certain section of advanced nationalists, others the really serious ones deplore this as is evidenced by the advertisement from Reynolds which is thus given, *slightly revised*, in big type – The ceremony of the presentation of the sword, the article goes on, will be attended by *continental anarchists* & by French nationalists of the Rochefort[7] Millevoye type. I haven't got a copy of this choice article or I would send it to you – Then there is another violent attack on me in Diamond's[8] Glasgow Observer, repeating all the lies about my being in receipt of a governt pension & asserting that I am English. A new Illustrated paper the *Tatler*[9] gives a very pretty portrait of me & of my sister & calls it Two beautiful sisters but

under it insists in a very *marked* way that I am English daughter of
English Officer & Kathleen the wife of Col Pilcher. I fancy all these
things are some way connected, the Glasgow Observer hangs its
article on the picture in the *Tatler*

Well I have written too much about these absurd little worries. I
tell myself that life is not long enough to worry about trifles, but all
the same they irritate & get on one's nerves & waste time & thought
– If only one's own party were solid & consistent it wouldn't matter
– but the London Doctors[10] are *still* supporting Frank Hugh, & the
Dublin Nallys & Co say that 'anyone who like Miss Gonne talks
open revolution from the platform deserves to be shot because it is
felon setting & must compromise whoever is seen speaking to her.'
Isn't it funny, such doctrines according to them must only be
whispered in the seclusion of the Club or at some mysterious meeting
where as in 'Madame Angot'[11] slouch hats & long coats are necessary
& the conspirators should have walked sufficiently round the town
with mysterious airs to have interested a good collection of
detectives.

I am tired & cross today that is all, because these things don't really
matter one bit. The people don't listen to them, & whenever I appear
in public all the men who spend their time whispering abuse of me
are obliged to come up & try & look as if they were my best friends
& confidants, in order to stand well with the people.

I lecture on the 21st for the Inginide na hEireann, & on the 22nd
on Nationalism & the situation generally for the Michael Dwyer
Club[12] in the Workman's Hall York Street, on the 23rd I leave for
France & will only come back for your play.

I went the other day to the haunted Glen. I saw Semias,[13] he is
still good to me but showed me several ways in which I have failed.
He promised me I should acquire the power of healing. Then I
followed him into the mountain by a long winding gallery & in a
small round chamber was a table, at the end was a veiled figure. I
could not see well. On the stone table was a cake of bread & a cup
of water. I was invited to eat & drink & though I do not know who
the veiled figure was or if I should have done so I eat[14] and drank
for I never err by caution. Then all disappeared. Standing by the
stream I saw but very vaguely a great figure of a woman clad in
dark shimmering purple & green with a veil that hid her face. I
think she was Dana[15] in her Nature aspect. Semias was with her.

I went a long way up the stream till I stood by stones marked with
7 & with 9. There standing in the middle of the stream dressed in
lily green was a beautiful girl. She stood still & presently sat down
by a rock & a laughing baby child came also dressed in green & leant
up against her. I don't know who they were. Once I heard the fairy
music quite distinctly with physical ears, it came from out the

mountain & was as if fiddlers were playing. At Westport I met a peasant man who told me he had often seen the fairies they are tall & sometimes walk *above* the ground, they are generally dressed in white. He often heard the fairy music at a fort near, he & his sister & many others have heard it together, they spend hours sometimes listening to it – Sometimes it is like a great brass band playing, sometimes like string instruments & sometimes like pipes, & it is always different –

I mustn't write any more now as I have so much to do. I am so glad you are well & contented dear friend & that you are working well.

Always dear Willie
Your friend
    Maud Gonne

Remember me to Lady Gregory. When is her book[16] coming out I am so looking forward to reading it.

Diarmuid and Grania was one of the final productions for the three-year experiment of the Literary Theatre. It was staged at the Gaiety Theatre, Dublin, on 21 October and performed by an English company. In Autobiographies *Yeats wrote: 'When Maud Gonne and I got into our cab to go to some supper party after the performance, the crowd from the gallery wanted to take the horse out of the cab and drag us there, but Maud Gonne, weary of public demonstrations, refused.'*

Yeats was pleased with the experiment. He wrote to the Freeman's Journal *on 14 November: 'We cannot have too much discussion about ideas in Ireland. The discussion over the theology of* The Countess Cathleen, *and over the politics of* The Bending of the Bough, *and over the morality of* Diarmuid *and* Grania *set the public mind thinking of matters it seldom thinks of in Ireland, and I hope the Irish Literary Theatre will remain a wise disturber of the peace.'*

102   Paris
                                             [October 1901]

My dear Willie
I will probably arrive in Dublin on Sunday morning & I shall stay at my rooms in the Province Hotel Cavendish Row & look forward very much to seeing you & seeing the 1st performance of Grania together –

In haste
Yours alwys
    Maud Gonne

Addressed c/o Lady Gregory, Coole Park near Gort, Co. Galway.
Postmark: Gort Oc 17 01.

1902

This was a difficult period for Maud Gonne. When in 1900 the Dublin
Metropolitan Police reported plans for an Irish Brigade for France,
they also remarked: 'Miss Gonne is using all the influence she possibly
can with the officials of the French Government to carry out the
project' which given 'the existing relationship between France and
England . . . does not seem practicable'. No such brigade materialised
and France was on the verge of an alliance with England. Maud's
political as well as romantic alliance with Millevoye had come to an
end, but she had formed a new Franco-Irish Committee in 1901.
While she was in America with John MacBride, Willie Rooney had
died at the age of twenty-seven. This left Griffith, already weary,
struggling alone with the United Irishman. *Three other friends died*
within a very short period. On 2 April 1902 Maud Gonne's
contemporary and friend, the poet Anna Johnston, died. John F.
Taylor was seriously ill and died in November, and Augusta Holmes
died in January 1903. Maud's letters to Yeats mention none of these
sadnesses; the deepest of all, perhaps, was the death of her old nurse
Bowie which would have stirred long-forgotten memories from as far
back as she could remember, but it was given only a passing reference
in a letter, so controlled were her emotions.

The letters themselves have become fewer; their paths seem to be
diverging. Where Yeats entertained revolution less, she, with John
MacBride, was prepared to use any opportunity to hand for immediate
action. At the same time she helped Griffith by promoting self-reliance
and by writing more for the United Irishman. *Things on the surface*
seemed normal.

Maud Gonne arrived in Dublin at Christmas 1901. Police reported
that she had left Holyhead on 23 December and had been 'seen off
at Euston Station by a man of Theatrical appearance and glasses,
presumably W. B. Yeats of London. She carried a dressing case, parcel
covered with green baize and left a copy of the United Irishman *in*
the sleeping car.'

103   8 Cavendish Row
                                                      [Dublin]
                                                      6th Jany [1902]

My dear Willie

Thank you for your letter & forgive me not writing sooner. I found so much worry & work waiting me here. I will be in London on the 13th & will have tea with you at 4 o'clock if you will have me & if I don't hear to the contrary.

My children's treat is on the 10 or 11th

Will you be so kind as to get the number of the King with the South African farm burnings,[1] it must be at least 2 months ago, probably 3 months since it appeared, don't trouble about asking for the photos, the number will do well enough.

Russell's Deirdre is very good. He & Miss Young acted it at Mrs Coffey's[2] last week – Miss Young is a VERY good actress quite exceptionally good. Moore was much struck by it. Martyn is not in town yet. Fays' company[3] is working hard but Miss Quinn[4] is very bad the rest are good & we have got a girl Miss Walker[5] who I think will act very well She has a beautiful voice –

Have you decided anything about Kathleen ni Houlihan yet? I think Fay will be able to manage it & I am sure it will be better than with English actors, possibly we might get Miss Young to act with Fay.

We will talk more over all this when we meet.

With every good wish for the New Year & that you may have peace & happiness

　　Alwys
　　Your friend
　　　　Maud G

104   [Paris]
                                                      Sunday [February 1902]

My dear Willie

Many thanks for your letter, I am delighted to hear you have given 'Cathleen Ni Houlihan' to Fay. Did you write him that I would act the part of Cathleen?[1] Have you got another copy that you could let me have as I would like to learn the words here & then go over them with you in London. If you haven't got a copy I will write to Fay to get one made for me. They must begin rehearsing it without me – as they are very slow & take a great time rehearsing a play & I would not be in Dublin long enough to do all that with them. I have a lot of work here – a lecture on the 4th, one on the 14th & one on the 20th Feb. & another on the 4th March besides a lot of other work.

Easter I think will be the best time for the plays but I will write

Fay as soon as I hear from you – What have you arranged with him.

The Society of St Patrick is having such a *handsome* & such a *comic* row that I thought it best not to go to the assemblé Generale this year as I didn't want to take sides. McGregor[2] wrote to me he wanted to see me, but I didn't answer his letter – I really can't afford to have Charlatans about – people don't understand it.

Martyn is ridiculous – it is too provoking, giving up the literary theatre.[3] I can't write more as friends have just come.

In haste,
Alwys your friend,
    Maud Gonne

Addressed to 18 Woburn Buildings, Euston Road, London, Angleterre.
Postmark: Paris 3.2.02; London FE 4 02.

Maud Gonne's Franco-Irish Society was working hard, and the 'brilliant series of lectures' at which Major MacBride spoke in halting French were reported in the United Irishman, *as were the soirées and St Patrick's banquet which they both attended.*

105   [Paris]
                                                 Sunday [February 1902]
My dear Willie

I am so sorry to hear you have been so ill. It is such wretched cold weather, do take care & not go out too soon – I am so glad Lady Gregory is in London & is taking care of you.

I have been terribly busy & a little worried over things in general. I had the biggest meeting I have ever had in Paris on the 14th in the Salle Wagram.[1] The enthusiasm was great, & à bas l'Angleterre was loudly cried – about *4000* people were present. It was presided over by M. Berteaux, Député,[2] who is a governmental député & reporter du budget de la guerre. Clovis Hugues recited a poem on the Transvaal he had written for the occasion.[3] MacBride said a few words, his French would not let him do more, & I lectured on *L'Oeuvre de l'Angleterre* illustrating it with magic lantern views of photos taken in Ireland, India & the Transvaal.

On the 20 I speak at another big meeting organised by the nationalists & on the 3rd March at a meeting organised by the very advanced socialists, so I cannot be accused of not being eclectique (however that is spelt.)

I keep getting a vision of a beautiful grey shrouded figure holding a wonderful jewelled chalice, which I think at times contains fire, for

I see flames sometimes rising for ⌊from⌋ it. Through the grey veils one can see the glimmer of precious stones & jewels. I don't think she has anything to do with the grey woman I used to see. She is very calm & seems to be great & holy. Do you know what it means?

Write soon & tell me how you are. I will stay a day or two in London on my way to Ireland to see you – it will be in the beginning of March –

Alwys your friend
Maud

106   [Paris]
                                          Sunday [February 1902]

My dear Willie

It is my fault that Fay wrote you about the dress for Kathleen, a brilliant idea had occurred to Inginide that they would invite Miss Milligan to come & help them design the costumes. Fearing the same storms which arose last year I hastily wrote that you wanted to design the costumes for your play & Russell was doing so for his – & that being the case they couldn't ask Miss Milligan just to come & sew like a dressmaker. I think I had better wear a black dress (one of my old ones cut shorter will do), & a long round dark blue cloak with a hood such as the country women wear. I shall make my hair grey & wear nothing on it but the hood, which probably I will push back in the house –

If you can suggest anything better please do so –

I hope you are quite well again now. I am as usual a great deal too busy for my liking.

My sister & Cousin are in London 28 Hyde Park Gate London S.W. I shall be staying a day or two with them on my way to Ireland first week March.

We have had great sorrow in the death of our old nurse Bowie – she died only a few days ago.[1]

Au revoir à bientôt

I hope you are quite well.

Affecly yours
In haste
Maud Gonne

Iseult is much better & stronger than she was, I hope she will keep so while I am away.

107   [March 1902]

My dear Willie
  I cross to London on Wednesday and will be staying with my
cousins, 28 Hyde Park Gate. If convenient for you I will come to
see you about *4 on Thursday* afternoon & we can go over Kathleen
ni Houlihan together.
  In great haste
  (I am lecturing tonight)
  Yours alwys
    Maud Gonne

I hope you are quite well again.

108   [Letterhead]
                                       An Cumann na nGaedheal
                                       (Celtic Literary Society Branch)
                                       32 Lower Abbey Street
                                       Dublin

                                       8 Cavendish Row
                                       Monday Night [March 1902]
My dear Willie
  We rehearsed Kathleen tonight, it went splendidly all but the end.
It doesn't make a good curtain – We are all of opinion that Michael
ought to go *right* out of the door instead of standing HESITATING. It
doesn't seem clear if he doesn't go out. If he goes out Delia can throw
herself on Bridget's shoulder in tears which makes a much better
end.[1] Please write at once and say if we may do that. *Russell* & Miss
Young[2] & the Fays & all the actors want it & think it is much better
indeed *necessary*.
  I am desperately busy, there is always so much to be done here.
  I hope you will come over & see the rehearsal of the plays in time
to make any suggestions you think fit. The Company is really good
& immensely improved.
  I remain, dear Willie
  Always your friend
    Maud Gonne

109   [Dublin]
                                            Saturday [March 1902]

My dear Willie

When are you coming over? They are all anxious you should be there for some of the rehearsals of Kathleen – I think it is going very well & will be a great success.

George Moore was at our second rehearsal when some of them didn't quite know their parts (they all know it well now) & he had many suggestions to offer which would have entirely changed the character of the play & which I think would have spoilt it, for instance he wanted Kathleen to get up when she talked about her beautiful green fields & to walk to the door & come back again, in fact he wanted her to be wandering round the cottage all the time & make most of her remarks from the front of the stage instead of from the corner of the fire.

I don't agree with Moore at all about this, for I think one must keep up the idea of the poor old weary woman who would certainly sit down & rock herself over the fire & not get up & walk about until the idea of meeting her friends comes to her.

Deirdre[1] is going well also. The 1st act is the one which seems to me to drag the most, the last acts well – Tomorrow Sunday is the first *dress* rehearsal. I have a beautiful untidy grey wig, a torn grey <flannil> flannel dress *exactly* like the old women wear in the west, bare feet & a big blue hooded cloak.

You would give me a penny in the street if you saw me & I look 60 at least.

Let me know when you are coming over.

I had a wild success with my meetings in the south.[2] Hundreds of people turned away at each of the three meetings for want of room.

In haste dear Willie

Alwys your friend

M

Yeats wrote to Lady Gregory on 22 March: 'Moore writes to me, by the by, that the acting in Russell's play is the silliest he ever saw. He wants Kathleen ny Hoolihan not to sit down. . . . However I have told Miss Gonne, to whom I have sent Moore's letter to do as she likes. One must judge of these things on the stage. I shall go over and see for myself on Wednesday.'

The plays were very successful. Inghínidhe na hÉireann combined the talents of the Literary Society and the theatrical experience of the Fays with their own enthusiasm and amateur ability in a completely native original production. After a slow start the combination, including as it did the giant figures of Yeats, Maud Gonne and Russell, filled the hall, with 'crowds turned away from the door every night'. Yeats wrote to Frank Fay suggesting he might join the new National Theatre Company.

Cathleen ni Houlihan, which had such an explosive effect in 1902, was billed in Dublin in 1916 for Easter Week (matinées at sixpence a seat), but when the theatre reopened it was not performed. Shortly before his death Yeats was to ask himself in his poem 'The Man and the Echo':

> *Did that play of mine send out*
> *Certain men the English shot?*

110   [Dublin]
                                          Monday [March 1902]
My dear Willie

Thank you for letter and enclosure – Don't be a bit anxious about Kathleen, it is going *splendidly*, last night we had a dress rehearsal. Russell & several others were present, they all thought it very good, & begged us not to alter anything, we have kept your stage direction exactly except that Michael goes right off at the end – George Moore doesn't the least understand the piece & would spoil it if we listened to him.

Deirdre is really going well, the first act seems to me to drag a little because Miss Quinn's acting is not, as you say, inspiring but she is very much *improved*. The last act goes very well. The dresses & scenery are very good.

Let me know when you are coming over.

In haste dear Willie

Yours alwys

    Maud Gonne

111   8 Cavendish Row
                                        Wednesday [?March 1902]
My dear Willie

Enclosed is a letter from my cousin about the [?planetary] colors in the Celtic system –

Please *keep* the letter *safely*.

I send it you to show you how *sincere* it is & that she knows nothing of the other system or even of those I got. I wouldn't tell her them rightly because I didn't want her to be influenced by what I see & yet she has got nearly the same.

Saturn seems to me to stand for the Formore[1] & black indigo or purple do equally well they are all storm colors, black is probably the outer purple the more actively dangerous & Indigo the inner & higher form, like the Akasa.

The gold dust may be a symbol of [?majesty] but I think is more something to do with the connection with the *Firbolgs*[2] or gnomes (In Greek mythology are not Vulcan & Saturn sometimes connected?)

It might also be that ♄[3] being the direct opposite of the sun, has the curious reflex quality, for she sees the gold of the sun with a cloud or smoke rising up.

Mercury being in a way air & the messenger of the gods it is natural she should see the divine blue with him but it is covered by his own orange color.

I think we can take these colors as correct now – keep May's letter, it will prove that we took no other system but that the Celtic Gods sent us.

I haven't time to write more now my friend.

Yours alwys

Maud

112   <Vendredi Soir>
                              Friday evening [?March/April 1902]

My dear Willie

Thank you for your letter. Your idea of writing me the letter about the UI for friends in America is excellent please do so by return of post if possible as time presses, I think your letter will have great weight. There is no time to be lost.[1]

I have had resolutions of congratulation passed by our Franco Irish Society & forwarded to Cuman na Gael of Cork & Dublin for their brave protestation against the *Daily* [?*People*]. I have also sent some money towards paying the fines & hope to get enough to pay all. It seems to me that the fact of the *Daily* [?*People*] being of a political character gave point to the protestation & a banquet to the boys fined & arrested would be very good. The time to do it would be when Liddy comes out of prison in three weeks' time. No doubt there will be other occasions of protesting England's vulgarity being rampant in the Dublin theatre & your idea is excellent –

I am very busy & I am only writing these few lines in haste to beg you to write to me the proposed letter without delay & to *register* it to me.

I will write again soon.

Alwys your friend
    Maud Gonne

113   Monday [?March/April 1902]

My dear Willie

I am so sorry to give you the bother of re writing your letter, but I think it would be more effective if it were addressed to Griffith, & the last sentence which I have crossed out omitted. Don't mind sending it to Griffith, return it to me by return of post if possible as time *presses badly*.

Major MacBride will forward it, it is better *not* for my name to appear in the matter –

Thank you so much for taking all this trouble but I know you are as interested in the success of the paper as I am.

In gt haste

Alwys yours
    Maud Gonne

Maud Gonne had rented a small house next door to George and Violet Russell in Coulson Avenue, Rathgar, Dublin. She was lecturing, writing for the United Irishman, *including an obituary for Anna Johnston, and organising a children's excursion to Tara.*

However, what is not apparent in these letters is that the soldier's daughter of whom the journalist H. W. Nevinson had said a few years previously, 'the first man of resolute action whom she meets will have her at his mercy', had decided to marry. In her own words spoken in America, John MacBride 'of all Ireland's living children' had served her the best by fighting 'for right and justice. . . . He saved Ireland's name from dishonor at a time when there was great need.' In June, Maud Gonne wrote to her 'darling Sister' from Coulson Avenue telling her of her intentions: '1st I am to become Catholic, 2nd I am to get married to Major MacBride, this last is not public yet.' Later she wrote again to her protesting sister: 'I am getting old and oh so tired and I have found a man who has a stronger will than myself and who at the same time is thoroughly honorable and who I trust'; 'as for Willie Yeats I love him dearly as a friend but I could not for one minute imagine marrying him.' In a strange way her letters to him seem kinder from now on. It is as if, having reached a resolution for herself, she wished to soften in some way the very hard blow she was about to deal him.

114
26 Coulson Avenue
Rathgar
Dublin
24th May [1902]

My dear Willie

I gave all the details to the Doctor.[1] Things over here don't look very bright but somehow or other they must be made to mend. I don't think Tynan[2] would be any use. I have seen Mr O'Leary.

Would not *Friday the 30th* do for Symons' dinner? there are only 30 days in June I think, & the 1st (i.e. Saturday) I want to go back to Paris. If Friday suits you make arrangements with Symons if not it will have to wait till I am in London some other time. Please thank him nicely for me.

I am so sorry to hear your eyes are still so bad. I am very glad you are going to consult an oculist. Let me know what he says. I think the rest in Galway will do you more good than anything, the quiet green woods will be so restful. Everyone is so anxious to get you to come & live in Dublin. Wasn't it strange of Moore he didn't invite the Fays or any of the Inginide to his garden party.[3]

Hoping your eyes are better,
Alwys your friend
Maud Gonne

115
[Paris]
Thursday [July 1902]

My dear Willie

I am crossing to Dublin today. I think all the work is done about Tara[1] thanks to you & Griffith but I will go to the meeting of the 13th as my children & Inginide want me with them.[2]

I haven't written you all this time, for one thing I haven't been well, I have had very bad rheumatism & was uncertain as to my plans, whether or not I would be able to come to Ireland before going to Aix les Bains. I am only coming over to Ireland for the 13th as I must not delay going to Aix any longer –

I have been staying a week at Laval in the Carmelite Convent there, the superior is a great friend of mine.[3] It is such a wonderful quiet restful place with an immense garden with huge cedar trees & fountains & all a tangle of roses & lillies. Iseult was with me, in fact she was the cause of my visit for she was baptised a Catholic. I felt a little inclined to be also but felt it would mean limitations of thought so didn't. Iseult looked too lovely in her white veil & wreath of white roses. She is now at the seaside with some friends on the coast of Normandy.[4]

I am so glad you are at Coole, the rest & Lady Gregory's care will do you good & your eyes will get stronger.

Alwys my friend

Yours

Maud Gonne

Write me Dublin. I will be there till the 14th

116   26 Coulson Avenue
                                                        Dublin
                                                        Tuesday [August 1902]

My dear Willie

Many thanks for your letter you must forgive me for not having written before – I received Celtic Twilight[1] for which many thanks. I have not had time to re-read the poem you speak of but intend doing so tonight in the train – for I leave tonight for London – What a lovely cover – Where did you get the symbol of the three arrows, Russell was telling me about it.

I am so sorry your eyes are still troubling you. It will take some time but I am sure it is *rest* you need to put them right. I am nearly in the same condition only not so bad as you. I cannot read for half an hour at a time without great difficulty. I expect a month's complete rest will put them all right again & as I have been very lame with rheumatism I am going to Aix les Bains at once – I hate the place & I hate the people I meet there, & the life & all, but the doctor says it is necessary if I don't want to become quite decrepit – What a hideous thing old age is!

It was a great mistake I think to have abandoned the public meeting at Tara. I don't think Groom & Brisco[2] are really beaten at all. In a few weeks I expect they will be digging away as merrily as ever. Griffith doesn't share my views on this subject.

Our Children's excursion was a great success, & every body enjoyed the day immensely.

Brisco had prepared an enormous bonfire to be lighted in honor of the king of England's coronation – We felt it would serve a better purpose if burnt in honor of an Independent Ireland so lighted it & sang A Nation once again.[3] The Constabulary didn't like it at all & danced & jumped with rage – they added greatly to the fun.

My room looks lovely with Russell's paintings all round[4] & I am very sorry to be going away so soon.

I must end now as I have all my packing to do.
I remain dear friend
Alwys yours
    Maud Gonne

My cousin got Celtic Twilight & wondered if it was for her or for me. She was afraid to write to thank you as she thought perhaps the book was *not* for her. Her address is
    Mrs Bertie Clay,
    28 Hyde Park Gate,
    London S.W.

I am going straight to Paris. Only one day in London

During the summer Maud Gonne had been in Roscommon helping the tenants on Lord de Freyne's estate. Apparently she also went to Westport, County Mayo, to meet Mrs MacBride and other members of John MacBride's family. This she had to do on her own, since John MacBride could not enter British jurisdiction because of his action in the Boer War, although in Ireland he was the hero of the day, with MacBride buttons and photographs of an illuminated address to him on sale.

This was the first year that Cumann na nGaedheal held its autumn festival, Samhain. It was a week of competitions and entertainment during which Cathleen ni Houlihan was played. In late November the Irish National Theatre Society had its first season.

117   Westport
                                   Tuesday [August/September 1902]
My dear Willie
    I go back to Dublin today. I have had a very pleasant time. Last night Joseph MacBride[1] took me out conger eel fishing, we didn't get back till one o'clock – It was too lovely among the islands in Clew bay. We went out in the golden sunset & the mountains looked all purple then the light & colors dried out & only grey & black surrounded us & the curlews cried & the sea seemed to sob & the Reek[2] looked black & terrible. Then the moon came out & made a silver way for the boat & the Herring sprat filled the sea with phosphorescent stars & flashes – It was the loveliest night I had ever seen. Joseph MacBride is very nice, he reads a great deal & knows all your books. He lives in a charming cottage on the edge of the bay, where we all went to tea yesterday. By the way he told me to tell you that any time it suited you to come & spend a quiet time in the

country, you would greatly please him if you would write & tell him you were coming to stay with him in that cottage.

I spoke to Cumann na Gaedhal executive[3] & they said you could have the ancient [Antient] concert rooms whichever afternoon suited you best for the lecture & Mrs Emery.[4] Monday there might be some difficulty as they will be putting up the stage – We would like to know as soon as you can which day you select because the other days we will be using the hall for reading the competition papers. I told them they might announce that you would speak at Monday's Concert on the art of chanting. May we announce Mrs Emery or not? Arthur Griffith was anxious at not getting the manuscript before I left Dublin, on account of sending you the proofs early. I hope it arrived safely.

I remain dear Willie
Always your friend
Maedbe[5]

118

26 Coulson Avenue
Rathgar
[Dublin]
Saturday [late September 1902]

My dear Willie
Many many thanks for that lovely little copy of Cathleen (which by the way we are to *rehearse* tonight) when for the first time since my return I meet the National Theatre Co[1] & will probably have much more to write to you about.

I saw Miss Quinn at Inginide meeting on Thursday. She is most indignant over the withdrawal of the Hour Glass[2] which was going splendidly & is far the best play they have. Fay has withdrawn it because he wants to keep it for the opening of their hall.[3] This is a great mistake as their hall is small, smaller than Clarendon Street, & at Samhain[4] in the ancient [Antient] concert rooms it will attract far more attention & a great many more people will be able to see it – I met Cousins[5] (I don't know how he writes his name) for a moment & he told me Fay had withdrawn the 'Hour Glass' as he wanted to keep it for the Theatre Co – Cousins didn't seem to mind. Miss Quinn was wild as she says it seems a slight on the general public who support us. All the Clubs[6] will be at Samhain, while she thinks only a comparatively few & those of a more educated class will go to the little hall. I am not sure that she is correct about the last as I think the Clubs ought to support the National Theatre Co as well as Samhain. Russell also thinks it a great pity that the Hour Glass is withdrawn & he thinks that if Fay gave 'The Land of Hearts Desire'[7] as the opening piece for the small hall, it would attract quite as much notice to the Co, never before having been produced in Dublin.

I also hear but this is only vague rumour that Fay is most anxious not to be thought too strongly political & has not affiliated with *Cumann na Gaedhal* but this I doubt. Any how, you are the president & Douglas Hyde & myself vice presidents of the National Theatre Co & both their acting ladies are Inginide na hEireann so I don't think we need be anxious on that score –

It might be possible for you to write & urge on Fay to go on with the *Hour Glass* & say that I told you I heard that the real reason of its withdrawal was to keep it for the opening of the National Theatre – & offer him the *Land of Heart's Desire* or something instead –

Don't mention Miss Quinn's name in the letter however. As a matter of fact Cousins was first one who told me & the whole Co know. It was only after it was withdrawn & some of the Co protested loudly that it was *said* to have been withdrawn through want of time.

I had a most interesting time both in Tralee & Cork – The parliamentarians got no reception from the enormous crowd in Tralee. The public spirit is good. Cork exhibition has been SAVED by the Department, it is doing wonderful work for encouraging industries & technical education if it only continues but I haven't time to write of all that.[8]

I suppose you will be up in town for Samhain? I will be in Ireland till after Samhain & then I go back to France for Nov & Dec –

I am sending you a case which I made & embroidered for keeping letters & loose papers in. I made it at Aix-les-Bains. You will begin to tremble for my brain when you hear I have taken to embroidery. I hope it is only a passing weakness – & I hear *you* are playing Ping Pong!

Hoping to see you while I am in Ireland
I remain
Alwys your friend
Maud Gonne

119
7 Avenue d'Eylau
Paris
26 Nov [1902]

My dear Willie
Miss Horniman has just been lunching with me & tells me you have improved 'Where there is nothing' a great deal.[1] I am looking forward to seeing it. I am so glad you have found everything quite smooth with the Fays in Dublin & that the Theatre Co is going on so well. I hope there will be no difficulty about production of the Hour Glass. I don't think there will Miss Quinn was delighted with it when I saw her last.

I have done little or nothing at the Psaltery[2] since I came home, for one reason I have had rather a bad cold (it is better now) & I have been frittering my time away with lots of little things. Then I was a week in the Convent with Iseult at Laval. She was very well & happy there. I have her with me now but shall send her back to the convent in Jany when I return to Ireland.

How are your eyes?

Are you happy at being back in London after your long stay in the West or do you find it horrid? I will be passing through London end of 1st week in Jany.

I remain

dear Willie alwys your friend

    Maud Gonne

120   [Paris]

                                        28th December [1902]

My dear Willie

The best of all wishes for the new year forgive me for not having written. I have been in trouble.

Iseult got diphtheria – she is well now but I had a fearfully anxious time & could think of nothing but nursing her & when she was well my nerves rather gave way from the strain – for the last 10 days I have been incapable of doing anything. I am better & beginning to take an intelligent interest in things again. I will be passing through London on my way to Ireland about 8th Jany & hope to see you then – I am so sorry your eyes are giving you so much trouble – The article [in] *fortnightly*[1] is very interesting. MacBride[2] has it – but I will return it in a day or two –

I will write the Fays about theatre & plays in a day or so. I wish they could play MacCollum's *The Saxon Shilling*[3] it is good from national point of view & would please Cumann na Gaedhal so much as it won the prize competition –

You are so good writing to me even when I am silent – Thank you, you are a kind, kind friend always.

May the new year bring you happiness & content.

Alwys your friend

    Maud Gonne

────── *1903* ──────

Though 1903 appeared to start normally with the preparations for the second season of the National Theatre Society, this year had a profound and painful significance for Maud Gonne, Yeats and John MacBride.

121   [Paris]
                                                2 Janvier [1903]

My dear Willie
   I quite agree with you now I have read Cussons' play 'Sold',[1] it is a horror – vulgar & full of bad jokes.
   I will be in Dublin about the 10th & will speak quite frankly what I think of it, in the meantime I am writing Arthur Griffith about it as he is great friends with the Fays, it will certainly come to them.
   In gt haste
   Alwys your friend
      Maud Gonne

I don't the least agree with you about the advisability of the Fay company playing anything but Irish plays. I think they have quite enough at present without foreign drama. They will have much more success if they keep to plays by Irish authors.

122   [Paris]
                                                3rd Jany [1903]

My dear Willie
   Miss Quinn writes to ask me if I will let her understudy & if necessary play Kathleen ni Houlihan. She says she doesn't think she would be let do it unless you & I agreed. As far as I am concerned I am delighted she should because I can't possibly act often. 1st because I am away from Dublin & 2nd because I don't want to get too much in the habit of acting it wouldn't do good for my work –
   If you don't mind Miss Quinn understudying & play[ing] Kathleen will you write her a note to 57 S. Richmond Street to say so –
   In great haste
   Alwys your friend
      Maud Gonne

I will probably be the 9th, possibly 8th in London.

In January Maud Gonne was lecturing in Ireland and did not leave until the end of the month. From Dublin she wrote about the controversy over the ending of Padraic Colum's one-act play The Saxon Shillin'. *In the published version the young soldier who has taken 'the Saxon shilling' by joining the English army is called on to help in the eviction of his family. Finding that even with the money he earns there is not enough to save them, he finally goes to their defence and is shot by order of his commanding officer.*

123   [Dublin]
                                                            Monday [January 1903]

My dear Willie

It is possible I may resign the vice presidency of the National Theatre Co –

They decided on acting the *Saxon Shilling* & then Willie Fay said the end must be changed. He gave many & various & conflicting reasons.

1st he said it was *inartistic*

2nd that it *couldn't* be acted

3rd that it was *impossible*

as to the 1st I don't think Willie Fay is a competent judge –

as to the 2nd, neither I nor most of the company can see the difficulty & Fay won't explain.

as to the 3rd, it is nonsense.

A soldier who mutinies & points his gun at his officer or comrades would at once be shot down – The real reason is, *I think*, that Fay thinks it is too strong & might vex certain people who he hopes to get such as Martin [Martyn] for instance or George Moore on account of his brother[1] –

The ending now which is joint inspiration of Colum & Fay is absolutely grotesque. At the moment when the young soldier say[s] he will get his gun & God knew which way he will fire, an old wound breaks out & he falls & the audience is uncertain if he is dead or not or if the eviction is carried out, it is simply absurd & entirely spoils the play.

This play was the *Cumann na Gaedhal* prize play, & there is much feeling over it being changed – Griffith declares it is spoiled from an artistic point of view & all openly say it is because Fay fears to vex the *respectable*.

If the National theatre is to be independent it *must* be *really* independent or it ceases to be interesting.

I went to one of the rehearsals & spoke out plainly & told Fay the piece was absurd like that. He blustered & was rude to me & to *Cumann na Gaedhal*, personally I don't mind & only laughed.

Last night in Russell's[2] the discussion came up again – the Fays both said that it was an affair for the stage manager & I had no right to give an opinion before the Company. I said I offered no opinion on the *acting* which was the affair of the stage manager, but that I or anyone had the right of expressing our opinion about the merit of a published play & as vice president I had certainly the right of expressing an open opinion before the Company, that the alterations made destroyed the play. It was only *one* individual opinion, but as *one* opinion it merited as that of Mr Fay's individual opinion. Mr Fay said it rested with no one but himself, that the rest of the Company's opinion didn't count, and finally he handed back the manuscript of the play to Collum saying it shouldn't be acted at all –

Collum had asked me before to try & get the original ending put back as he knew this last ending was very bad. He had also said the same thing to Griffith, but before Fay said he was willing it should be changed. The matter dropped there for I saw Russell was pained & didn't want the discussion to go on at his house. When Fay gave back the manuscript to Collum I merely said *Inginidhe na hEireann* will produce it as it appeared in the U.I. at their next public entertainment & I know my Dublin public well enough to know that it would have an immense success –

It is very foolish of Fay quarrelling with *Cumann na Gaedhal*, he forgets that the majority of his actors are members – I don't want to make trouble, but I cannot remain vice president of an Association where I am told only the stage manager's opinion counts not only as to acting but as to altering cutting & choosing plays, & which may as in this case involve a question of principle.

Wednesday is the 1st performance of '*The Lost Saint*'[3] it goes very well. I saw a rehearsal of 'Hour Glass' it is very good. Digges is perfect. He never objected on theological grounds nor did Miss Quinn. But a quarrel seems to have arrisen over the interpretation of the part of the *Wise man* & Digges backed up by Miss Quinn said he wouldn't act if he wasn't allowed to act as he understood the part. He carried the point & all is peace as far as that is concerned. Miss Quinn gave up her part to Miss Laird[4] for quite another reason – Theological *discussion* hinging on the play had been very lively among the Co & one member, Mr Caulfield (the boy who did Patrick in Kathleen) resigned *not because* of the play, as far as I can make out they all like that, but because of the religious discussions which were a danger to faith and morals. The Fays being converts have all the zeal of a convert for unbelief –

How are your eyes? have you seen an oculist yet?

I am very busy & can't write more now –

Alwys your friend

Maud Gonne

On her way through London to and from Dublin it is likely that Maud Gonne saw Yeats, as was her wont. The following is a draft of a letter he wrote in a vain attempt to dissuade her from marrying John MacBride, reminding her of their spiritual marriage in 1898, and warning her that she would lose political power and influence by marrying MacBride as well as betraying her own soul and her friends by abandoning her 'proud solitary haughty life'.

WBY 3 [? London]
[? late January 1903]
<I appeal to you in the name of 14 years of friendship to read this letter. It is perhaps the last thing I shall [write] you.>

Dear Friend
I thought over things last night. The thought came to me 'you are not writing to her quite fully what you think. You fear to make her angry, to spoil her memory of you. Write all [a line & a half cancelled & indecipherable] that you would have her know. Not to do so is mere selfishness. It is too late now to think of anything but the truth. If you do not speak no one will.' Then I thought that you had given me the right to speak. I remembered the passage in one of the diaries in which I have written all that was of moment in our dealing with spiritual things. (I have left out some expressions of feeling that might give you pain). Here is the passage it is dated December 12 1898. 'I will write out what has happened that I may read of it in coming years & re[mem]ber all the rest. <I have dreamed of my friend many times but only once when her spirit came to me at Coole & bent over me did her lips meet.> On the morning of Dec. 7 I woke after a sleep less broken than my sleep is commonly & knew that our lips had met in dreams. I went to see her & she said "What dreams had you last night?" I told her what had happened & she said "I was with you last night but do not remember much," but in the evening she said some such words as these. "I will tell you what happened last night. I went out of my body. I saw my body from outside it & I was brought away by Lug & my hand <outside it & I was brought> was put in yours & I was told that we were married. All became dark. I think we went away together to do some work." ' There are other entries [?similar] concerning this & earlier visions of mine. Now I claim that this gives me the right to speak. Your hands were put in mine & we were told to do a certain great work together. For all who undertake such tasks there comes a moment of extreme peril. I know now that you have come to your moment of peril. If you carry out your purpose you will fall into a lower order & do great injury to the religeon of free souls that is growing up in Ireland, it may be to

enlighten the whole world. A man said to me last night having seen the announcement in the papers 'The priests will <all triumph over for you> exult over us <us for generations> all for generations because of this.' There are people (& these are the great number) who need the priests or some other masters but [there] are a few bid me write this letter. You possess your influence in Ireland very largely because you come to the people from above. You represent a superior class, a class whose people are more independent, have a more beautiful life, a more refined life. Every man almost of the people who has spoken to me of you has shown that you influence him very largely because of this. <You are> Maud Gonne is surrounded with romance. She puts <away> from her what seems an easy & splendid life that she may devote herself to the people. I have heard you called 'our great lady'. But Maud Gonne is about to pass away <you are going to do> something which the people <did> never forgave James Stephens[1] for doing, though he was a man for whom it mattered far less, you are going to marry one of the people <you are>. This [?weakness] which has <has> [?thrust] down your soul to a lower order of faith is thrusting you down socially, is thrusting you down to the people, <you will have no longer any thing to give only those who are above them can [indecipherable] you to [?] rob & them of robbing you>. They will never forgive it – This [?they] [are] most aristocratic minded <people> the most thirsting for what is above them & beyond them, of living peoples. You have lived so much & you are of those for whom surrender of any leadership not that of their own souls is the great betrayal, the denial of God. It was our work to teach a few strong aristocratic spirits that to believe the soul was immortal & that one prospered hereafter *if one laid upon oneself* an heroic discipline in living & [?to] send them to uplift the nation. You & I were chosen to begin this work & <just> just when <you> I come to understand it fully you go from me & seek to thrust the people <down> further into weakness further from self reliance. Now on <on> a matter on which I must <say all> speak if I am to say & believe <that it is not many [?my]> that some are more than man [?know/now] now I appeal, I whose hands were placed in yours by eternal hands, to come back to yourself. To take up again the proud solitary haughty life which made [you] seem like one of the Golden Gods. Do not, you <who> seem the most strong, the most inspired be the first to betray us, to betray the truth. Become again as <the> one of the Gods. Is it the priest, when the day of great hazard has come who will lead the people. No no. He will palter with the government is [?as] he did at the act of union[2] <as he did when he denounced the Fenians>. He will say 'Be quiet, be good cristians, do not shed blood'. It is [?Is it] not the priest who has [?softened] the will of our young men – who has broken their pride. You have said all these things & not so long ago. For [it] is not only the truth & your friends but your own soul that you are about to betray.

The following letter was written from the convent in Laval, where she was being prepared for her baptism. Since she had spent so much time from early childhood in Ireland and in the Catholic countries of the continent, with their rich artistic religious heritage, the Catholic Church had never been alien to her. Iseult and Eileen Wilson were also with her. The next two letters are very crumpled and creased as if carried in Yeats's pocket and taken out and read many times.

124   5 Rue de Paradis
                                                     Laval
                                                     Mayeune
                                                     10th Feby [1903]

My dear Friend

I have your three letters[1] – they have made me sad, because I fear that you are sad & yet our friendship need not suffer by my marriage. You have known me for many years in the ups & downs of a rather agitated life, yet you have always found me the same as far as our friendship was concerned. So it will always be. I did not myself quite understand things but I *know* that I am fulfilling a destiny & but for the sorrow I have in giving pain, I am at peace with myself.

About my change of religion[2] I believe like you that there is one great universal truth. God that pervades everything. I believe that each religion is a different *prism* through which one looks at truth. None can see *the whole* of truth. When we do, we shall have merged in the deity, & we shall be as God but that is not yet. In the meantime <my> our nation looks at God or truth through one prism, The Catholic Religion –

I am officially a protestant & supposed to look at it from another & a much narrower one which is moreover the English one. I prefer to look at truth through the same prism as my country people – I am going to become a Catholic. It seems to me of small importance if one calls the great spirit forces the Sidhe, the Gods & the Arch Angels, the great symbols of all religions are the same –

But I do feel it important *not* to belong to the Church of England. You say I leave the few to mix myself with the crowd while Willie I have always told you I am the voice, the soul of the *crowd*.

I will be here at Laval for the next 10 or 12 days, it is a lovely peaceful place here where I can play with Iseult & forget for a little the worries of life.

Friend of mine au revoir. I shall go over to Ireland in a couple of months, if you care to see me I shall be so glad & you will find I think that I am just the same woman you have always known, marriage won't change me I think at all. I intend to keep my own name & to go on with all my work the same as ever.

Write to me sometimes for I want your news & I want to keep your friendship alwys.

Maud Gonne

Not many months after Maud Gonne was required to abjure the heresies of the Anglican Church, which she did in her own fashion, the nationalists of Dublin posted up the King's Coronation oath, which declared: 'the Invocation or Adoration of the Virgin Mary or any other Saint, and the Sacrifice of the Mass, as they are now used in the Church of Rome, are Superstitious and Idolatrous.'

The marriage took place on 21 February. It was a quiet affair with only a few friends present and had been arranged by MacBride's friend Victor Collins. Many good wishes and gifts arrived from Ireland, for to the nationalists in general this was a union of heroes, though many close friends and relatives on both sides thought it a mistake.

John MacBride wrote to his sister-in-law, Anthony's wife, from Saint-Laurent: 'We had to go to the British Consulate to have the civil ceremony performed and I kept my hand on my revolver while the deed was being done as I was under the British flag while there and I was not going to allow them to try any tricks. . . . Everything seems tinted by the golden rays of the sun and we are happy and enjoying ourselves.' In a note at the end Maud Gonne endorses this view.

125   Bayeux
24 Feby [1903]

My dear Willie

Please forgive me for not having answered your letter sooner. Our last letters crossed & in some way my letter answered yours – I had a fearful rush last week & no time for anything thank goodness ceremonies of all sorts abjurations baptism, marriage are over – I hated having to abjure anything – I refused completely to do so in the form presented to me. In it I was to declare hatred of all heresies. I said I hated nothing in the world but the British Empire which I looked on as the outward symbol of Satan in the world & where ever it came in I was to declare hatred of heresy I declared hatred of the British Empire & in this form I made my solemn Abjuration of Anglicism & declaration of hatred of England –

Dear Willie please do not for a moment think I was vexed at your letter, on the contrary I think you were quite right to write frankly to me – We are surely sufficiently old & strong friends to be able to be quite frank & open with one another. I do not think you will find much change in me –

Tell me when is the Hour Glass to be acted? & have you heard any more about the Theatre Co. I hear the rules with our amendments were adopted –

I received enclosed letter about Tara. Is anything possible do you think?

Will you thank Lady Gregory very much for me for her most kind & thoughtful letter. I was very grateful to her & will write her myself soon –

Write to me Paris as I am wandering about too much for letters to be addressed any where else. I hope to be in Ireland in April.

Alwys dear Willie

Your friend

    Maud Gonne MacBride

In later years Maud Gonne said that she and John MacBride had married at a stage in their lives when their work seemed to have come to a standstill. They were both depressed and decided to undertake one of those lunatic schemes the Fenians engaged in from time to time. John MacBride seemed to be linked with Clann na Gael in America; he had written to John Devoy from Paris in 1902, 'should my services be required for work you can promise for me', and spoke of 'the necessity of renewed activity'. Maud Gonne has written that the honeymoon in Spain was a cover for a journey to Gibraltar to assassinate King Edward VII on his visit there. This scheme had already been floated in America in 1901. Maud Gonne acted as a decoy for the shadowing police. MacBride went to meet his friends to carry out the mission, but that night he came back to the hotel drunk and would not say what had happened. This was the final blow in a honeymoon that from the start had not been auspicious. Next morning Maud Gonne packed her bags and announced she was going back to Paris, and he went too. In April, John MacBride wrote to his brother Anthony: 'Needless to say I did not put foot on Gibraltar and consequently do not know how the C.B.s are doing there. We were at Algeciras (opposite Gib) the day the king arrived and as he forgot to send me an invitation I did not go.'

On 28 April, Russell wrote to Yeats: 'My wife told me that Miss Young had a curious dream about Mrs McB., seeing her all grey with a darkness about her, and that she herself had a dream about ten days ago in which Mrs McB. came to her weeping, and saying she did not

*know what to do or where to hide herself. My wife in the dream
asked her was she not going to stay in her house in Coulson Avenue,
but she said "No, he would find me there".'*

126   St Laurent[-sur-Mer][1]
[Normandy]
Wednesday [April 1903]

My dear Willie
I have only just got your letter – I am so happy to get it – I will
be in London Sunday or Monday, Grosvenor Hotel. Will I come to
tea with you at 5 on Monday? Let me know to the Grosvenor.
I am here for two days getting house ready for Iseult.[2]
Thank you so much for your letter.
Alwys your friend
Maud Gonne MacBride

127   Dublin
7th May [1903]

Private

My dear Willie
I have been thinking over the Celtic rite you read to me & away
from the glamour of the musical words I see some defects which I
think I should [?signal] to you.
As I said at the time it is far too much influenced by Neiche
[Nietzsche],[1] not only as to expression but as to fundamental
thought, *for Neiche is not Celtic*, though his intense individualism &
his rushing fiery paradox & his impatience & his contempt for the
banalité & smallness of the many useless ones, appeal to us – Neiche's
central thought seems to be to do away with the Gods, & to reverence
& to recognise nothing greater than himself, this is most contrary to
Celtic thought.
The Celts have always worshipped & striven after an ideal purer,
more spiritual, higher than themselves & it is no abasement to them
to kneel before such an ideal. Then too – but this I think is far more
from what you *said* to me than from the *rite* itself – you should not
let any personal feeling of annoyance at my becoming Catholic
induce you to put in words which would make it jar or [?seem]
to take the obligation. The motive is unworthy & personal & must
injure the whole rite. I confess I saw nothing in it that would prevent
me taking it but then, to me it seems the spear of the soldier piercing
the side of Christ & letting the essence of God flow into the Graal
cup is the same symbolism as the spear of Lug piercing the night &

letting the essence of God the spark of fire of the soul flow down into the Cauldron of regeneration & rebirth, & the font of baptism & the holy water seem to me the same as the purifying Cauldron of Dana[2] which begins initiation, or the deep well by the tree of knowledge!

The altar of sacrifice & of glory is it not the stone of sacrifice & empire? & the sword which was to the warriors of old an inspiration as well as a defence is it not symbolised in the pure sword of Bridget the holy.

What do I care if the Great Mother is called Mary or Dana or Bridget[3] or the Captain of the Armies of Heaven is called Lug or Michael.

Why Willie it was you yourself who taught me these things.

I still think that for Celtic rites you should keep closely to Celtic names, for though the symbolism is the same the introduction of the foreign element in the names would injure the artistic unity.

I find the Ritual of the Catholic Church beautiful & inspiring. It has greater & more ancient tradition than the English Church & as the head of one's church I prefer the pope to Edward the 7th. Then the great reason the real reason I think though I don't think I reasoned much, I followed as usual inspiration, was that I felt for my work it was necessary for me to become more completely united to the soul of my people so that I could more completely understand their thoughts & help them better.

I hesitated all day yesterday about writing to Martyn about the committee you suggested. I don't like doing anything politically from a personal motive & it seemed to me for the reasons you gave me for acting it might be one, but on the whole the usefulness of such a committee has out-weighed all other considerations & I have just written to Martyn. I am also bringing the matter up before Cumann na Gaedhal & proposing the advisability of organising a series of free open air entertainments all bearing on the visit so as to prepare the public feeling[4] –

I am trying to get a very direct short anti king play written to be given at these entertainments. If you think of any other suggestions let me know.

The Saxon Shilling[5] is going splendidly, it will make a sensation. We have an entirely new set of actors who are wonderful in the parts. Miss Quinn cast them for it, & has displayed a really extraordinary judgement in choosing the types required for the parts & Mr Digges has rehearsed them – I was at rehearsal last night & the play was electric.

Russell is away just now I regret to say –

I like Lady Gregory's book so much but how like her style has grown to yours, especially in the Rafferty article[6] – I suppose this is almost inevitable.

I am very busy, & should not have written you this long letter as I am not sure you will like getting it but it seemed to me it was better to be frank with each other. You think I acted insincerely in changing my religion. I do not think I did, I know I did what I felt to be right both as to that & as to my marriage, but I never analyse or reason out personal things very deeply or at least not consciously.

I hope & I believe we will always remain friends & this banal phase [?phrase] is not the echo of a banal thought

Your friend

Maud Gonne MacBride

128   [Dublin]
                                          8th [May 1903]

My dear Willie

I saw Mr O'Leary, who approves & will join committee. I have just written to various prominent people some of whose names we mentioned in London & others who I have thought of since as possible sympathisers with the movement. I don't send you their names as I expect this letter will be opened – & I don't want to mention names until I *get replies.* I am not writing to any nationalists of whose adhesion I am certain till after I have the answers of these men. *People's protection Committee* is the name I would suggest.[1] Would Lady Gregory join? If so will you write to her or shall I? Are you going to join? I hope so –

I have thought out what I think will be a very successful plan of campaign, but will keep all details till we meet because of the insecurity of the post. I don't want to give them time to checkmate any of our plans –

I am followed about in the most open way by detectives. There is one always watching the house & they follow me in the streets & wait outside shops for me etc just as they did when Queen Victoria was in Ireland. It is all the more strange their doing this in this open blatant manner because they are pretending to be very conciliatory since the introduction of the land bill & I hear have taken off all the detectives who used to watch all the different Clubs and U.I. office etc.

I am very busy so won't write more just now. Let me know if you will be on committee as soon as possible.

Alwys your friend

Maud Gonne MacBride

George Russell's letters are opened in the post since my return!

The United Irishman *had made public the rumour that Timothy Harrington MP, now Lord Mayor of Dublin, was to be absent from the Corporation when plans were being made for the presentation of a loyal address to the King on the occasion of his visit in July. A deputation of nationalists opposing the visit went to a public meeting of the Irish Parliamentary Fund in the Rotunda to ask the Lord Mayor if he intended to vote against any proposal made by Dublin Corporation to present a loyal address. When he prevaricated, tempers rose on both sides and a fracas ensued. The Lord Mayor was seen throwing chairs from the platform at his citizens, ably abetted by other MPs in what George Russell described to Yeats in a letter as 'the most gorgeous row Dublin has had since Jubilee time'.*

It became known as the Battle of the Rotunda. No loyal address was presented, and the United Irishman *gives the impression that Mirabeau's dictum, 'The silence of the people is the lesson of kings', was indeed observed.*

Maud Gonne had her own private demonstration. The Pope had died and in protest against the unionist bunting decorating the little Victorian houses in her quiet cul-de-sac she hung a black flag of mourning out of her window, the flag being a black petticoat on a broom handle. Police arrived to remove it, loyalists gathered and sang 'God Save the King', nationalists came and sang 'A Nation Once Again'. The police cordoned off Coulson Avenue, but Maud Gonne was protected by a group of young hurlers with their sticks, and the black flag continued to fly bravely.

While in Dublin she realised she was pregnant. She wrote that walking in the hills south of the city to think over her situation she met a poor old man who offered her tea in his tiny cabin. While talking to him she realised he was mad, quickly extricated herself and fled. She said she had two phobias, madness and drunkenness; although she had struggled to conquer her fear of madness, she considered drunkenness 'a danger to the national movement', and so her horror of it had appeared quite normal and right.

129   [Dublin]
                                                    Tuesday [May 1903]

My dear Willie

I haven't time to write much but I send you papers with garbled accounts of last night's deputation of *People's Protection Committee* the Independent gives the account Mr Dixon[1] & I wrote of what occurred on platform – The M.P.s were finally left with about two hundred supporters. I think it will have taught them a lesson & I hope it will be reported in the London press. Please send me over any papers which comment on it – Harrington is completely

gone over to the enemy – He receives Officer[s of] English Fleet
& I hear frequents the castle.

Haven't time to write more

Alwys your friend

Maud Gonne MacBride

Mr Martyn was to have read question but at the last moment got
nervous about *speaking*, never having spoken at a big stormy
meeting, & handed the paper he himself had written to me. It was
only nervousness about speaking for he was quite fearless & held his
own splendidly.

George Moore got afraid & backed out on the grounds that he was
a man of letters & not a politician. I may be over end of week.

*John MacBride, struggling to earn a livelihood in Paris, cabled Maud
on the success of the demonstrations and wrote to the nationalist clubs.
Though she might want to run from the drunkenness she feared, it
was not a thing she was ready to do easily, nor did she wish to separate
father and child. She went back to her life in France.*

*The rest of the summer was spent in Colleville. John MacBride's
friends the Collinses were there too.*

130

Les Mouettes
Colleville
par Vierville
Calvados
[September 1903]

My dear Willie

I have been wondering all this time why I have had no letter from
you, but yesterday when I was looking through some papers I
brought with me from Dublin I found the enclosed letter, which was
one I wrote in answer to yours to me in Dublin – As it concerns my
position in regard to the National Theatre Co I send it, though it was
written in a hurry when I was very much over worked just before I
returned to France. I don't know how I forgot to post it & you must
have been wondering why I left your letter unanswered.

We have had the house full of visitors ever since my return from
Ireland, the last departed yesterday – the end of the month we go to
Paris where I have to house hunt. Hotel de Florence, Rue des
Mathurins 26 will be my address till we get a house –

I still think it will be best for me to cease to be the vice president
of the Theatre Co, I won't undertake any but National fights, & the
theatre Co does not seem inclined for such fights. I have no wish to

injure the Co, so please let me know how to gently withdraw without harming it – From all I can hear I think Synge's play[1] is horrid & I will have no responsibility for it – It was forced on the Company by a trick. They were told the reading Committee had accepted it & they had no choice in the matter & yet Russell tells me as far as he knows it was never submitted to the reading Committee. He certainly never saw it or was consulted about it.

I must end now, as I am very tired – Of course you have seen that the U.I. is turned into a Company, I hear the shares are being taken up very well.

I remain,
Always dear Willie Your Friend,
Maud Gonne MacBride

131

Les Mouettes
Colleville
par Vierville
Calvados
9th Sept [1903]

Dear Friend

Your letter & your beautiful book[1] gave me great pleasure. I was rather worried thinking you would misunderstand my last letter & think me unkind & unsympathetic about the theatre affairs.

Of course the theatre is a great disappointment to me & to all the nationalists interested in it, & it is entirely Fay's fault if he is considered anti-national or at least indifferent to national things; it is a little bit your fault also for having made Fay 'above himself' but it can't be helped. He openly discarded a national play, The Saxon Shilling, & repeatedly he spoke slightingly of the national societies, without which societies he would never have come under your notice at all. He openly boasted now that he had a better class of public & he didn't care for them & wouldn't consider them. As he made these remarks before members of these societies, it is very natural that Cumann na Gaedhal decided to dispense with his services for Samhain, and to leave him & his select audiences to themselves.

I think they are quite right. Fay drove hard bargains about money when playing for any nationalistic Society, while he played for *nothing* for the Unionists, to say the least it ought to have been the other way round with a National Theatre Co who owed its existence to the National Societies – As for playing *Kathleen*.[2] It is published, there is no copyright, any society has the right to play it, *besides* you gave it to me for the use of any of the National Societies & particularly said it might be played by any of them & was not to be considered Fay's particular property. With Miss Quinn & Digges &

174

Conally[3] & another girl[4] whose name I can't remember just now but who I know acts well, I think it will be quite competently played but enough of all this –

I like your book so much – I read it all yesterday morning & in the evening I read it out to Eileen,[5] the little girl you may remember once having seen with my old nurse & who is now living with me as governess to Iseult – She too was delighted – Especially at 'The Old Age of Queen Maeve'[6] – & we all love the song of Hanrahan the Red[7] – The Cuchulain play[8] is very much improved since I heard it, but I can't help regretting one of the previous endings, when the body of the young man was brought in & Cuchulain recognised him as he lay dying. This ending is more original but less strong I think – One other criticism on the cover – isn't it ungrateful when you sent it to me & when it has given me such great pleasure? but I don't quite like the title pasted across the way it is – The printing I think is quite beautiful –

I wish I could come to Ireland for the plays, but I fear it will not be possible just now – We go to Paris on the 20th & I have to house hunt. My husband has been ill nearly ever since my return. Iseult is more beautiful & wild & fairy like than ever, she would fascinate you if you saw her by her wildness & originality, there is nothing *banal* about her.

I must end as the postman is waiting for my letter. We are such a distance from civilisation here that it is the only chance in the day of sending a letter –

I hope your cold is better. I hate thinking that your eyes are troubling you so much. I am sorry if you are writing a National play with Lady Gregory[9] that you are not going to sign it, it would do away with some of the misunderstandings that Fay's ridiculous talk has caused –

Let me know about America,[10] of course I will give you any introductions you think of use & am sure you will have a VERY great *success*.

  Alwys your friend
    Maud Gonne MacBride

The following disagreements and the row over Synge's The Shadow of the Glen, *first performed on 8 October, when Maud Gonne and others walked out, led to some members, including Maud Gonne, leaving the Theatre Society and concentrating on Cumann na nGaedheal's Theatre Company.*

132

My dear Willie

I am so sorry I have once more to write to you a long & tiresome letter on the National Theatre affairs, but from your last to me you evidently do not understand or forget what has taken place.

Fay having succeeded in a certain measure through you & your friends (many of who are unionists) has lost his head & thinks he can insult the National Societies who created him. It was not 'hear say' reports I sent you, to *me* Fay said that he didn't care a D—— about the Nationalist Societies & other rude remarks. He made more of these remarks before the members of the N.T. Co. many of whom being Nationalists naturally resented them. He refused a national play that you yourself recommended, he acted for nothing for Unionists & drove hard bargains with National Societies, he naturally made it impossible for the National Societies to co-operate with him.

You forget the existence of the National Theatre Society was originally due to Inginide na hEireann & Cumann na Gaedhal. If these Societies had not taken Fay up he would still be contentedly playing vulgar English farces in the Union Jack Coffee Palace. It was after Inginide na hEireann passed a resolution forbidding any of their members to act for Fay in his English farces & for the Coffee Palace that he came to me & said he would rather act for Nationalists if he could get National pieces & we introduced him to Russell who gave him or rather gave us his 'Deirdre' to act. Have you forgotten how both Russell & I urged you to let us have your 'Kathleen'[1] how you said Lady Gregory thought you should not – & how at last to make things smooth I consented to act Kathleen. It was Inginide na hEireann & Cumann na Gaedhal who financed each of Fay's first attempts at National performances. On each occasion we not only gave him the dresses & scenery we had paid for, but also gave him more than the fair share of profits & even when there was a loss made up something for Fay, not for himself naturally but with the idea of helping the formation of a National Theatre Co – Members of Cumann na Gaedhal personally gave money & collected money for the Company & all this because we wanted a NATIONAL Theatre Co to help us combat the influence of the low English theatres & music halls.

It is absurd for you to say you did not know all this from the beginning though I will believe you have forgotten it now & have grown to think that it is you & Lady Gregory & her friends who started the National Theatre Co. Undoubtedly lately you have given

Colonel Thomas Gonne, Maud's father, who had great influence on Maud's life.

The Bailey lighthouse at the tip of Howth Head. 'We dined at a little cottage near the Bailey lighthouse where her old nurse lived and I overheard the nurse asking if we were engaged to be married.' W.B. Yeats, *Memoirs*

Maud and her sister Kathleen in their presentation dresses. 'Two beautiful sisters', Letter **101**
LEFT Maud 'But even at the starting-post, all sleek and new
I saw the wildness in her.'
W.B. Yeats, *A Bronze Head*
RIGHT Kathleen 'That beautiful mild woman, your close friend.'
W.B. Yeats, *Adam's Curse*

W.B. Yeats at the time of his first meetings with
Maud in 1889, a drawing by his father John
Butler Yeats

RIGHT Lucien Millevoye. Another of the men
who played a great part in Maud's life.

Georges Silvère 1890–1891

> ... 'You shadowy armies of the dead
>   Why did you take the starlike head
>   The faltering feet, the little hand?

> ... She had much need of some fair thing
>   To make love spread his quiet wing
>   Above the tumult of her days.'
>   W.B. Yeats, *On A Child's Death*

Maud in USA 1897.
'Onward alwys till Liberty
is won!' Maud's inscription
on the photograph
given to Miss Murphy,
19 November 1897.

James Connolly.
'Connolly took the reins
and we drove all round the
town ...' Letter **66,** 1899

BELOW RIGHT Arthur
Griffith. Griffith and
Connolly 'worked
successfully with her, and
were the most active
publicists for the separatist
ideal over those half dozen
years at the turn of the
century.'

TOP An artist's impression of the unveiling of 1798 memorial in Ballina, May 1899. '... crowds gathered once if she but showed her face.' W.B. Yeats, *Fallen Majesty*

ABOVE Madame Ghénia Avril de Sainte-Croix. A very close friend of Maud Gonne's.

Letterheads 1895–1902, showing Maud Gonne's different forms of address to Yeats

The leaders of the Transvaal Irish Brigade, Major John MacBride *left* and Colonel Blake *right*. (*The United Irishman,* 12 May 1900.)

'The Famine Queen'. Cover of the edition of Maud Gonne's journal, *L'Irlande Libre,* which was produced to mock Queen Victoria's visit to Ireland in April 1900.

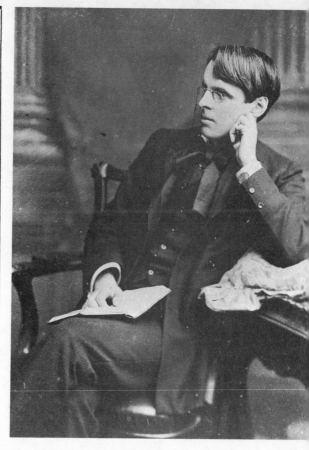

W.B. Yeats at the time of the first production of
Kathleen ni Houlihan in 1902.

Advertisement in *The United Irishman*, 29 March
1902, for *Deirdre* and *Kathleen ni Houlihan*. 'Maud
Gonne played it [the part of Kathleen]
magnificently and with weird power.' W.B.
Yeats, *Autobiographies*

Maud Gonne in *Kathleen ni Houlihan*

'Three Irish Irreconcileables in Paris': *The Tatler,* February 1904. (Maud Gonne, Seán, John MacBride.)

Premises of Honoria MacBride, Family Grocer, Tea, Wine and Spirit Merchant, The Quay, Westport. 'The house where Seagan's father was born.'

John O'Leary and John MacBride. Fontenoy, 1905. 'I was sorry to see poor Mr O'Leary's photo with MacBride just now in the papers.' Letter **153,** 1905

LEFT Mrs Honoria MacBride.

Seán, Maud Gonne and Iseult, 1905.

13 Rue de Passy.

Kathleen Gonne, later Mrs Kathleen Pilcher.

Maud's cousin, May Gonne, later Mrs Bertie-Clay.

it great *financial help* & all its *London* publicity for which last by the way we don't care in the least. There is another thing you forgot. Nationalists are fighting a hard up-hill fight against overwhelming odds. It is somewhat hard to see an instrument we fashioned at considerable sacrifice of time & money quietly taken possession of for another purpose by people who to say the least of it are not *militantly* national. The instrument we formed has been taken from us by you who are looked on as a friend; your conception is different from ours. In many ways you are our friend still, so I say nothing hard, but we have set to work to form another instrument to carry on the work of combating English stage influence. It will not have the London publicity of your theatre, it will not have writers like Shaw who look to England more than to Ireland, it will not have & *does* not want unionist patronage, but it will have the people with it – which is our object –

We have much of the up-hill work & toil to begin again; but the actors and actresses who put the National ideal above all others will join us & last year Fay said, they were the only ones who were any good, because their hearts were in their work – & they drew back at no sacrifice, & worked harder than any others.

Now about 'Kathleen' You forget repeatedly that in Dublin before members of Inginide & Cumann na Gaedhal you stated you had given me for them the acting rights of that play, & I hear it has repeatedly been acted in Ireland since. You remember you quite agreed with me formerly that a play like 'Kathleen' which would do national good should be allowed to be acted by all societies who wished to act it & that it would be selfish to confine it to one society. If I remember right you said this when some cooperative Society in the North proposed acting it & as it was not a National Society I asked you what I should do about the matter. A theatrical manager soon after our success in Dublin wrote to me asking me what terms I would take to tour Ireland & America as Kathleen; of course I never even answered the letter (so much for the copy right)

Soon after my return to France the Sec. of Samhain Committee [of] Cumann na Gaedhal wrote consulting me about Samhain prog-ramme. He stated they proposed acting Kathleen & Douglas Hyde's plays & one or two others. They knew you had given Kathleen to the National Societies subject to my approval & wished to know also if Dr Hyde's plays were copyrighted or were open to them to play & asked me if I would write to Dr Hyde about the matter. I answered I didn't know if Dr Hyde's plays were copy righted but I felt sure he would give permission any way for them to be acted, but it would be well to write to him at once & ask his permission as an act of courtesy. I said I know you would not mind any Nationalist Society acting 'Kathleen' & that I would be writing to you in a day or so &

would mention the matter. Just then my husband became very ill & letter writing went out of my head for the time. I regret this as it would certainly have been more courteous to have written to you about Kathleen – but if I had what could you have done? You gave it originally to Inginide & not to Fay. Would you have taken back a gift? I hardly think so.

I can't quite write the letter of resignation you suggest. I have no intention of narrowing in the future my activities any more than I have in the past – I don't think Cumann na Gaedhal N.T. Company intends to confine itself to purely political plays, for instance it would accept joyfully plays like Dr Hyde's or Deirdre or most of yours if you ever entrusted us with them, but shall play for Nationalists without any regard whatever for the unionists or the English. I enclose a copy of my letter.

I am sorry to write all this which I know will be distasteful to you but with me the National Ideal is a religion, & a Theatre Co unless it serves the National cause seems to me of little importance. I know your answer, Beyreuth, Christiania theatre etc.,[2] serve their Nation though not propaganda but the circumstances are so different. We are in a life & death struggle with England, most of the men & women who started the National theatre are engaged in that struggle & have not time & energy for purely literary & artistic movements unless they can be made to serve directly & immediately the National cause.

Alwys my friend yours very sincerely
Maud Gonne MacBride

Copy of letter

Dear Mr R[ussell][3]
I wish to resign my position as Vice-President of the N.T. Society.

When I joined the Society I understood it was formed to carry on National & propagandist work by combating the influence of the English stage.

I find it has considerably changed its character & ideals & while I shall always be interested and glad of its success, I can no longer take an active part in the direction & work.

I remain,
Very sincerely yours,
M.G. MacB.

133

Hotel de Florence
26 Rue des Mathurins
Paris
28th Sept [1903]

My dear Willie

About the wig, in my presence you asked Mr Fay who was going over to Ireland that same evening to take charge of it. I would be glad if he would give it to Miss Quinn who in my absence has charge of all the *very few* theatrical properties we have succeeded in getting together for the Cumann na Gaedhal National Theatre Co – ·

I have no objection in lending that wig to whoever plays Kathleen in your Co. if dates of production don't clash with ours but I wish it to be kept with our things it is the only *old* wig we have & we use it for other old parts in our repertoire.

After a desperate week of house-hunting I have at last found a queer charming little house in a garden at 13 Rue de Passey, but we shall not be able to get into it for another 3 weeks as it is in the hands of workmen –

What is the truth in the rumour, that a conference between the Irish parliamentary leaders & members of the Conservative government with a view, in return for Irish support of Chamberlain & Balfour's fiscal policy, of the introduction of a Home Rule bill, is to take place?

In haste
Alwys your friend
    Maud G. MacB.

In November, Yeats left for America, where he lectured until March. He wrote to Lady Gregory from New York: 'I have just heard a painful rumour – Major MacBride is said to be drinking. It is the last touch of tragedy if it is true. Mrs MacBride said in one of her last letters that he has been ill all summer.'

1904

Jean Seaghan (later known as Seán) MacBride was born on 26 January 1904. Newspaper reports in Ireland, France, America and England announced the arrival of the 'latest Irish rebel'. The London Tatler *carried a picture of 'Three Irish Irreconcilables in Paris'. Messages of goodwill for the infant poured in; the offspring of heroes, he was hailed as the saviour of Ireland.*

John MacBride left for America to tour for Clann na Gael and Maud Gonne went with her children to Ireland, where her son was to be baptised. However, the priest refused to accept John O'Leary as godfather on the grounds that he was a Fenian (though he had never taken the Fenian oath). After some confusion Joseph MacBride discreetly repeated the vows also; Mrs MacBride from Westport was the godmother.

In 1904 Yeats was busy forming the National Theatre Society into a limited company and preparing its premises in Abbey Street (part of which had formerly been a morgue), where the first productions appeared in December.

134   13 Rue de Passy
                                                  12th Feb [1904]

My dear Willie

This is the first letter I have been allowed to write, & I waited to thank you for 3 letters till I was able to write myself –

I was very ill for a couple of months before my baby was born, but did not write to any of my friends as I didn't want to make them anxious. I am very well now only rather weak & I hope next week to be able to get up[1] –

The baby is a treasure & of course I imagine all sorts of wonderful things for his future.

Your last letter was such a nice letter, thank you so much for it – The others I understood very well & though on one or two things we don't think quite the same, & I think you have ALTERED your views in National art you think I have in some way changed mine – it is possible that both of us have *unconsciously* modified our opinions still I believe we shall be able to work together for Ireland just the same as in the past.

I knew well that you gave the scenario to Dr Hyde for his plays & worked him up to write to them too, & it is exactly that last that seemed to show me the difficulty of producing purely National & original work when one is influenced by foreign schools & knows too much of cosmopolitan art & literature.

You get a purely Irish conception of a play, & as you work it out, it becomes less & less Irish – I have noticed this more than once in work of yours that you have read me in its various stages of development – You give an Irish scenario to Hyde & he who has been but little out of Ireland is influenced to a much lesser degree than you by the foreign schools – will work it out in a way which makes it more Irish, & more in affinity with the thought of the nation for whom it is written & yet I know well that Douglas Hyde cannot in any way compare with you as a writer – Kathleen ni Houlihan is more national than anything Hyde has ever written, but it was written rapidly as it came to you direct from the life forces of Ireland you hardly changed or altered a word of that play from your first dream conception of it –

I wonder if I am only making things worse by writing this or whether this will make you see a little what I tried to express in the letter you did not like & in the article of mine you refer to in the U.I. I did not mean to say anything to pain you & I would be *very* VERY sorry if I thought there was any serious misunderstanding between us. There would not be if we could talk things over but I find it hard to express my thoughts in writing.

I am glad your tour is such a success.[2] I look forward to hearing it all when you come home. As soon as I am well I am going to Dublin for a few months as my husband has to go to America & my work in Ireland has been rather neglected for the last 6 months.

With very good wishes for your tour & for a good journey home. Alwys your friend

Maud Gonne MacBride

The war news is very exciting is it the beginning of *the great war?*[3]

Eileen Wilson, who had been engaged to Joseph MacBride for some time, was married on 3 August at St Etheldreda's Church, Ely Place, London, and went to live in Westport, County Mayo.

In November 1904 John MacBride wrote to Devoy: 'Mrs MacBride got back from Ireland a few weeks ago – she gives a very encouraging account of the state of affairs there. She finds fault with our friends for not being as active as they might be; but women are never satisfied.'

A Phoenix
1905–1907

Thereon my phoenix answered in reproof,
'The drunkards, pilferers of public funds,
All the dishonest crowd I had driven away,
When my luck changed and they dared meet my face,
Crawled from obscurity, and set upon me
Those I had served and some that I had fed;
Yet never have I, now nor any time,
Complained of the people.'

W. B. Yeats, 'The People' (first published 1916)

 *1905*

*What had been building up for some time came to a head while Maud
Gonne was in Ireland in October 1904. She returned to find the
household at 13 Rue de Passy in a distressful condition. The women
of her household and Madame Avril de Sainte-Croix, to whom Iseult
had gone, had a sad story to relate. Whatever dreadful state John
MacBride had been reduced to by stress, anxiety and disappointment,
he was now accused of indecent behaviour while drunk towards
various members of the household including the cook and Miss
Delany, of 'tempting' Eileen Wilson and, most seriously of all, of
frightening the ten-year-old Iseult in the same fashion. Iseult was
vulnerable not only because of her childish beauty but also because
she was the unacknowledged illegitimate child of a prominent French
politician. The scandal could reach untold proportions not only in
Ireland but in France. Such behaviour towards a child was a criminal
offence carrying a sentence of over twenty years in France.*

*Wishing to keep the matter out of court, in order to protect her
daughter and to avoid causing her husband to be convicted on a
criminal charge, Maud Gonne first sought a peaceful settlement by
going to London to see her husband's brother, Dr Anthony MacBride,
whom she had known for many years. She was met with outrage,
disbelief and denial. After some negotiations, a peaceful settlement
failed. John MacBride did not contest the separation she had
requested, but they could not agree on the future of their child. Maud
Gonne had hoped there would not be much controversy if it was put
out that John MacBride had to go to America to look for work.*

However, she expected to have complete guardianship of the child, though after seven years she would not prevent her husband seeing Seán provided he had led a sober, decent life.

The counter-proposals were that the child should be brought up in Ireland in a good Catholic and nationalist atmosphere for nine months of the year and could live with his mother until six years old, when his future would be open to negotiation. The breaking off of negotiations came when Maud Gonne's final offer was refused on the grounds that it was not specific and detailed enough; in this she had agreed to the nine months in Ireland in the right atmosphere with the proviso that this could be changed if the health of mother or child required living abroad and a senior physician's certificate was furnished, or if her husband made it too difficult for her. If there was a dispute about Seán's future at the age of ten it should be referred to the Archbishop of Dublin.

The affair with 'E', as Eileen was only ever referred to officially, and how serious that was or was not, is not very clear. It was used as a last resort to keep the whole thing quiet, being originally referred to as something which 'would inevitably injure the reputation of a woman I should think he has every reason to wish to spare'. As such situations usually are, it was a nasty bitter game, but on the whole Maud Gonne's letters give a reasonable account, allowing for a certain obvious onesidedness, and so the story unfolds in her own words to Yeats.

On 7 January 1905 her family solicitor in London, Mr Witham, wrote to her: 'The whole position is a very unpleasant and very serious one and [I] should have been very glad if you could have got some friend whom you trust to go over the whole thing again for you and finally decide on your course of action. If you decide to have a judicial separation you had better make up your mind as soon as you can because evidently your husband grasps at every concession and uses them to try and get new terms.' It was then she asked her cousin May in London to tell Yeats, the friend on whom she knew she could rely, the whole tragic story.

135   13 Rue de Passy
                                               Paris
                                               Tuesday [January 1905]

My dear Friend

Thank you for your letter. It is generous & it is like you & I am very glad to get it. Of a hero I had made, nothing remains & the disillusion has been cruel. I am fighting an uneven battle because I am fighting a man without honor or scruples who is sheltering himself & his vices behind the National cause knowing that my loyalty to it in part ties my hands, – for instance it has prevented me allowing my lawyer to use the ordinary methods used in such cases for finding evidence.

Bad as my husband is, in one thing he is true I think, that is his fidelity to the National cause – as far as he understands it, though it will not prevent him disgracing it by drunkenness.

I am writing to May[1] to tell her she may tell you the whole story, you will be able to judge then better of the situation & understand why for the children's sake as well as from an Irish point of view I wish this thing if possible kept out of court. But Willie I tell you because of our old friendship, but be careful not to tell others. It is so serious I think you will be – The exact position of affairs is this. My husband has completely talked over Barry O'Brien[2] who thinks he is a fine fellow & does not believe the hideous accusations against him. He refuses to go into them & says his interest in the affair is not to know if John be innocent or guilty but only to save the Irish cause from scandal – I would be glad, if you would let him know the influence John is already having in the drinking way in Dublin, it will be very bad – but in a short time he will discredit himself so that my position will be vindicated without my saying a word.

I have offered terms my cousin told you of, & which she is perhaps right in considering too generous. They have been taken by John as a sign of weakness & he has asked for more concessions absolutely impossible which I have refused. Here is the last letter of my lawyer[3] to Mr O'Brien which I have received this morning. So it is possible this affair will have to go to court all the same & in the event I am having to get sufficient evidence of other matters to be able to leave the principal offence out altogether. There is plenty of other material though if the evidence is complete enough I am not yet sure – It is all horrible & a war fare I am not used to.

I think it will be better for you not to come to Paris, though I would very much like to see you as my husband is insinuating that every man who has ever been a friend of mine, is a lover – I learned this from something Barry O'Brien said, besides from his endless scenes of jealousy during our two years' married life.

I am so glad the theatre was so successful. I longed to be in Dublin for the opening.[4]

Alwys your friend

Maud Gonne MacBride

136
13 Rue de Passy
Paris
Friday [January 1905]

My dear Friend

I am glad you know all. Thank you for your letter & thank you for all the trouble you are taking for me.

My nerves are so shattered by all I have gone through, not only since I knew this horrible thing, but ever since my marriage, where insane scenes of jealousy, & an atmosphere of base intrigue have rendered life almost unbearable – that I find it hard to think out the situation fully. However as you say, Barry O'Brien says my husband has not accepted the terms I offered, things are shaping them selves & the only thing left is to apply for judicial separation or divorce, it seems to me indifferent which. Which ever is easiest to obtain, as I believe both give me complete security for the control of the children.

The French avoué[1] says I have quite enough evidence to go on without bringing in anything about little Iseult. This morning I have a letter from Mr Witham saying up to the present he has heard nothing from Barry O'Brien or from John MacBride as to the acceptance or refusal of terms offered. If the affair goes into court it will be necessary to have the best Counsel possible. I know nothing of the law or the bar – I wrote to Mr Witham that as John was trying so hard to get political & religious sympathy to cover his vices & is making a great point against me that I have been to an English solicitor, it would be well to get an Irish barrister. I enclose Mr Witham's answer about this. Would you make enquiries & advise me on this matter. You might tell Mrs Clay[2] to see Mr Witham about it if you think well. I don't think that could do any harm – your kind letters are a great comfort to me & I thank you for your generous sympathy – but Willie I don't want you to get mixed up in this horrible affair.

By my marriage *I brought all this trouble on myself*, and as far as I can I want to fight it alone. This is why I have spoken to none of my friends. Why should they who are engaged on noble work be mixed up with a sordid horror of this sort.

My husband is insanely jealous & utterly unscrupulous, he has accused, at some time or other, every man who he has ever heard of being my friend or whose photo he has ever seen at my house of having been my lover. On one occasion he told me he had intended to kill you – Even Russell he declared was my lover & that Mrs Russell was mad with jealousy!! I expect the unknown man Barry O'Brien mentioned to you is Arthur Griffith as he was one of those Barry O'Brien told me John mentioned to him & he was very much annoyed over £50 I sent to the U.I. a few months ago to make good money which in one of the periodical financial crises of the paper

Griffith and the trustees of the *Rooney* memorial fund[5] had used for the paper & which I had verbally guaranteed.

To have a really good counsel <barrister> is necessary, & if you will help me in this you will do me a great service, but apart from this Willie, for your sake for Ireland's sake & for your own work as well as for mine try & keep quite clear of this affair, don't even think of it too much. I know the generosity of your nature makes you want to help me & to defend me but it would only add to my trouble to know your life was touched in any way by this miserable tragedy – That I have your friendship what ever happens is a great comfort to me. I was angry with myself after I had written asking you to see Barry O'Brien for the less you think of it all the better – & it was failing in the resolution I had made to stand alone.

It is probable you feel it all worse than I do.

My nerves are a little stunned except at rare moments the horrible reality doesn't take hold of me. A sort of deadness prevents me thinking or suffering much & life goes on just the same so don't worry about me & don't think of me as very unhappy –

I received Samhain[4] & have not read it yet – but it looks very interesting – I shall read it tonight –

Again thanking you Willie for all your kindness.

I remain

Your friend alwys

    Maud Gonne MacBride

On 16 January Mr Witham wrote to Maud Gonne:

I want to know if you can get your French lawyer, M. Détroye, to take down an accurate statement from the witnesses shewing exactly what they will say. . . .

If we can prove before the Court what they assert, you will get your separation and the custody of your child.

The law does not take any notice of drunkenness unless a man knocks his wife about when he is drunk. . . .

If you were going to live in France altogether with the child, a French Divorce might, if you could get it, serve your purpose; but as you will want to come over to England or Ireland your only protection is getting the separation in England.

137

[Letterhead]
L'Oeuvre Libération
1 Avenue Malakoff
Paris (16e)

13 Rue de Passy
Monday [January 1905]

My dear Willie

Thank you so much for all your kindness, & all the trouble you have taken for me – I saw the French lawyer this morning & showed him the letter to Lady Gregory, he was very pleased, as it exactly confirmed what he had said, that the divorce should take place in France because of it being my husband's domicile. It has taken a great weight off my mind not having to appeal to English justice. My lawyer is getting up the case & will go on as soon as possible. It seems the only possible solution. Iseult was so pleased with the book you sent her. She wrote to you to thank you, but her letter was sent to London.

I am glad you are starting a publishing house in Ireland[1] & hope it will be a great success. It should be. When is Synge's play?[2] I wish I could be in Dublin for it, but alas for the present I must stay here. Will you thank Lady Gregory very much for me for having written to Mr Grey. His opinion is most valuable. It is very kind of her troubling.

Are not the massacres in Russia fearful![3] How could the Czar have lost such an opportunity as he had of winning the people by going alone among them. It is all too hideous. Thousands of unarmed people shot down because they trusted & believed in their Czar, for the majority of the crowd I think hardly understood what they were asking for, only they believed in the Czar & that he could make all right – It will be difficult for them to believe in him now, though with the terrible means of repression, & the unscrupulous use of them, I don't believe in the success of the revolution in Russia yet. Think of the massacre after the Commune in Paris! & Galifet who ordered them was made minister in France, & kept in power by the Socialists.

I must end for it is getting late. Once more thank you Willie for your sympathy.

  Alwys your friend
    Maud Gonne MacBride

138   [Paris]
                                Tuesday evening [January 1905]

My dear friend

I don't know how to thank you for all the trouble you are taking
for me. I suppose my husband is in Paris now but have heard nothing
of him. I was glad when I got your telegram saying withdrawn Dixon
proposal as I felt it would not do. I am not the least surprised that
John MacBride has talked over several people in Dublin, he is quite
unscrupulous & very plausible, when sober. Also I have not told any
of the facts of the case; in Dublin I have only written to Mr Russell,
to Ella Young and to Miss Machen[1] & to these I have merely stated
that I am separating from my husband for very serious reasons.

Miss Ella Young wrote me that Dixon & Griffith wanted to meet
me in London with a view to arriving at a settlement without scandal,
they told Ella that John was very reasonable & wanted settlement. I
wrote back that I had given him every opportunity of settling things
quietly, that he had refused, that now my friends in Dublin could do
no good by trying to arrange a settlement as I had already applied
for divorce in the French courts –

John has written to at least three friends of mine in France trying
to get sympathy for himself & asking them I think to intercede with
me in his favor – only one, a priest, tried to do so. I replied, that if
he knew the circumstances he would give different advice, & that it
was too late now for when John refused the terms I offered, I applied
to the French court. I shall make the same reply to any suggestion
of arbitration from whatever source it comes.

You are quite right in saying that the verdict of the court in my
favor will be the surest way of putting an end to the lies my husband
has been telling or may yet tell & my lawyers are quite certain I will
get the verdict. The French divorces are all tried in Camera, but I
think the judgements are public in any case, I shall always have the
judgement to show if John gives trouble after. The case has to be
made more heavy against him than I wished & the Eileen affair
<thing> will have to be gone into, because in case of John giving
trouble later & trying to get a control of the child under English law,
my lawyer says this case must be made to satisfy the requirements of
the English as well as the French divorce law. As the case will be
tried in camera I hope the Eileen part will not get to Ireland. Miss
O'Delaney's part of the evidence is very slight & is chiefly useful to
corroborate the shocking moral condition to which drink has
brought John. I don't think anyone over here would believe in his
talk about my mind being unhinged, besides the case will rest on the
evidence of others, not on mine.

Wednesday morning

I was interrupted last night & couldn't finish my letter – This morning post has brought a note from my lawyer saying that John has put his case into the hands of Mr Kelly the lawyer attached to the English Embassy here! Isn't that amusing after his indignation at my having consulted our family solicitor who happened to be an Englishman.

I will write you tomorrow about the plays, I am so glad they are succeeding so well. I still think 6 penny place[2] would get fuller houses & after all apart from the money point of view you want to interest the greatest number of our people possible – after reading Synge['s] play *In a Wicklow Glen*[3] I must say I quite agree with you as to his really remarkable force & talent as a dramatic writer, though still I think this play is not for the many in Ireland & not helpful to the movement as we were trying to carry it out at that time.

You are carrying a movement on another line. It is good & I wish you all success.

Again thanking you for all your kind sympathy
I remain
Yours alwys
    Maud Gonne MacBride

139   [Paris]
                                         [January/February 1905]
My dear Friend

Things are going on here satisfactorily. My lawyer says I have more than enough evidence for divorce. I hope not to have to use the Eileen affair, but it is being prepared also, so if John gives trouble it will be used.

Now things are decided I am much calmer & happier – I feel I have a force supporting me, it may be that it is the thoughts of my friends – I have got over the horrible time of groping in the darkness –

The details of the whole affair are miserable & sordid & I try to think of them as little as possible.

My husband evidently confided his affairs to a journalistic friend of his Mr Collins[1] who takes his side & who is a good friend to him but very indiscreet. He told several other American journalists & I believe the announcement of our separation is already in the *New York World* though I haven't seen it. The last thing I hear is that John has written to Mr Collins asking him to see his friends here & tell them his side of the case *as I have been* trying to secure the American press on my side – I have spoken to no one who has not first spoken to me on the subject, & I have traced all the rumours here to Collins

& to his son. I don't care much what is being said here as the divorce given in my favour will be the answer.

I am afraid it will take a long time however, 6 months at least, & most of that time I will have to remain here & I want so much to be in Ireland.

Again thank you very much for all you have done & for your kind thoughts.

Yours alwys
    Maud Gonne MacBride

140
                                13 Rue de Passy
                                Paris
                                Sunday [February 1905]

My dear Willie

By a stupid forgetfulness the telegram I wrote in answer to yours was not sent – I am so sorry –

Things are going on fairly well. I have the best lawyer in Paris Mr Crouppi[1] to defend me. He hopes things will go quickly. The confrontation was very painful, my husband sat & cried all the time & talked about wanting no scandal & wanting arbitration & at the same time trying to make insinuations against me – I think he did himself as much harm as possible in the eyes of the judge.

I hear Barry O'Brien is in Paris – I don't know for what purpose – John is going round with tears to most people saying he is an innocent man & very badly treated & that if I go on he will be able to blacken my character – but this of course does him more harm than it does me.

The judge has given me control of the child pending the judgement, but the father has always the right of seeing it once a week. This permission is very trying as so many precautions have to be taken. Except for this weekly visit which is not to exceed one hour & at which Madame Avril de Ste Croix is to assist, my husband is not allowed to come to this house –

It is an awful time I live through & I don't know what I should do without the sympathy & help of my cousin May. She is so good & kind.

Again thanking you for all your kind thoughtfulness for me
I remain
Alwys your friend
    Maud Gonne MacBride

141
13 Rue de Passy
Paris
25th Feb [1905]

My dear Willie

I haven't much news to tell, things are going wearily on here. I believe the assignation[1] has been sent, & John will then have to name a French lawyer who will state his line of defence but I think he has still 10 days' delay to do this. Then the tribunal fixes a day & our Lawyers fight it out between them & the judges decide whether or no the Court can pronounce at once or must order an enquiry. If John is at all wise he will let the divorce be pronounced then but he is not at all wise & he is being very badly counselled by Mr Collins the correspondent of the New York Sun who for some reason I don't know of, is a bitter enemy of mine.

Your telegram was badly transcribed here & May did not understand it wanted an answer so it was only on receiving your letter that I found it did, the telegram read 'All well here!' Barry O'Brien I hear, is in Paris a great deal with John. I am getting a fit of homesickness & would love to be in Ireland, but for the present I see no chance of being able to leave Paris. I am glad Mr Martyn is a friend of mine, for I like & respect him very much. As for the others when the verdict is given against John I suppose they will be convinced anyhow it is not for me to bother about convincing them – It is a private matter so it doesn't matter. All I care about is to safeguard my child. You are quite right in saying the Irish Cause is above being injured by the unworthiness of one of its servants. Though because of his love of that cause I would rather have spared him, if he would have made it possible – but between John whose usefulness is I should think over & little Seagan whose work has not yet begun there can be no hesitation.

Iseult sends her love. She also is always asking when are we going to Ireland?

Thank you my dear friend for all your sympathy, it has been a great help to me but I don't want you to think & worry too much over this wretched affair.

Always your friend
Maud Gonne MacBride

142
[Paris]
Friday [March 1905]

My dear Willie

Thank you so much for the book of Lionel Johnson's poems,[1] most of them I know. You read many of them to me long ago. They are very beautiful there is music in them I love. Iseult is learning some of them. The printing is quite charming. I wish they would get some thing more distinctively their own on the covers. It is a pity Althea² did not go on with her designs. She made some beautiful ones for you. What has become of her?

I send this to London. I think you are there now. I spent the day in Granié's studio.³ He lets me come down and draw with him. I don't draw much, but I like the Graniés, they are old friends of mine; I think you met them when you were in Paris. Jules Bois came in, he spoke of your poems he admires your work very greatly. In the mornings I work at Julian's Academy.⁴

As usual with me I am trying to fill my life so as not to think – for the present I can do nothing for Ireland, later on I expect things may come right with me & I may again be useful to the cause for which I have lived, but it may be the Gods have no more use for me & want a younger voice & energy to carry on the work –

I have no more news. Will you be in London for long?

Alwys your friend

Maud Gonne MacBride

143   [Paris]
                                          [March 1905]

My dear Willie

The correspondent of the *Morning Leader* is a Mr Cozens Hardy a great friend of the Collins' & he is in love with one of the daughters & is continually with Collins. It is his note that the Irish papers have reproduced. The French papers have not & *may* not publish the causes of divorce; they may publish nothing but actual judgments so John has again his own friends to thank for the glaring announcement in the Irish papers as he had for the announcement in the American press. It has caused great sorrow to his poor old mother in Westport for whom I feel very sorry, of course she says she believes nothing against her son but is terribly upset & miserable.

I think the effect of this announcement will be to make John defend himself to the utmost, as now it is more difficult for him to accept what my lawyers were willing to offer that the divorce should be pronounced without dishonoring considerations & on the minimum offence.

This will of course come to the same result in the end but will delay matters & make the wretched affair drag on longer.

Thank you so much for offering to stay in Dublin, but PLEASE don't alter your plans at all on my account. You have been so helpful & so kind all through this trouble, but I don't want you to do any more. It is such a horrid thing to keep one's mind on. My lawyer M. Crouppi's advice was very good when he said to me the other day 'don't be the least anxious about the result. You will have the divorce & the entire control of the child there is no doubt of that but it is possible that the affair may drag, so just put it out of your head & forget all about it.' This is easier said than done but I am trying to do so & as until the judgment is pronounced it is useless to think of political work I am taking to painting which is always a joy for which I never have time. I am going to draw in a studio.

I wish I was in Dublin. I should love to see the plays. I am sure *Kincora*[1] will be a great success with the people. You ought to try & make some arrangements by which the clubs can see it by letting *two* in on one ticket or some such thing. When one has 15/- a week to live on & belongs to Clubs & Societies where dues have to be paid 1/- is a big lot to pay for a theatre ticket – You ought to give at least one Saturday night performance at special prices, and play both *Kathleen*[2] and *Kincora*.

I have just received the *Independent* with sensational article evidently inspired by John. The *Daily Mirror* account is in Collins' best style, though I don't think he is the usual correspondent. I shall not reply a word to any newspaper's lies. The judgment in the Court will be sufficient answer – John evidently intends to publish lying accounts of what takes place in camera before the French Judges. I will consult my lawyers as to how far this is contrary to the law.

I must end now as I have a good deal of writing to do.
Alwys your friend
    Maud Gonne MacBride

144   [Paris]
                                        Sunday [March 1905]
My dear Willie
    It is good getting your letters. You always know the right things to say. I am glad some of my old friends like Dr Quinn[1] are capable of standing firm. As for the others they are like water & can be pushed aside but they will return again as surely. Of course there is no truth in the announcement in the Independent that an arrangement has been come to & divorce proceedings will be stayed. After the lies John MacBride has been telling & publishing about me nothing but the divorce judgment given in my favor can reply.

We heard from some friends of John's that Kelly[2] who is counsellor to the American Embassy was very unwilling to take up John's case, indeed he refused at first, & I think this was why Barry O'Brien was brought over to Paris to decide him to act for John. He is the one person who lends a semblance of respectability to John & is taken round among the journalists, shown as a representative of the Irish party, sent over to help John –

I have written Russell asking him to warn the Cumann na Gaedhal men who may have been staying with John (Griffith will know their names) in my absence that I don't know who they are & have in no way identified the Drunken men who stayed with John & helped him create a drunken scandal in the neighbourhood while I was away.

No one here knows their names, & John alone can bring their names into it. My servants & the neighbors only know they were English speaking men.

I see in the article in the *Daily Mirror* he says I accuse him of bringing tipsy *Irishmen* to the house, whereas the citation says 'bringing Drunken men to the house' & does not specify nationality. It is a small matter but John probably hopes to put the Clubs against me by saying I am accusing some of their members of drunkenness & of course it would injure the two men who were with John if their names came out – It would in any other country but ours. We seem to have such toleration for drink.

I think your idea of having song & poems between the plays very good, couldn't you get the author sometimes to come & recite their own poems, as they did at the *Chat Noir* in Paris.[3] It used to be very interesting.

I am longing for all the worry to be over, so as to come back to Ireland, until it is all over I don't think I shall be able to leave Paris at all, or only for a very short while at a time.

I am sending you Iseult's photo. She is growing so pretty & has an extraordinary appreciation of art, though she is such a child, & somewhat of a tomboy.

I shall never forget how good you have been to me & how your kind thoughts & words have helped me.

Your friend alwys
Maud Gonne MacBride

145   [Paris]
                                           Tuesday [March 1905]
My dear Willie

Thank you for your letter to me which I ought to have answered long since which I have answered in thought many times, thank you also for the letters written to May, which were also written to help me. When one is in trouble one finds out who are one's real friends.

Of men friends I have found few who cared or troubled & I have asked help of none – I asked help of no women either, except of my cousin May, but from a *great* many I have received help & sympathy, in a degree which surprised me – I have had letters from many Inghinide & Mary Quinn from America sent me letters from others who had not liked to write to me but who were warm in their sympathy. I send you one of these to read.

I am distressed about Inghinide. This is not the sort of fight I want them to be in & yet what can I do? If I sent my resignation as president just now it would I think make their position more difficult, as many of them wouldn't accept it, & even if they did it would weaken them & be used against them. I have written to some of them telling them not to fight at all on this matter & to refuse altogether to discuss it or to try & defend me, the verdict in the court will do that, but I know it is very hard for them. Mary Quinn will send me some valuable evidence of drunkenness from America. *Don't say anything about this*, however, as I shall only use it if *absolutely* necessary when the question of the guardianship of the child comes up, & it might do her harm with some of John MacBride's friends. Affairs here are stationary. My lawyer has just had scarlatina, which has helped delay things, he is well again now.

I had a queer dream last night or rather early this morning but as my dreams don't generally come true, I don't attach importance to it. I saw you standing in a doorway & looking very ill. I think it was the doorway of the house in Avenue Kleber where Miss Delaney lives & I woke up before I had time to speak to you. All the same I would be very glad to hear from you at once that you are well & all is well with you.

I am drawing hard & get a good many compliments from the professors. I was 4th in the weekly concours de composition of our studio which as I have never worked before isn't bad.

I rather agree with you that it is more amusing *making things* than *pictures*, but for every thing *drawing* is necessary & it interests me very much. I must end now.

Alwys your friend
Maud Gonne

146   [Paris]
                                        Thursday evening [late March 1905]
My dear Willie

I am so glad to read of the success of Kincora how I wish May & I could have seen it – we will one day I hope – All my congratulations to Lady Gregory. The book of the play arrived today & I have only had time to read a few pages. I am looking forward to reading it this evening.

About what May asked you to find out for me about Mrs MacBride's public house in Westport[1] – We heard that John MacBride is going to propose that my child should spend part of each year there with his grandmother. I don't think the French Court will consent to this but as the matter is of the utmost importance to me I think it would be well if I could get evidence as to the drunkenness which goes on there. I know nothing of it except that there is always a lot of drunkenness in every public house in Ireland, & I have heard John MacBride pleasantly recount how on several occasions he had in that same public house experimented on various drunkards of the neighborhood how much whiskey a man could drink at a time without dying.

Davitt, in the pamphlet attributed to him[2] which with the other one you & I succeeded in forcing the two unwilling sections of a certain Society to repudiate, stated that Mrs MacBride kept '*a low shebeen house*'[3] I haven't got that pamphlet. Poor old Mrs MacBride herself I like & respect & am very sorry for her. I am certain she does not drink but her son Patrick who now keeps the public house looks like a man who drinks. I have heard he drinks. He is in mortal terror of the police & wanted to present an address to the King of England.

It would be useless for my lawyers to write to the local police, because their barracks is next door to the MacBride public house & I expect the local police drink freely there – the higher police authorities would not wish to give me any help whatever – The priest also would I fear, say nothing against any publican for publicans are his best subscribers & the MacBride family being very pious are certain to subscribe generously – the bishop showed them marked favor at the Mayo Feis which also will make any priest of the diocese cautious of saying anything about them –

William O'Brien & the United Irish League however are bitter enemies of the MacBride family. United Irish Leaguers of the neighborhood would be sure to know everything against them that was why I thought Davitt likely to be well informed but United Irish Leaguers also hate me so I can't ask them directly. Dr Quinn could easily find out as he is friends with the United Irish Leaguers as I think Mr Russell might be able to find out.

Joseph MacBride (Eileen's husband) who lives in Westport is quite sober & [a] very different sort of man from his brother Patrick with whom he is not on the best of terms, but it is in Patrick's public house that MacBride proposes that my son should spend part of his time.

Forgive me for writing all these details, & for bothering you with all this. I hope & think I am perhaps worrying unnecessarily as I don't think the french court will give John MacBride *any* right on the child at all, but I know his whole case is to be based on this & as he feels he will never get the Court to give *him* the child he is going to try & bring forward his mother as a suitable person to take charge of the child.

I dreamed of you again last night, but it was a good dream, & I don't think you are ill & the world seemed full of success for you & I was very glad, the dreams of the other night had rather worried me though I do not believe much in my dreams.

Again thank you for your letters.

Alwys your friend

Maud Gonne

147   13 Rue de Passy
[Paris]
Monday [April 1905]

My dear Willie

Forgive me for not writing before. I have been so busy & have had a bad cold.

I wrote & telegraphed Miss Horniman accepting her offer[1] because my lawyer thought it of great importance. I don't know how to express my gratitude to her for her more than kindness. Kindness I would hardly have expected or ventured to ask from even a great friend –

I am not surprise[d] Sarah[2] refused. I knew she would, but it was too late to telegraph you not to trouble yourself to ask her.

I have little or no news. Things drag on here just the same. M. Cruppi's illness retarded things & the trial will now not come on till end of May.

J. MacBride announces his intention of returning to Ireland.

It must be so lovely in Ireland now – I am glad you have taken Colm [Colum] down to Coole, it will do him good. He is such a charming boy & his work is so interesting.

I sent you the illustrated catalogue of Gustave Moreau's exhibition.[3] The reproductions are unfortunately bad but Moreau's notes on the pictures are interesting & help to explain his work. I am copying some of his smaller things – I like his coloring so much –

I wish I were in the woods in Ireland they must be getting beautiful now even my miserable little Paris garden is beginning to smile & Iseult darts about & discovers treasures.

I hope your cold is quite gone now,

Alwys your friend

Maud Gonne

148   [Paris]
                                          Sunday [April 1905]

My dear Willie

I am so sorry to hear you have been ill with rheumatism, it is such a horrid thing I know from experience. I hope it is quite passed now –

I heard from Miss Horniman also, she has not succeeded but I am deeply grateful to her for the trouble she has taken, it was more than kind of her. I know how timid & suspicious people are in the country towns in Ireland, & it was only to be expected they would not speak out to a stranger. Also the fact of the bishop having shown favor to the MacBride family lately means that everyone will hesitate how they speak about them. Also I am sorry to say Drunkenness is so usual in the country towns that a man must be in the last stages before any one speaks of it. I think I must do without this evidence, I don't really think it is vitally necessary, I hope the American evidence will be good, Miss Quinn will say all she knows if she is home, or will write it if not. I have been expecting a letter from her for the last fortnight telling me her plans.

Of course it is a lie that MacBride visits Seagan every day. Once a week is all that is permitted by the Court. Madame Avril has been away in Switzerland & during her absence deputed Madame Dangien[1] (Iseult's governess) to replace her. John MacBride objected & said he wouldn't come until a new ordinance was got from the judge & Labori[2] wrote this to my lawyer, but in spite of this MacBride came every Monday & in the presence of Madame Dangien I allowed him to see baby. (In this I acted according to the advice of my lawyer.)

The incident (i.e.) the question of the visits as well as the divorce is to be pleaded end of May on the same day I think.

May wrote to you to Nassau Hotel last Tuesday, telling you how affairs were going on & that MacBride had left for Ireland.[3] I expect he is there now at Barry's Hotel Dublin.

I have had influenza but am well again & working very hard at my drawing. In the morning at Julien's Academy & in the afternoons I copy in the Gustave Moreau Gallery, his jewel like colouring is so fascinating.

Hoping you are quite well again
I remain
Alwys your friend
   Maud Gonne .

149

13 Rue de Passy
Paris
Thursday night [April 1905]

My dear Willie

Please read these two letters & return them to me. The one from Miss Quinn I wish you to read to show that there is much that would be useful to know of my husband's drunkenness in New York if only Mr Quinn[1] could get evidence of it, (I have written her suggesting she should go see Mr Quinn) & I also want you to read the last part about herself & Mr Digges, *but I want you to look on this as private*, because even to her own sister in Dublin she has not said how badly off she has been or what trouble she is in.

The New York climate in winter is deadly for any one inclined to consumption far worse than Dublin. If she & Digges come home would you give Digges employment in the theatre? I might be able to contribute (though I wouldn't like it known) to make up a salary for him he was only earning £1 or 30/- a week before he went away. Miss Quinn could live in Dun Inghinidhe[2] as caretaker & I am sure she would get employment before long (this last suggestion I have written to her but Digges is the difficulty).

The other letter is from another Inghinide written to Miss Quinn. I send it to show how good those girls are. I have found them in everything far more dependable than any of the men of the same class (but I don't want them to have to fight this sort of fight, & don't mean them to).

I am sending this letter to the Nassau Hotel as I think you may be back in Dublin for the plays. What are you writing now? Don't let the plays quite absorb all your energies, keep some for your books. The poems must not suffer.

I have no news. Every day I work at the studio it is an atmosphere where I can forget my troubles. Old Julian says I am getting on in quite a remarkable way I suppose it is my untiring energy which has to find expression somewhere – take me out of personal life which in this life at all events was never to succeed or bring me happiness.

I hope your cold is quite gone.
Alwys your friend
Maud Gonne

Parts of Miss Quinn's letter are so important. I think it better to keep it for my lawyer, am only sending you extracts copied from it –
Send me back Miss Quinn's letter & the other & treat it as private.

Extracts from Miss Quinn's letter.

She begins telling me the difficulty she has met with in getting men to say what they know about John's drunkenness and the failure of her efforts. She goes on, 'there is only one man I know that was constantly with J. in New York. Sergt Joe Wade of the Brigade he was looking for work, and as I cannot get any trace of him I fear he must have gone away again to South America whence he came & even if I could reach him, I doubt if he would do what we want as he seemed greatly attached to the Major, & *went after him & took care of him all the time when he was wandering about drunk & half insane.* Of course, the *Vanderbilt Hotel* people saw J *drink heavily* several times but he was often days & weeks that he did not show up at all & when we could not see him & then I presume he must have been on a spree at his own rooms on 24th Street or elsewhere. The few people that J. introduced us to here are mostly of a drunken set too, that I have no faith in.'

Then she goes on telling me of Inghinide & various suggestions as to Inghinide openly publishing a resolution of sympathy & trust in me which of course, I decline.

Then about her own affairs she writes that the climate in New York during the winter has been too hard for Digges & that 17th Feb he broke down with haemorrhage of the lungs & was in bed for a month with Doctor in daily attendance she was obliged to give up her position to act as nurse. Fortunately the firm Digges works for were kind & kept the place open for him and paid salary during his illness, but with doctor's bills & medicine etc., all their little savings, 'which were to take us home in joy next May, are scattered & we both started to fight the world again on the first of this month with not five dollars between us.' The worst of all is the Dr says Digges lungs won't stand another New York winter & he says, Ireland isn't good either. Digges has a starving father, mother & sister & brothers at home, to whom he sends help every week so he can't afford to give up the work he is in.

She writes 'The thought we may have to put in a longer exile than we ever thought of is preying upon both of us & we cannot trust ourselves to talk of home – – – This last blow is the worst one we have had from fate. We used to laugh over our misfortunes since we came to America, and say what did it matter so long as we had health but even that has been snatched from us now' –

150 [Paris]
Wednesday [April 1905]

My dear Willie

Many thanks for your letters and for the book of stories[1] it is charming & I am so glad to have it –

About Digges, I quite understand what you say about the difficulty, so let's say no more on the subject, I wouldn't have suggested it, if some time ago you had not asked me if I thought it likely that Digges would come back to Dublin & join your theatre, as you wanted him. Miss Quinn never for one moment suggested the possibility of such a thing in her letter to me – I wrote entirely on my own idea as I was trying to think what chance there was of getting them back to Dublin & what to advise them to do.

As I told you Miss Quinn's letter to me was private she has not told & does not wish her people to know of their difficulties – Digges has never even told his family of his illness. I think Fay's estimation of the Digges family is quite correct – I hope you didn't let Fay think either Miss Quinn or Digges has asked to return or be paid as it would hurt their feelings terribly if such a thing were said, & they certainly have done no such thing. I am delighted to hear things are going on so well with you –

I have no news. I am waiting anxiously for the affidavits Mr Quinn promised to get –

In haste & again thanking you for the stories

Alwys your friend

    Maud Gonne

Are you writing any new poems?

151   [Paris]
                                                                              [April 1905]

My dear Willie

The day I got your letter telling me of my husband's announced intention of asking for the transfer of the divorce case from France to England, I also got a letter from my lawyer saying he had had a visit from MacBride's solicitor Mr Kelly. On my husband's behalf he offered to let the divorce suit go undefended if I would take back the citation containing the charges & arrange some other charges not so dishonoring. He admits being drunk on *two occasions*! Also that I would sign a paper, which it was explained would not be even legally binding, to agree to the submitting the question for the custody of the child to arbitrators named by MacBride & by myself in seven years' time. Failing my agreement to these terms Mr Kelly said they would push the defence in such a way that my reputation & political work would be ruined completely.

I replied I would concede nothing whatever in regard to the complete custody of the child & as I knew it was always possible for MacBride to reopen this question in the English Courts (where French divorce is recognised but where the question of the custody of the child can be contested), I could not allow the charges against my husband to be made too light, though the one of adultery with E.[1] I would gladly withdraw though I have complete proof; if the other charges could be made to satisfy English as well as French law & that my husband allowed the divorce to be pronounced at once and undefended.

My lawyer said he didn't think Kelly would allow MacBride to give in without scandal. I replied that telling lies against me in open court unsupported by evidence & with a crushing verdict against him would do far less harm to me, to my work than the whispered lies he & his friends are circulating against me in Ireland & which would be strengthened by any sign of weakness or compromise on my part. My lawyer fully agreed with me. He is certain I will win my case, but says there is no means of preventing MacBride & his council telling what lies they like against me, or from getting these lies copied in the *foreign* press. The French press never publishes divorce affairs & in France a wife cannot attack her husband or her husband's lawyer for defamation – The verdict given however will be the answer to these lies. MacBride has no grounds for getting the case removed to England, he knows well he can't do it. I think it is only to prepare opinion for a verdict against him, or for possibly letting the case go by default that he is beginning to express want of confidence in French justice.

May has a cable from Mr Quinn saying he has sent by this mail two affidavits.

Mr Kelly is the legal adviser of the American as well as the English Embassys from his name he is Irish & MacBride & Collins have got a legend that he was a fenian & his father defended fenian prisoners on some occasions or some story of that sort – He was describing MacBride's heroism to M. Cruppi my lawyer who stopped him at once, saying oh yes of course a hero if you like but a drunkard & an exhibitionist, except for that a hero: The fenian lawyer Mr Kelly replied 'Well as for drunkenness what could she expect if she married an Irishman!' Maître Cruppi said 'It will be for your council to bring forward that excuse for your client in Court.'

I *know* that Kelly refused to have anything to do with John MacBride's case at first, I heard (but this last is only *hear* say & I am not sure of the source) that it was only at the suggestion of the English Embassy who wanted the scandal as big as possible that he took it up. I am afraid that I cannot comfort myself with the thought that by my stand against a blackguard & drunken husband I am doing more than protecting Seagan & Iseult & that I am helping other women in Ireland in similar circumstances. Several horrible cases of this sort have come to my knowledge in Ireland & I have never dared to tell the unhappy women to act as I am doing, for too often the drunken brute was the breadwinner & in each case the women had big families & no means of supporting them & no means of getting judicial assistance. One of these women wrote me the other day asking why I had given her different advice to that on which I myself am acting – I replied that in her case as in mine our lives are on the decline, & therefore of less importance than the lives of the children who still contain in them possibilities of great fulfilment, therefore the safety of the children must be our 1st consideration in such matters. In her case she would have to have left a helpless family to the tender mercies of a Drunkard as having to get a situation she couldn't have taken them with her – I on the contrary had the power of turning the drunkard out, & so saving the children the scandal of his presence, so I did it for the same reasons that she had to stay, *the protection of the children.* She wrote me she understood & wished me all success.

I think the horror with which drunkenness is regarded in France would do good if realised in Ireland. Here it is no excuse for a man who commits a crime to say 'I was drunk'.

What a dull letter I am writing my mind tends to be occupied with dull things just now. I have had to take a week off from my painting to devote to the full consideration of my affairs. I manage to get so absorbed in painting that I don't worry over things much, but at times I have to come out of that peace to see that things go on as they should.

I remain
my dear friend
Alwys yours very sincerely
Maud Gonne

On 6 May, John Quinn, finding it difficult to procure affidavits, wrote: 'I have been met by opposition and silence at every turn. MacBride has had his friends here notified and they apparently take his side of the case and those who do not say that the scandal is hurtful to the cause generally and that the sooner it is hushed up the better.'

152   [Paris]
                                                 1st June [1905]

My dear Friend
Thank you for your letter and enclosure – I had already written to Mr Quinn to thank him. I am writing again to tell him my gratitude & am sending £12 which I am begging him to allow me to pay for the outside expenses. I said I knew through you he had taken all this trouble out of friendship, but that I had written you begging you to

find out for me at least what the outside expenses were.

The trial is put off from week to week & this waiting is a fearful strain on my nerves. It is comparatively easy to pull oneself together for an ordeal but when that ordeal is put off & off & off the strain is bad. However it must end some time. I am quite certain John MacBride would have collapsed before this but for the encouragement & support he has got from fellow drunkards & from English agents. My lawyer told me, he was sure that Kelly, MacBride's lawyer, wouldn't let him give in & Labori who I hear is not at all enthusiastic about his case said, 'C'est les anglais qui le montent' it's the English who are stirring him up.

I am painting a great deal it absorbs me & helps me to live over this horrible time – I have just finished copying a lovely picture of Sirenes by Gustave Moreau, & am copying two others of his a Salome a Polyphemus & I have just done a sketch of Nieve[1] which I am rather pleased with.

Colum told me a lot about his play on the land & the tyranny of the old & I think it will be very interesting. It is cruel not to be able to see it.

Digges is better & has gone back to work. Miss Quinn has also got a good situation & wrote in good spirits.

Who is going to be [your] publisher in Dublin?[2] I am delighted you have found someone.

Mrs MacGregor[3] wrote to me the other day & I asked them to dine. She is working hard at art, & hopes to succeed. They are exactly the same as ever – She said they had passed through awful trouble & difficulties but she hoped things were getting better with them now. MacGregor is giving a series of lectures on occultism & the Mysteries. May & I went to the first. It wasn't very interesting.

It is very hot here too, but I like the heat & my little house is very cool & we have a tiny garden & a big tree to dine under, which is nice in Paris –

Tell me what you are writing.

We are expecting May's sister[4] who is coming to stay & paint for a couple of months.

Your letters are always so good & so comforting. Thank you.

Alwys your friend

Maud Gonne

153

13 Rue de Passy
Paris
Thursday night [June 1905]

My dear Friend

So many thanks for your letter & for the copy of Colum's play.[1]

It is hard to be away so long & to miss so much I am interested in –

However everything comes to an end & these weary months of suspense & anxiety will come to an end too. The trial is definitely fixed for the 26th July & Labori will not be able to obtain any further delay, though I suppose they will defend & insist on the enquête[2] which means that things will drag on till the Autumn but I should think after the first trial John MacBride's power for harm will be considerable diminished & he will not be able to get people to be photographed with him [as] he did at Fontenoy. I was really sorry to see poor Mr O'Leary's photo with MacBride just now in the papers.[3]

Mr Quinn sent me back the £12 I sent him & wrote me a very kind sympathetic letter – he has been more than kind taking so much trouble for me & I don't know how to thank him.

I know that his kindness is due largely to his friendship for you – so I should thank you too, but I have given up thanking you. I have *always counted* on your friendship, ever since I knew you & it has never failed me. In the terrible time I have been through it was a great comfort & a great support to me, it helped me in a wonderful way – one does not thank for help of this kind, only one can never forget it.

I have got back my nerves again & can look fearlessly at life as I always have done but last winter when you wrote to me after you had seen my cousin & heard all from her, I was not like this. I had been through so much that for the time my will even was stunned, your letters then helped me more than you know.

Once before, a long while ago in another terrible moment of my life,[4] your letters & your friendship helped & supported me in the same way.

It is so late I must end this long rambling letter – I think you are in Dublin so [I] write to the Nassau Hotel.

Alwys your friend
Maud Gonne

My cousin May & her sister <are> both staying here.

154

13 Rue de Passy
Paris
Sunday [July 1905]

My dear Willie

I wrote to you to Dublin, probably our letters just crossed –

I haven't much news. The hearing of the divorce case is fixed for 26th July. My lawyer is quite certain of success but thinks it probable that MacBride & his 5 lawyers will obtain an enquête which will drag things on till the autumn.

I heard from the superior of the convent in Laval[1] that Eileen had written her that she & her husband[2] intended coming to France for the trial. I am sorry for this for their sakes, as MacBride persisting in his defence & his claim on my son makes it unavoidable to bring Eileen's name forward. He has still not formulated the counter charges he says he has against me, this is probably to avoid my lawyer having time to prepare an answer to them but I think he will be bound to formulate them next week –

Last week with my cousins & the children I went to Samois, in the forest of Fontainebleau, for a few days. It was so lovely & made me long to be over in Ireland out of the heat of Paris. Though in my tiny garden, surrounded with ivy covered walls & full of tall holy okes [holyhocks] & lilies & one big tree under which we always dine the heat is really not unbearable.

I can make no Plans till after the 26th. I like Colum's play very much but I think he will do better work than that yet –

Will you be in London long?

Alwys your friend
Maud Gonne

155

13 Rue de Passy
Paris
15th July [1905]

My dear Willie

I wonder did you get either of my two last letters one addressed to Nassau Hotel & one to London?

There was nothing particular in them so it doesn't much matter & I dare say you are very busy.

I am working at painting all day long & trying to forget there is such a thing as divorce suit on the 26th.

Have you seen your poems in French in *Vers et Pros*?[1] They lose a good deal in the translation though they are always beautiful – Every poetry book of yours disappeared out of my house here. They were all on the bookshelf in my bedroom where I keep most of my favourite books – I hope one or two are in my house in Dublin, that

I had taken over with me last time, but all those that were here have disappeared. I think there is little doubt my husband took them, for their presence had always annoyed him considerably – my cook says that he spent his last few days in Paris in ransacking the cupboards in my room & in the room which Eileen Wilson used to have.

The only papers which I can find that have disappeared is a large bundle of very compromising documents. . . .
[End of letter missing]

156
13 Rue de Passy
[Paris]
Monday night [July 1905]

My dear Willie

Yesterday I got Labori's conclusions – he waited to the last moment –

MacBride denies all the charges & invokes testimonials of his industry & bravery & says he presided [at the] Bodenstown[1] meeting as showing the high esteem his compatriots hold him –

Asks for separation from me because of the unjust charges I have formulated against him, declares I am weak minded & given to credulity & listening to servants' gossip – offers to prove that I have said I believe in past incarnations most of them *royal ones* –

Alleges I am English & not Irish –

Says I <tried to> consulted an English solicitor with a view of obtaining a divorce from him last Nov. on much graver charges which charges I have made before members of his own family, says I should feel grateful to him for not bringing forward very serious charges against me, which he only refrains from doing for the sake of his son –

Requests the court to give him the custody of the child –

I know that he has had a very low class lawyer engaged trying to find out things against me for several months he has hunted up old servants of mine, old concierges etc – he <got no> has been able to find nothing against me – which is evidently the reason he says that for the sake of his son he refrains from bringing serious charges.

I have no difficulty in proving the Irish origins of my family[2] & I have never contested that my grandfather lived in England & that my father was in the English army, but as these conclusions were only shown to us in the last legal delay 3 days before the trial, I may not have all the papers I want but my cousin the head of our family telegraphed he is sending some & getting others.

This evening Labori has suddenly entered a new plea on MacBride's behalf. While the competence of the French Court is uncontested – he demands to be tried by that Court but according to Irish law which does not admit divorce only judicial separation. This is too late for Labori legally to enter this new plea, but if one brought this up it would mean the case would be remanded & not heard till after the vacation which would give MacBride another 6 months a[t] least to spread his lies about me, so we are making every effort to get knowledge of international law on this point & it is wonderfully difficult to get.

They are very afraid of the publicity of the trial & that we may carry it without enquête. Labori said this last difficulty would not be raised if my lawyer would agree to have the enquête without the public trial & statement of the case but my lawyer says I must in no way consent to this it would look bad for me – he doesn't think it likely that we will carry it without enquête but once the case is stated my position will be cleared of MacBride's lies & insinuations. I think this request for Irish law is a bluff on their part & once I can find out exactly how much is required by Irish law to get judicial separation (I fear drunkenness would be looked on as an extenuating circumstance which might be invoked to cover adultery & indecency etc.) if by judicial separation I can secure complete control of my child I would be inclined to tell my lawyer that I am willing to accept Irish law administered by French Judges & judicial separation with complete control of my child will please me as much as divorce – but I have got to be very sure what I am accepting first

It is very late & I am so tired. I can't write more.
Alwys your friend
Maud Gonne

157

Bellot
par Rebais
Seine et Marne
[September 1905]

My dear Willie

How interesting about the Slave Girl of Tara[1] – I am longing to hear the whole story –

I am trying to forget my worries for the time in this beautiful little country place surrounded by woods & what inhabitants call mountains, to me they seem hills. The inhabitants here are most charming. They all meet one with friendly greetings & insist on giving what they have in the way of fruit or flowers. It is such a little country place, they are not used to seeing strangers & have all the old ideas of hospitality & welcome. It is a peaceful place of small joys, small sorrows, & somehow the peace of it weighs heavily on me – I am not made for a peaceful life – We have taken three little whitewashed rooms. The Graniés & some other artist friends have also taken rooms here & we all eat together at the little inn & spend most of the day painting.

I wonder what people in Dublin are thinking now most of the hideous facts about MacBride are published? The French Press has not said a word except the little note I sent you.

Would John O'Leary get photographed with him still for the papers. I was sorry all the same that all those hideous things were published, for I fear it will prevent MacBride getting a chance of earning his living honestly even if he wants to – It is strange that the Foreign papers may report what the French Press may not, but it is because according to French law all judgements must be pronounced in a public Court so the press cannot be excluded though not admitted as the press. . . .

[End of letter missing]

158   Bellot
                                                                        par Rebais
                                                                        Seine et Marne
                                                                        30 Sept [1905]

My dear Willie

I have not answered your letter all this while as I have been very busy nursing Iseult who got an attack of low fever. She is well again now, so I can return to my painting for another 10 days when I shall have to return to Paris for the final settlement of my affairs –

It is possible I may have to get the opinion of an Irish Council as to the question of MacBride's right of claiming an Irish domicile & Irish Nationality. My French Solicitor would of course write to him the exact legal points he would want opinion on – but he will ask me what Council to write to & I thought perhaps you or Lady Gregory could advise me who it would be best to consult. Sir William Geary[1] wrote me most kindly & gave me his opinion unofficially, but he said if it came before the French Courts the opinion of an *active council* of the Irish bar would be necessary.

When I see Mr Martyn I could console him on the religious side of the divorce question by telling him that Canon Dissard,[2] who received me into the Catholic Church & has since been my confessor – when he heard of the divorce came to Paris from Laval expressly to ask me to forgo & be content with judicial separation but when he heard all the facts & my reason for asking for a divorce he said he could no longer advise me against it – it was a case where legal divorce was necessary, and after Labori's speech in defence of my husband saying that his, MacBride's conscience as a Catholic forbade him accepting the divorce & saying that I had turned protestant because I asked for it Canon Dissard wrote me a letter which he said

I could show to any priest or Bishop justifying my demand for legal divorce. He also suggested I should send a note to the papers refuting Labori's statement & stating my position in the matter, but as I have decided on not writing to the papers or correcting any lies until the whole affair is ended I have not done so –

Dublin *Evening Mail* had a fairly just account of the trial published & most of the charges against MacBride. It was sent to me by one of the Inginide. I think people in Dublin must know that there is more than drunkenness against MacBride though the *Freeman* & *Independent* kept these things out. The *Freeman's* position has been quite correct & what all newspapers should be in such matters – It has made no comment, has hardly mentioned the affair. The *Independent* on the contrary was full of it & only grew discreet since it has seen that MacBride will be quite impossible to defend – This has not prevented MacBride's legal advisers putting a note in the press threatening the *Independent* with libel action for having reproduced some part of Cruppi's speech – of course this was only bluff.[3]

I hope to be in Ireland for Xmas I am getting so homesick. The peaceful mediocrity of this place with its little hills, its little trees, its little houses, where no one is rich & no one very poor, no one very happy & no one very unhappy & all so nice & so well ordered, is getting on my nerves.

Granié who sees beauty everywhere gets indignant with me when I say such things –

May is going to India to join her husband![4] She starts [on] the 4th Nov. She is coming to stay with me on the 15th Oct.

Tell me more of the Slave Girl of Tara.

Alwys,

Very sincerely your friend,

Maud Gonne

159   13 Rue de Passy
                                                                 Paris
                                                                 24th Oct. [1905]

My dear Willie

Thank you so much for all the trouble you have taken in getting me names of Councils & for your letters & telegram – I think Sergeant Dodd[1] would be the best. He defended me in the action I took against Collis of the Dublin *Figaro*. Things legal move so slowly here that my lawyers have not yet decided on writing to him. My charges against John MacBride they say will have to be proved before the question of nationality is gone into – The enquiry will all take place in November but the final trial will probably not come on till Jany or Feby so I must make up my mind on spending another winter out of Ireland. Directly the verdict is given I shall return to Dublin.

I hear that MacBride got a friend of his, Hallinan[2] (who only for my forbearance in not providing the names of the two friends of MacBride's whose drunkenness created a scandal, not only in my house but in the neighbourhood would have had his name side by side with John MacBride's for drunkenness at the trial & in the newspapers) to propose that the prize I always offer for the Samhain competitions[3] should this year be returned I being an English woman & consequently not eligible as a member of *Cumann na Gaedhal*. It is rather amusing when one thinks it is I who created the organisation & drew up its rules – It was put to the meeting & Hallinan was voted out but I hear he intends (or other friends of MacBride) bringing the matter forward at the Samhain convention – John O'Leary is President of Cumann na Gaedhal so I have written him a letter saying I have heard of this & as I wish to save idle discussion I have sent him the pedigree of our family as I received it from my cousin Henry Gonne the present head of the family who possesses the letters, heirlooms & portraits & documents proving its exactitude – The family is in Ireland since 1560, they came from Caithness in Scotland. I sent a copy of the letter & pedigree to the Secretary of Inginide na hEireann who is on the Executive of Cumann na Gaedhal in case old Mr O'Leary was not present, if the matter was brought up. It seems so absurd that such a thing should be necessary. In my letter I said I was sorry for *them* that it should be.

In your last letter you seemed exasperated with things or rather people in Dublin – I know one does get exasperated sometimes for it's aggravating to have to waste time & energy in little struggles over details – but after all no-where else does one find people as capable of enthusiasm & devotion & work as in Ireland only we want a few energetic & practical wills to prevent all this devotion & enthusiasm being wasted on trifles.

My cousins are staying with me, but May leaves 4th Nov. for India – Write me when you have time.
Alwys your friend
Maud Gonne

Writing to John O'Leary Maud Gonne said:

I am writing to you as president of Cumann na Gaedhal. I have heard that the lies so freely circulated against me by John MacBride and his friends have so far gained credence that some members of Cumann na Gaedhal are deceived about my nationality and have announced their intention of bringing forward the matter at Samain Convention it being against the rules of Cumann na Gaedhal for any who are not of Irish descent to belong to the organisation. I was one of the principal movers in starting the organisation and collaborated in drawing up its rules and forwarding its objects and I must say that I am surprised that any of those with whom I have worked for so many years should be so ready to doubt me. To prevent any useless discussion on this matter I send you a copy of the pedigree of my family as I have received it from my cousin Henry Gonne, the present head of the family . . . the judge refused to go into the matter as being entirely irrelevant to the case. But John MacBride has succeeded in what he wanted, in getting articles in the American and English press throwing doubt on my Irish origin and consequently on my sincerity and truthfulness, for undoubtedly, if I were not Irish, the position in Irish politics which I have always taken, would be incomprehensible. I am sorry to trouble you with such a long letter, but I wish you to know facts, which in this case, cease to be of only private interest and affect my position in an organisation in which I have always been deeply interested. I am grieved and surprised that it is necessary for me to do so. I have remained away from Ireland all this time and I shall remain away until the verdict in my case against John MacBride leaves no opening for discussion as to who is right or who is wrong, in doing so and in refusing, as I have refused, to put the facts of my case before the many friends who have written begging me to do so, I have made a considerable sacrifice, for I am well aware that John MacBride has taken a quite opposite course and has used political organisations for his personal interest and defence. At least I will give no opportunity for my friends and fellow workers to waste valuable time in discussing matters unconnected with our work or through their friendship to be drawn into a personal quarrel unconnected with the Irish cause.

160   13 Rue de Passy
                                                    [Paris]
                                                    Wednesday night [November 1905]

My dear Willie

I hate to trouble you, but I want your advice & help.

I have just received enclosed letter. I heard that this matter was to be brought up at the Samhain convention so I sent copies of enclosed notes & pedigree to Mr O'Leary President Cumann na Gaedhal & in case of his absence to the Secretary – Mr O'Leary wrote the enclosed letter which please return to me –

According to the ruling of Mr P. T. Daly[1] the accident of birth is the test of Nationality so my Grandfather & Uncles are Portuguese, my father English, my sister Irish, my son French –

Could you get Mr O'Leary to write a letter which could be published saying he is satisfied as to my Irish descent & saying that the ruling of Mr P. T. Daly at the Samhain convention was wrong?

This thing pained me so much that I distrust my own judgement in the matter – I have worked with & for these people for nearly 20 years, I have sacrificed riches & position for this work & they say I am not Irish – it is bewildering & very saddening.

I created Cumann na Gaedhal – it became a power, it frightened the tea party because it destroyed *mysterious inaction*,[2] they set to work to affiliate its members. They have taken up John MacBride because he plays their game & helps them play it to perfection – Drunken orgies can be covered by secret meetings & idleness & cowardice by secret plotting for the cause & politicians & police help the game forward. It is the affiliated members of the tea party who elected MacBride –

To night I feel inclined at the next trial to give names of the Drunken delegates I refused before & who caused such scandal in the Rue de Passy when they visited MacBride, Cumann na Gaedhal could no doubt create a few more vice presidencys for them –

The enquiry into the divorce case begins on the 20th of this month, though I am quite certain of the result it will be a great strain as I am obliged to be present all the time –

I have been working hard at painting with some success for a picture dealer who saw some of my things offered to sell them for me & a lady who hardly knows me has asked to have her portrait done from seeing a little head I did of Iseult – but I don't sign or sell anything yet.

May has started for India. I miss her very much.

Write soon –

Alwys your friend

Maud Gonne

In November a member of Inghínidhe na hÉireann wrote giving her account of the Cumann na nGaedheal convention of which P. T. Daly was chairman:

Hallinan proposed MacBride [for vice-president] and I proposed you. The Chairman said he could not accept your name it being against the rules of the organisation to have anyone who was not of Irish birth or descent. . . . You could see by the people present that they were not your friends. One of the delegates said it was a very strange thing to bring up the question of your nationality now after you had been so long connected with the organisation . . . even if your name went forward I think you would not have been elected as they had the majority.

161   [Paris]

Tuesday [November 1905]

My dear Willie

Thank you so much for both your letters. I think you are right there is nothing to be done for the present in regard to what I wrote you about – I was very pained at the time but I am very philosophical over things generally. I worked for Ireland for Ireland's sake, not for my own. I always thought I was an instrument of force working for Ireland's liberty, it may be these forces need me no longer, that they have chosen others for their work – it does not matter, so long as that work goes on. I will never under any circumstances enter on a personal fight or campaign. When this horrible divorce is over I shall return to Ireland & see how things are & if I see any useful work to do – if not I shall return to France where the children will get a better education & live in a wider movement of ideas.

Yesterday for 5 mortal hours I sat opposite MacBride while my witnesses one after another gave their evidence of his drunken immorality – my lawyer said he never had a better case as the witnesses gave their evidence quite simply & it was impossible for MacBride's lawyer even once to put them in contradiction with themselves or each other. Next Monday his witnesses will be heard & the following Monday I have the right, if I wish, of calling other witnesses to refute anything his witnesses may say – this all takes place in camera – then the judge writes a report & next Feby this report will come before the 1st Judge in open court & our Lawyers will have one more opportuntiy for mud throwing. The only one thing I have to fear in all this is that MacBride will succeed in order to spite me in dragging little Iseult into the case. The only one thing he has been authorised to prove against me is *that I have calumniated him to members of his own family in London with a view to obtaining a divorce & that my accusations at that time were false because I have not brought them forward in the charges at present before the French Court.* Only after next Monday I shall know if he really *dare* go on with this. If he does I shall have to prove the whole horrible thing which for the sake of keeping little Iseult out of the witness box I have not brought forward.

I see by the *Independent* MacBride is bringing a libel action against them for having published (& only in a modified form) what took place in the French Courts last June – I enclose cutting. If by any extraordinary chance MacBride won the libel action & got damages he would be a rich man for he could repeat the action against *all* the English newspapers who reported even more fully than the *Independent* the trial which took place in June – but I expect he has no chance of winning, it is only bluff to throw dust in the eyes of his friends in Dublin – tell me if you hear anything about this –

Send me the account of your lecture in Oxford.

I am so tired I can't write more today

Alwys your friend

Maud Gonne

162
Paris
Tuesday night [November 1905]

My dear Willie

Monday week all my witnesses were heard, & the evidence was most conclusive against John MacBride. His own solicitor is reported to have said his case is lost – yesterday from 12 till 7 I sat & listened to his witnesses. Several of them had to admit his drunkenness & those who denied it were so manifestly lying & in such contradiction with the preceding ones that they did him more harm than good. The only one who made me feel very sad was Eileen, though she has behaved very badly, it was terrible to bring her into it & I regret very much having allowed it. I allowed it at first because I believed it would have made John MacBride accept my offer of a quiet separation – leaving me the child – but it did not & I thought her name in any case need not have been made public, but now they have brought her over as a witness there is no way of keeping her name out – I offered if he let the case go undefended to withdraw all charges except drunkenness but he refused & replied by threats through his lawyer that he would ruin me. I have never yielded to a threat in my life so I told the lawyer to go on. Eileen's husband seems quite convinced of her innocence which is the great thing, & I forbid my lawyer putting any questions to him in cross examination which would shake this belief – he declared that all those who slandered his wife were vile women in the pay of the vilest creature upon earth & after having stated this opinion he subsided into consideration of his family history which if the judge had permitted he said he could trace back into the dim ages of time, that the men were true & noble, & the women chaste & pure, defenders of the faith of their ancestors etc. etc.

The Judge translated all this 'famille honorable' & my lawyer with much difficulty illicited [elicited] that they kept a public house.

Hallinan, whom *Cumann na Gaedhal* has rewarded for his attack on me by naming him treasurer when they named MacBride vice president, gave himself away completely. He swore on his honor that he & his friend Mr Casey & Major John MacBride were perfect gentlemen & had *never* been drunk, that they were Irishmen while the opposite party was the SON of an English Colonel. The Judge couldn't understand. I suggested that his testimony should be inscribed textually, but I fear this wasn't done. He then described his visit to Major MacBride in Paris which he said was in the interest of the Irish cause & he proceeded to give an account of how they spent their time. They arrived at 6 & dined with Major MacBride & as they did not know Paris the major proposed showing them the places of interest, they went to Olympia (a big music hall) & after to another big restaurant in Montmartre but he did not remember the name.

They only drank coffee & then having heard the flower market was beautiful they visited that & went to *Notre Dame* & to *la Chambre des Députés* & got home at 8 o'clock in the morning perfectly sober & went to bed – As their return, owing to their scandalous drunkenness, had made a sensation in La Rue de Passy & had been attested by several witnesses beside the concierge & my servants, this witness & his friend Mr Casey who repeated the same story like a parrot, did not improve MacBride's case & caused considerable amusement to those present.

Several other equally truthful & reputable witnesses swore that MacBride never got drunk & several young girls out of the Collins family[1] swore he was incapable of any of the wicked acts of which he was accused. Miss Florence Collins aged 16 swore I told her that my husband adored me but was very jealous especially of Mr Yeats & a Spanish gentleman who followed me in the streets of Madrid, & that my husband wouldn't let me go out alone. Cross-examined she said she had been to my house 5 times in 6 years – Several witnesses said I was morphinomane but brought no proof – As this might influence the guardianship of the child I shall get a doctor's certificate & as a matter of fact I have taken morphine 21 *times* in all my life.

Barry O'Brien was announced as one of MacBride's witnesses but it was announced that professional work kept him in London & there is an application now before the court to allow him to send his testimony from London – My lawyer objects on the grounds of his being MacBride's lawyer & connected with the case & his deposition would be a breach of professional secrecy.

In cross examination Mrs Collins admitted that the London Lawyer (Mr B. O'Brien) had written them a full account of the *criminal charge* she said I made against my husband. It is an extraordinary violation of profession[al] secrecy as I only saw Mr O'Brien at the request of Dr MacBride & as my husband's lawyers, but Barry O'Brien's conduct has been extraordinary all through this case.

Will you be staying long in London?

Alwys your friend

Maud Gonne

The Dungannon Club[s][2] are doing splendid work – I have been reading of them in the U.I. for a long time & know most of the young men – I met them in Belfast.

Inginide na hEireann have just sent me a wire to say I have been reelected president & I have a letter from the National Player Society[3] branch Cumann na Gaedhal to say they have elected [me] president. This is evidently a protest against the rigged convention of Cumann na Gaedhal & the ruling of the Chairman. It is very good of them, but I would rather they did not I want to avoid any sort of personal fight being raised over me –

163   13 Rue de Passy
                                                                  [Paris]
                                                                  Dimanche [November 1905]

My dear Willie

One more hideous day of listening to MacBride's friends perjuring themselves by saying he never got drunk. 5 hours of useless talk & gossip but not one of them has ventured to say anything direct against my character though several vaguely insinuated things about Iseult but of no consequence. 2 have sworn that I take morphine & one that he heard I did. There was an effort made to bring forward the Iseult affair & drag her in but the judge absolutely refused to allow witnesses to disprove a charge that was not before him or to go into the matter at all – Barry O'Brien's name is still murmured at intervals. Some say he is sick in Bologne, some that his professional work prevents him attending, they are moving for the right of having him give evidence in London.

Tomorrow 11 more of MacBride's witnesses among whom O'Leary & Dixon are announced & then his case is done & I have one day to bring witnesses to disprove the lies that have been told. I do not think either MacBride or I are heard. We are supposed to be too partial I suppose. Only in February there will be the public trial & speeches of the lawyers & all the evidence read in open Court & the judge's verdict.

The latest lie that MacBride is whispering to his friends is that Eileen Wilson is my daughter but he won't dare to bring that into court as it is too easily disproved. There is no question of this.

I have been so taken up with the trial for the last month that I have hardly done any drawing. I return to my studio life on Monday & am going resolutely to forget worries until the verdict is given when I shall at once return to Ireland – The strain of the last month has worn me thin as a shadow. It was such a nightmare work having to sit in court day after day listening to my witnesses describing the hideous things I knew of, I found myself feeling glad & relieved when they forgot some ugly detail & then I had to shake myself up to the fact that I was there to remind my lawyer to ask some question that would bring it out & that the future of my son depended on it. Day after day I had to listen to MacBride's witnesses perjuring themselves & contradicting each other & sometimes the fighting spirit in me woke up & it amused me to suggest questions that I knew would accentuate the contradiction, but all the time at the bottom of my heart was the sickening fear that the name of my innocent little Iseult would be dragged into the sea of mud. For though agreement had been come to between the lawyers on both sides in the presence of the judge that the affair was not to be alluded to on either side, I knew I was fighting a *mad man* who when he realised he was losing would do anything for revenge. As I expected it came. The last day of the hearing of witnesses in spite of protest from the judge, in spite of remonstrance from his own lawyer MacBride insisted in calling his brother Dr MacBride to go into the whole affair, he ended by saying it was his belief that I & the British Government had concocted this to get rid of his brother –

Nothing was left of me then but to ask for another day's hearing of witnesses & getting Madame Avril & the other witnesses to give evidence in this affair. As I had the calling of witnesses in my hands I refused to allow Iseult to be called & she knows nothing at all of the affair. The judge quite understood & appreciated the reasons I think. It has damaged MacBride's case frightfully his baseness was so apparent that the judge spoke most severely to him when he tried to put questions to my witnesses, questions which he knew were groundless but which might perhaps leave a doubt in the judge's mind. The judge said 'You have had every opportunity given you for bringing charges against your wife & for bringing witnesses to prove them – you have not done so because you could not & I am not here to listen to insinuations not based on evidence' – My lawyers say the case is certainly won now. I think the case in the Dublin Courts has also settled the question of domicile & nationality which will save a lot of trouble – Is it not extraordinary that MacBride's Dublin lawyer Mr Henry[1] should ridicule the issues set forth by MacBride himself in his Paris case. Of course no one here sees the relevancy of his presiding at a meeting in Bodenstown, but as he asked to prove it, & as I raised no objection he was allowed by the court to do so. It is strange that his own lawyer in Dublin should repudiate it. The only people who ought to feel indignant are the Nationalists who MacBride should dare to try to shelter his shame & his vices behind the Irish flag but they don't seem to mind.

Your letter interested me very much. It is strange that clerical censor or any censor should break a man up so much. I am afraid Kettle[2] can't be very strong, but I am glad you are seeing him, it will be good for him & help him get back his balance for even if he is not strong, an active brain capable of original thoughts is always valuable.

I know what a help your letters & thoughts were to me last year when my nerves were in such a state of collapse that my will was irresolute. Now I have got back my old blessed indifference to circumstances, but I do not forget how you helped me then & I am sure you can help Kettle as few others could – & from what you say he is worth helping.

I haven't read Samhain yet[3]
I remain
Alwys your friend
    Maud Gonne

164   13 Rue de Passy
                                   [Paris]
                       Monday [November/December 1905]

My dear Willie

Thank you so much for your letter – Don't trouble about watching papers for me. I have ordered a press agency to send me every thing where my name occurs for the present & the bundle of cuttings I receive every day are surprisingly large & require a certain amount of resolution to read, however I always prefer to know exactly the facts & the dangers to be faced. All the London & English papers have had whole columns but with the exception of TWO *provincial* papers none have mentioned the Iseult incident & these very slightly – & yet I know that Collins who supplied the press association man with all the details he thought damaging to me particularly insisted on this. I suppose it was only the fear of a libel action which prevented them using it. The *Independent* didn't dare & it only showed its bias by glossing over some of my lawyer's statements about John MacBride which the other papers published – The great point which the English papers expatiate on is Labori's statement that I am an English woman – that I only became Catholic to marry MacBride & have now become protestant to divorce. They also gave my lawyers contradiction. I have quite decided to reply *nothing* until the divorce is quite over & I have a judgement in my favor.

When I return to Ireland people will see that I am Catholic – & I am having the whole affiliation of my family from the 16th Century which we have in old prayer books & family papers clearly made out by the Heralds' office at Ulster House, Dublin & when all is finally over I may perhaps publish this in one of the papers. These family papers corroborated by heirlooms & portraits etc. trace my family from father to son in Kerry & Mayo from the 16th Century, till my great grandfather William Gonne settled in Portugal & started a business between London & Portugal in Spanish wines – but I am not going to contradict any lies until after the verdict is given in my favor.

The impression of the Court I hear is quite favorable & my lawyer says I need have no anxiety – I hear also that Collins & Co are abusing Labori & saying that he pleaded so badly that John MacBride may lose his case – The enquête will probably have to go through & through, it is painful & will make a long delay as the holidays will intervene. Still I think it will be for the best because if ever the question of the custody of the child is raised in the future by the English Courts it will be better that all my charges against MacBride are fully & separately proved.

I shall of course try to keep Iseult from having to witness & I think I can do so.

Again thanking you for your letter

I remain

Always your friend

Maud Gonne

165   [Paris]
                          [November/December 1905]

[Beginning of letter missing]

American affidavits having been contested as far as I have heard, as Mr Quinn had had them all legally taken down before the French consul in New York I don't think they can be – The National Players which is one of the largest branches of Cumann na Gaedhal in Dublin at their annual meeting elected me President & Inginide at their annual meeting re elected me, both clubs telegraphed the fact to me so as to arrive on the day of the trial but though I wrote them my gratitude I explained that the question between John MacBride & myself was a question between man & woman – involving the duty of a mother to keep the home pure for her child, as well as of her own dignity of life, it was not a question which touched the Irish national Cause & though I thanked them & was deeply touched by their expression of confidence I did not wish to use the Irish cause as weapon for private & individual defence.

That if it was possible for the contempt which I feel for MacBride & men like him to be deepened it was when I heard him & his friends sheltering their drunkenness or their immorality behind the Irish flag –

Tell me where will you be at Xmas – I am going to send you a little drawing of Iseult I have done[1] – I shall send it by my cousin Miss Gonne who is going to London for Xmas. It is Iseult with her hair twisted up for the bath, it is like her but makes her look older than she is. Thank you so much for your letter. I only part agree with it, there is more good than you admit in the unconscious thought of the masses of the people.

Yours alwys

Maud Gonne

I am so glad the theatre tour has been so successful.

166   13 Rue de Passy
                                                                       [Paris]
                                                                       16th Dec [1905]

My dear Willie

I have just read the *White Cockade*.[1] Indeed you did not say too much about it! It is wonderful to read, & must be wonderful to see acted.

Lady Gregory knows the soul of our people & expresses it as no one else does. Through the surface of triviality, of selfish avarice, of folly which often jars on one, she never ceases to see & to express in her writing that deep passion which *only heroic* action or thought is able to arouse in them, & when once aroused makes them capable of sacrifice for ideals as no other people on earth are. It is a play that will live & I know I shall often have the opportunity of seeing it, which consoles me little for missing its first production. It is a play that will be popular – don't look contemptuous – such plays are needed for your work & for the public.

I sent off my little drawing of Iseult for you, tell me if you like it. She had her hair twisted up for her bath which makes her look too old but otherwise it is like her.

167   13 Rue de Passy
                                                                       [Paris]
                                                                       Monday [December 1905]

My dear Willie

I am so glad you like the little drawing of Iseult. It is very like her except that having her hair twisted up gives her a grown up air she has not got. She is only 11 & though very tall, is a real child. She will be very beautiful I think & she has a wonderful imagination & a love of art remarkable in a child & she would always rather go to a picture gallery or to see beautiful things than to the circus.

Dixon's compromise ideas crystalised into an offer to Ella Young to try & settle matters (*this is private*) Dixon practically admitted I was likely to gain my case in France through technicalities whatever that may mean & that he knew I would never consent to any arrangement which did not give me complete control of the child & he felt could undertake this should be conceded. He added that he was acting independently of MacBride, but he felt MacBride would take his advice – Ella didn't at all advise compromise but merely wrote the offer made to her – I replied by sending her a translation of the whole of the evidence in both sides & told her to let Dixon read that & after to ask him, honestly, in view of all the lies he has heard circulated against me, if he still would advise compromise. There is not a single thing against my character in all the evidence produced by MacBride except that Anthony MacBride said I told him that Iseult is my daughter – & that he believed me in league with the British Govt against MacBride which was a lie & can if necessary be disproved by Mrs Clay[1] who assisted at the interview – otherwise there is not one word that I would object to be[ing] published in the Irish papers whereas the evidence against MacBride is overwhelmingly terrible & complete – I thought it was good that Dixon who according to his lights is an honest man should have a chance of reading the evidence for though he witnessed for MacBride I am certain they did not show him the evidence of the other witnesses. If he & his friends continue to support MacBride once they have read this evidence they can no longer support the theory, which is one they love – of Irish intolerance of immorality – Of course there is no possibility of compromise now – After all that has been said a public verdict is the only possible ending to this miserable business.

You are quite right to address my letters to Madame Maud Gonne. In France I have always been Madame Maud Gonne before & since my marriage so the divorce makes no difference in this respect.

I am working very hard at the studio. I have been advised to go in for illustration because as Granié says '*imagination* which is ruin to real painting in the highest form, is very useful for illustration' – I am amusing myself by illustrating the life of Cuchulain,[2] I will send you the first illustrations, for I want your *opinion* on them – your *criticism* – There are very few things in English art that are as good as in French art, but English illustrations are on the whole I think better – certainly their books are better illustrated. I expect this letter will follow you to Scotland. I hope you will have an enjoyable time there – tell me about Fiona Macleod, is Sharpe's death the end of her as well as of his writings?[3]

I remain alwys your friend
Maud Gonne

1906

In 1905 the National Theatre Society had been reorganised into a limited company with Yeats, Synge and Lady Gregory as directors and subsidised by Miss Horniman, who accompanied the company on a tour to England. In 1906 the theatre still kept Yeats very busy; he was also working on his play Deirdre, *and he revised several other works.*

168

13 Rue de Passy
Paris
15 Feby [1906]

My dear Willie

I have waited to answer your letter till I had some news of my affairs – The date is at last settled for the final trial – the 28th of this month. It is likely that Major MacBride's lawyers will obtain a week or a fortnight's delay, as delay has been all along their tactics but this will be the limit of delay now possible I think – I shall not have to be present at this trial – & if it were not for my anxiety lest Labori will, to satisfy his client's desire for vengence, drag Iseult's name into it I should be fairly indifferent.

In the summing up of evidence on my side, which will be read publicly in court nothing is said about her & Eileen's name is not mentioned except by an initial, & very slightly mentioned at all, if she had not had the folly of coming over as a witness, no one would have connected her with the thing but since she gave evidence & consequently had to give her name in full, it may get into the papers. I hope not, but MacBride's drunken newspaper friends talk freely in bars & the English journalists will I am afraid be on the alert.

I have just heard that my cousin May (Mrs Clay) is coming home & will be here next month I think –

I am working steadily at painting all day & every day – As you like my work I am sending you another little pencil sketch – my master Granié says it is the best thing I have done, the model is rather old & worn but the drawing I think will interest you – In my spare time in the evenings I am working at illustrations for the Cuchulain Saga & have got some rather interesting studies but they all want being worked out with models & having no studio of my own it is rather difficult to manage so I am for the present leaving them in the state of projects rather than finished drawings.

Why are you rejoicing in unpopularity?[1] (It is only your own letter which says you are unpopular & I dare say it is not true) I know our people are full of prejudices many of which get on one's nerves & hinder work greatly, but many of these prejudices, wrong in themselves, spring from a good source & their intensity show a capacity for feeling & action which is hopeful – here in France at the present there is no capacity for strong feeling or action among the people, & I think this is a very bad sign – I would rather see the people wildly excited & moved over even a wrong ideal, than indifferent to every thing as they seem to be here just now –

I know when I return to Ireland I shall find all the forces of prejudice against me – & being used by dishonest politicians & cowards for all it is worth – I am not the least pleased by the thought it will mean a waste of time & energy to combat & I am not certain if I have the energy necessary for such a fight. The indifference which I complain of in the French people today, has taken a deep hold of me too, & if I find things hard for my work in Ireland I feel inclined to return to Paris & paint. I have always recognised the possibility that the forces or the Gods who used me as an instrument to work through in Ireland would suddenly find other instruments & my power over crowds would go – & yet I know I could still move the crowds if I could show them a fiercer & wilder way to freedom – but I am tired & if others are there to do the work I am glad to leave it to them. We will talk all this over when we meet. Why I am sorry, if what you say about unpopularity is true, is that the people who *need* your movement & the theatre will not benefit by it. The National Theatre *ought* to be *crowded* & it *might be* but we can talk of all this better than write of it –

Are you going to be in Dublin for long? Let me know where to send the drawing.

Always your friend,
Maud Gonne

169

13 Rue de Passy
Paris
Tuesday [March 1906]

My dear Willie

I have just got back from Marseilles where I went to meet my cousin May who has just returned from India & is staying with me for a fortnight & find your letter. Do send me the novel about me.[1] Even if absurd I would like to see it & it won't worry me. I am too indifferent. I had not even heard of it – I am sending you the drawing I promised – the Dectora design[2] was done entirely without models so of course the figure drawing is not good – If ever I intend to carry out my ideas for the illustration of the life of Cuchulain I shall have to get models – these I am doing now are merely ideas not worked out –

I am so glad the theatre is going on well & the audiences increasing –

I am still uncertain of the date of the final trial of my divorce case & of my plans after – I certainly shall go to Dublin immediately after, but whether alone & only for a short time, or whether with my family & to stay there is still uncertain.

May sends her kindest regards to you.
I remain
In haste
Yours alwys
Maud Gonne

170   [Paris]
                                            Friday [March 1906]
My dear Willie
   I posted you yesterday a drawing I have made for an illustration
of the wedding cup of Dectora, I cut out the drawing I had made of
the banquet where Conchobar[1] is handing the wine cup to Sualtim,[2]
because I was not satisfied with some of the figures of the warriors,
I had drawn them without a model & they looked wooden. I shall
finish the banquet scene with a model next week because though it
is only of secondary importance to the drawing I like the naif irony
of the idea [of] Sualtim drinking with the King while the bride drinks
with the Gods – Tell me just what you think of it – I am working
very hard. Drawing has been a great comfort to me & helped me to
get through this awful time. I am quite happy when painting and have
no time to worry over troubles.
   When do you return to Ireland?
   Alwys your friend,
      Maud Gonne

171   [Paris]
                                    Tuesday [March/April 1906]
My dear Willie
   All this time I have not written to thank you for sending me
Hyacinth,[1] but I was waiting to have news of my divorce to tell, &
even now I have none. In vain my lawyer tries to get MacBride's
lawyer to fix the date for the final hearing. My case is the 20th on
the rolls, but as the judge is amenable it could be heard at once,
without waiting its actual turn, if only the lawyers could agree.
   Last Wednesday, there was quite a scene in court between my
lawyer Cruppi & MacBride's lawyer Labori. Cruppi asked for the
case to be heard immediately, the Judge said he was willing to fix an
early date but Labori refused absolutely to allow the affair to be heard
before the elections (he is candidate), & they do not come till the 6th
May. Cruppi insisted but Labori said if he forced the date, he would
throw up the case, as he would not plead it till after the elections.
   MacBride evidently wants delay, in hopes of winning his libel
action against the *Independent* in the mean time, which, if by any
chance he does succeed in winning, would prevent the publication of
the trial & verdict in the English & French papers.
   My lawyer says there is no hope that the case will be heard now,
till the *middle of May*, as when the Lawyers don't agree the Judge
cannot fix a date out of turn. This waiting is most wearisome &
unsettling. [*Fragment*][2]
   What you say about the *weakness* in my drawing is probably right.

I feel it myself, & in all the work I do at the *Académie Julian*. I fight against it by using brushes the size of house painters & steadily ignoring fine detail – it is only in the little pencil drawings like those I sent you that I let myself follow my love of delicate line & detail. I am very dependant on my model. I cannot paint like Russell from memory but in the model I like to translate moods. In Iseult's head I wanted to show youth which is beautiful in every movement & can defy even hair twisted tightly up for a bath – In my portrait I wanted to give the idea of a face that has *out lived life & has no age* – I think I suceeded, for my cousin Mrs Clay when she saw it said though she did not know the idea I had when I drew it, 'you couldn't tell what age you are from that portrait, the face is beyond age' – I was very pleased because while I conscientiously put in every line and hollow I saw, I wanted to get that feeling into the drawing.

Mrs Clay has gone to Rome to stay with my sister for a couple of months – She was not happy in India & so came home, but she is not separated from her husband, or likely to be I think – & *doesn't want it to be talked about* – She has come home to avoid the hot weather & her husband will follow when he gets leave. On the whole, I do not think she would be happier if she separated, neither she nor her husband seem to know quite what they want. I am afraid he drinks or takes opium or some drug – he certainly does not make her happy & yet when she is away he has one idea only, to get her to return, & she doesn't like the thought of entirely abandoning him. She is very generous & won't give up the idea she may be able to help him to a happier life – I do not think she would be happy living alone, so it seems best for things to drift on as they are for the present.

Hyacinth was not *so abominable* as I expected, of course a great deal is absurd & grotesque & evidently written by a man who doesn't know me at all – what vexed me most in it was the infamous calumny on the Irish boys who went out to fight for the Boers, with one exception they were very fine young fellows, who were [*end fragment*]³ absolutely unselfish and patriotic.

What are you writing? It is so long since I have read anything of yours.

I must end this long rambling letter.

Alwys your friend

Maud Gonne

[Paris]
                                            29th April [1906]

My dear Willie

Thank you for your letter & the *Freeman*.¹ The *press cutting agency* send me most things where my name is mentioned & several Dublin friends send me items of Irish news but I am always glad to get the news from you as often the commentaries are very different.

Nothing but madness can have prompted MacBride to take a libel action against the *Independent* for having published a *very* modified account of what took place in the Paris Courts. The *Independent* up to that moment was distinctly favorable to MacBride, & used to publish all sorts of touching little paragraphs about his visits to my son, supplied by himself, & also how his name was applauded at all the meetings when it was mentioned etc.

I understand from the accounts in the papers that MacBride is now ordered by the court to produce all the evidence which was heard before the *private* enquiry court in Paris² – As far as I personally am concerned every word may be published & will do me no harm, but Eileen will be ruined & of course I would much rather have kept out of the press all the Iseult incident, which after Dr MacBride had insisted on breaking the agreement made before the Judge that this matter was not to be touched on by either side I was obliged to call witnesses to prove very thoroughly. None of this evidence will ever get into the press through the French courts as it is not read out at the final trial which is public & I imagine the judge's summing up & verdict is worded so as not to bring in matters that would injure outside parties more than necessary.

Then with a man like MacBride who lies for the pleasure of lying one never knows what false documents he may produce in this [indecipherable] case against the *Independent*. He has allowed his lawyer to file absolutely false affidavits & quite gratuitously without reason, as for instance when they declared he had paid the 1500 francs he was condemned to pay to my lawyer which he never has paid, & when his lawyer Mr Henry repudiated entirely the whole of his defence in Paris saying he had never said anything about being elected to preside at Bodenstown nor about his bravery in the Transvaal etc when these very things are set out at length in each official document concerning the case – For this reason I have written to Mr Friery the solicitor who prosecuted <defended me against> Ramsey Collis for me years ago – asking him if there is anything I can do 1st to keep out of the press the two things I wish for the sake of Eileen & Iseult to keep out & 2nd if he can watch the case for me & prevent or immediately contradict any false document MacBride may try & produce.

No I am not so thin & worn as I was when I drew the picture. I drew it at the beginning of the winter, soon after these long enquiries which were fearfully trying on my nerves. Now I am much stronger & am looking well again. It would have been nice to have seen you in Paris, but I didn't suggest it because I knew you were busy & I also expected any month to have been in Ireland. Now I don't think I shall be over until June. I went to Colleville for Easter with the children the Country was lovely & so spring like with the apple blossoms out everywhere. I painted a great deal. I am trying to sell my property there but haven't succeeded yet.

What courage you have to begin a great work like Deirdre[3] all over again – I don't think I could do that. In painting when a picture goes wrong I destroy it but seldom have the courage to begin it over again.

Paris is very charming now, the Salons are open – I don't believe a bit in all the talk of revolution the panic however is extraordinary.[4] Everyone is laying in provisions as if for a siege & the town crowded with soldiers. I, on the contrary have chosen the eve of the 1st of May to give a dinner party but few of my friends would I think have arrived if I had fixed it actually on the 1st, such is the state of alarm people are in here. It seems so funny to see them so frightened & I don't believe there is any cause.

Give my kind regards to Lady Gregory.

Iseult is very well & very charming. She is working hard at lessons I am afraid rather against the grain but with very good results.

In haste,

Very sincerely your friend

Maud Gonne

173   [Paris]

Monday [early May 1906]

My dear Willie

My plans are still vague my lawyer only returns from his election campaign today. I have a rendezvous with him tomorrow & hope to get the date fixed then. As soon as I know I will write to you – by the Irish papers I see that Major MacBride's libel action in Dublin is fixed for the 6th June. It is almost certain that Labori will ask a delay till after that date & as the law always seems ready for delays he may get it. I expect it will be nearly the end of June before the case is over.

I intend coming to Dublin directly it is over though the lawyers have not yet decided as to whether it will be safe for me to take my son out of France – much depends on the terms of the verdict. If I cannot bring him to Ireland with me at once, my stay there will be very short as he is very delicate & I shall have to take him into the country for the hot weather –

I will let you know as soon as possible the dates I am likely to be in Dublin & in London as I should like to meet you then & there is a great deal I would like to talk to you about.

As I am coming to Ireland shortly I think it would hardly be worth while you coming to France to see me as you have so much work, just now waiting for you.

I have a model waiting for me so must end in haste –

Thanking you for your letter

Alwys your friend
    Maud

I have just begun a picture of Deirdre as a child.

174   [Paris]
                                             Sunday [June 1906]

My dear Willie

'Can you by any chance find out why the Court of Appeal (Baron Fitzgibbon)[1] has reversed Judge Boyd's sentence obliging Major MacBride to find security for costs in his case against the Independent. Judge Boyd found very rightly that Major MacBride had no domicile in Ireland & as he expressed it a peripatetic residence in various hotels did not constitute domicile.

The question affects in a small way my case here, as MacBride who knows his case is lost on its merits here is asking to benefit by the fact that Irish law does not admit divorce & the fact that Judge Boyd treated him as an alien was of importance.

I think this question of finding security for costs rests on the fact of *Domicile* & the application of Irish Law here rests on the question of *Nationality* but the two questions touch very closely – the date of the final trial is not yet fixed.

I am scribbling this in a hurry so excuse more, hoping you are well. I remain

Yours alwys
    Maud Gonne

Are you in Dublin? Shall I send you the drawing to Dublin?

175   13 Rue de Passy
                                           Paris
                                   22nd July [1906]

My dear Friend

Many thanks for your letter I was wondering why I did not hear from you – I am very sorry you have had so much worry about the theatre affairs & hope things are satisfactorily arranged, for though

your theatre is not quite the theatre I wanted, still it is beautiful &
there is room for both – you will be able to make it much more
popular if you have got complete control. Popular in Ireland does
not mean the same as popular in England or in most other countries
– for in Ireland it is the *people* who guard the ideal & who will
sacrifice & strive for it.

Tell me what you see in the stars & don't be afraid of telling me,
I want to know –

I have been working very hard at my wretched law suit. The more
I see of lawyers the more I learn that one must do all the work for
them if one wants it well done.

Major MacBride's lawyers succeeded in getting delay after delay
but at last they have come to the limit of the judge's patience & when
Maître Labori got up last Wednesday & asked for the case to be
postponed till after the long vacation the judge said there had been
sufficient delay & ordered the trial to begin *at once* – The evidence
was read & my lawyer is to make his speech on the 26th & Labori
to reply on the 1st August & the verdict I expect will be given on
the 8th August.

Major MacBride is relying entirely on the point of International
law that if he can prove Irish domicile the French Courts cannot grant
divorce only separation but I think he will find it hard to prove Irish
domicile –

I will let you know the result at once –

I want so much to hear your Deirdre & I hope to when I am in
Ireland this autumn –

I have no time to write more now –

Alwys your friend,
Maud Gonne

176
13 Rue de Passy
Paris
Thursday [August 1906]

My dear Willie

The plaidoirie of Maître Labori was infamous, I hear though as it
is scarcely considered etiquette in France for a woman asking for
divorce to be present at the trial I did not go myself.

Labori openly spoke about Iseult as my daughter '*by a former
marriage I mean union*' & said I had dared to accuse the 'chivalrous
MacBride' of having made an indecent assault on the child. That I
had accused him before members of his own family but knowing this
accusation to be false I had not brought it forward in the divorce suit.
This may mean that I will have to prove this horrible thing, I shrink
from doing it because it means that poor little Iseult will have to

appear in court & be questioned & cross questioned on this hideous thing which I want her to forget. She is a nervous child & was ill for days after from the terror of it & used to wake at night screaming that MacBride with his 'eyes of an assassin' was running after her, even now she hardly likes going up stairs after dark alone because as she told me last week when I was laughing at her for being afraid, she is always afraid MacBride may be hiding & run after her. Still it is possible it will have to be proved.

Labori insisted I was English not Irish but this doesn't seem to have affected the French mind as today all the papers have rather sympathetic references to *la patriote Irlandaise* none of the French papers do more than mention the fact that I have applied for divorce from MacBride giving the names of our lawyers & saying it has been sent on till next Wednesday. MacBride's friend Mr Collins was in a front row taking notes, every insult that Labori addressed to me he laughed & rubbed his hands, he will probably send some ignoble copy to the *Independent* and *Freeman,* but I doubt the latter taking it.

I am very busy today & have much writing to do so won't write more.

Always your friend
Maud Gonne

177   13 Rue de Passy
                                                 Paris
                                                 Wednesday 8th August [1906]

My dear Willie

Here is the verdict as far as I can remember it not as yet having received the written copy. MacBride has succeeded in proving Irish nationality & domicile so that only separation & not divorce can be granted.

The Court now suits Mr MacBride in his petition of separation against me –

The Court thinks the charges of immorality are insufficiently proved, but that the charges of drunkenness are manifestly proved & that considering the position & education of the parties the Court notes '*L'Injure Grâve*' which in France gives right of divorce but as the Irish law doesn't admit divorce the Court grants Mrs MacBride judicial separation in her favor & gives her the right of guardianship of the child. It allows the father the right of visiting the child at his wife's house every Monday, & when the child shall be over 6 years old allows the father to have him for one month in the year –

I am very disappointed & I shall probably appeal against this verdict & change my lawyer for Cruppi neglected my affairs shockingly.

I am going to la Bourboule[1] with little Seagan who isn't very well in a day or two, but write to me here as letters will be always forwarded. I am too tired to write more now.

Alwys your friend
Maud Gonne

The verdict was given at 10 minutes after 12 today – I wonder if you could see anything in my stars for me on the matter.

While the divorce was in progress the ground rules had changed. Ironically John MacBride's appeal against the Independent *had fixed his domicile in Ireland. Also a change in governmental attitude after the Liberal landslide victory in the general election of January 1906 allowed him to return safely to Ireland, while Maud Gonne, in fear that her son might be taken from her, continued to live in France.*

Yeats was occupied with the theatre. In September 1906 he wrote to Florence Farr: 'I have had a bad time with Miss Horniman, whose moon is always at the full of late' and that 'Deirdre has me tied to the table leg'.

In October 1906 a young university student, later to marry the poet Padraic Colum, was sitting in the audience at the opening night of Gaol Gate *by Lady Gregory. There seemed to be a delay in raising the curtain, but, Mary Colum wrote:*

at last we saw Yeats hastily enter, accompanied, not by the short Queen Victoria-like figure of Lady Gregory, but a tall woman dressed in black, one of the tallest women I had ever seen. Instantly a small group in the pit began to hiss loudly and to shout, 'Up, John MacBride!'

The woman stood and faced the hissers, her whole figure showing a lively emotion, and I saw the most beautiful, the most heroic-looking human being I have ever seen before or since . . . she was smiling and unperturbed. Soon a counter-hissing set up, the first hissers being drowned by another group, and then I realized who she was. . . . She was a legend to us young persons in our teens.

At the end of the year Yeats wrote to Katharine Tynan: 'I have had a desperate three months of it, working for the theatre and doing its business. We are beginning to get audiences. Last winter we played to almost empty houses, a sprinkling of people in pit and stalls. Now we have big Saturday audiences. Last Saturday we turned away people from all parts of the house.'

The start of 1907 was turbulent in the theatre. Yeats went to
Aberdeen to lecture and subsequently wrote the following letter.

WBY 4
                                        18 Woburn Buildings
                                        Euston Road
                                        Jan. 14, 1907

My dear Friend

I was unable to write to you when I got your letter for I was up
to my eyes in business. I am putting a professional theatre manager
at a fair salary in charge of the Abbey Theatre and it has been a huge
fight.[1] Do not tell this in Dublin for I imagine that everybody except
Synge has been more or less in tears. Fay struggled hard to keep his
authority threatened even to go on to the music hall stage but it is
done now, I mean it is agreed to, and everyone seems quite content,
even I think a little relieved. Battles of pride are like that, it is a cloudy
thing and when the battle is over people know they have fought about
clouds. I have asked the Manager of the Court Theatre, the only
intellectual theatre in London to recommend a good man certainly
and an Irishman if possible. We will take whatever man he
recommends for I have great reliance in him and if he be an
Englishman and know his business, well, I shall be sorry, but I prefer
to enlarge the brain of my country where it is weakest in expert
knowledge, than to fill one Irishman's stomach and think myself the
better patriot for the choice. Fay is to produce all the Irish plays but
the new man is to stage manage them as distinct from production and
to produce classical and romantic work, which is outside Fay's
knowledge. I always knew this would have to come, for Fay is far
too excitable and hot-tempered for management. I know you will
agree with me in that though you won't like the Englishman, if
English he is to be. I saw Mrs Sharpe the other day and know a great
deal more about the Fiona MacLeod mystery.[2] It is as I thought.
Fiona MacLeod was so far as external perception could say a
secondary personality induced in Sharpe by the presence of a very
beautiful unknown woman whom he fell in love with. She, alas! has
disappeared from everyone's sight, no one having set eyes on her
except George Meredith[3] who says she was the most beautiful
woman he ever saw. Whether there was more than this I do not know
but poor Mrs Sharpe, though generous and self-sacrificing as I can
see does not want to enlarge that unknown woman's share. A great
deal, however, which Sharp used to give in letters as an account of

Fiona's doings were she insists a kind of semi-allegorical description of the adventures of his own secondary personality and its relation with the primary self. For instance in one letter to me he had said 'I will leave your letter where Fiona will find it when she wakes', and by this he meant that the secondary personality when it awoke in him would answer the letter which it certainly did in a much more impassioned way than that of the rest of the letter. I don't think there would be much of all this in the official biography for when I said to Mrs Sharpe that she should tell the whole truth, she answered 'How can I! Other people are so much involved.' She never talked quite openly about things, except it being a secondary personality, but told things in a series of hints and yet, at the same time, quite clearly. I noticed that each time she said this personality was awakened in him by a beautiful person she would add as if to lessen the effect, 'and by beautiful scenery'. She was evidently very fond of him and has sent me his birth date and her own to find out how their horoscopes interlocked. I would be rather glad if you would keep this letter, for I am fresh from seeing Mrs Sharp (I saw her a week ago) and this will be a record. Put it in some safe place and I may ask you for it again some day for it is a fragment of history. She told me that the morning William Sharp died she heard visionary music and indeed a good deal of one sort and another about the supernatural side of his talent.

I should think that your husband must have been badly damaged by the Dublin cross-examination and will gradually sink and disappear now. You never told me what happened at the Convention of Cuman-na-Gael. How was the temperance resolution met, and is there any likelihood of your being in Dublin in time for Synge's play on the 25th of this month, it runs for a week.[4] We are still doing rather well. We have matinées now, which are bringing us quite an audience. I have such great heaps of letters that I must dictate even when writing to you.

Your ever

W. B. Yeats

178   13 Rue de Passy
                                              [Paris]
                                              21st Jany [1907]

My dear Willie

Thank you so much for that very interesting letter. I have put it safely away & if you want it for reference at any time I will send it to you.[1]

It is very interesting about Sharp – I do think one can get so completely in touch with a spiritual force that all one's work is influenced by it & it takes some times a very different personal form, for years all my work was so influenced. I also think to one's imagination that spiritual force may seem to reflect round or almost incarnate in some individual but I should think any attempt at realising a material union on this plain would destroy everything. I should therefore think that Mrs Sharpe is probably right when she minimises the share of the unknown woman.

These spiritual influences are very strange & very powerful & one can seldom talk of them as Sharpe did & the result in one's work is seldom so extraordinary.

I only wanted to know about Borridge because if he had been the Dr you alluded to in Dublin I would have thought it only right to tell you something I had learned about him. Nothing very bad – but showing him a little unsafe as guide or knowledge giver –

I am working very hard at painting, & I think making some progress. It is very absorbing.

I don't think I shall come to Ireland till after my appeal case is finished, publicly I think it better to wait & I have so much to do here now that it is difficult to get away –

How long are you going to be in London? What a pity you never came over to Paris.

Write to me when you have time and tell me what you are doing
Alwys you friend,
    Maud Gonne

I think I am almost sure you are making a great mistake in getting a manager from England for the theatre, of course I won't mention it to anyone.

Rumours had been abroad that Synge's new play was shocking and an outrage to Irish womanhood. An expectant audience waited for trouble. Yeats received a telegram in Aberdeen saying, 'Audience broke up in disorder at the word "shift" ', and hurried back. The Playboy of the Western World was causing riots, which were prolonged by the advanced nationalists. When the police were called in, this angered the nationalists further. Yeats threw open the theatre to a discussion of the play on 4 February, claiming the necessity to call on the police to protect the right of free speech, and affirming his own nationalism with the words 'the author of Cathleen ni Houlihan *addresses you'. Mary Colum recalled: 'I never witnessed a human being fight as Yeats fought that night, nor ever knew another with so many weapons in his armory.' The* Playboy *and the Abbey weathered the storm.*

179   [Paris]
                                                 [February 1907]

My dear Willie

I have been thinking about you a great deal these days &
wondering how you are feeling over this theatre business. Of course
I am dreadfully sorry about the whole thing. I know you think you
are right – I know the men who are against you are equally sure they
are right are suffering for a good cause & this makes it tragic, as I
don't see the same as you over it I don't want to go into the matter,
except to say that I am feeling rather anxious & would like to hear
from you – Do you remember a vision you had once long ago about
the crowd & the stones – It worries me because all of those other
visions we had at that time have come so strangely true – Have you
still that book in which you used to note these things? If so some
day a long while off, we will look over it for some things I do not
remember, but some that I do, have been so startlingly true & when
we are both old it will be interesting to note them.

Will you be in Dublin for long? I am very busy with law affairs
just now, & every spare moment I am painting.

Alwys your friend
Maud Gonne

180   57 Grosvenor Square[1]
                                             Rathmines
                                             Dublin
                                             Wednesday [early 1907]

My dear Friend

Did you get a letter I wrote you posted on the boat before landing
in Ireland.

It is so good to be back in Ireland but I am so sorry you are not
here.

I went out to Howth the other day, it was lovely but rather sad
for I found my old servant dead & her little thatched cottage tumbled.

Yesterday I went up Slieve Gullion,[2] it is such a beautiful mountain
& the day was so lovely the sun shone so I wanted more than ever
to live in Ireland.

Is it true that you are going to Venice with Lady Gregory?[3]

I shall return to London on the 20th. My address will be

c/o Mrs Pilcher,

12 Milner Street, S.W.

Have you seen Mrs Campbell[4] & are you working at the Player
Queen? I must end as Colum has just come to see me.

Yours alwys,
Maud

181 [Paris]
Friday [March 1907]

My dear Willie

I was so glad to hear from you & very glad also to know that the theatre is likely to absorb less of your time in the near future – It has seemed to me for a long time that it was taking too much of your time from your real work which is writing. I dare say it has been good for you in some ways & has certainly taught you much about play writing which I should think only practical experience can teach, but on the whole it has been taking too much of your time & energy & I think your work will get on far better with freedom from worries it entails –

When one is actually working at a thing one often loses all sense of proportion & gets to think that particular thing the one all important thing in one's life & work if not in the universe. I, looking at things in my work in Ireland from a distance, wonder very much at the importance I attached to some of the details & the immense energy I expended on them – It is only from a distance we can get proportions right. I think looking back on things you will perhaps wonder at all the hard work & energy you have expended on that theatre –

Do send me some of that wonderful powder,[1] it seems most fascinating. I will write you full description of results if I get any –

When [do] you think it likely you will be in Paris. At the end of April I and my cousin May will probably go to Aix les Bains for 3 weeks, as I have been suffering a great deal from rheumatism the doctor wants me to go there as soon as possible – so let me know your plans in time so I can arrange to be in Paris when you come –

My law business is going on slowly as usual, it is impossible to make lawyers or judges hurry. MacBride has at last decided to defend which means things will take longer than I expected, but I am hopeful of success – beyond a paragraph in the Freeman's Journal contradicting a report of an Australian paper saying MacBride had committed suicide I have no news of him & do not know what he is doing if you hear anything in Dublin by chance let me know.

I have been painting hard – this is a secret – have sent a picture to the salon but have told NO ONE – it is more than likely to be refused as I have not recommended it to anyone so it will be pure good luck or its own merits if by chance it is accepted I shall know next week –

Iseult is getting very big & very beautiful. She is translating some Irish legends that Ella Young has written that I am illustrating.[2] She has done the translation so far wonderfully well & I hope to get it published here – I think she will write, she has great imagination & great taste. I have been seeing a lot of people lately & living more my own life than I have ever done before –

Write to me when you have time – I am always so interested to hear from you.

I remain
Alwys your friend
Maud Gonne

182   Hotel Thermal
                                                            Aix les Bains
                                                            Savoie
                                                            7th May [1907]

My dear Willie

It is very good of you writing for I know how hard writing is when one is travelling. You must be enjoying Italy very much. I remember it as a sort of land of enchantment & flowers, I wish I were with you there. Are you going to Rome? for lovely as Florence is I like Rome much better – If you go to Rome you must go to Frascati which is only about an hour by train from Rome & a most lovely place & see my sister who is staying there – She would be so glad to see you.

I wish you could send me that incense powder for just now I think I might get some very interesting results. I have been having some strange sorts of dreams lately seeming to foretell some hideous war in which England & France would take part, they were strange fragmentary sort of dreams & seemed wholly unconnected with my life & came without any reason I could think of. I had been invoking but for quite other sorts of things –

I have suddenly developed (without any effort or work or even wish on my part) a wonderful power of healing,[1] which would make my fortune if I turned doctor. I never fail in taking away pain instantly & even curing coughs & other things. The strange thing about it is that over 4 years ago when I was up in Kilmacanogue[2] the druid who I often see there instead of answering some question on the political future of Ireland which I wanted to know told me I would have the gift of healing. I was not thinking about the subject at all & didn't particularly want it & it didn't interest me very much. I am not sure if I <ever> told you of this at the time, probably not, then the hideous crash came in my life & for a long time my nerves were too shattered to do any occult work or see visions or any thing but now that my nerves are strong again I am able to see visions again & have suddenly found I have this power of healing to an extraordinary degree. It must be the fruit of work in another life, for I have certainly not worked for it here –

I & my cousin May & my son are here until the 23rd of the month taking the baths to prevent getting stiff & rheumatic. We go back to

Paris in time to hear Richard Strauss's & Oscar Wilde's Salomé[3] – I have heard Salomé *played* but not as an opera. I am told Strauss's music is a revelation – I don't know when I shall be in London, except that I should like to see you, I *hate* London & avoid it as much as I can.

How do you propose getting to London? Shall you not pass by Paris? Surely it is the most direct way from Italy I don't know how you can avoid it. Why do you not stay there a few days on your way back & see the Salons which are open now, then I should have the pleasure of seeing you & showing you Iseult. She is the despair of her governess & of the school where she goes every day, because of her laziness & because she will not learn what doesn't interest her. She is extraordinarily clever but won't work. I sympathise with her in my heart though I scold & try & remember all the scolding I used to get when a little girl to pass them on to her – not that they ever did me much good.

I am sorry the theatre affairs are still occupying you – Don't let them take too much of your time.

Do you know I think you are quite unjust in what you say about our people at home. They have taken up MacBride because they had been told he was a hero & because they *know* he *actually* fought England & because they *believe* (here they are wrong) that he will fight England again.

They considered that a woman's life should not count, if by sacrificing it they could keep their hero, *their one fighting man* intact.

It is not an ignoble idea, the only misfortune is that their hero is not a hero, that he has entered on the path of compromise & lies which has kept the *tea party* what it is an instrument of England's rule in Ireland, & this perhaps without direct open & retributed treachery –

If, knowing MacBride the Blackguard I know him, I thought he were a strong man capable of striking serious blows at England's rule in Ireland, as I once thought him, I should feel & say, that those in Ireland who support him against me are doing right & well, it is because *I know* him to be incapable of any strong action only a danger to the Nationalists, that I feel sad though not a bit indignant over the way they have behaved. And as to you Willie, we are such friends you will not misunderstand me when I say you have done things such as calling in the police[4] & witnessing for the Crown that give them cause to hate you & it is a healthy sign they do.

You can never expect people who do not know you personally very well, who are not in *the same atmosphere of thought that you are in* to understand subtle reasons for your actions. They see only the bald facts, & judge from them. A few years ago you openly *approved* & I *organised* the rendering impossible of English plays that we objected to on National grounds, in the theatres & music halls in Dublin. You start a theatre you call a *National* theatre, in the beginning at all events it was to be a theatre for the people – you put on a play[5] they hate & consider wrong. Naturally they look on it as their duty to stop that play & the men who were fined, many of them I know to be very good & earnest young fellows, feel proud that they have suffered for the national cause. I am quite ready to admit that in your case there are some few who may be personally jealous of your work, or some whom you may have wounded by too frank criticism of their efforts or by ignoring them, who profit of moments such as these to attack you bitterly & even treacherously, as in my case, the frauds who I had exposed, the publicans & drunkards I had driven out the cowards who I had made own their cowardice all join MacBride's party & whisper calumny against me – but in neither of our cases were the people generally to blame & even from a national point I think their action is a healthy sign[6] –

You who believe in the super man[7] why do you grow indignant with the crowd because they don't think as you do, because their virtue is not your virtue, you should not want them to think as you do. It would be a misfortune if the crowd began worrying over subtleties for it would be an end of action.

I have a great belief in our people & would not for worlds see them change their ideals which I think are wonderfully right as far as they go, but I would like to save them from the wretched creatures who exploit the National cause for their own ends & divert the energy of the people, from the direct object.

But I am writing much too long a letter – things are said so quickly & written so slowly & dumbly.

I am glad to know you are in Italy, I know you will enjoy it & it will do you good. My kindest regards to Lady Gregory & her son.

Always dear Willie your friend,
Maud Gonne

183   Hotel Thermal
Aix-les-Bains
Monday 26th [May 1907]

My dear Friend

We go to Paris on the 22nd so you will be sure to find us on the 23rd or any days soon after that. It will be nice seeing you & I have lots to talk of.

We have been up near the snows too & saw the countless little star like flowers like the one you sent me from the Appenines & deep blue gentians springing up wherever the snow had melted. Then it got very cold & we are down in Aix again going on with our

rheumatism cure – How I envy you in Venice or rather how I wish
I were there too.

Au revoir, à bientôt
Always your friend,
    Maud Gonne

I have not received the incense I suppose you found it too difficult
to send.

*In May and June the Abbey company was touring Scotland and
England. There was worry whether the English censor would object
to* The Playboy of the Western World, *which was included in the
repertoire; it was not played in Birmingham but was most successful
in London.*

184   Paris
                                              Sunday [June 1907]
My dear friend
    How can I make you see the proportion of things. I thought the
extraordinary & harmonious beauty of Italy would have brought it
back to you. How shall I put it? Do you consider Synge's literature
of equal value to your own? Do you consider its literary value to
Ireland comparable to the value of Lady Gregory's work? Do you
even think the Playboy at all the best of Mr Synge's plays? & yet –
for the sake of that mediocre play you & Lady Gregory are willing
to go to prison for 3 months i.e. cease all chance of work for 3
months.
    I know you will say *principle*! but what principle is involved for
Irishmen breaking English Law *in England*. One breaks law to
reform law, but why should Irish men want to reform English law?
We break England's law *in Ireland* to turn it into contempt & if
possible destroy it all together for the sake of Independence but there
is no logic in breaking it in England? Don't be annoyed with me for
writing just what I think. I am afraid it sounds unsympathetic, but I
do so hate seeing you waste time & energy which you owe to your
art & to Ireland.
    I have got the incense. I will try it in a few days when I can get
quietly in the country & will write you the results.
    In haste
    Alwys your friend
        Maud Gonne

185

Les Mouettes
Colleville
Par Vierville
Calvados
15th Juin [1907]

My dear Willie

I have tried the incense twice, my cousin May was with me. The first time in the drawing room here we had no result except a sort of drowsyness. I think I actually slept for a few minutes once or twice, but I could remember nothing clearly, the 2nd time I burned the incense one evening sitting close to the sea shore – I saw nothing except some wandering lights on the sea & once a pathway of light. My cousin saw this also & we both heard murmuring sounds all round us, sometimes like faint music, sometimes like the crying of a multitude, my cousin said she also heard what seemed to her like the howling or crying of animals. I didn't hear that. Again I got that strange drowsyness & kept waking with starts & trying to remember what I had heard & not succeeding, that was all. I shall try again for I felt I ought to be able to get better results with it – Tell me who gave you the incense? has an American woman? had anything to do with it? I ask this because since I have used it once or twice, while I have been painting, I heard a voice with I think an American accent saying, not very interesting things about the painting I was doing & I cannot account for it, for it is the voice of no one I know.

I go to Paris today to look after my legal business & to fetch Iseult but I shall only stay a week & return here where I am very happy painting. May will be in London in about a fortnight. I hope you will go to see her. How did the plays go off? I am afraid you found my last letter rather unsympathetic but I felt cross at the way you let the theatre in particular Synge's play[1] interfere with your work. In the old days I used to feel sorry when politics took you away from your writing but they never interfered with your writing as that theatre does.

Always your friend
Maud Gonne

All this year Yeats had been working hard at revision for the eight volumes of his Collected Works, *published in 1908; he also had portraits painted for inclusion in this. Miss Horniman was proving difficult. Writing to Florence Farr, Yeats reported: 'Lady Gregory says that Miss Horniman is like a shilling in a tub of electrified water – everybody tries to get the shilling out.'*

186
Les Mouettes
Colleville
Par Vierville
Calvados
Friday 6th July [1907]

My dear Willie

I don't like to hear of you not being well & feeling like nervous breakdown. I know so well what that means for I went through it two years ago & know how wretched & undecided & unlike oneself it makes one – Your journey in Italy ought to have done you good but it was too rapid, you tried to do too much in too short a time. To enjoy Italy one must live like its inhabitants a little & walk leisurely in the shady side of the streets. One can't shake off the dust & roar of the railway & get into the atmosphere of the living past which hangs round all those old Italian towns in 48 hours or the effort tires one too much. I always feel it is better to see only one or two places & to see them well & live in their life, than to rush from place to place – yet there is [are] always so many places one wants to see that one finally does rush –

The country in Ireland will do you good. If only you do resolutely let the theatre look after itself, or rather let Lady Gregory look after it for she knows just how you want it to go, only she shouldn't always be consulting you about it.

One gets caught in the wheels of work, & it is so hard to get out of them. It becomes a sort of tread mill one can't escape from. I got caught in it once before my marriage, the weariness of it made me lose all sense of proportion & all sense of life & I doubt if anything but the horrid crash in my affairs would have got me free of it –

You ought to make an effort to get free, for the sake of your writing & your poetry –

May left me yesterday. She is at 39 Alexandra Court, 171 Queen's Gate & would, I know, be very happy to see you though I told her you were going to Ireland soon & would perhaps not have time to call.

It is strange about the American woman,[1] I hardly think she can be the writer you describe for she seemed to me uninteresting & very crude, but of course the impressions I got were very vague – She seemed to me a woman who had realised that modern art is decadent & to be successful its decadent side must be exaggerated. This side *attracts* & *shocks* her at the same time. She would certainly try to put it into her work and put it in clumsily & heavily – I did not see her, but only heard her talking & got the impression – it occurred on one or two occasions while I was painting the day after I had used the incense & as I could not connect her with any one I knew I wondered if she had had anything to do with the incense.

I hope my law affairs will be terminated on the 18th of this month but am doubtful as the delays seem interminable.

Let me know when you go to Ireland & where to write & how you are & do try & take a real rest.

Alwys your friend

Maud Gonne

187   Les Mouettes

Colleville

Par Vierville

Calvados

[Summer 1907]

The post man came while I was writing & as he will never wait & we are so far from the post down here that I had to send your letter unfinished yesterday as I couldn't wait longer to tell you what I thought of your Deirdre.[1]

I haven't much news. I have been ill only just escaping rheumatic fever.

I came back from Paris tired & very disappointed at the delay in hearing my appeal (it won't be heard till end of October or beginning of November) I had been struggling against rheumatism for a long while & I felt so tired & disheartened that it was easier to go to bed & be ill than to fight against it & tell myself that I was well –

I am well again now or nearly so & I have begun painting again & I have friends staying here. It is a lovely country place on the sea shore the children are so well & happy here that I shall stay till the end of September when my affairs oblige me to return to Paris. Mr Anthony Mackay[2] who you may remember as a '98 delegate has got a situation for MacBride in the salmon fishery at Castleconor – I am very sorry for this as I hoped he would have drifted to America – which would have made it safe for me to bring my son to Ireland where I feel he ought to be at least part of each year.

Iseult is translating some Irish legends retold by Ella Young. She is doing it very well & I hope to get them published in Paris as a book for Children. Iseult has an extraordinary gift for writing & I think will do good work some day though she is a very lazy & very beautiful child.

Please give my congratulations & good wishes to Mr Gregory.[3] I hope he & his wife will come to see me if they are in Paris this winter. Have you decided if you are going to live in Dublin? I wish I could but at present it isn't possible. However Paris is quite interesting.

Au revoir & once more thank you for Deirdre

Always your friend

Maud Gonne

188

Les Mouettes
Colleville
28th Sept [1907]

My dear Willie

This is to tell you we return to Paris tomorrow. *13 rue de Passy.*

Where are you? I send this c/o Lady Gregory as she will forward it to you if you are not at Coole.

I hope theatre worries are not bothering you again –

Sinn Fein seems really succeeding in Ireland. I don't know why you feel depressed about things political – though I am away from it all I feel hopeful & see many signs of progress.

I started the Sinn Fein Movement, but I never thought it would progress as rapidly as it has. Griffith really has worked well at it which must make one lenient to many aggravating traits in his character, he has great tenacity of purpose.[1]

I am going back to law worries, but I hope they will all be over by the end of Oct. then I am coming to Dublin for a few weeks to stay with Ella Young.

Digges is making a success in America on the strength of it he & Miss Quinn have got married. They talk of coming home next year.

Iseult & I went to Mont St Michel. It is the most wonderful place, magically & artistically. You must visit it some day. It was once a great centre of Druidism then the Romans built a temple to Jupiter – then Michael the Archangel some where about 1000 ordered a pious bishop to build him a shrine & promised that it would be invincible & the monastery fortress has never been taken though all the country round was in the hands of the English.

The whole place is full of magic, not with standing the crowds of tourists. I would like to go there with you some time.

Since then we have been wandering about the great forest of Balleroy which is lovely & golden & now we are going back to work & Paris.

Iseult is low spirited at the thought of the Lycée.

I am looking forward to your collected edition & to reading the essays.[2] I am glad you don't attack directly those who annoy you in Irish life. I too am beginning to think that direct personal attack is GENERALLY a mistake.

I do not know if my direct work for Ireland is over or not – now as ever, in this matter I am in the hands of the gods, for the moment I am forming a wonderful instrument. I will tell you all about this when we meet. I am not good at writing of things that interest me very deeply.

Personally I am quite content with my life as it is & find so much that interests me. You know for years I wore blinkers so as to never cease working for the cause & only see the one end & object. Now

I have taken them off & find so much to look at –
I must end for it is late.
Alwys your friend
    Maud Gonne

189   Paris
                                        [September/October 1907]

My dear Willie

Thank you so much for your letter & for the trouble you are taking to get my horoscope.[1] The dates you ask I will only be able to give you with any sort of exactitude when I get the papers back from the lawyers after the appeal is heard. I have NO memory for dates – Time as one counts by days & years, it has never meant very much to me & I never can remember the dates, even of the most important things in my life. At the time of the divorce proceeding I was obliged however to get exact dates of some of the principal events of my life both before & after my marriage – but they are *on paper* not *in my head*. When I get my papers back I will note them for you exactly. Iseult's birth date is 6th August 1894. Her arrival that year in my house may be the event you see marked in my 27th year, it is the only marked change I can remember in my life that year – I think it must have been about 3 or 4 years before that that a terrible tragic event[2] occurred which shook & has certainly altered the whole of my life, but as usual I have no date for it.

It was as far as I can remember end of October 1904 I learnt the extent of MacBride's infamy or insanity, that date I can get accurately when my papers are returned to me. In Dec. 1904 I was in London trying to settle for a quiet separation without scandal & in February 1905 I think the divorce proceedings began in the French Courts. I was very unhappy all that time but in a dazed dull sort of way as my nerves had been so worn by the strain of the previous year that I was incapable of feeling anything *very* keenly.

I can't recollect any very fortunate thing happening in Jany, 1906 –

Ella Young writes me that she thinks the END of this year will be fortunate for me, but I don't know on what she bases this –

I have not the same impossibility I used to have of seeing Aengus. I see Lugh less frequently & less clearly than formerly, but I think I am still under his protection.

I have had another disappointment – the hearing of my appeal is again delayed. Labori has finally refused to defend MacBride who has named a new lawyer M[aîtr]e *Hild* to defend him & this has caused delay so the end of November or beginning of December will be the earliest I can hope that my case will be heard. This delays my return to Ireland & I am a little home sick. I have begun painting again to console myself & go every morning to the art school – the afternoons I work in my own studio.

I think what you say about *fate* (Saturn in mid Heaven) at the time of the discovery about MacBride should be correct, for months before it happened I was like one in a dream waiting for some event I knew not *what*, that would end my marriage. I waited quite calmly knowing only one thing that I must wait & be *quite still* & let fate work – It was one of the reasons I think that made me so reluctant to start divorce proceedings. I felt I ought to remain quite still & trust to fate, – even now I don't feel quite sure that I was passive enough at that time. MacBride had to disappear from my life because fate had ordered it – I need not have troubled about helping fate by going to law –

I am writing a very long & very egotistical letter, but there are so many horoscope questions in your letter, I can only answer at some length –

I am sorry you didn't send me your letter on the situation in Ireland, I would certainly not have found it dull though perhaps I wouldn't have agreed.

The apathy you speak of is every where at present, at least in our part of the world, it is appalling in France –

When will your essays appear?

Always dear Willie Your Friend

    Maud Gonne

190

        39 Park Mansions
        Knightsbridge S.W.
        Monday [November 1907]

My dear Willie

Your letter forwarded from Paris arrived this morning giving me your address which I had stupidly forgotten –

I am so glad you have found such nice lodgings – I cross to Dublin today & shall be staying with the Youngs, 57 Grosvenor Square, Rathmines. Come & see me tomorrow Tuesday at 5 o'clock or if engaged Tuesday come Wednesday.

I will keep all news till we meet.

Yours alwys

    Maud Gonne

I shall only be in Dublin till 12th Nov.

191   [Paris]
                                  [December 1907]

My dear Willie

Thank you for your letter & thank you for sending the photo of your portrait[1] which I think horrid. I shouldn't like you if you were like that & if you had not sent it I should never have recognised it at all.

'Discoveries' I like very much. I don't always agree with your philosophy, but it is very living. I am so sorry the theatre worries have again absorbed you, you will have to try & shake yourself free of them, or the flood of little jealousies & little quarrels & little but *vast* intrigues will prevent you doing your own work which is much more important –

I am not sorry you have postponed your visit to Paris as until my proces[2] is over I am so worried by absurd legal difficulties & complications that my mind is not free for intelligent thought. I have had even to give up my painting all through this month, by the end of Jany I hope it will be all ended. The hearing of the case is fixed for the 9th Jany. Is that a good date? I think it ought to be fortunate it was my father's birthday.

Ella Young is coming to stay with me. I expect her any day now.

Let me know where you are & what work you are doing & pull yourself out of theatre affairs. I see by the *Gaelic American* that your plays are having great success in America by the way, is Mr Quinn coming to Europe this winter? I want to see him to thank him for all the trouble he took for me.

In haste
I remain
Alwys your friend
    Maud Gonne

I am sorry you didn't send me the letter you wrote even if wrong about events it would have been very interesting & you know my nerves are very good & bad prophecies wouldn't have worried me overmuch

I have just realised that it is Xmas time so I reopened my letter to wish you all good luck & happiness for the New Year & may success be with you. Have you found good for yourself in your horoscope?

Thank you so much for having taken so much trouble about mine. I am sorry dates are so vague.

I have a little picture for you but it has to go to an exhibition first so I can't send it yet.

Fallen Majesty
1908–1913

Although crowds gathered once if she but showed her face,
  And even old men's eyes grew dim, this hand alone,
  Like some last courtier at a gypsy camping-place
  Babbling of fallen majesty, records what's gone.

The lineaments, a heart that laughter has made sweet,
These, these remain, but I record what's gone. A crowd
Will gather, and not know it walks the very street
Whereon a thing once walked that seemed a burning cloud.

W. B. Yeats, 'Fallen Majesty' (first published 1912)

 *1908*

As Maud Gonne recovered from the concentrated and preoccupying period of the legal proceedings which came to an end with the results of the appeal in January 1908, the need for a deep healing relationship found its expression in the revival of the mystical marriage with Yeats, but this time it was different, since the Celtic Order was not so apparent and the physical strain was lessened for him by his affair with Mabel Dickinson. The mystical marriage was confirmed during his visit to Paris in June; with his visit in late December it is apparent the relationship entered a new deeper phase.

In order to avoid divisions and partisanship Maud Gonne kept out of Irish politics, yet she kept her finger on its pulse, and she was in close contact with Inghínidhe na hÉireann and presided at the meeting when a little paper, Bean na hÉireann, was proposed. The first issue came out late in 1908.

Yeats was busy with the theatre as the Fays resigned from the Abbey in January. He was still working on his Collected Works (due out in the autumn), and having further portraits painted for it. Mrs Patrick Campbell played in his Deirdre in Dublin and London and he was working on The Player Queen.

251

192
13 Rue de Passy
Paris
8 Jany [1908]

My dear Willie
I had a strange vision this morning which makes me write to you. It is all very indefinite, only I seemed to feel after I ought to write to you. It seemed to me you had a choice to make on which much depended – I think it is in connection with your work – It is most important that you should choose the higher. I really don't understand, though I thought I did at the time for I forgot a great deal as when I stopped seeing & began to think & try & remember in words I was trying to go into the 3rd [?5th] world.

I got to a place of dazzling light where great titan forms of light & immense energy were moving. I thought they were the higher souls but I was not sure. Then suddenly I saw you & you seemed anxious & troubled about something, as if you were trying to see that world of light & energy & to get help & something was impeding you then things faded but I felt all day I ought to write to you, now when I come to write it down there seems so little & yet at the time it felt so important.

Write & tell me if you are well & what you are doing if you know at all what this means.

My appeal case comes on tomorrow & I am very busy so haven't time to write more now.

Alwys your friend
Maud Gonne

Ella Young is staying with me, she is a great help.

193
13 Rue de Passy
Paris
Saturday [January 1908]

My dear Willie
You are feeling cross with me for not writing & it must seem to you horrid & ungrateful of me not having written to thank you for your very kind letter of sympathy.[1] I began writing to you the day after I received it but was interrupted & the letter remained posted in my blotter. Since then life has been rather a rush for me. My sister & my two cousins are here & I have had to go about a great deal with them – then I am finishing off the pictures I am sending to the Salon des Independents & I have had a lot of law business to settle.

Things have not been quite as bad for me as the papers represented, the divorce is refused, but in such a way as to make it possible for me to get it in three years before the French Courts if I wish to. Then the monthly visit which Seagan was to have paid to his father each year when he will be 6 years old has been suppressed & the visits which MacBride by the first verdict had a right to receive twice a week have been reduced to once a week but my request that they should take place at my house or the house of the doctor has been refused. This is very great cause for upset & anxiety – for it facilitates MacBride stealing the child & I shall have great worry & expense to make things quite safe. However for the last 18 months MacBride has not once asked to see the child & as he is not likely to live in Paris I hope these visits will be a dead letter. Still they are always a nuisance & will prevent me living in Ireland for the present.

I was very sorry to hear you had undertaken to stage manage yourself – it must mean endless work & worry & will take you away too much from your writing – however I suppose it will not be for very long. What is it that May tells me you may be going to America with the theatre?[2] It is a startling piece of news, do write and tell me about it –

I can't write more today as I have to go out.

When we meet I must have a long talk with you about the horoscope. I am trying to get some dates. Thank you so much for all the trouble you have taken about it for me.

Wishing you luck if you go to America but rather hoping you will not for it will mean such horrible worry and struggle –

I remain

Alwys your friend

Maud Gonne

194

13 Rue de Passy
Paris
8th April [1908]

My dear Willie

I have had in my mind to write to you often for the last few days but have been prevented by the arrival of my sister's children & other things.

I dreamed of you last night. What are you doing? Still very busy I suppose over the theatre affairs – I wish you could get free of them – I heard the plays were a great success & was glad for I suppose the more prosperous the theatre gets the easier it will be for you to get free & be able to write again.

I had a letter from Mr Quinn the other day introducing an American woman Miss Coats.[1] She is intelligent & rather psychic, but I don't like American women generally though for Mr Quinn's sake I was very nice to her. She has wandered on to Italy now – Mr

Quinn says your Father is getting on splendidly & enjoying America very much.

The Fays, he says, have been giving him a good deal of trouble & he is sorry you & Lady Gregory gave them some of your plays to act, he says they are only fair amateurs, but no doubt he has written you on all this.

I wish you would write to me – I am doing a good deal of occult work just now & get visions sometimes which I don't understand & which when I have not heard from you for some time & know every thing is well trouble me. I don't mean I now see anything bad for you, only I like knowing you are all right. You & I having done a certain amount of occult work together, I often get things concerning you when I am trying to go into the higher plains.

I may go to Rome shortly, but only for a week & it is not certain yet. Kindly don't mention it to anyone –

I am working hard at painting but haven't much to show, as it has been chiefly at anatomy – but I feel it is necessary to get that knowledge thoroughly so as not to forget it after –

Write soon
Alwys your friend,
  Maud Gonne

195   Colleville
                                             par Vierville
                                             Calvados
                                             [April 1908]

My dear Willie
  I was so glad to get your letter & hear all is well with you. I don't think the visions I got refer in any way to your material life – One was, I saw you trying hard to climb a mountain, & some barrier preventing you. That came when I was doing some visionary work & not at all thinking about you – but you helped me so much formerly in occult work that it is only natural I get things about you when I am working but what made me a little anxious & was the reason I wrote to you was a dream I had (I don't trust dreams) I seemed to see you in some trouble you seemed *very distressed* & I had that sort of nightmare feeling of powerlessness. I didn't know how to comfort you or understand quite what was the matter. I woke up & dreamed again directly after, but then you seemed quite consoled & to have got over whatever trouble there may have been.

As I had not heard from you for such a long time I wrote to get news of you – The visions I feel sure refer to your occult life & work probably you have had some difficulty or failure there. Possibly the dreams did too though at the time I thought it was about something in this life, but anyhow *that* seemed to come alright – It may be that all the worry & very exterior work you have had to do in the theatre has hindered your occult work, as well as your writing, which used to be an expression of it – but I am quite sure you will get back to it all again –

It is most interesting about your pictures, I want to see them. Which Shannon[1] is painting you? the friend of Ricketts?[2]

I am not a bit surprised that Fay has behaved badly[3] – He is never to be trusted. I hope he will stay altogether in America. I should like MacBride to join him there & then I & the children could come to live in Ireland, which is always what I want to do though circumstances are against it just at present all the better perhaps for my painting. Has Moore's book[4] come out yet? he called to see me in Paris – he seemed thoroughly OUT with Dublin.

I am down here for a week with the children. They are both psychicly extremely interesting. Iseult wrote a letter to you to thank you for the book of greek stories you sent her at Xmas[5] – She sent the letter why I can't think – to Mrs Clay in London – their house was let & the letter remained there till lately when I heard of it – You must have thought her quite horrid not writing to you – She is mad on Greek stories & knows the Illiad & the Odysée better than her prayer book – I start for Rome next week & shall be away about 10 days.

Alwys your friend
Maud Gonne

196   Paris
                                                                26 June [1908]

Friend of mine

It was sad you had to leave paris so soon – there is so much I wanted to talk to you about & so much we had not time for – Next time you come you must arrange to have a little more time to spare.

I was so tired last night when I got home I could not do much, but several times I felt your thought with me quite distinctly.

I am thinking it would not be right for you to give up your London life completely yet – There are elements in it which you still need – The theatre is the millstone from which you must try to get free, or at least partially free. I understand how you feel about the responsibility towards the players who depend on you, – it is that recognition of responsibility which I always admire in you & which is such a rare quality in our country but for the sake of Ireland, you *must* keep your writing before all else – A great poet or a great writer, can give nobler & more precious gifts to his country than the greatest philanthropist ever can give – Your own writing, above all, your poetry must be your first consideration, any thing that takes you from it – or makes it less intense is wrong & must be shaken off.

You remember how for the *sake of Ireland*, I hated you in politics, even in the politics I believed in, because I always felt it took you from your writing & cheated Ireland of a greater gift than we could give her – & the theatre is just as bad, or worse for it brings you among jealousies & petty quarrels & little animosities which you as a great writer should be above & apart from – It is because you vaguely feel this, that you are exasperated & often very unjust to our people – It is this exasperation that has made you take up old class prejudices which are unworthy of you, & makes you say cruel things which *sound* ungenerous – though you are never ungenerous really. I *hate* hearing you speak of Russell's Deirdre as you do – of course Russell cannot write as you do, but all the same Russell is an artist & has a very noble mind, & his Deirdre did not hurt your Kathleen when they were first played together long ago. In painting your father might say hard things about Russell's technique, but in his lecture in America he spoke of what he saw great & beautiful in Russell's painting – it is not like you to speak like that of an artist & a great mystic.

Forgive me Willie for writing all this which may make you angry. I ought to have *said* it but I was so taken up by this thought when you were here that I had not time – every thing else seemed too unimportant to waste the short time we had together in discussing & indeed even now I know these outer things are of little importance, but even in little things I don't want there to be the least jar between us. I know on many things we think differently but only when you spoke of those two things I felt a slight surprise & disappointment, as though it was not you yourself who was speaking –

I think a most wonderful thing has happened – the most wonderful I have met with in life. If we are only strong enough to hold the doors open I think we shall obtain knowledge & life we have never dreamed of.

The meaning of things are becoming very clear to me, I shall work it all

[End of letter missing][1]

197   Paris
                                                                 26 July [1908]

Willie

It is not in a week but in a day that I am writing to you. I had such a wonderful experience last night that I must know at once if it affected you & how? for above all I don't want to do any thing which will take you from your work, or make working more arduous –

That play[1] is going to be a wonderful thing & must come first – nothing must interfere with it –

Last night all my household had retired at a quarter to 11 and I thought I would go to you astrally. It was not working hours for you & I thought by going to you I might even be able to leave with you some of my vitality & energy which would make working less of a toil next day – I had seen the day before when waking from sleep a curious some what Egyptian form floating over me (like in the picture of Blake the soul leaving the body)[2] – It was dressed in moth like garments & had curious wings edged with gold in which it could fold itself up – I had thought it was myself, a body in which I could go out into the astral – at a quarter to 11 last night I put on this body & thought strongly of you & desired to go to you. We went some where in space I dont know where – I was conscious of starlight & of hearing the sea below us. You had taken the form I think of a great serpent, but I am not quite sure. I only saw your face distinctly & as I looked into your eyes (as I did the day in Paris you asked me what I was thinking of) & your lips touched mine. We melted into one another till we formed only *one being, a being greater than ourselves* who felt all & knew all with double intensity – the clock striking 11 broke the spell & as we separated it felt as if life was being drawn away from me through my chest with almost physical pain. I went again twice, each time it was the same – each time I was brought back by some slight noise in the house. Then I went upstairs to bed & I dreamed of you confused dreams of ordinary life. We were in Italy together (I think this was from some word in your letter which I had read again before sleeping). We were quite happy, & we talked of this wonderful spiritual vision I have described – you said it would tend to increase physical desire – This troubles me a little – for there was nothing physical in that union – Material union is but a pale shadow compared to it – write to me quickly & tell me if you know anything of this & what you think of it – & if I may come to you again like this. I shall not until I hear from you. My thought with you always.

Maud Gonne[3]

These last two letters, written after Yeats left Paris, were pasted in a notebook given to him by Maud Gonne. He recorded that 'on the night of the 25th' he had made evocation & 'sought union with PIAL'. He also wrote in the notebook: 'We are divided by her religious ideas, a Catholicism which has grown on her – she will not divorce her husband and marry because of her Church. Since she has said this, she has not been further from me but is always very near.

She too seems to love more than of old. In addition to this the old dread of physical love has awakened in her.'

198

13 Rue de Passy
Paris
5th October [1908]

Dear Willie

We are back in Paris – Iseult at her Lycée I at my painting. I don't know if I already sent you a photo of a water colour sketch I did of Etain and Angus as Ildathach.[1] Tell me what you think of it.

Are you still in the West

In haste,

Alwys your friend,

Maud Gonne

199

13 Rue de Passy
Paris
Friday [December 1908]

Dearest

It was hard leaving you yesterday, but I knew it would be just as hard today if I had waited. Life is so good when we are together & we are together so little – !

Did you know it I went to you last night? about 12 or 2 o'clock I don't exactly know the time. I think you knew. It was as it was when you made me see with the golden light on Wednesday. I shall go to you again often but not quite in that way, I shall try to make strong & well for your work for dear one you must work or I shall begin tormenting myself thinking perhaps I help to make you idle & then I would soon feel we ought not to meet at all, & that would be O so dreary! –

You asked me yesterday if I am not a little sad that things are as they are between us – I am sorry & I am glad. It is hard being away from each other so much there are moments when I am dreadfully lonely & long to be with you, – one of these moments is on me now – but beloved I am glad & proud beyond measure of your love, & that it is strong enough & high enough to accept the spiritual love & union I offer –

I have prayed so hard to have all earthly desire taken from my love for you & dearest, loving you as I do, I have prayed & I am praying still that the bodily desire for me may be taken from you too. I know how hard & rare a thing it is for a man to hold spiritual love when the bodily desire is gone & I have not made these prayers without a terrible struggle a struggle that shook my life though I do not speak much of it & generally manage to laugh.

That struggle is over & I have found peace. I think today I could let you marry another without losing it – for I know the spiritual union between us will outlive this life, even if we never see each other in this world again.

Write to me soon.

Yours

　　Maud

1909

1909 was a difficult year for Yeats, who suffered some form of breakdown early in the year: Synge was dying, Symons was temporarily in a state of madness, Lady Gregory nearly died early in February, and probably the strain of the mystical marriage and the visit to Paris was taking its toll. Perhaps it had become a whole union at last. In his sixties, Yeats was to write:

> *My arms are like the twisted thorn*
> *And yet there beauty lay;*
>
> *The first of all the tribe lay there*
> *And did such pleasure take –*
> *She who had brought great Hector down*
> *And put all Troy to wreck –*
> *That she cried into this ear,*
> *'Strike me if I shriek.'*

200　　　　　　　　　　　　　　　　　　　　　　[Paris]

　　　　　　　　　　　　　　　　Wednesday [January 1909]

Dearest

You must have had a hideous journey! When the storm came on I thought of you all the time. I see by the papers that the boats all got in very late. The cold here is awful there is no way of keeping warm. I am afraid you will have another horrid journey to Manchester & to Ireland.

Lynch[1] was at the station seeing off his sister in law, he was so sorry not to have seen you. Hughes[2] last night was also full of regret at not having seen you before you left, he said you had promised to go & see him again. Not with standing there was nearly half a foot of snow on the ground all my guests arrived for dinner, it was very brave of them. We missed you very much.

I am feeling tired with this horrible cold weather that I can only write a few words today, I will write a better letter in a day or two.

This is only to tell you that my thoughts are with you & I am sad you are no longer here.

Alwys your friend
    Maud

201   [Paris]
                                                  9th Jany [1909]

Dearest friend

Thank you so much for your letter – you must have got mine before you left Manchester. I wrote a telegram, but being ill couldn't go & post it myself & I found the servant had forgotten it & I knew then that my letter would have arrived at same time.

I hope you are quite well again & not having too much worry over that theatre –

I think of you very often & I wish you were back in Paris. I miss you very much. I think you are right there was some sort of occult attack & this is what really made us both ill but whatever it is, it is passed for I feel quite different now & my nerves are getting alright again. There are many forces that seek to separate us –

I am interrupted & can write no more today, this doesn't count as a letter.

My thoughts are with you
Yours
    Maud

202   [Paris]
                                    Tuesday night [January 1909]

Dearest

I am so sorry you are ill, it is probably the result of this hideous cold weather, coming when you are probably worried over something – & the visit to poor Symons[1] must have been very terrible to you – I believe more & more that illness can only take hold of one when one is in some way out of harmony with oneself psychically – at least I know it is so with me. I will try & go to you and make you well – I have been too ill to go to you or to do anything since you left Paris, but I am much better today, & as the anxiety I spoke to you of when you were in Paris is now at an end I shall soon get alright. Today I have been able to work again.

I am so sorry for poor Mrs Symons I do not think she is to be blamed for their tragedy, at the worst she was ignorant, but I don't even think that had anything to do with the result. She must suffer even more than he does, for I suppose he is not really conscious of his condition. It must have been too dreadful for you, his friend to see him like that –

I will be able to come to London end Feb or beginning of March – I hope you will be there then. Don't let the theatre take up too much of your time in Dublin, your own work is so much more important for I suppose you have not done anything at the 'Player Queen' since you left Paris.² One day when you have time will you send me a copy of the Lyric you made for me, I want it written in your own hand to keep. Do you know you have not written anything in the books you gave me! It is so late, my friends stayed so late this evening & as I want to go to you I won't write any more now.

Always yours,
Maud

Remember [me] with all courtesy to Miss Horniman –

203   [Paris]
                                           13th Jany [1909]
Dearest

The horoscope is very interesting, I think you ought to heed what it says about marriage, I always feel that marriage for you would be a mistake, I always have felt this – I was surprised by what you said about health & am much more inclined to think that the astrologer is right – I think he has curiously mixed up me & Lady Gregory together in the description of the woman who will influence your life – in some respects I think he is very correct on the whole it is good.

I went to you consciously on the Tuesday night when you were in Manchester. I went about 12 or 2 o'clock at night after I had read your letter. I went with the intention of making you well, I went again Wednesday –

I will send you the photo soon & get the other one copied for you.

I wish you remembered more of your dream of 'le mage', it must have been most interesting.

I don't understand or rather I don't agree with the dream you wrote me of yesterday – Take the Greatest Masters – Raphael bowed down to sex till it killed him when he was only 30, his painting is the essence of prettiness. Michael Angelo denied the power of sex, *for a year* while he was painting the marvel of the Sistine Chapel they say he did not come down from the scaffolding where he worked, he had his bed arranged there & lived there – The only thing one knows of his love, are letters from some great Italian lady who was quite old & I think there are sonnets or letters written by him to her, but they only speak of spiritual love – & yet the passion of his work is terrible & makes Raphael's sink away into insignificance – About Leonardo I do not know, probably he held the balance of all things & was probably courtier, lover, soldier, painter in his hour, but holding always the balance & centre in himself. I think sex perversion may also produce strange unquiet haunting things in art – but not the greatest art.

Gustave Moreau cared little for love or that side of life. I believe he had only one mistress, to whom he was faithful for many many years.

I am well again now & next Monday I return to my studio life. Ella Young has left, my cousin is still here. Have you taken all the accounts of the visions we had together I can't find them? If you have the Initiation of the Spear you might send it me. I want to copy it into my book. I will write again soon.

Yours alwys
Your comrade
Maud

204   [Paris]
                                               [January 1909]

Dearest

I have just received the most beautiful volumes of your work.[1] Thank you so much it will be a joy reading them!

I didn't answer your last letter before for I have been so busy, little Seagan caught influenza from my cousin who has had it very badly, all my time was taken looking after them both, they are both up & much better today. The MacGregors & Dr Fauré[2] met at my house yesterday & had a most interesting & somewhat lively conversation on Druidism & Rosicrucianism – they are dining next Tuesday also senators Pauliat[3] & Bailly[4] & I think it will be quite interesting – Dr Faure's ideas on the occult currents & forces are most interesting –

I hope you are feeling better & not over working yourself with theatre, I feel inclined to quote your verses in the Sally Gardens which Iseult is always saying over – & bid you 'take life easy' as far as theatre goes.[5]

I don't feel I agree with a good deal of your last letter though I could not argue the subject having indifferent knowledge.

Tomorrow I have to have rather a nasty operation, the wretched dentist in London couldn't get all the tooth he pulled out or said he couldn't, a French one has also tried & not succeeded & tomorrow I am to have chloroform & an american dentist declares he will get it out somehow – I am afraid this means I shall be good for nothing for a day or two –

I took the portrait I have done of May to the art school this morning to show it to my master there. He & the students were all most encouraging. Humbert[6] praised it very much & he is not lavish with praise generally. He seemed surprised I had done so well.

Dear friend & comrade goodnight – I am so tired I can only write you such a dull letter –

My thoughts go to you my love.
    Maud

205   [Paris]
                                                   [January/February 1909]

Dearest if I have not written, it is because I was not well, since I had that operation & got the tooth out Saturday evening. I am better, though Sunday I was rather a wreck after it – I was able to go back to Studio work yesterday –

Thank you so much for your letters & the poem.[1] It is so good hearing from you. I have not yet got the review with the old poem.[2] This new one is beautiful, as all you write is but perhaps it is not QUITE as magical as some of your poems – Don't think me ungrateful because I say so, for I like it very much too, only your new poems have such terrible rivals in the old –

How interesting [?your] that manuscript book[3] of yours will be. I am longing to see it, we will read it together –

Dr Fauré, the MacGregors, Bailly and an occult senator are dining with me tonight. I think it will be interesting for Bailly's book will furnish them a good ground for discussion of Druidism & its bearing & connection with Rosicrucianism MacGregor may get fierce for I fancy he is on a different currant from Dr Fauré

How I wish you were here my love, my thoughts with you
    Alwys your friend
        Maud

206   13 Rue de Passy
                                                      [Paris]
                                                   [February 1909]

Dearest – I am sad for you. I know how deeply you must feel Lady Gregory's illness[1] – it would be horrid & unnatural if you didn't she being such a friend of yours –

I think you ought to go down & see her at once, leave that wretched theatre to take care of itself, it will get on all right – for a little – I went to see you last night – I saw you sleeping & tried to give you some of my vitality I also tried to find out something about Lady Gregory, the impression I got is that she is not dangerously ill, it is more caused by worry than by overwork, but I saw nothing clearly it was only an impression.

You ought to go to Coole & see her, & you might stay there & write your *Player Queen*, which is much more important than the theatre – Why don't you let the young man[2] who wants to take it on at end of patent period, try to stage manage etc in your place for a little. You could finish the *Player Queen* which I am sure would please Lady Gregory & you could help her get her own play right, which would also comfort her, for it must be very worrying to have a work one is not altogether content with & not feel well enough to put it right, & I think she needs your collaboration spiritually for any of her books – My love to you my friend & my thoughts

Your friend alwys
    Maud

Write soon and tell me how you are.

207   [Paris]
                                    Saturday [February 1909]

My dear Willie

Why don't you write? I am getting anxious, in your last letter you said you were not well I think you are down at Coole. It doesn't seem to me that you are ill but all the same I would like a few words from you to say you are well –

The St Patrick's Society here are very anxious for me to be here on the 17th March for the annual Mass for Ireland & banquet & ball of which I am hony president possibly I will come back for it before going to Ireland. Have you heard any thing from Shannon?

Iseult has been in bed with a bad cold, but is alright again now – Have you fixed your plans at all yet? I have been very hard at work painting finishing pictures for exhibition. What date is your lecture in London?

I can't write till I hear from you
In gt haste
Yours alwys
    Maud

208   [Paris]
                                                Samedi [February 1909]

Dearest friend

I am glad you *did* send me that letter for I was beginning to feel
anxious – I suppose you are right to go on with the theatre but you
are making a very big sacrifice for it & it does not seem to me half
so important to Ireland as your own work.

I wonder when we shall meet. I may be going over to London
about the 28th of this month to join my cousin Mrs Clay there.

Will Shannon really paint me then or later on? I may come over
to Ireland but only for about a week middle of March. I have some
work to see to there.

I went to see Isadora Duncan[1] & her school of dancing children
dancing here last week – She is quite wonderful, I am going to take
Iseult to see her next Wednesday. I wish I had seen Ruth St Denis[2]
with you in London –

It will be very sad if you can't be in London while I am sitting for
my picture & there was such a lot of things I wanted to go see with
you –

I hope Lady Gregory is quite well again. I did not think she was
dangerously ill. I have a different impression about poor Synge.

We have started an Irish class here. Iseult & I are both working at
it – it is very difficult & you will know French before I know Irish
I am afraid.

I must end for it is very late & I must be up early tomorrow –
write to me soon a few words just to say how you are.

Alwys yours
Maud

209   [Paris]
                                              Sunday 21st Feb [1909]

[Beginning of letter missing]
over here & not got on well how much more worried Lady Gregory
would have been thinking as she does of family, I expect she does
feel very grandmotherly over it, though perhaps she doesn't show
this side much to you & I expect that child will be a great interest &
joy to her.[1]

I think Feathers & Arrows[2] have been *wise*.

I can't think of letting you come over to London if you have only
a few days to stay. It is so much useless fatigue & time taken from
your work – later on you may have more time, & later on I may be
over in Ireland.

My plans are a little uncertain as I want to see my sister on her
way back from Davos – before I go to Ireland so when I come back

to Paris for the St Patrick's Celebrations I may only stay till end of month. Then for Easter I have to take the children to the country –

I do hope Lady Gregory is really quite recovered & at least that anxiety is over for you. I want so much to hear you are working at your play again. You must have had such an unsettled time lately that work must be hard.

Yours with all love
    Maud

210   13 Rue de Passy
                                   [Paris]
                                   Sunday [February 1909]

Dearest your letters are always a joy to me even though this one I have just received troubles me somewhat. Are you quite sure what you write about health is from *your own* experience, are you sure of it? It is so different from all I have ever heard – Is it not possible that it is something that has been put into your mind by some woman seeking to justify something that troubled her?[1] People do tell themselves strange tales sometimes till they end by believing them –

Is Lady Gregory's grandchild born yet that she is able to come to Dublin & take charge of the theatre? I think it is quite right of you not to leave Dublin till your work is finished, going from place to place is so distracting.

I am so glad your French is going on so well.[2] Are you going to Berlitz school or to a private teacher? My three neveus[3] have just arrived on their way back to England & the house is a pandemonium & will be till tomorrow night when they depart – I must go & keep order for I hear distressful voices of governess & servants.

Dear Comrade I think of you alwys & I long to see you.

Yours alwys
    Maud

211   [Paris]
                                   Sunday [February 1909]

Dearest I got your letter only on Sunday afternoon, my friend Madame Avril de Ste Croix is dangerously ill congestion of the lungs & I am nursing her, so I only got home today in afternoon & found your letter. I will telegraph to you tomorrow morning but I don't think I will be able to leave Paris for some days. Madame Avril is very ill & I seem to be the only available person to do much for her – she has so often taken care of Iseult for me & when I have been away nursed her for me, that I can't leave her now she has real need of me.

I hope this won't be a very great disappointment to you, because I will be coming to Ireland probably before Easter so we will meet then.

I am scribbling this in gt haste – as I have to go back to Madame Avril, I was up all last night & am very tired.

Yours alwys
  Maud

212   [Paris]
                              Wednesday [February/March 1909]
Dear friend

I am so sorry not to be able to write you any definite dates yet Madame Avril is still very ill. I sit up with her every other night & the Dr can't tell me any date for certain when she will be better. I *think* she is out of danger but am not sure. I can't leave her, for I know so much about her work I am able to help as no one else could.

I am so sorry to have to change plans like this & very disappointed.

In haste
Yours alwys
  Maud

I have sent your letter to my cousin & on receipt of your telegram have sent him R. G.'s address, also I have sent R. G. my cousin's address.[1]

213   [Paris]
                                        9th March [1909]

Dear Friend

It has been very disappointing missing our meeting in London. I am very sad about it, but I couldn't leave Madame Avril. She is better, out of danger I think, but is still in bed & so weak she cannot stand. Last night was the first I have not had to sit up with her – Now the St Patrick's banquet of which I am hon president is on the 17th so I can't leave before that – after it I have one or two things I would like to be in Paris for. The opening of the Salon des Independants where I am sending pictures etc. It would suit me best only to leave Paris about the 27th March. I have to be in Paris again by Easter the 11th April to take the children to Colleville for their holidays.

I may be able to come to Ireland, I have several reasons for wanting to be there. In that case you would not have to interrupt your theatre work –

If you were in London I would arrange to stay there for a week anyhow –

Do you remember if it was while you were in Paris at Xmas that I got back all my papers from the lawyer? Did I show you the evidence? I ask you this because I cannot find these papers & am trying to remember when I had them last –

I got a letter today from Miss Coates. She says your father has done two charming pencil sketches of her. She has been ill & seems in bad spirits.

I hope Lady Gregory is better. I was very sorry that her Kincora was attacked in Sinn Fein when she was ill. I hope it didn't worry her – I don't think it should for every successful dramatist is attacked – attacks are much better than silence in theatrical matters. I wish I could have seen it.

I am so glad you are working at the Player Queen again. It seemed so sad to leave off that when it was going so well.

Yours with love
Maud Gonne

214
13 Rue de Passy
Paris
23rd March [1909]

My dear friend

I got the first letter from abroad yesterday since the beginning of the strike![1]

While it was horrid being without letters & I fear many will have been lost yet all my sympathy was with the strikers & I think they have given in too soon, though they have got most of their complaints redressed.

How are you? & how is the theatre? & what is more important, how is the Player Queen?

I have been ill again – am still in the doctor's hands. I don't think I shall be able to get to England or Ireland till after the Easter holidays. Madame Avril is better though still in bed. She wants, if the doctors allow her, to come to Colleville with me & the children for Easter –

How is Lady Gregory. I expect you have been at Coole & are perhaps still there.

My cousin wrote me he saw Robert Gregory. I think he will be able to help him about the illustrations.

I have got so thin it wouldn't be a good time to have my picture painted but I always pick up quickly & I expect after a fortnight at Colleville I shall look alright again. I think we shall go down there for Holy week.

The astronomer said I was likely to be ill this spring – he was right.

The St Patrick's banquet was a great success this year in point of numbers & press notices. I got up from bed to go to it & had to take to bed again next day.

I will send you in a few days a book of Papus's on Masonry & the Rose Cross[2] which have just read & find very curious & interesting as bearing out ideas I had in my mind without any definite reason for –

Papus's style is not at all fascinating & I don't want you to wade through it all, Balzac is better for your French – but I have marked certain passages which I want you to tell me what you think of

Goodbye friend of mine write to me soon

Yours alwys with love
    Maud

215   [Paris]

Monday [March 1909]

My dear friend

I am so sorry to hear of poor Synge's death for I know how you will feel it – for himself with that awful illness it is the happiest thing that could have happened.[1] An invalid's life would be so terrible – Did he finish his Deirdre?[2] Have you read it?

I am glad Norrey[s] Connell is in Dublin to help you with the theatre, it is too dreadful you having to sacrifice your own work to it all this time. Has Norrey[s] Connell altered his Shakespeare play[3] & are you going to have it acted? I liked it very much indeed when I heard it in London. What a good evening we had at your house the night he read it.

It rains rains rains here with out stopping & my spirits are rather low, I want the sea air & its noise & battle to get into harmony with life again.

I am homesick & want to be able to live in Ireland – & that is out of the question for the present. I am only like this because it rains & because I am not very strong yet.

I won't write any more for it is only gloomy things I would write today, & when you get this letter perhaps the sun will be shining & I shall wonder why I ever felt sad or why anyone should.

Alwys dear friend with all love,

Yours
    Maud

216

Les Mouettes
Colleville
Par Vierville
Calvados
Holy Thursday [April 1909]

My dear Friend

We came here on Monday & already I feel much better & much happier – The country is so wonderful in the early spring, violets & primroses every where & the new shoots on the trees shining like jewels – I have been through rather a strange & troubled time spiritually lately but now I am at peace again – & consequently I am well. I believe more & more that illness always comes from moral more than physical causes – & can be cured also morally.

I am sending you a note book of yours which I only discovered the day I left Paris, it has notes for the Player Queen & you may need it – My sister has written asking to come to me on the 24th April on her way back from Davos where she has spent the winter fighting against consumption – she will only stay three days & we will travel to England together. When is the Shakespeare Festival?[1] I would like to go to it very much if dates can fit, it may be very interesting, though it is an *English* festival & the glorification of an English genius. I know that you say that it is the celebration of an England of the past which was not as horrid as the England of today, but even that England was the enemy & destroyer of our country.

You must have had a terribly trying time lately – it is so bad for your work. I do hope Miss Horniman will agree to Norrey[s] Connell becoming manager – How is Lady Gregory?

We stay here till the 21st & I want to do a lot of occult work it is so quiet & so calm here.

With all love
Your friend
Maud

217

[London]
[May 1909]

Dear friend

I got to London last night, & am staying with my cousin Mrs Clay. I want to hear from you very soon what your plans are, I want to go to Dublin very soon – if I can cross on the 3rd or 4th shall you still be there?

I am longing to be in Ireland again, it seems to me everything is more beautiful there –

I am so sorry you have been having such a lot of trouble with Synge's relations what an awful thought his brother in law suggesting revising his work!¹ You have read his Deirdre haven't you? Do you like it?

What a lot we have to talk of when we meet it will be so good seeing you.

In gt haste
Yours alwys
Maud

I couldn't write before when I should cross to England as it depended on my sister being able to go. My address is on other page.

c/o Mrs Bertie-Clay
39 Park Mansions
Knightsbridge
London S W

After Maud Gonne arrived in London, Yeats wrote to Lady Gregory on 27 May: 'Maud Gonne has struck up the most surprising friendship with Miss Tobin. They met at Arthur Symons's on Sunday (Symons had asked to see Maud Gonne) and Maud Gonne said afterwards "she is so good – it flows from her" and Miss Tobin wrote "she is the most glorious of human creatures" – I think that was the phrase – and sent her a string of pearls. They spent Tuesday morning in Westminster Abbey. Maud Gonne leaves to-day.' (Agnes Tobin was an American writer.)

Having left London, Maud Gonne wrote the following letter. What occasioned this renunciation and a gradual return to their former relationship?

218
Thursday
On the boat going to Ireland
[May 1909]

Beloved

I write to you things I wanted to say & could not. All last night I was with you in happy dreams, not that great spiritual union of which I once wrote, but I know we were together & at peace & I hope that peace came to you too. Dearest I have not come to the decision I have come to without struggle & without suffering though once that decision come to, in answer to my prayers, the suffering & the struggle ceased in a way I surely do not deserve. Beloved I will pray with my whole strength that suffering & temptation may be taken from you as they have from me & that we may gain spiritual union stronger than earthly union could ever be.

I want to thank you my own for being generous with me *as you have always been.* I have brought suffering to you so often, & you never reproach me. – Will I ever bring you happiness & peace to compensate? I pray to God that by holding our love pure it may be so.

Some of the things I said to you yesterday evening were unjust, *I had no right* to say them, and I am sorry I did – On me alone the blame lies for the forgetfulness of that spiritual marriage long ago,[1] which if we had obeyed would have saved us both from the long weariness of separation.

I was carried away on the wave of hate which I thought righteous, I sought a wild revenge which because impersonal I thought noble. I forgot that those who would distribute life or death must be purer than the angels & that I was full of human passion & weakness.

Willie your arms were not strong enough to save me for my eyes were too blind to see these things & all the crushing sorrow that came on me *I have earned.*

My loved one I belong to you more in this renunciation than if I came to you in sin. Did you not say yourself that our love must be holy?

Yours
Maud

While staying with Lady Gregory at the Burren in County Clare, Yeats wrote to his father on 17 July: 'I went to Paris for a few days before I came here, and met Sarah Purser at Maud Gonne's. She was characteristic as ever, as like herself as a John drawing. Maud Gonne had a cage full of canaries and the birds were all singing. Sarah Purser began lunch by saying "What a noise! I'd like my lunch in the kitchen!"'

219   [Paris]
                                          Saturday [June 1909]

My dearest friend

It has been horrid of me not writing all this time & not answering your letter which I liked so much. It is not because I have not thought of you but I know you were busy & your mind full of that theatre & all it means & I too was very busy preparing for shutting up my house for the summer.

We go to Evian on Monday so write to me to

l'Ermitage
Evian les Bains
Haute Savoie

I am glad that Mrs Campbell has insisted & got you to the point of signing the contract[1] as now I know you will finish the Player Queen & be free again to write poetry –

I am in great admiration before a picture, or rather three pictures in the Paris Salon (Société Nationale) of Joan of Arc by Boutet de Monvel[2] he has worked in *flat* colors, the drawing doing almost all of the light & shade – & the details of brocades in the dresses very elaborately painted. It gives the effect of the old missals. The intensity of the faces & figures is got by their extreme simplicity & flat coloring. I wish you could see it – I have been seeing a lot of pictures since my return, & how I wished you had been with me – I see things twice as well when we are together

I must end for I want to catch the post

Write soon

Yours alwys

    Maud

220
                                        L'Ermitage
                                        Evian les Bains
                                        Haute Savoie
                                        Friday [June 1909]

Dearest – I am so glad your Deirdre is being given again. How I wish I were in London to see it with you. Send me the papers about it. Also about Synge's Deirdre. Has it been played yet? I only heard the two acts you read but I hardly feel it will grip an audience. Synge being in love with rather an ordinary little girl,[1] it may have taken somewhat away from the prestige of his written Deirdre – but perhaps this is unjust, as those two first acts are so difficult to make living – it would take a d'Annunzio[2] to do that – you were not interested enough in them to try & only began at the third – Synge's third act you say is his best –

We are here in a beautiful quiet place among woods looking over a lake which takes such colors they seem unreal – I wish you were here, at the end of the month when Iseult has done her cure we will climb higher up the mountain.

I have just heard from Mr Quinn saying he is likely to be in Paris first week in July. I shall be sorry to miss him, it is quite possible that some business affairs may make it necessary for me to return to Paris for a few days soon and if so I will try & make it coincide with Mr Quinn's visit for I haven't forgotten how kind he was to me when I had all that trouble of the divorce & I want to thank him –

I know that the United Arts Club[3] is going to have a paid secretary (a *very* small salary) & I want you to use your influence on behalf of Miss Moloney the editoress of Bean na hEireann for it. She has a tiny income of her own some thirty pounds a year & this would make it possible for her to live in Ireland, & I *want her there very much*. She is a very intelligent girl & very conscientious & would certainly scrupulously <fulfil> do any work she undertakes. Please do this for me – I am writing to Mrs O'Grady[4] also about this – but you have more influence than any one on that committee I am told –

Let me know when you go to Ireland. Arthur Symons sent me a lovely poem before I left Paris on Ireland. I must write to thank him. Have you seen him again?[5]

My thoughts are with you very often, but I have not actually tried to go to you lately – I was very busy before leaving Paris & rather tired, & I knew your life was full of activities just then.

Yours alwys
Maud

221   Hotel de Midi
Bernex
Haute Savoie
12 July [1909]

My dear friend

I was so glad to get your letter. I had a strange dream of you about 3 nights ago. You had hypnotised me & there was a great deal I cannot remember. I woke rather startled.

We are in the most lovely mountain place just near the snows & with the most wonderful wild flowers everywhere. The children are so happy & we take long walks & live out of doors which makes me lazy about writing. The people here are so kindly & simple & remind me of our peasants it has made me long to be back in Ireland.

On the 15th I have promised to join my cousin May at Aix les Bains & I am so sorry to leave this, for I hate the fashionable watering places. The children stay on here till I come back to them in three weeks. This place is full of Irish souvenirs. St Colomban[1] founded a monastery near here. We are going to visit it tomorrow.

I am so sorry you have & are having so much worry with that theatre. Oh Willie DO get out of it, it is keeping you from your real work. What business have you to be wasting your time arranging all these petty squabbles. If Norrys Connell is no longer Manager the whole work will again be shifted on to you & you know what that means. It is far better the theatre should end than that you should waste another year over it –

Don't think I am unsympathetic writing like this, but it is really CRUEL to see you waste your time in that wretched theatre. I know how you feel that one cannot draw back from what one has put one's hand to, but your writing, your poetry is of so far more value to Ireland than the theatre – You didn't send me any paper notices of Deirdre which was very wrong of you, you didn't tell me if Synge's Deirdre was acted & how it was received I want to hear all that so much.

I have not heard again from Mr Quinn so I don't know if I shall see him.

I can't send you your books till I get back to Paris

Friend of mine goodnight my thoughts are with you

Maud

Address next letter to Hotel Thermal Aix les Bains Savoie.

222

Hotel Thermal
Aix-les-Bains
Savoie
27th July [1909]

Dearest – When I read your 1st letter from Burren[1] I did try & send you a thought of strength for I was afraid, not from anything you said in the letter, but from the feel of it, that you were dissatisfied with life, & almost ill. I am so glad to get your letter today & know that you are well & able to do your writing.

I was also very happy that there is a chance of the professorship,[2] I want that for you, for a time at any rate & you could do so much for our country, & you would get, I think, again in harmony with our people – I do not think it would keep you from your own work – Less I am sure than the theatre with its endless worries & petty quarrels does.

I got a cable from Mr Quinn, he will be in Paris on the 1st August, but does not say where he will stay – I have just begun a cure for rheumatism here & it would be rather bad to interrupt it, so I don't think I shall see him. I am very disappointed at this. In a letter he wrote me some weeks ago, he said he was going to stay with Hyde & with Lady Gregory for a few days so you are sure to see him. Tell him how sorry I am not to see him, & say I always feel most grateful for his kindness, & all the help he gave me in my trouble.

This is a very fashionable crowded place where one is obliged to wear hats & gloves when ever one goes out, which I hate doing in summer – other years gambling amused me very much, & it would this year I think, but I have let myself get so sensitive psychically to the atmosphere created by the people one meets that the proximity of jew bankers & enterprising fair ladies & fat vulgar creatures of all sorts gets so on my nerves that after the first day or two I have not been in the gaming rooms at all – & there is nothing else at all to do at Aix, for the baths make one so tired that long walks & excursions are forbidden. I spend most of my time reading Boehme,³ but he is difficult to read, for either the translations are not good or what is probable he had not the art of expressing himself – yet his book is wonderful, & there are the keys to unlock many doors in it if only one can understand. I wish we were reading it together – you would help me so –

I go back to the children at Bernex on the 10th August about the 2[?9]th we shall go to Colleville for a month then I am coming to Ireland, & I hope we shall meet.

Dearest another reason you are feeling better & able to work is that it is the beginning of the festival of Lug⁴ & the Sun influence must be strong in those who work in the spirit, to make it manifest in the earth –

My thoughts are with you
Yours alwys
  Maud

May who is with me sends messages to you.

Yeats had made indiscreet remarks about John Quinn's mistress, Dorothy Coates. Apparently Quinn accused Yeats of making overtures to her while she was in Paris, and Yeats's 'unrestrained sense of comedy' led him to reply: 'If it had been your wife, yes, but your mistress – never.' The ensuing quarrel lasted until March 1914.

223   Aix les Bains
                                          [August 1909]

                                          Private

My dear Willie
  What a long while it is since you wrote to me. If it is because you are working hard at the *Player Queen*, I am satisfied, but I am afraid it is the *theatre* and then I feel aggrieved. I saw in the Daily Mail that the Abbey theatre is going to produce Shaw's play.¹ If it can be done without you giving your time & energy to it – it is very good, but nothing is worth while doing that means taking you away from your own work.

  I was in Paris two days last week & saw Mr Quinn. Now Willie there is something I am going to write, which I feel perhaps I ought *not* to write because it goes near to breaking confidence which of all things *I hate doing*, but it seems to me so important to you that I must say a few words, but I do beg you will be serious & not mention the subject of my letter to your hostess or to anyone. Things you have said to & about certain Ladies have been repeated probably exaggerated & caused harm. Mr Quinn is very hurt about it & very angry with you, which if the things are as he thinks *he would have good right to be* but I am certain there has been misrepresentation & exaggeration & perhaps invention & I have asked him to speak to you quite frankly about the whole thing & give you the opportunity of explaining – otherwise your friendship with him is over & as I know you like him & value his friendship & it would be a great pity.

Remember if you talk to Lady Gregory or to anyone about this you may make things worse, I write this to you so that you may not let anything prevent you meeting Mr Quinn when he is in Ireland – I would prefer you do not tell Mr Quinn I have written, for though I gave no promise not to write it does seem a little like breaking confidence as he said he would see you himself –

My cousin May & I leave here tomorrow morning for Bernex where Iseult & the little golden heart[2] are waiting for us my address there is *Hotel de Midi, Bernex, Haute Savoie.*

We shall be there till the 17th or 18th when we go to Colleville – How is the play getting on?

I have much packing to do so end

Alwys your friend,

    Maud

224
                                         Bernex
                                      15th Aug [1909]

My dear Willie

I am so sorry you have so much worry just now. There was a want of *will* in your first letter I don't like – There *must* not be any doubt about you finishing your play for Mrs Campbell[1] – It is not so much from anything you said, as from the *feel* of your letter that I think you are just now a little too much inclined to let things drift – I believe if you *really want* the professorship you will get it but you would have to want it & *will* to get it in earnest, & just now you don't really want it & are rather glad that there are difficulties in the way yet it would have meant more liberty & independence than you have now & I don't think it would have interfered with your creative work. Besides, this new university[2] is so different from an ordinary professorship. Here the professors will be really working for Ireland. They will be *creating* what may become a thought centre for the world. If it is great, it may make Ireland great – O Willie, I did so want you to be in this – If it is still possible do try –

Don't be impatient at me for writing like this, but I feel you are at a time when you must make an effort & must not let things drift along –

About your 2nd letter – I don't know enough details to write fully, but I think you are right in supposing that the conversation with Miss Coates to which you refer is the cause of the trouble – but I am afraid other people to whom you talked have also repeated things but it is the conversation with Miss Coates that mattered & gave importance to the stories. I think from the things I noticed in Mr Quinn's way of writing about you that he must have heard this very shortly before he left America – Mr Quinn takes the matter very seriously – he didn't want to see you, I told him it would be too unfair not to have an explanation with you, as I felt certain things must have been misrepresented. He told me he would see you but feared you would talk it over with friends & he didn't want this, so *please* Willie don't talk to anyone till you have seen Mr Quinn. Think well what you did say to Miss Coates & if she has exaggerated as I think she must have, say exactly what you *did* say but be gentle in talking of Miss Coates for she is not well & any word against her would annoy Mr Quinn very much I think – Also I don't think you must say that it is an 'unrestrained sense of comedy' that made you indiscreet. If you cannot disprove the thing entirely & I doubt if you can do that you must make Mr Quinn see that any indiscretion was involuntary & that you are really distressed by it – You must try hard not to lose that friendship. I told Mr Quinn that to me who am one of your oldest friends & to whom you had often talked of him you had never referred in any way to any of his private affairs & naturally I never let him think I had heard or that I supposed Miss Coates was a particularly great friend – but he says he has gone into the matter thoroughly & is convinced you have talked to others – I am most anxious to hear when you have seen Mr Quinn. Nothing but your own personal influence & charm can make things right between you but I trust much to that.

We go to Paris tomorrow & on the 20th to *les Mouettes, Colleville par Vierville, Calvados.*

Alwys your friend,
Maud

225   Paris
                                                          19th August [1909]

My dear Willie

I found your letter last night on arriving in Paris.

I am so glad, I do hope Lord Aberdeen[1] will continue to support the Abbey it would be great this news has put me in great good spirits. It is worth the interruption of your work, even! –

I have not heard anything from Mr Quinn since he went to England to buy pictures – John & Shannon if possible – he then intended going to Ireland for three or four days – I do hope you will see him.

I am scribbling this note in wild haste in a noisy shop where I have to wait – we leave for Colleville tomorrow at 6 o'clock morning. Ella Young is coming to stay with me. We are going to Mont St Michel where there are wonderful fêtes & pilgrimages in honor of Jeanne d'Arc. I wish you could have come, but with your work that is quite out of the question. I hope to see you in October when I come to Ireland – I hope you were not vexed with my last letter. I was so disappointed that you were not going for the professorship[2] that I said perhaps more than I should, & if so forgive me.

Alwys your friend
Maud

Maud Gonne wrote to Quinn about Yeats: 'I thought a lot and the more I thought the more certain I became that you ought to see Willie and hear his explanation. . . . I know he is incapable of deliberately making mischief.'

In his Journal *(included in* Memoirs*) Yeats had written:*

Yesterday a most evil day . . . letter from MG saying that Quinn is offended at something I said or am said to have to or about some friend of Quinn's. I do not think I can have said the things he complains of, whatever they are, but I know myself to be utterly indiscreet.

On 17 August he recorded:

Have been to Dublin – saw Quinn and had whole thing out. Various incautious sayings of mine to a friend of his in Paris have been made the foundation for an architecture of lies. . . . I accepted the worst case possible against myself and did years' work of repentance in ten minutes. Quinn is between a bad woman and a good one and the bad can control nothing in her nature, least of all her imagination and her speech.

In the meantime Dublin Castle and the Lord Lieutenant had been putting pressure on the Abbey Theatre not to perform Shaw's play, The Shewing-Up of Blanco Posnet, *because it had been banned by the Lord Chamberlain in England. In spite of this, the play was put on in August and had a great success, making money and healing the rift with Sinn Féin caused by the* Playboy *riots.*

226

My dear Willie

I am delighted at the success you have had.[1] Delighted that you have made the viceroy ridiculous & that once more you are at heart with our people. I hated the theatre because it takes too much of your time from your own work & quite as much because it has been one of the great causes of estrangement between you & the people – for it, you have done things I can never understand but at last the Abbey theatre has been definitely against the English government in Ireland so of course I am pleased though I still would be more pleased to know you were free from it completely & able to write the wonderful poetry you used to.

I am so glad to see that German papers sent correspondents. It is very good that it should be known abroad that in art as well as politics Ireland is separate & distinct from England & ready to defy her on all occasions. Your firm stand will have done great good from this point of view also.

Thank you so much for the papers, they have interested me greatly.

I am so glad you saw Mr Quinn. I have had a letter from him the day before he sailed for America. I think you have made things better by the interview if only it is not undone again in America. Will you send me his address in New York. I ought to answer his letter & have not his address here. Please send it.

Monday

Rather strange things have been happening here, of which I can't altogether understand the meaning.

I don't know if you know a life size portrait there is of mine – painted by an Alsatian artist, standing in a white dress. It is much the best portrait there is of me –

The other day Iseult came to me with much excitement saying she had been sitting in the drawing room opposite this picture when suddenly she saw it move, the eyes opened & shut. Then the lips moved and the face became contorted. Then it became black then appeared again but quite changed. It seemed like a figure in stone with a green veil over the head, the eyes half closed and a strange smile on the lips, the hands instead of hanging down were together folded under the chin partly hidden by the green veil. It was like me yet different. Iseult got so frightened that she fled –

Next day some people were at tea with me suddenly I caught sight of the picture in a mirror opposite to it & sure enough the eyes opened & shut. I said nothing for the people there would have thought me mad if I had but that evening I told Ella Young & my cousin May, & we three went into the drawing room & invoked. *We all saw* the picture move & change in the most extraordinary way – Something has taken possession of the picture – I think it may be the grey woman who I had to get rid of – there have been several other rather curious manifestations which as it is very late I have not time to describe[2] –

I hope the Player Queen is going well & that you are happy & well
My thoughts go to you always
Your friend Alwys
Maud

227   [Colleville]
Monday [September 1909]

My dear Willie
On the night of the 10th to 11th did you try to come & see me. I dreamed of you very vividly. I think it was a good dream, though it referred to some past incarnation in India, of which I have never remembered anything before.

Tuesday I was interrupted yesterday – I have just got your letter this morning. Evidently you dreamed of me the night I asked you if you had tried to come & see me –

My picture here was quite extraordinary for some days. Iseult saw it first, then May & I & Ella, not once but many times. We all saw it move & change – I think it is connected with the grey woman – as she could not come to me she went to the picture. We have worked a good deal at it & I am sure now it will do us no harm even if she stays with the picture.

We went to Mont St Michel last week. How I wished you had been with us – you must come there some day – Tomorrow we are going to Coutance[1] which is a most fascinating old medieval town – These old sleepy towns in Normandy would please you. They have wonderful Gothic Churches & houses with strange carvings –

I am still very sad you are not trying for the professorship – still it may come later on.

It is good news that the Player Queen is going so well – I am longing to hear it.

I have been drawing a good deal. I have finished a set of illustrations for Maunsel which Roberts[2] is very pleased with & I have just done 4 symbolic figures with four jewels

It will be good seeing you again, but I am not quite certain when I shall be in Ireland, Iseult is going to stay with May in October, & I don't like leaving the golden heart while she is away.

Alwys dearest your friend
Maud

228
Les Mouettes
Colleville
Monday 27th Sept [1909]

My dear Willie

I too have been very careless this summer in writing down dreams & occult experiences, which I regret all the more as there have been rather interesting ones. I can't tell the date Iseult first saw the picture move. She did not tell me the day she saw it because she thought it might impression me & she first told my cousin May & I think it was the next day she told me. I thought it was probably only a dream or a hallucination of Iseult's & should probably not have taken any notice but a few days after as I was pouring out tea (the parish priest was paying a visit) I was sitting back to the picture but in front of me there was a mirror in which the picture was reflected. I suddenly saw the eyes of the picture move & open & shut several times. After the priest was gone & the children out of the way I told May & Ella & we three went & examined the picture, there is no doubt at all we *all* saw it move. We took a lamp & put it in several places to see if it was only a play of light. I went close up to the picture or stood away, it was always the same, *the picture moved*. Sometimes only the eyes, sometimes the whole face & it smiled a strange mocking smile & sometimes it looked very sad. May said she saw it breathing & we all saw it sway – occasionally a blackness seemed to come over it & the head disappeared altogether –

This happened not once but on four or five successive days. I believe if we had tried we could have got whatever was in the picture to come right out of the frame, but I would do nothing to give it strength, with children around one has to be so careful.

I think it is the Grey woman who I used to have with me who as you know I banished when I found she was evil. Something has given her strength to return & not being able to come to me she had gone to the picture. I knew for some time she was around but I would not let her appear. I also think she is my Ka out of the Egyptian Incarnation when I was a priestess.

One night while Ella was staying here she told me a woman had appeared in her room in the most terrible grief wringing her hands, just as that grey woman used to do – about that time also a lot of queer physical phenomenons happened.

One evening for instance while May & Ella & I were putting a guard on my room to prevent Bichon[1] getting nightmares of which he had a few, a water bottle standing on my writing table was suddenly broken though no one was near it. Doors were locked & things disappeared & were found afterwards in places no one had put them in.

I did all I could to quiet & banish on account of the children &

we took care not to talk of any of this before them.

We go to Paris on Thursday so write to me to 13 Rue de Passy. I thank you so much for papers & your letter.

Alwys dearest your friend
    Maud

229   12th Nov [1909]

Dearest as usual our letters have crossed. I knew you were feeling sad & lonely & I was too, but at the end of this summer it had seemed to me there was some barrier between us I did not care to write much.

It is hard to be so much apart & yet perhaps it is better for both of us until we grow very strong – When I know things are going well with you I am fairly content, but when I know you are sad, the temptation to write to you to come to me, or to go to you is terrible – Yet Willie I know we are doing the right thing. The love whose physical realisation we deny here will unite us in another life – If we did the easy thing & yielded to it now, very likely it would *part us here* & after.

I think what made us sad now was I stayed so short a time in Dublin & we had both so much to do we had little time to see each other – We are never sad when we know we are going to meet the next day & the next.

My hope is that we will both be very strong, so strong that we shall be at peace, & that one day we live near each other in Ireland –

You are quite right in saying in your note we have never been nearer than now – The love you have given me is so wonderful so pure so unselfish I want to keep it always bright & shining as the Sidhe gave it back to me. I want always to reverence in our love. Dearest in Art, in life in every thing the easy thing, is never the interesting thing. Only those who make an effort to surpass themselves are interesting.

What makes the extraordinary charm of your poetry is the terrible though unseen effort of its creation. This somehow makes the atmosphere of a precious jewel about it. Like a gem it is the outcome of a terrible & hidden effort. With human lives it is the same & only lives of great hidden effort are worth looking at. The least gesture of a saint I think must be more worth looking at than the whole life & agitation of those who take life easily because of the power which is behind even when that power is not manifesting. These things I have only realised lately – am I boring you with all this? Write to me from London & tell me what Mrs Cambell decides about the play.[1] I am afraid she will be very disappointed at not having it at once. Will you be long in London? I am in bed with a chill, but am already better

& will be up tomorrow – Iseult sends messages, she likes you very much she was much pleased at the thought of meeting poets at your Monday evenings.[2] She is growing very beautiful. This is her last year of school grind, after this I shall let her take up what subjects she pleases – She is so intilectual she ought to do something interesting, but she declares energetically that she hates the thought of working hard at anything.

My thoughts are with you

Yours

    Maud

230   [Paris]

                                Tuesday 2nd Dec [1909]

My dear Willie

A word in haste to say May is in London,

    39 Park Mansions

    Knightsbridge,

    S.W.

Kathleen is in Davos for her health – I am afraid she is not at all well.

How kind of you getting a fan for Iseult. She is delighted at the thought of having it. A few mornings before I got your letter Bichon woke me up with this question 'When is Willie Yeats coming?' I asked why he asked, 'Only because I was thinking of him & I like him'

There is a compliment for you.

I am working very hard at art school every morning, work at home in the afternoons. The day is never long enough – by the way did you get the letter I wrote to you to London in answer to yours from Dublin?

What a bore about Mrs Cambell and Tree.[1] What part did Mrs Cambell think Tree could do? Did she seem to want the play herself? The old obsessed man's part might be made wonderful but could Tree play it?

When do your lectures begin –

Alwys dear Willie

Your friend

    Maud

231   [Paris]
                                                  26 December [1909]

My dear Willie

I was so glad to get your letter & I knew you must be busy as you
did not write.

Buying the Abbey Theatre[1] is a big undertaking & means a lot of
responsibility & worry for you which I am sorry for –

What of the Player Queen? Is it finished yet? has anything been
decided about its production?

Are your lectures settled yet? I have been rather ill, or I would
have written before for I often think of you & wonder what are you
doing.

Iseult's fan is quite lovely. How clever your sister is! It is so kind
of you sending it to her – We are both going to Laval for the New
Year but I only stay a day or two & return to Paris leaving Iseult
with her Godmother for the holidays.

Your old astrologer[2] sounds very interesting. I *think* I have all the
dates you ask for but I must take a day to hunt them up in the papers
which my lawyer returned – I will do this in a day or two.

I always wondered why you didn't like the little drawing of myself
I made for you, I rather liked it & Granié said as a drawing it was
good. I am working hard and have got a very beautiful model. Granié
sent me a lovely pencil drawing of his as a Xmas present.

I must end for I have, for my sins, to go out to a big at home this
evening & must go & dress. I am getting very lazy about going out
unless there is someone very specially interesting I want to meet &
I shall be very glad when the New Year's festivities are over.

May the New Year bring you great good luck & happiness.

Your friend alwys
    Maud

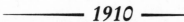

1910

*Radical politics behind him, Yeats was by now recognised as a leading
man of letters, being invited to join the Academic Committee of the
Royal Society of Literature and offered a Civil List pension. There
was a possibility of being appointed to a professorship of English
Literature at Trinity College, Dublin. Maud Gonne, however,
thought a post in University College, Dublin, a constituent college of
the new National University, for which he applied unsuccessfully,
would have enabled him to help in creating a thought centre for the
world. In September Yeats suffered another great loss in the death of*

his uncle George Pollexfen, with whom he had been very close, and this broke the link with his ancestral Sligo.

After her relief work during the Paris floods, the worst that Paris had experienced for 170 years, Maud Gonne launched another project close to her heart – the feeding of schoolchildren in Ireland. One day while she and Seán were feeding the ducks in St Stephens Green, Dublin, some poor children came and took the ducks' 'wet muddy crusts'. A little girl explained: 'When we get home from school and mother has no dinner for us I always bring my little brothers to the Green to get bits off the ducks.' Consumption and insanity, she thought, were among the results of such starvation.

Yeats visited Colleville in May. In the summer Maud Gonne brought her family to Mayo and in the autumn she was in Dublin tackling the issue of school meals.

232

5 Rue de Paradis
Laval
[January 1910]

My dear Willie

Your letter arrived just as Iseult & I were starting for this quaint peaceful place – Iseult is going to stay 10 days with her Godmother but I go back to Paris tomorrow. It was formerly a Carmelite Convent but owing to the persecutions in France the nuns had to put on secular dress. It makes them look much older. this morning in the chapel in the half light they looked like strange ghosts, but there is a strange peace & charm about the place & they all seem quite happy.

There is a wonderful garden with fountains & statues which even in winter does not quite lose its charm though the pomegranate trees & the roses look desolate & bare.

I don't think the date of Chantecler[1] has been announced yet. I will enquire as soon as I get back to Paris & let you know – it will be very nice seeing you.

Thank you for the poem.[2] I will write you a long letter from Paris, today I haven't time.

Alwys your friend,
Maud

I have not been able to do much drawing all Dec I have been ill but you shall have a head of Iseult soon. She is such a nice model.

233   [Paris]
[January 1910]
My dear Willie

Chantecler is announced for the 25th Jany tickets will be issued from the 13th. Let me know the date you are likely to be over for I expect one will have to buy the tickets a good time in advance at first if one wants good places.

It will be funny certainly but I can't imagine the piece really being a success, the theme is too slight – It will be really funny to see the actors *hopping* about like birds all the time, but I imagine the audience will get as tired of it as they will –

It will be very nice seeing you – I have a desperate lot of New Year's letters to answer so can't write more today.

Yours alwys
Maud

234   [Paris]
Friday [February/March 1910]
My dear Willie

a word in great haste in case you may be nervous at not hearing from me in so long, while all this hideous destruction is going on in Paris[1] – It really seems as if half of Paris is crumbling, today I took three hours in a cab getting from the Louvre to my house – so many streets were barred & flooded or the houses toppling – & the streets where one can pass being of course blocked with congested traffic. The telegraph service is almost entirely stopped, the electric light has failed in most places, the gas works are stopped, drains are bursting everywhere & houses threatening ruin, the newspaper accounts are not one bit exaggerated. All my time is taken up in relief committees trying to provide clothing & shelter for the hundreds of unfortunate people who have lost everything – I have lodged four in my own house and we have a great dortoir[2] in the stables of the Passy marketplace where we feed & clothe hundreds & give shelter to as many as our limited space allows, & Passy is one of the least affected quarters in Paris. It is all a horrible nightmare – On Sunday I am sending Madam Dangien with the children to Colleville. Paris is not a fit place for them just now – I shall follow when I can.

It was a great disappointment that you could not come to Paris, but as it is, it is just as well – Paris is appalling today.

I am glad Synge's Deirdre was such a success[3] – How I would have liked to have heard it.

In haste
dearest alwys your friend,
Maud

235

My dear friend

It was really bad of me not answering your last letter – you know what a bad correspondent I am. It is not because I don't think, but it never comes naturally to me to write of thoughts or impressions & of material events here there are few to tell of. We are living in complete solitude except for the peasants & the Parish priest, we are the only people in Colleville at this time of the year. The place is beautiful covered with white violets & primroses & wind blown leafless apple trees. Iseult & Seagan like it better than Paris & I am quite contented painting & reading – I am illustrating two more books of Ella Young's for Maunsell one booklet like the last & one big book.[1] It is work I find very interesting, for I can work in all sorts of symbols & I do a good deal of painting besides, about 4 hours every day.

Iseult & I read a good deal together – just now we are struggling with St Thomas Acquinas, the scholastic language of the 13th Century makes it hard –

I am quite sorry to have to go to Paris next Monday to preside at the annual Franco-Irish dinner on St Patrick's Day – I shall only stay a week – the children are going as far as Caen with me as there are some wonderful old churches there we want to visit & they will come & meet me at Bayeux when I come back where we are going to spend Holy Week for the religious services in the Cathedral, which I believe are wonderful. They have some old vestments dating from the 13th Century & one vestment has a real pearl embroidery in it which dates from the *4th* Century.

We are going to stay at a convent in Bayeux if only we can persuade the nuns to admit Seagan & because of his long curls to forget he is a boy.

May is coming to stay with me in May. If you could come at the same time it would be very pleasant – I have written to May to come in April but I am not sure she will be able to come so soon – I will let you know directly I hear from her. We shall be staying here till July or August as Paris is very unhealthy after the floods & I am making a severe attempt at economy with a view to a journey to Italy next spring which I have promised Iseult.

This is the only place I know where it is easy to be economical as there are no shops – & the peasants round are all so comfortably well off that one doesn't want to give them money.

I am so glad you have been lecturing for the Gaelic League[2] & that you liked your audience. I already knew that they liked you from letters & from the papers – What are you lecturing on in London?

It will be so good seeing you & having time for long talks, there

is so much I want to hear & to tell.
  Write soon to
  Your friend
      Maud Gonne

236

[Colleville]
Easter Monday [1910]

PRIVATE

My dear Willie
  This is a few words written in gt haste to tell you to be a little
careful & enquire a good deal before accepting an invitation you are
likely to receive to preside over a section on Anglo Irish literature at
a *Celtic Congress* which it is proposed to hold in Brussels this
Summer. The promoters wrote to me about the scheme a good while
ago & I thought it sounded very interesting & subscribed & also at
their request wrote a list of names of people who I thought would
be well to invite to attend the different Irish sections of the Congress
– I suggested yours.
  When I was in Paris for Patrick's day banquet I met M. de Courcy
MacDonald who seems to be the chief organiser & from a long talk
I had with him I fear the organisation of the whole affair will be *very
bad* – I hope I am wrong, but I write to tell you to make some
enquiries before accepting the invitation if you feel inclined to do so.
I think Mr *Graves* who MacDonald says is to preside over a section
of Irish folklore will probably be able to give you information on the
subject but please don't use my name in writing to him. I know he
went & had a long talk with Mr de C. MacDonald.
  I spent some lovely days with the children in Bayeux during holy
week – the Cathedral is so wonderful & the ceremonies so beautifully
done – We returned here Saturday & I am going to work hard at my
illustrations to make up for a fortnight's idleness.
  I presided at St Patrick's banquet in Paris this year about 80 people
at the banquet & several hundreds at the soirée afterwards. I never
saw so many people at the Patrick's Celebration in Paris before –
  Did you get the letter I wrote to Dublin just before I went to Paris
asking you to come here with my cousin May in April. I haven't her
date yet, but I expect it will be middle or end of April, as soon as
Kathleen's boys who she is looking after go back to their school after
the Easter holidays.
  I hope you are finding life interesting & that you are writing.
  Yours alwys
      Maud G.

Addressed to The Theatre, Abbey Street, Dublin – please forward.
Postmark: Vierville Calvados 21–3.

WBY 5   18 Woburn Buildings
                                                    Woburn Place, N.W.
                                                    April 13, 1910

My dear Maud

I am dictating this for no better reason that that I am at my typist's <and shall not be going home immediately afterwards> and that it saves time.

I called the other day on Mrs Clay[1] thinking to arrange with her about my visit to you, but she wasn't in London. I have since written to her.

I go to Manchester in two or three days and cannot get away from that or its neighbourhood till after the 22nd. If you have made any changes of plans will you tell me please. All is going well with my affairs. The New Manager[2] is apparently keeping the Abbey in good order and the money is coming in, slowly but I think steadily for our purchase or re-establishment of the theatre. I am going to Manchester because I have put a play[3] on against the protests of the local management, and I want to find out for myself how it goes. They will probably not tell me the truth. On the 22nd I am going to see a little Company[4] which made a success with my Kings Threshold in Birmingham. I want to see if it is worth working with at any time, as my own sympathies are rather with movements that arise outside the ordinary theatres. And this little Company is rather an imitation of our own. Yesterday, I was at Sir Hugh Lane's,[5] you know he has a wonderful house in Cheyne Walk, full of pictures, representing great wealth, in the one room a Velasquez, a Van Dyck, a Titian and a Goya and lesser masters. I met there a relation of yours, a clever talkative woman, who sees ghosts in the small hours, astral monkeys sitting by the fire and the like, a certain Lady Ward.[6] She was praising you, deploring your politics.

I have been lecturing and had a sort of fashionable success, and made enough money to pay most of my debts for the moment, and I am editing Synge,[7] doing a long Introduction and thinking about my long play,[8] but not writing at it.

I have written two or three short poems,[9] one or two satirical, but London is the devil of a place to write in.

Do not have anxiety about that Brussels Exhibition. Nothing would bring me there in the summer months, my best working time.

Do you remember that old astrologer[10] we paid in advance. Well, he has suddenly woke[n] up again after two years and sent me a small fragment of the work, unfortunately the fragment I least wanted, a rectification of my own horoscope. His letter is not as explicit as usual, but I judge that two years ago all his goods were seized by his landlady, including my letters and that he has only just got them back. Except for a passing wish that he were dead his letter is cheerful for him, and I think we may really get the work now. He is evidently quite honest.

Yours ever –
    W. B. Yeats

237   Les Mouettes
                                                 Colleville
                                                 par Vierville
                                                 Calvados
                                                 17 April [1910]

My dear Willie
    I have just returned from Laval where Iseult & I have been staying for a week with her Godmother.[1] Iseult has now gone with her Godmother to Tours for a fortnight.
    I found your letter & one from May waiting for me. She is coming on the 6th or 7th May, but if you find it more convenient to come sooner we shall be very happy to see you at any time that suits you – Find out at Cook's or at the Railway Station if the boats from Southampton to Cherbourg are running & which days, for that is much the cheapest & easiest way of getting here & you being a good sailor don't mind a 6 or 7 hour crossing. May generally comes that way & I think the boats may go three times a week – from Cherbourg you take the train to Le Molay Litry where I will meet you, for you have to change trains there & might get lost.
    I have so much to talk to you of, but as I hope to see you shortly & as I am alas, a very bad letter writer I will keep all news till we meet. It will be so nice seeing you.
    Alwys your friend
        Maud

While in Colleville Yeats was taken to see Mont Saint-Michel and wrote about it. He also wrote on Synge, who still preoccupied his mind. He revised old poems and wrote others with new perceptions of Maud Gonne which became part of 'Raymond Lully and his Wife Pernella':

> *Ah, but peace that comes at length*
> *Came when Time had touched her form.*

With the long summer days of sightseeing, and discussions old and new, the spiritual marriage seems to have faded back into the basic enduring friendship.

238

Les Mouettes
Colleville
par Vierville
Calvados
[7 July 1910]

Dear friend

Today only the 7th July your letter of the 2nd reached me. I was beginning to feel a little anxious even though I knew there was nothing wrong. It was written on the 2nd & the night of 2nd I sat for a long while looking at the sea & I felt our thoughts were very near together – I want so much to read your poem from the dream fragment.[1] Will you send it to me? or will you keep it to read to me? Saturday the 5th July I had a dream which seemed to me full of meaning, but waking I found I had forgotten most of it – I remember we were together – in some town I do not know, but which I think is in Ireland. We were engaged on some work which seemed of great importance & were filled with wild enthusiasm about it – I remember your sense of responsibility making you hesitate in the discussion of some detail, but I was quite reckless & happy as I knew the work was right – When I woke – I had forgotten what the work was though I remembered many details of the dream which I have written down – Why is it, I cannot remember, or get more clearly the work we have to do? I am angry with myself for not remembering.

I have been able to do very little occult work since you left – bringing the children to the sea & some dull & worrying business affairs have taken up a good deal of my time – I hope to work more now & shall come to you, which I have not done yet –

I am very glad you came

[End of letter missing]

239

May's hotel[1]
Ballycastle
Co. Mayo
[August 1910]

My dear Willie

I got your letter this morning. I have been meaning for days to write to you but in this place time passes so. It is so good to be back in Ireland that even the rainy weather does not depress me though Madame Dangien grows more & more desperate every day at the roughness of the hotel, the continual rain & the Eternal bogs. She can't see the beauty in them & to me they seem so extraordinarily lovely. Iseult does find them beautiful & she loves the peasants & as for Seagan he is quite happy riding a little turf donkey & learning Irish. Everyone here welcomes us, it is wonderful the memory they have, for it is 12 years since I was here but everywhere we go the people come out with a welcome & ask us to their houses & remember every little detail of my last visit. I think we shall stay here another week. I want to go up Nephin mountain & I want to go in a boat round to Belmullet & perhaps up to Sligo.

Mrs Meeking wrote asking me to lunch with her in London but she was leaving town that evening & I was leaving the next day. I was unfortunately engaged so we did not meet, better luck next time.

I am so glad the play is going on so well. I long to hear it – I like the few lines you quote immensely. We go back to France in September but I think I shall return alone to Ireland in November for a few weeks, as there are many people I want to see in Dublin & I have not time this visit –

Your brother & his wife[2] stayed here for two months last year & many of your sister's prints[3] adorn the hotel.

All good luck to the Player Queen & to the work –

Alwys your friend

Maud Gonne

I have your two books (manuscripts) & some collars and socks you left at Colleville. Shall I leave them in a parcel at the Nassau Hotel for you?

240   Paris
                                    Sunday [September 1910]

My dear Willie

A brother of your beautiful Indian Princess[1] is in Paris, & though I have only met him lately we have become great friends. He is very anxious to meet you & has read much of your poetry. I have been meeting a good many Indians lately & helping to work up a press campaign for Savakar,[2] to make the English respect the right of asile[3] in France.

Savakar is the Indian writer who was arrested in London & on his way to India managed to escape from the English ship at Marseilles. The English raised a cry of '*stop thief*' & a French policeman believing them arrested Savakar & handed him over by erreur to the English Captain. The French Govert has protested but in spite of their protest the trial of Savakar at Bombay has begun. So it is urgent to keep the facts well before the public in France so that the French government will insist in the treaty rights of France being respected

& Savakar handed over to the French. This has delayed our departure for Colleville but I hope to go there on Wednesday. I look forward to reading what you have written on Mont St Michel[4]

Poor old Mr Avril is dead & I have invited Madame Avril to come to Colleville with us.

Have the harvests been very much destroyed round the part of the country where you are & is it true that there will be serious want among the people this autumn?

I am so sorry to hear about your Uncle in Sligo[5] – The only time I met him he seemed to me quite interesting, perhaps from the many things you had told me of him.

It will be good seeing you in November.

Alwys your affecate friend
    Maud Gonne

241   Colleville
                                    29th October[1] [September 1910]

Dear Friend

I like the poems[2] so much, even more than when I first heard them, the slight alterations you have made are improvements I think – Iseult read them & is wild over the music of the rhythm in them. There is a danger of my growing very vain when I think of these beautiful things created for me – thank you –

Of all my work & all my effort little will remain because I worked on the ray of Hate, I think, & the Demons of hate which possessed me are not eternal – what you have written for me will live because our love has always been high & pure – You have loved generously and unselfishly as few men have loved – It is what remains to me out of the wreck of life, what I can take with me into the peace of the Sanctuary.

Tell me, are you quite sure that Pernella was the wife of Raymond Lully? My memory is so bad but I think Pernella was the name of the wife of Nicholas Flamel the Alchemiste[3] & two streets in Paris called one Nicholas Flamel & the other Pernelle named after them. I have no books here to look up, & can only do so when I go back to Paris on the *4th October.*

You are hard on poor Bow & Arrows![4]

I am longing to read what you have written on Mont St Michel. By the way did you call for your things – among others the bells from Mont St Michel, left for you at the Nassau Hotel.

I have been re reading the *Cathedral* by Huysmans,[5] which is all on Gothic Art & which I think you would like, what a pity you are not here for us to read it together.

Alwys your friend
    Maud

242   Paris
                                                  10th Oct [1910]
Dear friend

I have been looking up Raymund Lully in the French Encyclopedia
– he was a most interesting person, a catholic mystic who lived in
1235 – much more interesting than Nicholas Flamel the Alchemist
but there is no mention of his wife. He was a student of the Cabbala
& wrote a great number of philosophic & mystical books & had
wonderful ecstatic visions, he founded a convent at Majorca & finally
was stoned to death when a very old man by the muselmens who he
was trying to convert into Christianity.

Nicholas Flamel's wife was named Pernella – They lived in Paris
about two centuries later – & possessed great wealth which they made
some say by Alchemy & some say by usury but any how they used
it very generously and two streets in Paris are named after them –

Iseult & I go to Laval on the 14th for a week, I expect to cross to
England on the 27 & shall stay two or three days in London & come
to Dublin 1st November.

When will you be there?

I have lots I want to talk to you about

Your friend alwys
    Maud

243   13 Rue de Passy
                                                  Paris
                                                  18th Oct [1910]

My dear Willie

It is long since I have heard from you – I saw by the paper that
your uncle is dead & that you were at the funeral[1] – your last letter
said he was dying – so I was not surprised but a funeral is always a
terrible thing & must have been trying for you.

Here we are in the middle of strikes, dynamite bombs, & other
exciting incidents. Paris is somewhat too lively just now. One
always feels on a volcano & the combat of spiritual currents is rather
trying. I hope things will quieten down enough for me to feel I can
safely leave the children with Madam Dangien & come to Ireland
– I want to cross to England on the 27th & be in Dublin by the
1st Nov –

Enclosed is a poem by Delany which I like very much. Read it, it
is short & send it back if it does not bore you tell me what you think
of it – I think it is by far the best she has written. Iseult whose taste
in literature is really good has got most enthusiastic over it.

If you can think of any magazine where it would likely be taken
let me know –

I am looking forward to seeing you in Ireland, let me know your plans

I remain

Always your friend

    Maud

My old friend Canon Disard is very ill & wants to see me so I may have to go to Laval as soon as the trains will let me.[2] Did you get my letter about Pernella?

244
                          Laval
                         21st Oct [1910]

Dear friend

I shall only be in London 28th 29th & 30th. I must cross to Ireland on the 31st. It would be nice if we could travel together – I will be in Dublin about three weeks & a day or two in London on my return –

Kathleen, May & I will be staying at

    Queen's Gate Hotel

    Queen's Gate

    S.W.

Write to me there

In haste

Yours alwys

    Maud

245
                      Nassau Hotel
                      [Dublin]
                      Mercredi [November 1910]

My dear Willie

It is sad just to have missed you in this way, however I look forward to seeing you next week – Hope the lectures will be a great success, send me papers shall keep all news til we meet

By the way did you get a letter I wrote you to Coole enclosing a poem of Delany's? If you happen to have it, the poem I mean, send it to me here –

In haste

Alwys your friend

    Maud

—— *1911* ——

It was this winter that the work of providing school meals first got under way. Maud Gonne and Inghínide na hÉireann joined with new friends of the Women's Franchise League and her old allies James Connolly, with his trade union backing, and Father Kavanagh. It was in his school of St Audeon's that a pint of stew a day was first given to 250 children. The following year the number of children being fed doubled.

Yeats and Maud Gonne were not meeting as regularly as of old and somehow they seemed frequently to miss each other. She kept asking him to come and visit her in Paris, yet he went there with Lady Gregory in May while Maud Gonne was in Italy. Then he accompanied the Abbey players to America, returning after a short stay to look after the second company formed to carry on in Dublin. Lady Gregory and the Abbey continued the tour, the Playboy *causing more riots. A new manager, the playwright Lennox Robinson, took over at the end of the year, leaving Yeats freer of the theatre from then on. Yeats found much of his Dublin sociability in the United Arts Club, of which Mrs Duncan was the leading light.*

246
13 Rue de Passy
Paris
8 Feby [1911]

My dear Friend

What ages it is since I heard from you! Where are you? Are you in love? I think there must be something very interesting which keeps you from writing to me for so long. I hope you are not going to get married!

Well this letter besides to ask all those questions is to say that I am going to arrive in London on the 13th Feb next Monday & I shall only be staying two or three days on my way to Dublin – but I should very much like to see you. I am going to stay with my cousin Miss Gonne exactly where I don't know but please write to me

c/o Mrs Browning[1]
9 Cadogan Sq, S.W.

unless you have time to reply here.

I went to see some Irish members while in London to try & get the free feeding bill altered & extended to Ireland.[2]

Hoping to hear from you soon

I remain

Alwys your friend

Maud Gonne

247   [Paris]
                                                          [March 1911]
My dear Willie
    I can't help thinking Mrs Duncan is not going straight. She came
& asked me to join club[1] & *insisted* a great deal – I told her it wasn't
worth while as I was away so much. She spoke of *special* terms for
country members & finally said I shall put down your name. She
came back later when I was lunching with Madame de Markievicz[2]
& *asked her* to second me.
    Then she asked me to lunch a few days later which rather surprised
me but as she had promised to write an article on feeding school
children some time before I accepted. At that lunch Mrs Duncan
talked about the necessity for decorating the Club for the Royal
Visit[3] – She said her husband had spent sleepless nights over it,
shortly after her husband came in & I began to laugh at him over his
sleepless nights, he seemed surprised & as though he heard of the
whole question for the first time & Mrs Duncan hastily intervened –
I felt that Mrs Duncan was trying to sound me as to what I thought
would happen if they decorated & I of course tried my best to
frighten her & prophesied smashed glass – perhaps I am too
suspicious but I think Mrs Duncan may have proposed me knowing
there would be opposition & *asked* Madame de Markievicz to *second*
me thinking she would get angry & probably resign over this instead
of over loyal decorations & that she would be safely out of the Club
before July & the Royal visit.
    Perhaps I am suspicious, but that is how things seem to me.
Enclosed is a letter I have written which if you think well of it please
send to Madame de Markievicz to use as she thinks fit. (her new
address is
    15 Lr Mount Street,
    Dublin.)
Though the ground given for objection may not be political the
real ground is surely political. I have asked Madame de Markievicz
to write & tell *what* the ground of objection really is, because though
I divorced MacBride not one word in all the evidence brought was
against me.
    Thank you very much for writing to Mrs Duncan & to Madame
de Markievicz. I am so sorry to give you all this trouble.
    Alwys your friend
        Maud

248
Paris
21st March [1911]

My dear Willie

What a lot of letters this stupid affair is making us all write & we all so hate writing letters!

On receipt of your letter this morning I wrote the letter, the copy of which I enclose to Madame de Markievicz to be read or not as she thinks fit. I have not replied at all to Mrs Duncan as yet – It is too good of you taking so much trouble.

If you think the letter I sent you yesterday as a withdrawal better just send it to Madame de Markievicz saying you think it ought to be used. I told her I had written to consult you.

Yours alwys in gt haste
    Maud

249
[Paris]
[March 1911]

My dear Willie

That beautiful little ring arrived yesterday. It is quite the right size, thank you so much – I love it. The setting is quite beautiful –

Enclosed is a letter from Mrs Duncan which I received this morning. I shall not answer it till I get to Italy so *write* HERE to me to say what you think.

As I told you two days ago I got a letter from Madame de Markievicz saying that I must on *no* account withdraw if Mrs Duncan wrote & asked me to. Madame de Markievicz thinks it is Mrs Duncan's doing as she is intriguing for loyal decorations. I don't care a straw about belonging to the Arts Club & should never have consented if Mrs Duncan had not *insisted* a great deal.

Iseult wrote you a letter last week but forgot to post it setting out all the reasons which ought to bring you to Italy.

The Editor of *la Revue Poetique* who I met at the St Patrick's banquet again asked me if I would write a short account of you & your work & especially translate literally some of your poems which he would publish with the originals in English on the same page. (I told him to send you a copy of the review.) I said I would write this in Italy & I will send it you to read before it is published –

I have such a headache I can hardly see so must end now.

Alwys your friend
    Maud

250   Convent of San Carlo
                                                 Frascati
                                                 4th May [1911]

My dear Willie

I was surprised to hear you were in Paris.[1] I hope you are enjoying it as much as we are Italy.

The fascination of Rome is extraordinary. I wish you knew it – Frascati is a [village] in the hills just outside, with a tramway which makes going into Rome whenever we wish quite easy. It is a mountain village with a big Cathedral & old houses with wonderful gardens & fountains where the big Roman families come in Summer – Kathleen & I do a lot of paintings in these gardens & olive woods.

Last week we were received in private audience by the holy Father & admitted to receive Holy Communion from his hands, which is a great favor.[2] He was specially kind to little Seagan & gave him a medal with his portrait –

Alas we leave here tomorrow. We are sad to go, but there are so many places that we want to see that we *must*. We go to Tivoli, to Assisi, to Perugia & Sienna & Florence & Venice & Lugarno & will be back in Paris at the end of the month. Will you be there still? Write to me to Florence

    c/o Charles Eyre Esqre[3]

    Messrs French [?Leinan] & Co.

    Florence

I have not the exact address of where we will be staying.

How strange it seems to think of you in Paris just the time I am away! Are you learning French? I am glad Mr Hughes is there otherwise you would find it lonely – he must be glad too for he has such admiration & great friendship for you.

I have packing to do so must end

Hoping to find you still in Paris when we get there

Alwys your friend

    Maud

My kind regards to Lady Gregory.

We had a most exciting earthquake shock here the first week of our arrival. It did no harm beyond knocking down some ruins of Cicero's Villa but was quite a curious experience.

251

Colleville
par Vierville
Calvados
[June/July 1911]

My dear Willie

I am glad at least to know you are in the country during this great heat. It must be terrible in the town. By the sea we are enjoying it lazily.

But what I am not at all glad to learn from your letter is that you still seem to have all your time & thoughts taken up by business for the theatre. Really Willie you have no right to *waste* your time like that. There are a hundred of theatre managers & the coarser & rougher they are the better they succeed, but there are one or two poets at most in the world capable of producing literature that will live as a crown to their nation & you are one of these & it makes me quite wild to think you are going to America simply as advance agent to the Abbey Theatre Company.[1] You say you are going in August when the heat in America is so awful & everyone who can flies from the towns. What do you intend doing there? Business arrangements! Newspaper interviews! It is too hot for lectures – I think you have gone a little mad.

This is far worse than when you wanted to go into politics to help me, & you knew I always tried to prevent you doing that,

Don't think I under rate the value of your theatre but it is as NOTHING in comparison with your poems & while you are absorbed in the business management of the theatre you won't write a line of poetry. If you think over the things the only poetry you have written for several years since you became so absorbed in the business management of the theatre are the few lyric[s] you wrote while in France.[2]

Of course there is the verse of the Green Helmet – & the Player Queen which I haven't heard yet but as for the rewriting of your Abbey plays, you have not IMPROVED them at all & I hate to think of 'Countess Kathleen' being re-written[3] –

Now after all this long grumble written perhaps because I am tired having just walked from early mass in Colleville I must ask you not to be vexed at it.

May is leaving here on Monday, & Helen Laird & a young cousin whom you haven't met Michael Gonne[4] are coming, I expect Joseph Granié who has begun a beautiful painting of Iseult as the Angel of the Annunciation.

I am painting a good deal. I have one thing I am pleased with, a symbolic painting of the Sacred Heart which I saw in a vision.[5]

The postman is here & Brutus[6] is terrifying him & he won't wait. I must end.

Alwys dear Willie, your friend
Maud

252   Colleville
15th Sept [1911]

My dear Friend

I hope you had an enjoyable journey notwithstanding the heat & though I wish you hadn't gone to America I hope you will enjoy yourself & have a good time now you are there. Of course I am not angry with you. I only thought that a man like Rostand[1] who is not nearly such a great poet as you are wouldn't think of going touring with or for say Antoine's[2] Theatre Co. or any other theatre Co. who might be playing his pieces.

As the great poet of our nation if you lecture in America it should be on literature itself & its bearing on Ireland not on the theatre Co. which is but an incident, a beautiful incident, but still an incident –

It sounds so obvious & I am afraid to write it, but being as near things as you are to that theatre Co. makes one lose one's sense of proportion, it may not appear so to you – one of your beautiful poems enriches Ireland, indeed the world a hundred times more than the most successful theatre Co. that ever was organised & yet the Abbey theatre Co. has prevented you writing many beautiful poems, this thought has come to me out of my ill humour about your journey to America for the theatre, it may amuse you <to know> for its truth & strangeness.

Our children were your poems of which I was the Father sowing the unrest & storm which made them possible & you the mother who brought them forth in suffering & in the highest beauty & our children had wings –

You & Lady Gregory have a child also *the theatre company* & Lady Gregory is the Father who holds you to your duty of motherhood in true marriage style. That child requires much feeding & looking after. I am sometimes jealous for my children.

You will see your Father in America. Tell him to come home, that Dublin is lonely after him & is forgetting how to talk & be gay in his absence.

We return to Paris next week & I shall come to Dublin in the middle of October.

When do you return?

Write soon. Alwys your friend.
Maud

253

12 Milner Street
London
Saturday [?1911]

My dear Willie

I cross to Ireland on Monday and am staying with Ella Young, Temple Hill, Terenure.[1] Let me know if you are in Dublin. It will be nice seeing you.

In gt haste
Yours alwys
Maud Gonne

254

[Temple Hill]
Wednesday [?1911]

My dear Willie

I heard you were in town last Friday and wondered why you didn't write.

Yes I am free Friday evening. Come out here and have tea with me Friday afternoon. I want you to see my rooms here and then we will go into town and dine and go to the theatre together. This place is at the end of Terenure tram on the *Kimmage Road* about 4 minutes' walk from the tram.

In gt haste
Your friend,
Maud

255

[Temple Hill]
Saturday [?1911]

My dear Willie

I am not feeling very well today. I don't think I shall be able to come out this evening.

I generally go to 12 o'clock Mass at the Cathedral & will call & see what you are doing as I come back about 1.30. I suppose you are at the Nassau. Anyhow we will meet at the Cousins' tomorrow evening, so don't trouble to stay in if you have any thing else to do.

[?Meeting] last night was very interesting.

I am so sorry I can't come to the theatre tonight.

In haste
Yours always
Maud

256   Paris
                                                                                       Friday [?1911]
Friend of mine

I have been wanting to write to you continually for the last 4 days but travelling and many occupations and people prevented me.

I was sorry to see so little of you in Dublin and still more sorry because the last day you seemed depressed & gloomy. I hope the journey to Cork was good for [you] and that you had a great audience and came back feeling better.

I found people and things so interesting in Limerick that though I only spent 24 hours I came back refreshed.

Iseult & I returned here on Sunday – I am going to paint hard for the next few months – academy work in the morning and design work in the afternoon. I want to be able to draw all your Celtic symbols.

Let me know when you go to London and how long you are likely to stay there and if there is any chance of you coming for a little to Paris. I was so sorry not to have heard The Player Queen while I was in Dublin, I wanted so much to hear how much of it you had changed this summer.

Write soon and tell me that your cold is gone and that you are feeling more content with life. Do you remember it used to be you who used to tell me that life was good and worth living for *itself* apart from *causes*. Now I am fairly content and always interested but I still think that life without a cause to work for would be very dull and meaningless.

Write to me very soon.

Always your friend
        Maud

Sarah Purser is in Paris and lunches with me tomorrow.

1912

Freer from the theatre, Yeats began to lead a more varied and sociable life, which was in part to shape his future, for in 1911 he had met Georgie Hyde Lees, who was eventually to become his wife. His friendship with the American poet Ezra Pound grew, and he met and worked with the Indian poet Rabindranath Tagore before going to stay at Colleville in August. But the closeness of the relationship

seemed to be fading as their lives evolved separately. While in
Colleville he wrote:

> We sat as silent as a stone,
> We knew, though she'd not said a word,
> That even the best of love must die,
> And had been savagely undone
> Were it not that Love upon the cry
> Of a most ridiculous little bird
> Tore from the clouds his marvellous moon.

257
                                                        [13 Rue de Passy]
                                                        [Paris]
                                                        7th Jany 1912

My dear Friend

What will you think of me for not having written to you before
to thank you for that lovely book & the plays & for the picture of
St Michael & still more for your letters –

I have thought of you very often & have not written for two bad
reasons – 1st I have begun a series of pictures (illuminations) on the
meditations of St Bridget[1] which interest me so much & take up every
spare moment & thought –

Granié is nearly as excited about them as I am, for he says there is
something quite new & original about them & if only I can *execute*
them properly he thinks they will be wonderful but it is in the
finishing & executing where I fall so they won't probably be worth
anything in the end.

Granié calls *every* day to look at them.

The second reason is a worse one still. I am overwhelmed by
worries as the little house where I live in is to be torn down[2] & I
have to find another apartment & also get compensation for the
studio I built. This last part is very difficult – till the 15th Jany we
remain here after that our address will be

17 Rue de l'Annonciation 17.

Passy.

I have taken a little flat quite near here in the same house where
the Graniés are now living –

I would so like to have seen 'Countess Kathleen'[3] – it must have
been a beautiful performance from all I hear –

I expect it will often be played, so I hope I will have a chance of
seeing it next time I am in Ireland.

M. Piots,[4] an artist with a beautiful wife, who I think you met at
my house has just arranged the most wonderful scenery & dresses
for a Chinese play which has had a great success here at the Théatre

des Arts – I wish you could have seen it – It was most beautiful & weird. I have been twice & want to go again it is so lovely to look at especially the dances –

Your dream is very strange. I, once, a long time ago, thought of writing my life for you, but I can't express myself in writing & soon gave up – I am rather inarticulate as I expect you have discovered.

Iseult & I were both sorry you didn't come here for Xmas. It would have been nice seeing you –

M. Bourgeois[5] a young French man who was in Dublin & who has been writing on Bergsen[6] in the *Irish Review* is most interesting in all the literary & theatrical movement in Dublin. He has taken Synge as the subject of his agrégation[7] work. He is writing about him also I think for some French Review.

He asked me if I would ask you this question for him.

Had Synge been to the Arran Islands *before* he met you in Paris or was it you who first suggested him to go there?[8]

He says in some article, he thinks you said that it was you who advised him to go there, but in the same work of Synge's he thinks Synge speaks of having been there often & before he came in contact with your movement.

He attaches great importance to this, in studying the origin of Synge's inspiration – & of how far

[End of letter missing]

258   17 Rue de l'Annonciation
                                                Passy
                                                Saturday [January 1912]

My dear Willie

Thank you for your letter & for the beautiful poem[1] – I like it very much.

What a quite absurd thing arresting the players in Philadelphia.[2] How has it ended? Cannot they seek compensation for illegal arrest. I suppose they get compensation by extra full houses from the advertisement –

I have been so busy changing houses. It is terrible the amount of papers that have to be destroyed & of accumulated rubbish which has to be got rid of when one moves from one house to another. We had been in 13 Rue de Passy nearly 9 years.

This apartment is comfortable & modern & in a quiet street just opposite the Passy Church. It has electricity, central heating & a bathroom, lifts etc. but I miss my big studio – however I believe I shall get a small one on the top floor of this house soon –

My cousins May & Chotie arrive tomorrow. They have taken a tiny furnished *apartment* consisting of two rooms & a bathroom in this house for a month – it only costs under £10 – it might suit you well if you come to Paris sometime, for it is very quiet & comfortable.

My little Jean is making alarming progress at school I do all I can to inculcate idleness & have prevented the master putting him in a higher class than his age warrants. At his age Iseult was just the same, & it nearly resulted in meningitis, now alas she is idle enough & I complain so one is never satisfied.

Write soon
Alwys your friend
      Maud

259   17 Rue de l'Annonciation
                                           Paris
                                           Thursday [January 1912]

My dear Willie
Thank you so much for your letters & the new edition of *John Bull's Other Island*[1]

I am in great trouble & anxiety, little Seagan is ill & the doctors fear appendicitis which could mean perhaps an operation.

There is to be a consultation of Doctors on Monday. You know what all this means to me & you will forgive me if I don't write more.

It will be very good to see you if you come to Paris to meet Craig,[2] when all this horrible anxiety is over –

Alwys your friend
      Maud

260   17 Rue de l'Annonciation
                                           Passy
                                           Paris
                                           Good Friday [March 1912]

My dear Willie
forgive me not writing all this time. I only got home last Sunday, at the hospital, with all the nursing I had no time for letters – I was worn out & had to go to bed for three days as soon as I got home.

Little Seagan is going on all well now. He gets up every day & I think will be stronger than before at least the Doctors say he will be – but for the next month he requires constant care & watching to prevent him moving about too much so I shall not be able to leave him just yet – In almost three weeks we shall go to Colleville. You will be very busy I am sure with the return of the Abbey Company from America. Lady Gregory has succeeded wonderfully thanks to her courage & energy.[1]

I am so glad to hear you think Helen Moloney has the makings of an actress. If she gets interested, as I think she will, in her work on the stage, I shall be very glad, for I was rather unhappy about her. She was not fitted for the life she was leading & was getting wretched & unsettled – She has great power of throwing herself completely into different parts which should make her very useful, she is also, which is very rare in characters of her type, without jealousy & has a great power of working with others.

Of course though if she stays with you she must get enough to live on, for though she has simple tastes & no exaggerated idea of life, & cares little for money, she can't live on air & she is being constantly urged by her family who are in America to go out to them.

What of your writing? When are you going to get time for that?

I was painting a lot with Granié before Bichon got ill, & hope to again now – but I am not very strong. I had to see a doctor last week & he talked rather seriously but I have never worried over what doctors say, and I am sure that now my anxiety for Bichon is over I will get alright.

Iseult is going to Italy with May for a month when I go to Colleville – I envy her, don't you?

With all good wishes for Easter & thanking you so much for your kind sympathy & letters

 Alwys your friend
  Maud

261   [Colleville]
                 9th June [1912]

My dear Willie

Your account of the seance[1] is very interesting – I cannot however connect it with any special thought of mine at that exact hour – As far as I can remember I was painting some illuminated pictures on the Meditation of St Bridget, at 5 o'clock on the 4th June, but I think it must have been on the night of the 5 or 6th that I dreamed of you very vividly. It was a strange dream – you looked very young, we were engaged, people were congratulating us, everything seemed very happy, only all the time I had a sort of knowledge that it was not real & in my dream I said to my cousin May 'Of course this is not real it is impossible for us ever to marry' – & yet all the time we were engaged –

I have not been able to get anything with the violets as yet, partly I think because I am not at all well just now – I shall try again later –

I look forward to seeing the whole accounts of the seances –

I wish you could come & stay here a little this summer. It would be so nice seeing you –

Seagan is quite well again & looking stronger than before his illness – Iseult is more beautiful than ever –

I wrote to Miss Tobin,[2] I am so sorry she is ill, she wrote me a charming letter in answer but said little about her health.

I told M. [?Pelletier] secretary of the Celtic League of France to send you a copy of a revue called *la Poetique*, which is now going to become the organ of the Celtic League – in this no there is a translation of the *Triades of the Druid* which I find very interesting.

I think M. [?Pelletier] may be able to make a big movement in France.

M. de St Chamorand Editor of La Poetique is always asking me for translations of some of your poems or an article on you & your work.

I must end as the postman's visit is announced by the barking of the dogs –

Alwys your friend
Maud

262
Colleville
29th Juin [1912]

My dear Willie

I got your letter on my return here yesterday –

I had been to Paris to consult a Doctor for I was feeling rather ill.

I couldn't make out quite what he thinks, he said there was nothing serious, but ordered a course of *over feeding* which would make anyone ill. I shall only carry it out in a VERY modified way – as I do want to get strong – it is wretched not feeling strong enough for work or even for concentrated thought.

I don't really think there is anything very seriously wrong so don't worry about me –

Seagan's illness was a great strain on my nerves I am paying for it now –

I hope your new arrangement about the theatre will prove satisfactory & that the material & business worries will be off your hands for really you *must* put your own work first. I am very glad they are having such success in London.

Did you see Digges & his wife they came here to see me & crossed by Cherbourg to London. They are getting on splendidly in America & making piles of money – I am very glad, for it hasn't spoilt them a bit –

I will write you a better letter in a day or two. It is just possible I may have to come to London in a week for a few days to try & get [indecipherable] M.P.s to do something about feeding school children.

I will let you know.
Alwys dear Willie
Your friend
        Maud

How interesting those Seances must be! I want to read all your account of them.

263   [Colleville]
                                                    29th August [1912]
My dear Willie
    What has happened? I am getting weary at getting no news from you – I hope it only means that you have been very busy & interested in life, but please find time to send me a few lines.
    I have still the house full of people & have to do *Chaperone*, it wastes a lot of time.
    We go to Paris on the 15th Sept & I shall be in Ireland by the 25th. Have you written to May?
    In gt haste
    affectly yours
        Maud

264   Colleville
                                                    par Vierville
                                                    Sunday 1 Sept [1912]
My dear Willie
    I was so pleased to get your letter, I was worrying about you, thinking you were ill – I have finished *la messagère de la Celtique* & will bring it to Ireland when I come. I have also finished a design for your bookmark – it is full of symbols. It has the Trinity & the Sophia & the 4 talisman[s][1] & Celtic ornament & of course the SHAMROCK, you can't escape that!
    Mr Malya[2] stayed a fortnight & M. [Pelletier] only left us yesterday. While here M. [Pelletier] wrote a really remarkable essay on *Race & Patrie* based on the occult theory of the Restrictive & the Expansive forces & some verses to Iseult which are rather good. He has a lot of talent. The thunderclap of Iseult's growing up has not come yet – she is at present enjoying herself wildly playing hide & seek with Bichon & young Michael Gonne –
    I hope to see you in Dublin where I shall be from about the 25th Sept to 24th Oct looking after baby feeding. I am afraid this winter

is going to be a hideous one for the poor, I am dreading it. In France where the poor are comparatively rich the prospects are gloomy owing to the ruined crops, but in Ireland things must be *far* worse. –

Is there solid foundation for this article of Griffith's[3] which I enclose? It is certainly alarming –

I do hope you will be able to go to May in Florence – Hoping you are feeling quite well & strong again

[End of letter missing]

265   [Paris]
                                                            [?1912]

Dearest

I must send you on this letter I have just received from an Irish American. I had lent him your 'Poems 1899–1905' for though you must be used to getting many letters of this kind yet I think it must be always good to feel your art can give such pleasure.

M. Malya was here yesterday & I lent him a good many of your books, (not the new ones) for his thesis as he was obliged within 10 days to give an outline of it to his professor. He said the library, I think of the Sorbonne, have promised to order your works, but he hadn't the time to wait for that.

I am going this afternoon with Iseult to the matinée at the Odeon to see [?Cisina]. Are you back in Dublin yet?

Yours alwys with love
    Maud

266   [Letterhead]
                                           Hôtel de Belle-Vue et de Flandre
                                           Bruxelles
                                           [November 1912]

My dear Willie

I got your letter just as I was starting for Brussells where I have come to study the way school canteen[s] or as they call them here *Les Soupes Communales* are arranged. Last year, when I wrote I talked about the French *Cantine Scholaire* I was told by some pious adversaries that we in Ireland should not copy in any way Atheist France, so this year I want to quote for their edification Catholic Belgium –

I am going to visit the schools & see various officials tomorrow & on Friday I go to my sister 12 Milner Street & on Monday or perhaps Sunday night I hope to be in Dublin.

It will be nice seeing you there is so much I want to talk to you about. I am bringing your picture & also the design for the embroidery.

You have done a lot of work this summer good for you & good for Ireland.

I on the contrary have been rather lazy but am going to work in earnest now.

Iseult & Bichon are already with May in Florence. It will be sad if you cannot manage to come. I have been looking forward to visiting those wonderful galleries with you –

Mr Quinn has been in Paris for a few days only, on business & had to return to America without visiting Ireland, he bought a pencil drawing Granié had made of Iseult's head – a study for the Angel of Annunciation & also a reproduction of a drawing of Granié's which is in the Lyons Museum of the portrait of a Roman Rollier[1]

Iseult will be delighted to hear about Tagore,[2] & to get the beautiful book you have for her. How kind of you thinking of her – She has been breaking several hearts lately! but I hope her own is quite untouched as yet.

I must end
In haste
Alwys your friend
    Maud

267   Temple Hill
                                                 Terenure
                                                 Monday [?1912]

My dear Willie
    I just got this through dead letter office.
    The more I look at Tagore's book the more I like those illustrations.[1] He is a great artist for illustration. Iseult will love it.
    I am very busy, baby feeding is more difficult and more necessary this year as prices of potatoes & food generally have doubled.
    Here is rather a curious thing which I think may interest you in your psychical research. It is very well authenticated. A friend of mine & a mystic, Miss Fox,[2] used to live in a little cottage out of Dundrum near the hills, it was lonely & she was very nervous, she had the habit every night of going through certain protective ceremonies and formulas among them, she used to invoke & imagine a ring of white fire round her cottage through which no evil thing should pass. Some months ago she gave up this cottage and came to live in town. The cottage was left to a man she did not know and whom she had never seen. He only remained there a short time and left because he declared the place was haunted for he saw white fire round the house. Miss Williams who lived near there knew the man & told Miss Fox about this & asked her if she had ever seen anything.

I haven't time to write more now.
Yours always
    Maud

Don't forget to go to see Kathleen. 12 Milner St, Cadogan Square.

268
                         [Letterhead]
                         Great Eastern Railway
                         Harwich Route to the Continent
                         On Board S.S. 'Brussels'
                         Sunday 17th Nov.

My dear Willie
  This is too disappointing missing you everywhere.
  When I got your letter saying you were staying in London longer than you expected because you were not well, I hurried up my affairs, I telegraphed you I was crossing & telegraphed to Kathleen to ask you to dinner – When she told me she had received no answer I was afraid you were really ill & I went to your house where they told me you had crossed to Ireland on *Monday* – the day I got your letter saying you were staying in London! – Then Kathleen got your letter from Coole
  I hope you are better now.
  I am on my way to Italy, I suppose there is little hope of seeing you there as Lady Gregory & the theatre will not allow.
  Write to me
    Villa Castiglione
    Via Montughi
    Florence
& tell me how you are –
  The boat is just stopping & I must look after my luggage so goodbye for the present.
  Alwys your friend
    Maud Gonne

Postmark: Bruxelles 17–XI–12.

269
                         Villa Castiglione
                         Via Montughi
                         Florence
                         28 Nov. [1912]

My dear Willie
  It was very disappointing missing you in Dublin & in London –
  This is a wonderfully beautiful place – on a hill with olive groves

all round & beautiful views of Florence & of the mountains. It is an old Italian house with marble floors & great high rooms such as you love – The weather is rather cold but very bright & sunny.

It is sad you will not be able to come. We were all looking forward to having you – however it will be for some other time I hope –

Iseult is so pleased with the Indian book she will write to you about it. She & Bichon are both so well & so happy here.

I don't understand your dream very well.

You remember you were to have come up to tea at Temple Hill with Lucy Middleton[1] to investigate the ghost – you were ill in London & didn't come but a strange thing happened.

We were all sitting round waiting for the ghost, when you came in & sat down between me & Lucy Middleton & took my hand. Lucy turned to us asked if we had seen anything, I said – I think Willie has just come in – I expect he has just remembered his engagement & is thinking of us. 'Yes' said Lucy 'I see him he is sitting between us, I wondered if you saw him too.'

I did *not* see you with my *physical* eyes but I felt you were there & we talked together –

The rest of the seance was not very interesting, Lucy has a melodramatic mind & sees tragedies & I think sometimes suggests these tragedies to the ghost. I saw what she saw but I knew it was all from her mind – It is too long to write the description.

I hope you are feeling better. I am so sorry your eyes have been bad again. Write soon.

Alwys your friend
Maud Gonne

1913

The political atmosphere in Ireland was becoming increasingly tense. As the Home Rule Bill was about to be enacted, opposition from the Orangemen in the North was mobilised with the formation in January of the Ulster Volunteer Force, which was countered in the South by the formation of the National Volunteers in November to protect the rule of law.

In Dublin, from August onwards, there was a general strike and lock-out which lasted nearly a year and increased the already dreadful hardship of the poor in the city. Countess Markiewicz organised soup kitchens to feed the starving. There was civil unrest and strife, and James Connolly formed the Irish Citizen Army to enable the people to defend themselves against the police.

Late in September Yeats went to live in Stone Cottage, Coleman's Hatch, in Sussex, with Ezra Pound as his secretary. He was becoming increasingly interested in psychic research.

270

> Villa Castiglione
> Florence
> 4 Jan [1913]

My dear Willie

Thank you so much for that lovely book of Tagore's.[1] How I sympathise with your difficulty in making up parcels, it has often prevented me sending presents – In civilised countries like Italy at the big post office there is a special office where a man does nothing else but make up parcels & weigh & stamp them. You bring what ever you want to send & the man supplies paper, string etc. It was the man in the Florence post office who made up the book parcel I sent you.

Why, oh why did you let the theatre interfere with your coming here! Since I got well we have been having a lovely time & seeing beautiful things every day, living amid beauty & tomorrow I & my babies are going to Ravenna & to Bologna & then back to Paris & you might have been travelling with us & seeing all those divine pictures with us. Oh that theatre!

Well I suppose half of it is in America & when Lady Gregory is away the other half leaves you a little freer.[2]

I am so sorry to hear you have been ill again – I tried the sour milk cure some years ago & didn't find it did either good or harm – but it sounds cold & uncomfortable in winter –

How did the Hour Glass[3] go in Dublin? Write me to Paris & say you are feeling better –

May the New Year bring you happiness & joy in your work & time to do your own work –

Always your friend
Maud

271

> 17 Rue de l'Annonciation
> Passy
> Paris
> Sunday [February 1913]

My dear Willie

At last I am allowed to sit up & write a little so can answer your letter – I have been *very* ill for the last three weeks, I had a cold which got better & worse but never went away since the beginning of December, then my little boy got measles & of course I nursed him, he was almost well & able to get up when suddenly I got very bad congestion of the lungs & such high fever that for about three days it was doubtful which way things would go. I don't think I ever felt quite so near death & for myself I didn't care, but I had a terror of what would happen to the children as of course MacBride would make a fight to get Bichon on account of the money – for three days I was in a sort of torpor, conscious but not wanting to speak for fear of delirium – then gradually the fever went down & I was able to breathe easier – I had a nun to nurse me who was a great comfort, she is with me still, she is a splendid nurse but a dragon in the way of not allowing me to do anything or talk much or receive visitors.

Poor Bichon got a relapse & the nun is nursing him too now, but we are both going on well & there is no more excitement & I expect we shall both be allowed out at the end of the week. Poor Iseult has had a hard dull time –

What a dull selfish letter I am writing. I met Mabel Beardsley[1] twice or three times in London over at my cousin's studio & we liked each other very much & we wanted to meet oftener, but I am never in London – I am so sorry to hear she is so ill – she is most charming – I hope she doesn't suffer great pain, the doctors ought to be able to prevent that at any rate but what powerless useless creatures doctors are – I often wonder why I ever send for them.

Send me copies of your poems[2] to read

Iseult sends you messages & wonders if you got a letter she wrote you when I was so ill

Alwys your friend
Maud Gonne

272   17 Rue de l'Annonciation
                                             Passy
                                             Easter [March 1913]

My dear Willie

I have been meaning to write & thank you for your letters, but when one is so weak days pass by & one only *thinks* of doing things & doesn't do them.

I am well again, that is I don't cough any more & I am beginning to be able to go up & down stairs & take walks – I even presided at the annual St Patrick's Day banquet on the 17th & made a speech –

I have got so thin, you would be quite envious – I think I am as thin as I have ever been.

How interesting about Gordon Craig & the new theatre[1] – Though Florence is quite a charming place I rather wonder why he chose it as the centre for his theatre, for it seems a little out of the world. Rome has drawn much of the old Italian society from it – In this respect it seems to have changed a good deal since I was there as a girl, but it is a place full of beauty & fascination & ANCIENT art, for of *modern* there is none in Italy –

I do hope he will stage some of your plays, it would be so wonderful to see them really well done –

Isadora Duncan is starting a new Art theatre in Paris she wants music & poetry & dancing to complete each other instead of jealously ignoring or injuring each other. She thinks this can be done by following the example of the Greek chorus.

Iseult & I are going to see her dance at the Trocadero next Tuesday. She is giving a performance with [?Manet] Sully. Her own theatre is not built yet –

Have your players returned from America yet? What success have they had? I am so glad you are getting on so well with French. Iseult & I & Bichon will all talk to you in French next time you come here. We hardly ever speak any other language except before the servants –

We may be going for a week or ten days for a change of air to the Forest of Fontainebleau. We should be there now but for a sudden return of cold weather –

Kathleen & Thora[2] are coming here beginning of April for a month. They are staying with May in Florence at present –

Yours alwys
Maud Gonne

273

Hotel St Joseph
Samois
Seine et Marne
[March 1913]

My dear Willie

I think our letters must have crossed. I received yours yesterday just as I was leaving Paris for Fontainebleau where we spent three very interesting days visiting the chateau which is full of wonderful tapestries & furniture & art treasures.

Georges d'Esparbes[1] an old Friend of mine who I think you met when he was in Ireland in 1897 is Governor of the Chateau.

We came on here today, but it is too rainy to thoroughly enjoy the forest & the country & I shall not be sorry to return to Paris next Tuesday.

I am much better but I don't think I shall be strong enough for anything like a walking tour for some time yet –

It will be nice seeing you in Paris.

Kathleen & Thora are coming next week & will stay till the 1st of May.

I am so glad your lectures were such a success. I wish I had been in Dublin to have heard them.

We went to see Isadora Duncan dance.

She was as charming as ever in her old dances but not nearly so good in her more ambitious attempts to interpret by dancing Gluck's Orphée[2] – She attracted immense audiences. She will probably get her theatre for they say she is the bonne amie of the millionaire Singer of sewing machine fame[3]

In haste

Alwys your friend

Maud Gonne

Write to *Paris*

George Russell wrote to John Hughes, the sculptor, in Paris on 15 April: 'This is to introduce to you a dear friend of mine James Stephens. . . . He is the last and the best of the numerous band of poets and storytellers Ireland has been blessed with since our time.'

274   [Paris]
                                          [April 1913]

My dear Willie

It was a great disappointment to me & to Iseult to hear that you had changed your plans & would not have time to come to Paris – Paris is so charming just now with the salons open & the trees in leaf.

Mademoiselle Claire de Pratz[1] has asked me for an introduction to you for a friend of hers Mademoiselle Mispoulet who has taken all sorts of scholarships here & has now got some sort of university mission to write on Irish folklore – she came to see me yesterday & seems quite nice so I gave her a card for you –

I wish I could come over to Ireland, but I am not very strong yet & the Doctor forbids me doing anything tiring. Indeed I find chaperoning Iseult to be very tiring & I have to do a good deal of that here – but in Ireland I am always caught in a rush of work which I have neither the will or the courage to refuse – so I shall have to remain here for the present.

I have just begun painting again – I work a good deal with Granié. I would so like to see Tagore's play[2] – I have read his poems over & over, they are wonderful. Have you settled anything with Gordon Craig about the production of your plays? Will it be in his theatre in Florence?

I was at tea yesterday at the studio of rather an interesting artist Cohen, he had yours & Dunsany's books[3] & wants to meet you very much.

I hear Stephens[4] is coming to stay in Paris for a year.

Have you decided about the professorship,[5] I understand that you hesitate, but I think you should take it though I wish it had been in the other University. You would have made things LIVE there & it would have been so interesting. I think you should take this. You are strong enough not to let yourself get overwhelmed [by] the dull & sleepy side of scholarship & you could do so much for thought in Ireland, without I think, injuring your own power of work which is of course the 1st importance both to you & to Ireland.

I think I know what you mean by the period of *mental stocktaking* you have been through – I have been through it several years ago, for me, it was not pleasant so many things seemed fallen, so many toys broken but about that time I found a spiritual peace which made the broken toys & the fallen idols seem insignificant. In that peace I found I had not changed the ideals of my young days: only I saw that most of the efforts I had made to realise them had been mere playing with sand.

I must end this long letter or you will be tired of it – now that you do so little occult work I never know at a distance as I used to what you are thinking or what will interest or bore you – You did not even know when I was almost dying, & for three days nearly unconscious & when I wrote to you the words didn't convey anything to you. I think you were astonished yourself they did not.

It is not I think that you had ceased to like me but because a mood you were in wrapped you round completely.

You were perhaps trying to write a poem that was hard to find.

Kathleen has been staying with me for a month. She is in London now 12 Milner Street & would I know like to see you

Alwys your friend
Maud Gonne

275   17 Rue de l'Annonciation
                                             Passy
                                             Paris
                                             8 May [1913]
Willie dear

Thank you so much for your interesting long letter. I am so sorry theatre affairs are still so worrying & so absorbing. I was hoping you would be free to go on with your own work & that possibly you would have had time to come & see me in France.

I am feeling better though I still look thin & 'hungry' as Iseult says.

Bichon is looking much better than before his illness & I am no longer worried about him.

Iseult gets back from Italy on the 15th & on the 17th we will all go to Colleville. Will you be able to come & see me there this summer?

I am very much interested in a Celtic Movement which is starting in France. It is to be much wider than the Breton movement. Its object is to claim all in art, literature which belongs to the Celts, & show how all the art of the middle ages, of the wonderful 13th century is Celtic, & to remind the French people of their Celtic origins & to teach them to seek inspiration for their present work from the Celtic tradition.

It is much what we have tried to do in Ireland & I think it is the beginning of a big movement here.

I would like to see your rooms I am sure you must have made them beautiful for you have the art of making beauty, but you are thinking dangerously much about a wife, think how she would disarrange your things! Matrimony I think requires great space either a castle & vast rooms or a cottage where one only enters to sleep & all the wide world outside.

M. de St Chamarond editor of the Revue La Poetique, rather an interesting little literary review asked me to translate one or two of your poems in French. He wants to publish an article on you he would publish the English original & the translation side by side. I asked you once before about this & you said you had no objection, but I just mention it again in case there is anything in particular you would like said or any particular poem you wish cited.

I saw the McGregors the other day. He has a sprained ankle. She is doing some really beautiful drawings. They say order work keeps them very busy & that it is going on very well.

Are you doing any occult work? I am longing to have a talk with you & hear all the new theories you have been evolving. I don't share your desire for proof, not having perhaps a scientific or analytical mind & also because faith is such a real force & the exercise of it so useful.

I have a lot of ideas for painting which I am going to carry out at Colleville, it is so difficult to find time in Paris.

Write soon
Alwys your friend
Maud

276

[Paris]
Thursday [?June 1913]

My dear Willie

I have written to Mr Rummel to come to tea with me Sunday. I am grateful to him as he was the cause of your writing & I was anxious at your silence – Your letter still leaves me anxious & I prayed hard at mass for you this morning.[1]

I wish I coud be of any help to you.

About 4 years ago a Clairvoyant in the group with whom I am working in Ireland told me that a terrible crisis was soon coming which would shake your life to its foundations. She said you had brought it on yourself by forsaking old ideals & giving up spiritual life.

I asked her if it could be averted. She said she thought not, but that you would come out of it safely & do greater work than ever.

I asked if I could warn you. She said it would be useless, but to keep close to you, as I would be able to help you & you would need the help & spiritual strength of your friends. She seemed to think the trouble was very near & shortly after you were ill & worried & I asked her if it was this she had foreseen. She said *no* and didn't think it was to do with physical health.

I never spoke of this to you, as I never could get anything more precise or definite & as time went on & all was well with you I ceased to think of it.

I only mention it now because she said she was certain you would come safely through & gain spiritual strength & do great work after.

This is June, the month which the Catholic Church consecrates to the Sacred Heart, Divine Love which gives Divine Wisdom, to know how to love & make our love Divine.

Dearest write to me when you can, for I get very anxious when I don't hear from you.

Bichon has been ill again but is better. I am taking him down to Colleville next week where I am going to leave him with Miss Delaney in charge as the Doctor says I must not stay long at the sea.

Alwys your friend
Maud Gonne

277

Hotel des Baignots
Dax
Landes
[1913]

My dear Friend

As probably you have found out by now Iseult is no longer staying at Alexandra Court but has gone to Kathleen's, 12 Milner Street.

I am glad you are going to see her & take her to meet Tagore. It will do her good. I got to know in Paris Diva Brat Mukerjea[1] who translated the *Post Office*. We like him so much. There is great charm about many of the Hindous, they are so refined in thought & understand shades of thought & expression with wonderful delicacy. I took him to hear Mr Rummel's music,[2] I think he liked it but I had no opportunity of talking to him alone after as I left Paris the following day.

As I wrote you I was *very* ill this winter, for several days the doctor thought I would hardly recover, then I got well up to a certain point, but remained very weak & my nerves all to pieces. Rheumatism came as a result of this weakness & I could only walk & go about with great effort so the doctor advised me to come here for a month & to take the baths which are good for rheumatism & tonic as well

My general health is *much better*, chiefly I think owing to the rest & real quiet & the rheumatism I hope will go when I have finished the 21 baths. I am at my 12th now – I know nobody here & spend my time quite alone, & rather enjoy it. I paint a little chiefly illuminations. Last week I was the edification of the hotel for on the rare occasions

[End of letter missing]

WBY 6

18 Woburn Buildings
Upper Woburn Place
W.C.
Sunday [?July 1913]

My Dear Friend

When I got your card I asked a friend to look up the place where you are too see if I could get there but it seems [it] is a far long expensive journey off & I should never get through for all my Berlitz lessons. My period of trouble is over[1] – I was given a piece of false information that had an overwhelming effect on me & this trouble has gone side by side with the most irrefutable evidence of the survival of the soul & the power of the soul. Various spirits have come to a friend of mine & written their names & dates etc through her hand.[2] I have verified fact after fact – the last through nine lines in the *Times* of seventy years ago.[3] No thought reading theory can cover the facts – proof is overwhelming. In addition to this, this girl who only knows English and a little French and a few words of Italian, has written Hebrew, Greek, Latin, Provencal, Arabic, Chinese, Welsh, Irish, Latin, German. No telepathic theory covers this either for in numerous cases these languages contain sentences which refer to conversations & questions of the moment. On Thursday last for instance I quoted something from the second part of *Faust* & a few minutes later a question in German from another part of the same scene was given & signed by the name of a German poetess whom I have found in a [?biographical] dictionary. The spirits have admitted myself, & a friend to a series of experiments on the condition that we make nothing public. I am putting everything aside for this one study, as far as possible. My dear, you wronged me & vexed me by a letter you wrote some time ago in which you spoke as if phisical love 'was the one thing[']] I required of a woman. This is not true. My gloom this week was from lonliness. Mrs Emery is in Ceylon,[4] Miss Horniman & I have quarrelled. There was not a soul I could go to after nightfall & in the winter it is dark at four & after that I cannot use my sight except a very little. I should neither read nor go to the theatre which makes my eyes smart next day (here where stages are very brightly lit). The alternative is to dine out and last week I was ill – could not & even when I am well dining out every night leaves me worn out with nerves upset. A mistress cannot give one a home & a home I shall never have; but now that it is summer and I can work till late I do not mind. I am in spirits again. I shall call on Iseult today some time, but I want first to see Tagore. I want Iseult to meet him & hope to arrange for it here. Tell me how you are my dear. Tell me what it is that is wrong. In a strange way this spirit evidence has bound me near to you – for all things become so much more important. One day we got this message 'I have lost her. I have lost her. Tell her. Tell her. Sister Mary Ellen tell Sister Mary Aloysius. Tell her I have lost her. We were with Florence Nightingale.'[5] I believe I have found Mary Aloysius but am not sure. They are Irish I think dead & one is looking [?] for the others the controlls promise [?] to bring them together. It changes life to believe all the new intimate knowledge, not theoretical merely, that love & friendship last beyond the grave.

Yours ever

W B Yeats

278 Argeles

7th August [1913]

My dear Friend

Are you making up your mind to travel out here with Iseult & Seagan? If so let me know at once so I can find a room for you. I have taken two big bare but very clean rooms for us in a peasant's house on the edge of a mountain torrent at Arrens.[1] It is very wild & beautiful. We shall get our meals at the Inn – It is very cheap – 5 francs a day for board & 1.50 for a room but there are not many rooms to be had. Granié has just telegraphed me that he is coming –

Iseult says she spent a wonderful evening with Tagore.[2]

I am so glad you have introduced her to him. It does one good to meet such a man.

In haste
Always your friend
Maud Gonne

Address letter or telegram
Arrens,
par Aucun
Haute Pyrénées

279   [Arrens]
                                    5th September [1913]

My dear Willie

I was very disappointed you could not join me here. It is one of the most charming places I know, like Switzerland in the mountain scenery but with a charm which Switzerland has not. The people remind me of our peasants at their best they are dignified & very courteous & hospitable & they have a real artistic sense. The women drape themselves in the most beautiful black cloaks on Sundays the folds make me quite envious, & their houses are beautiful in their comfortable simplicity & nearly all have wood carvings on their doors or interesting chiselled bronze knockers. It is quite out of the way of tourists. We have two large white washed rooms with raftered ceilings a big chimney corner in a farm house. Life is quite beautiful & very inexpensive which is also a consideration for 4 francs a day one has everything one wants. We shall certainly return here next year – I came here feeling still very weak & unable to do much, but I have got quite strong & am able to take long walks. Iseult & Jean are also very well & happy – We join the Irish National Pilgrimage at Lourdes on the 12th & we shall be in Paris about the 20th Sept.

I am coming to Ireland in October. Where shall you be then? I think Iseult will be with me. Thank you so much for introducing her to Tagore –

I think Lane is behaving *very disgracefully* about the picture collection.[1] I don't see that the Dublin Corporation can do more than they have done. Lane has got his knighthood by pretending to give the pictures, now he is taking them back, probably to get some other advantage elsewhere – it is almost a swindle & I hope he will be made to feel it, by those whose society he desires – He seems to me to be violating every rule of honor, he is acting as after all one expects a jew picture dealer to do – he has lived & made his money in that world, so I suppose he has adopted their habits of mind & conduct.

The removal of the French picture[s] I regret, but I am delighted that Dublin will not be inflicted by the vulgarity of modern Italian art as shown by the Mancinis.[2] Lane will find those a white elephant anywhere –

I am longing to have a talk with you about your spirit experiences, they are most interesting. I want to hear what theory you are developing from them. Have you spoken of them to Tagore? It would be interesting to hear what he thinks.

Hoping to see you soon.

Always your friend

Maud Gonne

280   [France]
                                                                              [Autumn 1913]

[Beginning of letter missing]

money is needed for starving children. It is horrible to think of the misery & hunger in Dublin. Iseult & I are coming over to do what little we can to help the people – We start on Friday & I hope to be in Dublin by Sunday *Temple Hill Terenure* will be my address but I suppose your dislike of Rathmines extends to Terenure & to the streets of Dublin,[1] so I shall probably not see you & shall only hear later on of your spiritualist researches.

We have had a most interesting time at Alzonne, a small French town where half the inhabitants have seen since June last, visions of Jeanne d'Arc, of the Blessed Virgin & some have been able to take down long inscriptions in latin which they see on scrolls in the sky, though they are of course ignorant of latin. Scholars who have seen these writings taken down by uneducated people say it is good latin, the latin of Cicero & not church latin. But one day many people at Alzonne, including the parish priest, saw the devil & since a terrible doubt exists, are the visions divine or diabolical. We stayed 2 days but saw nothing ourselves, but were present when others saw. Iseult has taken notes which will interest & may be useful to you.

Yours alwys,

Maud Gonne

On 6 October the Irish Times *published a letter from George Russell addressed 'To the Masters of Dublin':*

I address this warning to you, the aristocracy of industry in this city, because, like all aristocracies, you tend to grow blind on long authority, and to be unaware that you and your class and its every action are being considered and judged day by day by those who have power to shake or overturn the whole social order, and whose restlessness in poverty to-day is making our industrial civilization stir like a quaking bog. . . .

Even in the Dark Ages humanity could not endure the sight of such suffering, and it learnt of such misuse of power by slow degrees, through rumour, and when it was certain it razed its Bastilles to their foundations. It remained for the twentieth century and the capital city of Ireland to see an oligarchy of four hundred masters deciding openly upon starving one hundred thousand people, and refusing to consider any solution except that fixed by their pride.

281
Temple Hill
Terenure
Dublin
Sunday [November 1913]

My dear Willie

I got your letters in London but have been so rushed by our arrival here last Wednesday I have not had time to answer.

I have no French paper with the latin inscription but Madame Louis the miller's wife at Alzonne – who took down three latin inscriptions has promised to send me copies she made, but which she had lent to a priest. I have not received them yet. If I do not soon I will write to her.

When will you be in Dublin? When is your play coming on?[1] I hope we shall still be here for it Iseult wants to see one of your plays acted so much.

Dublin is very sad just now.[2] The misery is bad & is getting worse every day.

The employers who are trying to starve the transport union are criminals & like most criminals are stupid as well. They will certainly not succeed in starving the union men who are getting support from England, Scotland & Wales, but they will succeed in starving & I am afraid very soon the unorganised labor the men who belong to no union who never thought of striking but who owing to general stopping of trade & of the materials of production are idle & of course receiving no strike pay, their case is terrible.

I have sold my diamond necklace, it is the last jewel I have left to keep up & increase the numbers of dinners for the children. Iseult is helping us in this work, but it is very discouraging for one feels it is so very inadequate to the need of the situation,

Russell's letter caused a great sensation & I believe has upset many of the employers very much. They are getting ashamed of themselves & many of them are longing to get out of the false situation Murphy has placed them in.[3]

I haven't time to write more now. Let me know when you will be in Dublin.

In haste
Yours alwys
    Maud Gonne

Iseult sends messages.

282
                                  12 Milner St
                                  [London]
                      Wednesday [?November 1913]

My dear Willie

Thank you so much for your letter & invitation. I am so tired I don't think we can come to Coleman Hatch this time.[1] I hope to return to Ireland before long & will see you on the way. Perhaps you will be in London then.

Before leaving Dublin I & Helen Laird had a most interesting & satisfactory interview with Archbishop Walsh[2] about School Dinners & I think now we will soon be able to get the Free meals act altered & extended to Ireland –

Yesterday on the train from Holyhead to London we met a man called Swift. He took us for French women & talked French all the time we did not undeceive him. He said he had once travelled from London to Holyhead with you & the long journey had seemed to him hardly ½ hour in duration, he was so under the charm of your conversation. He had travelled much in Persia & was rather interesting.

I am very sorry not to see your cottage & not to make the acquaintance of Mr Pound.[3] I look forward to that later

Bon souvenir from Iseult
Alwys your friend
    Maud Gonne

283
                            17 Rue de l'Annonciation
                            Passy
                            Paris
                      Thursday [November 1913]

My dear Willie

It was sad not seeing you on your way through London but I was so tired I hadn't the courage between two long journeys to take a short one which would have meant a good deal of travelling with the return journey.

I found poor little Seagan in bed on my arrival here but he was so cheered up by my return that he is now up & about again.

I lectured before a rather a big & fashionable audience at the Parthenon & the lecture was such a success that I have been asked to repeat it at the Maison de Balzac next Sunday.[1] People take a great deal of interest in Irish affairs over here just now, & I have interviewers from the newspapers calling all the time.

I met Miss Dickinson in London & liked her very much. She has written me several letters about the strike & sent help for the children's dinners –

Pierce[2] of St Enda's College, is very anxious to go to lecture in America – He wants to lecture on Education, & on the heroic literature of Ireland, both of which subjects he would be very good on. He is a great Gaelic scholar & has translated many of the old texts himself. He is one of the finest orators I have heard but he is little known in America. Devoy[3] says the clan would support him but will not *run* his tour because they are *pledged* not to run anyone's lecture tours until the money for the Wolfe Tone Monument is collected. Do you think Pond[4] would take him up? Have you Pond's address? I think you said you were going to him.

I think Pierce would be a success & I am sure he would do good he has great nobleness in his way of speaking – I heard him speaking in the Rotunda at the Wolfe Tone Anniversary. He held that huge audience spellbound for nearly an hour – except Taylor[5] who was very very different, I don't think I ever heard anyone speak so well.

How are you liking life in your cottage? I would so have liked to have seen it. Is it a good place to work?

Iseult & I & Helen Moloney & Miss Gifford[6] played planchette one evening. A spirit called Teig O'Driscoll of Bantry who lived in 1691 communicated. He said he had been a sailor & talked a good deal about ships & the sea, he told us to take a bible & open it & read. I did so & it opened at a most warlike passage in the old testament but I was not very interested & shut the book & don't remember the place. Teig got quite excited & said 'open the bible at *Numbers & read & ponder*' I did so & read 'Behold the people riseth up as a Lioness, as a lion doth lift himself up, He shall not lie down until he eat of his prey & drink the blood of the Slain'

We asked him if these verses referred to the men locked out, or was it personal to himself. He answered 'It is all the same battle'. Asked what he would advise he said 'Draw bloody swords on the black ones', asked who the black ones are he said 'I am not one of Cromwell's Whelp', asked to be a little more clear & explicit he said 'Look for them, I am not there, I have no ship, fight them on the water, on the waves, you are the fighters, I have no knowledge', asked who are the fighters he said '*The Red ones* there are two of them. They know what they pray for. *Red second number I will fight along with you*', asked his opinion of the English he said Bodachs,[7] which at first we didn't understand, & when we did it made us laugh so much that the séance ended.

Now the strange thing is that Red 2nd number, is actually my designation in a certain mystical society which few people know of[8] – It only occurred to me after the seance was over & made me think the thing much more interesting.

Stephens dined with me last night. He is going to London shortly, he recited some very interesting new poems he has written, one he says he stole from you, he means he wrote it when very excited after reading some of your poems, another he says he stole from Tagore – I saw Mukerjia also.

Write soon, or get Mr Pond [Pound] to write if your eyes are still troublesome.

Alwys your friend
Maud Gonne

Have you been doing any more work with your medium –

284   17 Rue de l'Annonciation
                                                 Passy
                                                 Paris
                                                 29th Nov [1913]

My dear Willie

Thank you so much for your generous subscription to the children's dinners. It is very kind of you. I hope this will be the last year I shall have to beg for this object. Now that Archbishop Walsh has expressed approval of our work & will help getting the permissive act through Parliament I hope it will not be long till we get the whole thing on a municipal basis as it is in other countries. This year I think EVERY school in Dublin where there are poor children are getting some sort of dinners from charitable funds. I may have to go over to Ireland about all this again before long. I would like to put off till after Xmas if possible.

About Teig O'Driscoll. We all four had our hands on the planchette most of the time though part of the time Iseult & I began taking notes & then one or the other of us had our hands off & Teig talked just the same. I think it was a little quicker & better when we all had our hands on.

Helen Moloney could not have known 'Red no 2' neither Miss Gifford nor Iseult did. We none of us made up our minds as to who Teig meant by 'the Black ones' but I think were inclined to take it as meaning the employers, especially as he kept repeating 'attack them on the sea on the waves' & to talk of ships. This may have been because he used to be a sailor – Iseult with her usual sceptical mind said she thought Miss Gifford capable of having made *planchette* move, but personally I don't think she did.

I have had great encouragement about my illuminations, I have been *asked* to expose them at a small but rather *recherché* exhibition of water colours & illuminations, where they are likely to get a good deal of notice. I shall have a good deal of work to finish them in time.

At the same time I have been asked by [?Jean de Bonnejou] a very well known Catholic writer to collaborate with him on a book on Ireland. I don't think I will have time for both, for when I am painting I get very stupid & incapable of doing anything else.

When do you start for America I am sending Pond's address to Pierce

I would love to see the Comedy on the police.[1] Who is it by? I am sure it will be popular, so I shall most likely have chances of seeing later –

I suppose it wouldn't be possible for you to come & spend Xmas with us. I can offer you quite a comfortable little room next to my studio among the chimneys, so expenses would only be about £2 price of return ticket to Paris. It would be so nice seeing you & you could exercise your French – Iseult says she hopes you will come

In haste
Yours alwys
Maud Gonne

285
                                                17 Rue de l'Annonciation
                                                Passy
                                                [Paris]
                                                Sunday [December 1913]

Dear Willie

It is a great disappointment you not being able to come to spend Xmas with us in Paris. There is so much I wanted to talk to you about & I never have time when we meet hurriedly in Dublin or London.

I was at 1st performance of [?Bourgeois] translation of Synge's Playboy yesterday & hated & loathed it more than words can say. It was received with puzzled coldness by the French Audience, who went away thinking that the Ireland they had dreamed of was after all only a dirty place filled with drunken criminal people little better than savages.

A piece I saw at the Theatre des Arts last week, & which really interested me very greatly was *Eugénie Grandet* by Balzac.[1] It was extremely well adapted for the theatre by Monsieur Albert Arracett, very literal & gripped one the whole way through. It might be a piece you might like to get translated for the Abbey. Stephens went there last night & is dining with me tomorrow to tell me what he thinks of it.

Iseult was very proud of your idea of her wisdom – She is a strange mixture almost like two people, one, the embodiment of youth & childhood almost, the other one full of old wisdom & often cynical. The OLD Iseult disconcerts & alarms me though I have to admire her. She has intense imagination but lacks the energy & will to use it, & it often makes her sad & restless.

I am lecturing here again next Thursday. I think I shall have to go to Dublin middle or end of Jany but only for a short time. When do you start for America.

Alwys your friend
Maud Gonne

All Changed, Changed Utterly
1914–1918

We know their dream; enough
To know they dreamed and are dead.

W. B. Yeats, 'Easter 1916' (written in 1916)

─────── 1914 ───────

The next few years would see the old order, not only in Ireland but in the world, completely changed.

The strike came to an unhappy end with a gradual return to work in January when English trade union support was withdrawn. Poverty in the city was startling.

On 31 January Yeats left for his lecture tour in the USA, where he was finally reconciled with John Quinn in March.

286   [Paris]
                                                    3rd Jany [1914]

My dear Willie

Are you coming to Paris before you go to America? When do you start for America? I will try & time my visit to Ireland if possible so as to see you either here or in London. It would be pleasantest here.

Kathleen & Thora have been staying here for New Year, they left yesterday for Cairo. The room they had is ready for you if you can come –

I had a long talk with Lugné Poe – Theatre de l'Oeuvre, today.[1] I told him he ought to give some other play of the Irish theatre to do away with the bad impression left by the Playboy.[2] The critics have all been bad on it – & Lugné Poe is somewhat cross in consequence & not over anxious for another Irish play – I spoke to him of Kathleen ni Houlihan & gave him Mallya's translation of it to read[3] – The translation is very good & very literal – Mallya read it to Stephens & to me the other day and we both thought it excellent –

Lugné Poe asked if I had your authority to have it played. I replied I thought you would give it me, but I would write & make quite

333

sure. It is really a NECESSITY to have a play like that played here after the Playboy which has been understood by nobody & has certainly done harm to Ireland here among a large number of people – It was not played enough as a farce to show people who had never been to Ireland that it was a caricature or an extravaganza & not a picture of Irish life. I know enough press people here to be able to ensure that *Kathleen* would be fairly reviewed & properly understood – Please let me have it for l'Oeuvre if Lugné Poe wants to act it –

Poor Helen Moloney has again broken down & is in hospital. I fear it will have to come to an operation – I am very sorry for I am very fond of her & she is terribly depressed about everything.

I can't write more now for I am tired, this evening after having given a children's party Xmas Tree & Snapdragon[4] etc for Seagan & a lot of his friends.

Do you like life in your cottage isn't English country rather drear & cold? Here in Paris we have some difficulty in keeping warm this year –

Iseult joins me in all good wishes for 1914, & hopes that you will find time to come to Paris a little before America.

Yours alwys
　　Maud Gonne

287
　　　　　　　　　　　　　　　　　　　　　[Paris]
　　　　　　　　　　　　　　　　　　　　　[January 1914]

　　　　　　　　　　　　　　　　　　　　　Private

My dear Willie
　　I wish you had sent me the article in the *English Review*[1] or at all events the *date*. I have written for it, but abroad it takes time to get things, newspaper articles should be answered at once. My answer, if, as from your letter I infer, I am *personally* insulted, will be very simple. I shall dog whip the author, but of course first I must see the article & see how far it *directly* refers to me. If the insult is put as supposed words of yours, it makes things more complicated unless you have denied them. I cannot tell till I get the article – kindly don't mention this letter of mine or my intentions *to anyone*, as such things are ridiculous when talked of, though not at all ridiculous when done. As you have already written a poem – which sounds a very good one, on the emotions of that article I fear it must have appeared some time ago – however as I am abroad the dating doesn't matter as much – Kindly send me G.M.'s address[2]

In haste
Yours
　　Maud Gonne

*In answer to George Moore's taunts Yeats wrote 'Closing Rhymes',
originally entitled 'Notoriety/Suggested by a recent magazine article':*

> *Those undreamt accidents that have made me*
> *– Seeing that Fame has perished this long while,*
> *Being but a part of ancient ceremony –*
> *Notorious, till all my priceless things*
> *Are but a post the passing dogs defile.*

288   [Paris]
                                                    [January 1914]
My dear Willie

I succeeded in getting a copy of the *English Review*. Moore is more
yellow journalist than ever. It is extraordinary that people tolerate
him after *Ave*. Personally there is nothing in this article which affects
me but it is outrageous & if Lady Gregory really thinks she has a
chance of winning this case she will be quite right to prosecute.[1]

I don't think it will injure the theatre at all.

I am afraid it has given you a great deal of worry & annoyance but
if it has made you write a fine poem that is some consolation. It is
generally out of the hard things in life that the best comes.

I can't write more now, as I receive this evening and people are
beginning to come & Iseult doesn't like being hostess alone – I had
to scribble this in haste for my letter of this morning may have made
you anxious – from your letter I thought Moore had attacked me
personally. Now I have read the article, I see I have no cause to act
– *Please treat that letter as* PRIVATE

When do you start for America? I am very sorry you hadn't time
for a visit in Paris first. Iseult joins me in good wishes for your
journey. She has been so taken up with New Year festivities she
hasn't had time to look out the ghost yet but she will do so.

In haste
Yours alwys
    Maud Gonne

289   [Paris]
                                                    [January 1914]
My dear Willie

Thank you so much for your letter & for Lady Gregory's book
on the Irish Theatre.[1] The subject interests me & there are bits of
charming writing in it but it seems to be a little long & tedious &
egotistical & I doubt if it will do her personally much good. It may
be that I care seldom for autobiographies.

I received a letter asking me if I wouldn't like to have the real facts about Inghinide na hEireann's connection with the starting of Irish plays & Samain festivals & with the 1st performance of Kathleen ni Houlihan made public,[2] I replied I did not think it worth while. I have never minded other people taking credit for my work why should I this time? – but I must say I was amused when I remembered how I engaged Fay for Inghinide na hEireann to stage & produce for us & how much I paid for those first performances & Russell painted most of the scenery, that Lady Gregory thought it worth while to mention the small cheque she sent to Russell *some time* after, when they had the Camden St Hall – She was not I think once on our committee at that time but as far as I am concerned I don't mind & refused to give the facts for publication –

Our letters again crossed. As soon as I had read Moore's article I wrote to you saying there was nothing that needed answering as far as I am concerned & I think I agree with you that your poem[3] is the best & most dignified answer you could give. The lines of that poem on your old sailor grandfather are particularly fine, at least Moore's scurrility has had that good result, it has made you write that poem. Everyone must be shocked at Moore's want of taste & manners & his disdain for all the ordinary decencies of social life. Social life would be impossible if there were many Moores, if one had to think, in talking to one's friends of how they could twist & turn one's words & gestures into material to sell to the public –

I will try to get over to Dublin when you are there, or at all events I will see you in London before you start for America –

Again thanking you for your letter. In haste

Yours alwys

Maud Gonne

I will see Mallya & Lugné Poe about Kathleen next week & let you know at once.

Monday

I have opened my letter this morning to add this. I don't want you to think that because I don't care much for Lady Gregory's *book* on the theatre, I underrate her work – I think she has done great work & has shown great courage & *staying* power – her perseverance under difficulties has been wonderful – I also think her books on Cuchulain & Finn[4] most valuable & most charming. I have read & reread them many times & always with delight.

In haste

Yours alwys

M.G.

290
17 Rue de l'Annonciation
[Passy]
[Paris]
19th Jany [1914]

My dear Willie

Stephens was here on Tuesday & as he had seen the article in the *English Review* was indignant over it. I showed him your poem, he was enthusiastic over it. It is the best of all Yeats' later poems he exclaimed. I am so glad he has written it, & he asked me when writing to you to tell you how much he admired it. ('Not that he cares a bit for what I think but I should like to tell him all the same') He has a great love & reverence for you.

I was coming to Ireland next week but the 26th is Seagan's birthday & there was great wailing at the idea of my going away just before it, so I decided on staying till after. I will be in London on the 28th, 29th, 30th so I shall see you before you start for America.

I am bringing over piles of clothing to distribute to the children of the locked out men in Dublin & in the schools, my studio is piled up with it. I lectured twice & suggested people sending me things for the children & I am getting bundles every day –

I hope your cold is quite gone –

Yours alwys
Maud Gonne

291
Paris
Friday [January 1914]

My dear Willie

We shall cross to England on Monday & hope to arrive London Tuesday evening.

I have written to May <Gonne> Bertie Clay to take rooms for us at an hotel in Queen's Gate. Don't know exact address but letters to c/o May, 39 Alexandra Court, 171 Queen's Gate will always find us.

I think we shall stay in London about a week.

Looking forward to seeing you.

In great haste

I remain

Alwys your friend
Maud Gonne

292   [Paris]
                                                      [January 1914]
My dear Willie

for the last 5 days I have a bad attack of bronchitis, fever etc &
have to stay in bed. The doctor who has just been, says that there is
no possibility of my being well enough to travel on the 28th & I am
afraid he is right as though I am better I have been pretty bad & still
cough a great deal. I still hope I shall be able to travel 30th but it is
uncertain – I think you said you start for America on the 31st. Do
you mean you leave London that date, or Queenstown? Please let
me know. I shall be very disappointed if I don't see you before you
start –

I hope you will have a most successful tour. How long will you
be away? Write to me some time & send papers.
     Always your friend
          Maud Gonne

293   [Paris]
                                              Thursday [January 1914]
My dear Willie

I spent yesterday in packing several big trunks of clothes for the
strikers children & had everything ready to leave here on Friday
morning when last night, without any apparent reason, I got a high
temperature again & the doctor who came this morning says that I
may on no account travel tomorrow. He says not for a fortnight.
This I think is exaggerated caution but it is certain I don't feel able
to travel tomorrow. I am very disappointed. I would so have liked
to have seen you before you start for America.

This is to wish you a very pleasant voyage & great good luck with
the lectures – How long will you be away. My kindest regards to
your Father. I have met quite a number of Americans here who know
& admire him in New York. Tell him we all want him back in
Dublin.
     Iseult joins me in best wishes.
     Always your friend
          Maud Gonne

Don't worry about my health. I am not dangerously ill, only if I got
fresh cold the bronchitis might turn to congestion of the lungs like
last year – so I have to take care. I expect to be able to get up in a
few days.

294

[Letterhead]
17 Rue de l'Annonciation
Paris XVI
Sunday. 19th March [1914]

My dear Willie

On my return from Dublin where I spent a month I was so glad to find your letter waiting for me here & to know you are well & on the whole enjoying your tour in America in spite of all the hard work. I am very glad the tour is so successful. You might send me paper[s] occasionally with accounts of your lectures.

Iseult has taken your advice & is learning Bengali. She is very interested in it & a charming Hindu Mr Mukerjea who translated the *Post Office* who is teaching her, says she is making quite outstanding progress. She has communicated her enthusiasm for Bengali & for Tagore poems to a friend of hers, Mademoiselle Cherfils,[1] who has also started learning. Together with the help of Mukerjea they have translated some of Tagore's poems into french very beautifully.

If they could get permission from Tagore to publish a translation of *The Gardener*[2] or the Crescent Moon in French, signed *translations direct from the Bengali by Mukerjea & his pupils*, I believe they would have a very great success for the translations by Gide,[3] & a few by [?Davray][4] that have appeared are only translations from translations. I think there would be no difficulty in finding an editor here if Tagore would give permission. Could you write a word to him on the matter? Perhaps the best thing would be for them to send some of the translations to Tagore. M. Mukerjea says he thinks a brother of Tagore's knows French well so he could judge them.

I feel they ought to get the permission *quickly* as many people are wanting to translate the poems though I don't think any of them have taken the trouble to learn Bengali –

I saw a good many of the Irish M.P.s on my way through London including Mr Redmond. All seemed confident that Home Rule would pass before the Election, the only really pessimistic one was Lynch – They all seemed to think that the election would come directly after the bill was passed & before it came into effect.

You remember my friend Marinette Granié.[5] She died quite suddenly the very day I came home. We miss her very much. Poor Granié is quite overcome, he spends much of his time with us.

We are going to Florence for a fortnight at Easter but return here after. You must come & see us when you get home.

Remember me to your father. When will he come back? We are getting jealous of America!

Iseult joins me in best wishes, & hopes of seeing you soon.

Alwys your friend
Maud Gonne

[Two notes written on the letter: (1) an address in New York in different handwriting; (2) Carl Jung, The Journal of Abnormal Psychology [?] published by Clark University Press.]

295
17 rue de l'Annonciation
Paris
Wednesday
16th [?Avril/Août] [1914]

Dear Willie

I have just received your letter forwarded by Kathleen, I fear with some delay, as she was not sure if we were back in Paris.

Diva Brat Mukerjea or in Bengalee Mukhopadhyaye's address was *Hotel Nicole 19 Rue Pierre Nicole Paris* but I don't know if he is back yet. He told me he was going to London in August & would return to Paris in the autumn. *Chattopadhyaya (Sirosone brother) 4 Rue Dupont des Loges, Champs de Mars Paris* would probably know where he is.

James Stephens' address is *11 Rue Campagne 1ère*. I am so glad he has got the prize it will be a great thing for him.[1]

I am very busy getting ready to start for London on Friday, where I shall stay with Kathleen for two nights & be in Dublin on Monday.

I won't write more now
Very sincerely your friend
In gt haste
    Maud Gonne

296
Villa Castiglionie
24, Via Montughi
Florence
20th April [1914]

My dear Willie

Thank you so much for the letters & papers sent before you left New York. They were forwarded to me here. I cannot tell you how glad I am that you and Mr Quinn are friends again.[1] Thank you so much for writing to Tagore's Agent. A strange thing has happened about Mukerjea, he has suddenly disappeared without writing to us – I cannot help suspecting that Mr Mallya a young French writer who would love to translate Tagore's poems himself & who beside was very much in love with Iseult & *very jealous* of her friendship with Mukerjea (Mallya proposed & was refused a year or more ago) may have made mischief in some way.

Iseult will write to you all the particulars about Mukerjea who is in London now & whom I would very much like you to see & if possible, find out from, what has happened. Mallya who has also been in London staying at the same [?pension] as Mukerjea & wrote to Iseult the most strange letter the other day, accusing Mukerjea of drunkenness in public houses & all sorts of vague evil things, telling her to keep all this to herself & he would tell her more when we return to Paris. Iseult would not believe me when I said that I thought Mallya had had something to do with Mukerjea's sudden departure, since she has received this letter begins to think that I am perhaps right in my suspicions.

Mukerjea is the last man I could imagine drinking in public houses –

He is *very* sensitive & if Mallya told him that Iseult & Christiane[2] had laughed at him or any silly lie of that sort I think it would be enough to account for his sudden disappearance. He was staying on in Paris on purpose to keep on the work with them. He used to be at my house almost every day & seemed quite eager to do the translations into French with them. He asked me to write to Tagore about it which I did. His sudden disappearance, without a word of explanation, is most unaccountable. Mallya came instead of Mukerjea one evening & announced that he had left & had asked him to return some books he had borrowed from us –

We came here to spend Easter, & my boy took the opportunity to get chickenpox, so I am busy nursing him & can't get out much.

He is better. I think we shall go to Assisi for a week at the end of this month before returning to Paris – where I expect to be till the end of June when I think we shall go to the Pyrenees – but my plans are a little vague. I would much like to see you. Is there any chance of you coming to France? I have a room for you whenever you care to come.

I am so glad you had such a successful tour of America. You must be glad to get back for those tours get very exhausting

I won't write more now –

Alwys your friend

Maud Gonne

Kathleen & my cousins send their kind regards

Yeats left America in April. At the end of May or early June he went to France with Everard Feilding, and invited Maud Gonne to join them to investigate a supposed miracle at Mirebeau, near Poitiers, where an oleograph of the Sacred Heart, belonging to the Abbé Vachère, had apparently begun to bleed. They were allowed to dip their handkerchiefs in the supposed blood.

[Paris]
8th June [1914]

My dear Willie

forgive me for not answering sooner. My sister & Thora have been here for 5 days & left today – then Iseult who has continued NOT to take care of her foot has been a great worry. In spite of her & of the Masseuse I got in another doctor, a specialist. He at once said what I had said from the first & which the first doctor denied that there was a fracture. We then had her foot radiographed which showed *3 fractures*. The doctor was most urgent & told her that if she will not rest the foot *entirely* she will be lame for life. In spite of this she continues just as when you were here. I am worn out trying to persuade her to keep quiet. She is really a little mad. I hope now that Thora has left she will take to writing again, if she would it would fill her time & keep her quiet.

Thank you so much for sending her the book, she is writing to you herself.

I have had no answer from Mukerjea. Iseult's first story was true, there was something she was trying to hide, I have not yet found out what it is; she thought she had put me off the matter by saying she had invented it all, but there really is something.

I send you a no. of the Croix[1] poor Abbé Vacher is excommunicated for disobedience to his superiors. I wonder what he will do I expect he will go to Rome. Has Feilding got the analysis of the blood yet?[2]

It is indeed a stroke of luck that the Censor has again interfered with your plays.[3] It will fill houses & revive interest in the theatre.

I am longing to hear the new poem.

Kathleen has taken two bottles you left here belonging to your dressing case. Her address is 12 Milner Street. I told her you would call for them – you must often be at the Court Theatre & it is quite near to Milner Street. Kathleen will I know like to see you –

I will find out about Claudel's publisher agent tomorrow & let you know at once.

In haste
Your friend
    Maud Gonne

I hope you got your cheque book & various letters & papers safely.

298 Paris
9 July [1914]

My dear Willie

forgive me for not writing all this time, I have been & still am very much worried over business affairs & over Iseult's health – & hadn't the courage to answer even your letters – We are starting for the mountains on the 14th which I feel sure will do Iseult good – I am going to try & forget all worries for the present –

Mukerjea arrived in Paris a day or so after your first letter – I sifted the mystery down – It was after all as you supposed when here, a literary invention of Iseult's, complicated by her having told it with wonderful amplifications to Christianne Chirfil who in her turn repeated it in half confidence & much excitement & it came round again to me, but I believe the whole thing originated with Iseult's imagination – & poor Mukerjea had never even heard of it –

The Bengali lessons have been going on ever since his return & they are really working very hard. Mukerjea has given up the bar & wants a professorship – In the mean time he is very hard up & has with great difficulty at last consented to receiving a very small remuneration for the lessons – He is coming to Arrens with us but will not consent to be my guest entirely – He insists on paying his lodging but consents to take his meals with us. He is extraordinarily delicate about money matters, & but for old Mr Chirfil's intervention I don't think he would have ever consented to take money for the lessons. They hope to do a good deal of translations this summer. Mukerjea is also going to let them teach him French which will certainly be of use to him – the Chirfils are coming to Arrens also so my duties of chaperone will be lightened.

Mukerjea just applied for a professorship of literature & history. I took down the enclosed particulars & send them to you, in case you might be able to recommend him usefully – I believe recommendations tell a great deal in such appointments. I would be very glad indeed if you could help him. Lady Gregory knows so many powerful people it is possible you or she could recommend him –

Helen Molony is with us. She is looking ever so much stronger & better & from what the Doctor writes here I believe the cure is complete. She is also coming to Arrens & I hope I shall be able to tell you that she is really quite recovered & able for steady work again in the Autumn – I hope I shall be able to see Abbé Vacher some time during the summer. I have promised to go & stay with my old friend Dr Fabre at Poitier[s] later on.

It was quite interesting your Medium's account, but as you say she may have got it from your mind. Iseult alarmed us very much by getting one or two faint fits last week – & several very severe nose bleedings. The Dr is rather anxious about her, says her heart is weak.

He orders her to give up smoking, to eat meat & keep her windows open – all of which she refuses to do. I think the country will do her good & she will find it harder to get the cigarettes she likes there.

I suppose you will soon be going to Ireland. How I envy you – be charitable, return good for evil & write to me soon in spite of my long silence.

 Always your friend
  Maud Gonne

When shall we see your new poems?[1] Quinn sent me a photo of you & of himself taken last time you were in America. Quinn has come out better than you have in it, some how you never photograph well.

299
           ·Arren
           Pyrenees
          25 July [1914]

My dear Willie

We are in these wonderful mountains. How I wish you were here with us. You would love this country & the life here!

Mr Mukerjea is with us. He & Iseult are working hard at the translations. They have already translated a good many poems of Tagore's direct from the Bengali – some from the Gardener – some that have not been translated into English, some of them are very beautiful & I think their translations are very good. They have tried to translate as literally as possible & they have obtained wonderful beauty & freshness of expression. I think you will think their work very good. I can't tell you how glad I am to find Iseult really working & interested in the work.

Now we want you to write to Mr Tagore as soon as possible, saying what you think of Iseult's style & asking permission for them to bring the poems out as a book if they can find a publisher in France – This is rather urgent, as we have heard of a jewess, a Mlle Carpetis, who has been in India & who knows the Tagores (especially the artist[1]) & who wants to get the right of translating Mr Tagore's work in French. She is trying to make a speciality of translating Indian things, but Mr Mukerjea says she is quite incapable of doing it well. She does not know as much Bengalee as Iseult & I doubt her having much literary ability or style but she is very intelligent & very pushing. She tried hard to get hold of Mr Mukerjea & get him to work for her & help her translate, but she said some very cruel & false things about Madame Cama,[2] who Mukerjea reveres as an Indian nationalist & Mukerjea said he would not go to her house again. She then turned her anger against Mukerjea & abuses him to everyone, among others Iseult, who she hardly knows.

She has now gone to Cambridge to work [at] Bengalee with Mr

Anderson,[3] professor of Indian Language, but who Mukerjea says does not know very much Bengali. She may of course pick up some Bengali student who would translate for her & there is danger that she may get from Mr Tagore permission to translate his works before Iseult does.

Your recommendation of Iseult would carry real weight with Mr Tagore. I hear that Tagore, or Tagore's agent, has quarrelled with Gide about the financial arrangements of the translation of Gitanjali so he is not likely to want to do any more. Iseult is sending by next mail some specimens of her translations to Mr Tagore, but I fear he doesn't know French well enough to really appreciate the style.

Your opinion would weigh a great deal with him I think. I will tell Iseult to copy out some of her translations for you, so you can say you have seen them. I think it is important you should write to Tagore soon, on account of the activity of Mlle Carpetis.

We went to Lourdes for two days to the Eucharistic Congress. It was a most wonderful sight & most impressive. Cardinals & Bishops from all countries in their crimson & purple robes & the heads of most of the great religious orders & thousands of priests & thousands and thousands of people of all classes & all countries, all met together at Lourdes to affirm their belief in the supernatural & in the highest form of manifestation of spiritual life.

It was wonderful & very beautiful. I & Helen Molony as Catholics were deeply moved & Mr Mukerjea, who is a Brahmin, was equally so – I wish you had been there. It was an extraordinary & very inspiring sight –

I have a long letter from Mr Feilding[4] which I must answer soon. I may be able to go to Poitier[s] on my way back to Paris. Dr Fabre who lives near Poitier[s] has asked us to stay. I will probably be able to get much information about Mirebeau there.

When are you going to Ireland? Kathleen wrote me you dined with her & greatly interested everyone with your talk. I am longing for the papers to know the result of the conference.[5] Have you much inside news. From the French papers it looks as if a split in the Liberal party was inevitable. It seems strange to an outsider that Asquith[6] should have allowed the King's speech. Is he playing straight, or does he want an election before Home Rule?

Helen Molony is here, She seems *perfectly well & strong again.* I am going to make her practise her voice. I hope she will be able to join the Abbey again in the Autumn.[7] She is a charming companion. We are all fond of her –

Write soon

With love from Iseult I remain

Alwys your friend

    Maud Gonne

Did you get the letter I wrote before leaving Paris asking if you could get Mukerjea recommended for an appointment as professor in India.

The Government of Ireland Act (1914) had been passed on 14 May. It allowed six northern counties to be excluded for a period, but subsequent events kept this exclusion indefinitely suspended.

The Ulster Volunteer Force had practical plans for declaring independence and forming their own provisional government. At Larne in April they had openly imported large quantities of arms to augment their already existing stocks. The National Volunteers, drilling with dummy weapons, in preparation to defend Home Rule, followed suit with a far less profitable gun-running on 26 July at Howth, where arms were landed from Erskine Childers's yacht Asgard. *The troops were called out, and in a confrontation with a jeering Dublin crowd three civilians were killed and thirty-eight wounded.*

The long-expected Armageddon was at hand. The Great War broke out on 4 August.

300

Arrens
Pyrenees
30 July [1914]

My dear Willie

Once more I am going to bother you about Iseult's work. M. Mukerjea has just received enclosed letter. He has written proposing Iseult should do the work. He will help her with it – they will collaborate – he thinks your recommendation would again be most useful & if possible would like you to write & say you think Iseult competent.

He asked if you would write at once as here again there is a danger of Mlle Carpetis getting before them –

The Gardener is almost finished – they do not intend doing all the poems, only those that they have got written in Bengalee. Iseult is copying them & will forward some to you tomorrow –

When I read of the splendid coup of the Volunteers & of its tragic sequel I nearly rushed over to Dublin to be at the funeral of the victims, but the difficulty of leaving Iseult & Bichon alone in France with the chance of war being declared which would probably make my return to them impossible stopped me.

How I love & *reverence* the Dublin crowd. They are always fearless & heroic whenever a national or religious idea is before them – They never fought like that all through the labor war last winter. They stood dejectedly listening to orators telling them to fight for themselves to better their conditions, there was no enthusiasm though they starved and suffered silently & bravely & stood to a blundering leader loyally as people of no other country would have done. I have written to the Freeman but I do not know if they will publish my letter. The war scare & the sacrifice of those poor Dublin men & women & children should make it possible for Redmond to obtain a great deal for Ireland.[1] I am waiting for the paper with breathless anxiety & can hardly sleep for thinking of it all –

How are you, where are you, & why don't you write to me? In spite of the condition appearing as promising for Ireland I had a haunting sort of vision of death & famine which put me in very low spirits, but today I try & explain it to myself by thinking I was desperately moved & excited by the thought of what had happened in Dublin, & by my powerlessness to help or to be with the people & this may have drawn to my mind thoughts & memories of the famine & misery I have witnessed long ago. I think it must be that.

Write to me soon.

Always your friend

Maud Gonne

What are you writing? You probably know about Balganadhar Tilak[2] the great Indian scholar & nationalist leader who wrote the Age of the Vedas, the Origin of the Aryans & edited *Kasari* a paper written in English & in Marathi. Mukerjea says that apart from politics he has done wonderful work in rousing his countrymen to study their heroic literature & in teaching the value of spirituality.

The English put that man in prison for 7 years – he was only liberated last month. A meeting to celebrate his release is being organised by the Indians in London & probably they will ask you to raise your voice to welcome back to liberty the distinguished nationalist & scholar.

Maud Gonne said that she heard the tocsin ring in the little mountain village for the young men to come in from the harvest fields and go to war.

301

Arrens
Pyrenees
26 August [1914]

My dear Willie

You seemed to have escaped the obsession of this war – I cannot; night & day I think about it *uselessly*. I cannot work, I cannot read, I cannot sleep – I am torn in two, my love of France on one side, my love of Ireland on the other for I know what we should have done just the contrary apparently from what we have done – Redmond seems to have wasted a glorious opportunity & Ireland seems too confused & inarticulate to redeem his mistake –

This war is an inconceivable madness which has taken hold of Europe – It is unlike any other war that has ever been. It has no great idea behind it. Even the leaders hardly know why they have entered into it, & certainly the people do not – (I except England from this, she, as usual, is following her commercial selfishness getting others to fight so her commerce of existence shall be ensured by the weakening of Germany).

Is it the slave & Germanic race trouble? If so, what logically has France to do with it?

If it goes on, it is race suicide for all the countries engaged in it who have conscription, only the weaklings will be left to carry on the race; & their whole intelectual & industrial life is already at a standstill. The victor will be nearly as enfeebled as the vanquished. And who is to end it? In France, in Germany, in Austria only the old men & children & women are left, these are not necessary elements for a revolution which might bring peace.

Could the women, who are after all the guardians of the race, end it? Soon they will be in a terrible majority, unless famine destroys them too. I always felt the wave of the woman's power was rising, the men are destroying themselves & we are looking on – Will it be in our power to end this war before European civilisation is swept away – The press is busily engaged working up race hatred in the interest of war – to make the people who are fighting confusedly fiercer. Every day in the French papers there is a column of *German attrocities* most I should think invented, though in all war there are attrocities enough, two days ago an official order from Viviani[1] or the minister of war not to treat German prisoners *too well* as they were barbarians – ! Before the war is over there will probably be atrocities on both sides to make the Bulgarians envious[2] –

The post takes a long time to distribute letters – about 7 to 10 days from Ireland. Have you got Iseult's letter with the translations yet? She was very slow sending them, as she & Mukerjea had both got a spell of idleness on them. However, they were really sent off to you about a week ago –

Helen Molony practises voice production regularly & with very good results on the edge of a mountain torrent. She is very well & in good spirits & *quite strong* again. I think you will be quite safe in taking her back to the Abby – she will not break down again – Let me know *when* she ought to be back in Dublin – It may be difficult to get there just now. Are the channel steamers running regularly between France & England. I hear the mail goes regularly once a day to & from Ireland, travelling in France is slow & difficult but *possible* now. Write to me often & send news. I want it *badly*. Also send me an Irish paper occasionally, those sent by friends seem to come through alright, with considerable delay, but *The Freeman* which I have subscribed to has ceased to arrive & want of Irish news makes me very restless.

Though we are in a such a quiet place, so far from the war, the weather is really *war weather* strange thunderstorms, & floods – a house was nearly swept away yesterday, the people say they have not seen things like that since 1870 during the war[3] – We have all heard strange sounds in the hill, drums beating, bells ringing, hammering etc. I got up twice last night & opened my window I was so certain the church bell was ringing – but it was not.

Always your friend
Maud Gonne

Kathleen & I are very anxious about Toby[4] who has voluntered & gone as despatch carrier with the English force to Belgium.

The wounded were being brought to the Pyrenees by train from the front, many dying on the long journey. Because the hospital in the resort of Argelès-Gazost was soon filled, the casino was converted into a temporary one, and the mayor of Argelès went to the nearby village of Arrens seeking help to organise and run it. Refused a passport home, Maud Gonne took rooms in a small house in Argelès and undertook the work for which she later received commendation from the doctor in charge. She and Iseult were given the rank of lieutenant, which enabled them to travel with the army and nurse where required.

On 20 September, at Woodenbridge, County Wicklow, John Redmond, leader of the Parliamentary Party, believing that joint action against Germany would weld Irishmen together, pledged the National Volunteers to support the war. All nationalists had worked under the umbrella of the Volunteers, but now they divided along the old familiar lines. The separatist IRB nationalists formed the anti-war Irish Volunteers, who grew in numbers over the next few years, carefully fostered by a new breed of IRB. Urged by their leader, many of the Redmondite Volunteers went to fight for the rights of small nations in Flanders, believing in the words of Tom Kettle:

> *Know that we fools, now with the foolish dead,*
> *Died not for flag, nor King, nor Emperor,*
> *But for a dream, born in a herdsman's shed,*
> *And the secret Scripture of the poor.*

Argelis
                                             Pyrenees
                                             25 September [1914]

My dear Willie
  Thank you so much for your letter.
  1st about Iseult's translations probably the faults of *spelling*
signaled by Mabel Beardsly are there for though Iseult does not spell
badly generally, she is very lazy & careless & I had to lecture & scold
a great deal before I could get the copies of the translations made to
send to you & even then Mukerjea whose french is very imperfect
copied a good many of them, but luckily printers spell better than
writers – As to the faults of grammar Mabel B. signals, it is she who
is wrong not Iseult. Of that I am *sure* & any french person would
say the same – About the appropriate wording that is more difficult
to pronounce on for nearly all the poems were translated direct from
the Bengali & only the english version consulted after. For instance
to *growl* does not quite correspond to the French *gronder*, for one
can say la mer gronde but to say the sea *growls* would be ridiculous
– I will ask Mukerjea to write you on this. They have perhaps
attempted to be too *literal* & as of course the languages are so
different, the result may sometimes be strange, but I must say I like
the translations very much better than those of the *Gardener* (English
translation)[1]
  Mukerjea is returning to India next week if he can get a boat,
travelling anywhere is so difficult during war time – He & Iseult are
very lazy & I have hard work to keep them to translating. They prefer
reading Plato or Pater or talking metaphysics. All very good in their
way if they would only work as well.
  Of course Mukerjea has fallen in love with Iseult, which has
complicated things a bit – We have come down to Argeles to help
nurse the wounded soldiers of whom the numbers are simply
appaling. Every hospital is overcrowded & every public building
throughout France is turned into a hospital. I have been taken on as
a regular Red X nurse & Iseult & Helen Moloney as helpers & even
Bichon is employed as page.
  It may distract her from her writing but on the other hand it brings
her into contact with real life & anyhow in such a terrible upheaval
it is too awful to stand idly by & watch suffering –
  This war seems to me to mean destruction for both Germany &
France, if it goes on only England, where there is no conscription,
will profit by it – Thank you so much for the papers. It is consoling
to read of the rage of the Unionists, for I certainly thought Redmond
might have made a better bargain. It is so kind of you sending the
papers they are great treasures here, for even on war news they are
so much better informed than the French where the censor is *terrible*.

I wonder if you could take Helen Moloney back at the Abby *without* salary while things are so bad it would keep her working & learning parts & prevent her getting rusty. She is quite well & strong now & is longing to get back to work.

I must go off to the hospital so can't write more now –
Alwys your friend
Maud Gonne.

303
Argelis
Pyrenees
7 November [1914]

My dear Willie
Vassily's account[1] is fairly correct. I had the draft of the treaty with me. It had to be in St Petersburg by a certain date. I think I told you long ago how I was stopped at the Russian Frontier because my passport was not *visé*, how I only got through thanks to a Russian diplomat who was carrying papers from Shuvalov[2] of the Russian Ambassador in Berlin who was proposing a Russian German alliance.

At that time Russia was England's greatest political foe. She was supposed to have designs on India & you remember all the virtuous indignation of England over Russian tyranny & barbarism. The only man in England who, at that time, had realised that Germany was England's real commercial rival & the advantages to England of a Russian Alliance was Stead.[3] He was in Petersburg at the same time as myself – & with the help of Madame Olga Novikoff[4] was trying to create a current of Anglo Russian sympathy & to use the panslavist movement to this end by saying that Russia should logically possess Constantinople which was the key of her own door & that England could help her to this.

England had checkmated Russia to France & Germany's undoing, for however this war may end, France & Germany will be of little account in Europe after it is over – at least for some generations –

Ireland should help every chance she has at home. She has nothing to gain in this war, except perhaps extra tillage & employment for her people.

I am nursing the wounded from 6 in the morning till 8 at night & trying in material work to drown the sorrow & disappointment of it all – & in my heart is growing up a wild hatred of the war machine which is grinding the life out of these great natures & reducing their population to helpless slavery & ruin, among all the wounded I have nursed I have only met one man who spoke with real enthusiasm of returning to the front. The greater part are resigned to the inevitable, they accept patriotic duty, but all pray for the end of the war & hope it will be before they are recovered, & in the hearts of some there is a terrible secret bitterness. Among the workers it is the same.

Have you seen Mukerjea? He was to call on you in London on his way to India. Thank you so much for writing to Doctor Lecky about Iseult. She has got very lazy about her Bengali & after the first few weeks this summer it was very hard to keep her & Mukerjea at their translation. Is there any chance for Helen Moloney getting back to the Abbey. She is very serious about it. She would work even without a salary while times are bad, if you would only take her back. She is perfectly *well* & strong now & I am sure she will keep so. She & Iseult are both helping in the hospital here, but without enthusiasm & I would much rather see her at her own work.

I love the verses you send.[5] I think you told it me once, it seemed familiar to me. Iseult to whom I read it was enthusiastic & said 'Ah how much more interesting than writing about the war!'

I wonder when we shall meet. My plans are vague – I want to be in Ireland but don't see how I can manage it.

Alwys your friend
Maud Gonne.

304   17 Rue de l'Annonciation
                                                         Passy
                                                         Paris [December 1914]

My dear Willie

We are back in Paris – after 3 months' hard red cross nursing. I feel that I would like to go & stir my hungry children's potato pot a little. It has been allowed to go slightly off the boil lately, in spite of the fact that we have now got the free meal act passed.[1] I feel it would be more useful work for me than to go on nursing soldiers patching them up in order that they may be sent back again, to be gored again, by the War bull.

I have no military enthusiasm & can see nothing but misery in this present war – a wind of folly & fatality is driving Germany & France to their ruin. Conqueror or conquered these two great nations will find themselves after this war second rate powers & for this they are sacrificing their strongest & bravest & no one dare raise a voice of protest. It would be unpatriotic, but the dumb misery of the people is very tragic.

Paris is very sad everyone seems in mourning. There is little traffic in the streets, numbers of the shops are shut, hospitals seem the only civil activity, people console themselves by nursing the wounded & they deaden their thoughts by rolling bandages & knitting stockings.

If I bring Bichon over to Ireland will MacBride try & interfere? This is my great preoccupation for I cannot make up my mind to have him in a war country, with the possibility of my return being cut off or delayed. I would love to send him to St Enda's.[2] Here I feel school education will be bad for a long time all the young professors are at the war & the classes are being carried on by old men & scratch teachers & the classes of course are over crowded.

Then I think there is a very serious danger of epidemics in the spring. Only 40 or 50 kilometres from Paris in the North & East the fields are vast cemetries of hastily buried dead – already the military hospitals are crowded with typhoid enteric & dyptheria.

Where are you? What are you doing? How is the Abbey? What are you writing? Write soon & tell me your news.

It is Xmas day but it is a treachery talking of Xmas.

How I wish we could meet – Where are you likely to be? Iseult joins me in friendly greetings.

 Always your friend
  Maud Gonne

Isn't it monstrous the suppression of all the independent Dublin newspapers.

How have people taken it

Addressed to 18 Woburn Buildings, redirected to Coole Park.
Postmark: Paris 26–12–14; London 28 Dec 14; Gort 30 Dec 14.

1915

Yeats spent the early part of the year at Stone Cottage and in London involved in the problems of Sir Hugh Lane's will and his picture collection. He also endeavoured to procure a grant for James Joyce, caught in Switzerland as a result of the war. He spent the summer at Coole. On being asked for a war poem he wrote:

> *I think it better that in times like these*
> *A poet's mouth be silent, for in truth*
> *We have no gift to set a statesman right.*

Political attention in Ireland appeared to be focused on Home Rule and the war; the vigilant police were not reporting anything untoward. In Dublin in August in his funeral oration at the graveside of the old Fenian O'Donovan Rossa, Patrick Pearse said: 'Life springs from death, and from the graves of patriotic men and women spring living nations.' The poetic and mystical stage was set, and the hard-

headed new men, with the old grey-haired Treason Felony prisoner Tom Clarke, were planning carefully in secret.

305   17 Rue de l'Annonciation
                                                             Passy
                                                             Paris
                                                             3d Jany [1915]

My dear Willie

Maurice Bourgeois called on me yesterday in his uniform as a French officer. He was going to the front tomorrow – he has the rank of sous-lieutenant he asked me if I would write to you to ask if you could recommend him as interpreter to any of the English generals. He is most anxious to get that position, as he says he would be more useful that way, he says very incompetent men who know English very badly are getting named. He knows German as well as English. He says an English General would have to write to ask for him as interpreter to Colonel Huquet, Chef de la Mission Francaise, au Grand Quartier Général Britannique.

I have decided to stay in France for the present, as I am afraid that MacBride will give me trouble if I brought Seagan to Ireland & I can't leave him here alone – So I expect I shall take to red cross nursing again, as one cannot remain idle when there is much suffering, but I would rather be working in Ireland.

Where are you? Do write soon – Did you hear from Mukerjea since he left us? He has never written to us since he left Lourdes on his way to Paris.

The Stephens are back here. They & Captain White[1] are dining with me tomorrow. Capt. White has been *'body snatching'* in an ambulance car of his, picking up wounded on the battle fields, but I think he is tired of it, he feels rather like I do that when you hate the war even ambulance work is rather encouraging it, & yet & yet, one cannot remain with hands folded before suffering –

Write soon
Always your friend
    Maud Gonne

Helen Moloney has gone back to Dublin.

306

My dear Willie

It was nice getting your letters. I am longing to read your memoirs.[1] Your descriptions of Ireland & your childhood will be fascinating.

I wish you could come over to Paris. It would be very interesting to talk over the 2nd Vol – possibly I may remember things, or even find some notes of our early work together that may be of use. One day I will have to hunt among old papers, but I have kept very little, always feeling my papers were liable to be seized by the police.

Bichon has returned to his school here again, so I have decided for the present at all events to remain on here. Life is very quiet & sad, most of our friends are at the war & everyone is more or less ruined. I have a good deal of money in France & get no dividend from it, so I have to live very quietly.

We are all ordered to shutter & curtain our windows at nightfall so as to let no light pass & only a few of the street lamps are lit so Paris looks strange & gloomy at night. They seem to expect air raids but I think Germany's attentions in this line are for England, & there is not much danger here.

Captain White is in Paris, we see a good deal of him he is interesting from a philosophical & mystical point of view. He is very much impressed by the writings of the Russian philosopher Wronsky,[2] who he is studying in the Bibliothèque Nationale.

I hope to meet Ezra Pound & his pretty wife[3] some day. Iseult is very lazy & is not working at all at Bengalee I am sorry to say.

Friends have just come into tea so I must end.

Hoping to see you soon.

Yours alwys
    Maud Gonne

307

My dear Willie

forgive me for not having written sooner. I have had many anxieties & troubles lately of which I may tell you when we meet, unless indeed which is likely we find so many more interesting things to talk of that I forget them.

First about Iseult. She is lazy & beautiful & unsatisfactory as ever, she can't be got to think of Bengalee at all. I don't think it is worthwhile writing to Tagore – I say this very sadly, for she might have done really interesting things, as it is I fear she will do nothing. She has written some strange & very beautiful fragments of her own, very living & I think sincere, but they are all unfinished, all fragments. She has never the will to finish anything – She is destroying her health by endless smoking of cigarettes & inhaling the smoke & with it all she is unhappy & bored.

How I wish you were over here. You did seem to have an influence on her. She has an intense admiration & respect for you.

Last Sunday my nephew Tom Pilcher was killed leading his platoon on a charge near La Bassie. He was only 21. I don't know how poor Kathleen will bear this, it may kill her, she adored that boy. He was very handsome & charming.

In the streets here everyone seems in mourning – & the number of maimed people is terrible –

I was nursing in a military hospital in the South, but since Xmas I have been at home since I find it hard to leave the children, & all the places where they want me to go & nurse are outside Paris so I have been doing nothing but painting lately with Granié, who like you, refuses to discuss or think about the war which he hates & loathes. I can't do this, with me it is an obsession from which I cannot escape, though I know it is not Ireland's war & that she ought to keep quite out of it –

I can't place Doyle[1] just now, my memory is bad. I don't remember him being a companion or a friend of MacBride. I know it was always a cherished dream of Tom Kelly's[2] to build a theatre at the back of the Sinn Féin premises & I think the idea is good & I hope they will succeed.

I hope your theatre will get on, I don't see why the war should injure it, for up to the present at all events Ireland does not seem to have been much injured materially, indeed some tell me she is better off this year than last, though if the price of living goes up I am afraid that won't last. Still there must be more employment. There should be a great opening for Russell's Co-operative Societies.[3]

How I wish I were in Ireland. I feel I could forget the war there for there is always living work to be done & people think & feel so intensely.

My poor Seagan is again ill, but is getting better. I took him out today for a drive to see the havoc caused by the Zeppelin raid of last night. There were crowds of sightseers like ourselves & no one seemed to be alarmed or impressed. Really the French people have wonderful calm & courage. Some of the houses looked like the houses I used to see in our villages after the English battering ram had been at them –

I have never thanked you for the poem.[4] To me you are too kind – You have often tried to defend & protect me with your art – &

perhaps when we are dead I shall be known by those poems of yours –

Have you seen James Stephen's new book of poems.[5] They are very charming & some of them I like very much – 'A Song for Lovers' & 'The Satyr' I liked particularly.

Shall you be long in Dublin?

Hoping we shall meet soon

Alwys your friend

    Maud Gonne

308   17 Rue de l'Annonciation

                                       Passy

                                       Paris

                                       Sunday [May 1915]

My dear Willie

This evening's papers give[s] Sir Hugh Lane's name among those drowned with the Lucitania.[1] I am afraid this will be a great blow to Lady Gregory & indeed to you also, for though during this war one gets so familiar with death, hardly a day but some acquaintance is killed, it is always a shock to lose someone with whose work one was so much associated as you were with Sir Hugh Lane's. Is Lady Gregory back in Ireland? Please tell her of my sympathy –

What I cannot understand is how after that warning the Lucitania took any passengers, or if she did, why was she not convoyed by some English war vessels who at least if they failed in stopping the submarine, could have been ready to pick up passengers. The English boasted enough that they had destroyed or shut up all the German transatlantics. How could they not foresee that the Germans would try to do the same with theirs, even if there had been no warning given. In the face of that warning to take passengers seems to me madness, but I suppose the constant familiarity with Death will end by making everyone reckless or indifferent. It seems quite natural now to have a Zeppelin or an airship overhead & to watch for the falling bombs as one would watch a display of fireworks & to listen to shrapnel rattling on the roofs of the houses like hail stones, & to open the windows & get a better view. My charwoman who is nothing of a heroine does this.

I have been staying at Etaples with my poor little sister whose son her greatest treasure was killed at Neuve Chapelle. I am afraid he has taken all the joy of life that was left to her with him.

She had gone to nurse at a Military Hospital near Etaples so that in case he was wounded she might nurse him but he was killed. She is very brave, but the bravery of her forced smile makes her face so wan & shadowy I am afraid to look at her. Iseult is still with her, helping her in the ward to nurse the wounded.

Redmond & all our Irish Parliamentarians have found the courage to defend the publicans[2] which they lacked when it was a question of making Home Rule a reality & not a sham. Nothing O'Leary or Taylor or Sein Fein ever said of them in the past seems to me bad enough for them tonight!

Though for the sake of the French I would have liked to, I could not bring myself to go near any of them, or to assist at their banquet in Paris last week.

I have never spoken to T. P. O'Connor[3] since I turned my back on him when he refused to defend the Irish political prisoners, long ago, because it would embarrass the Govt

Have you heard where those 25,000 noble Ulster Volunteers have been safely hidden from the eyes of the Nationalists & safely kept out of reach of the German bullets? It would be interesting to know. It would interest people very much.

I wish you could come over to Paris sometime. There is so much I would like to talk over with you. How is the biography[4] getting on?

Write soon
Your friend
    Maud Gonne

309
                      Infirmière Hôpital
                      Militaire 72
                      1 Village Swisse
                      Paris Plage
                      Pas de Calais
                      Thursday [Summer 1915]

My dear Willie

I was so glad to get your letters & have been wanting to reply all this time, but the real hard absorbing work of nursing makes letter writing very difficult, from 8 to 12 & from 2 till 6 every day at the hospital & when one gets home one is so tired one can do nothing but eat & sleep – Kathleen, May & Iseult & I are working in two French Military hospitals here. It is a strange absorbing life. Sometimes it seems abrutissant[1] for there is little or no place for intellectual life, sometimes it is an exciting struggle for life against death. It brings one in contact with awful suffering & heroic courage & a great deal of the waste & squalor of war.

Peace seems to be the only thing worth working & striving for but HOW?

I would love to have a long talk with you – but I don't seem to be able to pull myself away even for a few weeks – & yet, & yet, perhaps in Ireland I could be doing much better work.

When I wrote to you from Paris I was worried over several things, money was the least of these though as a great part of my fortune is in France, of course my income has reduced by about half, but in the midst of this general ruin & bloodshed, material loss seems unimportant. I was worried seriously about Iseult but now that she is keenly interested in nursing & is fully occupied worry has gone for the present.

How is your biography getting on? I am longing to read it –

It is a beautiful thing that Dublin is going to get all the pictures & endowment for the Gallery. Sir Hugh Lane will indeed have given great gifts.[2]

I will try again & write soon when I am less tired – tonight I am stupid with tiredness.

Alwys your friend
Maud

It was a *real joy* getting your letters.

310
                                        17 Rue de l'Annonciation
                                        Passy
                                        Paris
                                        1st Oct [1915]

My dear Willie

We have just returned to Paris after 6 months hard nursing in Paris Plage within sound of the cannon. I am rather worn out & had to take a rest.

All I want to do now is to work for peace – It is the only thing worth working for – How to begin? What to do? I don't know. I feel so bewildered & helpless & yet I know a great wonderful movement might be started if the Pope with his immense spiritual power could work through the great material force of Socialism – It might mean the reformation of the world. It would mean the saving of European civilisation which seems doomed at present.

I am very sorry Mr Gregory has decided to go to war.[1] It seems so outside his life & duty, but one cannot tell how others feel things. It must be a terrible anxiety to Lady Gregory.

Life is so tragic now & when one says goodbye to friends one feels the chances are one will never see them again –

I was having tea 5 days ago with Millevoye & his son.[2] Today I just received a telegram from Millevoye his son is killed – & I knew it two days ago, at prayer in Passy Church I saw him dead but I did not dare say it to anyone. The horror of this war has made me strangely sensitive & clairvoyant. I feel the great battle & the thousands of souls going out before I read of it in the papers – I think it was to escape from this that I took up the material work of nursing, & now that that is over it is beginning again.

Iseult has taken position of Secretary to a big Aviation Society[3] – it means £100 a year & meeting a good many people chiefly engineers & politicians & aviators. There is only about 3 or 4 hours' work a day at most. I think for a time at least it will be good for her – though I would rather she had gone in thoroughly for literature, but I don't think this need prevent her.

How I wish we could meet. There is so much I want to talk with you about.

    Alwys your friend
      Maud Gonne

311
                    [Letterhead]
                    Hôpital Auxiliaire No. 117
                    Lycée Janson-de-Sailly
                    106, Rue de la Pompe

                    Croix-Rouge Française
                    Union des Femmes de France
                    Telep. Passy 86–63
                    Cabinet du Chirurgien-Chef
                    [early November 1915]

My dear Willie

It is long since I heard from you – Are you in London? Are you able to work? I got rather worn out nursing at Paris Plage, the work was very hard there, so I am taking a rest, i.e. I am only doing night nurse work & that only twice a week.

I am trying to paint again, but I find it very hard to concentrate my mind on anything. I can't get away from the thought of this war – How is it possible for any art or literature or beauty to exist? In France all the vital forces & young strength of the nations are in the trenches forced to kill or be killed. No criticism of any sort is allowed; I heard of a woman being arrested because in the street she ventured to throw doubt on the result of the war – The only expression of opinion tolerated is a blind admiration for one's own side & an equally blind & furious hatred of the enemy.

Romain Rollin[1] is the only man courageous enough to write & speak openly in favour of peace.

I got a quaint hysterical letter from Miss Coates. She wants to do *real work* for the allies & asks me if I will find a child who has been mutilated by the Germans & she will send money for it!

I am writing this at 1 o'clock in the morning at the hospital [End of letter missing]

312

My dear Willie

I wrote you a letter at the hospital over a week ago, & did not post it – Then Sunday I had this strange experience, which I wrote down at once intending to send you but didn't do so – I send it now.[1]

A small circle of people in Ireland, many of whom I do not know personally, keep the Celtic festivals, which correspond wonderfully with those of the Catholic Church. I enclose the paper which they sent me for the Samhain festival as it may have some bearing on the experience – The 'Samhain thoughts' at the end of the paper was part of something I wrote to Ella Young about a month ago and I don't know just why they incorporated it, in the *Samhain* paper.[2]

Let me know what you think of this experience – The war has got on my nerves & made me at times clairvoyant – I have on several occasions seen deaths of friends who have been killed & get horrible impressions of the great battles – I hate all this, but cannot get away from it. I fully realise what you say of the danger of becoming [?'A nerve air which do creep'] for in this passive state one does no good to others or to oneself.

It is alright when it leads to action & if I were in Ireland working I would get the same careless peace I used to have – but Ireland would mean work that would perhaps cut me off from my life in France, which till Seagan is grown up would be disastrous, & for Iseult too it would be hard.

Hospital life though tiring does not supply the activity I need. It is not work I *ought* to be doing.

I believe by great spiritual concentration & effort one might do much but I have not the strength & courage for that concentration – on the spiritual plane I seem to be passive.

Can one be positive & active at once on the Spiritual & on the material plane? I think not. The great contemplatives are rarely active themselves in the world, though they cause great activities – & the great leaders of world movements are probably quite passive on the spiritual plane. They receive currents & forces which they put in motion by material activity in the world. It is part of that old truth you taught me long ago, of the reversal of things in the two worlds –

I am speechless with rage over the refusal of the English lines to carry Irish emigrants of military age to America.[3] There is no conscription, therefore why should they not go? I hope the American lines will take up the traffic with energy – not that I want Irish emigration to increase, but it is simply diabolical to force men by starvation into this war – Have Carson's volunteers[4] gone yet?

I am longing to see the poems[5] Do get them typed & send me copies. I wish we could meet & have a long talk, there is so much I want to hear about. How is your autobiography going on? Where are you in it?

Passport difficulties are getting so great that my cousin May had great difficulty in returning to France where she is nursing in a hospital. If I went over to London I don't know if I should get back here easily.

Did you see that Victor Collins, MacBride's Friend, was refused permission to go to Switzerland. He was arrested at the English boat & refused to land in France. Was it to white wash him for further use in Ireland. He wrote reams about it in the advanced Irish papers.

Write soon
Alwys your friend
    Maud

Send me back the Samhain papers.

313   7th November [1915]

Samhain has been for me a terrible confusion of effort. I felt I could grasp nothing with my conscious mind. I could hardly pray connectedly for the Souls of the Dead.

For three days I have been haunted by an air with the Rhythm of a dance reel. I hummed it unconsciously, I walked to its measure, in spite of me my feet beat time to it. I could not get away from it. It exasperated me, it seemed so futile. At moments it brought a feeling of exaltation & of unnatural triumph – but chiefly the feeling of confusion prevailed.

Suddenly this morning I understood & at Mass was able to translate into consciousness scraps of the experience I have been going through –

1st I suddenly remembered where I had heard the air before – It was, as I with a few friends rested on Slieve Gullion – It seemed then to come out of the heart of the mountain & was accompanied by the beating of hammers on anvils. It had seemed to me to be connected with the Smiths, also the no. 16 & perhaps of its connection with the smiths it reminded me of the music of Wagner's *Siegfried* & of the song of the Sword. I told all this to my friends at the time – I heard also an air like, but not exactly like it, though the rhythm was identical at a Gaelic league Feis, it was played for the 8 hand reels.

This morning as I went to church this dance air sounded with terrific persistency & with a sort of wild triumph. I could hardly keep my feet from dancing.

In church I prayed to be able to keep my thoughts on the Divine Sacrifice, but during the sermon, of which I heard nothing, things became clear –

I have been seeing, I think I have been among, masses of spirits of those who have been killed in this war, they are being marshalled & drawn together by waves of rhythmic music, it draws them into dances of strange patterns.

The thousands of Irish soliders who have been killed are being drawn together in this wild reel tune I have been hearing. They are dancing to it, some with almost frenzied intensity & enthusiasm while others seem to be drawn in unwillingly not knowing why, but the rhythm is so strong & compelling they have to dance. It is leading them back to the spiritual Ireland from which they have wandered & where they would find their self realisation & perfectionment & to whom they would bring their strength.

On the whole as they got far into the dance current there was a freshness & innocence & joy that was good to see – They had killed & been killed without hate & they had gone inconsequently into this war, they were being brought back in this dance rhythm which is young & inconsequent but very strong & appeals to them irresistibly.

Others have died with a definite idea of sacrifice to an ideal, they were held by the stronger & deeper Rhythms of the chants, leading in wonderful patterns to a deeper peace, the peace of the Crucified, which is above the currents of nationalities & storms, but for all that they will not be separated from Ireland for as an entity she has followed the path of Sacrifice & has tasted of the Grail & the strength they will bring her is greater.

Scraps
which I am writing things which I thought I understood clearly are getting dim & confused.

The Rhythms have colors, that dance tune was green, the German Rhythm which is most powerful I think was red purple by their rhythm they should conquer.

I saw a group of scarlet trumpeters very triumphant & beautiful which was connected with England & yet my general impression was that England was going down because she has no great Rhythm.

I thought one ought to hold on to air [?our] dance Rhythms even though they are not great like German Rhythms for some day out of their freshness, their primitiveness and their inconsequence a great deep power may be revealed or evolved.

314   [Paris]
                                              Thursday [11 November 1915]
My dear Willie
   Claire de Pratz has exaggerated. When I came back first from Paris-
Plage I was very worn out – Hospital work is very hard, one is
standing all day long – that & the sea air had brought on an attack
of rheumatism & the Doctor said I must rest, but though I had a
very swollen knee I was able to walk & am now nearly all right,
though I get tired easily. It would be lovely if you could come over
to Paris, for there is much I want to talk to you about & it would
do me great good to see you, but my physical health is alright. It
would do Iseult also a lot of good to see you.
   I wrote you a long letter or rather *letters* yesterday. I hope you
will get them safely – as they were about a strange psychical
experience they may worry the censor but I hope he will let you have
them in the end.
   Thank you so much for your letter
   Yours alwys
       Maud

315   17 Rue de l'Annonciation
                                              [Paris]
                                              14th November [1915]
My dear Willie
   knowing your love of the Shamrock! I am sending you this little
design[1] which I rather like.
   Our National Emblem is the greatest symbol of the world but
because there is no art discipline, it has become banalised It ought to
be a punishable offence to degrade a symbol.
   You must not worry about my health I am really better
   Alwys your friend
       Maud

Iseult has got the book on India & will write you soon. Thank you
for her.

316   [Paris]
                                              Saturday [November/December 1915]
My dear Willie
   I am so sorry you have a cold & are feeling so tired.
   I would much like to hear Mrs Manus music. Does she know
Bailly, the French theosophist, MacGregor's friend, who I think you

met at my house, he plays an extraordinary instrument he has invented which has the quarter tones on which he gets curious Indian music which he says is Deva music.

I don't think the music I heard has anything to do with India.

It is the music of a reel almost exactly like one that is played for the 8 handed reels at some of the Gaelic league festivities, only the music I heard seemed wilder & with infinite variations, though always on the same primitive air. I hummed it to Iseult at the time. Now it has completely gone from me that I can not even hum it. But I know I can get it when I shall hear again the music played for the reels.

I think you are too well known to be arrested for an anarchist by mistake, like your artist friends & there is I think no difficulty in getting to Paris, my cousins come backwards & forwards, so if you find yourself free, do come. I have no longer my little studio at the top of the house; times were too hard to keep it on, but I can get a nice room for you near & you will take your meals with us.

Does Lord Loriburn & Lord Courteny's[?] speeches in the House of Lords[1] mean that a glimmer of reason is dawning?

Send me a copy of poems when you get them typed

I hope you are better

Affecaly your friend

Maud Gonne

317   17 Rue de l'Annonciation
                                                                        Passy
                                                                        Paris
                                                                        14th Dec [1915]

My dear Willie

I am anxious at not hearing from you. I only hope it means you are busy & interested in things, but as in your last letter you said you had asthma & a cold, I would very much like to have a few words to say you are well.

Also when you think of it, I would like to have the Samhain notes back.

Is the Player Queen finished?[1] Is there any chance of seeing you in Paris?

How are the biographical notes[2] progressing. I am longing to read them. Where have you got to in them?

It would be lovely if you could spend Xmas with us.

Iseult is taking a rest from hospital work till the New Year. I am still doing night work, but only twice a week, so we have lots of free time at present.

I am painting again, but find it hard to do regular work.
In haste
Your friend
     Maud Gonne

318   Rue de l'Annonciation
                                                 Passy
                                                 Paris
                                                 Sunday [December 1915]

My dear Willie
    Thank you so much for the book[1] which arrived safely one post
earlier than your letter.
    I wanted to read it & then to write you at once but in answer to
your letter I send this in haste & will write again as soon as I have
read it. The first chapter which I read last night delighted me – I read
it with all the greater interest as it is that part of your life about which
I know the least.
    It must be very hard to select out of the mass of one's child
memories, the essential things to note, the things which have really
influenced one's life – I have tried in a desultory kind of way to note
down child memories & I found they crowded back in an
extraordinary way – much more vividly than memories of later life –
    It will be nice if you can come to Paris. Iseult & I are both looking
forward to it. There is so much I want to talk of with you – & I am
longing to hear the poems – Iseult got knocked up with hospital work
& has had to give up nursing for the present. I am still working but
shall take a rest when you come over –
    I will write in a day or two when I have read more of Reveries
In haste
Alwys your friend
     Maud Gonne

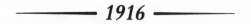

1916

319   [Paris]
                                                             [early 1916]

My dear Willie
    I like the last part of your book even better than the first. The first
is interesting but it does not tell of the things that were really vital
to you *as a child*, from it I could not tell what sort of child you were

there was much about others & little about yourself – you have written about what might have importance for you now not what had importance to you then – It must be very hard not to do that, to get back into one's child's skin. Once you get to the part where your father's influence played on you & you accepted or differed from his thought it became very real & living.

· I like all you have written of your meetings with Dowden[1] – & I am very glad you wrote about Taylor & quoted his wonderful speech[2] – I think you have feared being egotistical & so have not made yourself – especially in the beginning, enough the centre of your own book.

Now having said all these critical things because you ask me to tell you exactly the impression it makes on me, I must tell you that the whole gave me great pleasure. I read it quickly & eagerly at first & then slowly afterwards – & I liked it immensely, but I often wished for a greater detail especially as to your first beliefs.

Iseult is not doing very much – she has given up hospital work, of which I am glad, it was too hard for her. She still retains her secretariat at Millevoye's aviation association for the material reason that the £8 a month enables her to dress well & the work is so light. a couple of hours in the afternoon covers it, true she has been brought into contact with a nasty side of life & has had some nasty moral shocks – on the whole I think they have done her no harm, & it has given me great confidence in her, for she has shown great moral dignity combined with tact & gracefulness – a really rare combination & quite surprising in anyone so young & in some ways such a child as Iseult.

I am longing more than ever for life in Ireland – France after this war will not be a possible place to live in.

Please send me back the Samhain papers when you can. I want to return them – I should have done so already, I would rather not say I have lent them because it is understood we do not lend them – I have the Beltaine[3] ones now, which are interesting too.

It will be very nice if you come to Paris.[4] Have you heard for certain of Lady Gregory's dates yet?

Kathleen & Thora arrive here today but only for a few days, they are going to Switzerland, as Kathleen's lungs are again giving her trouble.

Write soon –
Yours alwys
    Maud Gonne

320   Rue de l'Annonciation
                                             Paris xvi
                                             16th March [1916]

My dear Willie

Thank you for your letters & Joyce's book[1] – I have been meaning to write, but I have again been ill & a return of influenza. I am still voiceless – It has made me lazy – Paris is terribly unhealthy just now. We are all going to Colleville for the Easter holidays from the 24th to the 15th April. I am going to supervise the sowing of the potato fields & garden as famine precautions. It will be needed. If only we were in Ireland I would be so much happier.

I have read Joyce's book – I read it with wearyness & difficulty, it seemed to me so *deadly dull* – It sent me to sleep several evenings. I struggled on with it because of what you said & generally, even when I may not always like I admire what you recommend. The childhood part was the best. One can understand a child being articulate & searchingly hesitant – it may develop something interesting, but when that goes on indefinitely into manhood, one wonders why it was worth anyone's while writing dreary chapters about him, or worthwhile reading them. There is no character vividly drawn except the careless self satisfied drunken father.

I think Willie you have not yourself read the book – or only glanced at it for I can't find Skeffington[2] – & there is no mention of me in the '98 procession as you said there was, though the laying of the Wolfe Tone Memorial stone was mentioned & a French delegate.

There are little bits of coarseness dragged in unnecessarily, because so called realist writers who seem to me to miss the real essence of life, think they may get an effect by shocking their readers which will make them forget the monotonous dullness of the pages.

To have lived in Dublin & seen nothing but its uglyness & squalor, to have associated with those eager intensely living people & to have been able to describe nothing but dull futility & boredom seems to denote a nature to whom the stars would look like bits of tinsel paper –

Tell me the truth – confess – you have not read the book yourself? Pound has perhaps read you extracts – isn't that so?[3]

He has done a kind act in getting a pension for a man in need[4] & has to defend this act of charity on literary grounds. That is respectable & don't damp him by telling him how dull I find the book – I have passed it on to Iseult, but I hardly think she will have the courage to read it. She is working hard & has written some lovely fragments. She never finishes or completes anything, that is her stumbling block.

Have you got the [?indecipherable] back for the poor magician? I hope so. It is a most amusing story. Did you yourself get any interesting communications on it? Can any one work it or must it

Letter from Les Mouettes, 1907.

ABOVE Les Mouettes, the house at Colleville-sur-Mer that Maud Gonne purchased.

TOP RIGHT Portrait of Seán, aged four, by Maud Gonne in 1908.

RIGHT A self-portrait of the artist Granié. 'I spent the day in Granié's studio, he lets me come down and draw with him.' Letter **42,** 1905

Constance, Countess de Markiewicz.
'. . . long ago I saw her ride
Under Ben Bulben to the meet,
The beauty of her country-side
With all youth's lonely wildness stressed.'
W.B. Yeats, *On A Political Prisoner*

Comte de Crémont, MacGregor Mathers, and
Maud Gonne outside Notre Dame des Victoires,
Paris, on St Patrick's Day, *circa* 1909.

John Quinn and W.B. Yeats after their
reconciliation. 'Quinn has come out better than
you have in it, somehow you never photograph
well.' Letter **299**, 1914

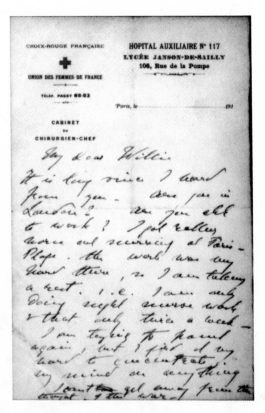

Letter sent by Maud Gonne to Yeats from the Red Cross hospital in France in November 1915 (see page 360)

Military Government of Paris Railway Pass, August 1915.

'Knowing your love of Shamrocks! I am sending you this little design which I rather like.' Letter **315,** November 1915

THE SINN FEIN RISING AS IT AFFECTED PROPERTY

The damage to property is estimated at £2,500,000. One hundred and seventy-nine buildings were destroyed by flame and shell, the area that suffered most being Lower Sackville Street, where the General Post Office stood. It was the rebels' central stronghold, and was entirely burnt out.

A BARRICADE AT THE FOUR COURTS   RESCUING VALUABLES FROM THE SMOKING RUINS   A BARRICADE MADE OF MOTORS

FROM THE TOP OF THE NELSON COLUMN: BOTH SIDES OF SACKVILLE STREET, SHOWING THE BURNT-OUT IMPERIAL HOTEL, AND POST OFFICE

THE CENTRE OF THE DEVASTATED AREA: A CORNER OF SACKVILLE STREET AND EDEN QUAY, VIEWED FROM O'CONNELL BRIDGE

'I am fearfully anxious for my friends and for news of what is taking place. Of your charity Willie quickly send me some London papers.' Letter **323**

DARE HUNS' BATTLE-CRUISERS RAID OUR COASTS AGAIN ?—P. 2.

DAILY SKETCH.

GUARANTEED DAILY NETT SALE MORE THAN 1,000,000 COPIES.

No. 2,237.   LONDON, WEDNESDAY, MAY 10, 1916.   [Registered as a Newspaper.]   ONE HALFPENNY.

IRISH REBEL CHIEF'S SURRENDER : FIRST PHOTOGRAPHS.

Major McBride, on the left in uniform (who was shot), being marched away after sentence.

Patrick H. Pearse (shot), the " President of the Irish Republic," surrendering to the military.

The Countess Markievicz leaving in charge of a wardress after her court-martial.

Two of the brothers Plunkett (in slouch hats) under escort.

These photographs are the first to be published showing the scene of the surrender of the Irish rebel chief, and the leading figures in the insurrection leaving after being sentenced by court-martial. To psychologists the faces of these men and the woman who played her part with them reveal them more as misguided fanatics than as desperate revolutionists.

'The whole tragedy is so appalling I can hardly collect my thoughts.' Letter 325

Maud Gonne some
months after her release
from Holloway Gaol.

RIGHT Iseult and Francis.

73 St Stephen's Green
after a house raid during
the Civil War. 'The CID
were raiding everywhere
for him.' Letter **368**

Seán MacBride in the early
twenties around the time
he was 'on the run' during
the Civil War and after.

Senator W.B. Yeats at Punchestown Races.

Letter **WBY 16.**

Charlotte Despard on the steps of Roebuck House. (1921–1932)

Maud Gonne MacBride at a Women's Prisoners' Defence League meeting in the 1930s.

Madame and Anna at Roebuck House.

'Oh how you hate old age – well so do I, . . . but I, who am more a rebel against man than you, rebel less against nature, and accept the inevitable and go with it gently into the unknown.' Letter **373,** 1928

'Boldly decrepitude is wisdom; young
We loved each other and were ignorant.'
W.B. Yeats, *After Long Silence*

have a medium? I expect the presence of a medium is necessary – Horton's story is strange & pathetic.[5] Did he go back to the hotel again & enquire for the lady, or if his letter had been delivered? Even if the lady was a living person it is possible that Miss Lock[6] appeared through her to him & smiled through the other woman's face – I think the dead do sometimes send us messages in this way.

We see a great deal of the Rummels they are charming, one likes them more & more as one knows them. His music really helps one out of the horrid obsession of this war –

I hope you will get your castle.[7] It seems to suit you so well. It is a dream which should be realised – It would help you with your work I think –

How soon will the picture controversy be settled?[8] I do hope you will succeed.

Tell Joyce to write his next book about Redmond & his colleagues. He might do them justice.

Always your friend
Maud Gonne

---

321 Hospital de Lycée Janson
2 o'clock in the morning
21st March [1916]

My dear Willie

I am writing this from the hospital where I am on night duty taking care of some terribly mangled wrecks from the Verdun battle – for the moment all are calm & more or less asleep so I fill up my time writing letters.

I began a letter to you at home but was interrupted. I am sending you my Bealtaine thoughts, as you said you liked the Samhain ones. I get these thoughts generally at mass. I find concentration very hard alone. I could get it when you invoked & I can get it often in the extraordinary atmosphere of peace & purity & effort which surround the Mass. I have sent back all the other Bealtaine papers or I would send them to you also. If it doesn't bother you too much please return the paper to me when you have read it – I am so sorry you had such a lot of bother over the last. Hunting for things is such a devil's waste of time & so aggravating.

Iseult has been writing some really VERY remarkable things lately. I am longing for you to see them.

They are very personal perhaps too personal to be published if not I am sure they would have great success – Her style is really wonderful & she gets a living quality into what she writes which she used not to have – She has also written a critique on d'Annunzio & his work which is full of originality & in a few words seems to go straight to the root of things in an astounding way. She is now writing on Huysmans, who is a great favourite of hers but I have not seen yet what she has written. I want so much for you to see her work & it would be great encouragement to her, & she needs this, for she has little or no confidence in herself –

I did not feel at all surprised when you told me about the Hawk influence[1] – I always knew it in a vague way that you & I are both connected with a hawk. It has been my symbol which I designated in a certain occult work – & I think it has been in several of the visions we have had together though when I tried to find it in some of our old records I could only find it in one.

You had been told you had received the initiation of knowledge & were about to receive the initiation of power – Then when we were trying through the initiation of knowledge to get back the knowledge of our past lives, we were told we should find it at the *meeting of the winds*. The sword then became a fiery pyramid & at its apex was the meeting of the winds & there hovered a *great bird* like an eagle.

Though it appeared in this initiation of the Sword, I think the hawk would belong more to the spear & to the sun. How I would like to see your play.[2] I hope it will have great success & send me paper cuttings about it.

My poor little boy has had a very bad attack of influenza – he is better but still weak & thin so we are going to Colleville for a month about the 1st of April

Write soon
Alwys your friend
Maud Gonne

322   Paris
                                                          Monday [April 1916]

My dear Willie

Miss Delaney has just come in, in a great state of excitement saying she fears Mlle de Pratz was on the Sussex[1] & that at her home in Paris there is no news of her – She also says that she sent you a wire yesterday, *in my name* asking if you knew if she had started on the Sussex. She had heard me say you thought perhaps of crossing to France with Mlle de Pratz so she thought you would know her movements. She used my name because she thought you would not trouble to answer her – She is so excited I have difficulty in making out if it is some psychic intuition that makes her suppose Mlle de Pratz with whom she has made great friends, was on the Sussex, or any fact of date. As far as I can make out Mlle de Pratz said she was crossing about this time, so I hope she was not on the Sussex. I have told Miss Delaney that it is unlikely that you have received the telegram as probably you are in the country. I am glad you have decided not to come to Paris just now for travelling is certainly dangerous, though it is a disappointment not to see you. We are going to Colleville on Friday for a month May Berti-Clay is with us. She has worn herself out nursing & wants a rest. I also shall be glad to forget hospitals for a time –

When is your play to be acted. I am longing to hear about it.

In haste

Your friend

 Maud Gonne

Write to me

 Les Mouettes

 Colleville

 par Vierville

 Calvados

On Easter Monday, 24th April, members of the Irish Volunteers and the Citizen Army took over key buildings in Dublin and read a proclamation declaring a Republic 'in the name of God and the dead generations'. The buildings were held for about a week, but, with artillery clearing street barricades and a gunboat in the river, the centre of the city was reduced to ruins. On 27 April the French papers carried a report from London stating that martial law had been proclaimed and rigorous methods were being employed in Dublin. On 30 April Reynold's Newspaper *announced: 'Rebels in circle of Steel'. It was on Saturday, 29 April, that Pearse and the wounded Connolly called a ceasefire and agreed to an unconditional surrender.*

323   Colleville

                 par Vierville

                 Calvados

                 Friday [April 1916]

My dear Willie

Your poems[1] reached me here. Thank you so much. They are a great joy to me. – I agree with you they are not well brought out. What a contrast to your sister's printing, but the poems themselves *are* so beautiful –

I wish you were here with me for the country is looking so beautiful & it is so good to be away from the sadness of men among the songs of birds & the joy of life & the flowers – we all dread having to return to Paris for Bichon's school & my hospital work of the 5th of May. We hate leaving the lovely country loveliness.

The papers have just arrived & I have just seen about the troubles in Ireland. It is awful to be so far away. I am fearfully anxious & distressed.

I have only the French papers with Birell's[2] answers in House of Commons saying that troops from the Curragh have quelled the disturbances in Dublin & 12 people are killed & that the authorities are now masters of the situation – but he also says that communications with Ireland are not yet regularly established & one wonders if the authorities are as victorious as he pretends. He also says 12 people have been killed. I am fearfully anxious for my friends & for news of what really is taking place. Of your charity Willie quickly send me some London papers. They will reach me I think though probably nothing sent from Dublin directly will get through.

If only the Irish M.P.s will pluck up their courage & make a decent stand in England. It is their lamentable weakness that has brought the trouble about. Casement's arrest is also announced but no details given.[3]

PLEASE send me papers quickly – It is awful not knowing what is happening.

Write soon. It is possible Iseult & I will be in London soon if I can get over passport difficulties.

 Alwys your friend
  Maud Gonne

On 4 May the Daily Mirror *announced that 'Three Rebel Ringleaders were shot' on 3 May after trial by court martial. They were Patrick Pearse, Thomas MacDonagh and the old Fenian, Thomas Clarke. On 5 May the papers reported that four more of the leaders had been shot on 4 May after court martial.*

324   Colleville
                      [May 1916]
Dear Willie
Thank you for your letter & paper forwarded from Paris where we return tomorrow.

I am overwhelmed by the tragedy & the greatness of the sacrifice our country men & women have made. They have raised the Irish cause again to a position of tragic dignity. They will have made it impossible to ignore Ireland or to say that she is satisfied at the conference where at the end of the war, much will be heard about the Right of small nationalities.

If materially they have failed, & I think that failure must have been inevitable for the whole of this war has proved that inferiority of arms & scarcity of ammunition condemns the bravest to inevitable failure – their courage & determination in the cause of freedom has equalled that of any of the soldiers of the belligerents & has surpassed the courage of most of them, who are fighting poor devils because they *cannot* do anything else. Practically, & *politically* I do not think their heroique sacrifice has been in vain.

You are quite right in saying the English Government should have, after passing Home Rule, at once given power to an Irish executive & if they had this tragedy would not have happened. They would have done it, if they had been sincere but Irish parliamentarians *themselves* have told me in Paris that they considered Home Rule was betrayed & that after the war another government would rescind the Home Rule bill.[1] I heard this opinion also from a french journalist who generally know things English pretty well, though of course it is the fashion up till now in France to say that Ireland is now quite satisfied & that England has granted her all she wants.

The disgraceful trick of trying to dishonor Roger Casement[2] is already beginning, little notes in the French press pretending to come from a *Dutch source* couple his name with that of [?Enlenberg],[3] & said that it was reported he was arrested in Germany. In Ireland at least no one will believe this.

At the beginning of the war I had a horrible vision which affected me for days. I saw Dublin, in darkness & figures lying on the quays by O'Connell Bridge, they were either wounded or dying of hunger – It was so terribly clear it has haunted me ever since. There must have been scenes like that in the streets of Dublin during the last days.

I hope to see you for I am going to try to get to London with Iseult in a week, my difficulty is always leaving the boy –

Have you news of Helen Moloney? Perhaps you will hear through the players. One feels anxious for every friend one has in Dublin –

Thank you for writing, our letters crossed, & the newspapers – I go back to Paris tomorrow.

Alwys your friend
Maud Gonne

On 7 May the French papers announced that the eighth rebel, John MacBride, had been executed on 5 May. At the Jesuit school of Saint-Louis-de-Gonzague in Passy a roll of honour was called every morning of pupils' relatives killed in the war. John MacBride's name was included.

On 8 May four more were executed. On 9 May the thirteenth execution took place amid mounting protests in Ireland and England.

325

17 Ave de l'Annonciation
Passy
Paris
Tuesday 9th May [1916]

My dear Willie

Thank you for writing so often & sending me the papers – I am ill with sorrow – so many of my best & noblest friends gone – I envy them for this world does not seem a place to live in when such crimes can go unpunished. The shelling & destruction of an open town like Dublin[1] seem to me one of the greatest crimes of this awful war – It has disgusted every French person I have spoken to, though with the alliance the French press cannot voice this disgust – 'It is so difficult to understand the cynicism of their photos' one man said to me as he looked at the English illustrated papers exhibited at some of the kiosques & he added, 'what effect will this have on Irish troops at the front?'

On Sunday morning I read in the papers the announcement of Major MacBride's execution he has died for Ireland. Yesterday the *Daily Mail* Paris edition had a vile attack on his memory – I sent the enclosed letter to the French press, I could not bring myself to reply to the *Daily Mail* –

The arrest of Count & Countess Plunkett astonishes me – It is well, for it will stir some who are not easily stirred – & unite them in the common indignation –

I am glad you have news of Lady Gregory but of course she would have no cause for fear – Even the English panic could not go to the length of arresting her! I am returning your sister's interesting letter –

I am anxious for news of so many. The accounts of the coffinless & unidentified dead alarms me – The papers say we shall probably never know the number of victims of the shells which have destroyed half Dublin.

I can't write more now –
Always your friend
Maud Gonne

Among the prisoners taken were many friends, including Countess Markiewicz, who had her death sentence commuted to penal servitude for life, and the sixty-five-year-old Count Plunkett, whose death sentence was commuted to ten years' penal servitude.

326 [Paris]

Thursday [11 May 1916]

Dear Willie

I forgot to return your sister's letter yesterday & also to enclose the letter I sent to the French papers & which appeared yesterday – all but the first three lines which I have marked & which I thought the censor would stop!! –

The whole tragedy is so appalling I can hardly collect my thoughts. I feel stunned & stupid. I shall stay in France for the present, where everyone is kind & sympathetic & thoroughly shocked at the brutality & *folly* of their ally –

I would like to go to Dublin to nurse the wounded there, but from the polite references to myself in the *Times*,[1] & one or two other English Papers which Miss Delaney brought me, I do not think I should get a passport –

Thank you for so much for you kind letter – Major MacBride by his Death has left a name for Seagan to be proud of. Those who die for Ireland are sacred.

Those who enter Eternity by the great door of Sacrifice atone for all – in one moment they do more than all our effort. Thank you again for all your kind thoughtfulness for me.

You too must be much shaken, by the death of friends & the shattering of dreams, but your work will go on & is more necessary than ever now.

Alwys your friend

Maud Gonne

Copy of the letter which I sent to the French papers

Dear Sirs

The *Daily Mail* (Paris Edition), <in order to dishonour the memory of one of those who gave his life for the Irish cause>, while announcing the execution of Major MacBride, said that during the Boer War he went to Paris without [?an excuse] wanting to raise an Irish Legion to fight against England, and that Colonel Villebois-Mareuil refused to have anything to do with him, and that in the end in the Transvaal the Boers were glad to get rid of him because he stole some horses.

I separated from my husband for personal reasons, but I don't want the memory of him to be dishonoured. Major MacBride was in the Transvaal long before the Boer War. He had grouped together his fellow countrymen who were working in the mines in a patriotic Irish association. He had, therefore, everything at hand to get together an Irish regiment which he presented to President Kruger, by whom he was named Major. It was only at the end of the

Transvaal war that Major MacBride came to Paris and received unanimous praise, which I heard, from President Kruger & Steyne, both for himself & his regiment. General Botha thanked him publicly for the services he had given.

 Maud Gonne

On 11 May John Dillon, speaking in the House of Commons, said to the government: 'You are letting loose a river of blood and, make no mistake about it, between two races who, after three hundred years of hatred and strife, we had nearly succeeded in bringing together.' The House was also informed that the medical authorities had been consulted before the trial of James Connolly, that he had been certified as in a fit state to undergo his trial, and that there was no reason, in the interests of humanity, why his execution should be delayed. James Connolly, suffering from gangrene, was tried in bed, brought to be executed on a stretcher, and shot sitting in a chair, on 12 May.

327   [Paris]
            Wednesday night [May 1916]

My dear Willie

Iseult & May started for London on Sunday, & I suppose forgot to wire me on arrival for I have heard nothing yet & am getting anxious. She is looking forward to seeing you. Get her to show you some of the things she has been writing especially one on her walks & conversations with Mukerjea at Arrens. There is something charming & fresh about it – & unexpected.

I am glad she will be seeing you, it will do her good & inspire her to write more – She is not at all strong & has grown very thin. She has had some nasty heart attacks brought on, the doctor says, by over smoking. She gets nicotine poisoning & yet I can't induce her to give up or even moderate her smoking & *it is killing her* – she smokes a paquet of cigarettes a day. I tell you this in case you can get her to stop.

I am afraid Mabel Beardsley's death must have been a great grief to you. She was such a beautiful & charming woman.

I sent translations of Shaw's letters[1] to several French papers. The Editors took them with avidity but the censor forbid it. The censor in its wisdom, has decreed that France is not to hear the truth about its ally's doings in Ireland.

Pearse's poem, written the night before his execution is beautiful.[2] He was a great spiritual power, & his love of Ireland is so very great.

The deaths of those leaders are full of beauty & romance & 'They will be speaking forever, the people shall hear them forever.'[3]

Mahaffy's letter to the *Times* on Mr Dillon & Sein Fein is a disgrace.[4] It is vulgar & commonplace besides being untrue. To think a contemptible creature like that should have the Education of young men in his hands! I am sorry for Trinity. It must feel ashamed of its provost.

I should like to talk with you very much, & I may still join Iseult in London soon.

I must end now for it is very late, but I am suffering badly from insomnia just now, & go to bed late & get up early. I am, with meritorious industry, collecting from the English papers accounts of the Rebellion & English methods of dealing with it. I am going to translate it into French for publication, if a day ever comes when the Censor will disappear – though this war, which we are assured is a people's war, a war for Liberty, is doing away so thoroughly with all vestige of liberty everywhere that I doubt, in our time, ever having a free press or free speech again. In the meantime the dead are lying so thick round Verdun that they will soon hide what is left of the battlements & when all the men are killed & disabled I hear talk of conscripting the women

Always your friend
Maud Gonne

Thursday Morning. Still no news of Iseult!

George Bernard Shaw wrote:

My own view is that the men who were shot in cold blood, after their capture or surrender, were prisoners of war, and that it was therefore entirely incorrect to slaughter them. . . . an Irishman resorting to arms to achieve the independence of his country is doing only what an Englishman will do, if it be their misfortune to be invaded and conquered by the Germans in the course of the present war. . . . The Military authorities and the English government must have known that they were canonising their prisoners.

What Shaw said was true. Gradually public opinion in Ireland turned in favour of the executed men and what they stood for. Relatives were cheered by crowds as they left the numerous masses held throughout the city to commemorate the dead.

Home Rule was again under discussion in the House of Commons. In June, George Russell, himself of Ulster Protestant stock, wrote to Balfour, whom he deemed to have influence with the northern Unionists, making various proposals, and ended by quoting Arthur Griffith: 'If a good Bill accepted by Ulster had been introduced I and

*my party would have disappeared from Ireland. Nobody would have
listened to us.'*

WBY 7   18 Woburn Buildings
                                             W.C.
                                             Sunday [May 1916]

My dear Friend
    I send you a charming essay on *Sinn Féin* by Robinson[1] (I shall
write [?]& try [?]& persuade him to do a history of the movement)
and an article by Healey.[2] Healey prints for the first time the rumour
that the troops used poison gas. There are sure now to be questions
in parliament. If they have done so they have played into our hands
but we must not take it on his word. He says all the fine Dublin
buildings are in ashes which is nonsense, the only public building
destroyed is I think the Post Office & that is a dull affair of 1820 or
so. He is always exaggerated. There is no news. I brought Iseult to
meet Shaw but she was very shy & only began to talk when lunch
was over. She dines here tomorrow, she & Mrs Clay,[3] to meet the
Pounds.
    If you come to London I shall of course be well pleased but Dublin
would hardly be a good place for you just now. The authorities are
it seems in a panic & there is martial law which is no law. Mrs
Chetwynd[4] the novelist told me a couple of days ago that Bailey[5] &
a second rate novelist called Vere Stackpole[6] who had just come from
Ireland told her that new and worse trouble was brewing. I don't
believe them for Ireland has neither the ammunition nor the folly but
while official nerves are in this state Dublin will be no place for those
who like to speak their mind. In England somebody is arrested from
time to time for speaking against recruiting or the like in some Hotel
bar, in Ireland the whole Hotel would probably be arrested also.
When it is over there will be a new Ireland to build up. Till it is over
Colleville would be a quiet place & Iseult tells me that she is going
to bring me there. She is quite a commanding person now, no longer
a fanciful child.
    It does really look like Home Rule almost at once. Asquith will
feel [?]later it has been [?]evident that his position is weakened in the
coming peace conference. I do not think he was responsible for the
Dublin executions though he had to defend them. They were I think
the work of the military & of Irish officials. The man who shot
Sheehy Skeffington was the son of [?Lord] Colthurst.[7] He is Irish &
a friend of Horace Cole, the practical joker who is hardly sane. As
the mad attract their like one can measure him. His relations say his
shooting of Skeffington was 'the first sane act of his life' which
suggests that he shot him because he disliked his opinions. Skeffing-

ton perhaps had made himself unpopular with the military. Asquith evidently stopped the proposed secret trial of Colthurst on his arrival in Dublin.

Yours affectionately
W B Yeats

328   [Paris]
                                                  MONDAY [May 1916]

My dear Willie

Thank you so much for taking Iseult about & introducing her to your friends.[1] I am so glad she is so much admired & is having such an interesting time, it will do her a great deal of good. She has had much too dull a time lately – She can stay as long as ever she likes, for though I shall be very glad to have her back, I think it would be a pity not to stay on in London now she is enjoying herself.

I got my passport with amazing facility – what is called an *emergency passport.* & will have to get another in London to return here. I was asked no questions & was told I could *start* the *same night* I made the application which was a great surprise, after all the difficulties & delays I have seen made about other people's passports, or what Cook's agency told me to expect! They knew who I was & didn't ask me to produce any papers! merely said they supposed I wanted to go to Ireland but the passport is only available to London. Does one have to get passports for Ireland now?

My poor boy has got one of his bad attacks of enteritis & has been in bed for the last week. I could not start until he is able to get up –

When are you going to Dublin? I want to go there, because I feel I ought, but I dread it – it will be so changed – so much that I loved has disappeared – I shall not be able to stay long, for war time has diminished my income very much & I shall have to remain quietly at Colleville & live on the potato field for the summer. – In the autumn I think I shall go to live in Dublin & arrange for Seagan to be educated there. Paris doesn't suit him & I have always wanted him brought up in Ireland. I want that more than ever now – I think Iseult also would be better in Ireland than in France & she has got over her objection to leaving Paris –

I am very anxious for a talk with you over everything & as I hope to see you soon either in London or Paris – for to go to Colleville now you will have to come to Paris first – I am not going to write anything. My mind is growing a little clearer on what has happened, & I think my friends acted with political wisdom as well as courage.

I hope the theatre will be able to go on in spite of financial difficulties. It will be so necessary to keep strong & alive every intellectual movement in Ireland.

In the peace & quiet of Colleville we will be able to talk everything over –
Thanking you for all the newspapers
Alwys your friend
   Maud Gonne

letters arriving vary from 4 or 6 days to 2 days I suppose according to the industriousness or the dilatoryness of the Censor.

329   17 Rue de l'Annonciation
                                                 Passy
                                                 Paris
                                                 4th June [1916]

My dear Willie
   Seagan is still ill in bed. He is over 10 days in bed now, & I can't leave until he is well enough to return to school. So much as I want to go to Ireland I think I shall probably now remain here till you & Iseult arrive – Thank God for Bishop O'Dwyer's letter,[1] at last someone of authority has been found to voice the conscience of the country. In the interview of the *Manchester Guardian* Maxwell[2] says that though in a general way he has done with the Drumhead courtmartials, he reserves himself the liberty of judging 9 or 10 more rebels who are still in hiding *as he thinks fit*. One knows what that means! Why do not the Irish M.P.s insist on Maxwell's withdrawal & Civil Law being put into force again. They would I think have a great part of English opinion with them in this. I am very sorry you have had to close the Abbey but I hope it is only temporarily closed. Everyone will regret it & want it started again. The *Evening Mail* which Ella sent me had an article in this sense. Please send me Irish papers.
   I am looking forward so much to seeing you – I am better now & manage to sleep 5 or 6 hours a night – which is nearly enough – I don't want to take sleeping draughts again for once before when I had insomnia I had terrible difficulty to sleep without them after.
   I shall go & live in Ireland now as soon as I can arrange it & only keep a *tiny* flat in Paris, or perhaps only Colleville. I must see what Iseult wants about this. How is she? I am sure the change has done her good.
   In haste
   Yours alwys
      Maud Gonne

What is the date of your play?[3]

330   [Paris]
                                                 Sunday [June 1916]

My dear Willie

Thank you so much for your letters & for the papers. You tell me
so much I want to know. Arthur Lynch is here but has no news, can
you believe he wanted to discuss Greek literature today! That is a
wonderful poem of Pearce's. I translated the other one of his you
sent me for the *Mercure de France* & also for a Dutch paper

Poor Seagan has been very ill, he got up yesterday for the 1st time
& today I took him out for a little but he is very weak & I don't
think he is fit to go to school this term, so as soon as you & Iseult
arrive we will go down to Colleville – You will I believe have to
apply for your passport some days (a week even) before you need it,
as sometimes, the Lynches say, there are great delays in getting it.

I am looking forward to seeing you & hearing all the news. It is
so lonely here being away from all who care for things I love.

Here it is natural each one has his own terrible anxiety & can think
of little else – I am so glad you have decided only to close the Abbey
for a while. It will be necessary for Ireland to keep up every side of
her National life & thought.

Thank goodness our people have more character than Redmond.
His weakness & affable conciliation has been *disastrous*. England's
NECESSITY to settle the Irish question before peace negotiations begin
should get us good terms if only we had a leader worth the name.

It seems to me foolishness to make concessions to Ulster, or rather
to the protestant minority of Ulster. It is monstrous that they should
be allowed to stand forever in the way of National progress.

I would like to see the Well of the Hawks.[1] You will give it in
Ireland later & I shall then see it.

Always your friend
Maud Gonne

Let me know soon as you decide dates for coming to France.

*On 13 June Yeats wrote to Robert Bridges: 'All my habits of thought
and work are upset by this tragic Irish rebellion which has swept away
friends and fellow workers. I have just returned from Dublin where
of course one talks of nothing else, and now, if I can get a passport,
I must go to a friend in Normandy who has been greatly troubled by
it all.'*

331   [Paris]
                                                  Monday [June 1916]

My dear Willie

I have not answered your last letter for I was expecting every day
to hear from you or Iseult the date of your arrival in Paris, but not
hearing from either of you & yesterday getting a letter from May
saying Iseult had a cold & not mentioning the date for her crossing,
I think I may as well write.

I am sure Kerrigan[1] was misinformed about my husband's last
words & refusal to see a priest, it would be so unlike all I know of
him & why should he? for all his life he had been, with occasional
lapses perhaps, [a] practical Catholic & a very convinced one, even
when he failed to act up to the teaching of the Church.

Besides I have a very nice letter from Father Aloysius, prior of the
Franciscans which I will show you when I meet, speaking of Major
MacBride's bravery & promising that Father Augustine a monk of
his order who assisted Major MacBride at the last to write to me.[2] I
have not yet received his letter.

I am very distressed at the news of Kathleen. I am afraid she is
very ill. It is dreadful she & little Thora being so far away, especially
during the war when passport difficulties make it impossible to go
quickly to anyone –

I have just got letters from you & Iseult announcing your arrival
Thursday. It will be good seeing you both – I suppose you will arrive
sometime in the dead of night, Kathleen & Thora arrived at 3.30 in
the morning. I shall enquire Thursday evening at the station & if
possible meet you.

I will engage a room for you at a little private hotel near here, Rue
Gavarni, where any of our family who come to see me stay.

The proprietor speaks English & it is clean & comfortable & of
course you will have meals with us. We will go to Colleville very
soon after your arrival, if you have nothing which keeps you in Paris.

Looking forward to seeing you

Alwys your friend

Maud Gonne

*Yeats stayed in France throughout the summer. He started his poem
'Easter 1916' and studied the French Catholic literary movement and
the work of writers such as Péguy and Jammes which Iseult translated
for him. He proposed to Maud Gonne, asking her, on the advice of
Lady Gregory, to leave politics and saying he could build a beautiful
life for her among writers and artists where she could still work for
Ireland in a different way. As always she refused him; he then*

requested her permission to ask Iseult to marry him. She gave it, but warned him it was unlikely she would accept. Iseult, with mixed emotions, was honoured, moved and yet amused, and does not appear to have given a clear answer.

332

[Letterhead]
Etablissement Thermal
et
Grand Hôtel des Baignots
Dax
Landes
3 Nov [1916]

My dear Willie

I am much better & return to Paris on the 8th Nov & I hope a week later we shall be able to start for Ireland – Thank you for your interesting letter. I am longing to be in Dublin again.

Iseult has probably written to you about our rather unsatisfactory interview with Madame Péguy.[1] I shall try & see her again before we leave Paris. She knows little I should think of literary matters, & is probably very badly off & is afraid naturally of not doing the best she can for her husband's work – She said the French Editor was publishing a collected edition of his work, & was afraid an English translation of part of it would prevent English readers from buying it – She also spoke vaguely of some young man in the trenches who had known her husband & was writing on him, who might want to translate him into English. She also said that someone called Dease who writes in the *Irish Rosary* had written asking to translate but she had not replied. Iseult was very disappointed at not getting an answer as she likes the idea of translating Péguy very much – Her article on this movement in France is still unfinished but what she has read to me of it is VERY good & requires very little more to finish it. Suggest to her to send it to you, that perhaps will make her finish it. I think it might also help her to get the translation right.

I have succeeded in getting a couple of sketch portraits to do, which has paid for my stay here, which is a comfort, for our money affairs are still unsettled though promising –

I hope you are feeling better. Do you know who is now the Editor of *New Ireland*? It is really very good.

Dax is not a place for news so you must excuse this dull letter. I spend my time studying Miss Evelyn Underhill's[2] book on mysticism which is very remarkable. Mr Rummell tells me she is a friend of Mrs Shakespear's. You ought to get to know her. She is a great scholar

& must be a very interesting woman
 Looking forward to seeing you soon
 Alwys your friend
   Maud Gonne

Yeats sent her his poem 'Easter 1916':

> *Hearts with one purpose alone*
> *Through summer and winter seem*
> *Enchanted to a stone*
> *To trouble the living stream.* . . .
>
> *Too long a sacrifice*
> *Can make a stone of the heart.*

333   17 Rue de l'Annonciation
                                          Passy
                                          Paris
                                          8th Nov [1916]

My dear Willie
   No I don't like your poem,[1] it isn't worthy of you & above all it
isn't worthy of the subject – Though it reflects your present state of
mind perhaps, it isn't quite sincere enough for you who have studied
philosophy & know something of history know quite well that
sacrifice has never yet turned a heart to stone though it has
immortalised many & through it alone mankind can rise to God –
You recognise this in the line which was the original inspiration of
your poem 'A terrible Beauty is born' but you let your present mood
mar & confuse it till even some of the verses become unintelligible
to many. Even Iseult reading it didn't understand your thought till I
explained your [?retribution] theory of constant change & becoming
in the flux of things –
   But you could never say that MacDonagh & Pearse & Conally[2]
were sterile fixed minds, each served Ireland, which was their share
of the world, the part they were in contact with, with varied faculties
& vivid energy! those three were men of genius, with large
comprehensive & speculative & active brains the others of whom we
know less were probably less remarkable men, but still I think they
must have been men with a stronger grasp on Reality a stronger
spiritual life than most of those we meet. As for my husband he has
entered Eternity by the great door of sacrifice which Christ opened
& has therefore atoned for all so that praying for him I can also ask
for his prayers & 'A terrible beauty is born'
   There are beautiful lines in your poem, as there are in all you write

but it is not a great WHOLE, a living thing which our race would treasure & repeat, such as a poet like you might have given to your nation & which would have avenged our material failure by its spiritual beauty –

You will be angry perhaps that I write so frankly what I feel, but I am always frank with my friends & though our ideals are wide apart we are still friends.

I am writing this in the confusion & wearyness of a déménagement.[3] Our new apartment is small but has a wonderful roof terrace from which one sees the chimney pots of all Paris & gorgeous clouds & sunsets. Money affairs are worrying & may prevent us leaving Paris for another month. I will let you know as soon as dates are settled. I would like to see the Hawk's Well, but fear we shall be late for that. However you will bring it to Ireland will you not –

How nice really getting your old Castle.[4] I hope you will succeed in that. It sounds very fascinating & it would be lovely to have a place you could put all your treasures & make really beautiful –

Alwys your friend
Maud Gonne

334   17 Rue de l'Annonciation
                                                Paris
                                                4th Dec [1916]

My dear Willie

Why do you not write! We are feeling anxious at not hearing from you. Are you ill? Iseult has written 3 times. I have been very ill with congestion of the lungs & am still in bed.

Iseult told you of the horrid disappointment we had the day before we were to have started for Ireland. Major Lampton after duly signing our passports said he had orders from the war office to inform me I might go to London but would not be allowed to go to Ireland –

He also said that it was probable once in England I should not get a passport to return to France, as they were discouraging travellers as much as possible.

There was nothing for it but to put off our journey till we can get this absurd & monstrous order reversed – I have written to several Irish M.P.s who are taking the matter up for me, in the meantime we all got bad colds from living in a cold attic where my furniture is stored, with me it turned to congestion of the lungs.

It is all very worrying & disappointing.

Do write & let us know how you are & where you are. Iseult wrote you of our interview with the Editor of Péguy. It is all quite satisfactory on this side, if arrangements can be made with the London editor.

Iseult wrote you all particulars.

Last week their was a strong peace wave & I hope we were really going to see the end of this hideous war, but a fresh war wind seems to have arisen with the appointment of Trepoff in Russia[1] & everything is gloomy again.

Very gloomy because *famine* seems inevitable all over Europe, beginning of course with the smallest & poorest countries, but even here the economic situation is very serious & I doubt that food supplies will hold out till the rippening of next harvest.

This may end the war, & if so even famine will be blessed.

Alwys your affecate friend

Maud Gonne

Your castle looks lovely. Have you really bought it. It will be nice visiting you in it.

335   17 Rue de l'Annonciation
                                           Paris
                                           29th Dec. [1916]

My dear Willie

I think we have received all but two of your letters. I hope the censor enjoys them. Perhaps he wanted your autograph so kept two.

Now that the Irish prisoners have been allowed to return to Ireland,[1] surely we, who have been out of Ireland since before the war ought to be allowed to return – I read the correspondence in the *Observer* about the Lane pictures.[2] You are doing splendid work & of course if there was any sort of honesty in England you ought to succeed in restoring them to Ireland – but – censor –

Life is becoming very difficult in Paris. My washing woman came yesterday & told me she was very sorry but she could no longer do the washing, & she could get no coal – & the two big public wash houses near her had been taken over as ammunition factories – then we are so limited with gas & electricity, that – I have had to have all the electric burners changed to the feeblest kinds & we cannot sit up late, for there are all sorts of pains & penalties threatened if we burn more than the absurdly small regulation allowance – our gas cooking stove has also to be so carefully watched that inviting friends to dinner will I think be an impossibility unless we live on salads & cold dishes.

My coal man I only induced to give me ONE sack of coal after half an hour's entreaties & he said he thought it would be the last he would be able to supply. One sees long lines of people standing outside the milk shops waiting for their turn of milk which is very much rationed & one can seldom get as much as one needs. These crowds stand for hours on the streets waiting for coal & for sugar.

It will be strange if you are asked to do labourer's work – Will it be ammunition making? Or agriculture? I wish I were in Ireland, it is the one nice quiet place to live in.

We often see your friends the Rumells – Mrs Rummell has translated your *Countess Cathleen* into French & a friend of theirs Mr Krause the actor – (he has a great talent) is so pleased with it he wants to act it – after the war of course – in Paris. He has some most interesting & excellent ideas about the way it ought to be staged. He says the scenery should not be realistic at all, it should be kept like a painted [?panel] I told him these were your ideas & he was very interested in hearing about all the scenery experiments you had made in the Abbey & your last experiment with the masks in drawing-rooms[3] – He is very intelligent & I wish you could meet – He is most anxious for Mr Rumel to write music for the Countess Cathleen, music that would be played softly while the play was acted & as both Mr & Mrs Rumell are very fond of the play I think Mr Rumell is inclined to do so, he talked to us about it yesterday & asked me if I had heard that you had given the rights of making the play into an opera to an Italian? I did not know but said I would ask you – but even if you had I think this need not prevent Mr Rumell writing music for it for his would not be to be sung, it would not in any sense be an opera – You might tell me this when you write – I dare say Mr Rumel will write to you himself on this matter –

I am much better, but still cough a good deal – I am most anxious to get to Ireland on account of Seagan. Mr Law[4] & Baily[5] & a few other friends are doing their best. If you can hear anything let me know.

Wishing you all good things for 1917 & hoping to meet soon.
I remain
Vy sincerely Your friend
Maud Gonne

1917

336

My dear Willie

Baily wrote me what he told you. I answered thanking him for the trouble he has taken – & stating very clearly my reasons for wanting to return to my country which are 1st I want my boy to go to school there & 2nd I want to make sure that the school children feeding bill which after three years' work I succeeded in getting passed, does not remain a dead letter, for school meals will be hideously wanted this winter if all I hear about the conditions of the poor is true. At the same time I said that of course I could give no undertaking of any sort to England for it would be aquiescing in a monstrous tyranny – I have never heard of Germany or Austria requiring written declarations from any of their people abroad who want to return to their homes. It only shows what England's idea of national & personal Liberty amounts to – The unfortunate Irishmen confined in Frongogh[1] though they were shockingly treated all refused to sign any such declaration & in the end have been allowed to return to Ireland without doing so. French people to whom I spoke of the conditions offered to me to return home, all were shocked & quite agreed with me that I could never sign any such paper – I want to return home very much it is most inconvenient remaining on in Paris under present circumstances after having given up my apartment but I would go through a great deal more than that rather than give way on a matter of real principle –

Possibly I may find useful work to do here – I believe with you that after one more hideous *offensive* & useless butchering that makes me sick to think of the nations will make peace before next summer. The economic conditions *everywhere* will oblige them to do so – It will be of paramount importance that Ireland shall be properly represented at that peace congress & her national status fully recognised. Our country men at home & in America are fully alive to this, & my knowledge of the French press & of the foreign newspapers correspondents here may be very useful later on –

I am leaving no stone unturned to return to Ireland for I know it is the best thing for Iseult & for Bichon but if I do not succeed it may be all for the best in the end as I may have more important work to do here – I am very philosophical.

You are making a splendid fight for the pictures & ought to succeed if you were dealing with people who really knew what honesty meant but – subject nations are made to be robbed & small nations to be bullied.

Have you heard anything different from [?Meynal][2] yet? Iseult is very anxious to know, as she would like to begin her translations.

By the way when you write to her ask her to send you the article she wrote on french Catholic writers & the earth – I think it is VERY good, but she won't finish it, if you write for it she will have to, & I think you will like it.

She is just now very much taken up with Steiner's philosophy[3] – I haven't read much but I think I should find him too dogmatic & assertive.

With best wishes for the success of your efforts for the pictures
Alwys your friend
Maud Gonne

337   Colleville
par Vierville
sur mer
[April 1917]

My dear Willie
I enclose letters I have received from Moirín Fox (who is going to
be married next month to Mr Chevasse[1]) I have told her that I do
not think you will do the preface, as you dislike writing prefaces &
have refused so many people – but that I have sent on the letters –

We are at Colleville for Easter, & I am feeling much better. I was
ill most of the winter – We go back to Paris on the 17th alas – needs
must if I don't want Seagan to be quite a dunce.

I have written twice to the War Office & have written through my
Solicitor to know for what reason I am refused the right of returning
home but cannot even get the courtesy of an answer from the
Champion of Liberty.

Joseph MacBride has again been arrested, though he had taken no
part in politics his wife said since he returned home at Xmas after his
9 month imprisonment in England – No reason was given for his
re arrest & deportation – he was sent first to Oxford, where having
some introduction to the Jesuit Fathers he succeeded in getting work
in the Bodlean Library – most necessary for him, as he has no means
& a wife & 5 little children dependent on him – some two months
later, again without any alleged reason being formulated he & 10
other deported Irishmen who were living at Oxford, were re arrested
& conducted to a little village in Gloucestershire & left there without
any provision being made for them with the orders that they were
not to move out of a five mile radius. Of course in that village there
was no means of getting employment. I have always heard that the
Germans provide board for the deported people though the French
& English press complain that it is scanty.

After some complaints in parliament I think the English Government are considering the provision of board for the deported
Irishmen. The *Freeman's Journal* is hopeful on the matter –

I have a long & interesting letter from Quinn, who is most anxious
for America to take real part in the war! Strange.

I fear Submarines will prevent you paying a visit to Colleville this
summer – 5 fishing ships from Port en Bessin were sunk last week
but no lives were lost luckily & several coal ships have gone down
so that the whole district is without coal – We pick up bits of coal

on the seashore & everyone has to bring in his basket of coal or wood every day if they want dinner. One has not far to go & find one's basket ful. Casks of rum & oil & wine & other things are also often thrown up, but these have to be given up to the Coastguard.

Havard is busy planting potatoes in the garden, so I hope we shall not have to starve this summer – In England I am afraid you will be hungrier then we shall be in France – M le Curé is coming to lunch & is at the cabane du [?douanier]² so goodbye.

 Yours alwys
  Maud Gonne

338   Paris
                  25th April [1917]

My dear Willie

How kind of you sending a book to Seagan. He will write & thank you himself tomorrow. It is a great joy to him, he loves reading books of adventure –

We are back again in Paris. It is still winter & the war is a pall over everything – It will be nice if you come over to France to lecture, but sea travelling is really very dangerous just now & one is often kept 2 or 3 days or even a week, at the port of departure waiting for the possibility of the boat starting with reasonable chances of safety.

Are the boats between England & Ireland also subject to these delays? I imagine much less so, as there is not the same movement of troops. How charming your Western castle looks in the photo you sent Iseult. We are longing to see it. Can it really be possible you got it for £35?

Kathleen & Thora will be returning from Switzerland towards the end of this month & I hope they will stay a long time in Paris.

I am reading Russell's book *National Being*¹ & find it is very interesting. It starts so many ideas – He is doing great work. James Stephens has been very ill with pneumonia –

I wish I could have been at the Mansion House meeting convened by Plunkett. The programme was really good – all now depends for Ireland on the way she is represented at the peace congress. She should compromise nothing of her claims before that for America is bound to support her. To be in a hurry for settlement before the peace congress would be a great folly.

[End of letter missing]

Having first been at Coole in July, Yeats went to France early in August. He wrote regularly to Lady Gregory from Colleville, once saying: 'I would be glad of a letter of counsel.' He had hoped that

Iseult would marry him but he wrote: 'Iseult and I take long walks, and are as we were last year affectionate and intimate and she shows many little signs of affection.' He worked on the lectures he was to give in Paris in December.

Back in Paris in September, Maud Gonne finally got permission to travel as far as England. An old friend of her father's whom she had known as a child was in charge of the English Passport Office in France. He went to great trouble to get her a passport but advised her not to travel, as she might not get to Ireland or back to France; he told her she was well liked in France, where she was doing useful work in the hospitals. Maud Gonne said that all the Sinn Féin prisoners, even Constance de Markiewicz (who had been sentenced to death), had been released and were back in Ireland, and asked why she, who had been out of Ireland since 1914, could not return. His answer was: 'Perhaps the authorities do not want to have two such mad women on the loose in Ireland.'

Probably suffering the aftermath of the past year's events, Yeats badly needed calm and the resolution of his problems. He wrote to Lady Gregory that, though less upset than he might have been, he was determined to return to England and ask Georgie Hyde Lees to marry him; he said his only concern for Iseult was about her future, adding: 'Maud Gonne on the other hand is in a joyous and self forgetting condition of political hate the like of which I have not yet encountered.'

Maud's calm of the pre-war years was utterly shattered by the relentless course of events which had deprived her of many of her friends and endangered others, and which was rapidly shaping all she had worked for while she was held helpless in France unable to participate or help. She had packed her belongings and realised her assets.

On 18 September Yeats wrote to Lady Gregory from London:

Mrs Tucker [Georgie Hyde Lees's mother] has asked me down to where she and her daughter are. I am however in rather a whirlpool. Maud Gonne and the harmless Iseult have been served with a notice under the defence of the realm forbidding their landing in Ireland. Their getting back to Paris is also doubtful. We had a difficult time in Southampton. They were searched as possible spies by the order of polite and plainly shamefaced officials who kept the train waiting for us. I am just going to see them. Poor Iseult was very depressed on the journey and at Havre went off by herself and cried. Because she was so ashamed 'at being so selfish' 'in not wanting me to marry and so break her friendship with me'. I need hardly say she had said nothing to me of 'not wanting'. Meanwhile she has not faltered in her refusal of me but as you can imagine life is a good deal at white heat. . . . Maud Gonne will certainly do something wild.

A few days later he wrote, 'I have seen Iseult and am doing as she wishes', and went to propose to Georgie Hyde Lees. They were married on 20 October, 1917.

Still distraught over the whole affair and feeling he 'had betrayed three people', he received a letter from Iseult saying 'an abruptly new condition is bound to have a little of the fearfulness of a birth . . . all I know is that I share your sadness and will share your joy when you will tell me "All is well".' But it was not long before he was relieved of worry by his wife's automatic writing which told him: 'with the bird [Iseult] all is well at heart.' In December a contented Yeats wrote to Lady Gregory: 'My wife is a perfect wife, kind, wise, and unselfish. . . . She has made my life serene and full of order.' He was writing verse again.

In the meantime Maud Gonne, now virtually imprisoned in London rather than Paris, was restless. She finally escaped to Ireland in January 1918, disguised, with the help of Eva Gore-Booth and the Pankhursts. Iseult remained in London where she was working in the School for Oriental Studies and had decided to share a flat in Beaufort Mansions with a friend, Iris Barry, who worked with her. It was from there that she wrote to her mother telling her 'the heart breaking news' that she had read of Millevoye's death in the papers.

By the end of March, Maud Gonne had purchased a house on St Stephen's Green, Dublin, and had become politically active, primarily in her capacity as a journalist and in public-relations work with visiting foreigners and press. The situation was becoming increasingly tense, with Sinn Féin contesting by-elections amid heated arguments on Home Rule and rising objections to the proposed extension of conscription to Ireland, which united all shades of nationalists, and the extension of martial law to various parts of the country.

339
265 Kings Road
Chelsea
[London]
Wednesday [?October 1917]

My dear Willie

I think your betrothed charming & I am sure we will be great friends. I am so glad of this, it would have been dreadful if you had chosen someone who would have broken our friendship, I feel Georgie will not, I think she will enter into it & add to it. I find her graceful & beautiful, & in her bright picturesque dresses, she will give life & added beauty to the grey walls of Ballylee.

I think she has an intense spiritual life of her own & on this side you must be careful not to disappoint her.

I am glad we are going to see her again on Friday. Iseult likes her very much, & Iseult is difficult & does not take to many people – Yes I think you have chosen well – I am so glad, for I want you to be very happy –

I hope you will be back in London soon. I expect you will. Iseult & I were at Leighton House this afternoon where three little grey ladies in old fashioned shot silk dresses played 18th Century French music with great charm – but in England nothing seems to me to be alive except air raids. I wish we were in Ireland.

Alwys your friend
Maud Gonne

—— *1918* ——

WBY 8

Ballinamantane House
Gort
May 13 [1918]

My dear Maude

I have cancelled my lecture & put off my play. It is not possible to prepare a lecture when one does not know under what condition of the public mind it will be delivered. At the same time I think there is only one chance in a hundred that the government is mad enough to attempt conscription. I think they are afraid of something else & are preparing for that & not for conscription.

Since I saw you I have read much Catholic economics. I can now recommend you one Catholic book which is a most able survey of the whole of political economy including Carl Marx. It is *Distributive Justice* by Father Ryan of the Catholic University at Washington[1] & can be got from the Catholic [indecipherable] Guild. If you get the book & consider its arguments you will not start any movement which would bring you into hostility with Catholicism & when Catholicism is right. You will find for instance that your quotation from St Ambrose (that on your leaflet) is not considered to carry the meaning (considering the circumstances of its delivery) which you suppose. You will find the whole historical development of Catholic economics in this book. The book however is difficult & rather dry – at least my non economic head finds it so. A book which I will send you if you wish is *The Housing Problem* by Leslie Touche. If you cared to take up housing in Dublin you would find it a help from the Catholic point of view.

We hope to be in Ballylee in a month & there I dream of making a house that may encourage people to avoid ugly manufactured things

– an ideal poor man's house.[2] Except a very few things imported as models we should get all made in Galway or Limerick. I am told that our neighbours are pleased that we are not getting 'grand things but old Irish furniture'. Now that I am not tied to London (or some place in Ireland where I can get eyes to help my blindness) I shall do much more in Ireland than ever before. Perhaps when the present crisis is over you may help me in the work we planned in Normandy ten years ago.[3] For the moment you would help by attending Rahilly's lecture[4] next Sunday & getting socialists to come & speak. I wish I had asked you to go to Finlay's[5] & speak. I expect to open the Autumn lectures course myself possibly with *Claudel*[6] if I can arrange for performance.

Yours

W B Yeats

On 11 May Field Marshal Lord French, as a military man, was made Lord Lieutenant in order to put conscription into force when needed. His proposed proclamation was approved by the cabinet and on 17 May almost the entire leadership of Sinn Féin and the Volunteers were seized. The following day the newspapers printed the proclamation, which said that Sinn Féin had been engaged in a treasonable conspiracy with the Germans. The authorities did not produce the evidence on which they acted.

Maud Gonne was returning from an evening at George Russell's house with her son and Joseph King, an English MP in Ireland on a fact-finding mission, when they were accosted on their way from the tram to her house on St Stephen's Green. She was taken to the Bridewell and next day was put on the boat to England. Many times during her long political life the authorities had been on the brink of arresting her, but this was her first time in prison as a prisoner.

The original intention was to send her to Frongoch in Wales, but she ended in Holloway Prison in the VD wing with Countess Markiewicz and Mrs Kathleen Clarke, who was ill. In the end she did not go on hunger strike, since her two companions said they would join her and she felt that Kathleen Clarke would not survive. But she maintained that with self-hypnosis she willed herself to lose weight – which she did rapidly.

340

> [Holloway Prison]
> c/o Chief Postal Censor
> Strand House
> Portugal Street
> London W.C.
> 14th June [1918]

My dear Willie

I need hardly tell you that the German Plot[1] exists only in the panic disordered imagination of the English Government. Outside my cell is a card *unconvicted prisoner* yet here are kept Countess Markievicz[2] Mrs Clark[3] & I *au secret*, no visits, no solicitor allowed, no charge made. I live, eat & sleep in a cell 7 feet by 13, a small window so high one can't see out, only about ½ foot air opening. We meet in exercise yard, & while cells are cleaned & about one hour in the afternoon, we are allowed to write & to receive 3 letters a week, but I have received no answers to those I have sent. Each letter must not exceed 20 lines & reply 30 lines. I am wild with anxiety about Seagan, this day week I hunger strike unless I am allowed to see him. If I die my death will give America & the world a striking example of English justice. I don't mind solitude, & am getting quite interested in meditation. Send me small English translation of the Summa of St Thomas Acquinas for one needs very sound doctrine to prevent imagination going wild in meditation. Do what you can for Seagan & Iseult.

Goodbye love to George & yourself
Your old friend
Maud Gonne

WBY 9

> Ballynamantane House
> Gort
> Co. Galway
> August 18 [1918]

My dear Maude

Iseult will have told you that, owing to what I heard from Seagan, George and I went to London and separated Iseult and Barry.[1] Iseult had feared to be unkind but was grateful to be rid of Barry by the act of others. She can stay at Woburn Buildings until March next without rent to pay as we are moving to Oxford. I came back at once but George is waiting a few days, so Seagan & I are alone here. He went to Martyn while I was away. I have made many enquiries about Irish schools. I think Clongowes[2] would be best as it is not so rough as most & the teaching is good. Castleknock[3] is a good school but to[o] near Dublin & its political excitement. Sweetman's[4] is ruled out by Collins who has said many things against you in Ireland. I hear

[?] you have decided for London & Tutor (The alternative would be a French school in England and I don't know if there is a French day school in London. I have asked for an introduction to a well known London priest that I may make enquiries by letter). If Seagan has a tutor all will be well if you insist on his working regular hours. Iseult would be firm on that point. I am very much struck by Seagan. He is the most remarkable boy I have met – self possessed and very just, seeing all round a question and full of tact. Ezra[5] thinks he has literary talent. I am asking Hatchards to send you *Studies* a very able Irish Catholic Review & *The Times Literary Supplement*. The last because it will tell you what books are being published. I will send you any book you want. I have not written as I knew you are only allowed three letters a week & will not write unless there is something important. I am asking Stephen Gwynn's help for you.
    Yours Affectionately
        W B Yeats

It seemed that Iseult and Iris Barry were not getting on. Seán had been spending the summer with the Yeatses in Galway, where he was being tutored by the Gort schoolteacher. His future education was of major concern to his mother, and her friends were actively helping while she was imprisoned. Seán insisted on returning in the autumn to London, where he and Iseult carried on a campaign for her release, as did Yeats, King, John Quinn in America and many others. Some time during this period he was tutored by Ezra Pound, who had an affair with Iseult.

WBY 10   Stephen's Green Club
                                          Dublin
                                          [1918]

My dear Maude
    I did not write to you as I knew how few letters you were allowed. I have waited to have some definite thing to say. When I got your alarming letter I had the contents laid before Short.[1] Russell I think did the same with his letter. I am told that an examination by doctor has taken place. I have asked Gwynn[2] to arrange for me to meet Short and discuss and I hope for good results. I think of asking for examination by a doctor chosen by your friends. George & I have taken your Dublin house at £2–10–0 a week – the price Delaney[3] named – for four months. Should you be released & allowed to live in Ireland we will move out which strangers would not. George was not well enough to go to England and to manage a move to Oxford.[4] She is now at Ballylee Castle, which has all the charm I hoped for. I

hear from Iseult at times and I know she is writing beautiful things and but for her shyness might have great personal success. My own sorrow at not getting to Oxford is that I can do little for her from so far off. I think she is learning a great deal and growing more confident. It is often the best thing that can happen to a timid sensitive nature to be forced to rely upon itself for a while.

Yours affectionately
W. B. Yeats

WBY 11 St Stephen's Green Club
Dublin
4/10/18

My dear Maude

Stephen Gwynn brought me to-day to see Shortt. I asked him if you could be released but confined to some district in England and without being asked for your parole. We both explained that with you it was a matter of conscience not to give your parole. He said that if you were confined to a district in England the Home Office would have to give its consent as it would depend upon the Home Office to keep a watch etc, and he made it quite plain that the Home Office would be unlikely to consent. I then asked him if you would be allowed to return to France without giving any parole. He said that it would be more easy as it would only be necessary for the French Embassy to consent and he thought it probable that they would do so. He then undertook – if it was your wish – to bring that matter before the Government and there is no doubt, I think, that he can assure their consent. I know that you will hesitate thinking of Iseult and of Seagan especially of Seagan's schooling for they may both accompany you. Seagan could go to that school of his in Paris where he did so well and you would all return at the end of the War. The matter of most importance to them in the world is that your health shall not break down and that you will be able to watch over their start into life. Even if Iseult should be much away writing and studying, it would always be of you she would think and you that she would wish to please. If, therefore, it is necessary for your health to be set free do not hesitate to accept this offer. I then asked the Chief Secretary if he would allow your friends to select a Specialist to examine you. I said we were all very anxious about your health and that we felt that a doctor chosen by the Government might feel anxious to take what he might suppose to be the Government view. We discussed the possibility of the Government being afraid that a doctor chosen in that way might carry a message from within the prison to the outside world. I suggested that someone – Bernard Shaw for instance – trusted by the Nationalists and not distrusted by the Government might name the specialist. Shortt, however, said that they would accept any specialist recognised as such by the profession, and chosen by yourself. I then asked him could he manage that my letter to you would not be restricted to the thirty lines allowed by the Regulations and he very kindly offered himself to forward the letter. I am, therefore, sending this letter to him but not open, for I don't want you to think that I am giving the interview any colour from the knowledge that he will read what I write. In both matters I hope you will think of your health as the one great consideration not on any selfish ground but because your health is necessary to the two children.

I will show this letter to Stephen Gwynn that I may be quite sure that I do not misrepresent the Chief Secretary in anything and I will send a copy to Iseult. I would not but for the importance of the matter have so soon again written to you for I know that besides the two letters from your family you can only have one other letter. I shall ask the Chief Secretary if this letter can be an extra one but I am not certain that he will be able to grant that.

Yours affectionately
W B Yeats

341

[Letterhead]
73 St Stephen's Green
Dublin

Nursing Home
Welbeck Street
write to 18 Woburn Buildings
1st Nov [1918]

My dear Willie
It is such a joy to be with the children again, & I thank you for all the trouble you have taken for me – perhaps you will have to take a little more & get us all permission to return to Ireland.

On Tuesday night as I was just going to bed the Governor of Holloway came to my cell & told me to get ready at once as I was to go for a week to a Nursing Home to be under Dr Tunicliffe's[1] care – Warden was sent with me in a taxi. At the home I found Seagan & Iseult waiting for me – next day I heard from Miss Allen, the head of the establishment that the Warden had asked her to sign a paper saying I was handed over to her from Holloway – She was surprised. Mr King[2] called & said he didn't know if I was free or not Mr Short had promised my release & Sir G. Cave[3] had said he would sign it. Mr King went to the Home office for it, was shown the Document which only needed Sir George's signature he was asked to return for it in a hour's time. When he did so he was told there was no need for it, as orders had already been sent to Holloway to send me to Nursing Home. Later Mr King was rung up by the Home Office to make it quite clear to him that though the government was sending me to the nursing home, they wouldn't pay for me there. Mr King foolishly but amicably said – 'If it comes to that I will pay myself' – of course I wouldn't allow him to do so. I wanted to go to 18 Woburn Buildings at once. Mr King asked me to wait till the next day when Dr Tunicliffe would call & examine me again. I consented to this & next day Dr Tunicliffe telephoned he could only come the following day & wanted to see me in Bed. This morning his secretary telephoned he is down with influenza. So I am going to 18 Woburn Buildings – This place is too expensive for a war pauper like myself £10.10. a week!

Mr King said much would depend on Dr Tunicliffe's next report as to whether I should be allowed return home.

It appears that Kathleen had written Mr Shortt asking for me to join her in Switzerland which I should have liked almost as well as returning home, as I am very anxious about her, she has had another haemorrhage from lungs – but that has been refused – it is said by Swiss Govt! also it is said that French Govt has refused, but Seagan who went to French Consulate says this is not true & I am sure it is not true about Swiss Govt either. Seagan got a letter from Home Office saying I was only *temporarily* released.

It is monstrous to refuse me to return to my home. Iseult needs care. She is terribly thin & says she feels London climate for so long is doing her harm. She wants to go to Dublin. It appears she was in bed for several days & only got up to receive me – As to my health, I am *very thin* & rather shaky & sometimes breathless but have less fever – I have a bad pain in base of left lung whenever I get the least tired, – even writing this letter is tiring me, but I hope to [?fatten] up again now I am free, but it will take time & I shall have to live quietly for a time. Dr Croften, the Dr who was treating me for Rheumatism in Dublin is a great specialist for lungs & is over the Peamount Sanatorium.[4] I would consult him as to treatment if in Dublin. Wherever I am, I *must* have Iseult & Seagan with me. Seagan's education must go on which makes any country place in England impossible. I can't afford such expensive vagaries as nursing homes, hotels or Sans. My home in Dublin is best place for all of us, with Josephine[5] to cook for us. Please try & arrange that – How is George? Best love & thanks to you both.

Always your old friend
  Maud Gonne

Please forgive this rambling egotistical letter but I am still weak &
my brain doesn't work quickly –

*On 6 November Dr Tunnicliffe reported that her condition was
somewhat improved, though her night sweats continued, her nutri-
tional condition was bad and the condition of her chest was as in his
last report. He recommended she be looked after by Dr Crofton
of Dublin.*

*Maud Gonne left the nursing home and went to Woburn Buildings
where Iseult, Seán and Josephine were living, but she was not given
permission to leave England, though the war was at an end. Iseult
described her to Yeats as 'not really bitter, but very tired and needs
a lot of looking after', and in a postscript added: 'How alarming . . .
if they drag her away now, it would really be a bad shock to her
nerves.'*

*In late November Maud Gonne again disguised herself and,
eluding her watchers, made her way unannounced to Dublin and
arrived on the doorstep of her house. The Yeatses were still living
there and George, expecting their first child, was recovering from
pneumonia. Yeats, fearing the upset to his wife, would not admit
Maud because of the likelihood of police raids in a search for her.*

Somehow the situation was resolved.

*In the general election in December, Sinn Féin won a resounding
victory at the polls. The majority of the candidates were still in gaol,
including Countess Markiewicz, who was the first woman to be
elected to the British Parliament. The elected Sinn Féin candidates did
not take their seats at Westminster, but formed their own Parliament,
Dáil Éireann, in Dublin on 21 January 1919. Two policemen were
killed in an ambush in Tipperary that day.*

*On 2 January 1919 Maud Gonne's nephew Pat Pilcher wrote from
Switzerland to tell her that the doctor had said his mother had only
a few weeks to live. She died shortly afterwards.*

Face to Face We Stood
1920–1938

Hidden by old age awhile
In masker's cloak and hood,
Each hating what the other loved,
Face to face we stood.

W. B. Yeats, 'Meeting' (first published 1929)

1920–1921

I slept on my three-legged stool by the fire,
The speckled cat slept on my knee;
We never thought to enquire
Where the brown hare might be,
And whether the door were shut.
Who knows how she drank the wind
Stretched up on two legs from the mat,
Before she had settled her mind
To drum with her heel and to leap?
Had I but awakened from sleep
And called her name, she had heard,
It may be, and had not stirred,
That now, it may be, has found
The horn's sweet note and the tooth of the hound.

W. B. Yeats, 'Two Songs of a Fool'
(written in the summer of 1918)

The War of Independence, which with hindsight had started with the killing of the policemen in Tipperary on 21 January 1918, was building up from small-scale incidents to a situation where shootings and arms raids were met with berserk retaliations on the civilian population from mid-1920 onwards, the police being augmented by reinforcements of the Black and Tans and the Auxiliaries.

Sinn Féin, though outlawed since September 1919, had put into force its long-planned operation of withdrawal and had formed a Government of the Republic which worked in hiding. Among her other activities, Maud Gonne assisted Desmond Fitzgerald, Minister for Propaganda, whose department produced the government paper the Irish Bulletin, *started in November 1919.*

Yeats gave up his rooms in Woburn Buildings in June 1919, and he and his wife spent the summer at Ballylee, County Galway, before moving into a house in Oxford. He lectured in America from January to the end of May 1920, and came to Ireland early in August to help to disentangle Iseult's marriage.

By 1919 Iseult Gonne, now twenty-five, was in Ireland living with her mother, with whom she had a very close relationship from which she found it difficult to separate. She met Harry Francis Stuart in Dublin that year. Harry was seventeen and having just left his English public school, Rugby, was preparing for a university entrance examination. He had much promise as a poet; Iseult recognised this and thought to mould it, writing to Yeats that 'he could be your spiritual child'. She saw in him genius and beauty. However, in spite of her literary intelligence – cool, detached and full of subtlety – she failed to see his attraction to the negative and to understand the unawakened adolescent in him, ready to break all bounds, aspects that would be triggered off by his resentment of her strange mixture of sophistication and simplicity, for in the practicalities of life she was as immature as he.

Planning on marriage, Harry was received into the church on 30 January 1920 at the Catholic University Church, St Stephen's Green, with Seán as godfather in absentia (he was probably in hiding) and Mary Barry O'Delaney registered as godmother. It seemed to be a small family affair. Then he received his first communion on 15 March.

Lady Gregory wrote in her journal on 13 April that Lennox Robinson had met them on their way to the boat to England and 'sees nothing but disaster'.

342   [Letterhead][1]
                                          73 St Stephens Green
                                          Dublin
                                          June [1920]

                                          Private

My dear Willie

I am very glad to know you are safe home & well & happy & educating the parrot[2]

Iseult *Stuart* is at present lodging 5 Ely Place but I think is leaving there in a day or two to get into a flat she is thinking of taking in Harcourt Street but it is safer to write to her here, she comes in every day. The marriage is a tragedy & I don't like to speak or think of it. She certainly took your advice of taking no notice of what I might think or advise.

The boy[3] is utterly selfish & takes no thought for Iseult in any way – he is madly jealous & makes the most hideous scenes about everything.

His family are a queer lot from Antrim who, though well connected, have drunk themselves into degeneracy.[4] He has talent of a queer morbid kind, but no education & no power or will to work. He gives you as an example that college is unnecessary when one is a genius. – I pointed out that your father had educated you vigorously & that with your extraordinary brain activity you had read & studied more than most college men – He says he has £350 a year, but as far as I can see intends spending this on himself – & expects Iseult to *take* & *pay* for the flat – He has been most unpleasant about money with her. Iseult has about £100 a year from me & I fear will have to dress, feed & lodge herself on this – With her disregard for ordinary worldly matters she refuses to have any settlement made.

He & his mother manoeuvred her into that position & she would not allow me to interfere – when I tried to, they bolted to London, before the marriage, his mother seeing them off & providing the money for the escapade. For over a fortnight I was left without an address – his mother had it all the time, but she pretended to me she didn't know where they were – Then she announced to various people in Dublin that they had been married in London, so as to make the marriage inevitable, finally they returned & were married here.

Knowing the horrible life Iseult has prepared for herself, I have refused to quarrel with them, for Iseult will need all the help & support her friends can give her –

I am going to Glenmalure[5] on the 1st July I hope as I am longing for the country.

I heard that George was over at the Arts Club[6] but I have not seen her. You must be eager to see Ann[7] – Children change so rapidly, & she must be getting at her prettiest & most fascinating age now –

I have let the top of the house[8] as it was too big for Seagan & me –

When are you going to your Castle? I would like to see you on your way through, but I fear I shall be in Wicklow. I have one of the big brass Normandy milk cans for you. Where shall I leave it when I go? for you will probably like to take it down to Galway.

Love to George & Ann if they are back with you now

Alwys your friend

Maud Gonne MacBride

343

[Letterhead]
73 St Stephens Green
Dublin

Glenmalure
21st July 1920

My dear Willie

Thank you for your letters. I would like to see you & talk things over with you for I am very anxious about Iseult. She arrived here yesterday looking fearfully thin & worn –

It is quite true what you have heard that her husband has a great admiration for you & imitates you & wants to know you. It is very possible you might influence him. To do so I think you should know all the facts & therefore I shall write things which I should otherwise not talk about.

Stuart's conduct towards Iseult is shocking. While they were staying with me in Dublin he struck her & one day knocked her down. He threw her out of her own room with such violence that she fell on the landing half dressed at the feet of Claud Chevasse who was staying in the house at the time –

After they left my house & went into lodgings at 5 Ely Place, his conduct must have been just as bad for Mr Purser[1] who lived in the flat beneath theirs complained to the landlady he could not sleep because of the violence of the scenes above at night – & the disputes.

They stayed three weeks here in Glenmalure by themselves, all the people in the Glen are full of pity for Iseult. One woman told me he tried to set the house on fire, her little girl saw the flames through the window & rushed to get her mother to help – They found Iseult in her dressing gown outside. Stuart had locked himself in her room from where the flames where coming. They could see him pouring petroleum. Finally he opened the door – he had been burning Iseult's clothes to punish her! Frequently he locked her up without food. He behaves like a lunatic – or perhaps only like a vicious English public school boy would behave to a fag. He is only 18. He refuses her money to buy food. The flat they have taken is paid for by Iseult. The char woman is paid for by Iseult. He has never given her a penny for her clothes or personal expenses, she has never asked him to. Sometimes he buys the food himself, at other times he gives her a few shillings to do so, never enough, often she goes hungry. He keeps the money, some £350 a year his mother allows, entirely for himself.

Iseult has had to provide all the furniture for the flat –

His father died in a lunatic asylum. He may have talent that doesn't interest me much. He certainly has cunning of a low kind. The family curse[2] is working with terrible violence in Iseult's case –

I have so far avoided a regular break with Stuart for Iseult's sake, but it is hard to do –

I can write of nothing else today for I am so worried about Iseult. Excuse this hasty & untidy letter.
Alwys your friend
    Maud Gonne

344
                                  Ballinagoneen[1]
                                  Glenmalure
                                  Co Wicklow
                                  29th July [1920]

My dear Willie

Thank you very much for your two most kind letters received together 24 hours after your telegram, & after I had sent reply to telegram. I was uncertain if the two letters you referred to in telegram were the two previous letters you had written about Iseult's marriage so can not say I had not received them.

You are the only person I know who could help, & your letters are very wise & helpful. If you have not already started for Ireland, I don't think there is any need for you to hurry or inconvenience yourself – though I should be very thankful to be able to talk the whole situation over with you when you do come – & I think Iseult would be also. She is still here with me, but has promised to meet her husband in Dublin on the 5th August, though she would rather remain longer in the country & indeed needs the rest badly –

It is possible however that Stuart may not return to Dublin by the 5th for he writes that he is going to London for a short time, & Iseult wrote to tell him not to hurry back as another week in the country will do her good – Still this may bring him back sooner than if she said she wanted to see him.

I do not think Iseult wants a definite break with him. I think she still cares for him, though she says it is quite possible his conduct will make it impossible for her to go on living with him –

She is looking very ill & worn & is very tired & has little physical energy left. There may be another cause for this because I think there is a child coming. On this account it is necessary that there should be no more violent scenes & starvation.

She realises this too & it is possible this may give her strength of will & firmness which her own passivity would not.

Cecil Salkeld[2] came down to see me a short while ago, & told me in confidence how alarmed he & his mother felt for Iseult. He said he called on her one day about 6 o clock. Her husband had gone out to dine she said – after about an hour's talk as he was going, Iseult suddenly said 'Could you lend me 2/6, I have eaten no food today & am feeling so weak' – Francis *deprives* her of food to punish her for any little difference of opinion they may have. He takes all the food he can find in the house & locks it in his room where he goes & eats himself – or he goes out & eats at a restaurant & leaves her without food or money –

As I told you the money I give her he manages to make her spend on rent or other things so she shall have nothing left & be entirely in his power –

It is as you say absolutely impossible for her to go abroad with him under the circumstances – his one idea is to get her away from her friends so that he can treat her as he likes – In Dublin she has always one or two houses where she can take refuge & get a meal though from a shrinking of letting people know of the misery of her life she has not availed herself of this as much as she should have done.

I explained to you how Stuart & his mother manoeuvred to get her married without settlement. It was of course her own fault, but now that a child is coming, & that she knows the incredible meanness of Stuart about money she realises what a mistake she has made & would be willing I think to adopt the suggestion in your letter of refusing to live with him altogether unless some satisfactory arrangement about money could be made for her & the child – I think you could help her in this perhaps by speaking to his mother, or his Aunt Miss Montgomery[3] who seems the best business woman of the family and manages the mother's affairs – The mother is considered by her own relatives as weak minded. She seemed to me an amiable liar entirely led by her son. Since she arranged the flight to London *before* the marriage I am barely on speaking terms with her, so Iseult thinks I am not the best person to speak or write to her – as her son is not of age he has an allowance from her of £350 a year – part of this might be paid to Iseult direct – sufficient to cover rent & half house keeping expenses so that any money Iseult gets from me she can keep for food when her husband takes in his head to starve her –

Another torture he has invented is that of preventing her sleeping. The wooden door panel of my room here is broken & a piece hacked out with a knife or battered out by Stuart one night when Iseult wearied out had gone into another room & shut herself in to try & get a little sleep – He, on these occasions stays in bed all day to rest, but having no servant, Iseult is obliged to get up & do housework –

I believe a break will be inevitable – but Iseult doesn't seem ready for it yet – & all we can do is to try & make arrangements for her safety.

As I write this word it seems a mockery, what safety can there be for her with a semi-lunatic of this type –

She says he does not drink she says he is not mad she says I don't see the good there is in him. She says he has charm & great will power

& possibility for genius. I see will power & Northern cunning & selfishness. He MAY have talent.

George's idea of asking them to Oxford & trying to influence him is both kind & wise – He admires you greatly. He would be immensely flattered at being asked & quite possibly you would have great influence on him – He would also see that you could make things pleasant or unpleasant for him in the literary world according to how he treated Iseult. His Northern self interest might enable his will to dominate his perversity – & of course for Iseult it would mean peace to be with you & George. On the other hand I am not sure that she ought to travel – & he would try & drag her abroad after –

Let me know when you are coming over – If you could come down to this primitive cottage & lovely country it would be nice, if not I will go to see you in Dublin – I hope Anne is better. Chickenpox is not generally a serious illness, though very tiresome.

My love to George & again many, many thanks for your letters
    Maud Gonne

I read your letter to Iseult. *Except to George*, don't mention to anyone that I think there is a child on the way. Iseult would hate it talked of.

Yeats arrived in Ireland on 30 July and went straight to Glenmalure, where he found Iseult worn out and ill. He heard from her and the neighbours of the incidents Maud Gonne had described, though Iseult defended her husband. Wisely Maud Gonne accepted that Yeats was a better intermediary than she could be, considering Iseult's reactions and the apparent irreconcilable antipathy between herself and Harry. Yeats suggested that Iseult go to a nursing home and not return to her husband until a satisfactory settlement could be reached. Iseult agreed, and he arranged the nursing home, putting her under the care of a gynaecologist, Dr Solomons, whom he had already consulted.

345
        73 St Stephens Green
        Dublin
        Thursday [5 August 1920]

My dear Willie

I saw Iseult this morning. She had seen Dr Solomon.[1] He confirmed my opinion about the child. There is no doubt about it. He finds her very run down & has ordered her to stay in bed completely for 2 or 3 days & then only get up to wander a little in the garden. He has written to Francis to come & see him, & after the interview he will let him see Iseult. The matron of nursing home said

Dr Solomon says she is to have no visitors at present *except me* & *you* if you call. I think Iseult would very much like to see you. Miss O'Delaney called with me this morning but the matron was quite firm & would not let her to go up without permission from the Dr even though I said she had been Iseult's Governess & might be useful to get her books or things she wanted –

If you could find her a book or two she would be grateful for the present choice of books in the nursing home is very limited & dull.

I have an appointment with Mr Friery[2] tomorrow morning at 10 o'clock. He was away today when I called.

Iseult said she felt glad to rest & on the whole was very reasonable & calm. Tomorrow is her birthday & she said she found it sad to pass it in this 'reformatory'. Dr Solomon has allowed 6 cigarettes a day! I am just going back to take her some things she needs.

Thank you so much for all your kindness in this matter
Yours alwys
    Maud Gonne

346
                                       Glenmalure
                                 10 Aug [1920]

My dear Willie
    We are still at Glenmalure Iseult is I think a little better, but gets tired very easily & is far from strong. Her nerves are very much on edge & at times she says she wants to go away from here, but as she wants to go to her flat in Dublin I do my best to dissuade her – & want of money is a great argument & unfortunately a true one – On the whole she is very reasonable – I am glad to say she is writing again, a good deal & seems interested in that. She has some philosophical thoughts on the 'Veil of Veronica'[1] which are interesting. She even vaguely talks of trying to follow your suggestion of getting the best of her things together into a little volume called *'Dreams'*. It is the first time I have heard her talk seriously of publishing anything. If she writes to you about it encourage her, it will occupy her mind & be very good for her –

She feels I think that she must try & establish her own personality & be less vague & *floating*. Whether she will have the strength of purpose to do it I don't know –

I went to Dublin & had a long interview with Miss Montgomery, Stuart's aunt. A nice amicable person with no illusions about her nephew – She had never got the letter I sent her, probably he had stopped it, as he was staying in her house with his mother & she had been away. I wrote a [?registered] letter asking if she had received it & as she had not she arranged an interview. The financial arrangements are much as I told you. Mrs Clements[2] has 500 a year in trust funds. Miss Montgomery is a trustee of this. Mrs Clements gives 250 a year to her son but seems to have been giving him rather more lately – she sends him a cheque every month. Her 2nd husband spent all available money that he could get of hers. He has just died, leaving his affairs very much involved but a few weeks before his death he inherited a fairly large sum of money, but made a will leaving it all to his sisters & away from his wife. There is some chance of her getting some of it through the decency of one of the sisters – Mrs Clements was evidently counting on this when she increased her son's allowance – All these details I got from Miss Montgomery. She quite realises that Iseult & the future child must be provided for & that arrangements must be made to make it impossible for Francis to go on starving her – She is to talk things over with her sister & write to me. She says her sister is terrorised by the boy who has an uncanny influence over her. Francis wrote Iseult that he was ready to make settlement for the child & was discussing them with his mother & that they would take time owing to the involved state of his step father's affairs, he said he would not see her or write to her again, but he wished arrangts made that would give him the child for some part of the year – His aunt told me that only a few days before – about the time Iseult got this letter Mrs Clements wrote her that she & Francis were taking a house in Cushendal[3] as it would be good for Iseult's health! I told Miss Montgomery that Iseult was quite firm in her resolve of not returning to Francis until proper settlements were made. Miss Montgomery seemed to agree that this was the right course – of course the waiting & inaction is very trying on Iseult's nerves. If she could get away for a visit to England it might be best but there are so many difficulties in the way.

I don't think we half thanked you for all the trouble you took to help us. You were most helpful & kind.

Lennox[4] motor cycled down to see us a couple of days ago & Seagan was home yesterday. Helen Molony is coming on Friday. I try to keep Iseult amused but it is not easy She is still too weak to walk much. Give our loves to George & Ann. It will be nice seeing you all when you come over.

Yours alwys
Maud Gonne

347   Glenmalure
                        Wednesday [?August/September 1920]
My dear Willie

Iseult got so restless she insisted on returning to her own flat in Dublin, 67 Fitzwilliam Square. I feel sure it is a mistake but I could not prevent it. The waiting & inaction was telling on her nerves; of course Francis counts on that. If Francis goes to Dublin she says she will see him & she wishes to talk to him, but says she is determined to keep firmly to her refusal to live with him until settlements are made.

She is rather stronger but still far from well & looks very thin & worn.

His aunt wrote me her return home had been delayed a few days but promised to write when she had seen her sister at the end of last week. I may get a letter today & will let you know at once if I do.

If the delay continues Iseult suggests writing herself to Mrs Clements. If there is no satisfaction then, we shall have to get Mr Friery to write & claim maintenance. Iseult doesn't want this, but I see nothing else for it. I cannot afford to keep up two separate establishments & she doesn't seem to want to return to live with me altogether, in any case Stuart must provide for his wife & for the child.

When do you expect to be in Dublin? I shall stay here another 3 weeks, unless obliged to go to Dublin earlier.

Love to George & Ann
Alwys your friend,
Maud Gonne

348   In gt haste

[Glenmalure]
Wednesday [?September 1920]

Dear Willie

I just received yours & Lady Ottoline's[1] letters. I am sending Lady Ottoline's on to Iseult. I don't think she will go, Mrs Clay asked her for a fortnight & she refused though I advised her to go. She says she wants to stay in Dublin in other words she wants to meet Francis – Seagan writes me this morning that he thinks she is already tired of Dublin – so it is possible she may accept – I have written her that if she does I will find the money for her journey.

Most unsatisfactory letter from Miss Montgomery – She says there is no doubt my first letter to her fell into the wrong hands, that her sister & her boy were going tomorrow to a house in Cushendall that they have taken, but refuse to discuss plans with her – She thinks they have invited Iseult to stay, this from what they wrote her previously.

I am sending on the letter to Iseult by same post I am forwarding a letter to Iseult from Mrs Clements & have written her to let me know the contents as soon as possible.

Postman waiting so can say no more.
Yours alwys
   M. G. MacB.

349 Glenmalure
8th Sept [1920]

My dear Willie

Iseult writes me very sad letters. She has now almost decided to go & stay with May. I think that will be good for her. May writes she can have her & she will be in her own flat. Also Iseult has committed another blunder. She got impatient & when she got on her own in Dublin & wrote to her husband saying that as he had written he wished to separate from her she quite agreed with him & she also wished to say that to cut every link she would not accept a penny from him!

Mrs Clements wrote her – the letters crossed – that she had taken a house at Cushendal with her son & they would both be so happy if Iseult would come & stay with them, it was a most affectionate letter as if there was nothing wrong. She also said that she had proposed after that for economy sake, the three of them should take a house together wherever Iseult wished, & that she would make settlements for the child, if Iseult would say just what she wanted & how it should be done. Iseult replied amicably that she would like to be with Mrs Clements & thanked her for the invitation but that as her husband had written it was best for them to part & as he had shown such callousness during her illness she felt he had no real affection for her & was going to take him at his word & remain on her own in Dublin; no word about settlements.

If Iseult goes to London it will be within a few days, she wrote me for the money which I have sent her.

When will you be in London & when in Dublin?

In haste
Yours alwys
   Maud Gonne

350[Glenmalure]
24th Sept. [1920]

My dear Willie

Iseult I think crosses to England Tuesday morning her address is c/o Mrs Bertie Clay, 40 [?Lexham] Gardens, Flat A. London W.8.

She is going through a terribly bad time & I am afraid she is suffering terribly. In reply to the foolish letter I told you of, Francis wrote her, she says a most affectionate letter asking her to come &

stay with him & his mother at Cushendal, saying he was broken hearted & would go to America if she didn't come. She replied if he were ready to make the settlements he might come & *fetch her* in Dublin. She received a wire from him to join him & his mother at Cushendal, she wired back that he could come & arrange things with her in Dublin if not she intended going to England on Monday. Her letter to me dated Monday says he had not come & she thinks his pride won't let him give in so far as to come to her & if he doesn't arrive she is going to start for London as arranged Tuesday morning. She is suffering from insomnia & I have heard from friends she is looking very worn & ill. The terrible thing is that she still loves this cur – Why, why do I insult an honest dog in this way? A change is the best thing possible for her, anything to get her mind off her present troubles.

She writes me she has not got good clothes enough to stay with Lady Ottoline. I know her amiable husband burned some of the dresses I gave her in the Spring but still I think she could arrange her things quite well, only she is so tired & miserable she is afraid of meeting strangers & having to make an effort. I am sure it would be the best thing for her & I have written urging her to go if only for a few days but I fear she will have already written to Lady Ottoline declining her invitation. I think May will be good for her – the more people she sees the more her mind is occupied better.

I am sorry you are not coming to Dublin. It would have been so nice seeing you & George & Ann but I dare say you will be over a little later. I hope the operation won't make you feel ill.[1] I believe it is a very slight thing & does not make one ill for more than a day or two.

If you see Iseult let me know what you think of her. I am very anxious.

Alwys your friend
Maud Gonne

Police & Military raided this peaceful glen on Saturday & took all guns for which people had permits & took the permits as well, thereby making good Sinn Feiners of people who were not so before.

P.S. If you see Iseult encourage her to write, work is the only thing to keep one from the auto suggestion of sorrow – She is writing a little & I believe Lennox[2] has sent some of her things to a publisher – urge her to go on – if once she begins I think she will go on. Encourage her for she is over diffident & over critical of her own work. She has always a strange want of confidence in her own ability. When she was a little child she used to ask me in all seriousness if I thought she would ever be as intelligent & interesting as the dogs!

Francis has also done his best to destroy the small amount of self esteem she had.

The greatest kindness one can do her is give her confidence in herself & try & get her to work. I know you have always tried to help her in this way but lately she said to me that now even you were convinced she was not capable of doing any good work –

Have you seen in the papers the accounts of the Bleeding Statue in Templemore.[3] It is very like *Marbeau.*[4]

1st a man call[ed] Dwane a contractor had a statue of the Blessed Vergin & noticed that it had drops of blood on it, then a statue of the Sacred Heart also began bleeding. He did not talk of this except to a very few for several months. Then a nephew of his, a boy of 18 called Walsh who lived several miles away saw a vision of Our Lady who told him that his uncle was wrong to hide the statues & that he should tell people about them, she also told him if he dug a spade full of earth out of the floor of his room he would find a miraculous spring. He did so and a tiny spring appeared. Our Lady also is said to have appeared to several people at Templemore among them a soldier. Young Walsh had given a little statue of the Blessed Virgin some time previously to a policeman & that statue also showed drops of blood. All the country people here are very excited about it. Thousands visit Templemore & there have been many cures – Young Walsh has been sent for to Rome. Your friend, the Rev. Innocent Ryan[5] has written to the papers denying the miraculous cures, but admitting the bleeding statues & telling people to put their faith in the sacraments of the church & not to look for or run after wonders –

351   73 St Stephen's Green
                                              [Dublin]
                                              Thursday [October 1920]

My dear Willie

Thank you for your letter. It is a horrible anxiety having Seagan in Prison & for such a childish stupidity – driving Mr Friery's car without a military driving permit! He had the ordinary driving licence & Mr Friery had a permit for the car – but did not know that Seagan had taken it without his leave – He has missed his exam in consequence which means a whole year's work lost.[1] He had been up for it on Friday & Saturday – & was arrested on Sunday, so could not attend on the Monday & Tuesday – Mr Friery has not yet got back his car!

Seagan met Maurice Bourgeois who we used to know in Paris & who is over here on a mission for the French Govt of collecting material for the *Musée de la Guerre* also writing for *Le Temps* – Bourgeois wanted to see me & asked Seagan how to get to

Glenmalure & the idea occurred to Seagan of driving him down – all would have been well, if Con[2] had not heard of the excursion & insisted on coming too. They were all arrested on their return to Dublin as they were driving her to the house where she was staying in Highfield Rd. The police & the military ignored Bourgeois's Diplomatic passport & treated him like a mere Irishman, shut him up in the Bridewell[3] without food on a plank bed & refused to let him communicate with his consul. He was rescued by an officer who had known him in France & happened to hear about it. He now knows English methods from actual experience which is so much to the good.

Seagan may be kept months or he may be let out any day. There are boys waiting trial in Mountjoy prison for months. Sometimes they are tried sometimes they are just put out without any explanation –

This house was raided, but nothing taken away – but the military said they would return! Why I don't know –

I wonder if the Museum or the Art Gallery would take one or two pictures & ornaments for me till times are better. I have put my silver at the bank, as often the military & police raiders are very destructive & thieving.

Iseult is looking shockingly ill. She is not very reasonable about her affairs. I cannot get her to answer Mrs Clements' letter asking for the name of the trustee, for she says if she & Francis do not come together she will accept nothing for herself or for the child. Of course this is absurd, for I am nearly ruined & *cannot provide.* Iseult will only see the beauty of the geste & not the consequence & will not bring her mind to the practical details of life, & crys when I try to make her! She is obviously too ill at present to think of starting work even if work could be found for her;

Life is very difficult just now & I am very tired, but one has just to go on & keep one's nerves in hand.

Politically, time is on our side, no country could go on ruling another as England is doing here indefinitely those who survive will see Irish freedom.

I hope you are feeling better. Love to George & to Ann –

Yours alwys

Maud Gonne MacBride

352   73 St Stephen's Green
Dublin
[October 1920]

My dear Willie

I have just seen Seagan in Mountjoy. He is well & hopeful of his release in a few days. I am less hopeful for under the present tyranny they will punish him for being his father's & his mother's son –

He was driving the motor car without a permit & Con Markievicz & a French journalist were in the car – They had been visiting Smith Gordon[1] & something having gone wrong with the engine or lamps they were late returning it was 11.35 when the police held them up in Highfield Rd. They said they would have to wait till an inspector came up. They kept them till *12.5* after curfew hour & then handed them over to the military wagon which was collecting the curfew prisoners of whom there are some taken every night.

I don't know when the Courtmartial[2] will come off. In the meantime it has ruined his exam. He was at it Friday & Saturday & thinks he did well. He should have been there on Monday & Tuesday as well.

Iseult got nervous for me this morning & arrived over here very tired & worn out.

When are you coming to Dublin? I am glad you are going to have Gogarty for the operation, he is so very skilful.

My house was raided by the military before I arrived but little damage was done – but the raiders said they would return which is an unpleasant prospect. I am lucky in having Unionists on each side of me, for they won't perhaps fire the house on that account. People are expecting every sort of horror from the military & black & tans[3] until Parliament meets.

In haste,
Yours alwys
Maud Gonne

Before having his operation, Yeats stayed in Glenmalure, where he wrote 'On a Picture of a Black Centaur by Edmund Dulac'. After it he wrote to John Quinn: 'Gogarty, with his usual exuberant gaiety, removed my tonsils. As long as I retained consciousness he discussed literature, and continued the discussion when I awoke. He would probably have continued it most of the afternoon (he came 6 times) but I had a hemorrhage and was preoccupied with my possible end.'

353
73 St Stephen's Green
Dublin
22nd Oct. [1920]

Dear George

I am writing to ask you to be kind enough to send me a card to say if you have got home safely & without too much trouble & delay on journey, & how Willie is feeling. It is a pity he had to travel so soon after the operation for he must have felt very weak & uncomfortable. As things are over here at present you may be thankful to be out of it.

Life is made hideous by raids & rumours of raids & indiscriminate shootings by the military & if you are not feeling strong it is very trying. I hope Willie will pick up quickly – I thought he looked very tired last Monday. I should have written before but I have been ill ever since. My cold developed into fever & high temperature & I am still in bed; though much better & hope to be up tomorrow.

I wrote to Mrs Clements & she has written me address of her solicitor in the North, before she told me he was in Dublin. She says she sent it to you, but was not sure of your address.

You must be glad to be back with Ann. I hope you found her well & joyful.

I want to thank you again for being so kind as to take all this trouble about Iseult's affairs – Love to you & Willie & hoping to hear soon that he is quite recovered.

I remain
yours alwys
Maud Gonne MacBride

354
[Dublin]
[November 1920]

Did you or George get my last letter? I am anxious for news of you both. I hope you were none the worse for the journey. I am anxious at not hearing. Iseult writes me that she has also written but has no answer. She & her husband are coming to Dublin next week & going to her flat 67 Fitzwilliam Square.

Alwys your friend
M. G.

Postcard addressed to: W. B. Yeats Esq, 4 Broad Street, Oxford, England.
Postmark: Dublin 8 Nov. 1920.

355 [Dublin]
Wednesday [November 1920]

My dear Willie

I was so glad to get your letter & know that you are well – I was getting very anxious. Things are so bad here, they can't be worse, no one's life or liberty is safe from the military, police or auxiliaries.[1]

The lying in high places is so bare faced, it takes one's breath away, it is making even conservatives & old unionists blush – I am very busy with Mrs Erskine Childers[2] getting up an *All Ireland Relief for the Devastated Areas Committee*. The Lord Mayor will take the lead in it.[3] Something must be done to help the thousands who are homeless & starving as a result of military depravation – Something to show the Solidarity of the Nation before common terror is necessary.

As relief work is exactly countering the English Govt's design against the people, if we succeed, as I believe we shall, in a great movement we may prepare for arrests raids etc – I have put all my pictures & treasures away am now going to work night & day to help the people – I wish Seagan was in a calmer atmosphere for work; it is hard for students to work with such happenings. Miss Hayden (prof) said to me after the raid on the university – 'of course none of the students will do any work this week – they are all too excited'[4]

The sight of the mild Dr Coffey[5] marched off between two tommies with trench Helmets & fixed bayonets followed by an armoured car while mounted guns on cars were trained on the wandering students & shots fired in the air to alarm the girl graduates was typical of English rule here. Dr Coffey was only marched to his own house which was searched for the register of the University, which for some reason he had taken there the day before – I have not seen any adequate protest made against the violation of the dignity of the University – but then Dr Coffey is a peaceable timid man, not a Sein Feiner unless his late experience has made him one – I wonder what the Principal of a foreign University would have said to such treatment.

Every male student in the University was searched by the military. It took hours – They didn't search the women only fired off shots to frighten them, & the girls weren't frightened.

Yesterday Eason's a central book & paper shop came in for their attention 2 raids in the day!

I sent you today's *Freeman* for I don't think you or any other Irishman has the right to 'try & avoid a too painful contact with the bitter present' for remember the unspeakable war fare being carried on by Government orders by the most debased riff raff of English jails & war drunk soldiers & officers these torturings of prisoners, these floggings & shootings of unarmed men & burning of homes of women & children is not directed as Lloyd George says against a 'Murder Gang' but against the Volunteers, those young men who you yourself have often said are the hope of the country & who form the arbitration courts that you so much admired. As often as not the looting murderous soldiers fall on men unconnected with the movement, they don't care but the objective of the Govt is against the volunteers & against all that is cleanest & bravest in our Nation.

I know what power you have. It seems to me that every power should be used now for Ireland. Forgive me writing like this

Love to George

Yours alwys

    Maud Gonne

A captain who you know but whose name I hesitate to mention in a letter lest he should be murdered by his own friends, in my presence the other day told an amazing story giving names etc. of what an officer he knew had done to a school master supposed to be a Sein Feiner. This officer & the other who accompanied him were disguised & dressed like workmen. The schoolmaster fainted under torture. The school master was not officially arrested & while in fainting condition was taken on a lorry & left at his own door.

356
        73 St Stephen's Green
        Dublin
        24th Dec. [1920]

My dear Willie

I agree with most of what you say about my poor Iseult.

The beauty of this gest out-weighs any other consideration when it suddenly strikes her, & strange & almost incredible as it seems to most of us who know Harry Stuart she is in love with him.

You mustn't be angry with her for her present most inconsequent behaviour she will suffer for it terribly later on – She has not written me even a post card since she left on Saturday – I have no address to forward letters to. If you hear from her let me know.

Dorothy MacArdle[1] is in London staying at the Stanhope Hotel, Stanhope Gardens till 10th of Jany. If you & George are in town try & see her. I want you to talk to her about her plays, she is by far the most promising of the young play writers I have met but needs encouragement. You could help her greatly, & she merits help. She is worth it – She is not self assertive & is very easily discouraged –

A little play she sent up lately to the Abbey was refused by Lady Gregory because it was 'too slight' & her more ambitious play 'Atonement' was never put on again, though much better than most of the new plays put on this year, & from this she is inclined to let herself believe that she has no real gift for writing, & absorb herself in her college work or in helping on other people who have not half her talent.

Xmas wishes to you & George & to Anne & my love.

Your old friend

Maud Gonne

Addressed to 2 Broad Street, Oxford.
Postmark: 26 Dec 1920.

Though the War of Independence continued with the ferocity it had reached during the latter part of 1920, when reprisals became official and draconian measures of search, arrest and sackings were the order of the day, in England there was mounting pressure against the war. Because of this and the exhaustion of the army there was talk of a truce.

The pre-war plans for Home Rule now came to fruition in the Government of Ireland Act, passed in December 1920 and allowing for a separate devolved government for six of the Northern counties. George V opened the Northern Parliament in April 1921. A general election gave Sinn Féin a mandate in the rest of the country. Of 128 members elected to the Southern Parliament under the Act, 124 were Sinn Féin members, who abstained, forming the second Sinn Féin Dáil. A truce was signed on 11 July; negotiations continued until a treaty between Britain and Ireland was signed on 6 December 1921.

With the arrest of Desmond Fitzgerald in March, Erskine Childers took over the Sinn Féin government's Department of Publicity, for which Maud Gonne continued to work. She also served as a judge in the Sinn Féin parish courts and organised relief work which developed into the White Cross, formed in February 1921.

357   73 St Stephen's Green
                                                     Dublin
                                                     [January 1921]

My dear Willie

I enclose letter re Iseult's affairs I have just got from Mr Friery.

Things were not going at all well lately, much the same as the summer but yesterday they have made up their quarrel & Iseult with a quixotic generosity which makes me very angry & very anxious says she will not allow any settlements to be made & has promised to trust herself & her child completely to her husband.

As it seems impossible for the present to get *real* settlements & it is perhaps not as important as later we may be able to get them done, for I doubt if the present mood will last –

Iseult & her husband are going over to England tomorrow to stay with friends of his in Bournemouth & after with Thora.[1] They mean to stay away till Feby when Iseult must return for the baby to be born.

Perhaps this is not altogether bad for the atmosphere in Dublin is so terrible. Day & night are made hideous by shots & raids.

I hope you & George are well & that Ann is growing in charm & beauty.

Alwys yours
    Maud Gonne MacBride

Please return Mr Friery's letter to me.

358   73 St Stephen's Green
                                                 [Dublin]
                                                 22 Feby [1921]

My dear Willie

Thank you so much for that lovely book[1] your sister left for me last night. I will write to you about it in a day or two for last night I was so tired & my eyes so bad I could not read.

I am working very hard, starting White Cross[2] work & trying to save the lives of those boys unjustly & wickedly condemned to death by Courtmartial on evidence which no civil tribunal would possibly condemn on –

Iseult returned from London to find her furniture all removed from her flat in Fitzwilliam Square, by landlord & an army tutor, evidently having taken the black & tans' view of property, Mr Friery had succeeded in getting it returned & it is at present dumped in my hall & she is looking for another flat – Iseult is of course staying with me for the coming advent of the child – I am sorry to say Francis is here also but I hope to get rid of him as soon as the new flat is found for I have no room for him having let the top of the house – He appears to be behaving fairly decently to Iseult but I think this is the case when no money is involved –

Their money affairs are as unsatisfactory as usual – Mrs Clements writes that as she cannot legally make settlements till Francis is of age she will give Iseult £100 a year as soon as the child is born & Iseult insists on being content with this – Iseult's health is as good as possible under the circumstances but as the event is so near she must not be worried over anything –

I am so sorry to hear George's mother[3] has been so ill, I hope George herself is as well as she can be not withstanding the discomforts which are I fear inevitable – when is the child expected?

I sat next to Jack & Cotty[4] at a very good performance of 'The Witch' by the Drama League at the Abbey produced by Elizabeth Young – The production was very good. Dolan's acting as the old husband was very wonderful[5] – He is a very good actor. Lady Gregory was there, but I did not get a chance of talking to her – Iseult saw her, & suggested a thing I am very anxious for, i.e. that the Abbey should revive Desmond Fitzgerald's play, *The Saint*.[6] This is a beautiful little play & had splendid houses when it was on before, & now that Desmond is in prison would be a graceful thing for the Abbey to do. Lady Gregory seemed pleased with the idea – I have heard yesterday that Desmond is in Arbour Hill Barracks, that not even his wife was allowed to see him or send parcels since the escape of Frank Teeling & 2 other prisoners from Kilmainham.[7]

The treatment of prisoners is getting worse & worse & there are a number of cases of torture. We believe that many of the boys sent over to scattered English prisons for long times are sent over to prevent *injuries* they have received under torture getting known about. One man, Harte,[8] a volunteer who was tortured with pliers is now insane in consequence <of prolonged torture> in Broadmore Lunatic Asylum – Another boy called Barnett[9] was tortured but I have not got full details yet. He is in Richmond Lunatic Asylum[10] today –

There are a great many cases of torture to extract names of the officers of the I.R. Army.

It is well known that Kevin Barry[11] was tortured in the Castle & underwent medical treatment as a result, before he was hung. His arm was twisted & I believe dislocated. A volunteer called Edmonds was taken from his home in Tipperary & was found with *both shoulders* dislocated & a bullet through his head.

I was so glad to see your speech at the Oxford Union[12] & the big majority for Ireland obtained in the debates – It must be uphill work in England, but all the same it is telling & the forces against us are falling apart in their desire to shirk odium & responsibility & shift the blame on one another. I believe we are at the worst point now – The courage of the country is magnificent – no one thinks of surrender – & victory is certain.

My love to George & Ann

Alwys your old friend

Maud Gonne

[Dublin]
4th March [1921]

My dear Willie

I enclose a letter from Jean Malya he has lost the letter you gave him authorising him to translate & get played Kathleen ni Houlihan in Paris, he wants you to send him another authorisation –

The poem I like best in the new book is the one to the prisoner,[1] I like all the part about the seabird. Poor Con, she must indeed be patient & endure these long months of imprisonment. I am glad you wrote it.

I hear that Desmond Fitzgerald is being treated shockingly. He is in Arbour Hill prison in a cell so dark that even at midday he cannot read without a candle – The heating arrangements are bad & he suffers greatly from cold he is in solitary confinement & is not allowed to exercise in the open air at all. He is only allowed out of his cell for 20 minutes into the corridor – He has not been charged with anything.

Curfew is at nine o'clock in Dublin now.

Is there any way of getting some influential person to write in *The Times* about the scandal of Courts martial. All the offences brought before them are offences against the military or police therefore the military are at once judge & party in the case – They flout & set aside all civilian evidence. The word of the most respectable citizen even a protestant clergyman, dont count a straw against the word of some drunken shell shocked soldier. The identification in all these trials where boys' lives are at stake would not have satisfied any civil tribunal. The judge advocates are out for blood the officers are mostly inexperienced or prejudiced – There are 9 boys under death sentence in Mountjoy Prison – 4 Conway Porter Whelan & Moran are well known to be innocent & 5 others were convicted of *High Treason* by which any republican could be sentenced to death.[2]

In actual fact they were taken near the scene of an ambush, where no one was injured, several of the boys are said to have had arms on them when arrested. Unless the High Treason charge had been brought they could not have incurred the death penalty as Dublin so far is not a martial law area – & the possession of a revolver does not incur death, & no one was wounded at ambush.

Even Unionists are scandalised at the Courtmartials' sentences & their disregard of evidence for the prisoners.

How is George? Give her my love & a kiss to Ann.

Iseult is well. Seagan has just passed a small law exam with credit 76 marks out of 100. Do you get the Irish papers in Oxford?

The White Cross work is taking up all my time –

Always your affecly
    Maud Gonne MacBride

360 [Dublin]
Sunday [March 1921]

My dear Willie

Many thanks for your letter. Desmond is in Arbour Hill Military Detention Barracks. Since question in the house his treatment has been improved. He is now allowed to exercise in the open air though he is still in the dark punishment cell. I hear it was by Hamar Greenwood's[1] special orders that he was put into solitary confinement! The military disavow all responsibility – Hamar lied when he said that Mrs Fitzgerald was allowed to visit him. I think it is probable that she will be allowed to do so now. His solicitor has seen him – I saw her yesterday – She said she did not wish more to be made about her husband's case than about the cases of the thousands of Irishmen who are suffering in the jails –

As you may have seen by the papers my house was raided by the military in the middle of the night. As raids go, it was a quiet raid & the officers were civil. They only took away Carson's Handbook of Rebels[2] & an appeal of the Women Workers of Ireland to English Women – Iseult did not seem at all frightened at the time & put on her dressing gown & smoked cigarettes quite placidly during the search, but her baby which was not expected for at least a fortnight was born a couple of days after. She did not have a bad time & both she & the child are going on as well as possible. The baby is a girl.[3]

Luckily Seagan was dining the night of the raid & on account of 9 o'clock curfew was sleeping with his friends or he probably would have been arrested, as they arrest most boys of military age & are particularly down on university students.

Iseult will write to you herself in a day or so. I am scribbling this in bed as I am wearied out – have not paper near – so excuse scraps[4] –

I telegrammed you last night about condemned boys as a last chance – I am trying everything & everyone to save those innocent lives. The despair of their mothers is terrible, they all come to me. A. E. telegraphed – made a splendid statement in the press

Iseult's rent was paid, as I paid it & up to date in advance – Her furniture was seized by the army tutor I suppose because he thought the army can do whatever it likes. There is no law for it. However a few letters from Friery got it back & they have taken another tiny flat – I believe in the house of a policeman this time!

Stuart calls to see Iseult every day & spends a few hours with her – she is still in love with him – no settlement, no money arrangement of any sort – Iseult refuses to discuss this even –

When is George's baby expected? Give her our love. I hope she will have as good a time as Iseult.

Yours affecy
Maud

361
Dublin
[21 March 1921]

My dear Willie

I hasten to tell you that on Saturday Mrs Desmond Fitzgerald was at last allowed to visit her husband in Arbour Hill Prison. She wants me to thank you very much for writing about this. She told Desmond of your intervention. He has much admiration for you. It pleased him greatly I think. He is well & though still kept in a dark cell does not complain. He is also now allowed to exercise in the open air which is an improvement –

I went on St Patricks Day to see Lady Gregory's new play The Bellows of Aristotle[1] – It is a most charming fantastic little play, introducing numbers of old Irish songs. It has the good humoured gaiety & fantasy & charm of the best of Lady Gregory's work & should prove a great favorite at the Abbey.

After the terrible week we had lived through I don't think I could have endured an ordinary comedy. I went to the Abbey that afternoon in some dread, chiefly because I wanted to talk to the chairman of the American Relief Delegation[2] who had asked me to meet him at the Abbey – but I was quite charmed & felt much better for it –

I am desperately hard at work with White Cross Committees, & terribly anxious about my Seagan as the raids & arrest of every boy particularly of students is going on worse than ever – & the treatment they get after arrest is shocking – He got through his law exams very creditably 76 out of 100 marks – he was one of the first four – Iseult sat up for a little yesterday. She & the baby are both doing well – Love to George & Ann

Affectionately yours
Maud Gonne MacBride

362
73 St Stephen's Green
Dublin
3rd April [1921]

My dear Willie

What is the mysterious message about an anonymous letter? How can I know anything about it? Please tell me.

I got back from Glenmalure last night. Seagan & I spent three days' holiday there. The weather was lovely & the Glen in the spring is very charming. I longed to stay longer but had to come back to work. The White Cross is taking up my whole time.

Iseult & the baby are very well. They are going tomorrow to Bettystown[1] to stay with Mrs Clements.

Mrs Despard[2] has returned to Ireland & is staying here. It is nice having her –

Love to George & Ann. When is the 'new one' arriving?

A strange man who said he knew you in Oxford, a Mr McQueen called on me

[End of letter missing]

363   73 St Stephen's Green
                                                 Dublin
                                                 19th April [1921]

My dear Willie

I want to write to you again about Desmond Fitzgerald I suppose you got the typewritten statement I sent you showing how he had been *tricked* out of the visits promised in the House of Commons

His wife actually received a permit from the Castle for *three* visits a week – After the 1st visit Desmond was removed from Arbour Hill to the Curragh Prison camp[1] where *no visits* are allowed. Mrs Fitzgerald applied for permission to visit him there, & explained she had an official permit for 3 visits a week, but was told that *no* visits are allowed at the Curragh.

She went with Mrs Despard to the Curragh, but Mrs Despard was also refused though she had been permitted to visit prisoners in Enniscorthy & in Galway.

In the Curragh the prisoners are confined in huts 25 in each hut. They form a sort of camp. The cold is bitter, even in the *crowded conditions, 25 sleeping in each hut,* last week Desmond writes that the water in the jugs froze.

It must be terrible for a literary man like Desmond never to be alone – to have no place where he can be quiet to write or read. He is always an *untried, uncharged prisoner* – Could you do anything for a writer, a dramatist, to obtain at least that he should have a private cell – He would not wish to try & get better treatment than the rest & therefore will not make any personal appeal, but all his friends know that his health will suffer under the strain & that a promising writer may be destroyed – He is not at all strong & feels the cold terribly, but I think it must be the overcrowding & the impossibility of never being alone to work or read which must be the hardest for him.

Iseult & the infant are still at Bettystown with Mrs Clements.

I am working very hard at White X work. It is very interesting. Are you coming over to Ireland soon? It would be good to see you, but of course the conditions of life here are trying –

Have you any news? How long will this hideous situation last?

Love to George & Ann

Always your old friend,

Maud Gonne

364   [Dublin]
                                          Wednesday 27th July [1921]

My dear Willie

forgive me for not answering sooner.

Yes, the truce[1] is a great relief to everybody, but no one as far as I can see is very confident as to settlement. We all distrust the English Govt so much that until we see the jails & internment camps opened & the ships carrying away the English forces we cannot believe in peace however much we may hope for it. There are still 36 members of an Dail in prison mostly without trial.

Still the truce is satisfactory. I can go to bed without stockings on[2] & Seagan can sleep at home & it will be hard after the published terms of truce to call the Irish army the murder gang etc – again.

The real reason of my delay in answering your letter was that besides my usual work I have been very much taken up with my poor Iseult. Her baby got ill about two months ago. She came to Dublin with it to consult a doctor. It died of meningitis three days ago & Iseult is heartbroken – She had grown to adore the child & will miss it terribly. She has been extraordinarily brave & gentle throughout, but suffers terribly. We buried the tiny thing yesterday.[3] It was a wonderful little creature, too understanding & wise for a baby that means to live –

We buried it in a very beautiful place in Deans Grange Cemetery, from where the Mountains look quite near – The tiny grave is among the roots of a very old yew tree –

Iseult's husband only came after the child was dead. He seemed very much moved & he & Iseult have now gone up to Loch Dan.[4]

I must end.

Alwys your friend

Maud

365   [Dublin]
                                          24th Aug [1921]

My dear Willie

Congratulations to you & George on the arrival of the son[1] – I know it is a joy to both of you. Ann will also be pleased to have a brother

Poor Iseult is still very sad & very broken at the loss of her baby. She misses it terribly but she is very brave & charming as usual – she is in Dublin still.

We hope to go to Glenmalure for a week or so in Sept if I can get away & if the truce holds. I am very busy with White X work – The B. and Tans raided my Glenmalure cottage the night before the truce commenced.

Dublin is full of Americans.

Mrs Despard is staying with me. We paid a flying visit to Donegal.[2]
I had not been there for 30 years.

When are you coming to Ireland?

With much love to George & the babies & best wishes.

Your old friend

Maud

*Thora Pilcher, Iseult's cousin and closest friend, said that the light
died in Iseult at this time*

1922–1928

Hurrah for revolution and more cannon-shot!
A beggar upon horseback lashes a beggar on foot.
Hurrah for revolution and cannon come again!
The beggars have changed places, but the lash goes on.

W. B. Yeats, 'The Great Day' (first published March 1938)

*The treaty offered more than had the Government of Ireland Act –
still not the visionary free and undivided republic, but, for twenty-six
counties, dominion status within the British Empire, including an oath
of allegiance to the King. From December 1921 to January 1922 there
was a bitter and tragically divisive debate in the Dáil, the Irish
legislative assembly. Michael Collins, one of the negotiators and
signatories, said that the treaty gave 'not the ultimate freedom that
all Nations aspire and develop to, but the ultimate freedom to achieve
it' – what he saw as stepping stones. The vote was 64 in favour and
57 against. Arthur Griffith became the new President on the
resignation of de Valera, and Michael Collins became Chairman of
the Provisional Government with the job of executing the transition
from British rule, including the evacuation of the troops and formal
takeover of the seat of government in Dublin Castle.*

*The Volunteers, now known as the Irish Republican Army, who
were semi-autonomous of the Dáil, also divided, so the takeover of
barracks throughout the country was in accordance with the views of
the IRA battalion executing the operation. In April 1922 the Four
Courts in Dublin were occupied by anti-Treaty IRA, whose aim was
to achieve, by reassertion in arms, the indivisible republic. In June*

there was a general election which the pro-treaty candidates won by a slim majority. There were also raids across the new border, where sectarian violence broke out in June and July, and 23,000 were forced to leave their homes.

Collins struggled to hold together the divided elements in this deteriorating situation which was poised in the balance while the IRA considered hastening to the assistance of the beleaguered Northern Catholics. After pressure from Britain, Collins finally decided to shell the anti-treaty forces out of their headquarters in the Four Courts on 27 June. Some 400 prisoners were taken, including Seán MacBride. This finally polarised the conflict, and the anti-treaty IRA, known as the Irregulars or Republicans, were gradually pushed close to defeat by August. However, by 22 August, within ten days of each other, both Arthur Griffith and Michael Collins were dead – Griffith suddenly collapsing unconscious, and Collins being killed in an ambush carried out by Irregulars in his home county of Cork.

Consequently it was their successors, William Cosgrave, Kevin O'Higgins and Richard Mulcahy, who were finally to establish the Free State, with the opposing anti-treaty deputies abstaining. In September 1922, within a month of being formed, the new government introduced a Public Safety Act to enable it to deal with the continuing strife, so the vicious cycle of violence continued. The new state's representatives had been threatened with death by its opponents; on 7 December two Dáil members were shot at and one killed. The government, after a night of terrible heart-searching, decided on drastic hard-line tactics by ordering four of the leaders – Liam Mellows, Rory O'Connor, Frank McKelvey and Joe Barrett, imprisoned after the taking of the Four Courts – to be shot that morning. Seán MacBride shared a cell with Rory O'Connor. This method of retribution was continually repeated.

In May 1923 a cease-fire was agreed but arms were not surrendered, and diehard republicans continued to work for an undivided, uncorrupted republic.

In this uneasy peace, after four years of strain, the government tried to settle down to govern the infant state. It was a government of able, conservative, hard young men. One of the ablest of these was Kevin O'Higgins. In November 1926 he felt it necessary to introduce another draconian Public Safety Act. He was assassinated on 10 July 1927.

Maud Gonne, unlike many of her friends, including her fellow prisoners in Holloway, Constance de Markiewicz and Kathleen Clarke, had at first believed that the treaty was something that could be worked with, and continued her long-established method of working as a freelance. On 15 June 1922 she went to Paris, sent by Griffith on behalf of the Provisional Government to help the Bulletin

Irlandaise *with her contacts and to publicise the pogroms taking place in Belfast. She was succeeding, as is shown by* La Petite Gironde's *heading of 28 June: 'Les Horreurs d'Irlande – Le massacre des enfants en Ulster – Une menace de Saint-Barthélemy orangiste – Un appel de la grande patriote irlandaise Maud Gonne MacBride'; but the next day the French papers reported that the Four Courts had been shelled and her son taken prisoner. She returned to Ireland, and took part in the peace initiative undertaken by Lord Mayor O'Neill as a member of a delegation who called on Collins and Griffith. The initiative took place just before Griffith died, and it failed.*

Her final disillusionment came when four of the Four Courts prisoners were shot out of hand in December, and, seeking news of her son, she met the broken-hearted mothers outside the gaol. It was then that she started the Women's Prisoners' Defence League, mainly composed of prisoners' mothers. Marches, meetings, protests, publicity, collections for the relatives, meals and parcels for the imprisoned followed and continued for the next two decades.

With foreboding about the political situation, Yeats decided his place was in Ireland and lived in Dublin from March 1922 onward. His father died in New York early in February. He was now becoming 'a smiling public man', his long labours bearing the fruit of public acknowledgement. In July 1922 he received an honorary degree from Trinity College, Dublin, and one from Queen's College, Belfast, straddling the political divide of the two new states; there were other honorary degrees to follow, from Aberdeen and Oxford. In December he was made a senator of the Irish Free State. 'I feel I have become a personage,' he wrote to Olivia Shakespear with satisfaction.

He confined his work as a senator to matters concerning the arts and culture, chairing the committee which selected the state's new coins. Apart from this and his writing, he worked for Dublin's right to the Lane pictures and remained on the board of the Abbey, where controversy could still excite, now over the new playwright Sean O'Casey. The greatest accolade was when he was awarded the Nobel Prize for Literature in November 1923. However, his sense of having arrived gradually became clouded by increasing ill health, and because of this he resigned from the Senate in 1928.

When the deadly phase of reprisals spiralled, Maud Gonne was arrested. On 5 January 1923 Yeats wrote to Olivia Shakespear: 'The day before her arrest she wrote to say that if I did not denounce the Government she renounced my society for ever. I am afraid my help in the matter of blankets, instead of her release (where I could do nothing), will not make her less resentful.' The old friendship was at a low ebb, but not completely broken, for his kindness could always be relied on, as when Iseult too was arrested in the general sweep of arrests in 1923.

WBY 12   82 Merrion Square
                                                             Dublin
                                                             Oct 21 [1922]

My dear Maud
   I send you my memoirs – *The Trembling of the Veil*. I hope you
will read & that perhaps Iseult will read it. The early part which you
know in another form has been re-written a good deal, & there is a
new chapter with our first meeting. On the things that seem to me
essential I do not think my memory has failed me anywhere. When
I give anybody's thought I believe I do so accurately, but in things
that have not so much interested me, in the names of places, & in the
dates of events, I am probably inaccurate. Indeed it can hardly be
otherwise but I have never consulted an old letter or adopted any
means of verification. You will remember that Goethe called his
memoirs truth & fiction so little did he think accuracy possible. My
accounts of the 98 celebration of which I read you a long rough draft
will interest you, but read the other chapters too. Whatever I have
of wordly wisdom is in this book. The book was all subscribed many
days ago. Booksellers in some cases subscribed & have no doubt a
few copies, but it will soon be unobtainable. By my agreement I must
not reprint for I think three years as by that time all copies will be
selling at four or five pounds. You will find that I use my philosophy
throughout but in a summary way & without the mathematical
foundation which gives it precision.
   Yours
      W B Yeats

WBY 13   82 Merrion Square S.
                                                             Dublin
                                                             May 3 [?1923]

Dear Maud
   I have had a phone message from MacGrath's office[1] as follows
'Mrs Stuart & several others were made ill by the shaking of the
lorrey that brought them to the North Dublin Union.[2] These lorreys
bump about a good deal. She is now perfectly well.' I said 'There has
been no scrap or anything of that kind' The answer was 'No nothing
of that kind'.
   George will take this out to you, as I hope for a chance of speaking
to Mulcahy[3] again about her. I am afraid of her being offered a form
and of his [?her] refusing & so getting lost among the general mass
of prisoners till there is a general release. A form was suggested this
morning in a spirit of kindness, as a way out of all our difficulties;
& I was urgent against it.
   Yours Sincerely
      W B Yeats

WBY 14

82 Merrion Square, S.
Dublin
Sept 27 [1925]

My dear Maud

I send you a copy of latest book *Early Poems & Stories* – all work you know or think you know. Some of the poems, however have nothing of their old selves but the titles. I am especially pleased with this on page 117. You may perhaps recognise the model for this particular portrait.[1] I felt as I wrote that I had recalled the exact expression of that time & that I had seen it at last as I could not when I was young & dimmed the window glass with my hot breath.

You will find the stories better written than they were – I have cleared out needless words – they sometimes startle me so much do they seem to prepare for my present thought. Strange to write enigmas & understand them twenty five years later.

Yours Sincerely
W B Yeats

366

Roebuck House[1]
[Clonskeagh]
12 Jany 1926

My dear Willie

I heard from Iseult that your little girl has been ill, & I trust she is better. I know how fearfully anxious one always is when a child is ill.

I enclose a statement I am sending to Senator Dowdal[2] who is the Free State Commissioner in the Compensation Claims Committee & who recommended my case & made the amount of £125.

Mrs Sheehy Skeffington[3] tells me that Bowen Colthurst the murderer of her husband & several other Irish people in 1916 has returned to live in Ireland & that Blythe[4] has made no objection to paying him a large compensation for the burning of his place in Cork – he will no doubt get his 10% extra. Such is Imperial Free State justice.

Many official & militant Republicans have had compensation paid for damage done by the English – I have never been official, & I have only been militant for peace & for prisoners

Very Sincerely yours
Maud Gonne MacBride

After Seán's arrest in 1922 he planned his escape, making a number of abortive attempts before he finally succeeded in jumping from a

lorry which was moving a number of prisoners. From then on he remained on the run and occupied with IRA activities. For a while he acted as de Valera's international secretary, and early in 1925 he accompanied him to Italy to meet the Irish nationalist, Archbishop Mannix of Melbourne, who urged de Valera to enter constitutional politics (which he did in 1926). Seán was married in January 1926 and lived abroad for a year, working for the IRA and as a journalist. In July 1927 Seán had been travelling to the continent when a member of the government, Kevin O'Higgins, was shot. A number of people were arrested on suspicion of his murder, including Seán.

367
                                                    Roebuck
                                                    [Clonskeagh]
                                                    [Sept 1927]

Dear Willie

Enclosed is the Dr's certificate. 3 months ago it was discovered that Josephine[1] has cancer of the stomach. Dr Moore told me then she would not be likely to live for more than 2 months – She has lasted longer than he expected but the end is very near now. Dr Neary who is the local doctor attends & has given the certificate. She was annointed by Father Fennelly of Donnybrook an hour ago – for the past 2 days she has been constantly calling for Seagan & says she would die happy if she could see him. He is the only thing she loves on earth – She was his nurse when he was a baby – & loves him as if he were her own child.

I am sending you also a statement of how the Public Safety Act[2] is being worked against Seagan – If that is considered justice in Ireland one is sick & ashamed of being Irish!

Thanking you for trying to get this last wish for Josephine –
I remain
yours alwys
    Maud Gonne MacB.

368
                                                    Roebuck House
                                                    Clonskea
                                                    Wednesday 28th Sept [1927]

My dear Willie

After your hopeful message we were expecting Seagan all day, alas he has not come –

Josephine rallied a little after she was annointed & today has been in much less pain. She lies looking like death & sometimes her mind wanders, but she is always muttering about *Le Patron* her name for Seagan – she says she would die happy if she could see his face.

I had a stupid accident last Friday, I slipped getting out of my bath & broke a rib – as ribs are supposed to mend themselves I took no notice & went about just the same – there is such a lot of work to be done trying to keep Seagan's business going[1] as well as my own work – but on Monday the pain got bad & so I am in bed for a day or two till the bone knits. It is a great nuisance –

I hear that Mr Bulfin Seagan's wife's uncle[2] [who] is a Free State T.D. went to see Seagan today in Mountjoy. He has been trying to get Seagan released he says. He says that they all admit that Seagan had nothing to do with O'Higgins' death,[3] but they are keeping him *on account of his past record!* – whatever they mean by that –

Of course he fought with great daring during the Black & Tan war. He was taken in the Four Courts in July 1922 & imprisoned for 2 years when he was 18, so he had no possibility of taking part in the Civil War –

He escaped when they were moving him from Mountjoy to Kilmainham during the great Hunger Strike[4] & as the C.I.D. were raiding everywhere for him & the other escaped prisoners he had to go on the run.

He got married while on the run & he & his wife[5] went to France where they lived for a year & she came home for his baby to be born in England [Ireland]

Sean did not come home till Xmas when Mr Bulfin had got a guarantee from Kevin O'Higgins that he would not be arrested.

O'Higgins' colleagues have not respected the guarantee.

Sean went into business & was working very hard & making a success of it when he was arrested. It is an attempt to destroy a republican [?indecipherable]

A Free State Officer gave himself away badly when talking to some friends of ours about Sean's arrest he said 'He is much too dangerous a man to release. He was over the Brunswick Street[6] areas & we always knew whenever he was seen there that there would be *trouble & ambushes* –' Sean was over the Brunswick street areas during the Tan War & he certainly kept things lively. The Free State officer forgot that he was not supposed to be an ex Black & Tan now he is in the F.S. Army. The Free State now punishes those who fought England & honours ex Black & Tans –

Of course both Seagan & I are Republicans & I still believe what I believe ever since I was [a] girl that Ireland has a right to be independent. You believed that too once long ago – but what is the use of writing this long letter to you who by your vote made yourself responsible for the Public Safety Act & put the Police above the magistrates & made law a mockery & derision.

In the Public Safety Act the Free State legislators have given their measure. They will be remembered by it for all time.

Poor Ireland! What has she done to be afflicted with such contemptible rulers –

My only satisfaction in the trouble & anxiety & loss occasioned by Sean's outrageous arrest is that it lost the Free State more votes than perhaps anything else –

I am tired & you will be tired of reading before you come to this so Goodnight.

Kindest regards to your wife

Vy sincerely yours

  Maud Gonne MacBride

I thank you for having tried to give peace to a dying woman even if you have not succeeded.

WBY 15   82 Merrion Square
                        Dublin
                        Sept 29 [1927]

My dear Maud

I am sorry that I have had no more success. I dare say you are right about [?Shawn's] formidable reputation, but of one thing I am sure. The heads of the Free State do not want to be unjust to the son of John MacBride. Your husband was never one of my heroes – his brave death did not abolish his treatment of you – but he is a hero to these men. Cosgrave[1] was in the next cell to him in 1916 & was to have been the next executed.

You are right – I think – in saying I was once a republican, though like you yourself I would have been satisfied with Gladstone's bill.[2] I wonder if I ever told you what changed all my political ideas. It was the reading through in 1903–4 of the entire works of Balzac.[3] To day I have one settled conviction 'Create, draw a firm strong line & hate nothing whatever not even <the devil> if he be your most cherished belief – Satan himself'. I hate many things but I do my best, & once some fifteen years ago, for I think one whole hour, I was free from hate. Like Faust I said 'stay moment' but in vain. I think it was the only happiness I have ever known.

Yours [ev]er

  W B Yeats

I am very sorry about your accident.

369   Roebuck House
                                          [Clonskeagh]
                                          Saturday 1st Oct 27

My dear Willie

Your letter interested me, but is it sincere? Certainly the part where
you say 'The heads of the Free State do not want to be unjust to the
son of John MacBride' is not. Cosgrave repeats ad nauseum at
election meetings where he thinks it may suit, that he was in the next
cell to John MacBride in 1916. The Mayo papers answered his cheap
heroics well by asking 'Is this the reason why he is now persecuting
his son?'

But the part of your letter where you attribute your change of
thought to the study of Balzac is interesting. I have only read a little
of Balzac. We both have come to the same philosophical conclusion
– the all power of love & the sterility of hate; – the firm strong line,
by different roads, you through Balzac, I through St John. What is
strange is that having the same philosophical idea, it works out
through us in such opposite directions. It leads you to vote for
flogging bills & Treason Acts & Public Safety Acts. It leads me to
found the Women's Prisoners' Defence League.[1] In the inaugural
meeting of the League in the Round Room of the Mansion House in
1922, where I had gathered thousands of anxious mothers who I had
met outside the gates of the prisons where our sons were confined,
I told them we were invincible because we relied on the greatest
power in the Universe, love. God is love, & love's human
manifestation is threefold, like the Trinity. Divine love, creative love,
the spring of life – & fostering love – the mother's love, & like the
Trinity they are co-equal & indivisible, each could not exist without
the other. I told them, we with our mother's love, would be
invincible because the power of the Trinity is with us & these broken
women understood me & it made them strong so that they stood
calmly against machine gun fire, & rifle volleys & faced all night vigils
in the bitter cold outside Mountjoy & Kilmainham. No power on
earth can move the Mothers – the police know this.

Only once in all these dreadful years, have I doubted the divine
power on which we rely – & that was when I stood by the side of
the mothers whose sons had been murdered in the prisons. 'My God
My God, why hast thou forsaken me' We had failed to protect the
sons of those mothers, what could we say to them? & it was the
mother of Liam Mellows[2] who said 'Dear Women, why do you cry?
I am very proud of my son' but she nearly died in the weeks that
followed & 3 mothers whose sons had been executed lost their reason
& one drowned herself in the canal she went there looking 'for the
face of her son' she had not been allowed to see for a last farewell.
It was for this reason that the women of the Defence League swore

in the name of love & of motherhood that none of the reprisal murderers should ever address a meeting without being made to answer before the people for their crime. On several occasions in Dublin & Donegal I put that question of the Mothers to Mulcahy & I saw him hooted off the platform. No doubt that is why it is Mulcahy, minister of Public Health & local Govt who signed the internment order for Sean. That is probably the reason why a poor old peasant woman whose one love in life is the child she nursed must die without the sight of him – & you talk of their *Goodwill* & say there is no injustice.

I am still in bed but hope to get up tomorrow to take the chair at the meeting in O'Connell Street which every Sunday for 5 years we have held at first for Peace to try & prevent the Civil War & when that failed for the political Prisoners –

As Redmond[3] told Asquith years ago, about the Treason Felony Prisoners & my campaign for them, you might tell the Staters today – 'The only way to stop the meetings is to release the prisoners'

Good night

Yours very sincerely

Maud Gonne MacBride

WBY 16

P.S. I have just finished a poem in memory of Con Markievicz & her sister Eva.[1]

> 82, Merrion Square
> Dublin
> Oct 3 [1927]

My dear Maud

One does not vote for 'treason bills' and the like, out of hatred of any one, but because one believes they are necessary to protect many harmless people against anxiety, danger, poverty & perhaps death. I have sometimes come up from the country to vote for such bills, when I might quite well have stayed at home, out of sense of duty. Not to vote was the easy, popular thing but I would have despised myself. I am puzzled to find that you think that [?]loving compelled the driving of Mulcahy or others from their platforms. I wrote when fresh from the study of Balzac a comparison between Balzac & George Eliot in which I showed that he knew, and she did not, that we may judge acts, but individuals never. I put it all in these lines[2] once

That on the lonely height where all are in God's eye,
There cannot be – confusion of our sound forgot –
A single soul that lacks a sweet crystalline cry.

I was moved to write it by listening to the cry of curlew. A Saint can see his murderer, or the murderer of his dearest, without hate, & the rest of us can try to be just – alone we must see to it that murder does not lead to murder.

The great political service that Balzac did me was that he made authoritative government (government which can, at need, be remorseless, as in his *Cathedral Des Médicis*) interesting in my eyes – that is what I mean by the 'strong line', a line drawn upon the fluctuating chaos of human nature – before I had read him only movements for liberty – movements led by lyrical idealists – seemed to me interesting. In some ways you & I have changed places. When I knew you first you were anti-Drefusard[3] all for authoritative government, – Boulanger – & so on; and I was Drefusard & more or less vaguely communist under the influence of William Morris. Today if I lived in France I would probably join your old party – though with some reservations – & call myself a French nationalist. You I imagine would join the communists.

Yours ever

W B Y

I offered to be personally responsible for your son. To go with him to Roebuck House, to wait there for him & to bring him back – I am sorry it was useless. It was the best I could do.

370

Roebuck
[Clonskeagh]
Tuesday 4 Oct [1927]

My dear Willie

In the old days when you were Dreyfusard you used to think it fine the thesis 'Better France perish, than one man suffer injustice'!

I held that Dreyfus was an uninteresting jew & too much money was spent on his cause for it to be an honest cause & that greater injustice triumphed everyday when poor men were sent to jail for the theft of food or clothing for their families & I would prefer to raise the cry for them.

Being a nationalist, I sympathised with French nationalists who objected to the Jews & international finance interfering in their country & upsetting their institutions –

I also held – & still hold, that on matters I am not prepared to study deeply – the safe rule is to look on which side England ranges herself & to go on the opposite.

I have always been instinctively nationalist, though I admit philosophical limitations of nationalism – Connolly helped me greatly to reconcile nationalism & communism.

I have very strong views against murder. I am convinced this country can never prosper so long as openly avowed & unrepentant reprisal murderers receive a large number of votes from the people –

The press of this country being the most tied press in the world, the only way to inform the people is by public meetings, posters & demonstrations –

It is through the fostering spirit of mothers' love & in the interest of the race that the Women's Defence League say that murderers must not rule.

We do not descend to the level of those murderers by killing them, we hope they may expiate their crime in this world, but for Ireland's sake they must be driven out of the country they have disgraced.

I did not get Mulcahy chased from platforms out of hate of Mulcahy who I have never as far as I know spoken to privately – any more than you voted for flogging bills & public safety bills out of individual hate – but I am not sure you did not vote for them out of *class fear* – & fear is a bad councillor too –

The real anarchists in Ireland are the people who voted for flogging bills, Treason bills & Public Safety bills for they held the law up to the hatred & contempt & derision of the people –

The magistrature subservient to the police! Your strong line grows very wobbly when it depends on the suspicion in the mind of a policeman & on the guns in the hands of C.I.D. to defend it!

Though my son is at present the solitary victim of the public safety act – & we are suffering a great pecuniary loss by his enforced absence, & from a patriotic & national point of view I know I ought to rejoice for what has brought Cosgrave's government down, & what has turned the country against it are just these flogging bills Treason bills and Public Safety bills; *The Irish People will not forgive them* –

Josephine is now in a state of semi-consciousness. I doubt if even the presence of Seagan would matter much to her now though she still mutters his name at times –

The fact that parole was refused to Seagan, though granted to the Plunkets who were equally fantastically arrested for Kevin O'Higgins' murder – & it has always been largely granted under British & Free State coercion regimes & even your personal offer of guarantee & accompaniment was refused must show you how your friends' STRONG LINE is based on vindictive hate.

Very sincerely yours,
Maud Gonne MacBride

WBY 17

82 Merrion Square
Dublin
Oct 7 [1927]

My dear Maud

I have not answered your letter because we will never change each other's politics. They are too deeply rooted in our characters.

I have however taken advantage of having a typist for the day & dictate what may I think interest you – an abstract impersonal statement of what I believe to be the ancient doctrine – which must soon be modern doctrine also – of the effects of hate & love. The whole of mystical philosophy seems to me a deduction from this single thought.

Yours
W B Yeats

As things only exist in being perceived (or, as Bergson puts it echoing Protinus [?Plotinus],[1] 'The universe is itself consciousness') when we forget a thought or an emotion, which we will recall perhaps years later, it does not pass out of existence. It is still somewhere, still a part of some mind. I will add to that commonplace of philosophy this further thought that when we forget something for ever, or die, that thing – thought or emotion – still remains in some other mind, all the bad passions so remain and only come to an end through those minds, who are in the mystic sense of the word Victims. A Victim is a person so placed in life that he would be excited into the most violent hatred or into some other bad passion, if he did not dissolve that passion into the totality of mind, or to use the common language into God. Until that act of Victimage takes place, an act not of simple renunciation, but of santification, the passion remains passing from mind to mind from being to being among the living and the dead. In so passing it arouses everywhere its like just as do the good passions, those who hate receiving the influx of hate, subjecting themselves as old writers believe to streams of disaster, those who love receiving the influx of love, human and divine.

I said the victim 'would be excited' and I should perhaps have said 'is excited', for the struggle to 'sanctify' – to make 'holy' or make 'whole' must be the greatest possible to the human mind. Think of St Lydwine of Schiedam[2] who cured diseases in others by taking them upon herself.

371   Roebuck House
                                                                           Clonskea
                                                                           13 Oct. 27

My dear Willie

I read your statement with great interest & all the more as I have thought much along the same lines but it is difficult for me amid the stress of work & anxiety caused by Sean's outrageous arrest & imprisonment to put down these thoughts coherently.

You say 'Things only exist in being perceived' I gather from the rest of your statement that you mean perceived by the *human* mind. I believe things exist in being perceived in the *Divine* mind, that is why we are apt to talk at cross purposes.

If things exist through human mind Balzac is wise & the gospels are a dream, but if things have their being from the breath of God their Creator, then Balzac is only a mouth piece of the world & of the power of this World, while St John gives testimony to the light.

If things exist in being perceived by the mind of man, emotional love is the greatest good, & emotional hate the greatest evil, for man left to himself only feels emotions, the mind becomes their servant, the blind minister of material needs.

But if God is the life of things, spiritual love is the highest & spiritual hate the worst – for spiritual hate means the cutting off of man from God.

A man mad with resentment or jealousy or some other passion kills another – he has yielded to his emotions, but he has not necessarily cut himself off from Divine Love, the surface is clouded but the depth may remain pure & not being cut off from the purifying source, the clouded surface will grow shining again. A sane dispassionate man, accompanied by the ritual of certain formalities decides that the murderer must die & gets him killed, the world approves, but God sees the whited sepulchre, spiritual sin, *hate so deep that is has passed to the very core*, leaving the outer layers free – the emotional surface is unruffled but the depth is stagnant, cut off from the Divine source – as the reverse happens to the greatest saints who lose all sensible devotion, even all outer joy to plunge into the depths of spiritual love.

Why do you who are not really one of them, choose to ally yourself to the deadly quiet exterminators of love?

Always your old friend

Maud Gonne MacBride

On reading this over I see I have writen more of what I think to be your *ideal* free state politician than of what most of them are in fact, for though underlying hate of the Irish nation & distrust of the Irish people is in the core of those who conceived flogging bills, treason bills & public safety bills – (which will stand forever in judgement against free state legislators) the deputies & *most* of the ministers who voted them were swayed by incoherent surface emotions of fear, jealousy & hate. The source was poisoned & the surface was muddy.

Josephine died this morning, her heart's wish ungratified. One more witness before God to Free State infamy.

WBY 18

I have [been] out for a few minutes this morning

> 82, Merrion Square
> Dublin
> [?October 1927]

My dear Maud

Your letter came yesterday – it had been left by postman at Dr Cahill's house No. 80 & he was away. This is my first letter since my illness and it will not be very vigorous The question of Immanence or Transcendence does not really affect the issue. A monk of the Thebaid or the Mareotic Sea – 400AD or thereabouts – spoke of his fight with the beast & the Daimon[1] – the beast being the sins of the flesh & the Daimon those of hatred & these were of course the worst. The desert monks were victims – their perpetual struggle lightened the struggle for those in the world – 'we keep the ramparts' one said. Hatred unlike any other form of lust has no good whatever. It may have been it that Newman thought of when he said 'it were better that the whole human race perished in agony than that a single sin were committed'. No the judge does not hate. He decides by precedent & law & so by an act of knowledge. I have known an Irish judge to give a case against a poor woman & to send her the amount the law had taken from her out of his own pocket. The famous Galway judge[2] – an historical character – sentenced his own son to death. The Head of your own Church has again & again – in the Papal States – confirmed sentences of death. One historical case gave Browning the theme of 'The Ring [&] the Book'. In the famous Xth book the Pope gives the argument for capital punishment in most noble poetry. Balzac was not modern in philosophy but, as he thought, the embodiment in all that affects the stability of society of the historical doctrine of his church. What you say is logical perhaps in Madame Despard's mouth but not in yours. You can deduce it or something like it – as Tolstoy did – from the practice of the early Christians & from certain passages in the Gospels – if you pick & choose – but Christianity both to you & me is a human-devine experience which has enfolded [?unfolded] itself through the centuries – to you in your Church to me in that Church & outside it. You can no more ignore the Encyclicals which have defined the relation of the individual to state than I can the effect of the Incarnation upon modern philosophy.

You have not put the issue between a certain Church philosophy and modern philosophy fairly though nobody could in a sentence. The orthodox church philosophy made God so self sufficing that it left no reason for the creation of man, while the modern philosophers like the great Indians and Chinese make god & man necessary to one another. A Dominican monk of the 13th Century – Eckhart[3] – said 'The eye with which man sees God is the same eye as this with which God sees man' That is the modern thought. It is by this eye that things are 'perceived' & so 'exist'.

Yours
W B Yeats

372   Roebuck House
                                                                          Clonskea
                                                                          [?October 1927]

My dear Willie

I am so sorry you have been ill. I only heard of it through Iseult & I am very glad to hear that you are now much better.

I naturally thought when I did not hear from you that it was owing to your illness & I am sorry you thought it necessary even now to write, writing is often so tiring, though I know that sometimes, with you letters are a game like playing at ball –

I hope you are really recovered & that you will enjoy the sunshine & beauty of Spain though you must go far south in Spain to feel the warmth of the sun at this season –

Unless I am to look on your letter as a game of ball forgive me if I say it is not sincere.

You hate the Catholic Church with the hate of the Daemon condemned by the old monk of the Mariotic Sea[1] & when you take your stand on certain papal Encyclicals you always remind me of Satan rebuking Sin.

I agree with you & that old monk that the Daemon is more dangerous than the Beast & in that connection I know that a poor prostitute would have a good right to refuse to shake hands with let us say Ernest Blyth or any murder minister –

It is difficult to see Tommy O'Shaughnessy[2] or Judge Byrne[3] in the role of the Christian *Victim* 'keeping the ramparts' by taking on themselves the sins of humanity & in their persons expiating those sins.

The concrete image of your thought suggests a cartoon for Dublin Opinion.[4]

To me judges seem the well paid watch-dogs of Capitalism, making things safe & easy for the devil Mammon.

But that is a common place – One can hardly accept Browning great poet though he is as a reliable exponent of Catholic Theology.

The church never asks us to defend all the acts of all the Popes & it may well be that popes have signed death warrants – any more than the Church obliges us to accept the changing orders of Bishops as Catholic doctrine.

Sean was released last night without explanation, excuse or compensation.

As I point out in today's paper under the amazing Public Safety act of yours which you made law – & which according to you is therefore an *Act of Knowledge & without hate* anyone may be arrested & charged with the most appalling crimes, he may be imprisoned, deported even under it – *he can never be acquitted.*

Surely not an Act of Knowledge & without hate!

Go away into the Sun & reflect on it, write poetry & pray to God to send men who understand what *love of Ireland & of their fellows* means to undo this mischief you – unwillingly perhaps have helped to do. For your poetry you will be forgiven, but sin no more

Your old friend

Maud Gonne MacBride

WBY 19   Hotel Reina Cristiana
                                                Algeciras
                                                Spain
                                                [November 1927]

My dear Maud

A multitude of white herons are beginning to roost among the dark branches of the trees just outside my windows. They fish in the Mediterranean on the other side of Gibraltar which is some ten miles off, & then fly home to the gardens here for a night's sleep. In a few days we motor to Saville [Seville] where on the feast of the Immaculate Conception I shall see the sixteen boys dance in front of the high altar, a ceremony of your church I do not 'hate'.

We have argued again the old problem we have fought over since we were in our middle twenties. You were about 26 when I gave you a symbol & tried to make you see your heavens but the spirit said you were in Hell – I had nothing to do with him, you talked it out between you – & that your third or lowest Hell was revenge (labour from hatred). Months afterward I tried again with the same symbol, & this time the spirit showed you the circles of Heaven possible to you, of these the third & highest was 'labour from devine love'. Then in 1909 or 1910 when you were working on the feeding of school children I met you in Paris & you told me that you were convinced that all the misfortunes of your life had come upon you because you had taken up movements which had hate for their motive power.

Do you remember the old priest[1] with the miraculous picture of the 'Sacred Heart' who said that you would serve the Heart of the Devine Man & I his Brain. The Devine Man is the central conception of every philosophical or mystical faith – Buddhist Mohomedan, Christian. In that image – Blake's 'Devine Image' – there can be no negation. At the end of Faust Mephistopheles (negation) is driven from the stage by a shower of roses that burn him like flame – [2½ indecipherable lines] but why should I go on – you will reply that I do not believe these things which are the study of my life, & perhaps there is nothing to be said – a Buddhist Saint once sang at the moment when he attained Nervana – 'He comes no more, amid sweet incense, from behind the brocaded screen, he goes with pipe-players & singers & he [is] so drunk that they hold him up, one on either side. Something very nice has happened to the young man, but he will not tell it to anybody but his sweetheart.'

If you answer which you may not, write to 82 Merrion Square & they will forward it. I seem in excellent health, but soon get tired & the lung is not quite healed. However I enjoy life. I shall begin to write verse again next week in Saville. Here there is beautiful summer weather.

Yours affectionately
   W B Yeats

WBY 20
                           Hotel Chateau St George
                           Route de Frejus
                           Cannes
                           Jan 14 [1928]

My dear Maud
   Yes I wrote a longish letter from Seville in which I spoke of the old miracle-working priest you, & I & Fielding investigated & like things.

The doctor has been explicit at last. I asked why I was so exhausted & he said 'You have broken down because of the over work of years. I will not hold out false hopes; your recovery will be very slow.' I shall get a second opinion, but I am afraid he is right.

The prospect of long inaction, when I must even 'get into the habit of turning my mind from any too exciting thought' bores me beyond words, & yet I am a little proud, like a wounded man after the battle.

444

I have always hated work & now I can permit myself a good conscience.

Write but of peaceful things as in your last charming letter.

Yours affectionately

W B Yeats

WBY 21

82 Merrion Square
Dublin
June 13 [1928]

My dear Maud

I send a fresh copy of book. You will find a reference to your self in 'Among School Children'[1] – a Waterford School I went over – I do not think it will offend you. The book seems to me the best I have done, it is certainly the most successful.

Your explanation about the loss of the book may be near the truth but it does not account for several letters of mine to other people not having arrived. I am exceedingly puzzled.

Yours

W B Yeats

373

[Letterhead]
ROEBUCK INDUSTRIES
Roebuck House
Clonskea
Co. Dublin

SHELL AND FELT FLOWERS
For Millinery and
House & Table Decoration

First Communion Wreaths
Funeral Wreaths
Made from Irish Shells

Saturday 16th June [1928]

My dear Willie

Very many thanks for again sending me your book[1] – It arrived safely this time, & I am very pleased to get it. Why should I be offended at the references to me in Among school children? It is very kind. Oh how you hate old age – well so do I, I see no redeeming features in it, but I, who am more a rebel against man than you, rebel less against nature, & accept the inevitable & go with it gently into the unknown – only against the sordidness & cruelty of small ambitions I fight until the long rest comes – out of that rest I believe the Great Mother will refashion beauty & life again. While we sleep she will work in the stupendous energy of Creation – but till sleep comes our souls & bodies fight – in wearyness which is old age – at the awakening it will be with the glory & joy of youth again.

You musn't feel puzzled about letters not arriving – Free State methods in the post office as in all these departments are British in brutality but minus the efficiency.

Did you ever know a time in Ireland where one felt certain one's letters were not opened & read by the police? Generally the English used to send them on with envelopes more or less damaged – sometimes written across '*opened in post*'. The Free State gets muddled & loses the letters or the envelopes so they don't arrive – that is all – it is provoking.

Though you voted treason bills & flogging bills for them, they don't trust you.

Please excuse business paper.² I have no other at hand.

Again thanking you,

Your old Friend

    Maud

WBY 22

                                 42 Fitzwilliam Square
                                 Dublin
                                 Monday [7 August 1928]

My dear Maud

I have just learned that Mrs MacGregor¹ died a few days ago. She was 'seedy' for a couple of weeks, then suddenly collapsed. That is all I know. Please tell Iseult² – I would, but I have left my address book with her new address at Howth where the children are.

This is our new flat. We have given up the Merrion Square House as I must winter abroad.

Yours

    W B Yeats

WBY 23

                                 82 Merrion Square
                                 Dublin
                                 Sept 6 [1928]

My dear Maud

Of course you may sell your Blake.¹ Remember it is one of the large paper edition – limited I think to 50 – & should fetch more than ordinary editions. I will write in it for you I can put an account of the origin of the book in say a dozen lines which make it worth more than a mere inscription would. It is probably best, for you are selling it, that I should not put your name in it. I can inscribe it to some imaginary person if you like & set the collectors [?guessing]

Yours

    W B Yeats

I will come out to Roebuck House & write in Blake. It is too heavy for you to send it in. I am longing to be away in Rapallo[2] but shall be kept here for some weeks more by Colnagi & by a revival of my *Player Queen* which I have so modified that the new Abbey Ballet[3] can dance abundantly in the middle & at the end. When I get to Rapallo I am a honey bee – here I am a wasp.

1929–1938

> Like a long-legged fly upon the stream
> His mind moves upon silence. . . .
>
> Like a long-legged fly upon the stream
> Her mind moves upon silence.

W. B. Yeats, 'Long-Legged Fly' (first published 1937)

The next decade brought changes. Lady Gregory died in 1932. Mrs Despard decided to leave Dublin and live in Belfast, so Roebuck, with its large garden and trees, became the sole property of Maud Gonne. Yeats moved to Riverdale outside Rathfarnham, below the Dublin hills – some consolation for the sad loss of Coole. It was also a decade of imperceptibly growing stability; the old friends continued to adopt opposing positions. Yeats longed more and more for 'levelled lawns and gravelled ways where slippered Contemplation finds his ease', and 'for traditional sanctity and loveliness' returning to that which 'gives our blood and state magnanimity of its own desire'. Tired of fanaticism, he thought the 'despotic rule of the educated classes' good, flirting briefly with an Irish-style fascism, yet still a man of contrasts. He could have been talking to Maud Gonne when he wrote:

> You think it horrible that lust and rage
> Should dance attention upon my old age;
> They were not such a plague when I was young;
> What else have I to spur me into song?

Maud Gonne had not lost her spur; though fighting on a smaller stage, she went indomitably on. De Valera decided not to work against the situation but to work with it, as Collins had ten years previously. The IRA supported him vigorously, and he was elected to power in 1932. Afterwards there was a growing disenchantment; the IRA and a small band of irreconcilables felt their ideals had been betrayed and retook their old stand, so repression started again. As before, Maud stood back for a while but, once there were political prisoners, she went into action with her weekly meetings, protests, letters to the papers and her own bulletin Prison Bars. *She was also writing her autobiography, which was published in 1938. This was the year that de Valera brought in his new constitution, which was republican in all but name, leaving the way open for complete separation from the Crown by the External Relations Act: one of Collins's stepping stones.*

WBY 24   Savile Club
                                                          69 Brook Street, W.1.
                                                          June 16

Dear Maud

I was so glad to get your letter. Here are the European Parties now everywhere upon the march.

First Party platform: Thought created the brain, soul (or God) created nature. The conscience is older than the universe. All is memory.

Second Party platform: The brain secrets thought, nature creates the soul (or God). The conscience is a deduction from facts. Let us look and hear.

First Party platform: We can no more submit the decrees of conscience to a popular vote than the results of the multiplication table. We set the state above the party.

Second Party platform: The conscience approves <anything> . everything that helps the rising class to power (this class is now the proletariat). We set the party above the state.

First Party platform: we approve the past because it is the means by which God brought us into existence. All that is real is reasonable.

Second Party platform: we approve nothing except what we are about to make: all that is reasonable is real.

First Party platform: we are Hegelians of the right.

Second Party platform: we are Hegelians of the left.

First Party platform: we are Fascists, nothing is true that does not strengthen the State.

Second Party platform: nothing is true that does not help our own party.

First Party platform: Hurrah for Platonic reminiscence.

Second party platform: Hurrah for [?]evolution (& Shaw's 'black girl')

I dislike both parties as I like liberty but we shall all have to join one or the other or take to a begging bowl

Yours

W B Yeats

WBY 25
Riversdale
Willbrook
Rathfarnham
Dublin
March 23 [?1933]

My dear Maud

I have just come from the phone with a horrible thought. Can it have been your grandchild that has died? I assumed while speaking it was some stranger's child – I know you are surrounded with the people you befriend – & may well have seemed to you heartless. Forgive me if you are plunged in personal grief. I know Sean has a ten or twelve months old baby.

My number is in the new telephone book. Please ring me up when you are able to say when you can come. I am not often out.

Yours affectionately
W B Yeats

WBY 26
Riversdale
Willbrook
Rathfarnham
Dublin
Dec 25 [1933]

My dear Maud

Your letter followed me to London and found me, at the Savile Club, in bed with a very bad cold, & when I got up I had still to struggle with exhaustion. I was able to get through some necessary activities but had no energy left after. I am back about four days and almost normal. I had gone to London partly for business, partly because the doctor had told me to stop work. My second night there was a social disaster. I was the guest of the evening at 'The Pen Club'. Blood pressure was very high & as a result I was very cross. I looked round, saw several Indian authors & a lot of refugees from Germany, got the impression every woman there was a Britannia and was suckling a little Polish Jew. Result I devoted my speech to denouncing the Indians for writing in English & England for compelling Indians to conduct government business and all higher education in English 'Go back to India,' I said, 'boycot the English language. Compell your masters to talk Pigeon Bengali, Pigeon Hindi, Pigeon Marratti. Thrust upon them the indignity they have thrust upon you.' As I looked round the room I saw a few delighted faces – all others glum – the delighted faces were those of Polish Jews. Much as they hate Germany for baiting Jews they hate it more for putting down the Polish language. I have been ashamed of myself ever since, just as if I were a cat and had eaten the canary. And I had accepted the invitation thinking it a pleasant way of letting people know I had arrived – like sending round cards.

I have not your letter near me at the moment – it is still unpacked. I know you were so kind as to ask us to lunch. May I write a [little] later when I am quite well & the Xmas excitement is over.

Yours
W B Yeats

WBY 27

Riversdale
Willbrook
Rathfarnham
Dublin
March 14

My dear Maud

Can you lunch with me on Thursday or Friday next week at 1.30, either here or at Jamet's Restaurant[1] which ever is most convenient to you.

Yours
W B Yeats

WBY 28

Riversdale
Willbrook
Rathfarnham
Dublin
Friday

My dear Maud

I don't suppose I shall again write to the papers or make a speech. I am ordered to avoid all strain or excitement. I do not even go to the board meeting of the Theatre & the Academy, or even go to see my friends. I am writing poetry & thinking of nothing else – I have written more in the last few months than in any similar period of my life. Think of me as [a] monk of some strict order.

I thought Iseult looked very charming the other day. I have a portrait you made of her years ago on a little easel on my study table.

Yours
W B Yeats

WBY 29

The Chantry House
Steyning
Sussex
June 16 [1938]

My dear Maud

Yes of course you may say what you like about me.[1] I do not however think that I would have said 'hopeless struggle'. I never felt the Irish struggle 'hopeless'. Let it be 'exhausting struggle' or 'tragic struggle' or some such phrase. I wanted the struggle to go on but in a different way.

You can of course quote those poems of mine, but if you do not want my curse do not misprint them. People constantly misprint quotations.

I do not know if Agnes Tobin is living. She went melancholy mad was shut up <somewhere> I doubt if she knows what is going on in the world. She is probably dead. A week ago I was talking to Mrs Moody,[2] the great tennis player, about the Tobin family. She lives in San Francisco and knows them well, but she had never heard of Agnes Tobin.

When I came back from the South of France in, I think, April I was ill for a time. When I got better I thought of asking you to dine with me, then I put it off till *On the Boiler* is out. *On the Boiler* is an occasional publication like my old *Samhain* which I am about to bring out. The first number will be published in about a month. Perhaps you will hate me for it. For the first time I am saying what I believe about Irish and European politics. I wonder how many friends I will have left. Some of it may amuse you.

I am staying now with an old friend Miss Shackleton Heald,[3] once the best paid woman journalist in the world. She found she had no leisure & so gave up most of it. On Tuesday I go to Penns in the Rocks, Withyham, also in Sussex, and stay with Lady Gerald Wellesley,[4] another good friend, then back here and then to Ireland for the first performance of my one-act play *Purgatory*.

God be with you
    W B Yeats[5]

WBY 30

Riversdale
Willbrook
Rathfarnham
Dublin
August 22 [1938]

My dear Maud

I want you & your friend to come here to tea at 4.30 on Friday. A motor will call for you at 4 or a little after. I have wanted to see you for a long time but –

Yours
W B Yeats

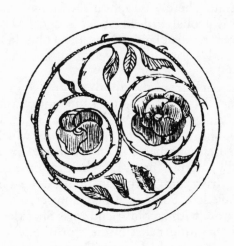

Epilogue

In November 1945 Maud Gonne wrote to Ethel Mannin:

Politics had separated us for quite a long while, we got on each other's nerves over them & neither wanted to see the other, but at the last we had come together & the last time I saw him at Riversdale he was planning things we would do together when he returned – but he seemed to me so ill, I felt unhappy for I didn't think we would meet again in this life – not that one should feel unhappy about death for the pattern will be clearer to us I think after.

Olivia Shakespear died in October 1938; she and Yeats had been friends for more than forty years. He left for England the same month and at the end of November went to the south of France and spent Christmas with his family there. His health was deteriorating but he was happy writing poetry.

> Many times man lives and dies
> Between his two eternities,
> That of race and that of soul,
> And ancient Ireland knew it all.
> Whether man die in his bed
> Or the rifle knocks him dead,
> Brief parting from those dear
> Is the worst man has to fear.

Yeats died on 28 January 1939, having been writing up to a few days before.

His body was temporarily buried at Roquebrune in France. Maud Gonne was one of those anxious to see that his remains be brought home. She wrote to de Valera, to the President, their old friend

Douglas Hyde, and to F. R. Higgins at the Abbey, who comforted her with his answer:

We are making every endeavour to have the remains brought home to Ireland; and while various appeals are being made to us for a burial in St Patrick's Cathedral, Glasnevin or Mount Jerome, because of their associations with W.B.'s work, I know personally that he had a passionate desire to rest in Sligo. He told me so frequently, and I do think that eventually that will be his resting place. We are using whatever pressure we can marshall to have his wishes carried out.

The war came before full arrangements were completed for his return home.

Maud Gonne started on her second autobiography but after a few chapters found it too painful to continue. She wrote reflective essays she intended to put in book form at a later stage; in these she said, 'I try to express the livingness of the Land as part of the national Trinity, the People, the Land and from their love proceeding the Spirit of the Nation.' She also worked on a series of articles on the Orange Order, published by the *Irish Press* in April 1939, and on the penal system and corporal punishment. In 1947 she wrote to Ethel Mannin that, recovering from pneumonia, 'mental lethargy prevents me finishing the three books I have begun'; yet extracts from these frequently found their way into print or were used for broadcasts.

Just before the Second World War, Seán had finally taken time from his political activities to complete his legal studies and was now practising at the Bar. As ever, England's difficulty was Ireland's opportunity, and the IRA decided on a bombing campaign in England. De Valera introduced emergency legislation, including censorship, rounded up any suspects he could find and interned them for the duration, establishing military courts which could only decide on either acquittal or the death sentence. Seán acted as defence lawyer in these cases.

At that time many Irish people, in the time-honoured tradition, were pro-German. Maud Gonne was one of these, but how much because she was fascist or merely anti-British is hard to judge. The great economic benefits that fascism brought in the early days and the strong sense of nationalism were certainly an attraction. The country remained neutral: at the end of the war Churchill said that it was with restraint that 'His Majesty's Government never laid a violent hand' on Ireland. De Valera broadcast his answer: 'It is indeed hard for the strong to be just to the weak' and 'By resisting the temptation to invade Ireland, Churchill, instead of adding another chapter to the bloodstained record of relations between England and this country, has advanced the cause of international morality.' No one was more in heartfelt approval of the nation's dignified answer than Maud Gonne.

At the end of the war she was active in a movement known as Save the German Child, which campaigned to allow Irish people to adopt war orphans.

When censorship was removed, a particularly emotive IRA hunger strike death took place. In the aftermath a new political party, Clann na Poblachta, was formed with Seán MacBride as leader. He contested the next by-election in 1947 and won. An irate de Valera called a general election in February 1948. By this time he had been in power for sixteen years. He lost his majority and a coalition was formed which included the old Free State Party, now Fine Gael, and the new Clann na Poblachta, which had attracted republicans who wished for constitutional action and many who were dissatisfied with the long years of de Valera's government and were generally experiencing post-war disillusion. Seán MacBride was made Minister for External Affairs. One of his first actions was to work for the return of Yeats's body. In September 1948 the Irish corvette, the *Macha*, brought his body back to Galway. The coffin was piped ashore and, accompanied by his wife and children, brought in funeral procession to Sligo, where it was met by Seán MacBride and other members of the government, the Mayor and Corporation of Sligo and a large crowd. After a Church of Ireland service at Drumcliffe he was buried in the graveyard beside the church, where his great-grandfather had been rector.

In 1948 the inter-party government repealed the External Relations Act and, breaking all Commonwealth ties with England, declared the twenty-six counties an independent republic, formally inaugurated on Easter Monday 1949. Frail but determined, Maud Gonne attended the religious ceremonies.

The five more years that were left to Maud Gonne were ones of steadily decreasing physical strength, but she had a mind still clear and a hand still able to wield a pen. In January 1951, when she had been preparing a series of recordings for radio, she wrote to Ethel Mannin:

How lucky Willie Yeats was to escape into the freer life of the spirit beyond the limitations of time and space.

I think Ireland is not doing too badly – when I compare it with the Ireland of my girlhood with the periodic famines & the wholesale destruction by the battering rams during the evictions of the little houses of the people. There has been tremendous progress and reconstruction work going on relatively quickly. I think Ireland is going to produce a *3rd Golden Age* which will probably make her a leader of the Peace thought in this world of confused thinking.

On 27 April 1953 Maud Gonne went 'gently into the unknown'. Dignitaries and friends attended the church service and people lined the streets as her funeral went through the city to Glasnevin Cemetery where she was buried in the Republican Plot.

Brigid Boland, whose father had been MP for South Kerry, in her biography *At My Mother's Knee* (1978) wrote:

From that world one face I never saw remains with me; the face of Maud Gonne. A lifetime after those Dublin days when her beauty reigned supreme, my father was in bed with a cold when I brought the morning paper with his breakfast and said as I gave it to him: 'It says here Maud Gonne died.' He was in his eighties then, but as he heard me his face changed as I should never have believed a face could: the lines of age were smoothed clean away, the eyes, a little misted, shone a clear and startling blue, and a young man was staring up at me. 'Maud Gonne,' he said, 'she couldn't!' And then the years flowed back. 'Ah, well,' he said, 'I suppose, come to think of it, she must have been getting on.' He had never approved of her politics which were far too extreme for him; but another aspect of her hold on the period struck me that same night. I had been down to Brighton to see the opening of a new play, and was coming back on the last train, alone in a carriage with a very drunken old Irish workman, who was singing rebelly songs as he lay full length along the seat opposite me. We had an hour's journey ahead of us, so – 'Been celebrating something good?' I asked, in my best Kerry accent. He squinted across at me. 'You wouldn't understand at your age,' he said. 'Maud Gonne died, and it was to her I was drinking.' 'She was a friend of my father's,' I said, fascinated, 'did you know her?' 'I did,' said he. He had been on the run after the 1916 Rising, and she had given him shelter. 'She washed my socks and she gave me a second pair. And says she to me, "Do you keep those washed now, every night one pair or t'other. A man on the run needs to look after his feet." And I did, and here I am to tell you: Maud Gonne died to-day.'

Anna MacBride White

Notes

A	W. B. Yeats, *Autobiographies* (London: Macmillan, 1955)
ASQ	Maud Gonne MacBride, *A Servant of the Queen: Reminiscences* (London: Gollancz, 1938; 1974)
Cardozo	Nancy Cardozo, *Maud Gonne: Lucky Eyes and a High Heart* (London: Gollancz, 1978)
CBS	Crime Branch Special Papers
CP	W. B. Yeats, *Collected Plays*, 2nd edn (London: Macmillan, 1952)
FJ	*Freeman's Journal*
L (K)	*The Collected letters of W. B. Yeats*, vol. I: *1865–1895*, ed. John Kelly (Oxford: Clarendon Press, 1986)
L (W)	*The Letters of W. B. Yeats*, ed. Allan Wade (London: Rupert Hart-Davis, 1954)
LTWBY	*Letters to W. B. Yeats*, ed. Richard J. Finneran, George Mills Harper and William M. Murphy, 2 vols (London: Macmillan, 1977)
M	W. B. Yeats, *Memoirs*, transcribed and ed. Denis Donoghue (London: Macmillan, 1972)
SVV	*Shan Van Vocht*
UI	*United Irishman*
UId	*United Ireland*
UPWBY	*Uncollected Prose by W. B. Yeats*, vol. I. ed. John P. Frayne (London: Macmillan, 1970; New York: Columbia University Press, 1970); vol. II, ed. John P. Frayne and Colton Johnson (London: Macmillan, 1975; New York: Columbia University Press, 1976)
YANB	A. Norman Jeffares, *W. B. Yeats: A New Biography* (London: Hutchinson, 1988)
YANC	A. Norman Jeffares, *W. B. Yeats: A New Commentary on the Poems of W. B. Yeats* (London: Macmillan, 1984)
YP	*Yeats's Poems*, ed. and annotated by A. Norman Jeffares, with an appendix by Warwick Gould (London: Macmillan, 1989)

Shining Days 1893–1899

1893

In the 1840s the Young Ireland paper *The Nation* and its 'Library of Ireland', under the editorship of Sir Charles Gavan Duffy and disseminated through Daniel O'Connell's Repeal Association's reading rooms, had produced throughout the country a lively intellectual activity which had died between the ravages of the Famine and the Land War. Political life, the Parliamentary Party and evicted tenants' associations were in a shambles after the death of Parnell, yet there was a growing interest in Irish culture. The Gaelic Athletic Association had been founded in 1888 with great success, and an exciting body of ancient history and literature was being uncovered. This provided inspiration for men such as Douglas Hyde and W. B. Yeats, who wished to develop a literature drawn from Irish sources, as the Young Ireland movement had in the 1840s, but one aimed at higher literary standards.

For this purpose the Literary Society of the National Club in May 1891 called a convention of all the literary societies which was held in the Rotunda in Dublin on 17 September 1891, reported by police as 'purely a meeting of Fenian Delegates of a dangerous class'. One jaundiced report suspected it of being a forerunner of some Fenian move similar to that which occurred at the time of the Invincibles, undoubtedly because many known Irish Republican Brotherhood men were present. The general opinion among the police, however, was that it would not be heard of much longer (CBS 501S/4629, 501/3994). It was presided over by the Young Irelander John O'Leary, and many of those who were present played a considerable part in literary nationalism in the following years. From this convention was formed the Young Ireland League.

From the discussion and organisation that followed, WBY revitalised the Southwark Irish Literary Club, renaming it the Irish Literary Society, London, in December 1891;

then, returning to Ireland, early in 1892 he organised the setting up of the National Literary Society, Dublin, with Douglas Hyde, whose presidential address on 'The Necessity for De-Anglicising Ireland' was given in November 1892. A plan was formed to set up village libraries and to publish a series of Irish books. This scheme did not succeed because, apart from lack of money, there were differences of literary opinion between WBY and Sir Charles Gavan Duffy, who had returned from exile in Australia, where he had become Premier of Victoria in 1871. The Irish Literary Society, London, is still in existence, and the National Literary Society, Dublin, flourished into the early twentieth century. It was under its auspices that the Irish Literary Theatre and the dramatic movement grew. Douglas Hyde went on to found the Gaelic League for the revitalisation of the Irish language in 1893. These three – the Gaelic Athletic Association, the Gaelic League and the literary movement – formed the basis of the Irish revival.

WBY1

1 'Scotia' was a name WBY used for MG in the early days of their friendship. See *L* (K), 341.

2 John O'Mahony (d. 1904), a journalist and later successful barrister, was a member of the National Literary Society and married Nora Tynan, sister of the poet Katharine Tynan, in 1895.

1

1 George Noble, Count Plunkett (1851–1948), created a papal count in 1884, was a member of the Irish Bar. A poet, he wrote under the name of Killeen and was founder editor of *Hibernia*, a short-lived journal. He became a vice-president of the National Literary Society in August 1892 and Treasurer of the Society's Libraries Sub-committee in September 1892.

2 Charles Hubert Oldham (1860–1926), a barrister and distinguished economist, founded the Contemporary Club in 1885 and the following year established the Protestant Home Rule Association. MG was introduced to him by her friend Ida Jameson on her return to Dublin in 1888. He helped her to become active in Irish politics.

3 Presumably she means that the accounts of the Libraries Sub-committee should be kept separate from those of the National Literary Society. See WBY, 'The National Literary Society – Librar-

ies Scheme', *UId*, 24 Sept 1892.

4 MG's first lecture resulted from her article 'Un Peuple Opprimé', published by Madame Ratazi in *La Revue Internationale* from which she received further publicity. She lectured not only in France but in Holland and Belgium, receiving at least 2000 notices and articles in the French press, according to the *UId*. See WBY, 'New Speranza', *UId*, 16 Jan 1892, and 'The New Speranza', the *Boston Pilot*, July 1892. 'Speranza' was the pen name of Lady Wilde, Oscar Wilde's mother, who wrote for the *Nation*.

5 The three-volume edition of *The Works of William Blake, Poetic, Symbolic and Critical*, ed. Edwin Ellis and WBY and published by Quaritch in 1893. WBY also edited *The Poems of William Blake*, published by Lawrence and Bullen in 1893.

6 MG's grey woman was a vision, familiar to her from childhood, which MacGregor Mathers and WBY decided was her Ka, their theory being that part of her personality survived the death of a former incarnation; the priests in ancient Egypt used to preserve mummies as a means of keeping their Kas in order to use them to perform the priests' magic. MG had the idea of sending her grey woman to influence people, but on learning that she admitted to having killed a child denied her existence. But she still managed to appear whenever people with mediumistic faculties were present (*ASQ*, 254–5). WBY (*M*, 48–9, 62–3) says she showed herself 'very evil'.

7 Probably the article in the Journal of the Amnesty Association of America's pamphlet published in New York, June 1893, which may also have appeared elsewhere. It is an interview account by MG of her visit to Portland Gaol. WBY took MG to the London Amnesty Association meeting in Chancery Lane, many of the members of which belonged to the IRB. There she met Dr Mark Ryan, at whose suggestion she visited Portland to see the Irish prisoners there about 1892 (*ASQ*, 156).

An amnesty association was first started in 1869 to help the Fenian prisoners including O'Donovan Rossa and John O'Leary when Isaac Butt and Richard Pigott were prominent in the movement, which commanded massive meetings of 250,000 to 300,000. MG belonged to both the National Amnesty

Association of Ireland and the English-based Amnesty Association of Great Britain, formed in 1892. The associations worked for the release of all prisoners 'incarcerated in English and Irish prisons on charges arising out of political struggle in Ireland, to protect their interests, and to give such aid for the support of their families as may be necessary; and also to secure that the prisoners shall be visited when permission can be obtained' (Rules of the Irish National Amnesty Association, 1896).

Undated fragment

1 *La Société Nouvelle* was a bi-weekly review published in Brussels. The founder editor was Madame Adam, *née* Juliette Lambert (b. 1836), an extreme French nationalist. See Winifred Stephens, *Madame Adam* (1917).

2 *United Ireland*, a paper founded by Parnell, had as its first editor William O'Brien in 1881. When the majority of the Parliamentary Party voted against Parnell as leader in December 1890, William O'Brien directed that the paper should go with the majority. Parnell started another paper, the *Irish Daily Independent*, while the *UId* became the organ for the National Party and was later run by Timothy Harrington.

2

1 Kathleen Gonne (1868–1919) at 21 married an army officer, Captain (later Major-General) Thomas David Pilcher (1858–1928), who commanded a flying column in the Boer War. They had three sons, Toby, Tommy and Pat, and a daughter, Thora. Since her childhood Kathleen always had an attachment to Ireland; she was musical, studied art at the Slade and was an accomplished artist. She divorced her husband in the first decade of the century. It was Kathleen and not Maud, as their father had feared, who developed tuberculosis; she suffered recurring bouts of illness and eventually died in Switzerland early in 1919. The two sisters were very close, and in spite of her husband's dislike Kathleen always insisted on seeing Maud whenever she passed through London, and MG always went to her aid when needed.

2 Annie Horniman (1860–1937), the daughter of an English MP and chairman of a firm of tea merchants in Manchester, had joined the Order of the Golden Dawn in 1890. She supported MacGre-gor Mathers, first by employing him as curator of the Horniman Museum until 1892, then by making him an allowance until 1896. She later financed the purchase of the Abbey Theatre in Dublin, to which she gave a subsidy until 1910, when she had a disagreement with WBY and Lady Gregory.

3 By this time MG was a practised journalist. In 1892 she wrote a series on 'Le Martyre de l'Irlande' for the *Journal des Voyages* with a front-page illustration of the attempted arrest of Father MacFadden in Donegal in Feb 1889. Acting in a public relations capacity, she kept in contact with editors who were frequent visitors to her soirées. In 1897 she started her little paper *L'Irlande Libre* in preparation for the French–Irish commemorations of the 1798 rebellion.

4 Florence Farr (1860–1917) was an actress; she married Edward Emery, an actor, in 1884 and they were divorced in 1894. Also in 1894 she acted in WBY's play *The Land of Heart's Desire* at the Avenue Theatre, which was sponsored by Annie Horniman. She joined the Order of the Golden Dawn in 1890, becoming Praemonstratrix in 1895. After disagreements with WBY and Annie Horniman she left the Order in 1902. In the first decade of the twentieth century she collaborated with WBY in his experiments with verse speaking to the psaltery. In Dublin she appeared as Aleel in the first production of WBY's *The Countess Cathleen* in 1899 and recited to the psaltery at the Antient Concert Rooms in 1902. In 1912 she went to Ceylon to become the headmistress of a girls' school; she died there of cancer.

5 $3°=8°$ is one of the degrees in the Order of the Golden Dawn, into which MG was initiated on 2 Nov 1891. The Golden Dawn was founded in London in 1888 for the study and practice of ritual magic, drawn from the ancient Hebrew occult writings of the Kabbala with an infusion of Egyptian magic and freemasonry legend, by three freemasons who asked MacGregor Mathers to join them and work on its rituals. MG went through four grades in the First Order which began at $0°=0°$ and went to $4°=7°$ (WBY was a member of the Second Order by Jan 1893 and in Oct 1914 took the $6°=5°$ grade, becoming an adeptus major). Her motto was *Per Ignem ad Lucem*, 'Through fire to light'. WBY often refers to MG in his diaries as PIAL; his motto

was *Demon est Deus Inversus*, 'The
Devil is the converse of God'. She
resigned from the Order in Dec 1894,
suspecting masonic influences.

1895

3

1 WBY wrote a number of symbols at the
end of this letter which may mean that
he had been doing some occult work
concerning her, and also mentions 'the
story of SR'. MG's intuitive feeling about
Mrs Shakespear makes itself apparent in
some of the following letters. Olivia
Shakespear (1863–1938), the 'Diana Ver-
non' of WBY's *Memoirs*, was disappointed in her marriage to a solicitor
Henry Hope Shakespear; she wrote several novels and her home was a centre for
musicians and writers. WBY first met her
in 1894, and had an affair with her when
he left Fountain Court for 18 Woburn
Buildings in Feb 1896. The affair ended
in early 1897: 'Maud Gonne wrote to
me; she was in London and would I
come to dine? I dined with her and my
trouble increased – she certainly had no
thought of the mischief she was doing.'
See *M*, 88–9, and 'The Lover mourns the
Loss of Love', *YP*, 95.

2 WBY's *Poems* (1895).

3 John Hughes (1865–1941) was a student
at the Metropolitan School of Art, Kildare Street, Dublin, when WBY was
there. He became a well-known Irish
sculptor. From 1903 to about 1920 he
lived in Paris.

4 WBY wrote to John O'Leary on 15 April
1894: 'For a couple of years it has been
getting more & more difficult for me to
do any steady reading as my eyes begin
to get uncomfortable in a few minutes. I
find now that I am never to read more
than a quarter of an hour at any time. I
have then to stop and rest for a few
minutes – the same in a less degree
applies to writing. I have "conical cor-
nea" in the left eye and "stigmatism" in
the right. The left eye is now practically
useless.' (See *L*(W), 230; *L*(K), 385.)

4

1 MG had begun to take chloroform after
the death of Georges in 1891 and became
addicted to it for a time, but she broke
the habit when Millevoye was sarcastic
about her ability to find the bottle which
her cousin, May, a nurse, had hidden in
the ashes of the fire; '"Yes," he said, "it

is just as wonderful as a drunkard who in
a strange place can always find the pub"'
(*ASQ*, 255–6). Both she and WBY took
hashish in Paris in 1894; she said it gave
her the ability to leave her body and go
where she wished, but when she
discovered it was happening without
conscious volition she gave it up (*ASQ*,
250–4).

2 See *Visions Notebook*. (There were two
volumes; for convenience they are here
alluded to as *Visions Notebook*.) This
roughly means earth and spirit symbols
meeting the fire symbol. Tatwas or
Tattwas are Hindu symbols of the elements, Prithivi, earth, represented by a
yellow square, Akasa, spirit, by a black
egg shape, Tejas, fire, by a red triangle,
Apas, water, by a silver crescent, and
Vayu, air, by a blue disc. These were
used in the Order of the Golden Dawn
as the basis for all forms of meditation,
astral travelling and *scriving*. Members
made cards with the five basic symbols
drawn on them, or combinations of any
two symbols. See *WBY, A*, 339, for an
account of his using the Tattwa cards in
Paris.

3 MG was probably in Belfast for a meeting; later she would stay with her friends
the Johnstons there.

4 The Irish National League was founded
by Parnell in 1882 at the instigation of
Michael Davitt to replace the old Land
League, but it was more a parliamentary
political organisation for the Irish Party.
It formed a basic structure throughout
the country for political action.

6

1 An article by Lionel Johnson entitled 'A
Poet', *Daily Chronicle*, 8 Nov 1895.

2 Lionel Pigot Johnson (1867–1902), a
cousin of Olivia Shakespear (whom he
introduced to Yeats), was a member of
the Rhymers' Club, founded by WBY
and Ernest Rhys in 1890. He developed
an interest in Irish Literature, visiting
Ireland in 1893, and wrote two books of
poems. As WBY put it, 'he loved his
learning better than mankind'. In the
mid-1890s he began drinking heavily and
died as a result of a fall from a chair in a
Fleet Street public house.

3 The rose was used frequently as a symbol
by WBY in his poetry of the nineties: it
could suggest MG, or Ireland, or spiritual or intellectual eternal beauty. (See
YANC, 32–3.)

4 Althea Gyles (1867–1949) was a student

at the Metropolitan School of Art in Dublin with WBY; she then trained at the Slade. She designed the covers of WBY's *The Secret Rose* (1897) and *The Wind among the Reeds* (1899). He wrote an article on her work for *The Dome*, Dec 1898, and described her in *A*, 237–8.

7

1 There was a feeling of approaching doom over these years as a result of tension between the colonial powers. The *Freeman's Journal*, 8 Dec 1895, carried news of a possible war between Britain and the USA over the boundary between Venezuela and British Guiana. The US President, Grover Cleveland, had invoked the Monroe Doctrine on 17 Dec in a message to Congress. WBY wrote to Florence Farr in Dec 1895: 'Has the magical Armageddon begun at last?' (*L* (K), 477).

2 In *ASQ* (244) MG mentions a portrait by a French artist, Kreder, which she likened to her grey lady. In later letters the grey lady seems to appear in a portrait in Colleville. MG also left a portrait behind when leaving France; whether these are all the same portrait or different ones is not known.

3 Alfred Percival Graves (1846–1931) collaborated with Stanford, publishing *Songs of Old Ireland* and *Songs of Erin*, the former including the well-known 'Father O'Flynn'. He was the father of Robert Graves, to whose autobiography *Goodbye to All That* (1929) he responded in *To Return to All That* (1930).

1896

8

1 This may be 'AM' 's review, 'Mr Yeats's Poems', *The Bookman*, Dec 1895.

2 John Davidson (1857–1909), a Scottish poet known for his *Fleet Street Eclogues* (1893), was a member of the Rhymers' Club and reviewed for *The Speaker* and the *Daily Chronicle*. He committed suicide.

3 MG gave lectures at Verdun, Rheims and Nancy, the proceeds from which she sent as subscriptions to the Amnesty Associations in London and Dublin. (See *SVV*, March 1896).

11

1 Samuel Liddell MacGregor Mathers (1854–1918) was one of the founders of the Hermetic Order of the Golden Dawn

in 1887. Becoming powerful within the organisation, he turned it towards the study of magic. He married the painter Moina Bergson (sister of the French philosopher Henri Bergson) in 1890. When he lost his post as curator of the Horniman Museum in 1892, he and his wife went to Paris, where he lived until he died. He became a supporter of Scottish nationalism, adopting the title of Comte de Glenstrae and dropping the name Mathers. When he became too autocratic he was expelled from the Golden Dawn in April 1900 and the rift between him and WBY was never healed: 'I thought him half a lunatic, half a knave, / And told him so, but friendship never ends.' MG met the Matherses occasionally in Paris, where Mrs Mac-Gregor Mathers tried to earn a living by painting and he was ill, believing himself bewitched.

2 The St Patrick's banquet was held every year on St Patrick's Day, 17 March, by l'Association de St Patrice. According to O'Donnell in *The Irish Abroad* (1915), the association was founded in 1893 and presided over by Viscount O'Neill de Tyrone. The members of the Association were mainly the descendants of the Wild Geese, the Jacobite exiles who formed the Irish Brigade which won renown in the armies of Louis XIV and XV.

3 This comment and the remark about 'meeting with the highlanders' in the following letter may refer to meetings at which Mathers and Scottish nationalists were introduced to advanced Irish nationalists in Scotland.

12

1 Mlle Ghénia de Sainte-Croix (1856–1939), later Madame Avril, a journalist who wrote under the name Savioz, was MG's closest friend in Paris. Primarily she was a reformist feminist, and was secretary of the National Council of French Women (founded in 1900), an affiliation of 67 societies concerned with questions affecting women and children. In 1901 she founded *L'Oeuvre Libératrice* to help prostitutes. She assisted MG with her writing and with the paper *L'Irlande Libre*, and frequently took care of Iseult, who adored her. She accompanied the French delegation to Mayo for the '98 centenary celebrations.

2 Dr Mark Ryan (1844–1940), the guiding spirit of Irish nationalists in London for 40 years, was a member of the Supreme

Council of the IRB and helped to form the Parnell Leadership Committees through which the IRB supported Parnell in his last fight. In 1892 he founded the Amnesty Associations.

In the USA, Clann na Gael, under the leadership of Sullivan and two others called the Triangle, had become a powerful political machine with jobs and power for Sullivan in the US Republican Party. John Devoy strenuously opposed Sullivan and his successor Lyman, who founded the 'New Movement', the Irish National Brotherhood (INB) or Irish National Alliance (INA). The resultant split in Clann na Gael had its effect on the IRB across the Atlantic. Most of the Supreme Council of the IRB would have nothing to do with the 'New Movement', but Dr Ryan and many of the London IRB joined it around 1894. Ryan formally set up the INB in Dublin in 1895, becoming the European leader. He features frequently in subsequent letters, mainly referred to as 'our gentle and conciliatory friend'.

3 MG was in Belfast speaking at the Kickham Literary Society on 'Humbert's invasion of Connaught' on 29 May and at an Amnesty meeting on 30 May.

14

1 Kathleen was pregnant.
2 Arthur Symons (1865–1945), English poet and critic, and a member of the Rhymers' Club.
3 MG loved Wagner's operatic cycle of the Ring and went frequently to Beyreuth. In *ASQ* she mentions being taken there by her father, and also having planned to go with Millevoye, but they 'never found time'.

15

1 In a letter to John O'Leary written between June and July, WBY mentions writing 'a rather elaborate series of essays on Blake for the Savoy' (*L* (W), 264). They were published in *The Savoy* in July, August and September 1896; the third essay appeared in *Ideas of Good and Evil* (1903).
2 Madame Rowley was a friend of MG's. She stayed in Dublin for two years and then lived in Paris, where she joined the Paris Young Ireland Society on its formation in 1897.
3 Mary Barry Delaney was a faithful friend of MG for many years. She left Ireland for France in 1883 and earned a living at

journalism, writing feature articles, stories, poetry and, being an earnest and devout Catholic, on religious matters and the lives of saints. After meeting MG in Paris, she became her devoted helper, assistant and researcher, and was the secretary of the Paris Young Ireland Society when it was formed in 1897. She reported on MG's activities in all the nationalist papers for which she wrote. She adored the family, particularly MG's son Seán, followed them back to Ireland in 1918 and looked after MG's affairs in Ireland while MG was in Holloway Gaol. Her knee was shattered by shrapnel during the Black and Tan war. Finally she went to live in MG's house in Clonskeagh and died there in 1947. Her surname was sometimes written as Delany or O'Delan(e)y. She used the pseudonyms MB, MO'D, MD as well as Joseph May and others.

16

1 Possibly the stories of *The Secret Rose* (1897), but the description of them as 'wild dreamy stories' may indicate two stories not included, 'The Tables of the Law' and 'The Adoration of the Magi', which were published separately in 1897.
2 Probably *The Speckled Bird*, a novel not published in WBY's lifetime. It dealt with his experiences in the Order of the Golden Dawn, his hero trying to combine artistic ideals with magic by creating a mystical brotherhood. In a letter WBY described it as a novel 'which moves between the Island of Aran and Paris'.
3 Mabel Gore-Booth of Lissadell, Co. Sligo, the younger sister of Constance and Eva, was about sixteen in 1896 when she helped Eva organise a meeting at Drumcliffe, Co. Sligo, to increase the awareness of the legal and social inequalities affecting women. She married Charles Percival Foster of Coombe Park, White Church, Berks, in Dec 1900 and died in 1955.
4 Sarah Purser (1848–1943), a Dublin artist, was a friend of the Yeats family. WBY described her as 'so clever a woman that people found it impossible to believe she was a bad painter' (*M*, 43–4). He recorded her comments on MG: 'Maud Gonne talks politics in Paris, and literature to you, and at the Horse Show she would talk of a clinking brood mare' (*M*, 61). He had earlier disliked one of her portraits of MG, and she had met him 'with the sentence, "so Maud Gonne

is dying in the South of France and her portrait is on sale", and went on to tell how she had lunched with Maud Gonne in Paris and there was a very tall Frenchman there [probably Millevoye] – and I thought she dwelt upon his presence for my sake – and the doctor had said to her "They will be both dead in six months"' (*M*, 44). As a founder member of the Friends of the National Collection in 1924, she was instrumental in securing Charlemount House as the Municipal Gallery of Modern Art, where the Lane Collection was housed when it came to Dublin.

5 Possibly Henri Davray's notice of WBY's poems in the *Mercure de France*, for which WBY wrote to thank him on 12 Aug, adding that he looked forward to his 'essay in *L'Ermitage* with expectant pleasure'.

1897

17

1 This refers to the Dublin meeting of 4 March called by the Young Ireland League, with John O'Leary as president, to plan the celebrations for the 1798 centenary. From the outset there were dissensions in the '98 centenary movement. According to Inspector Mallon of the Dublin Metropolitan Police, the idea and the money came from Lyman in America, Lyman being the founder and president of the 'New Movement', the INB; but the plans were taken over in Dublin by the IRB – who supported Lyman's opponent John Devoy and whose secretary was F. J. Allan – working under the auspices of the Young Ireland League. Inspector Mallon thought it was an attempt to strengthen the IRB and block the inroads of the INB (CBS 13419/s). MPs were not admitted or allowed to use the movement for their party-political aims, and the clergy too were banned.

The London Young Ireland Society, strongly pro-INB, formed its own '98 Committee, WBY and Dr Anthony MacBride publicly declaring that the Dublin organisation was unrepresentative. The London and Paris Young Ireland Societies joined together to form the Centenary Association of Great Britain and France, with affiliated branches throughout Britain, which could send delegates to Dublin. WBY was president and Ryan was treasurer.

At the end of November the Dublin '98 Executive Committee issued a circular announcing the formation of an All Ireland Reception Committee to receive overseas visitors; it invited 'every Irishman willing to participate to prove in an emphatic manner' that every nationalist desired to honour Wolfe Tone and '98. Among the signatories were John O'Leary, Henry Dixon, Count Plunkett, F. J. Allan and Maud Gonne, who described O'Leary at this time as 'a noble figurehead but too old to grasp and make use of a situation' (*ASQ*, 280). Three days later a letter from Lyman's INB in America was published saying MPs should be allowed to participate but only according to their worth. Michael Lambert, president of the Amnesty Association, and Patrick Tobin (a member of the INB on the '98 Executive) called for co-operation of all nationalists and appealed to the Lord Mayor designate to form a Citizens' Committee. From this was formed the United Irishmen Centennial Association.

The police, apparently sitting on the fence watching these 'squabbles' were expecting 'an outrage' in the form of a murder before the New Year (CBS 14706/s, 14719/s), and Major Gosselin, in charge of Irish Secret Service work in the Home Office, wrote in a memo on 4 Nov (CBS 14537/s), 'There are not wanting signs that this '98 movement will be split up into local sections with no binding or controlling authority to secure unity of action', and wrote on another memo of 12 Nov marked 'Secret and Confidential' (CBS 14537/s): 'I have worked hard in Great Britain to split up this movement and at present have good reason to be satisfied, but one can never be sure how such matters will end.' Major (later Sir) Nicholas Gosselin (1839–1917) had a large estate in Donegal, hence his discreet description as a 'farmer'. Known as 'the Gosling', he had, after an army career, joined the Home Office in 1882. As chief Secret Service official for Irish affairs, he commented on all police reports on political agitation and revolutionary organisations in Ireland. His remarks suggest that he took MG seriously but WBY not at all seriously.

2 The first Society of United Irishmen was founded in Belfast in 1791. It consisted mainly of Ulster Protestants, and included Wolfe Tone from Dublin; it had

strong connections with France and was originally in favour of constitutional reform. In 1794 the United Irishmen were suppressed, and in 1795 Tone went to France where he procured from General Lazare Hoche a fleet of 43 French ships and 15,000 men for the open war which he advocated. They set sail for Bantry in December 1796, but storms prevented a landing. In 1798 the leaders were arrested and tried. In early summer an angry and frustrated population broke out into unplanned insurrection in Antrim, Down and parts of Leinster, especially Wicklow and Wexford, but it was crushed by the end of June. In August a French expedition of three ships carrying 1036 men led by General Humbert, accompanied by the United Irishmen Bartholomew Teeling and Wolfe Tone's brother Matthew, landed in Mayo, and the local population rose to join them. (It was this background that Yeats used for his play *Cathleen ni Houlihan*.) After a legendary success at Castlebar, a Republic of Connaught was declared, having as its president John Moore, the younger brother of George Moore of Moore Hall. They were finally defeated at Ballinamuck and the Irish insurgents were slaughtered. Soon afterwards another French expedition of nine ships was intercepted near Lough Swilly and one captured. Wolfe Tone was on board in French uniform. Court-martialled and sentenced to be hanged, he managed to commit suicide before the unsoldierly sentence was carried out.

In the traumatised aftermath, Pitt pressed for parliamentary union with Britain, and with the Act of Union (1800) the Dublin Parliament joined Westminster by voting itself out of existence. In 1803 Robert Emmet of the United Irishmen, who had been negotiating for French support, organised a rebellion. Napoleon had ships standing by at Brest but the rebellion fizzled out. Emmet is remembered, however, as one of the great romantic martyrs.

3   According to WBY's account, MG, passing through London in the spring of 1897, was puzzled because the 'Dublin Nationalists' had failed to give her authorisation to go to America to collect money for their proposed Wolfe Tone statue, but he succeeded in getting it from the 'London Nationalists'. He says it was only after she had sailed that he discovered the reason why (*A*, 353).

4   *L'Irlande Libre*, issued in connection with the Paris '98 Centenary Committee and the Paris Young Ireland Society, was designed to further the nationalist cause in France with information and articles. The first issue appeared on 1 May 1897 with articles by Jean Richepin, A. Saissy, Emile Duboc and John Daly. The paper was one sheet, four pages of four columns of average newspaper size; it appeared on the first of every month until Oct 1898 (eighteen issues in all). On 20 Nov 1898 a notice to subscribers stated that future issues would have to be restricted, the journal's main aim of commemorating the centenary of 1798 having been achieved. In 1900, on the occasion of the Queen's visit to Ireland a 'numéro exceptionnel' was produced.

5   L'Association Irlandaise, the Paris Branch of the Young Ireland League founded by MG and WBY early in 1897. It had rooms at 6 rue des Martyrs, also used as the office of *L'Irlande Libre*. Mary Barry Delaney, the secretary, sent reports of its activities to the nationalist papers.

6   Charles MacCarthy Teeling, a vice-president of the Young Ireland Society in 1885, was expelled by the committee of the Society. He expected to play a part in the '98 celebrations as he was the great-nephew of Bartholomew Teeling of the United Irishmen (who was aide-de-camp to General Humbert and was hanged in Dublin in Sept 1798). He appeared at nationalist demonstrations on a white horse. In *ASQ* (171) MG says she learned later the reason for his attack on her was that she had invited Amilcari Cipriani, the friend of the Italian revolutionary leader Garibaldi, to the '98 celebrations in Mayo. As an ex-member of the Papal Guard and a conservative Catholic, Teeling would have had an extreme dislike of independent women and of Italian revolutionaries who had threatened the Papal States.

18

1   Entitled 'The Work of the United Irishmen', it appeared in *UId*, 3 April 1897. MG ended it: 'The people will never let England know what security and peace mean until our country is free.'

2   Jean Richepin (1849–1926), French poet and dramatist, wrote poems about tramps and vagrants, notably *Les Chansons des Gueux* (1876). His play *Le Chemineau* (1897), a drama of country

life, was extremely popular.

3 François Coppée (1842–1908), a Parisian, was a Parnassian poet and dramatist, and an anti-Dreyfusard. *La Bonne Souffrance* (1898) reflects his religious conversion.

4 William H. K. Redmond (1861-1917), the son of a Wexford MP, succeeded to his father's seat in 1883 and became a follower of Parnell. He was elected MP for East Clare in 1891 and held the seat until his death. When his brother John called for Irish volunteers at the outbreak of war in 1914, William joined the British army; he was killed in action at Messines, 7 June 1917. His article in *L'Irlande Libre* appeared in March 1898 and was entitled 'L'Irlande, la France et l'Angleterre'.

John Edward Redmond (1856–1918), William Redmond's elder brother, became MP in 1881, championed Home Rule in 1886, led the Parnellite minority of the Parliamentary Party in 1891 and the reunited party in 1900 which finally secured the introduction of the third Home Rule Bill in 1912. He supported the British government during the 1914–18 war, encouraging Irishmen to join the British forces. He opposed Sinn Féin and deplored the 1916 Rising.

5 Michael Davitt (1846–1906), whose family was evicted from a smallholding at Straid, Co. Mayo, and emigrated to Lancashire, lost an arm in a factory at the age of eleven. He joined the IRB in 1865 and became organising secretary; sentenced to 15 years' penal servitude in 1870, he was released in 1877. He left the IRB, formed the Land League of Mayo in 1878 and the National Land League in 1879, and led the Land War. After the Land League was suppressed in 1881 he persuaded Parnell to found the Irish National League. At the time of the split he opposed Parnell, was returned as Anti-Parnellite MP for N. Meath (1892) but was unseated on grounds of clerical intervention and was returned for South Mayo (1895–9). He resigned this seat in protest against the Boer War. He was co-founder with William O'Brien of the United Irish League in 1898, and was in favour of collective ownership of land. He sought to combine constitutional and revolutionary nationalism.

19

1 The Comte de Crémont, a Frenchman said to be lineally descended from the ancient MacGrian clan of Leinster, was a

royalist. He thought he had been a tiger in a previous existence and regarded MG as his tigress mother (*ASQ*, 169). He was said to be one of the founders of L'Association de Saint Patrice, of which he was at various times secretary and president. MG attended the association's annual banquet every year when she was in Paris (*ASQ*, 165).

2 Nemours de Godré, editor of *La Vérité* and a writer on the Catholic paper *L'Univers*, was a member of the St Patrick's Association and, for a period, also acted as its secretary. The 'old legitimists' were monarchists who supported the Comte de Chambord, as opposed to the Orléanist claimant to the throne, after the fall of Napoleon III when the monarchists held a majority in the Assembly of the Third Republic.

3 In fact the basis of MG's political alliance with Millevoye was their joint enmity of England, and Millevoye opposed Germany for its annexation of Alsace-Lorraine.

4 Albert Monniott, a journalist who worked on *Libre Parole*, was *secrétaire de rédaction* of the committee of the St Patrick's Association.

5 Lazare Hoche (1768–97) was the French Republican general who commanded the abortive invasion of Ireland with Wolfe Tone as Adjutant-General on his staff. The Paris Young Ireland Society placed a wreath at the foot of Hoche's statue in his home town, Versailles.

6 WBY wrote to John O'Leary on 31 March, telling him he had written to Crémont and asking him to do likewise (*L(W)*, 282).

John O'Leary (1830-1907) became editor of *The Irish People*, the organ of the IRB, in 1863. After 20 months the paper was suppressed and its editors and many IRB leaders arrested and tried under the Treason Felony Act. O'Leary was sentenced to 20 years' penal servitude in Portland Gaol. In 1870 he was released on condition that he went into exile. After living in Paris, he was allowed back into Ireland in 1885. He became influential in the Young Ireland Society, with WBY and MG as his disciples. MG praised his sense of duty and fearlessness, WBY 'the moral genius that moves all young people'. Major Gosselin judged that he was 'looked on by the IRB as a fossil, useful at times, but he is no leader and is an old crank full of whims and *honesty*' (CBS 15336/s).

WBY 2

1 WBY wrote this letter to the Comte de Crémont; it was translated into French.

21

1 Augusta Holmes (1850–1903), born in Paris of Irish descent, was a composer of symphonies, operas, choral works and songs. She studied under César Franck. Her symphonic poem *Irlande*, ending with the triumphal march of 'Let Erin Remember', was first performed in 1882 and subsequently in many European cities and, with the help of MG, at a Feis Concert in Dublin.

2 Monseigneur l'Escailles was Dean of the Metropolitan Chapter and a member of the St Patrick's Association.

3 Timothy C. Harrington (1851-1910) was an MP, a barrister, editor of the *Kerry Sentinel* and the leading Land League organiser in Kerry. He devised the Plan of Campaign with William O'Brien in 1886. In 1897, through his organ, *United Ireland*, he pursued a campaign for national unity. In 1898 he became a founder member of the United Irishmen Centennial and joined William O'Brien and Davitt in founding the United Irish League. He was Lord Mayor of Dublin (1901–4).

It was Harrington who involved MG in the Plan of Campaign and the Gweedore evictions, and also in her first electioneering in England. She campaigned for Duncan, his candidate in Barrow-in-Furness, Lancashire, in 1890, and helped to defeat the Chief Secretary, John Morley, in 1895.

4 *The Secret Rose*, a volume of stories by WBY, was published in April 1897.

22

1 In WBY's 'Rosa Alchemica', published in *The Secret Rose* (1897), the narrator longs for a life transmuted into art; the character Michael Robartes urges him to be initiated into the Order of the Alchemical Rose which involves the worship of the old gods, but the local people stone Robartes and his friends to death.

2 On 8 May *The Nation* and *United Ireland* published notes sent by Mary Barry Delaney from the Paris Young Ireland Society which included a letter from Crémont, of the Artistic and Literary Association of St Patrick, saying Teeling had been expelled from the society. On 29 May both published a correspondence sent by MacCarthy

Teeling which seemed to contradict this. On 26 June *United Ireland* published a conclusive letter from Crémont, listing letters from prominent nationalists denying Teeling's claim to be a nationalist representative.

3 Probably mescal, a drug distilled from the American aloe and used by the Mexican Indians. In the *Contemporary Review*, Jan 1898, Havelock Ellis commented on experiments he made on two poets (WBY and Arthur Symons): 'One [WBY] is interested in mystical matters, an excellent subject for visions, and very familiar with various vision-producing drugs and processes. His heart, however, is not very strong. While he obtained the visions, he found the effect of mescal on his breathing somewhat unpleasant; he much prefers haschisch, though recognising its effects are much more difficult to obtain.' WBY recorded the effect of Indian hemp in *Discoveries* (1907), remarking that 'some stray cactus' could convey 'immortal impartiality and simpleness'. He mentions mescal in his *Visions Notebook* in 1898.

4 Writing to John O'Leary in May 1897, WBY said that his eyes had 'been rather tired of late. I have to be very careful and find any steady reading almost impossible.' He added that his eyes seemed to be dependent on his general health; he had had many colds and small ailments and thought that when he got rid of them his eyes would improve (*L*(W), 284).

24

1 The inquest on Mrs Fitzsimon's death was reported by the *Daily Nation*, 30 June, and *UId*, 3 July. The police, asked why they charged, said the crowd had sticks and stones, and that they heard shots and saw smoke from the Orange Hall. Mrs Fitzsimon, on her way home when knocked down and trampled by the crowd, was put on a car from which she fell on her way to hospital. She died a few days later. The police reports of the incident were quite short and non-committal (CBS 13807/s). WBY gives an account of the demonstrations in *M*, 112-14, and *A*, 366-8. MG devotes most of ch. 10 of *ASQ*, 272-7, to 'Victoria's Jubilee'. These disturbances did not earn the title 'riots' until the trial of a few men charged with breaking glass and throwing stones.

2 WBY proposed that the Convention of Irishmen assembled on 22 June 1897

'declares its beliefs in the right of the freedom of Ireland'.

25

1 Samois-sur-Seine is six kilometres from Fontainebleau on the right bank of the Seine, bordered on either side by the river and the forest. It is likely that MG and Millevoye used it as a quiet retreat and that for this reason she chose to bury Georges there. In July 1895, when her daughter Iseult was a year old, she rented a house in Samois on rue Barbeau. Behind the house, which opened on to the street, there was a courtyard with a well and a walled garden beyond.

2 This may be WBY's *The Countess Kathleen* (published 1892), which he said in 1889 he would write for MG. Since this letter later refers to returning the manuscript it may have been a version written for the stage. If this letter does refer to *The Countess Cathleen* (spelt *Cathleen* after 1895) then the comment that MG was hoping to meet the author could be a joke. It is possible, however, that he could have sent her one of the plays by Martyn (whom she may not have met at this stage) which he envisaged for an Irish theatre. *The Heather Field and Maeve* was published in 1899. *The Heather Field* was performed with *The Countess Cathleen* in 1899.

3 Probably a general view of the writings grouped under the 'Celtic Twilight', the phrase made memorable by WBY's *The Celtic Twilight* (1893). A great impetus was given to the movement by Yeats's discussions with Martyn and Lady Gregory in the summer of 1897.

26

1 It is likely that while in Foxford, Co. Mayo, MG visited the Sisters of Charity at the Convent of Divine Providence. In 1891 the Sisters had started a school in Foxford, and to provide work for the children they set up the Providence Woollen Mills, with help from the Congested Districts Board. Their work spread to the surrounding countryside, raising the standard of the husbandry and industries of the cottagers, and it became a showpiece.

2 Standish James O'Grady (1846-1928) was a barrister and leader writer in the *Dublin Daily Express*, whose writings were a basis of the literary revival, notably his *History of Ireland: Heroic Period* (1878, 1880), *Early Bardic Literature of Ireland* (1879) and *The Coming of Cuchulain* (1894). He bought the *Kilkenny Moderator* in Jan 1898, but he could not use this paper to promulgate his views about the need for the Irish landlords to establish an Irish Convention. He then founded the *All Ireland Review*. He had a profound effect on WBY. The 'new enterprise' may be the *Kilkenny Moderator* or his book/ pamphlet *All Ireland* (1898).

3 Lady Isabella Augusta Gregory (née Persse; 1852–1932), born into a Co. Galway landed family, married Sir William Gregory (1817-92), a neighbouring landlord and politician, in 1880. Fiercely opposed to Home Rule in 1893, she came to realise that the position of Irish landlords was in danger but wished to save Coole for her son Robert. Her views were moving towards nationalism when she met WBY. She was co-founder of the Irish Literary Theatre in 1898 and director of the Abbey Theatre from 1904 to 1928, and wrote about forty plays produced at the Abbey.

28

1 Jules Bois was a well-known dramatist and novelist as well as a semi-public figure in France from 1890 to the First World War. He wrote books on transcendental magic, met MacGregor Mathers and, through him, WBY and MG. He was president of the Society for Psychical Research and wrote *The Little Religions of Paris* (1893).

2 A reference to WBY's plan for a Celtic mystical order.

3 The '98 Convention was held in the Free Trade Hall, Manchester, on 1 Oct, and chaired by WBY. There was a public meeting that evening at which WBY, MG and Frank Hugh O'Donnell spoke. In a letter to Lady Gregory WBY said: 'I have been chairman of a very noisy meeting for three hours and am very done up. I have a speech to prepare for to-night' (*L*(W), 287–8).

4 Probably 'The Lover [originally Poet] pleads with his Friend for Old Friends' (*YP*, 106), first published in the *Saturday Review*, July 1897, with its reference to MG's 'shining days' and her 'new friends' – Willie Rooney, James Connolly, 'Ethna Carbery' (Anna Johnston) and Alice Milligan, among others.

29

1 From the context the date should be 22 September, and the letter has been placed in this position.

2 All along the western seaboard from Donegal to Kerry people were living below subsistence level. Too many were trying to live on too little and too poor land. A Congested Districts Board, set up by Arthur Balfour in August 1890, purchased and redistributed land, built houses and various amenities such as bridges, harbours, piers and roads, encouraged local industry and endeavoured to improve agriculture.

3 24 Hyde Park Gate was where MG's cousins May and Chotie Gonne lived at this time.

30

1 Or possibly written from France or England.

2 Moran's Family, Commercial and Temperance Hotel, 71 Gardiner Street Lr and 20 Talbot Street.

3 This refers to the split in Clann na Gael in America between Lyman and Devoy. While Mark Ryan and the London IRB supported Lyman's INB, the Dublin IRB remained pro-Devoy. As the '98 Executive Committee, run by F. J. Allan, was primarily IRB, they were not prepared to support her visit to America which was being sponsored by Lyman and the London INB.

4 At the '98 Centenary Convention on 22 June in Dublin, Councillor Seagrave of Wigan, 'a very bad class of man' – Inspector Mallon's typically vivid description of an extreme activist – was reported to be anxious to find the true relations between the IRB and INB (CBS 13874/s). Over the next months he organised the North of England separately, in opposition to and bypassing London, and affiliating with the Dublin Executive directly. London and Dublin wished to have control of the strong '98 groups in Liverpool and Manchester. Seagrave attempted to hold a convention in Liverpool before the main London-organised one in Manchester in Oct. Finally he had an impressively successful convention on 14 Nov, to which he invited London delegates (CBS 14268/s, 14781/s). Both Mallon and Geoffrey Lavelle, one of the secretaries of the '98 Executive, considered the 'mischief' was brought about by F. J. Allan, the IRB secretary (CBS 1478/s).

31

1 James Daly (*c.* 1836–1910) was a farmer, journalist, town commissioner, poor law guardian, and editor and owner of the *Connaught Telegraph* of Castlebar, Co. Mayo. He raised money for the erection of a monument at French Hill outside Castlebar in 1875–6. This was to commemorate Humbert's French soldiers, killed in a rearguard action at the battle known as the Races of Castlebar in Aug 1798. He was one of the initiators of the land agitation, a constitutionalist and nationalist, but not considered a Fenian, except by the police. He was president of the Connaught Provincial '98 Executive and was elected to the new Mayo County Council in 1899.

2 A meeting calling the people of Connaught to prepare for the '98 centenary was held at French Hill, near Castlebar, on 9 Jan 1898, and presided over by James Daly. MG was one of the speakers; 'the proceedings, voicing the opinions of 10,000 men' were 'practically boycotted' by the Dublin papers (*SVV*, Feb 1898).

3 Patrick Tobin, a member of the IRB, joined the INB at its inception around 1894 and withdrew from the '98 Centenary Executive to form (in Nov 1897) the United Irishmen Centennial, becoming one of its secretaries.

4 The London committee chaired by WBY which had authorised MG's US visit.

1898

32

1 This may refer to plans for the banquet of the Executive of the Centenary Association of Great Britain and France, which was held at the Holborn Restaurant on 13 April 1898 and at which WBY gave an address. There was also a banquet at Frascati's on 9 Aug, when MG was principal speaker.

2 The convention held by the Executive of Great Britain and France on 20 Feb was in Liverpool, not Manchester.

3 Geoffrey Lavelle was secretary to the Executive of the Centenary Association of Great Britain and France.

4 WBY contributed two articles to *L'Irlande Libre* under the title 'Le Mouvement Celtique'; in the issue of April 1898 he wrote on Fiona Macleod and in June on John O'Leary. These were written in French; no translator's name was given.

33

1 Henry Dixon was a secretary and later vice-president of the '98 Executive Committee. A senior member of the IRB, he was one of the first members of the Young Ireland League and according to the police was anxious for increased secret society work.

2 The town commissioners of Nenagh, Co. Tipperary, invited Michael Lambert and another delegate from the United Irishmen Centennial Association to a meeting in the town hall. It was decided that the Town commissioners act as a provisional committee. Two delegates from the Dublin Executive Committee, told they were not invited and therefore could not speak, held a meeting in a private house in the town and formally inaugurated a branch (*FJ*, 23 Feb 1898).

3 This refers to the Dublin '98 Executive Committee which met in the City Hall, often referred to as Cork Hill because it is situated there.

4 Michael Lambert was president of the Amnesty Association of Ireland and one of the secretaries of the United Irishmen Centennial Association.

5 Frank Hugh O'Donnell (1848–1916) was MP for Galway (1874) and Dungarvan (1877). His renomination was refused by Parnell in 1885. He was castigated by Michael Davitt as a 'distinguished self-seeker and egoist'. He was introduced into the IRB by Dr Mark Ryan. When WBY developed his 'grandiose plan' to stop the centenary movement from dividing 'into its elements', and presented his idea that the Dublin Committee should become 'something like an Irish Parliament' (*M*, 109), 'a certain mad rogue', O'Donnell, his fellow delegate from the Centenary Association of Great Britain and France at the convention in March 1897, outsmarted him by giving a dishonest account of it to the London Committee on their return.

34

1 Belmullet is an isolated town on the Belmullet isthmus in Erris, on the northwest coast of Mayo.

2 Charles Guilfoyle Doran (d. 1911) was secretary of the Supreme Council of the IRB in the 1870s and a member of the '98 Centenary Committee.

3 Patsy (Patrick) Gregan, a Dublin-born town councillor, was a member of the IRB who had joined the INB. He left the '98 Executive Committee and later

became a secretary of the amalgamated associations. On 13 June police commented: 'Gregan and Allan fell out some months ago and go in fear of each other' (CBS 16515/s). Gregan had written on 30 Dec 1896 to the *Irish Daily Independent* to suggest a committee to co-ordinate celebrations of the 1798 uprising. J. Birmingham, a builder, was treasurer of the Amnesty Association of Ireland.

4 According to the police, MG's lecture in Ballina, Co. Mayo, on 12 March and the public meeting at which she spoke on the 13th were not well attended, but the *Western People* of 19 March reported that the public meeting was 'the largest and finest . . . seen in North Mayo for a long number of years'. A police report related the rumour that she was a detective in the pay of the British government (BSC 15660). On MG's arrival, the horses were taken from her wagonette and the crowd drew her to Thomas B. Kelly's house.

35

1 The great bogs of Erris west of Ballina in Co. Mayo are the wildest and most desolate part of Ireland. Belmullet had made a special request to the Chief Secretary, Balfour, for a railway to the town to provide relief works and access which had been turned down. The local Boards of Guardians were helpless to alleviate stress except by appealing to the Government. On 4 March MG spoke at the largest meeting ever held in Erris, which took place in Belmullet in protest against Balfour's attitude and 'the barbarous relief system'. On 9 March the *Freeman's Journal* published a letter written by MG from Belmullet and on 30 March published another letter when she wrote on her return to Dublin. She described the illness and debts and hopelessness, saying that much more was needed than could be supplied by the Manchester and Dublin Mansion House funds. She called especially on the women of Ireland. MG also had articles in the *Irish Daily Independent* and the *Daily Nation* (10 March 1898). The 'numéro exceptionnel' of *L'Irlande Libre* in 1900, known as the 'Famine Queen' number, reported that 32,000 emigrated that year.

2 The leaflet that MG and James Connolly wrote, 'Rights to life and the Rights of Property' (reproduced in Connolly's *The Workers' Republic*, Aug 1898), quoted St Thomas Aquinas, Pope Clement I, Greg-

ory the Great and Cardinal Manning: 'In case of extreme need of food all goods become common property' and 'no human law can stand between starving people and their right to food', including their right to take it.

3 William O'Brien (1852–1928) joined the *Freeman's Journal* in 1875, edited *United Ireland* from 1881, was Secretary of the National League (1882) and an MP (1883–1919). He devised the Plan of Campaign with Harrington in 1886, edited the *Irish People* (1899), supported the All Ireland League in 1910 and voted against the third Home Rule Bill in 1914. O'Brien founded the North Mayo United League in Westport, Co. Mayo, at a public meeting on 23 Jan 1898, with MPs Tim Harrington and John Dillon. Famine had accentuated the poverty of the smallholders compared to the large graziers on cleared land. The United League aimed at redistribution, using methods similar to those of the Land League (such as agitation, boycott and intimidation) to put pressure on the government. The organisation became the United Irish League and worked with the Parliamentary Party for the next two decades. The police watched its development closely and anxiously, ready with coercion and proscription (BSC 17425/s).

4 This could be J. W. O'Beirne, who was on the commercial staff of the *Independent* newspaper, a secret society man, and therefore part of F. J. Allan's organisation. He was on the executive of the Dublin '98 Committee.

5 Dr Ryan wrote apologising that circumstances prevented him coming to Mayo at that time.

36

1 At the Dublin convention on 12 March a motion was passed unanimously to the effect that no rule ever existed to preclude MPs, and that any Irishman could be eligible for membership of the '98 Executive Committee if elected by any of its branches. WBY suggested that a committee of experts should seek designs for the Wolfe Tone monument from Ireland, France, the USA and the Irish in England.

2 Gurteen was on the route of General Humbert's march through Mayo and Sligo in 1798. A meeting was held there on 17 March, organised by John O'Dowd, chairman of the Tubercurry

Board of Guardians, and contingents came from surrounding districts.

37

1 Tubercurry, Co. Sligo, is twenty miles from Ballina on the road to Gurteen, which passes the lake in Glen Eask in the Ox Mountains.

2 'The Federation' is probably a code name for the IRB. The 'advanced men' on United Irishmen Centennial were Patrick Tobin and Patsy Gregan of the INB, who were 'really bad men' in Inspector Mallon's terms.

38

1 WBY used the tarot cards frequently for fortune telling and divination, and according to his *Visions Notebook* they were apparently also used for the Celtic rites.

39

1 Newgrange (3rd millennium BC) is one of the finest manifestations of Neolithic culture, predating Mycenae and Stonehenge by nearly a millennium and older than the pyramids of Egypt by several centuries. The greatest of the prehistoric monuments of the Boyne valley, it is a passage grave with a cruciform chamber situated on a hillock overlooking the river Boyne in Co. Meath. Petrie, who with O'Donovan and O'Curry brought together ancient literature, folklore and modern scholarship in the 1830s and 1840s, attributed the mounds on the Boyne to the Tuatha De Danann, the mythical semi-divine ancestors of the Gael, and to the Bronze Age culture; it was within this context that Standish O'Grady, WBY and MG worked and by which their imagination was fired.

40

1 Either 'He hears the Cry of the Sedge' (*YP*, 102), alluding to their spiritual marriage (which she had not written about):

> Until the axle break
> That keeps the stars in their round,
> And hands hurl in the deep
> The banners of East and West,
> And the girdle of light is unbound,
> Your breast will not lie by the breast
> Of your beloved in sleep.

or 'He Thinks of Those who have Spoken Evil of his Beloved' (*YP*, 103), which reacts to the rumours and criticisms levelled against her:

And dream about the great and their pride;
They have spoken against you everywhere,
But weigh this song with the great and their
pride;
I made it out of a mouthful of air,
Their children's children shall say they have
lied.

The May 1898 issue of *The Dome* also included 'The Lover Mourns for the Loss of Love' (*YP*, 95), written to Olivia Shakespear.

2 Newgrange (Brú na Bóann) is the House of the Dagda, the supreme god of the people of Dana, the good god of the otherworld and the sun god; he married Bóand, the goddess of the river Boyne.

41

1 On 11 July, while staying at Coole, WBY commenced a diary, his *Visions Notebook*, two vellum-covered manuscript notebooks covering the period up to March 1901. They contain accounts of visions, prophecies and tarot divinations, in which many people took part with WBY, especially George Russell, MacGregor Mathers, Florence Farr, George Pollexfen and, of course, MG. He stuck some of MG's occult letters and mythological arrangements into the book in envelopes, and there are also pastel designs of some of the symbols and colours that were being used for evocation. MG records: 'Willie and I had tried sending messages to each other [on the astral plane]. At a fixed hour he would try to send me a thought, or I to send him one, and we would both note down on paper any thought which came into our minds and compare them when we met. We were not very successful though once or twice I did get something vaguely resembling the thought he was trying to send.' MG also describes leaving her body and going to see people (*ASQ*, 249–52). One of the first entries in *Visions Notebook* is an account of a trance he had had the previous week in which he had seen PIAL (MG's occult motto) and been aware that she wished to give him a message. He wrote to her in France about this.

2 This did not appear in *L'Irlande Libre*.
3 Most likely May Gonne.

42

1 Dr Mark Ryan.
2 Beside the first paragraph WBY had written: 'Executive Irish Revolutionary Organisation'.

3 A leaflet against Michael Davitt by Frank Hugh O'Donnell. With the support of John O'Leary, WBY and MG got the Dublin and London committees to repudiate it. The second leaflet attacked 'the mother or near relation of a London doctor supposed, wrongly, to have written the first leaflet', presumably Dr Anthony MacBride. The two secret societies were forced 'to sign and print at their own expense a document eating words they had accepted as their own'. See WBY, *M*, 115–16.

4 The French delegation included Cipriani, the Italian revolutionary. They were watched closely by the police until they were all safely out of the country, and the English police in Holyhead were telegraphed to expect their arrival, Major Gosselin remarking that he saw no further use in following such people. The police reporting from Castlebar commented that the French 'left a very bad impression on the people here. The general impression is that they were picked up about Dublin and brought on by Miss Gonne' (BSC 17115). Inspector Mallon suspected MG and Cipriani of 'hatching some new scheme' and said they required watching (BSC 17139). See also WBY, *A*, 410.

5 It was reported at a meeting of the '98 Executive Council that MG, honorary treasurer, had lodged that day for the Wolfe Tone and United Irishmen memorial the sum of £233 in the Executive's account. Inspector Mallon, always interested in what became of money collected, usually remarking that it was pocketed, commented that 'the money was in the Munster and Leinster Bank' (BSC 17200/s).

6 Two reports from Castlebar on 29 Aug and 3 Sept 1898 to Dublin Castle mentioned Charles MacCarthy Teeling's letter, which said that the police and commissariat of Paris were keeping a close watch on MG, that they suspected her of giving information to the English Government, and, as a nephew of Bartholomew Teeling, asked the people of Mayo to beware of her. The Roman Catholic clergyman who reported the letter said he was also using it to damage William O'Brien for joining MG at the Castlebar '98 celebrations in August (BSC 17115/s).

43

1 The holy well is just outside Ballina on the road to Killala. Dathai was a fifth-century Irish king who led a raid into Gaul; he was killed by lightning at the foot of the Alps and was supposed to have become a Christian before he died. Wells were attributed supernatural powers, fish had a symbolic significance both in Irish mythology and Christianity.

2 The Sídhe are the fairy hosts. WBY's note (dated 1899–1906) on 'The Hosting of the Sidhe' (*YP*, 89) reads: 'The gods of ancient Ireland, the Tuatha de Danaan, or the Tribes of the goddess Dana, or the Sidhe, from Aes Sidhe, or Sluagh Sidhe, the people of the Faery Hills. Sidhe is also Gaelic for wind, and certainly the Sidhe have much to with the wind.' The Faery Hills are prehistoric mounds, frequently on hill tops.

3 Possibly 'He thinks of his Past Greatness when a Part of the Constellations of Heaven' (*YP*, 108); this was published in *The Dome*, Oct 1898, and refers to the spiritual marriage: 'Knowing one, out of all things, alone, that his head / May not lie on the breast nor his lips on the hair / Of the woman that he loves, until he dies.'

44

1 Dr Mark Ryan.

2 Presumably this refers to the pamphlets against Davitt and Dr MacBride.

3 MG began her American trip in Jan 1900.

45

1 Queen Maeve comes into one of the four groups of stories, the Ulster Cycle, which appear in various manuscripts written down from ancient oral tradition. As the warrior queen she invades Ulster in a cattle raid to take possession of a famous bull. See WBY, '"Maive" and Certain Irish Beliefs', *UPWBY*, 204–7, reprinted from his 'The Literary Movement in Ireland', *North American Review*, Dec 1899. See *UPWBY*, 191–2.

2 William Sharp (1855–1905), a Scottish poet, wrote under the name of Fiona Macleod. Until Sharp's death she was thought to be a separate individual, a Celtic mystical writer. The 'poem' is probably 'La Tristesse d'Ulad', a story published in *L'Humanité Nouvelle*, Nov 1898. This is 'The Melancholy of Uladh', the first part of 'Uladh of the Dreams', collected in *Spiritual Tales*, reviewed by WBY (see *LTWBY*, 42–3) in *The Sketch*,

28 April 1897. See *UPWBY*, II, 42–5, and also 108–10.

3 'Uladh' (pronounced 'Ulla') is Irish for Ulster.

4 MG attended a '98 meeting in Manchester with James Stephens, the old Fenian leader, for the Manchester Martyrs' anniversary in November; 100,000 people attended. In 1867, after the Fenian rising, a policeman was accidentally shot during the rescue from a prison van of one of the Fenian leaders. On dubious evidence three men, the 'Manchester Martyrs', Allan, Larkin and O'Brien, were executed.

5 MG's occult motto in the Golden Dawn, *per ignem ad lucem*.

46

1 This appears to be code and connected with the INB and Dr Ryan, and perhaps O'Donnell.

2 Kathleen Pilcher and May Gonne.

47

1 Notation of a horoscope, tarot divination or vision.

2 This was probably part of the rituals of the proposed Order of Celtic Mysteries, which MacGregor was helping WBY and MG to create.

48

1 Sent with the preceding letter of late December, this part was placed by WBY in an envelope stuck in his *Visions Notebook*, just after an account written on 21 Dec when he and MG had taken the initiation of the spear. He wrote that Lugh said they were given the initiation of the spear before the sword that they might have inspiration to attain knowledge.

2 The Cauldron of Plenty was one of the four treasures of the Tuatha dé Danaan; belonging to the Dagda, it could never be emptied and was kept in his house of hospitality at Brú na Bóann (New-grange). The stone, another treasure, was the Lia Fáil, the Stone of Destiny or of Sovereignty, which cried out loud when trodden on by the lawful king of Ireland. It is said to be the Coronation Stone under the throne in Westminster Abbey. WBY and MG considered the possibility of removing it and returning it to Ireland. In 1950 it was temporarily removed to Scotland by Scottish nationalists.

MG went through the ceremony of the Dagda's Cauldron of Reward, accompanied by his druid Estras, and that of the Stone of Destiny, accompanied by the druid Semias, associated with Anna (Dana) 'of regeneration, the Great Mother, of life & death, of purity'. Then, coming to the place of the Sword, she invoked Brigid 'of knowledge', but her druid, Usces, would not accompany her. Having gone through the ceremonies of three of the ancient treasures and their associated gods, she next invoked Lugh, who held the Spear of Light. His druid was Mórfessi. (Clarified by a diagram of MG's.) In Geoffrey Keating's *History of Ireland* (tr. J. O'Mahony (1857), 136–9) Semias is the druid of Murias where the Dagda's cauldron was originally kept, Erus the druid of Gorias where Lugh's sword was kept, Mórfios (MG's Mórfessi) the druid of Falias where the Lia Fáil was kept, and Arias the druid of Finias (or Findrias) where Lugh's sword was kept. See note 3, letter 89.

3   Lugh (pronounced 'Loo') was thought to be the sun god, master of all arts, who possessed a spear of light, a lightning weapon, one of the four magic treasures that the Tuatha dé Danaan brought to Ireland. He was also the hero who overcame the god of darkness.

4   Brighid is the triple-quickening goddess Brigit, variously the mother of the Dagda, his wife or his daughter, worshipped by poets as Brigit of Poetry. She was also goddess of healing and smith-craft. Her name is derived from a word meaning 'fiery arrow'. Christianised, she is St Brigid, a prophetess whose perennial fire was never allowed to go out.

1899

49

1   This was probably a high official at the prefecture who had warned her about her servant, who, with her son, had been opening MG's letters for Clemenceau. See *ASQ*, 204.

50

1   Thomas Patrick Gill (1858–1931) was MP for South Louth (1885–92); on the staff of Sir Horace Plunkett's Irish Agricultural Organisation Society, he was editor of his Dublin *Daily Express* from July 1898 to Dec 1899.

2   Presumably a Breton Celtic association.

3   The Dreyfus Affair began in 1894 when a Jewish officer in the French army was court-martialled for treason and sentenced to imprisonment on the basis of

evidence that was later found to be forged. It came to a head in Jan 1898 when Zola openly accused the War Office of a judicial crime; he was tried, found guilty and sought refuge in England. Anti-semitism was widespread in France and combined with pro-Catholic feelings. There were bitter conflicts between Dreyfusards and Anti-Dreyfusards, and the situation was aggravated by the French humiliation over the Fashoda agreement in March 1899. The country seemed on the verge of civil war.

4   Elathan or Elatha, son of Delbaeth, a Fomorian king whose land lay under the sea, was a man 'of fairest form' (unlike most Fomorians). Eri, wife of Cethor, slept with him and gave birth to Bres, who became king of the Tuatha dé Danaan.

5   The Fomorians appear in the Mythological Cycle of Irish tales as the enemies of the Tuatha dé Danaan; they were evil demons, the forces of dark who fought the forces of light. The *Book of Invasions* describes them as pirates attacking early settlements in Ireland.

6   A Hindu term meaning an essence pervading space, something similar to the aether.

7   The Sword of Nuada was one of the four treasures of the Tuatha dé Danaan, the symbols of which could be obtained in visions; the others were the spear, the stone and the cauldron. See *A*, 253, and *YANC*, 23.

8   Edmund Edward Fournier d'Albe (1868–1933), an English physicist interested in psychical research, was Oireachtas literary prizewinner in 1899. A member of the councils of the National Literary Society and the Society for the Preservation of the Irish Language and editor of *Celtia*, he compiled an English–Irish dictionary and phrase book (1903). He was honorary secretary of the Pan-Celtic Congress in Dublin, which was planned for 1900 but postponed until Aug 1901.

51

1   WBY wrote to Lady Gregory on 14 Feb 1899: 'I hear that there is an article, very friendly to me, about Irish Literature in *Débats*. It is by a French journalist [Charles Legras] who was at my second '98 dinner in London.' WBY's letter, 'Important Announcement – Irish Literary Theatre', was published in the Dublin *Daily Express*, 12 Jan 1899; it was the

first public notice of the national dramatic project. See *UPWBY*, II, 137–9.

2 WBY insisted that no arrangements should be made to welcome or give special seating to Lady Cadogan and other members of the vice-regal party who came to a lecture by Margaret Stokes at the National Literary Society on 14 Jan 1899. See review by 'Rosicrux' (WBY) in the Dublin *Daily Express*, 28 Jan 1899 (*UPWBY*, II, 142-5).

3 Edward Martyn (1859–1923), a wealthy Catholic landlord who lived at Tillyra Castle, Co. Galway, was co-founder, with WBY, Lady Gregory and his cousin George Moore, of the Irish Literary Theatre in 1898. He was president of Sinn Féin (1904–8). He withdrew from the Abbey in protest against the peasant plays produced, and in 1914 founded the Irish Theatre in Hardwicke Street, Dublin. The plays referred to here are Martyn's *The Heather Field and Maeve*, published in Jan 1899 with an introduction by George Moore, which WBY gave to MG on 21 Jan 1899. For the Irish Literary Theatre's first season (it began as a plan in 1897) *The Heather Field* was produced with WBY's *The Countess Cathleen* in Dublin in May 1899.

52

1 Code probably referring to Robert Johnston (1833/5–1937) of Belfast. He was a prosperous timber merchant who had represented the North of Ireland on the Supreme Council of the IRB and was president of the Belfast Amnesty Association. He joined the INB and was a prominent member of the Cumann na nGaedheal from its foundation in 1900. His daughter Anna was the poet 'Ethna Carbery'.

53

1 Iseult was MG's second child by Lucien Millevoye, born in Paris, 6 Aug 1894. This is the first mention of her; she was four at the time. WBY probably only became fully aware of her when MG told him her story in Dec 1898 and during his visit to Paris. Whether he knew of the child as an adopted relative before that on previous visits to Paris is hard to say, but from now on Iseult is mentioned freely. WBY (*M*, 132) says MG fell in love with Millevoye when she was nineteen (that is, in 1885), but she suggests (*ASQ*, 289) that the affair had lasted thirteen years (that is, from 1887). She

may have met Millevoye before the meeting in Royat (described in *ASQ*, 62–77), but not been able to proceed further with the relationship until after her father's death (in 1886) and her discovery that she was financially and psychologically independent. See Prologue, pp.12–14, and Introduction, pp. 18–20.

54

1 Ballycastle, on the north coast of Mayo, is about twelve miles from Ballina, where MG was staying with T. B. Kelly. She was concerned with evictions there.

2 Collooney is a village in Co. Sligo where Father O'Grady was planning the unveiling of a '98 monument to Bartholomew Teeling.

3 At this National Gaelic Festival, the platform was thrown open by the nationalists to the non-political Gaelic League who took part with singers and speakers in Irish. It was presided over by Robert Johnston and addressed by MG.

4 The large public meeting was on 12 March at Lacken (about twelve miles from Ballina), organised by the United Ireland League and T. B. Kelly for an evicted tenant, Nealon, who described how, having built his house, fenced and drained the land and struggled to pay the rent, he saw his 'roof tree burned' over him. The landlord, Palmer, finally settled with Nealon and he was reinstated. MG contributed to the reroofing of his house (*Western People*, 18 March 1899).

55

1 William Sharp had been writing strange letters about the beautiful Fiona Macleod to WBY at this time. See *M*, 105–6.

56

1 Martyn consulted an ecclesiastical authority who disapproved of *The Countess Cathleen*; two other authorities consulted by WBY and Lady Gregory approved. George Moore, a cousin of Martyn, disapproved of subjecting a work of art to theologians' judgements and Martyn decided to resign, but WBY talked him round. See William Sharp's letter of 30 April 1898 (*LTWBY*, 35-6), which indicates 'an intense emotional crisis'. See also *M*, 105–6.

2 WBY's play, published in 1892, was staged with Martyn's *The Heather Field* on 9 May 1899 in the Antient Concert Rooms, with Florence Farr as Aleel and

May Whitty as Cathleen. MG attended the first night.

3 Having recently returned from the Gaelic Festival in Belfast, MG was probably fired with new enthusiasms suggested by the Gaelic League, which advocated Irish drama. In Dec 1898 in Letterkenny a historical play, one act of which was in Irish, had been produced at Aonach Tir-Conal. Douglas Hyde's *Casadh an tSugain* was the first Irish play to be staged, in 1900.

4 Alice Milligan (1866–1953), a poet, was a member of the Gaelic League and for a while involved with the INB. With Anna Johnston (the poet 'Ethna Carbery', Robert Johnston's daughter) she founded and edited the *Shan Van Vocht*, a nationalist monthly published in Belfast from 1896 to 1899. She wrote *A Royal Democrat* (1892), a novel; a life of *Wolfe Tone* (1898); *The Last Feast of the Fianna*, a play staged in 1900; and the *Daughter of Donagh* (1920).

5 This was held in the Rotunda, Dublin, on 30 March 1899 and was confined exclusively to evicted tenants, MG being the only non-evicted tenant present, since it was due to her that the meeting took place (*FJ*, 31 March 1899). The action of the Woodford tenants against their landlord, the paranoid and eccentric Marquis of Clanricarde (1832–1916), had sparked off the Plan of Campaign in 1886. Francis Tully, a farmer and boat builder, refused to pay his rent because of the treatment of the other tenants and was evicted in a famous siege. In 1899 Francis Tully was again to the fore in fighting for the rights of evicted tenants. At the convention MG promised to seek help for them when she went to America. Clanricarde continued to fight his tenants and the Congested Districts Board through the courts to the Court of Appeal and the House of Lords until final judgment was made against him in 1915.

57

1 WBY's *The Wind Among the Reeds*, published in April 1899.

2 This was an attack on WBY's *The Countess Cathleen* which led Cardinal Logue to condemn the play without reading it. Called 'Souls for Gold', it was published in the *Freeman's Journal*, which refused to publish his next article. He had both articles printed as a pamphlet and had it put into letterboxes throughout the city.

3 MG's and WBY's efforts to get Dr Mark Ryan to deal stringently with O'Donnell over the Davitt pamphlet had, obviously, not been very successful; or bitterness had in part prompted 'his merciless methods' as described by the *United Irishman*.

58

1 People who took over land from which tenants had been evicted.

2 The tramway around the wild haunts of their childhood probably seemed an intrusion and a desecration. The tram ran from Sutton on the isthmus of the peninsula, around the south coast to the summit and down to the fishing village of Howth on the north coast, where it joined the railway. It was discontinued with equal lamentation in 1958.

3 Thomas J. Clarke (1857–1916) took part in the Clann na Gael dynamite campaign of 1883, was arrested and sentenced to life imprisonment under the Treason Felony Act, and served fifteen years. In March 1899 he was presented with the Freedom of the City by the Mayor of Limerick, his friend and ex-fellow prisoner, John Daly. He lost the election for the clerkship of a Poor Law Union and at the end of 1899 he went to the USA where he worked with John Devoy. He returned to Dublin in 1907 to act as a link between the IRB and Clann na Gael. He kept a tobacconist's shop in Parnell Street, where as part of the IRB's undercover military command he planned the 1916 Rising from 1911 on. He was elected to the Supreme Council of the IRB in 1915, was taken prisoner and shot on 3 May 1916.

4 The last of the Treason Felony prisoners (or as the police referred to them, 'convicts') in Portland, Heneghan from Westport, was released in March. The *Freeman's Journal* on 30 Aug 1899 announced that the Irish National Amnesty Association was winding up. It published its final report and balance sheet in the *United Irishman* on 16 Dec 1899; in the last two years MG had made by far the largest contribution as a result of her 1898 American tour. The London Amnesty Association balance sheet was published in *UI* on 11 Nov 1899: 'of all the collections and contributions received over the years from its foundation the largest was collected by Miss Maud Gonne on the Continent.'

59

1 WBY had had a rheumatic attack. See *L*(W), 321.

2 Madame de Bourbonne was an elderly French widow who presided over MG's household and minded Iseult.

3 Jack Butler Yeats (1871–1957), famous Irish painter and author of plays, novels and volumes of poetry.

4 *The Dominion of Dreams* (1899) by Fiona Macleod. WBY reviewed it in *The Bookman*, July 1899.

5 The unsettled state of France caused by the Dreyfus Affair came to an end on 22 June 1899 with a cabinet formed by Waldeck Rousseau, who drew his ministers from the range of republican politics. Though not universally popular, it was to prove a stable government and ensured the continuance of the Third Republic up to the Second World War.

6 Jean-Marie de Lanessan (1843–1919), French naturalist, doctor and politician, became Governor-General of Indo-China in 1891 and was recalled after a dispute with Admiral Fournier. He was Minister of the Navy from 1899 to 1902 and was political director of the *Siècle* (1906).

7 Pierre Marie René Waldeck Rousseau (1846–1904) supported the republican, Gambetta, in the reform of the judiciary in 1880 and became minister in his government of 1881; Gambetta's party abandoned its original radical programme of 1876 and so earned the name of Opportunists given to it by the journalist Rochefort.

8 Alexandre Millerand (1859-1943) was charged with betrayal by the socialists when he accepted office – which his social reforms did nothing to mitigate. 'Collectiviste' means a supporter of the idea of common ownership.

9 At the end of the Franco-Prussian War and the fall of the Second Empire, extremists of the left revolted in a class war and from March to May 1871 the Commune ruled in Paris. It was savagely suppressed by Gallifet (1830–1909), who as Minister for War undertook a reorganisation of the army, badly needed as the Dreyfus Affair had shown.

10 The false god of materialism; see eg Deut. 9:16, 1 Kings 12:28 and Psalms 106:19.

60

1 Manannán mac Lír, the shape-shifting god, son of the sea, travelled the oceans in his copper craft; he gave his name to the Isle of Man. His wife was Fand, with whom WBY later identified MG.

63

1 At the Ballina Petty Sessions in October, John Durkan was accused of assault and of retaking forcible possession of a holding he had been evicted from seven years before. He had not caused any disturbance, living in a little house with no land until September at the time of the evictions meetings; he reclaimed his house, letting the pigs out of it, and took possession, saying the land was his. At the Quarter Sessions in Sligo he was convicted but released on his own cognisance. According to the *Times* report (Dec 1899), MG was reprimanded by the magistrate for encouraging Durkan.

Durkan's landlord, Arthur Sanders William Charles Fox, Fifth Earl of Arran, was Lord Lieutenant of Co. Mayo, with a residence at Castle Gore in Ballina. He was descended from one of the Gore brothers who founded the future Gore families in Ireland, Earls of Arran, and the Gore-Booths of Lissadell in 1600.

Two other prisoners were Arthur Muffeny of Ballina and his brother-in-law, Anthony MacGuire of Ballycastle, charged with having delivered speeches on 17 September at the Knockmore meeting and being party to general intimidation. MG had taken part in the meeting, and it had been rumoured that she too would be charged. She was present in court for the two-day trial. The meetings were all part of the land agitation of the United Irish League. At Sligo all Catholic jurors were challenged by the Crown and after two days' trial as first-class misdemeanants Muffeny and MacGuire were sentenced to six months' imprisonment.

2 George William Russell (1867–1935), whom WBY met at the School of Art in Dublin, was a mystic. He wrote poetry and plays under the pen name AE, and his mystical paintings represented some of his visions. He became an official of the Irish Agricultural Organisation Society in 1897, WBY having recommended him to Sir Horace Plunkett (see *L*(W), 291–2). He edited *The Irish Homestead*, its journal (1905–23), and was editor of *The Irish Statesman* (1923–30).

3 The plans for the second season of the Literary Theatre were for the production

of Martyn's *Maeve* and his *Tale of a Town*, rewritten by Moore, and Alice Milligan's *Last Feast of the Fianna*, early in Feb 1900.

4 George Augustus Moore (1852-1933) was the son of a wealthy Catholic landowner with a racing stable. A great-uncle, John Moore, joined Humbert and was declared president of the short-lived Republic of Connaught at Castlebar in August 1798. George Moore went to Paris, hoping to become an artist, but returned to his estate in Mayo in 1879 and moved between there and London. His first novels, *A Modern Lover* (1883), *A Mummer's Wife* (1885) and *Esther Waters* (1894), show Zola's influence. He returned to live in Dublin in 1901, having helped Lady Gregory and WBY in the establishment of the Irish Theatre, though there were frequent misunderstandings and quarrels. In his fictionalised memoirs, the trilogy *Hail and Farewell* (1911–14), he satirised life in Dublin. His Irish fiction included *A Drama in Muslin* (1886; *Muslin*, 1915), *The Untilled Field* (1903), *The Lake* (1905) and *A Storyteller's Holiday* (1918). He left Dublin for London in 1911. The play to which MG refers was *The Bending of the Bough*, originally Edward Martyn's *The Tale of a Town*, rewritten by WBY and Moore and first produced in Feb 1900. The process is described in Moore's *Hail and Farewell*.

5 WBY's play, which he had 'a chance of getting done in London in autumn' (*L(W)*, 320). He was working on *The Shadowy Waters* from June to Nov at Coole Park, finishing it in Dec 1899. It was published by Hodder & Stoughton in Dec 1900. It was first produced in mid-1905 but not in Dublin until Dec 1906.

6 The South African (or Boer) War broke out in Sept 1899. Tension between the Boer republics of the Transvaal and Orange Free State and the British colonial territories of the Cape and Natal had existed for many years, coming to a head with the 'Jameson raid', an armed attack on the Transvaal in 1895. The issue in 1899 was that of giving votes to the Uitlanders, the non-Boers. Up to the end of 1899 the British forces fared badly.

7 Octave Mirbeau (1848–1917) was a French dramatist, novelist and journalist. A radical and one-time anarchist, he wrote with some violence. *Jardin des Supplices* was published in 1899.

64

1 A Transvaal Committee was proposed after a large public meeting held in Beresford Place at which MG was among the speakers with Davitt and O'Leary (see *UI*, 7 Oct 1899). MG and WBY were listed among the members of the organising committee present. An anti-enlistment campaign quickly got under way. The police reported that 'from the date of Maud Gonne's meeting at Beresford Place on Sunday 1st instant there has been perpetual effort made to incite the people against soldiers leaving Dublin for South Africa. These efforts were not attended with success until the end of last week.' The *Independent* offices in Trinity Street had a limelight display, on a large illuminated screen outside, of the progress of the war and the America's Cup which caused 'regular pandemonium' between the Trinity students and pro-Boer sympathisers. The police believed that MG had 'some hand in the business' (J. Jones, C. Commissioner, BSC 20225A/s). Soldiers were forbidden to frequent the main city streets at night in uniform, and police were ordered to pull down the bright green posters and confiscate the bright green leaflets being distributed throughout the country proclaiming that 'Enlisting in the English Army is Treason to Ireland'. A fund for the wounded was started and an Ambulance Corps was being organised. The police said that Miss Milligan and Miss Johnston were working with MG as well as her 'ally' Connolly (BSC 20142/s).

2 Irish nationalists had met in Johannesburg to consider what steps should be taken by the Irish in the Transvaal. At a public meeting a resolution was passed empowering a deputation to offer services to the Boer government. A thousand men enrolled in the Transvaal Irish Brigade formed on 3 Sept 1899, with Col. Blake as its commandant, and Thomas Menton and John MacBride as majors (*UI*, 7 and 28 Oct 1899). It took part in Joubert's invasion of Natal, was among the attacking force at Dundee, was at the siege of Ladysmith and participated in the battle of Colenso in Dec 1899.

3 John Redmond had launched a campaign for a Parnell monument, and the foundation stone was laid opposite the Rotunda at the annual Parnell procession, amid protests from those still struggling to raise money for the proposed Wolfe Tone monument on St Stephen's Green

(*FJ*, 9 Oct 1899).

4 The Lord Mayor, Daniel Tallon, was hissed at the laying of the foundation stone for the Parnell monument because of his absence from the meeting at Beresford Place to sympathise with the Boers.

65

1 Sir Horace Plunkett (1854–1932) was a commissioner of the Congested Districts Board (1891–1918) and Unionist MP for South Dublin (1892–1900). He started the agricultural co-operative marketing movement in 1889 and founded the Irish Agricultural Organisation Society in 1894, later becoming first vice-president of the new Department of Agriculture and Technical Instruction in Ireland (1899–1907). His journal, *Irish Homestead*, was founded in 1895. Among the books he wrote were *Ireland in the New Century* (1904) and *The Unsettlement of the Irish Land Question* (1909).

2 The nationalists in the Dublin Corporation put forward a resolution that they protest 'against a policy which involves the loss of many valuable lives, and entails such an enormous expenditure of money, an undue proportion of which Ireland will have to bear'. The Transvaal Committee with MG were present at the meeting on 11 Dec when there was no quorum and the resolution could not be passed.

3 The *United Irishman* commenced publication as a nationalist separatist weekly on 4 March 1899. For the next few years MG worked closely with its founders, William Rooney and Arthur Griffith. The paper, acting as a propagandist organ, was educative, informative and literary, endeavouring to build up the self-respect and national identity of its readers. It ceased publication in 1906 and was followed by *Sinn Féin*.

William Rooney (1873–1901) was from a Dublin working-class nationalist background and left school at twelve to work as a clerk, continuing his education at night. He started the Celtic Literary Society in Feb 1893. One of the few at that time making speeches in Irish, he toured the west and spoke on many platforms with MG. When the *United Irishman* was founded, Rooney and Griffith wrote most of the paper themselves, Rooney using at least eight pseudonyms. With Griffith he launched the Cumann na nGaedheal in Oct 1900.

He died aged 27 in May 1901, mourned as a charismatic figure, his full potential unrealised. He had a great influence on his generation including MG. His *Poems and Ballads* were published in 1902, his *Prose Writings* in 1909. WBY dedicated the first edition of *Cathleen ni Houlihan* (1902) to his memory.

Arthur Griffith (1871–1922) was, like Rooney, from a Dublin working-class background and was educated by the nationally minded Christian Brothers. He became an apprentice printer and worked as a compositor. For a while he and Rooney were supporters of Mark Ryan's INB. In 1896 he went to South Africa, working in the mines with John MacBride. He returned to Ireland in Oct 1898, when he and Rooney decided to start the *United Irishman*. It was reported by the police that on a visit to Dublin in June 1899 Mark Ryan had said that his organisation adopted the *United Irishman* as their organ of opinion (BSC 1944492/s). Griffith's influential articles were published as *The Resurrection of Hungary; or a Parallel for Ireland* (1904). His advocacy of independence and self-sufficiency led to the formation of Sinn Féin (Ourselves Alone), a non-violent separatist organisation. Griffith remained aloof during the 1916 Rising but was arrested several times and was elected Sinn Féin MP for East Cavan in 1918. He was civilian leader of the Irish Provisional Government and headed the Irish delegation in the negotiations of 1921 which led to the establishment of the Irish Free State, of which he was the first President. He died suddenly on 12 Aug 1922.

66

1 James Connolly (1868–1916), born of Irish parents in Scotland, was self-educated; he joined the British army at 14 and deserted in 1889. He joined the socialist movement while working in Scotland. He went to Dublin in 1896 and developed the Irish Socialist Republican Party. MG was working closely with him and his party during 1897 at the time of the Jubilee riots. In America in 1902, Connolly founded the Irish Socialist Federation. In 1910, he became Ulster organiser of the Irish Transport and General Worker's Union. He joined James Larkin in the Dublin strike and lock-out of 1913, out of which activity he formed the Irish Citizen Army. He

was acting secretary of the Irish Transport and General Workers' Union in 1914, and military commander of the Republican forces in Dublin in 1916. He was shot on 12 May 1916. His publications included *Erin's Hope* (1897), *Labour in Irish History* (1910) and *The Reconquest of Ireland* (1915).

2 WBY's letter apologising for his inability to attend the protest meeting in Beresford Place was published in *FJ* on 8 Dec.

3 Joseph Chamberlain (1836–1914), a Liberal Unionist MP, was Colonial Secretary from 1896–1902 and came to personify the imperial ideal; he opposed Home Rule. In 1899 Trinity College presented him with an honorary degree – an action that was unpopular with all shades of nationalists. The *Freeman's Journal* reported that he was brought into Trinity College by a side entrance to avoid the crowds and that the meeting at Beresford Place on Sunday 17 Dec, called by placard days in advance, was only proclaimed by the police late on Saturday night, but at noon Beresford Place was occupied by the police.

Of a Hero I had Made 1900–1904

1900

67

1 An article on the literary movement in Ireland, first published in *The North American Review*, Dec 1899.

2 Cúchulain and Diarmuid were heroes of the Ulster Cycle and the Fenian Cycle of tales respectively.

3 Griffith gave two and a half columns to WBY's article in *UI*, 6 Jan 1900.

68

1 WBY's mother, Susan Yeats, née Pollexfen (1841–1900), died on 3 Jan. She had had a first stroke in 1887 and had remained an invalid after it.

2 John Butler Yeats (1839–1922) was educated at Trinity College, Dublin, and became an artist. After moving from Dublin to London in 1867, the family went to Sligo in 1872. From 1874 to 1881 they lived in London, then in Ireland until 1887, when they moved again to London, returning to Dublin in 1901. John Butler Yeats went to New York in 1908 and lived there until his death. A fine portrait painter (whose pencil sketches are impressive), he was not financially successful.

3 MG had placed herself under the protection of the god Lugh, who was master of all the arts and sciences.

4 The second season of the Irish Literary Theatre. George Moore's *The Bending of the Bough* and Alice Milligan's *The Last Feast of the Fianna* were played on 19 Feb 1900 and Edward Martyn's *Maeve* on 20 Feb 1900.

69

1 Dr Mark Ryan.

2 A fellow member of the organising committee for MG's tour in the USA with O'Donovan Rossa, who was not reconciled with John Devoy. The split in the Clann na Gael came to an end this year, but animosities lingered.

3 Not identified.

70

1 Boston, Massachusetts.

2 WBY was anxious about possible disturbances over George Moore's play *The Bending of the Bough*, a rewriting of Edward Martyn's political satire *The Tale of a Town*; after various rows Edward Martyn had handed the play over to Moore. See *L*(W), 334.

3 WBY had been 'quite incapable of moving with influenza' (*L*(W), 334).

4 MG collected $3000, which, after expenses were met, went largely to Arthur Griffith for the *United Irishman*, while some paid the costs of the 'Queen' edition of *L'Irlande Libre*. She visited twelve cities in addition to lecturing in the Grand Central Palace and, to an overflow audience, in the Academy of Music, New York.

71

1 WBY's letter (in *FJ*, 20 March 1900) suggested that a great meeting should be summoned in the Rotunda, Dublin, on the date of the Queen's departure for Ireland, 4 April, to 'protest against the Union and to disassociate Ireland from any welcome that the Unionist or the time-server may offer to the official head of that Empire in whose name liberty is being suppressed in South Africa, as it was suppressed in Ireland a hundred years ago.'

72

1 WBY wrote to Lady Gregory telling her that the parliamentarians had decided to protest against the Act of Union, and added: 'Maud Gonne is seriously ill with

enteritis and will hardly be well in time to do anything with the crowds.'

73

1 *L'Irlande Libre* of March/April 1900 contained MG's article 'The Famine Queen' and a chronology of the unedifying events of Victoria's reign in Ireland. The article was translated into English and published in *UI*, 7 April 1900, and the chronology was reproduced in sections over a number of weeks.

2 According to his letter of 10 April to Lady Gregory, WBY had suggested that Harrington, MP for the Harbour division of Dublin, stand down in favour of John MacBride at the next general election.

John MacBride (1868–1916) was educated at the Christian Brothers, Westport, and St Malachy's College, Belfast. He worked for 2–3 years in the drapery business in Castlerea, Co. Roscommon, returned to St Malachy's for a further year and then joined the staff of Hugh Moore & Co, a wholesale druggist's and grocer's in Dublin. He took the Fenian oath at 15 and was an early and active member of the Young Ireland Society. He was a friend of John O'Leary and Arthur Griffith before he left Ireland in 1896 to work as an assayer in the Robinson goldmines near Johannesburg. In 1897 he organised a west of Ireland famine relief fund. He was joined in South Africa by Arthur Griffith and they organised 1798 clubs and commemorations. In 1899 he formed the Irish Brigade, was given Boer citizenship – an honour for an Uitlander – and commissioned a major by President Kruger, and fought with Boer commandos in Natal in the first action of the South African War. While in South Africa he was defeated as a candidate for Davitt's seat in Mayo in Feb 1900. After the Irish Brigade was disbanded he went to Paris, then lectured in the USA before returning to Paris. He married MG on 21 Feb 1903. The marriage was not happy, and MG fought for divorce. On his return to Ireland – made easy, for one considered to be a treasonous British citizen, by a change in policy after the Liberal landslide of Jan 1906 – MacBride continued to be active in nationalist affairs and was on the Supreme Council of the IRB in 1911. He worked on the Shannon Eel Fisheries in Athlone and as water bailiff for Dublin Corporation. He joined Thomas Mac-

Donagh in holding Jacob's biscuit factory in the rising of Easter Week and was executed on 5 May 1916.

3 Mary Barry Delaney put forward the idea of the Queen's number of *L'Irlande Libre*. Stephen McKenna (1872–1934), a translator (notably of the *Enneads of Plotinus* (1917–30)) and journalist who lived in Paris for some time, was a leader writer on the *Freeman's Journal*. Both he and Mary Barry Delaney were active members of the Paris Young Ireland Society.

4 WBY's letter in *FJ*, 20 March 1900. WBY also wrote a letter, published in the Dublin *Daily Express* on 3 April 1900, the eve of the Queen's visit, advocating Mirabeau's dictum: 'The silence of the people is the lesson of kings'; anyone who cheered for Queen Victoria would cheer for Empire and dishonour Ireland; anyone who attended the meeting on the 4th to protest against the welcome from Unionists would honour Ireland. In a letter to Lady Gregory of 29 March he stated that the Irish Party had accepted the proposal for a meeting against the Act of Union (*L*(W), 337).

5 Edward Martyn had sent the Dublin *Daily Express* correspondence between himself, Lord Clonbrock and Lord Ashbourne, concerning his resignation as Deputy Lord Lieutenant of Co. Galway (and as Commissioner of the Peace). The letters were published on 24 March 1900. Lord Clonbrook had rebuked Martyn for disloyalty – he had refused to allow a band to play 'God Save the Queen' and 'The Absent-Minded Beggar' at a private party at Tillyra Castle. Martyn defended his decision on political grounds, essentially declaring his conversion to nationalism. Both Martyn and Moore lost Unionist friends because of their stand on the Queen's visit.

74

1 Dr Mark Ryan. She is referring to some as yet untraceable verse which Frank Hugh O'Donnell, 'the enemy' of the first sentence of the letter, seems to have written.

2 The INB in London.

3 Ramsey Colles, managing director and editor of the *Figaro* ('a kind of society paper and very loyal as you may imagine', as WBY described it to Lady Gregory, *L*(W), 339), was countering MG's anti-recruitment campaign. He claimed that Griffith had entered his

office and struck him on the head with a stick which got broken in the scuffle. Griffith then said, 'you arrest me'. The allegations on a *Figaro* poster and in the editorial reference were that as the daughter of a deceased British officer she was entitled to a pension and was in receipt of one, with the inference that she was a spy; she said both allegations were untrue.

4 Dublin Gaol.

5 Inspector John Mallon, head of the Detective Division of the Dublin Metropolitan Police, was, in view of the heightening tensions over enlistment and the Queen's visit, taking extra precautions.

6 James Napper Tandy (1740–1803) was the first secretary of the Dublin United Irishmen. He accompanied the French expedition to Ireland in 1798 and was arrested. Napoleon threatened to execute British prisoners unless Tandy was released to France, where he died a general in Napoleon's army, in 1803.

75

1 MG had made an application for criminal libel against Ramsey Colles, alleging that his statement could cause a breach of the peace. She was represented very skilfully by J. F. Taylor QC and Serjeant Dodd, instructed by Christopher Friery. John O'Leary, Arthur Griffith and other friends were present in court. The case was used as good nationalist propaganda.

2 John MacBride's brother Anthony (*c.* 1866–1942) received his medical degree from the Royal University of Ireland, practised in London and returned to Ireland about 1905. He was the Mayo County surgeon attached to Castlebar Hospital (1907–40), where he worked unstintingly for the improvement of the hospital and the conditions of the poor. While living in London he was an active member of the IRB and INB, and took part in all nationalist activities. MG was probably anxious to consult him as he was implicated by O'Donnell.

76

1 This was a *Figaro* poster for which Colles was responsible.

2 This may refer to a letter that Frank Hugh O'Donnell sent to the Celtic Literary Society through the post (even though he had been warned that his letters were being opened) in which he implicated a 'lady' who went to Dr

Leyds followed by detectives, and had called on 'a leading Irish Doctor' in London, thereby supplying 'the English Government with grounds for a charge that the Transvaal Embassy was violating Belgian Neutrality by intriguing with Irish Rebellion. At the same time her conduct pointed out the Irish doctor to the detectives in pursuit.' (See note 5, letter 88.)

3 Dr Mark Ryan.

4 WBY's 'Noble and Ignoble Loyalties', *UI*, 21 April 1900.

5 Anna Johnston (1866–1902) as 'Ethna Carbery' had a poem in this number of *UI* entitled 'The Suppliant' on the suppliant but heartless queen, mother of a starving race. The daughter of Robert Johnston of Belfast, Anna Johnston was co-editor of *Shan Van Vocht* (1896–8). Her work included *The Four Winds of Eirinn* (1902), the short stories of *The Passionate Heart* (1903) and *In the Celtic Past* (1904). She wrote the well-known ballad 'Roddy MacCorley'.

77

1 A reference to the trouble in the Order of the Golden Dawn. MacGregor Mathers had accused Florence Farr of attempting to create a schism in the Order and had charged Dr Wynn Westcott with having forged documents on which the Order was founded. Enraged by the setting up of a committee to investigate these charges, Mathers sent Aleister Crowley to take possession of the London premises and documents of the Order. Crowley was ejected and took out a summons. The case was settled out of court, Crowley paying £25 costs. See *L*(W), 339, 342, and *YANB*, 123–7.

2 WBY was doing tarot divinations.

3 This possibly refers to the Nally Club, an advanced nationalist club (called after P. W. Nally, who died in prison; the inquest said his death was due to ill health following the treatment he had received on refusing to give evidence against Parnell at the *Times* Special Commission trial). There may have been some enmity between members of the club and MG resulting from INB/IRB differences or because of O'Donnell.

4 Frank Hugh O'Donnell.

5 *Légèreté* means 'rashness', 'thoughtlessness'.

78

1 On 26 April the case against Colles was adjourned until Friday 4 May.
2 *The Immortal Hour* (1900) by Fiona Macleod.
3 The lawsuit.
4 The trouble in the Order of the Golden Dawn.

79

1 The warnings came from WBY's spiritual investigations and were recorded in his *Visions Notebook*. One spirit had said that it was going to seek her destruction, another that her adversaries were trying to bring about circumstances that would cause her to adopt certain actions that would seem wise but would destroy her. Fiona Macleod had warned that she would disappear from sight and never be seen again.
2 Mathers was ejected from the Golden Dawn and a new Order formed. See *YANB*, 124–7.

80

1 Jane Francesca Wilde, née Elgee (1826–96), contributed to *The Nation* under the name 'Speranza'. She married Sir William Wilde and was the mother of Oscar Wilde. MG refers here to Lady Wilde's *Ancient Legends of Ireland* (1887).
2 WBY stuck this letter in his *Visions Notebook*, recording his view that MG's letters were for a while more friendly than usual; he also mentioned that she had had an evil vision.

81

1 Colles's counsel said in a statement: 'There is no foundation for the suggestion that Miss Gonne has ever been in receipt of pension or pay of any kind from the Government. We now unreservedly withdraw and apologise for the mistake.'
2 Richard Barry O'Brien (1847–1918), born in Co. Clare, a lawyer and journalist, was on the editorial staff of *The Speaker* in London and wrote several historical and biographical books. He was president of the Irish Literary Society in London (1906–11).

82

1 Dr Mark Ryan.
2 This may mean that Frank Hugh O'Donnell had been rendered relatively harmless by being exposed in London and Dublin and could take part in activities where embezzlement was not possible.
3 The Paris exhibition opened in April 1900.
4 This relates to the suppression of the *United Irishman*.

83

1 Because of the regular interception of the *United Irishman* in the mail, Henry Dixon had posted the issue of 7 Feb 1900 to himself from the GPO. When he did not receive it he wrote to the Secretary-General of the Post Office, to be told that the Post Office had acted on the orders of the Lord Lieutenant, Lord Cadogan. He then wrote to the Lord Lieutenant. Receiving no satisfactory answer, he wrote again on 24 May and published the full correspondence in the *UI* of 26 May 1900. This issue was suppressed. Dixon challenged the Lord Lieutenant to prosecute him. No further action was taken by the authorities, though sporadic postal harassment continued. MG tried to get Irish MPs to ask questions in the House of Commons.
2 Possibly either WBY's *The Wind Among the Reeds* (1899) or his *Poems* (1895, revised and reprinted in 1899).

84

1 The Irish MPs did not take up the matter of the interception of the *United Irishman* by the Post Office. *Reynold's Newspaper*, an English democratic and socialist paper, however, did so (see *UI*, June 1900).

85

1 The Patriotic Children's Treat was the first large-scale activity carried out by what became Inghínidhe na hÉireann (Daughters of Erin), the organisation (founded from the ladies committee who met on Easter Sunday 1900) of which MG was elected president. This treat was to reward children who had refused to go to Queen Victoria's celebration in April. WBY later wondered about the result: 'in a field beyond Drumcondra and in the presence of a priest of their church, they swear to cherish towards England until the freedom of Ireland has been won, undying enmity. How many of these children will carry a bomb or a rifle when a little under or a little over thirty' (*A*, 368).

86

1 It may have been proposed that Davitt should be a member of the Irish nationalist delegation going to Paris.
2 Frank Hugh O'Donnell.
3 The remainder of this letter is in the Berg Collection, New York Public Library.

87

1 At the invitation of the French Friends of Ireland, a delegation of Irish nationalists (including Rocky Mountain O'Brien from New York) arrived in Paris on 11 July. They were entertained at a banquet at which 500 guests were present, visited the Paris exhibition, attended receptions and were received by the Municipal Council. The five days were covered by many of the French newspapers including Millevoye's *La Patrie* and in detail by *UI*, 21 July 1900. The event was probably organised by MG and the Franco-Irish Society.
2 This possibly refers to the second Irish Brigade, which broke up in July 1900, having been formed by Arthur Lynch in Jan 1900; it never took part in any major action. Alternatively it could refer to the French reception for the Irish ambulance volunteers going to the Transvaal.
3 Frank Hugh O'Donnell.
4 Dr Walsh was possibly a member of the Irish delegation to Paris.

88

1 Dr Mark Ryan.
2 Relating to the Order of the Golden Dawn.
3 WBY's letter 'The Freedom of the Press in Ireland', in *The Speaker*, 7 July 1900 (reprinted in *UI*), was an attack on the Lord Lieutenant for seizing the *UI* issues.
4 Robert Johnston.
5 There is one typescript page extant which would appear to be part of this pamphlet (see also note 2, letter 76). It ends by saying: 'I do not put this passage before you because it is malicious and lying, though it is all this, but because it is a singularly clear case of that offence which Ireland has agreed to call "Felon setting". I do not accuse him of deliberate treachery, but I do accuse him of being entirely reckless whether his words are helpful to the government or not so long as they satisfy that insanity of malice that has made him notorious. No precaution was taken to see that none but discreet eyes should see this passage.'

89

1 Because of its Celtic symbolism this letter was in the *Visions Notebook*. The symbol is a trefoil, with another trefoil within each leaflet, and with three colours assigned. The letter goes on: 'in each world there is a trinity the divine three children of Anna and the Dagda, Aed, Angus, Brighid, the heroic three children of Anna & [?In] demi gods or heroes the [?element] MacCecht Mac[?Cuill] Mac[?Grene] from Human waters earth [?grandson] of the Dagda – in the centre is a white crystal which I think is the symbol of the [?vision/union] I believe the 4 great symbols have their correspondence in each of these worlds.' (MG was always interested in the trinity of things; some of the last pieces she wrote were on the trinity of Ireland – the people, the land and the spirit.)
2 William Larminie (1849–1900), a civil servant, collected folk stories and wrote poetry. His books include *West Irish Folk Tales and Romances* (1898) and his volumes of poetry *Glanlua* (1889) and *Fand, and Other Poems* (1892), in which 'Moytura' was included. Moytura, a plain in Co. Sligo, was the site of a battle in which the Tuatha dé Danaan defeated the Firbolgs. WBY alludes to the great battle of good and evil, life and death, 'which was fought out on the strands of Moytura, near Sligo', in *Poems* (1895).
3 Falias, Findrias, Gorias and Murias, whence the Tuatha dé Danaan, the ancient gods, came to Ireland.

90

1 Marie Henri d'Arbois de Jubainville (1827–1910), a French scholar and founder of the *Revue Celtique*, was author of *Introduction à L'Etude de la Littérature Celtique* (1883); *Essai d'un Catalogue de la Littérature D'Irlande* (1883); *Le Cycle Mythologique Irlandais et la Mythologie Celtique* (1884) and *L'Epopée Celtique en Irlande* (1892). MG was probably alluding to the third of these.

91

1 May Gonne and Kathleen had joined the Order of the Golden Dawn on 13 July 1900. Kathleen took as her motto *Ferendo et Sperando*, the Gonne family motto, and May had taken *Ultra Aspicie*. MG associated freemasonry and Semitism with hidden power, privilege and wealth used destructively.

92

1 Oliver Bond Young Men's '98 Club (named after Oliver Bond, a leader in the 1798 revolution) held classes and lectures. MG spoke on 'Irishmen in the English army'.

2 Thomas Osborne Davis (1814–45) founded *The Nation* in 1842 and was a leader of the Young Ireland Party. He wrote prose and poems of a popular patriotic kind, and *The Nation* had a considerable influence in shaping nationalist ideas in Ireland.

3 At the invitation of the Limerick Young Ireland Society MG gave a lecture on 'Ireland and her foreign relations' in the Athenaeum Hall. It was reported in full on 15 Dec 1900 in *UI*, taken from the *Limerick Leader*. In a plan worked out between Griffith and herself it was decided that she, a more frequent and practised public speaker, would promulgate the policy of self-reliance of the newly formed Cumann na nGaedheal, as well as the anti-recruitment stand, her speeches being prepared jointly. Cumann na nGaedheal (Federation of the Gaels) was the umbrella organisation for all nationalist clubs, set up in an attempt to unify and direct their efforts, and launched by Griffith, Rooney, MG and others. Its basic policy of independence through self-sufficiency ('ourselves alone' or *sinn féin*) was set out in *UI*, 6 Oct 1900.

4 Anna Johnston probably wanted her to attend the Belfast Feis.

5 The general election was the 'khaki election' held on 16 Oct 1900 which the Conservatives won. Nationalists were advised to abstain from voting.

6 Máire Killeen, then engaged to William Rooney, was one of the founder members of Inghínidhe who had gathered on Easter Sunday 1900; she became a vice-president. She contributed Connaught stories and legends to the *United Irishman* as 'Máire' and later to *Bean na hÉireann*, writing on industries and reminiscences. She married Patrick Bradley, a close friend of Rooney. As a member of the Gaelic League she acted as examiner with P. H. Pearse in Irish for Fr Anderson's national schools at John Street, Dublin, which had 560 pupils on the rolls (*UI*, 1902).

7 George Moore.

93

1 When the Redmonds' *Independent* papers were taken over by William M. Murphy, J. W. O'Beirne, an IRB man on the commercial staff of the paper, lost his job along with the rest of Fred Allan's IRB clique working there. He had been on the Dublin '98 Executive Committee. Mrs O'Beirne was a member of Inghínidhe who held their socials in the hotel.

94

1 H. M. Kennedy (b. 1839), ordained 1868 to a Donegal curacy, became Vicar of Plumpton in 1879. On reading Anglo-Irish history, he became a fearless advocate of reform and was popularly known as the 'Radical Parson'. He was a regular contributor to the *United Irishman*. In a letter to Lady Gregory of 12 Aug 1898, WBY described him at the banquet at Frascati's in 1898, recommending everyone 'to buy a breech-loader and prepare for the day of battle' (*L*(W), 303).

95

1 Seamus MacManus (1861–1960), a schoolteacher who married Anna Johnston, published many collections of short stories and wrote some plays for the Abbey Theatre, including *The Townland of Tawney* (1904) and *The Hard Hearted Man* (1905). Able to make a living from his writing in the USA, he settled there, returning to Donegal every year. His autobiography, *The Rocky Road to Dublin*, was published in 1938.

2 W.J. Stanton Pyper, a journalist on the *United Irishman*, who knew Yeats from the days when WBY visited Katharine Tynan at Clondalkin, from 1885 on. See a letter from Stanton Pyper *LTWBY*, 80.

3 *The Dome* appeared as a quarterly magazine from March 1897 to May 1898, as a monthly from Oct 1898 to July 1900. Its editor, E. V. Oldmeadow, was a Nonconformist minister who later became a Roman Catholic, and editor of *The Tablet*. It published WBY's 'The Irish Literary Theatre, 1900' in Jan 1900.

4 The performances began on 19 Feb 1900 in the Gaiety Theatre, Dublin.

5 A Christmas party held by the Inghínidhe in the Workingmen's Club in York Street, Dublin, for the children attending their classes in Irish language, dancing and culture. To accommodate the numbers, the treat was held for two nights and consisted of a magic-lantern

show of the Boer War and illustrated Irish legends, 'with a goodly supply of cakes, sweets, and fruit'.

96

1 WBY's dramatic poem, *The Shadowy Waters*, was finished in Dec 1899, the main text appearing in the *North American Review* in 1900. The 'introductory lines' (*YP*, 143–4), published in *The Speaker*, Dec 1900, formed part of *The Shadowy Waters* (1900). The acting version was first published in book form in 1907.

1901

97

1 MG went out under the auspices of Clann na Gael. Before going she wrote informing them she would make the trip only on the understanding that she would receive the earnings at the time, since she did not want to be left waiting months, as had happened previously. She informed them that she had business offers of tours which she could undertake at any time, but preferred being of use to the cause they were all interested in. It was a gruelling and apparently highly organised tour lasting 48 days, with 27 stops including Boston, Chicago, St Louis, Kansas City, Cincinnati, Pittsburg and Philadelphia.

2 Presumably *Diarmuid and Grania*, in which WBY and George Moore collaborated with much quarrelling. It was apparently finished on 12 Dec 1900, though they revised it at Coole in the summer of 1901; it was produced at the Gaiety Theatre, Dublin, in Oct 1901. The love story of Diarmuid and Grania is in the Fenian Cycle of tales.

98

1 John A. Finnerty of Chicago attacked John MacBride in the *Chicago Citizen* in 1901 (*UI*, 28 Dec 1901).

2 Pat Ford was editor of the *Irish World*, which was at that time supporting the united Parliamentary Party. There was a five-column attack on MG, Major MacBride and John Daly, Mayor of Limerick, who was with them in Chicago on 9 March 1901 (the *UI* reported it). The *Irish World* was an influential New York Irish-American weekly founded by Patrick Ford in 1870. Ellen Ford had collected money for MG for the famine victims of Erris in 1898. In 1931 MG

helped to organise the circulation of the paper in Ireland for Thomas J. Ford.

3 *Diarmuid and Grania*.

99

1 This letter is in the Berg Collection, New York Public Library.

100

1 MG said it was when she was in Switzerland, 'in a flowery meadow ... at the foot of Mont Blanc', that she ended her relationship with Millevoye. This could have been now or in 1900. Yet he continued to attend her meetings in Paris.

2 Douglas Hyde (1860–1949), a poet, scholar and translator, founded the Gaelic League in 1893 and became first President of Ireland in 1937. *Casadh an tSugain*, his first Irish play (translated by Lady Gregory as *The Twisting of the Rope*), was published in *Samhain* (1901). Her translation of his *Teach na mBocht* ('The Poorhouse') was published in *The New Ireland Review* in 1903. *An Cleamhnas*, another one-act play, was published in the *Gaelic Journal* in 1904. The play mentioned here is probably *An Posadh* ('The Marriage'). Hyde wrote it at Coole in 1901, with input from WBY and Lady Gregory in its redrafting. The story hinges on the help given by Blind Raftery, the Connaught poet, to a poor newly married couple. The play was performed at the Galway Feis (pronouced 'fesh'; a festival) in Aug 1902.

3 Inghínidhe na hÉireann (pronounced 'In-nee-nee na hErin' – Daughters of Ireland) grew from the ladies' committee that organised and ran the Patriotic Children's Treat. Most of the women who joined were relatives of men involved in the movement. The organisation was formally inaugurated in Oct 1900. Each member took a Gaelic name of some famous Irishwoman, and researched and wrote a paper on her which was published in the *United Irishman*. The name was used as an alias to protect jobs. Each member had a sash of green-and-blue poplin ribbons and a replica of a Tara brooch as a badge. Their aims were to encourage the study of Gaelic, Irish literature, history, music and art, especially among the young, to support and popularise Irish manufacture, to discourage the reading and circulation of 'low English' songs and entertainments, and to combat English influence. To this end

they ran classes, put on their own entertainments and took a very active part in all nationalist activities. With the formation of Cumann na nGaedheal they could now, for the first time as women, be political activists and wield an official voice in political affairs, with the right to send delegates to Cumann na nGaedheal conventions. Apart from all the work they did, this in itself was a major advance from the time when MG, as a young girl, was not accepted into any of the societies she tried to join. Many of the members continued in active public life for many years.

101

1 WBY's 'Magic' was published in *The Monthly Review*, Sept 1901, and was later included in *Ideas of Good and Evil* (1903).

2 *The Deliverance of Red Hugh* by Alice Milligan was produced in Aug 1901 by the Inghínidhe in the Antient Concert Rooms, Dublin, with *Elís agus Bhean Dheirce* by P. T. MacGinley. The 'Brian thing' was *King Brian Ború at Clontarf* – the Battle of Clontarf (1014) – which was performed at the Inghínidhe entertainment at Easter while MG was in America; the author was not named. Both entertainments also had *tableaux vivants*, and a ceilidh, the children from the Inghínidhe classes performing in these. Alice Milligan and MacGinley had been doing this kind of work in Belfast and Donegal. The Fay brothers, originally in the Ormond Dramatic Society, now in the Irish National Dramatic Company, were called in for their professional assistance.

3 Katharine Tynan (1861–1931), a poet and novelist, was a friend of WBY in his youth.

4 Luke Patrick Hayden (b. 1850) was an MP from 1892 and proprietor of *The Roscommon Messenger*. The occasion was the unveiling of a memorial at which both MG and Hayden spoke. He pleaded for toleration among nationalists. She wrote an article for *UI*, 21 Sept 1901, on the poor of Castlerea.

5 Frank Hugh O'Donnell.

6 IRB.

7 Henri Magnis de Rochefort (1831–1913), a French political journalist, founded *La Lanterne* (1868), a weekly pamphlet which attacked the Empire; he became a fervent nationalist under the Third Republic.

8 Charles Diamond (1858–1934), born in Ireland, was MP for North Monaghan (1892–5) and founded many provincial newspapers.

9 'Two Beautiful Sisters', *The Tatler*, no 9, 28 Aug 1901, 416–17. The photographs were by Chancellor, Dublin. The captions read: 'Miss Maud Gonne, who is an enthusiastic supporter of the most extreme phase of the Irish Nationalist movement, and is sometimes called by her admirers "The Irish Joan of Arc", is of English origin, although her life has been passed principally between Dublin and Paris. Mrs Pilcher was a Miss Gonne, and is a sister of Miss Maud Gonne. She is the wife of Colonel T. D. Pilcher, extra ADC to the King, and now commanding the Bedfordshire Regiment in South Africa. She is also the daughter of an English officer.

10 Presumably Dr Mark Ryan and Dr Anthony MacBride.

11 Either *Madame Angot ou la Poissarde parvenue* (1796) or *Madame Angot au Sérail* (1809), popular French plays by Maillot (1747–1814) containing the adventures in foreign countries of simpletons given to boasting, verbal confusion and vulgarity.

12 Another club named after a famous Wicklow rebel of 1798, with whom Robert Emmet took refuge in July 1803 before his arrest. Dwyer's niece was Emmet's housekeeper. See WBY's address on Emmet in New York, 28 Feb 1904 (*UPWBY*, 317–18).

13 He has the function of a guardian angel in *Visions Notebook*, but is the druid of Murias (see note 2, letter 48).

14 This may be the Anglo-Irish usage of 'eat' (pronounced 'et') for 'ate'.

15 The mother goddess of the Tuatha dé Danaan.

16 Probably *Cuchulain of Muirthemne*, published April 1902.

1902

103

1 *The King*, 22 Dec 1900, p. 810, contained an article 'Farm Burning in South Africa' (with five photographs). MG probably required this for writing her articles and speeches.

2 Two acts of George Russell's *Deirdre* were played privately (informally without a stage) in the Coffeys' garden on 3 Jan 1902 for their son's twelfth birthday, with Elizabeth Young as Deirdre. She

was an actress who played in London under the name Violet Mervyn. The play was produced on 2 April 1902 at St Teresa's Abstinence Hall, Clarendon Street, Dublin, with WBY's *Cathleen ni Houlihan*. Mrs Coffey was the wife of George Coffey (1857–1916), Keeper of Antiquities in the National Museum of Ireland. The tale of Deirdre is a tragic love story from the Ulster Cycle.

3 At the National Dramatic Company William Fay (1872–1947) was producing plays when asked by Inghínidhe to help in their work. With the success of *Cathleen ni Houlihan*, he and his brother Frank were asked to join the newly formed National Theatre Society (eventually the Abbey Theatre), from which he resigned in 1908. His brother Frank was dramatic critic for the *United Irishman*. They were the only members with professional experience. See W. G. Fay and Catherine Carswell, *The Fays of the Abbey Theatre* (1935).

4 Máire T. Quinn, secretary to Inghínidhe, working in the accounts department of the Unionist firm of Alex Finlater, took the Inghínidhe pseudonym of Cliona; she was one of the first secretaries of Cumann na nGaedheal, and later was on the executive committee. A founder member of the National Theatre Society, she became an actress, playing the lead in George Russell's *Deirdre* in the Fays' Dublin production. She went to the USA with Dudley Digges, a fellow member of the company; they subsequently married. At the time of her death MG wrote an article on her and Inghínidhe in *The Irish World* (18 Oct 1947).

5 Mary Walker was a member of Inghínidhe, took the name of Deirdre, worked at the Yeats family's Dun Emer Industries for a time, and as an actress with the National Theatre Company, which she left after a row with WBY. She joined the Theatre of Ireland (with Martyn as president and directors including Padraic Colum, Frank Cousins and Padraic Pearse). By 1907 she had rejoined the Abbey Theatre company. She became a member of Constance Markiewicz's Cumann na mBan in 1915 when Inghínidhe was amalgamated with it, and was in Jacob's factory in 1916. See her *The Splendid Years* (1955).

104

MS Berg Collection, New York Public Library

1 MG agreed to play the title role in WBY's *Cathleen ni Houlihan* in April 1902. (The spelling in the first edition's title was *Hoolihan*, in the text of the play 'Cathleen ny Hoolihan'. MG generally spelt it 'Kathleen', not 'Cathleen'.) The Inghínidhe had decided to put on more ambitious plays to maintain theatrical interest now that the Irish Literary Theatre's three-year experiment was at an end. This they did in conjunction with the Fays' National Theatre Company.

2 It is not clear whether MacGregor Mathers was involved with the 'comic' row which probably resulted from the fact that the 'Shamrock League', which recruited for the British Army, gave a St Patrick's Day banquet in Paris to which many were invited and at which shamrock was to be distributed. Millevoye (in an article, 'Le Masque Anglais', in *La Patrie*) and Cumann na nGaedheal set about disillusioning the French of this apparently nationalist occasion.

3 Edward Martyn became president of the Theatre of Ireland because he had not enjoyed collaborating with George Moore and had not been happy with the way in which the Literary Theatre was developing.

105

1 The lecture in the Salle Wagram was one of a series of three which MG gave on 'La Tyrannie Anglaise'; the others were in the Salle des Agricultures de France, organised by the Franco-Irish Committee (where 2000 were present, including Député Millevoye), and at the Université Populaire. At this time she attended other functions in Paris at which MacBride was present with her, and he was introduced as a new member to the St Patrick's Society.

2 Maurice Berteaux, a wealthy radical deputy, became Minister for War; he was killed while officiating at the start of the Paris–Madrid air race at Issy-les-Moulineaux on 21 July 1911.

3 Clovis Hugués (1851–1907), French poet, politician and deputy for Paris, was imprisoned for supporting the Paris Commune in 1871. He killed a rival journalist in a duel in 1877. He became a Boulangist. See WBY, 'Clovis Huges on Ireland', *UId*, 30 Jan 1892, which gives Edwin Ellis's translation of Hugués's oratorical 'A Toast to Ireland', dedicated to MG. At the Salle Wagram he recited

'Pour les Boers', composed especially for the occasion.

106

1 Bowie, Mary Ann Meredith, who had been with MG and Kathleen from before the death of their mother, travelled with them everywhere. When MG's life became too hectic for her to be able to follow, she lived in a cottage in Farnborough, supported by the sisters. They sent those needing care to be looked after by her, including their half-sister, young Eileen Wilson. She and Eileen had visited MG in Paris.

108

1 The scene of WBY's one-act play, *Cathleen ni Houlihan*, is set near Killala in 1798 at the time of the French landing. Michael Gillane, the son of Bridget and Peter, is about to be married. A wandering old woman comes to the house and they offer her hospitality. She talks of the strangers in her house and her 'four beautiful green fields' which they have taken from her. She says the only help she needs is from those who will give themselves for love to get the strangers out of her house. Then she goes away to meet her friends; cheering can be heard, and she is like 'a young girl' with 'the walk of a queen'. Michael follows her, leaving his parents, his bride Delia and his prosperous future to join the French. The dramatic moment comes when the bent old woman, whose mind seems to be wandering, stands straight and beautiful as a queen.

2 Possibly Ella Young (see letter 181, note 2).

109

1 George Russell's play, staged on 2 April 1902.

2 MG's meetings in Cork, Skibbereen and Limerick resulted in increased membership of Cumann na nGaedheal and Inghínidhe.

111

1 The Fomorians.

2 The Firbolgs were supposedly prehistoric invaders of Ireland, a short dark people. WBY describes them as 'warring mainly upon the Fomorians or Formoroh before the coming of the Tuatha de Danaan'.

3 This symbol (*Saturn*) in the Celtic Rites referred to *Lir* and the colour indigo according to MG's notes.

112

1 The references in this letter have not been traced, so it is not certain that this and the following one should be placed here, but at this time the *United Irishman* was in serious financial trouble and about to close down. Early in June John MacBride wrote to John Devoy saying that money for *UI* had not arrived and stressing the importance of helping it, since it supplied the place of organisers in Ireland. Then on 10 June he wrote: 'your cheque for 2,540 francs has arrived'.

114

1 Dr Mark Ryan.

2 Possibly P. J. P. Tynan, an INB man, thought to be No 1 of the Invincibles, whom MG prevented being arrested in 1896 when he was accused of plotting to assassinate the Tsar. 'Things don't look very bright' may refer to political action from the IRB.

3 George Moore gave a famous garden party in 1902 at Ely Place, Dublin, where he had taken up residence in 1901.

115

1 The Hill of Tara, Co. Meath, the seat of the High Kings of Ireland, is an important prehistoric site. On Christmas Day 1900 MG and Griffith, walking on the Hill of Tara, discovered excavations and started a campaign in the *United Irishman*, commencing with an article by MG (*UI*, 5 Jan 1901). The excavators were supposedly looking for the Ark of the Covenant to present to Edward on his coronation. The *United Irishman* intervened again later. WBY, George Moore and Douglas Hyde wrote a letter to *The Times*, 27 June 1902, opposing the excavations in progress there which were set in motion 'apparently that the sect [British Israelites] which believes the English to be descended from the ten tribes [of Israel], may find the Ark of Covenant'. See WBY, 'In the Seven Woods' (*YP*, 129). The *United Irishman* had notes on the vandalism reprinted in foreign journals; MG, d'Arbois de Jubainville, O'Donnell, Duke of Tetuan, and Wilfred Blunt had also written on the subject abroad, and the Royal Society of Antiquaries stepped in to protect the site.

2 Inghínidhe na hÉireann organised a chil-

dren's excursion to Tara in which 300 children took part. (See *UI*, 19 July 1902).

3 MG's old friend, Canon Dissard, who was secretary to the Bishop of Laval, had sought her assistance when the Carmelite nuns in the town were being secularised in 1901. Some of the nuns left but others, headed by Suzanne Foccart, who founded the Association des Dames de Sainte Thérèse, remained. In order to continue to exist, contemplative orders had to have a *raison sociale*, to appear secular and earn a living. These nuns specialised in embroidery (*ASQ*, 267). Madame Foccart became a friend and Iseult's godmother, and when MG was going away she sometimes left Iseult and Eileen under her protection. (Later she and the nuns had to leave the convent after a dispute with the bishop, and she died in Brittany, in poverty, in 1921.)

4 MG has written that a friend of hers who had a house on the coast of Normandy took Iseult for a holiday there and later urged her to buy one nearby that had become vacant; this house was Les Mouettes, at Colleville. MG bought it with an unexpected legacy she had some time previously received from her Great-Aunt Augusta. She did not, however, use the house until after her marriage.

116

1 *The Celtic Twilight*, first published in 1893, was reissued in expanded and rewritten form in 1902, containing material WBY had collected with Lady Gregory, who had had a hand in the rewriting. The spine of the 1902 edition was certainly designed by Althea Gyles. It resembled that of *The Secret Rose* (the spear of the moon dipped in the cauldron); this is reproduced on the jacket of *YANB*. The top board was most likely by her also, with its three flèched arrows through a half-moon; it may have been part of an abandoned design.

2 Groom and Briscoe were responsible for the Anglo-Israelite Society's excavations at Tara. Groom was described as an English pork butcher in *UI*, 5 July 1902; *UI*, on 15 Nov 1902, called Briscoe a Meath squireen, a Tory landlord.

3 A patriotic ballad by Thomas Davis (1814–44), co-founder of *The Nation*; it was used as a nationalist anthem.

4 George Russell had done paintings of fairies on the walls of MG's house. He painted many visionary murals in Dub-lin, notably in the Theosophical Society's rooms in Ely Place.

117

1 Joseph MacBride (1860–1938) was the eldest of the five MacBride brothers. After boarding school at St Malachy's, Belfast, he worked in a bank there but because he came too much under the notice of the authorities on account of his activities in politics and the Gaelic League he emigrated to Australia for five years. Eventually he returned to Westport, where he farmed and became secretary to the Westport Harbour Commissioners. He married 18-year-old Eileen Wilson in 1904. He stood, unopposed, for South Mayo as a Sinn Féin candidate in 1918 while in gaol and retained his seat until his death.

2 The Reek, or Croagh (pronounced 'Crow') Patrick, St Patrick's Mountain (2510 ft) in Co. Mayo, where there is an annual pilgrimage in honour of the saint to the summit. It is a landmark on the southern shores of Clew Bay, which is said to have 352 islands. Westport is at the head of the bay and was a large distributing port before the coming of the railways.

3 At the first convention of Cumann na nGaedheal (Federation of the Gaels) in Nov 1900, John O'Leary was elected president, with MG and John MacBride (*in absentia*) as vice-presidents. From the ferment of nationalist discussion Cumann na nGaedheal had emerged in the autumn of 1900. Its inauguration meeting was held at the end of 1900. Starting from a loose federation of clubs with nationalist, cultural and economic aims, backed by the IRB it gradually moved towards a complete abstentionist and passive-resistance policy, which Griffith aired in the *United Irishman* from late Nov 1902, and finally to what he called the 'Hungarian' policy, using as an example the Hungarian nationalist representatives' struggle and abstention from the Imperial Austrian Diet in Vienna in the late nineteenth century, which led to separate parliaments for Austria and Hungary with a common monarch. He published this policy under the title *The Resurrection of Hungary* (1904).

4 A lecture by WBY, accompanied by Florence Farr on the psaltery, was given at Clifford's Inn Hall, Fleet Street, London, in June 1902. See *L*(W), 274, 373.

This performance was to take place in the Antient Concert Rooms, Dublin, at the Irish Concert – the first entertainment of Cumann na nGaedheal's Samhain week on Monday, 27 Oct (*UI*, 1 Nov 1902), though the announcement was not featured in the advertisement.

5 Maedbe (Maeve) was the Inghínidhe name that MG took, after the warrior queen of Connaught in the Ulster Cycle. For MG's article on her, see *UI*, 5 Oct 1901.

118

1 MG played Cathleen in performances of WBY's *Cathleen ni Houlihan* on 28 Oct and 1 Nov during Samhain week. The National Theatre Society was formed after the Inghínidhe performances of *Cathleen ni Houlihan* and *Deirdre* in March. WBY was president; Hyde, MG and Russell were vice-presidents. It finally found a permanent home in the Abbey with the aid of Miss Horniman.

2 WBY's play *The Hour Glass*, originally entitled *The Fool and the Wise Man*, was first performed on 14 March 1903 with Lady Gregory's *Twenty-Five* at the Molesworth Hall, Dublin. See *L*(W), 378. It was founded on a story, 'The Priest's Soul', recorded by Lady Wilde in *Ancient Legends, Mystic Charms and Superstitions of Ireland* (1887).

3 The National Theatre Company moved into the Camden Street Hall, Dublin, in 1902.

4 Samhain (pronounced 'Sow-on') was the ancient Irish festival of All Hallowtide on 1 November, the feast of the dead in the Pagan and Christian past and the beginning of winter. It is also the Irish word for November. In spring 1902 the executive committee of Cumann na nGaedheal decided to hold a gathering and a series of competitions to coincide with their annual convention at the end of October each year. The competitions, open to the whole country, were for essays on Irish history, economy and politics, for one-act plays in Irish and English, and for songs. The Inghínidhe assisted the executive in the preparations for this event which first took place from 26 Oct to 1 Nov 1902 with a ceilidh, concert or plays held each night.

5 James Henry Sproull Cousins (1873–1956) acted in minor parts with the Irish National Theatre Society; his play, *The Racing Lug* (1902), was a huge success. He wrote poetry, became a theosophist

and went to India in 1913.

6 The member clubs of Cumann na nGaedheal.

7 WBY's play *The Land of Heart's Desire* was first performed at the Avenue Theatre in 1894.

8 MG spoke on self-reliance in Tralee, Co. Kerry, where she laid the foundation stone for a '98 memorial on 21 Sept. In Cork she visited the exhibition run by the Department of Agriculture and Technical Instruction for Ireland, of which Horace Plunkett was vice-president, writing an article about it, 'Ways of checking emigration', for *UI*, 11 Nov 1902.

119

1 The play *Where There is Nothing*, written in a fortnight by WBY, Lady Gregory and Douglas Hyde 'to keep George Moore from stealing the plot' (*L*(W), 503), was first published as a supplement to *UI*, 1 Nov 1902, and performed at the Royal Court Theatre, London, on 26 June 1904. It was reworked largely by WBY and Lady Gregory as *The Unicorn from the Stars*, first performed at the Abbey Theatre, Dublin, 23 Nov 1907.

2 A stringed instrument similar to the lyre, but with a trapezoidal sounding board. It originated in the Near East and was popular in medieval Europe. Arnold Dolmetsch made one for WBY and Florence Farr.

120

1 This may be 'Away', the last of a group of six articles dealing with folk material that WBY and Lady Gregory gathered in Galway. It appeared in the *Fortnightly Review* in April 1902.

2 John MacBride, then living in Paris.

3 Padraic Colum (1881–1972) was a poet and playwright whose plays, particularly *The Land* (1903), *Broken Soil* (1903) and *Thomas Muskerry* (1910), brought an effective blend of peasant realism and Ibsenesque technique into the Abbey Theatre. He went to America in 1914, returning to Ireland in old age. *The Saxon Shillin'* was a propaganda piece against recruiting. Lady Gregory's *Twenty-Five* had been vetoed by MG in 1902 on the grounds that it made emigration seem financially over-attractive. *The Saxon Shillin'* was substituted for it and revised by Willie Fay into a form more suitable for staging. After George Russell had suggested a democratic system of

voting in which plays and casting were to be settled by a three-quarter vote of all the members, a compromise was reached by WBY when Colum withdrew his play and Lady Gregory revised hers. At this time Colum was signing his work 'Padraig MacCormac Colm' and had not yet settled on a distinct form – hence MG's added confusion in accommodating to the spelling of a new name.

1903

121

1 *Sold* by James Henry Cousins was blocked by WBY 'as rubbish and vulgar rubbish' when offered to the National Theatre Company. He wrote to Lady Gregory: 'I hear *Sold* has been given up, and that they are rehearsing Colum's *Saxon Shilling*. I am very glad of this as it will encourage him and be nothing against our dignity. Maud Gonne also wrote and protested against *Sold*' (*L*(W), 395).

123

1 George Moore's brother Maurice was a colonel in the British Army at that time. Later he was Inspector-General of the Irish Volunteers and was working for the Bureau Irlandais in Paris when MG was there in June 1922 for the Provisional Government.

2 Russell's house was next to MG's in Coulson Avenue.

3 *The Lost Saint* was a play by Dudley Digges (1879–1947), who started acting with the Fays in the Coffee Palace, then with the Fays and Inghínidhe, later with the Abbey Theatre. He went to the USA with Máire T. Quinn to act in an Irish play at the St Louis World Fair. They remained there and married. He made a successful career in acting.

4 Helen Laird was a member of Russell's Theosophical group, a friend of Ella Young, and joined Inghínidhe na hÉireann. In 1905 she married Constantine Peter Curran SC, but continued in Inghínidhe and acted as honorary secretary for the school meals project.

WBY 3

1 James Stephens (1824–1901) was active in the Young Ireland Party and was one of the founders of the Fenian movement. He founded the *Irish People* to urge armed rebellion, was arrested in Dublin in 1865, but escaped to New York. Deposed by the Fenians, he lost political influence and was allowed to return to Ireland in 1891.

2 The Act of Union, passed in 1800, amalgamated British and Irish Parliaments at Westminster; this led to agitation for the return of Home Rule. See Roy Foster, *Modern Ireland 1600–1972* (1988), 283, who argues that Catholics 'hoped for emancipation under the Union, and constituted an important Unionist lobby'.

124

1 Only one letter survives, and it is a draft.

2 MG received instruction for her baptism into the Roman Catholic Church from Canon Dissard at Laval (see *ASQ*, ch. 19). In a letter to her sister Kathleen, MG, while repeating the idea that it mattered little whether one called the great free spirits archangels or the Sídhe, also said she wanted to look at the truth 'from the same side as the man I am going to marry'. The baptism was performed by Monseigneur Pierre-Joseph Geay, Bishop of Laval, in the chapel of the Convent of the Association of the Ladies of Sainte Thérèse. Victor Collins was godfather and Mrs Collins stood for Honoria MacBride as godmother. The certificate was signed by eleven people, including the godparents, Suzanne Foccart and John MacBride.

126

1 Saint-Laurent-sur-Mer is a small village with a hotel a few miles west of Colleville-sur-mer on the coast road to Vierville.

2 MG's house, Les Mouettes, was about a mile from the village of Colleville. It stood right on the beach, which was known as Omaha beach in the Second World War, when the house was demolished to give German artillery a better field of fire.

127

1 WBY was avidly reading Nietzsche at this time.

2 The mother goddess of the People of Dana.

3 MG was responsible for the central branch of Inghínidhe na hÉireann being under the patronage of Brigid in her 'dual character of Goddess and Saint'.

4 On her way through London MG apparently discussed and made plans with WBY in connection with Edward VII's visit to Ireland in July 1903. The commit-

tee was possibly the 'People's protection Committee' mentioned in the next letter.

5 *The Saxon Shillin'* was produced by Inghínidhe na hÉireann in the Rotunda, Dublin.

6 Lady Gregory's *Poets and Dreamers* (1903) contains a chapter on Anthony Raftery (Antoine O Reachtabhra; *c.* 1784–1835) the Mayo wandering poet. Her first article on him was 'The Poet Raftery', *Argosy* (1907).

128

1 The People's Protection Committee was the name adopted for the committee whose purpose was to protect people from being forced, through intimidation, to take part in loyal demonstrations during the King's visit. The first action of the committee was to make a public challenge to the Lord Mayor of Dublin which resulted in the 'Battle of the Rotunda'. The committee extended into a National Council (see *UI*, 23 May 1903), attracted a growing list of names, and prior to the visit in July it organised one of the largest meetings to be held in Dublin for years at which Edward Martyn presided and MG spoke. The council continued to function after the King's visit and became more effective as a unified political force than Cumann na nGaedheal's loose federation of clubs. At its first convention in 1905 it produced a detailed policy, in pamphlet form, published as *The 'Sinn Féin' Policy* (1906).

129

1 Henry Dixon.

130

1 *The Shadow of the Glen* by John Millington Synge (1871–1909), produced in Oct 1903.

131

1 *In the Seven Woods*, the first book published by WBY's sister Elizabeth Corbet (Lollie) Yeats's Dun Emer Press, Churchtown, Co. Dublin, in Aug 1903.

2 *Cathleen ni Houlihan.*

3 'The player Connolly' of WBY's 'Three Songs to the One Burden' was an Abbey actor who was shot in the fighting on Easter Monday 1916.

4 Probably Helen Moloney (1884–1967), known as Helena by her family and as Emer in Inghínidhe na hÉireann, which she joined in 1903, editing *Bean na hÉireann* ('Women of Ireland'), the first

women's paper in Ireland, started in 1908. She helped Constance Markiewicz to found Fianna Éireann in 1909, the year she joined the Abbey Theatre Players. In 1915 she was secretary of the Irish Women Workers' Union (of which she was an organiser in the 1930s), joined the Irish Citizen Army, took part in the attack on Dublin Castle and was imprisoned in 1916. She opposed the treaty in 1922, was president of the Irish Trades Union Congress (1922–3), and continued to be active in trade-union and political affairs.

5 MG's half sister, Eileen Wilson, was born shortly before the death of her father, Col. Gonne, and died at the age of 86. Happily married to Joseph MacBride from Aug 1904 she had 5 children and lived most of her life in Westport, Co. Mayo.

6 See *YP*, 111.

7 'The Song of Hanrahan the Red' first appeared in the *National Observer*, 4 Aug 1894; it was drastically rewritten and entitled 'Red Hanrahan's Song about Ireland'. It was MG's favourite Yeats poem. See *YP*, 133.

8 WBY's *On Baile's Strand*, included in *In the Seven Woods* (1903), was first performed on 27 Dec 1904 by the Irish National Theatre Society.

9 Possibly *The Unicorn from the Stars* (1908), a reworking of *Where There is Nothing* (1902), a play 'almost wholly hers in handiwork' but so much WBY's in thought that Lady Gregory did 'not wish to include it in her own works'.

10 WBY left for his first lecture tour in the USA on 4 Nov 1903. The tour was largely arranged by John Quinn.

132

1 *Cathleen ni Houlihan.*

2 The Festival Theatre at Beyreuth for which Wagner raised funds, opened in 1876 with a complete programme of the *Ring* cycle. Ibsen was the director of the National Theatre at Christiana, Oslo, from 1857 to 1862, when it went bankrupt; he returned there in 1891.

3 Russell resigned his position as vice-president of the National Theatre Society the following year, and, after helping WBY to reorganise the society as a more professional body in 1905, he resigned altogether.

1904

134

1 MG's sister Kathleen and her midwife Mrs Gun both came to stay for the confinement. The baby was born on 26 Jan 1904 and named Jean Seagan. (In Gaelic script, the 'g' in 'Seagan' carries a dot over it to silence it which is signified by an 'h' in roman lettering in the form of 'Seaghan'; modern spelling simplified the name to 'Seán'.)

2 WBY was in the USA at the time the letter was written.

3 Early in 1904 the Japanese had attacked the Russian fleet at Port Arthur, in China, landed troops in Korea and attacked the Russian forces in southern Manchuria. The Russo-Japanese war lasted until Aug 1905.

A Phoenix 1905–1907

1905

135

1 MG's first cousin May (Mary Kemble) Gonne (1863–1929) married N. S. Bertie-Clay on 29 May 1902. MG asked her to tell WBY of the break-up of her marriage. May spent considerable time with MG in France during the legal proceedings, supporting her and dealing with correspondence, much of it with WBY. She returned to London and later lived in Italy.

2 Richard Barry O'Brien was a member of the English and Irish Bars, living in London, and he seems to have been fairly balanced in this difficult situation.

3 MG's family lawyer in England, Mr Witham, who had chambers in 1 Gray's Inn Square and administered the Gonne Trust.

4 The Abbey Theatre opened in Dublin on 27 Dec 1904. The plays staged were WBY's *On Baile's Strand* and Lady Gregory's *Spreading the News*.

136

1 M. Détroye, her French attorney or solicitor.

2 MG's cousin May.

3 The Rooney Memorial Fund was for the erection of a Celtic cross on his grave. There was a regular collection, and fund-raising functions were organised by clubs including Inghínidhe, who contributed takings from some of their theatrical and social events.

4 *Samhain: an occasional publication edited by W. B. Yeats*, appeared in Oct 1901, 1902, Sept 1903, Dec 1904, Nov 1905, Dec 1906 and Nov 1908. MG is referring to the Dec 1904 number here. Yeats explained its title as the old name for winter, used because 'our plays this year [1901] are in October and our present theatre is coming to an end in its present stage'.

137

1 The new publishing firm, Maunsel & Co Ltd, started in 1905 with George Roberts as managing director. He had acted in WBY's *The King's Threshold* and *On Baile's Strand* and contributed poems to AE's anthology *New Songs*.

2 *The Well of the Saints*, first published 1905 by Maunsel & Co as volume 1 of the Abbey Theatre Series.

3 The Russian Revolution of 1905 has been described as beginning on 9 Jan 1905 with the shooting down by troops of a procession of workers and their families in St Petersburg on their way to present a petition to Tsar Nicholas II. This was followed by mass political strikes and street demonstrations.

138

1 Mary Macken was for a time honorary secretary of Inghínidhe with Máire Quinn, executive member of the National Council from 1906, a member of Cumann na mBan and a professor of German.

2 According to Joseph Hone, *W. B. Yeats 1865–1939* (1942), 205, MG told WBY that, because he would not yield and provide sixpenny seats in the Abbey Theatre, the Sinn Féin clubs regarded him as 'lost to nationalism'.

3 *The Shadow of the Glen*, from the first performance of which on 8 Oct 1903 MG, Máire Quinn and Dudley Digges had walked out. They and Douglas Hyde resigned from the National Theatre Society because of it in 1904. In Oct 1905 WBY, Lady Gregory and Synge became the Board of Directors of what was now a limited company, a development brought about by George Russell's help.

139

1 Victor Collins was the Paris correspondent of the *New York Sun* and a close friend of John MacBride. MG suspected him of being an *agent provocateur* because of his influence over MacBride.

Collins remained friends with the Mac-
Bride family until the 1921 Treaty, electioneering for Joseph MacBride in the
1918 Sinn Féin election.

140

1 Maître Cruppi, MG's lawyer.

141

1 French for 'summons' or 'subpoena'.

142

1 *Twenty-One Poems by Lionel Johnson*,
selected by W. B. Yeats (from *Poems* and
Ireland and Other Poems), was published by Dun Emer Press in 1904.

2 Althea Gyles who had designed covers
for WBY's *The Secret Rose* (1897) and
The Wind among the Reeds (1899).

3 Joseph Granié (1866–1915) was a graphic
artist living in Passy, Paris.

4 Julian's Academy was a famous atelier in
Paris, immortalised in the diaries of
Marie Bashkirtseff; both Sarah Purser
and Constance Markiewicz had studied
there, about 1878 and 1898 respectively.

143

1 Lady Gregory's play *Kincora* was first
produced at the Abbey on 25 March and
published by Maunsel (probably in
April) as volume 2 of the Abbey Theatre
Series.

2 WBY's *Cathleen ni Houlihan*.

144

1 Dr Joseph Patrick Quinn (?1863–1915)
was an old political friend of WBY and
MG. See *M*, 71, and *L*(K), 303.

2 Kelly was legal adviser to the UK and US
embassies in Paris. He was reputedly an
old Fenian.

3 The Chat Noir was a club opened in
Paris in 1881 by Rodolphe Salis as a
centre for 'decadent' bohemian writers,
with its own paper of the same name.
Like other similar Parisian clubs of the
1880s, it aimed at a mixture of the comic
and serious.

146

1 Mrs MacBride was born Honoria Gill,
daughter of Joseph Gill, whose family
came from Island More in Clew Bay;
they ran a successful family business in
Westport, being importers and exporters
of merchandise. She inherited the family
business of ships' chandlers, general
grocers and licensed premises at Westport Quay. She married the captain (and

owner) of a merchant schooner, Patrick
MacBride, from Glenshesk in Co.
Antrim, who then settled in Westport.
He died when his youngest son was six
months old. Honoria, a formidable and
capable woman, carried on the business,
which was eventually taken over by her
second son Patrick. Patrick, mindful that
much of his business depended on the
local gentry, was not involved in politics.

2 O'Donnell's libellous pamphlet, which
Davitt was supposed to have written,
seems to have castigated the MacBride
family. This would have stirred the
already troubled waters surrounding the
by-election in 1900 caused by Davitt's
resignation of protest over the Boer War.
The advanced nationalists put forward
John MacBride, also as a protest, knowing he could not safely take his seat; they
wanted William O'Brien's United Irish
League to stand down temporarily on
that understanding. They eventually
decided not to and the election campaign
was a bitter one, with Davitt supporting
the League. MacBride lost badly.

3 The phrase was a calculated insult by
O'Donnell. A shebeen (Irish *síbín*, illicit
alcohol) is an unlicensed public house.

147

1 Annie Horniman had offered to go to
Westport to look for some evidence of a
'shebeen house', but her mission had
little success.

2 Sarah Purser had apparently refused to
be drawn into the affair.

3 Gustave Moreau (1825–99), part of the
symbolist movement to which WBY
belonged, was a French mystical and
spiritual painter of elaborate biblical and
mythological subjects. WBY had a copy
of his painting *Ladies and Unicorns* in his
Dublin house, 82 Merrion Square, and
later at Riversdale, Rathfarnham (see
L(W), 685).

148

1 Madame Dangien was Iseult's governess,
and later Seán's, until 1913.

2 Labori, a famous French lawyer, acted
for John MacBride. He successfully
defended Harriette Caillaux, who was
charged with the murder of the director
of *Le Figaro*, Gaston Calmette.

3 On 18 April P. T. Daly wrote to John
Devoy in New York: 'John MacBride
has come again from Paris . . . How have
Miss Quinn and Digges got on? And is
she backing her goddess very much?'

149

1 John Quinn (1870–1929) was a most successful Irish American lawyer who became a patron of Irish writers and painters. He was exceptionally kind to (and often exasperated by) WBY's father, John Butler Yeats, during the artist's stay in New York from 1908 to his death there in 1922. Máire Quinn and John Quinn were looking for evidence in the form of signed affidavits against John MacBride when he was in the USA in 1904 at the time MG was in Dublin for their son's baptism, and the money she offered was probably for out-of-pocket expenses.

2 *Dún* means fort, secure residence or refuge. This was 22 North Gt George's St for which MG had signed the lease on 30 Oct 1904 for Inghínidhe classes and general activities. (Before that they had used rooms in 196 Gt Brunswick Street.) The signing of this lease meant that when the question of domicile came up in the case it was shown that MG also could be said to live in Ireland.

150

1 Possibly WBY's *Stories of Red Hanrahan* (1904).

151

1 Maud's half-sister, Eileen.

152

1 Nieve or Niamh (her name means brightness, brilliance, beauty) was a fairy princess who, in the Fenian Cycle of tales, spent 300 years with Oisín in the otherworld. She was the daughter of Aengus, the Gaelic god of love, who reigned in Tír na nÓg, the Land of the Young, and Edáin, a legendary queen who went away and lived among the Sídhe. See *YP*, 5–6, 202, 531.

2 See WBY's letter to Lady Gregory of 30 May 1905, in which he discusses Bullen's bringing out *Poems, A New Series, 1899–1905*, of which he would print enough copies to last until 1907: 'I have heard nothing more about Hone. Bullen liked him very much and would have liked him still better if he could have got that thousand pounds for his own business.' Joseph Hone was about to finance Maunsel & Co Ltd, which began in 1905. See *L(W)*, 449, 451.

3 Moina Bergson, the wife of MacGregor Mathers; a painter and fellow student at the Slade with Annie Horniman, she is the 'Vestigia' to whom WBY dedicated *A Vision*.

4 Chotie (Katherine) Gonne (1861–1931), who remained unmarried.

153

1 Possibly *The Land* (1905).

2 Legal inquiry.

3 In June 1905 a group of nationalists from Dublin paid a commemcrative visit to Fontenoy, where the Irish Brigade's charge had decided the French victory during the war of the Austrian Succession in 1745. There was a pictorial record of the visit in the *Independent* of 17 June 1905. Among those present were O'Leary and MacBride, who gave an account of the battle. O'Leary liked MacBride and they often drank together.

4 Possibly the death of her son Georges in 1891.

154

1 Suzanne Foccart.

2 John MacBride's brother Joseph.

155

1 'Trois Poèmes d'Amour'; 'Les Chevaux de l'Ombre'; 'Le Travail de la Passion'; 'O'Sullivan Rua à Marie Lavell' (trans. Stuart Merrill), *Vers et Prose* (March–May 1905). These were translations of, respectively, 'He Bids his Beloved be at Peace' (originally 'The Shadowy Horses; Michael Robartes Bids his Beloved be at Peace'); 'The Travail of Passion'; 'Michael Robartes Remembers Forgotten Beauty' (originally 'O'Sullivan Rua to Mary Lavell').

156

1 Wolfe Tone (1763–98) was buried at Bodenstown in Co. Kildare; it is a place of homage for nationalists of all hues, each with their day of pilgrimage when someone of distinction is asked to give an oration.

2 William Gonne, being disinherited, left Ireland in the mid- to late eighteenth century and went to Portugal, starting a wine export business between Portugal and England. MG's grandfather, Charles Gonne, was born in Oporto in 1803, and some of his ten children were born there and the rest in England. His third surviving son, Charles (the father of May and Chotie), served in the Indian Civil Service for a time. His fourth surviving son, Thomas (MG's father), born in England in 1835, was educated abroad with a view

to working in the foreign department of the business, but, not fancying such a career, he took a commission in the 17th Lancers, served in India during the Indian Mutiny in 1859, married in 1865, and from 1868 to 1876 served in Ireland, where he felt he had roots. At this time speaking six languages, he was sent as military attaché to the Austrian court, then went to India in 1879 at the end of the Second Afghan War as colonel of his regiment. He went to Russia as military attaché in 1881, finally being posted back to Ireland, where he is still remembered in military circles. He died in Dublin of typhoid fever at the age of 51 in 1886. His funeral 'was the most imposing that had been seen in Dublin for many years' (*Irish Times*, Dec 1886).

157

1 In a letter from WBY to Florence Farr/ Emery from Coole in Aug 1905 he records that a fellow guest, Lady Cromartie, remembered a past life: 'She remembers people so beautiful looking that the people now seem ugly and trivial. . . . She was at Tara and describes curious details of that old life' (*L*(W), 456).

158

1 Sir William Geary (1859–1944), 5th and last baronet, had a career in the colonial legal service. Since he was a member of the English but not the Irish Bar, his advice to seek the opinion of an active counsel in Ireland was sensible. MG may have been put in touch with him by Lady Gregory, who possibly had Galway connections with his wife, a Burke from Danesfield, Co. Galway.

2 MG met the then Abbé Dissard at a meeting of Boulangist friends at Royat in the early 1890s. He was from the Auvergne and claimed a Celtic heritage. He was born in 1860 and ordained in 1886. He went with Bishop Geay as his secretary from Lyons to Laval in 1896.

3 On the main news page of the *Irish Daily Independent* of 27 July 1905 was a two-column report of the previous day's proceedings in the French court, quoting speeches of lawyers on both sides on the question of domicile. This report was cited in the libel case. At the end of the report was a statement from representatives of MacBride's legal advisers in Ireland saying that, as publication was not allowed in France, publication of

proceedings was not covered by the libel law. An editorial comment stated that the report was furnished in the normal way by a news agency, and that Major MacBride was at that time in Dublin.

4 May had married N. S. Bertie-Clay in London in 1902; he was a civil servant in India.

159

1 The Rt Hon William Huston Dodd, third Serjeant at Law, Ireland (1829–1907); Judge of the High Court of Justice, Ireland (1907).

2 Hallinan was a friend of John MacBride and possibly a member of the IRB.

3 Part of Cumann na nGaedheal's autumn week established in 1902.

160

1 P. T. Daly was a prominent member of Cumann na nGaedheal and the IRB. When acting as IRB secretary he was expelled for embezzlement in 1910. He was an active organiser during the 1913 strike.

2 MG probably meant that the tea party (IRB) behaved in a secret, mysterious way, giving the impression they were doing a lot when they were doing nothing.

162

1 The family of MacBride's friend, the journalist Victor Collins.

2 The Dungannon clubs, separatist in intent but not secret, were founded in 1905 by Bulmer Hobson (1883–1969) and Denis MacCullough, two Ulster IRB men. Hobson said that he was strongly influenced by Anna Johnston and, through her, MG and others, and also by the 1798 commemorations. These young men were some of the new breed now ousting the old IRB men. Hobson and MacCullough played an influential part in the events of the following years. In 1907 the Dungannon clubs and Cumann na nGaedheal came together as the Sinn Féin League which joined with the National Council in 1908 in a body known simply as Sinn Féin. (The name 'Shinner' was applied by many people and succeeded 'Fenian' as an abusive term for nationalists.)

3 A branch of Cumann na nGaedheal which put on plays during Samhain week; they played Hyde's *An Posadh* in 1905.

163

1 Denis S. Henry SC acted for John MacBride in the libel action, instructed by P. Lavelle.

2 Thomas Kettle (1880–1916) was Nationalist MP for East Tyrone and first Professor of Economics, University College, Dublin. A member of the Volunteers, he was in Belgium buying arms when the war broke out; thinking Germany more dangerous than England, he joined the Royal Dublin Fusiliers and was killed in the Battle of the Somme. His works included *The Open Secret of Ireland* (1912), *The Ways of War* (1917) and *The Day's Burden* (1918). In 1905, as a King's Inn student, he was the fighting editor of the *Nationist* (a penny weekly review first published on 21 Sept 1905), but in November when the owners criticised a controversial anti-clerical article he published, he apparently had a collapse and ceased to be editor, his brother-in-law Francis Sheehy Skeffington taking over from him.

3 Presumably the issue of Nov 1905.

165

1 The drawing is reproduced in Joseph Hone, *W. B. Yeats 1865–1939* (1942), 239, and in Cardozo, 148.

166

From Berg Collection, New York Public Library.

1 Lady Gregory's play, *The White Cockade*, produced on 9 Dec 1905 at the Abbey Theatre.

167

1 MG's cousin May.

2 Cúchulain (pronounced 'Koo-hullan'), the Hound (*Cú*) of Culann the Smith, was a warrior hero (half god, half man) of the Red Branch or Ulster Cycle of Tales, so called because as a boy he killed Culann's hound and offered to take its place. Single-handed, he protected Ulster from Maeve of Connaught. He was King of Muirthemne in Co. Louth, married to Emer, daughter of Forgael. The 'life' here refers to *Cuchulain of Muirthemne* by Lady Gregory.

3 William Sharp died on 12 Dec 1905. See letter WBY 4, note 2.

1906

168

1 As a result of the split in the Irish National Theatre Society, now control-led by WBY, Lady Gregory and Synge, WBY wrote to George Russell on 8 Jan 1906 that he 'deserved the love of very few people, my equals or my superiors'. He knew he could never have the support of the nationalist clubs in the theatre; he was trying for a general public. See *L*(W), 466, in reply to Russell's comment that there probably was not one of the younger people in Dublin about whom he had not made some stinging or contemptuous remark, adding that he had few or no friends in Dublin. By May various members of the National Theatre Company had left to form Cluctheóri na hÉireann (the Theatre of Ireland) with Edward Martyn as chairman. They included Máire ni Shuiblaigh, Padraic Colum, James Cousins, Patrick Pearse and Thomas Kettle. On 13 June 1906 WBY wrote to Stephen Gwynn that what Dublin wanted was some man who knew his own mind and had an intolerable tongue and a delight in enemies.

169

1 Possibly *Hyacinth* (1906) by George A. Birmingham, pseudonym of Canon James Owen Hannay (1865–1950).

2 The inspiration for MG's designs for the life of Cúchulain, of which the marriage of his mother Dectora was the first, was Lady Gregory's *Cuchulain of Muirthemne*.

170

1 Conchobar was King of Ulster in the Red Branch Cycle of tales.

2 At her marriage to Sualtim of Muirthemne, Dectora, drinking from a wine cup, swallowed a fly. Later the god Lugh appeared in a dream and told her he had been the fly. He took her away with him and fathered Cúchulain.

171

1 Possibly the novel by George A. Birmingham.

2 The first part of this letter is a fragment from Berg Collection, New York Public Library.

3 This end fragment is from the Berg Collection, New York Public Library.

172

1 The *Freeman's Journal* of 22 Feb 1906 reported that the plaintiff (MacBride) was suing the *Irish Daily Independent* for innuendo implied in its reports of Feb

and July 1905.

2 The *Independent* of 21 April reported that the plaintiff had delayed in producing the documents requested by the court, in orders of discovery of 21 and 28 Feb. It went on to say that Mrs MacBride had charged the major with cruelty, infidelity and drunken habits. The case before the Lord Chief Justice, Mr Justice Johnson and Mr Justice Boyd was then adjourned until the order of 28 Feb was complied with. On 26 April it was stated before the Lord Chief Justice that the defendants could not prove fair comment as the plaintiff could not produce documents in his possession, which were prohibited from publication in France. John MacBride won the appeal but received no damages and had to pay his costs.

3 WBY's play *Deirdre* was first performed at the Abbey Theatre, Dublin, on 25 Nov 1906. The story was taken from Lady Gregory's book *Cuchulain of Muirthemne*.

4 The colliery district of northern France was in a state of revolution, with the army on the alert. With the approach of May Day (Labour Day) and the general election the following week the political situation looked very serious.

174

1 Gerald Fitzgibbon (1837–1909), for over thirty years a member of the Irish Court of Appeal (an exceptionally strong tribunal when he was sitting with Palles and Holmes), became Solicitor-General for Ireland (1877–8), Lord Justice of Appeal in Ireland in 1878. According to Prof. R. F. V. Heuston, his opinion on a legal point would have ranked far above that of Mr Justice Boyd, who specialised in bankruptcy cases.

177

1 La Bourboule, in the Puy-de-Dôme, not far from Royat, had thermal baths which were used particularly by children.

1907

WBY 4

1 In March 1907 Ben Iden Payne (b. 1881) became a director of the Abbey Theatre and in May was installed as manager; he resigned after five months. His appointment was largely engineered by Annie Horniman who had given the money to create the theatre. She considered the Fay

brothers unsatisfactory, and they resigned in protest against her reorganisation of the theatre. See W. G. Fay and Catherine Carswell, *The Fays and the Abbey Theatre* (1935).

2 Elizabeth A. Sharp (1856–1932), William Sharp's widow, herself an author, wrote to WBY on 28 Dec 1905 to send him an enclosure. She commented: 'As you will see, he and he only, was and wrote as Fiona Macleod.' The letter from William Sharp read: 'This will reach you after my death. You will think I have deceived you about Fiona Macleod. But, in absolute privacy, I tell you that I have not, however, in certain details I have (inevitably) misled you. Only it is a mystery. Perhaps you will intuitively understand or may come to understand. . . . It is only right, however, to add that I, and I only, am the author – in the *literal* and literary sense – of all written under the name of Fiona Macleod.' The name is spelled Sharp or Sharpe in WBY's letter, which was dictated.

3 George Meredith (1828–1909), the English novelist and poet.

4 Synge's play, *The Playboy of the Western World*, led to riots in the theatre. See WBY, 'The Controversy over the Playboy', *UPWBY*, 348–52.

178

1 The fact that MG put this letter away separately ensured its survival.

180

1 The address of Ella Young's parents.

2 Slieve Gullion (the Holly Mountain, also known as Slieve Fuadh), a mountain in Co. Armagh, is rich in folklore and legend. With a prehistoric passage grave and the remains of ancient fortifications, it forms part of the boundary between north and south. Here MG first heard the strange fairy music that she heard again in Nov 1915.

3 WBY visited Italy for the first time with Lady Gregory and her son Robert in May 1907 (Lady Gregory sometimes stayed with Lady Layard at La Cappello Layard on the Grand Canal); they visited many cities and towns, WBY being particularly impressed with Urbino.

4 Mrs Patrick Campbell (née Beatrice Stella Tanner, 1865–1940) married in 1884. She went on the stage in 1888, achieving fame in *The Second Mrs Tanqueray* (1893). She married George Cornwallis-West in 1914 and had a long,

very close friendship with George Bernard Shaw. She acted the title role in WBY's *Deirdre* in Oct 1907; she was interested in *The Player Queen*, which WBY probably began in 1907. (See WBY's amusing account of reading it to her in Nov 1909, *YANB*, 175.)

181

1 Some form of incense, the effects of which are alluded to in letter 185.

2 Ella Young (1867/8–1956), a mystic poet, was a member of George Russell's Theosophist group, became a member of Inghínidhe and later of Constance Markiewicz's Cumann na mBan; she remained a close friend of MG until she became a Professor of Celtic Mythology in the University of California at Berkeley in 1925. Ten years later she moved to a Theosophy colony in Oceana, called Halcyon. She wrote both poetry and stories, which were published in Ireland and the USA. Her autobiography, *Flowering Dusk*, was published in 1945. MG illustrated her *The Coming of Lug* (1909), *Celtic Wonder Tales* (1910), with another (unidentified) book at this time, and *The Rose of Heaven* (1920). Iseult was presumably translating into French the versions on which Ella Young was working. It is not known whether anything came of these translations.

182

1 The prophecy of the gift of healing for her was recorded in the *Visions Notebook*. She does not seem to mention it again, even during the war.

2 A village (St Mochanog's Church) at the foot of the Rocky Valley, lying between the Great and Little Sugar Loaf mountains in Co. Wicklow, near Dublin. The druid may have been Semias.

3 Richard Strauss (1864–1949), German composer, invited to conduct at Beyreuth in 1891, based his opera *Salomé* on a German translation of Wilde's play. It was produced in 1905 and led him to concentrate on opera.

4 On the occasion of the troubles in the Abbey Theatre in Jan 1907, over Synge's *The Playboy of the Western World*.

5 *The Playboy of the Western World.*

6 This paragraph is the source of WBY's 'The People', written on 27 Jan 1915, first published Feb 1916 (see note, *YP*, 360).

7 A reference to WBY's reading Nietzsche

and being very influenced by his idea of the 'Superman'.

185

1 *The Playboy of the Western World.*

186

1 In response to MG's previous letter, WBY must have suggested some American writer, possibly Agnes Tobin (1863–1939), a minor poet and playwright who was living in London. WBY met her in San Francisco. She wrote *On the Death of Madonna Laura* (1906), translated from Petrarch, and other books of poems. She later suggested to Edmund Gosse that WBY should receive a Civil List pension, and MG threatened to disown him if he accepted. He did accept it and was subsequently sneered at by some nationalists as 'Pensioner Yeats'. See *L*(W), 542.

187

1 WBY's *Deirdre*, already performed at the Abbey Theatre, was first published in 1907.

2 Anthony Mackey, of Castleconnell, Co. Limerick, was a member of the IRB.

3 Robert Gregory (1881–1918), Lady Gregory's son, married (Lily) Margaret Graham Parry on 26 Sept 1907 with Augustus John as his best man. There were three children of the marriage. Gregory enlisted with the Connaught Rangers in 1915, transferred to the RFC in 1916 and was shot down over North Italy in error on 23 Jan 1918. *YP*, 234, 237, 244 and 553.

188

1 WBY described Griffith as 'the founder of the Sinn Féin movement' (*A*, 416). MG's reference to his 'many aggravating traits' may have been intended to palliate WBY's dislike of him, exacerbated by Griffith's attack on Synge's *The Playboy of the Western World*.

2 WBY was preparing his *Collected Works*, published in eight volumes in 1908 by A. H. Bullen under the Shakespeare Head Press imprint in Stratford-upon-Avon. His volume of essays, *Discoveries*, was published on 15 Dec 1907, by the Dun Emer Press.

189

1 WBY had consulted James Richard Wallace, who lived in Manchester, about MG, 'the 1866 case'.

2 Probably the death of her son Georges on 31 Aug 1891.

191

1 Possibly the Augustus John portrait painted at Coole in autumn 1907. See *L*(W), 496: 'He exaggerates every little hill and hollow of the face till one looks like a gypsy, grown old in wickedness and hardship. If one looked like any of his pictures the country women would take the clean clothes off the hedges when one passed, as they do at the sight of a tinker.' It was also included in WBY's *Collected Works*.
2 Legal Case.

Fallen Majesty 1908–1913

1908

193

1 The letter referred to the refusal of the divorce.
2 WBY did not go to the USA with the Abbey Players until Sept 1911.

194

1 Dorothy Coates, John Quinn's mistress. See William M. Murphy's account of her in *Prodigal Father – The Life of John Butler Yeats 1839–1922* (1978), 612, n. 105.

195

1 Charles Hazlewood Shannon (1839–1919), English artist and friend of WBY, commissioned by John Quinn to paint the poet in 1907. WBY thought it 'by an unlucky accident most damnably like Keats'. The portrait was included in the *Collected Works*.
2 Charles de Sousy Ricketts (1866–1931), called 'the magician' by WBY, was an artist, illustrator, painter, stage designer and writer known for the fine design of the Vale Press books and *The Dial* (1880–97).
3 The Fays resigned from the theatre on 13 Jan 1908.
4 Possibly the first volume of George Moore's trilogy *Hail and Farewell*, which he was then writing, the first volume of which, *Ave*, was to appear in 1911. Moore is described as reading part of it in Jan 1910 to WBY, some of it not included in the published version. See *L*(W), 547.
5 Andrew Lang, *Tales of Troy and Greece*

(1907), inscribed with the date 24 Dec 1907.

196

1 MS Yeats from *LTWBY*.

197

1 Probably WBY's *The Player Queen*.
2 Blake's illustration, 'The Soul hovering over the Body reluctantly parting from life', in Robert Blair, *The Grave* (1808).
3 MS Yeats from *LTWBY*.

198

1 Angus the many-coloured (Ildathach), god of love and son of the god Dagda, protected Etáin in a house of glass when, in the form of a butterfly, she fell from the Land of the Ever Young, Tír na nÓg. The illustration, which appeared in Ella Young's *Celtic Wonder Tales* (1910), shows Angus surrounded by kisses represented as birds, gently bearing Etáin through the air.

1909

200

1 Arthur Lynch (1861–1934), an Irish-Australian journalist and a long-time member of the Paris Young Ireland Society, had gone to South Africa and formed the 2nd Irish Brigade which never took part in any major action. Elected MP for Galway (1901–9), on arriving in England to take his seat in Parliament he was arrested on charges of high treason and condemned to death, but was later reprieved. He was MP for West Clare (1910–18) and a colonel in the British army (1918).
2 The Irish sculptor John Hughes.

202

1 Arthur Symons suffered a nervous collapse in 1908–9, from which he recovered with the aid of various friends and the Royal Literary Fund.
2 WBY began work on *The Player Queen* probably in 1907; it was almost finished by Sept 1914, but he was still working on it in 1916, and was revising it a year later. It was first performed on 25 May 1919 by the Stage Society at the King's Hall, Covent Garden, London, and repeated at the Abbey on 9 Dec 1919. It was first published in *The Dial*, Nov 1922, and in *Plays and Prose and Verse* (1922).

204

1 *The Collected Works* in eight volumes published in 1908: I and II in Sept, III and IV in Oct, V and VI in Nov, and VII and VIII in Dec.

2 Dr Henri Fauré had been physician to George Sand. MG painted two portraits of him.

3 Louis Paulliat.

4 Possibly Edmond Bailly, editor of *Isis Moderne*.

5 See WBY, 'Down by the Sally Gardens' (*YP*, 55), 1. 3; 'She bid me take life easy, as the leaves grow on the trees', and 1. 7; 'She bid me take life easy, as the grass grows on the weirs'.

6 Possibly Ferdinand Hubert (1842–1934), a French painter, who was appointed Professor at the Ecole Nationale Supérieure des Beaux-Arts in 1898. Influenced by Italian Renaissance art, he painted many portraits, his colours somewhat modelled on those of Manet.

205

1 Unidentified, but possibly 'No Second Troy', written in Dec 1908, or 'Words', written on 22 Jan with revised verses added 23 Jan 1909.

2 Possibly the *English Review*, Feb 1909, which included 'Three Poems: *I* On a Recent Government Appointment in Ireland; *II* Galway Races; *III* Distraction'. The 'old poem' could be 'All Things Can Tempt Me', called 'Distraction' in the *English Review*.

3 This is the vellum manuscript book, begun in Dec 1908, at the head of which was the poem 'No Second Troy'. It was published in *M* as 'Journal'.

206

1 Lady Gregory was very ill in late Jan 1909, probably suffering a cerebral haemorrhage. See *M*, 160–3.

2 Norreys Connel, pseudonym of Conal Holmes O'Connell O'Riordan (1874–1948). He revived *The Playboy of the Western World* despite strong opposition. He wrote several plays and many novels, among them a soldier series dealing with David Quinn from the end of the eighteenth century to the 1880s and another with a character called Adam as the central figure. He took charge of the Abbey Theatre in 1909. His plays produced there were *The Man Who Missed the Tide* (1908), *The Piper* (1908), *Time* (1909) and *An Imaginary Conversation* (1909).

208

1 Isadora Duncan (1878–1927), the American dancer who based her work on figures in Greek vase paintings, founded schools in Berlin, Vienna and elsewhere.

2 Ruth St Denis (1878/9–1968) was an American dancer. See WBY, 'His Phoenix', written in Jan 1915 (*YP*, 255).

209

1 Lady Gregory's first grandchild, Richard Graham Gregory, was born on 6 Jan 1909.

2 The reference is obscure, but see letter 241, note 4.

210

1 MG may be suggesting that WBY's remarks about health were influenced by Mabel Dickinson. Possibly MG knew about her, or was intuitively aware of a new influence.

2 WBY was again attempting to learn French. (As a young man he had attended classes given by May Morris.) See *L*(W), 513 (27 Dec 1908), where he describes going to a French class in Paris every afternoon.

3 Kathleen Pilcher's sons, Toby (1890–1966), Tommy (1893–1915) and Pat (1896–1963).

212

1 'R. G.' is Robert Gregory. The 'cousin' is probably either Henry (1860–1933) or Arthur Gonne (1864–1938), brothers of May and Chotie. They ran the family business and also did etchings – which was probably the link with Robert Gregory.

214

1 A French postal strike (which involved the cutting of various international phone lines) began on 16 March and lasted until 25 March 1909.

2 Papus was the pseudonym of Gerald en Causse. This book may have been *Willermosisme, Martinisme et Franc-Maçonnerie . . . avec un résumé de l'histoire de la Franc-Maçonnerie en France* (Paris, 1899).

215

1 Synge had been ill for some time and died of Hodgkin's Disease in Elpis, a nursing home in Dublin, on 24 March 1909.

2 *Deirdre of the Sorrows* was still uncompleted at Synge's death; it was published in Sept 1910 by the Cuala Press.

3 See Conal Riordan, *Shakespeare's End, and Other Irish Plays* (1912). This verse play was never performed, but its author read it to the Irish Literary Society in 1911. The characters included Shakespeare, his wife and Judith, as well as Jonson, Drayton and others.

216

1 WBY had attended the Shakespeare Festival at Stratford-upon-Avon in 1901 and wrote 'At Stratford-upon-Avon', describing the plays. There may have been a suggestion that MG should attend the 1909 festival with him.

217

1 Synge's brother-in-law, Stephens, was possibly offended, WBY suggested (*L*(W), 528), that his son Edward had been made Synge's executor instead of himself.

218

1 It began in 1898.

219

1 In March 1909 WBY complained to Florence Farr that Mrs Campbell had sent him no agreement for *The Player Queen* (*L*(W), 526), which he was to finish by Nov or Dec 1909 (*L*(W), 528); Mrs Campbell had obviously signed a contract for it later. See also *L*(W), 539, for her reception of it.

2 Louis-Maurice Boutet de Monvel (1851–1913) was a French artist who painted portraits and religious scenes and produced drawings for book illustrations. His son Bernard (1884–1949) was an artist known for his society portraits and, later, his drawings and book illustrations.

220

1 Molly Allgood (1887–1952), Synge's fiancée, and her sister Sara Allgood were both members of Inghínidhe and became Abbey actresses. Molly joined the Abbey Theatre company in 1905. Her stage name was Maire O'Neill, and her great success was as Pegeen in *The Playboy of the Western World*. When Synge died she married an Abbey actor, Arthur Sinclair (1883–1951), but left the Abbey in 1912 to act in New York.

2 Gabriele d'Annunzio, Prince Monte Nevoso (1864–1939), Italian nationalist poet, novelist, dramatist, soldier and airman. In Sept 1919 he seized the Adriatic port of Fiume (now Rijeka) while its future was under discussion at the Paris Peace Conference.

3 The United Arts Club was founded in Dublin in 1907 by Mrs Duncan, wife of James Duncan, a civil servant. See Patricia Boylan, *All Cultivated People: A History of the United Arts Club, Dublin* (1988); see also Page L. Dickinson, *The Dublin of Yesterday* (1929).

4 The wife of Standish O'Grady.

5 Symons had a mental breakdown in autumn 1908. He was confined in an asylum in Clapton, where Yeats visited him – 'a very painful experience'; see *L*(W), 523, 529. Later he recovered, though not completely, and was able to return home.

221

1 St Columban or Columbanus (543–615) was born in Leinster, went to Britain as a missionary and then to Gaul. He settled in the Vosges and founded monasteries at Annegray, Bernex and Fontaine. He moved to Switzerland (where his pupil Gall stayed) and on to Bobbio where he died, having founded his greatest monastery.

222

1 The Burren (Irish, 'grey rock'), a desolate, windy area famous for the profusion of its rare alpine spring flowers, stretches from Ardrahan, Co. Galway, to the coast of Co. Clare. There the Gregorys had a house which they referred to as Burren, where Robert Gregory was 'sketching and his wife getting health' and WBY was working on *The Player Queen*. Letter to J. B. Yeats, 17 July 1909, *L*(W), 532.

2 There was a possibility that WBY might be given the Chair of English Literature at Trinity College, Dublin, held since 1867 by Edward Dowden (1843–1913), who was a friend of John Butler Yeats from his undergraduate days and seemed to be inimical to the Irish Literary Movement. Dowden took leave of absence in 1910, recovered his health and did not retire. See note 2, letter 224, and note 2, letter 225.

3 Jacob Boehme (1575–1624) was a German Theosophist and mystic. WBY was impressed by his ideas of contraries, of the will fashioning itself a mirror, of the mentality of change.

4 The Irish name for August is *Lughnasa* (after the sun god, Lugh), the first of the

month being an ancient Celtic festival, surviving as Lammas.

223

1 George Bernard Shaw's play *The Shewing-Up of Blanco Posnet* was staged very successfully in the Abbey Theatre on 25 Aug 1909. Dublin Castle tried to prevent the production. See Lady Gregory, *Our Irish Theatre* (1913), 163, and note 1, letter 226.

2 MG's son Seán.

224

1 *The Player Queen.*

2 Originally named the Royal University of Ireland (an examining body only), it was founded under the Universities Act of 1908 and became the National University of Ireland, composed of colleges in Dublin, Cork, Galway and Maynooth. (Queen's University, Belfast, resulted from the same Act.) WBY was an unsuccessful candidate for a lecturership at University College, Dublin, in 1909. MG wrongly thought he had the chance of a professorship there. See J. B. Yeats's letter of 9 June 1909, *LTWBY*, 215–16. See note 2, letter 222, and note 2, letter 225.

225

1 The 7th Earl of Aberdeen (1847–1934) was Lord Lieutenant of Ireland in 1886 and from 1905 to 1915. His wife was interested in feminism and the condition of the Irish peasantry.

2 WBY had decided, despite the temptation of having rooms in Trinity College, not to apply for the chair there because he thought his eyes would not stand up to the concentrated reading the post would involve (letter to Prof. H. J. C. Grierson of 12 Oct 1909, *L*(W), 536; see also 555 and 557). He may also have been affected by the award in Aug 1910 of a Civil List pension of £150 p.a. See note 2, letter 222.

226

1 Rehearsals for *The Shewing-Up of Blanco Posnet* were proceeding in the Abbey when Lord Aberdeen threatened to withdraw the theatre's patent if the play was performed. WBY and Lady Gregory decided the production should go ahead. They stated that they could not give away any of the Irish Theatre's liberty by accepting the English censor's ruling, nor could they accept without

protest the revival of the Lord Lieutenant's claim at the bidding of the censor, because he was a political personage and what would sooner or later form into a political censorship could not be lightly accepted. The play was produced without hindrance.

2 Although she does not refer to the moving picture, Ella Young in her autobiography mentions some of these disturbances and attributes them to a poltergeist who had accompanied her from Dublin.

227

1 Coutances, on the Cotentin peninsula in Normandy, is known for its thirteenth-century cathedral.

2 Maunsel & Co Ltd was the recently established Irish publishing firm; George Roberts was its managing director.

228

1 Pet name for Seán meaning curly-headed puppy (French *bichon*, a lap-dog with silky hair).

229

1 *The Player Queen*, which WBY read to Mrs Campbell in Nov 1909. See *YANB*, 175.

2 Yeats entertained his friends on Monday evenings at Woburn Buildings 'from eight until two or three in the morning'. See John Maesfield, *Some Memoirs of W. B. Yeats* (1940).

230

1 Sir Herbert Beerbohm Tree (1853–1917), English actor-manager (half-brother of Max Beerbohm), who ran the Haymarket Theatre (1887–97) and, with the success of Du Maurier's *Trilby*, built His Majesty's Theatre (rivalling there Irving's Shakespearean productions at the Lyceum). On 26 Nov 1909 WBY wrote to Lady Gregory: 'I have just written to Mrs Campbell refusing to consider Tree in writing my play. His ideal of beauty is thrice vomited flesh' (*L*(W), 539).

231

1 Miss Horniman asked WBY and Lady Gregory to buy her interest in the Abbey Theatre for £1428.

2 Presumably James Richard Wallace.

1910

232

1 *Chantecler*, by Edmund Rostand (1868–1918), French dramatist and author of *Cyrano de Bergerac* (1897) and *L'Aiglon* (1900), was a verse play (first performed in 1910) in which the characters were animals. Yeats did not go to Paris at this time.

2 Probably 'King and No King', written 7 Dec 1909. See *YP*, 186.

234

1 The rivers Seine, Yonne and Marne had overflowed their banks, causing great damage. MG described Paris to John Quinn as 'a wrecked city'.

2 Dormitory.

3 Synge's *Deirdre of the Sorrows* was produced at the Abbey Theatre in 1910 and later in London in the summer. The title role in the first production was taken by Synge's fiancée, Molly Allgood.

235

1 Probably *Celtic Wonder Tales* and the unidentified publication.

2 The Gaelic League was founded by Douglas Hyde in 1893; he was the first president and resigned in 1915 when the League became politicised.

WBY 5

1 MG's cousin May.

2 (Esmé Stuart) Lennox Robinson (1886–1958), an Irish dramatist, was appointed manager of the Abbey Theatre in 1910; he was a director from 1923 to 1956.

3 WBY's *The King's Threshold*.

4 Presumably the Pilgrim Players, a group founded and directed by John Drinkwater (1882–1937), the dramatist, poet, critic and actor. They eventually became the Birmingham Repertory Theatre. See *LTWBY*, 225, where Drinkwater discusses plans to bring the company to Dublin.

5 Sir Hugh Lane (1875–1915), a nephew of Lady Gregory, later founder of the Dublin Municipal Gallery, had been a successful dealer in pictures, and was to leave his collection of French Impressionists to Dublin. For an account of the controversy this caused, see *YANC*, 105–14.

6 Lady Warde (CBE 1950) was the wife of John Roberts O'Brien Warde TD, of Squerryes Court, Kent. Born Millicent Anne Cook, she was the daughter of

Ralph Montague Cook of Roydon Hall in Kent and descended from Edwin Adolphus Cook, MG's maternal great-uncle.

7 Yeats had stopped Synge's family destroying manuscripts of which they disapproved; he wrote prefaces to Synge's work, praising it generously.

8 Presumably *The Player Queen*.

9 Possibly these include 'The Fascination of What's Difficult' (*YP*, 188), written between Sept 1909 and March 1910.

10 James Richard Wallace.

237

1 Suzanne Foccart.

238

1 Possibly 'His Dream', published 1908 (*YP*, 183).

239

1 Miss May, who ran the hotel, was a member of Inghínidhe and an old friend of MG from the time when she was active in that part of Mayo in 1897–9.

2 Jack Butler Yeats and his wife Mary (née White, called 'Cottie' from her second name, Cottenham).

3 Produced by the Cuala Press, which was run by WBY's sister Lollie Yeats; it succeeded the Dun Emer Press.

240

1 Possibly Sarojini Naidu, née Chattopadhyaya (1879–1949), Indian poet and feminist, educated at Madras, London and Cambridge. She wrote verse from 1905 to 1917. The first woman to be chairman of the National Congress in India (1925), she became governor of the United Provinces in 1947. As leader of the women's movement in India, she did much to remove the barrier of purdah.

2 Vinayak Damodar Savakar (1883–1966), from a middle-class Brahmin family, formed a secret society to free India and in 1910 was extradited to India from London, where he had studied law. He escaped from the ship near Marseille but was brought back and tried in India. He was transported and spent ten years in the Andaman Islands until 1921, was released from gaol in India in 1924, and campaigned for social reform. In 1937 he became president of the Hindu Mahasabha Session.

3 Political asylum.

4 See WBY, *M*, 249, and *Essays and Introduction* (1961), 340. See also *L(W)*, 666, where he mentions having read Henry

Adams, *Mont St-Michel and Chartres* (1858).

5 George Pollexfen (1839–1910); WBY had told MG he was dying.

241

1 MG seems to have confused the months.

2 Probably from *The Green Helmet and Other Poems* (1910). This volume was not published until Dec 1910, so WBY may have sent MG manuscripts or proofs of the first eight poems. However, since her letter of 10 Oct prompted an erratum slip, the book was probably set and printed by then, so he may have sent her an advance copy of the book.

3 MG was quite right. The first eight poems from *The Green Helmet and Other Poems* (1910) were grouped under the general title 'Raymond Lully and his Wife Pernella'. Lully (c. 1232–1315) was a Spanish theologian and philosopher. He led a dissolute life but became an ascetic from 1266, devoting himself to a crusade to convert the Muslims. He was stoned to death in Bugia in Algeria. An erratum slip pointed out that WBY had put Raymond Lully's name by a slip of the pen 'in the room of the later alchemist Nicholas Flamel'. Nicholas Flamel (1330–1418), of the University of Paris, with his wife Pernella, was said to have found the Philosopher's Stone and thereby discovered the secret of transmuting base metal into gold. This was supposedly the source of their wealth, which they kept secret, living modestly but spending their fortune on works of mercy and charity.

4 The bow is a sexual symbol in WBY as in Blake. In their edition of *The Works of William Blake* (1893) WBY and Ellis commented that the bow had sexual symbolism, the arrow was desire, the spear was male potency and the chariot of fire was joy. See WBY's poems 'The Arrow' (*YP*, 129) and 'No Second Troy' (*YP*, 185), where MG's beauty is like 'a tightened bow'.

5 Joris Karl (Georges Charles) Huysmans (1848–1907), a French novelist of Dutch origin. His *A Rebours* (1884), with its hero Des Esseintes, is anti-naturalist and anti-bourgeois. *La Cathédrale* (1898) analyses the religious symbolism in the art of Chartres Cathedral.

243

1 WBY described the funeral service in 'In Memory of Alfred Pollexfen' (*YP*, 259).

See also *L(W)*, 553–4.

2 A rail strike had threatened to spread to a general strike, but on 10 Oct the troops were called in and the railwaymen resumed work on 18 Oct.

1911

246

1 Elizabeth Gonne (1836–1922), MG's aunt, married Henry Browning.

2 The 1906 Act granting free meals for schoolchildren, which covered the rest of the UK, was extended to Ireland in an Act of Sept 1914 as a result of the campaign carried out by Inghínidhe and their friends. During those years MG wrote articles on the subject, including ones in *Bean na hÉireann* and the *Irish Review*, and held a large public meeting in the Mansion House in Nov 1912 calling on the Dublin Corporation and the MPs to have the Act extended without waiting for Home Rule. The corporation agreed to strike a rate for the purpose but was advised it could not proceed without legislation from Westminster. Hanna Sheehy Skeffington drafted the bill and MG presented it to Stephen Gwynn MP.

247

1 There is no record of MG being proposed as a member for the United Arts Club (founded in 1907), or of any loyal demonstrations by the club for the royal visit. Mrs Duncan was the honorary secretary and the Markiewiczes were founder and active members. Mr Duncan was a civil servant and a Unionist. Countess Markiewicz and Helen Moloney were arrested for their part in the Sinn Féin protest against the royal visit on 8 July. It would appear that something of what MG surmises in her letter was making Mrs Duncan regret her invitation to her to become a member, either because of MG's reputation in anti-monarch demonstrations or because she was separated from her husband (an ostracisable matter in those days).

2 Constance Gore-Booth (1868–1927), of Lissadell House, Sligo, in 1900 married Casimir Dunin de Markiewicz, a fellow art student and Polish landlord. They settled in Dublin in 1903. She entered politics through Inghínidhe na hÉireann, which she joined early in 1908. She designed the title page of *Bean na hÉireann* (first published Nov 1908) and was one of its chief contributors. She

became an executive member of both Inghínidhe and Sinn Féin and took charge of the Inghínidhe boys' classes from which grew her nationalist boys' organisation, Fianna Éireann, which she formed with the help of Bulmer Hobson and Helen Moloney. While she spent her money helping the poor, her first political action against poverty was with the Inghínidhe school meals campaign. She organised soup kitchens during the 1913 strike and joined Connolly's Citizen Army. In 1914 she started Cumann na mBan (Women's Organisation) from the Inghínidhe, and it grew rapidly. As one of the leaders of the 1916 rising she was sentenced to death, but reprieved and released in 1917. Rearrested in 1918, she was the first woman to be elected to Westminster, but with the rest of the Sinn Féin candidates did not take her seat. She was a member of the Sinn Féin government, opposed the 1921 treaty, supported de Valera and was re-elected to the Dáil in 1927, the year she died. She suffered many imprisonments during her political career.

3   A post-coronation royal visit to Ireland took place between 7 and 12 July. King George V and Queen Mary crossed to Ireland in the royal yacht and attended various functions in Dublin.

250

1   WBY had gone to Paris 'for a rest as I know so few people in Paris I would not find it distracting' (*L(W)*, 538). Lady Gregory and friends of hers were there, and WBY visited Ezra Pound.

2   Pius X encouraged early and frequent communion for young children. Seán had received his first communion in Passy on 11 March. Through a fortuitous meeting at the convent where they were staying, the family were invited to attend the Pope's private mass at a time when he was not giving public audiences because of ill health.

3   Charles Eyre was the son of an old family friend; he was the romantic young man who had proposed to MG in the Colosseum by moonlight (see *ASQ*, 27, 29).

251

1   WBY went to the USA on 13 Sept with the Abbey players and returned on 23 Oct.

2   Possibly 'The Dream', 'No Second Troy', 'Words', 'Peace' and 'Against

Unworthy Praise'.

3   A fourth version of WBY's *The Countess Cathleen* was published in 1912, and he was presumably working on it at this period.

4   Michael Gonne (1898–1918) was the younger son of May's eldest brother, Henry. He joined the Royal Flying Corps and was killed in Aug 1918.

5   The Sacred Heart was a decorative design for a hanging with a border motif of roses and vines, the centre in shades of cerise. Its theme was the Trinity – bread and chalice, the Son of Man crowned with thorns, his heart flowing into the chalice, the dove of the Spirit and above all the golden sun of God.

6   Brutus was a large black dog, part of whose function was to guard Seán from any kidnap attempt.

252

1   The French poet and dramatist Edmond Rostand.

2   André Antoine (1858–1943) greatly influenced French drama as an actor, manager and founder of the Théâtre Libre (1887); he was director of the Odéon from 1906.

253

1   It is not clear exactly what year MG took rooms with Ella Young, who had rented a large old house, called Temple Hill, with a big garden, between Rathgar and Kimmage. It had a ghost, and an underground passage where she hid guns for the Irish Volunteers. MG took rooms there and moved in her furniture which had been in Coulson Avenue. This and the following two letters give an idea of WBY's and her communication and activity while both in Dublin, and demonstrate the rapidity of the post at that time.

1912

257

1   'The Meditations of St Brigid' were highly decorative and symbolic pieces showing Brigid in her different roles, (such as Brigid of the Gaels), with a pictorial insert in each of her meditations on the life of Christ, the Annunciation, the Nativity, and so on.

2   The house at 13 Rue de Passy was not demolished and still stands, with MG's studio, behind the tall buildings on the street.

3 The third version of *The Countess Cathleen* appeared in *Poems* (1895), the fourth was published in 1912. A simplified ending had been adopted for the Abbey Theatre's production on 4 Dec 1911. See WBY's long note in the 1927 edition of *Poems* (1895).

4 René Piot (1869–1934) was a French painter who studied under Gustave Moreau. Jacques Rouché, director of the Théâtre des Arts, invited him on many occasions to design settings and costumes.

5 The French critic Maurice Bourgeois published his Sorbonne thesis as *John Millington Synge and the Irish Theatre* (1913). He also wrote on Henri Bergson.

6 Henri Bergson (1859–1941), the French philosopher, brother of Moina MacGregor Mathers, became a professor at the Collège de France in 1900 and won the Nobel Prize in 1927. He believed that 'l'élan vital', a vital creative impulse, is the basis of evolution. See his *Essai sur les Données Immédiates de la Conscience* (1889), translated as *Time and Free Will* (1910), and his *L'Evolution Créatrice* (1907).

7 The *agrégation* is the examination for a teaching post.

8 WBY first met Synge 'in the autumn of 1896' when they were both staying at the Hôtel Corneille in Paris. WBY had visited Inismaan and Inismor with Arthur Symons in the summer of 1896, and advised Synge (who had studied Irish at Trinity College, Dublin) to go to the Irish-speaking Aran islands and find 'a life that had never been expressed in literature' (*A*, 343). Synge knew of the islands already, his uncle, the Rev. Alexander Synge, having been Protestant incumbent there in 1851.

258

1 Possibly 'The Cold Heaven' or 'Fallen Majesty' (*YP*, 227 and 226).

2 The Abbey Theatre Company players touring in the USA were arrested on 18 Jan but acquitted on 22 Jan, having been successfully defended by John Quinn.

259

1 George Bernard Shaw's play *John Bull's Other Island* was first staged in 1904, its object 'to teach Irish people the value of an Englishman as well as to show the Englishman his own obscenities'. The Abbey did not perform it but Granville Barker staged it as his second play at the

Court Theatre, London. The 'Home Rule edition' was published in 1912.

2 Edward Gordon Craig (1872–1966), English stage designer, son of the actress Ellen Terry. An actor with Sir Henry Irving until 1897, he met Isadora Duncan in 1905 and travelled in Europe with her. He settled in Italy, published *The Mask*, a quarterly (1908–29), and greatly influenced theatre design in Europe and America. He designed screens for use in the Abbey Theatre; WBY appreciated his scenery's simplicity as 'a new and distinctive art'.

260

1 Lady Gregory had stood up to Irish Americans who had attacked Synge. The presence of Theodore Roosevelt on 29 Nov at her *The Gaol Gate* and Synge's *Playboy* in New York helped the success of the tour, despite the company's being arrested in Philadelphia. Lady Gregory, who lectured at various places during the tour, was in the USA from 29 Sept 1911 to March 1912.

261

1 After WBY's first youthful (and terrifying) experience of a séance in Dublin (*A*, 103–5), he did not attend one until 1900. After 1911 his interest in spiritualism increased in intensity.

2 The American writer Agnes Tobin, whom MG had met at Arthur Symons's in May 1909.

264

1 The Christian Trinity (exemplified by the Shamrock), Sophia (wisdom) and the four treasures of the Tuatha dé Danaan (cauldron, spear, sword and stone) are all symbols of wholeness.

2 Jean Malyé was author of *La Littérature Irlandaise* (1913), based on a series of articles in *Entretiens Idéalistes* entitled 'La Renaissance Celtique en Irlande', 25 Dec 1910, 25 March, 25 April and 25 May 1911. WBY asked Bullen to sell Malyé (then a Sorbonne candidate with a thesis on WBY) a set of the *Collected Works* at cost price. Malyé's book deals with WBY on pp. 53–70.

3 Possibly the leader in *Sinn Féin*, 24 Aug 1912, concerning the promise of the Ulster Unionists to enter into a covenant to resist, by force if necessary, any attempt to include the north-eastern counties in a Home Rule Bill.

266

1 Probably Romain Rolland (1866–1944), who in 1910 became Professor of Music at the Sorbonne and published *Beethoven*, the first of many biographical works. *Jean-Christophe*, a ten-volume novel, was written between 1904 and 1912. He was awarded the Nobel Prize for Literature in 1915. There is a drawing of him by Granié in the Lyon Museum.

2 Sir Rabindranath Tagore (1861–1941), an Indian poet and philosopher, received the Nobel Prize for Literature in 1913. He was knighted in 1915 (and resigned this honour as a protest against British policy in the Punjab). He wrote a novel and dramas. In 1907 he founded a communal school to blend Eastern and Western systems; in 1931 he wrote *The Religions of Man*. WBY was introduced to him by Sir William Rothenstein.

267

1 Possibly an advance copy of Tagore's *Gitanjali* (1913), or else a book illustrated by his nephew Abanindranath Tagore.

2 (Olive Alice) Moireen Fox was English, the daughter of Henry Fox (of the Earl of Ranfurly's family), but decided to learn Irish and become Irish. She was apparently clairvoyant, and published some poetry. She lived at Temple Hill with Ella Young and married Claude Chavasse in 1917.

269

1 One of Yeats's Sligo cousins who had second sight and with whom he shared or invoked visions when he was staying with George Pollexfen.

1913

270

1 WBY wrote an Introduction to Tagore's *Gitanjali* (1913).

2 Lady Gregory was in the USA with the Abbey players from Sept 1911 to March 1912 and from Dec 1912 to May 1913; the second company stayed in Dublin.

3 WBY's play *The Hour Glass*, first produced in a prose version on 14 March 1903, was reprinted in 1904 and in 1911 after a new production undertaken with Gordon Craig. A new version in verse and prose was staged at the Abbey Theatre on 21 Nov 1912, published in *The Mask* in April 1913 and revised for another version, included in *Responsibilities: Poems and a Play* (1914).

271

1 Mabel Beardsley (1871–1916), sister of the artist Aubrey Beardsley, was dying of cancer. See WBY's 'Upon a Dying Lady', seven poems written between Jan 1912 and July 1914 (*YP*, 261–3). See *L*(W), 574–7). The cousin referred to was probably Henry Gonne, who made prints of some of MG's work, including a portrait of Seán when he was about four.

2 Possibly the poems which were to appear in *Poems Written in Discouragement*, published Dec 1913.

272

1 Craig founded a theatre school in Florence in 1913. WBY thought of joining it, but Craig thought he could learn nothing there: 'What you've learnt you've learnt already – and how much you have learnt about the theatre is positively appalling.'

2 Kathleen's daughter Thora Pilcher (1892–1983) and Iseult were close friends all their lives.

273

1 Georges d'Esparbès (Thomas Auguste Esparbès; 1863–1944) was a French author of historical works, keeper of the château of Fontainebleau and one of the French guests to go to Ballina in 1898. His *Le Briseur de Fers* was an account of Humbert's invasion of Ireland which he dedicated to Arthur Lynch, 'poet and soldier, condemned to death for treason'. He inscribed the book: 'To a woman who is more than a woman, who is a nation! I offer this book that she inspired in me, her enthusiastic admirer, Palais de Fontainebleau, 28 March 1913.' This was one of a number of books she had inspired.

2 Christoph Willibald Gluck (1714–87) the Austro-German composer born in Bavaria, worked in Prague, Vienna, Milan, London and Paris. His *Orphée* (1774) was a revised version in French of his earlier *Orfeo* (1762), a landmark in modern musical drama.

3 Isaac Merritt Singer (1811–75), American inventor of, *inter alia*, the single-thread chain-stitch sewing-machine. The Singer referred to here is presumably a descendant of his.

274

1 Mademoiselle Claire de Pratz was a journalist, a friend of Oscar Wilde, and a contributor to *Petite Parisienne* and *Daily News*.

2 Tagore's play *The Post Office*, translated by Devabrata Mukerjee, was staged at the Abbey Theatre on 17 May 1913, directed by Lennox Robinson. It was published by the Cuala Press in 1914.

3 Lord Dunsany (Edward John Moreton Drax Plunkett, 18th Baron; 1878–1957), who lived at Dunsany Castle, Co. Meath, wrote short stories (he was the creator of Jorkins), novels and plays.

4 James Stephens (1882–1950) wrote poetry and short stories; his main work was *The Crock of Gold* (1912). He was registrar of the National Gallery of Ireland, lived in Paris for a time and became a successful broadcaster.

5 WBY's interest in the Chair of English Literature at Trinity College, Dublin, was renewed when Dowden, the holder, died on 4 April 1913. See letters 222, 224 and 225.

276

1 This letter may refer to WBY's 'period of trouble'; see letter WBY 6. However, the date of this letter is uncertain.

277

1 Devabrata Mukerjee (Mukhopadhyaya), an Indian who had studied in Calcutta, Exeter and Cambridge, was applying for a professorship in India having given up the idea of a career at the Bar. He translated Tagore's play *The Post Office*.

2 Walter Morse Rummel (1887–1953) was an American composer and pianist, the grandson of Samuel Morse (the inventor of the Morse code); his father Franz Rummel (1853–1901) was a distinguished German pianist. He had met the Shakespears by 1911 (when he shared a house with Ezra Pound in London).

WBY 6

1 WBY's mistress Mabel Dickinson had sent him a telegram when he was at Coole, saying she was pregnant. This was not true and they had a violent quarrel at the Victoria and Albert Museum on 6 June 1913; a truce was patched up but WBY was greatly shaken by the episode.

2 The automatic writing of Elizabeth Radcliffe (whom he met in the spring of 1912) was studied closely by WBY at Daisy Meadow near Brasted in Kent, a house belonging to Olivia Shakespear's friend Mrs Eva Fowler. In this automatic writing she had prophesied the trouble between WBY and Mabel Dickinson.

3 A reference, possibly, to the death of a London policeman, Thomas Emerson, who committed suicide in 1850. WBY made enquiries about him at Scotland Yard via political contacts.

4 Florence Farr (Mrs Emery) had gone to live in Ceylon in 1912.

5 Florence Nightingale (1820–1910), the English hospital reformer.

278

1 Arrens is a village near the thermal resort of Argelès-Gazost, 32 km from Lourdes, in the Pyrénées.

2 Iseult was in London and WBY introduced her to many of his friends, including Tagore.

279

1 Sir Hugh Lane offered to give his collection of French paintings to Dublin if they were properly housed. See WBY's 'To a Wealthy Man who Promised a Second Subscription to the Dublin Municipal Gallery if it were Proved the People Wanted Pictures', 'September 1913', 'Paudeen', and 'To a Shade' (*YP*, 208–12).

2 Antonio Mancini (1852–1930) was an Italian artist who painted WBY (see *Collected Works*) and Lady Gregory. WBY's portrait is in the Municipal Gallery, Dublin. See 'The Municipal Gallery Revisited' (*YP*, 438).

280

1 Many Protestant families affected to find Rathmines vulgar, but Rathgar, about a mile further from the city centre, more desirable. WBY had greatly disliked living in Ashford Terrace, Harold's Cross, nearer to Terenure Cross Roads than Rathgar Cross Roads! Temple Hill was a large house in Rathgar, on Terenure Road.

281

1 This may refer to *The Player Queen*, which was not finished before Sept 1914, or *The Hour Glass*, which WBY was revising at this time.

2 This refers to the Dublin lock-out, masterminded by William Martin Murphy, who led a cartel of the main Dublin employers.

3 William Martin Murphy (1844–1919) was proprietor of the *Irish Independent*

and the *Evening Herald*. WBY described him as 'an old foul mouth' in 'To a Shade' (*YP*, 212). WBY thought the lock-out was inhumane and an unprincipled attempt to stir up sectarian passion. He wrote a letter in *The Irish Worker*, 1 Nov 1913, to this effect. George Russell supported the Irish Transport and General Workers' Trade Union in their struggle with the employers, who had locked out about 24,000 workers in nearly five months. He and WBY, whose relations had been strained since 1907, restored their friendship after WBY's letter to *The Irish Worker*.

282
1 WBY was renting Stone Cottage at Coleman's Hatch in Sussex.
2 William Joseph Walsh (1841–1921), Catholic Archbishop of Dublin (1885–1921), supported the Land League, Parnell and the Parliamentary Party.
3 Ezra Pound (1885–1972), the American poet, was acting as WBY's secretary at Stone Cottage from Nov 1913. His *Cantos* first appeared in 1913.

283
1 MG covered the lock-out, poverty in Dublin and Home Rule in these lectures and interviews.
2 Patrick Pearse (1879–1916), writer, orator and a member of the Irish Bar, joined the Gaelic League in 1895 and edited its paper. Having advanced educational ideas, in 1908 he founded St Enda's, a bilingual school, which later moved to larger premises at the Hermitage in Rathfarnham, Co. Dublin. He joined the IRB in 1913, was co-opted to its Supreme Council and elected to the Provisional Committee of the Volunteers. He delivered a historic oration at the grave of O'Donovan Rossa in 1915. In 1916 he was commander-in-chief of the forces and president of the Provisional Republican Government, which he proclaimed. Court-martialled, he was executed on 3 May 1916. His fund-raising tour in 1913 was for St Enda's and the Irish Volunteers.
3 John Devoy (1842–1928), born in Co. Kildare, masterminded Fenian infiltration of the British army in 1862. Arrested in 1866, he was released on condition he went into exile. In the USA he became influential in Clann na Gael, and later opposed Lyman and the New Movement. He edited *The Gaelic American*

from 1910 until his death and assisted nationalists in many ways, including support for the *United Irishman* and St Enda's school.
4 J. B. Pond, manager of Pond's Lyceum Bureau, had organised WBY's lecture tours. He organised the tour in the USA that WBY began in Jan 1914.
5 John F. Taylor (1850–1903), an Irish barrister, journalist, orator and nationalist whose influence on MG was resented by WBY. The two men had quarrelled over the new Irish Library. MG counted him among her close friends. Taylor acted for her in her successful libel action against Colles of the *Figaro* in 1900.
6 Probably Sydney Gifford (1889–1974), a journalist who took the pen name of John Brennan. She was a member of Inghínidhe, contributed to *Sinn Féin*, *Bean na hÉireann* and other nationalist journals, was on the Sinn Féin executive (1910 and 1911) and in Cumann na mBan. While in America she married Czira, a Hungarian émigré. On her return at the end of the war she continued to be active in politics and journalism. Two of her sisters, Muriel and Grace, were married to MacDonagh and Plunkett respectively, both executed in 1916.
7 Irish for churls or louts.
8 MG mentions this society in a few letters (eg 277, 312). It may have been a society she was involved in with Ella Young, possibly Moireen Fox and other friends, but nothing is known about it.

284
1 Possibly *Duty*, by Seumas O'Brien, produced at the Abbey Theatre.

285
1 *Eugénie Grandet* (1833), the novel by Honoré de Balzac (1799–1850). WBY's father used to tell his children stories from Balzac; WBY had read two of his novels by 1886, and in 1905 bought the 40-volume edition, of which he had read nearly all by Oct 1909. For his effect on WBY, see Warwick Gould, 'A Crowded Theatre: Yeats and Balzac' in *Yeats the European* (1989).

All Changed, Changed Utterly 1914–1918

1914

286

1   A. F. Lugné-Poe (1870–1940), a French actor born in the USA, was founder (1892) and manager of the Théâtre de l'Oeuvre in Paris. He conducted tours for many actors and actresses, including Eleonora Duse and Isadora Duncan. He had produced Alfred Jarry's *Ubu Roi* in 1896, a performance WBY attended with Arthur Symons which prompted his remark 'After us the Savage God' (*A*, 348–9).

2   Synge's *The Playboy of the Western World.*

3   Jean Malyé translated WBY's *Cathleen ni Houlihan.*

4   Snapdragon is a game usually played at Christmas, in which the players try to snatch raisins out of a bowl of burning brandy and eat them when alight. In this case it may have been some kind of dipping game for presents.

287

1   Part of George Moore's *Vale*, the last volume of his trilogy *Hail and Farewell* (1911–14), his autobiographical and mischievous account of his stay in Dublin from 1901 to 1911, appeared in *The English Review* in Jan and Feb 1914. In these extracts he attacked Lady Gregory and WBY, regarding Yeats's work as finished and his love of MG as 'the common mistake of a boy'. The article provoked WBY. See the 'Introductory Rhymes' of *Responsibilities*, an account of his forebears, and the 'Closing Rhymes' of that volume, published on 7 Feb 1914 in the *New Stateman*. WBY's final retort came after Moore's death in *Dramatis Personae* (1935), where he gave a sharply malicious picture of Moore.

2   George Moore moved from Dublin to a house in Belgravia, 121 Ebury Street, where he lived until his death in 1933.

288

1   Because of the implicit accusation that she was a proselytiser, a 'souper', Moore skilfully altered the passage in question in *Vale*. (See 1947 edition, 122–31, 145–7.)

289

1   *Our Irish Theatre* (1914).

2   *Cathleen ni Houlihan* was first per-

formed by the dramatic group formed by Inghínidhe na hÉireann, directed by William Fay.

3   'Introductory Rhymes' *YP*, 197. See *YANC*, 99–102.

4   *Cuchulain of Muirthemne* (1902) and *Gods and Fighting Men* (1904), which retold the stories in the Ulster and Fenian Cycles.

294

1   Christiane Cherfils was a friend of Iseult and presumably the daughter of Christian Cherfils, a writer whose works included *Un Essai de religion scientifique* (1898) and *Mimes et Ballets Grecs* (1908).

2   *The Gardener*, translated by Tagore himself, was published by Macmillan in 1913.

3   André Gide (1869–1951) published a translation of *Gitanjali* in 1914. Gide was the author of over fifty books, fiction, poems, plays, criticism, biography, belles-lettres and translations. He was awarded the Nobel Prize for Literature in 1947.

4   Possibly Henri-Durand Davray (1873–1944), on the staff of the *Mercure de France* for many years, translated Wilde, Wells and WBY, who, with Arthur Symons, took hashish with him in Dec 1896.

5   A graphic artist and wife of Joseph Granié.

295

1   James Stephens was awarded the Polignac Prize (the gift of the Princess Edmond de Polignac) for *The Crock of Gold* in 1914.

296

1   John Quinn wrote to WBY on 9 Feb 1914 to say Dorothy Coates, who had been very ill – almost at the point of death – for months, had written to him expressing the hope that he and WBY would be friends again. He offered to 'shake hands with you and let by-gones be by-gones'.

2   Christiane Cherfils.

297

1   *La Croix*, founded by Le Père Vincent de Paul Bailly (1832–1912).

2   Feilding wrote to WBY on 10 July to say the Lister Institute had reported that an extract from the handkerchief gave no precipitate with anti-human serum, 'which therefore excluded the possibility

of its being human blood'. In Rome, Abbé Vachère was able to refute many of the charges against him, and Feilding never believed he had perpetrated a conscious fraud.

3 George Alexander Redford (d. 1916) was Examiner of Plays, 1895–1911. The Abbey was having a London season at the Court Theatre that June.

298
MS Yeats, from *LTWBY*.
1 Presumably *Responsibilities*, published on 28 May 1914.

299
MS Yeats, from *LTWBY*.
1 Abanindranath Tagore (1871–1951), Indian artist and author, whose grandfather was a distinguished portrait and landscape painter, was a nephew of Rabindranath Tagore. He gained an international reputation; his early works were exhibited in Paris and London in 1913 and in Tokyo in 1919. He held various academic positions.
2 Bhikaji Cama (1861–1936), from a wealthy Parsee family in Bombay, moved from social work to revolutionary activity. She smuggled arms and revolutionary literature into India, had her headquarters in Paris from 1909, was imprisoned in France in 1915–18, and was refused entry to India, returning there in 1935.
3 James D. Anderson, then lecturer in Bengali at the University of Cambridge.
4 Feilding had asked MG to visit Mirebeau again, to get further samples of the blood.
5 The conference called at Buckingham Palace on 21 July 1914 by King George V discussed fruitlessly with maps and figures areas of Ulster to be excluded from the Home Rule Bill; it failed to negotiate the political impasse. The King's speech was written by himself or one of his close aides, not by Asquith. It urged compromise and settlement, emphasising the threat of civil war. The breakdown was announced on 24 July, two days before the Howth gun-running. On 3 Aug Redmond eased Asquith's dilemma by pledging Ireland's support for the war.
6 Herbert Henry Asquith, 1st Earl of Oxford and Asquith (1852–1928), was Prime Minister from 1908–1915. When the First World War broke out he decided to postpone Home Rule, though

the bill had been passed in May 1914.
7 Helen Moloney acted in two Abbey Theatre productions in 1915.

300
MS Yeats, from *LTWBY*.
1 Redmond had forced Asquith into putting the Home Rule Bill through Parliament. In Sept the Government of Ireland Act (1914) went on the statute books with two provisos, that it would come into operation not until after the war and not without proper provision for amending legislation for the exclusion of Ulster. MG had hoped for more, and many believed that the Home Rule Act would never come into operation.
2 Bal Gangadhar Tilak (1856–1920) controlled two newspapers, *Kesari* and *Mahratta*, served eighteen months for sedition (1897–8), was transported to Mandalay (1908–14), campaigned for Home Rule for India and set up the Congress Party in 1920. Known as 'the father of Indian independence', he wrote *The Age of the Vedas* and *The Origin of the Aryans*.

301
MS Yeats, from *LTWBY*.
1 René Viviani (1862–1925), French statesman, was Prime Minister at the outbreak of war and withdrew French forces from the German frontier to demonstrate France's peaceful intentions.
2 A reference to 'the Bulgarian atrocities' committed by the Turks against the Bulgars in the Sanjak of Philippopolis who had joined a revolt of Bosnia and the Herzegovinians against the Turks.
3 The Franco-Prussian War.
4 Kathleen Pilcher's son.

302
MS Yeats from *LTWBY*.
1 Presumably a reference to Tagore's translation of *The Gardener*, 1913.

303
MS Yeats, from *LTWBY*.
1 Count Paul Vassili, the pseudonym of Princess Radziwill, who had published her memoirs, *France from Behind the Veil: Fifty Years of Social and Political Life* (1914), gave an account of MG's visit to Russia. In her book *My Recollections* (1904) she recounts how she met MG and 'through an introduction which I procured for her, the documents were handed over to M. Pobedonostev, the

Procurator of the Holy Synod, and by him put under the eyes of Alexander III'. See *ASQ*, 77–84.

2 Count Petr Andreyevich Shuvalov (1827–89), Russian diplomat, head of Russian secret police and Russian Ambassador in Berlin (1885–94).

3 William Thomas Stead (1849–1912), English journalist, editor of the *Pall Mall Gazette* (1883–9) and founder of the *Review of Reviews*, was drowned on the *Titanic* in 1912. MG had met him in St Petersburg and he called her 'one of the most beautiful women in the world' (*Review of Reviews*, Jan 1892).

4 Olga Novikoff was a well-known Russian journalist, the author of *Russia and England* (1880), who lived in England for many years. MG met her in Russia.

5 Possibly 'The Fisherman' (*YP*, 251), written on 4 June 1914; eleven lines of it, headed 'subject for a poem', were written between 18 and 25 March 1913 in the MG manuscript book.

304

1 The Free Meals Act was passed in Sept 1914.

2 The school set up by Patrick Pearse.

1915

305

1 Captain J. R. White (1879–1947) was the son of Field Marshal Sir George Stuart White (1835–1912) of Broughshane, Co. Antrim, who relieved Ladysmith during the Boer War and whose sister was Francis Stuart's maternal grandmother. Captain White was a member of the Ulster Protestant Home Rule movement with Roger Casement in opposition to the Ulster Volunteers. In Nov 1913 he was drilling Connolly's Citizen Army.

306

1 WBY's *Reveries over Childhood and Youth*, the first volume of his autobiography, was published 20 March 1916. Presumably WBY had discussed with her *The Trembling of the Veil*, part of which was published by Werner Laurie in 1922; this second section of his autobiography began in 1887 and ended in 1891.

2 Jozef Maria Wronski (1778–1853), a Polish mathematician and Kantian philosopher who devised his own system of philosophy which he termed 'messianism'.

3 WBY was staying with Ezra and Dorothy Pound at Stone Cottage in Jan and Feb 1915. Ezra had married Olivia Shakespear's only child Dorothy (1886–1973) on 20 April 1914.

307

1 Possibly Gerald Doyle, an actor in Dublin.

2 Alderman Tom Kelly, active member of Sinn Féin, vice-president from 1910 and a Dublin town councillor. He was a member of the Citizen Protection Committee at the Battle of the Rotunda.

3 The Irish Agricultural Organisation Society, founded by Sir Horace Plunkett in 1894. George Russell was an official of the society, and edited its journal, *The Irish Homestead*, from 1905 to 1923. He edited the *Irish Statesman* (1923–30).

4 Possibly 'The People', written on 10 Jan 1915. See *YP*, 254.

5 James Stephens's *Songs from the Clay* (1915).

308

1 Lane drowned when the *Lusitania* was torpedoed by a German submarine; he gave his lifebelt to a woman passenger.

2 On 29 April the Chancellor had proposed increased taxation on spirits, wine and beer to combat drunkenness among munitions workers. As this was a serious threat to the Irish drink trade, the Irish Parliamentary Party had worked hard to have the proposals dropped, and had succeeded in this by 7 May. A delegation of the Irish MPs were on a visit to Paris from 30 April to 2 May to convey their sympathy and support to France in the war and were entertained by the President and legislature, returning to vote on the division in the House on the drinks trade (*FJ*, 29 April–8 May).

3 T. P. O'Connor (1848–1929), an Irish journalist, was elected MP for Galway in 1880, MP for Liverpool in 1885. Living for a long time in England, he was regarded by nationalists as very much to the right of a party they felt was in any case too biased towards the establishment.

4 WBY's autobiography.

309

1 *Abrutissant* is French for 'brutalising', 'stupefying'.

2 Sir Hugh Lane left his collection of pictures 'in momentary irritation' to the National Gallery in London in a new will made in 1913 after his plans for a gallery

in Dublin had been rejected. He subsequently became director of the National Gallery in Dublin and in Feb 1915 wrote a codicil to his will, bequeathing the pictures to Dublin. This codicil, however, was not witnessed, and the Trustees of the National Gallery in London stood on their legal right to reclaim the pictures. From 1916 on, WBY and Lady Gregory fought a campaign to have the pictures in Dublin. See letter to the *Observer*, 21 Jan 1917, and the numerous references in Lady Gregory's *Journals* to their efforts. In 1959 an agreement was reached; the pictures are now shared on a loan basis between London and Dublin.

310

1 Robert Gregory joined the 4th Connaught Rangers in 1915, then transferred to the Royal Flying Corps in 1916. He became Chevalier of the Légion d'Honneur in 1917 and was awarded a Military Cross that year for conspicuous gallantry and devotion to duty. He was shot down in error by an Italian pilot on the Italian front on 23 Jan 1918.

2 Lucien Millevoye's only son, Henri, was killed in battle on 30 Sept or 1 Oct 1915. He was married but had no children. Lucien (1850–1918) came from a wealthy family, was the grandson of the poet, Charles-Hubert Millevoye, a magistrate, and respectably married. He became a member of the House of Deputies in 1889 as a representative of the National Party and was editor of *La Patrie* from 1891 until his death. The loss of Alsace-Lorraine to Germany after the Franco-Prussian war in 1870 was a burning question with him, as was his dislike of England, responsible for the defeat of Napoleon; this was the political basis of his alliance with MG, whom he first met when General Boulanger was in ascendance. By that time he was a politician, publicist, orator, a specialist in foreign affairs interested in a Franco-Russian alliance, and had been to Russia for General Boulanger. He was chairman of the French army's committee on aviation. He died on 25 March 1918.

3 Iseult's father, Millevoye, probably procured her a job in the aviation society.

311

1 The French writer Romain Rolland.

312

1 The letter (313) dated 7 Nov.

2 Possibly produced by the mystical society MG refers to in letter 282.

3 According to *The Times*, 8 Nov 1915, some of the crew of the *Saxonia* refused to sail from Liverpool to the USA with Irish passengers. The Cunard line sent notices to its agents that the company could not accept the bookings of British subjects who were fit for military service. This occurred at the height of Lord Derby's recruiting campaign and about 650 Irishmen were refused passage; 200 were, however, carried from Glasgow by the Anchor Line. *The Times* reported that about 500 Irishmen a week were arriving in Liverpool en route to the USA.

4 Edward Henry Carson (1854–1935), an MP from 1892 to 1921, was Solicitor-General for Ireland (1892) and for England (1900–6), Attorney-General (1915) and a member of the War Cabinet (1917–18). He became 1st Lord of the Admiralty in 1917. Having been admitted to the English Bar in 1894, he had been retained by the Marquis of Queensberry in 1895 in the action against Oscar Wilde. Violently opposed to Home Rule, in 1912 he organised the Ulster Volunteers. In the Battle of the Somme in July 1916, 5500 of the 36th Ulster Division, most of them recruits from Carson's Ulster Volunteers, were killed or wounded in the worst single day of the war; this provoked a complete stoppage of work in Belfast on 12 July. Of the 40,000–50,000 Irishmen who died in the war, about half were from Unionist Ulster.

5 Possibly some of the poems relating to MG published in *The Wild Swans at Coole* (1917). Those written in 1915, up to and including Nov, include 'Her Praise', 'The People', 'His Phoenix', 'A Thought from Propertius', 'Broken Dreams', 'A Deep-sworn Vow' and 'Presences' (*YP*, 253-8).

315

1 A simple design of trinities. The reference to shamrock is a joke. WBY had attacked the banal patriotic use of shamrocks and other stock symbols of Irish nationalism, 'the harps and the pepper pots'.

316

1 On 8 Nov 1915 Lord Loreburn said: 'It is no exaggeration to say that if this

conflict goes on indefinitely, revolution and anarchy may well follow; unless the collective common sense of mankind prevents it before the worst comes great portions of the Continent of Europe will be little better than a wilderness peopled by old men and women and children.' He spelt out what a war of attrition meant. Lord Courtney of Penwith said: 'Two great lines of military array have been drawn up against one another, of each of which it may probably be said that it is unconquered and unconquerable.' He raised the question 'whether there is not an alternative to this unceasing strife' (*The Parliamentary Debates*, 5th series, XX: *The House of Lords* (1916), 185–6 and 195).

317

1 *The Player Queen* was almost finished in 1914 but worked on again in May 1916 and revised in 1917.

2 Presumably the second volume of Yeats's autobiography, *Four Years 1887-1891*, included in *The Trembling of the Veil* (1922).

318

1 WBY's *Reveries over Childhood and Youth* (1916).

1916

319

1 Edward Dowden (1843-1913), Professor of English Literature at Trinity College, Dublin, from 1867, a friend of John Butler Yeats. He opposed Home Rule and did not support the Irish Literary Revival, for which WBY attacked him. He achieved an international reputation with his critical and biographical studies, notably *Shakespere: A Critical Study of his Mind and Art* (1875) and his *Life of Shelley* (1886). For WBY's comments on Dowden, see *A*, 85–9.

2 An attack on Fitzgibbon, the Lord Chancellor (see *A*, 96–7). Joyce quotes a different version of it in *Ulysses* (see *A*, 234 ff.).

3 Bealtaine was the Irish May festival.

4 WBY was to stay with MG in Normandy in July and Aug 1916.

320

1 James Joyce's *A Portrait of the Artist as a Young Man* (1916).

2 Francis Sheehy Skeffington (1878–1916) was an Irish journalist, reformer, femin-ist, and pacifist, editor of *The Nationist* and *The Irish Citizen*. He resigned from the Irish Citizen Army when it became militarised, was imprisoned in 1914–15 for opposing recruitment, but released after a six-day hunger strike. He supported the third Home Rule Bill. During the 1916 Rising he was arrested while trying to restrain looting and was shot out of hand with two journalists by Captain Bowen-Colthurst, who was later tried and found guilty of murder while insane.

3 WBY was staying with the Pounds at Stone Cottage, Coleman's Hatch, from Jan to March 1916.

4 According to Joseph Hone, *W. B. Yeats 1865-1939* (1942), 293, Pound 'procured that Yeats, Moore and Edmund Gosse should separately make representations to Asquith, and these resulted in a royal bounty of £100 being granted to an almost entirely unpublished author.' WBY wrote to Edmund Gosse on 6 July to suggest Joyce, living in penury in Zürich, should get a grant from the Royal Literary Fund. On 8 July he wrote again to Gosse about Joyce's work, then on 29 July wrote formally to the secretary of the Royal Literary Fund, stating his conviction that Joyce 'is the most remarkable new talent in Ireland today'; to Gosse on 21 Aug he wrote that he believed Joyce was 'a man of genius'. Joyce was awarded £75 by the Royal Literary Fund and WBY wrote on 28 Aug to Gosse to thank him for what he had done.

5 William Thomas Horton (1846-1919), an Irvingite whose mystic drawings appeared in *The Savoy* and in his *A Book of Images* (1896) with an introduction by WBY. See G. M. Harper, *Yeats and Horton: The Record of an Occult Friendship* (1980), and *The Making of Yeats's 'A Vision'*, II, 316 and 344. Horton appears in 'All Souls' Night' (*YP*), where Yeats alludes to his platonic love affair. See WBY *A Vision* (*A*), x, and *L*(W), 250–1.

6 Audrey Locke (1881–1916). Horton saw her as an apparition after her death. WBY wrote to Horton after Audrey Locke's death: 'the dead are not far from us ... they cling in some strange way to what is most deep and still in us.'

7 Ballylee Castle, near Gort, Co. Galway, which WBY bought for £35 in April 1917.

8 The controversy over Lane's pictures.

321

1 WBY had recently written *At the Hawk's Well*. See his note in *CP* on 'Meditations in Time of Civil War': 'I have a ring with a hawk and butterfly upon it, to symbolise the straight road of logic, and so of mechanism, and the crooked road of intuition; "For wisdom is a butterfly and not a gloomy bird of Prey".'

2 *At the Hawk's Well*, the first of WBY's new-style *Plays for Dancers*, was performed in London in Lady Cunard's drawing room, 1916.

322

1 The loss of the ship *Sussex* was reported in *The Times*, 6 April 1916. Later it was acknowledged that the ship had been sunk by a U-boat, the commander of which was reprimanded after an inquiry.

323

1 *Responsibilities and Other Poems* (1916). WBY's 'sister's printing' was the Cuala Press edition, *Responsibilities: Poems and Plays* (1914).

2 Augustine Birrell (1850–1933), politician and author, MP for Fife (1889–1900) and Bristol (1906–18), was Minister for Education (1906) and Secretary for Ireland (1907–16). He resigned after the Easter Rising.

3 Sir Roger Casement (1864–1916), a British Consular official (1895-1913), joined the Irish Volunteers in 1913, went to Germany to seek armed aid for Ireland in 1914, and returned to Ireland in a German U-boat. Arrested in south-west Ireland, he was tried on a charge of high treason in London and hanged on 3 Aug 1916. See Brian Inglis, *Roger Casement* (1973).

324

1 Cf. WBY's 'Easter 1916' (*YP*, 288):

Was it needless death after all?
For England may keep faith
For all that is done and said.

2 Casement's diaries were circulated at the time of his trial to suggest that he was a 'degenerate', a homosexual. See WBY's poems, 'Roger Casement' (*YP*, 423) and 'The Ghost of Roger Casement' (*YP*, 424), and notes, *YP*, 635–6.

3 The handwriting is unclear, and it is possible that the name should be Hindenburg. Paul von Hindenburg (1847–1934), a German officer who retired in 1911, was recommissioned as Commander in Chief with Ludendorff in 1914. Later Field Marshal and Chief of the General Staff (1916–19), he was president of the German Republic from 1925 to his death.

325

1 The *Helga*, a gunboat, as well as land-based artillery, shelled the centre of Dublin, occupied by rebel forces in the Rising.

326

1 *The Times*, 8 May 1916, referred briefly to John MacBride's execution the previous day and continued: 'John Mac-Bride was the famous "major" who fought in the Irish Brigade on the side of the Boers. . . . He married Miss Maud Gonne, but for some years they have lived apart and the woman is believed to be at present in France. It is recalled that on the occasion of Queen Victoria's last visit to Dublin, Miss Maud Gonne organised a procession of slum children and led them through the streets singing the songs then popular among the disloyal section.' The piece concludes with a reference to MacBride's career as a water board official.

327

1 After twelve of the insurgent leaders had been shot, Shaw stated: 'the men who were shot in cold blood, after their capture or surrender, were prisoners of war.' He published letters in the *Manchester Guardian* and the *Daily News* urging a reprieve for Casement in July 1916.

2 Patrick Pearse, chosen as President of the Provisional Republican Government during the Easter Rising, was taken prisoner, court-martialled and shot. His *Collected Works* were published in 1917, his Irish writings in *Scribini* (1919). The poems he wrote in gaol were 'To My Mother', 'To My Brother' and 'A Mother Speaks'.

3 The last words spoken by Cathleen in WBY's play *Cathleen ni Houlihan* (1902). They repeat part of a song she sings earlier, which begins, 'Do not make a great keening'.

4 A letter to the editor headed 'Mr Dillon and Sinn Féin', *The Times*, 16 May 1916, by John Pentland Mahaffy (1839–1919), provost of Trinity College, Dublin, 1914–19. His writings included histories

of ancient Greece and Rome as well as *The Art of Conversation* (1887). He held strong Unionist views, expressed in a subsequent letter, 'Facts to be Faced', *The Times*, 27 June 1916, which proclaimed that, owing to 'miserable misgovernment and the outbreak of a savage insurrection', Ireland was 'less fit for a sudden settlement than it ever was for the last 150 years'.

WBY 7

1 Presumably Lennox Robinson.
2 John Edward Healy (1872–1934), a barrister, edited the Dublin *Daily Express* and was appointed editor of the *Irish Times* in 1907.
3 MG's cousin May Bertie-Clay.
4 The Hon. Mrs Henry Weyland Chetwynd (Julia Bosville), who wrote novels from 1868 on.
5 William Frederick Bailey (1847–1917), Irish jurist and man of letters, Irish Land Commissioner, and Governor of the National Gallery of Ireland.
6 Henry de Vere Stackpole (1863–1951), an Irish popular novelist, known for *The Blue Lagoon* (1909) and *The Pearl Fishers* (1915).
7 The officer who shot Skeffington was Captain John Bowen-Colthurst (1880–1965) of Dripsey Castle, Co. Cork. He served in South Africa (1900–2), suffered shell shock in the First World War, retired in 1916 and was later found to be insane. He went to live in Canada.

328

1 WBY introduced Iseult to various fashionable friends in London, notably Lady Cunard, who said: 'never in my life have I seen such a complexion.' He wrote to Lady Gregory that he thought Iseult 'looked very distinguished' and was 'full of self-possession'.

329

1 Edward Thomas O'Dwyer (1842–1917), Catholic bishop of Limerick (1886–1917), was the first member of the Catholic hierarchy to defend the rebels of 1916. Hostile to land agitation and the Plan of Campaign, he had refused to sign Archbishop Walsh's condemnation of Parnell on 3 Dec 1890.
2 General Sir John Maxwell (1859–1929) was Commander in Chief in Ireland in 1916. After the Rising and the court-martials he was removed from Ireland by Lloyd George, to become Commander

in Chief, Northern Command (1916-19).
3 The play was probably *At the Hawk's Well*, staged in London in Lady Cunard's drawing room on 4 April 1916 and some days later in Lady Islington's at Chesterfield Gardens, London.

330

1 *At the Hawk's Well*.

331

1 Possibly J. M. Kerrigan (1885–1964), an Abbey actor.
2 Four monks from the Franciscan Capuchin Friary of Church Street, Dublin, attended the condemned men. Father Augustine, who was with John MacBride when he was shot, reported that he requested not to have his hands tied or be blindfolded; on orders, the soldiers had to refuse both requests. MacBride turned and said, 'You know, Father Augustine, I've often looked down their guns before.'

332

1 Madame Péguy was the widow of Charles Pierre Péguy (1873–1914), French neo-Catholic poet and nationalist, who was killed in action. His works include *Le Mystère de la Charité de Jeanne D'Arc* (1909), *L'Argent* (1912), *La Tapisserie de Notre-Dame* (1913) and *Eve* (1914).
2 Evelyn Underhill (1875–1941), who married H. S. Moore in 1907, was an English poet, novelist and writer on mysticism. MG is probably alluding to her *Mysticism* (1911).

333

1 'Easter 1916' (*YP*, 287). Yeats seems to have sent MG a copy of 'Easter 1916' when he had it finished. It was first printed in an edition of 25 copies in 1917.
2 See 'Easter 1916':

> Too long a sacrifice
> Can make a stone of the heart. . . .
> MacDonagh and MacBride
> And Connolly and Pearse . . .
> Are changed, changed utterly.

Thomas MacDonagh (1878–1916) was a poet, dramatist and critic. He helped Pearse to found St Enda's, taught literature at University College, Dublin, joined the Volunteers in 1913 and the IRB in 1915.
3 A removal: in view of her plan to return to Ireland, MG had given up her apart-

ment and was living in the attic of 17 Rue de l'Annonciation where her furniture was being stored.

4 Ballylee Castle, Co. Galway, which Yeats bought in April 1917.

334

1 Trepov, a former army officer and right-wing politician, previously Minister of Communications, was appointed Prime Minister by Ukase on 24 Nov 1916 and formed a new Russian cabinet.

335

1 The first interned Irish prisoners were released on 22-23 Dec 1916.
2 The letter from WBY in the *Observer*, 21 Jan 1917, sums up the arguments put forward in other letters he wrote between 1916–17 about Sir Hugh Lane's will, its codicil and his intentions about the ultimate location of his French pictures. See *L*(W), 616–23.
3 WBY wrote in a Preface to *The Hawk's Well*, *Harpers Bazaar*, March 1917, that the masks 'forced upon us by the absence of any special lighting or by the nearness of the audience who surround the players on three sides, do not seem to us eccentric'. The masks, suggested by Japanese Noh drama, helped the stylisation of character; Gordon Craig had advocated their use in his magazine *The Mask*.
4 Possibly Hugh Law, author of *Anglo-Irish Literature* (1926).
5 William Frederick Bailey.

1917

336

1 Frongoch in Wales, an internment camp.
2 Possibly Wilfrid Meynell (1852–1948), author and journalist, who co-edited several periodicals with his wife Alice Meynell, née Thompson (1847–1922), the English essayist and poet.
3 Rudolf Steiner (1861–1925), Austrian social philosopher, the founder of anthroposophy (knowledge of the nature and wisdom of men). He thought myth-making faculties had been divorced from practical life; his educational principles have been the basis of many Steiner schools in Europe and the USA.

337

1 Claude Albert Chavasse (1885–1971), whose family were of French origin, was born in Oxford, where his father was a don at Balliol. Being interested in every-

thing Gaelic, after graduating he went to stay with a distant cousin, Henry Chavasse, in Co. Waterford about 1912. He wore kilts, taught Irish and would speak only Irish or French. He and Moireen Fox were married in Dublin in 1917. The book referred to here is probably a long poem *Liadain and Curithir* (1917) written by Moireen Fox.
2 Possibly a customs or coastguard hut.

338

1 George Russell's *The National Being, Some Thoughts on Irish Polity by AE*.

1918

WBY 8

1 *Distributive Justice: The Rights and Wrongs of our Present Distribution of Wealth* (1916), by (Father) John Augustus Ryan (1869–1945).
2 WBY restored Ballylee Castle as a summer residence. See *YANB*, 219. He and his wife were staying in Ballinamantane House to supervise the work; Lady Gregory had lent it to them.
3 During the period of the second 'spiritual marriage'.
4 Given by Thomas Francis O'Rahilly (1883–1953), who became Professor of Irish at Trinity College, Dublin (1919–29), and then Research Professor at the National University of Ireland (1929–40). He founded and edited *Gadelica*, and worked extensively on the Irish language.
5 A lecture by Fr Thomas Aloysius Finlay (1848–1946), the first editor of the *Irish Homestead*. He was Professor of Political Economy at University College, Dublin, and wrote several novels.
6 WBY had been introduced to the French Catholic poets Claudel, Jammes and Péguy by Iseult Gonne in Normandy in the summer of 1916. Paul Claudel (1868–1955) was a diplomat, poet and dramatist.

340

1 This attempt by the British government to defuse opposition to conscription and to discredit Sinn Féin worked against the authorities in the long run, as it won sympathy votes for the prisoners in the ensuing by-elections and general election in Dec 1918.
2 Countess Markiewicz had been released from Ayleword Prison in June 1917 and had a triumphal return to Dublin; with de Valera still in prison, she was the only

surviving leader of 1916. While in Hollo-way she was elected MP, and made Minister for Labour in 1st Dáil Éireann (1919–21). She was released in March 1919.

3 Kathleen Clarke (1878–1972), the niece of the Treason Felony prisoner John Daly of Limerick, married Tom Clarke, his fellow prisoner, in New York in 1901. On their return from America in 1908 they continued their political activi-ties. Her uncle died in 1916, and her husband and brother Edward had been executed in 1916. Immediately after the Rising she set up the Volunteers' Depen-dent Fund, which joined with the Irish National Aid Association; together they gathered £107,069 for aid not only for widows and orphans but for the returned jobless prisoners. Elected to the Sinn Féin executive in 1917, she was a city councillor, and on the executive of the White Cross. She was released from Holloway in Feb 1919, and as member of the Dáil took part in the treaty debates, chaired a Dáil negotiation committee attempting reconciliation and finally took the anti-treaty side. She was on the Fianna Fáil executive, became a senator in 1927 for ten years, and was the first woman Lord Mayor of Dublin in 1939.

WBY 9

1 Iris Barry, a friend of Iseult.
2 Clongowes Wood College, at Clon-gowes Abbey, Co. Kildare, is a Jesuit school.
3 Castleknock College is a school run by the Vincentian Order at Castleknock, beyond the Phoenix Park near the river Liffey.
4 Mount St Benedict, a school near Gorey, Co. Wexford, was founded by Fr John Sweetman, a Benedictine, with a loan of £5000 from his cousin John Sweetman, one of the founders of Sinn Féin. It was closed in 1925 through opposition from both church and state. Victor Collins, John MacBride's friend, was teaching there at this time but had left by 1919, when Seán spent a few terms at the school preparing for matriculation, in the company of the sons of other well-known nationalists. Fr Sweetman also grew tobacco and made excellent cher-oots.
5 Ezra Pound.

WBY 10

1 The Rt Hon. Edward Shortt (1862–1935) was MP for West Newcastle (1910–22), Chief Secretary for Ireland (1918–19) and Home Secretary (1919–22).
2 Stephen Lucius Gwynn (1864–1950), literary journalist, novelist and bio-grapher, was Nationalist MP for Galway (1906–18).
3 Mary Barry Delaney had followed the family from France and was in Dublin looking after MG's affairs. The lease was signed on 7 Oct 1918.
4 WBY's wife George (née Bertha Georgie Hyde Lees; 1892–1968) had influenza, then pneumonia, and was pregnant at the time. They moved to 45 Broad Street, Oxford, early in 1918 (but were in Ireland from March). From Oct 1919 they lived at 4 Broad Street, a house now demolished; they let it from spring to autumn 1921 and left it in March 1922, when they purchased 82 Merrion Square, Dublin.

341

1 Dr Francis Whittaker Tunnicliffe MD (d. 1928) was physician of King's College Hospital, London, and Professor of Pharmacology, King's College, London. In his first report on MG, dated 22 Oct, he stated that he had examined her on 21 Oct in Holloway prison and that she was suffering from 'a recrudescence of her former pulmonary tuberculosis' and required suitable medical treatment and climate 'without delay'.
2 Joseph King (1860–1943), MP for North Somerset (1910–18), wrote various books and pamphlets sympathetic to the Irish nationalist cause. On a fact-finding mis-sion, he was with MG when she was arrested and was active in helping while she was in prison.
3 George Cave, 1st Viscount Cave (1856–1928), MP (1906–18), Solicitor-General (1915–16), Home Secretary (1916–19) and Lord of Appeal (1919–22).
4 Peamount Sanitorium, in Newcastle, Co. Dublin, specialised in the treatment of tuberculosis.
5 Josephine Pillon (1865–1927), from Nor-mandy, accompanied the family when they left France, living with them in London and Dublin, at St Stephen's Green, where she acted as cook, and finally at Roebuck House.

Face to Face We Stood 1920–1938

1920

342

1 From the time of her return to Ireland, MG abandoned the Gonne crest on her notepaper, using ordinary printed letter-heads.

2 The Yeatses had a green parrot in a cage on the landing of their house in Oxford, 4 Broad Street.

3 Henry Francis Stuart (b. 29 April 1902). His father was Henry Irwin Stuart and his mother Elizabeth Montgomery, of Benvarden, Dervock, Co. Antrim. Born in Australia, he was reared near Coleraine in the North of Ireland, went to various English preparatory schools and Rugby (1916–18). He married Iseult in April 1920 and commenced his writing career as a poet. In 1924 he won a Royal Irish Academy Award for *We Have Kept the Faith* (1923). After the bombardment of the Four Courts in Dublin he joined the IRA and was arrested in Aug 1922, spending six months in Maryborough and nine months in the Curragh internment camp. From poetry he moved to novels. He went to Germany to lecture before the Second World War, not returning to Ireland until 1957. See his *Black List, Section H* (1971) and Geoffrey Elborn, *Francis Stuart: A Life* (1990).

4 The Stuarts, who traced their descent back to the seventeenth century, had an estate near Dervock, Ballyhivistock. They had a family habit of emigrating to Australia, where Francis Stuart's father, Henry Irwin Stuart, committed suicide while in Callan Park Asylum in Sydney on 14 Aug 1902; he had married Elizabeth (known as Lily) Montgomery on 28 Jan 1901 in the parish church at Dervock; her father, Captain R. J. Montgomery, had died of alcoholism.

5 MG had bought a house in Glenmalure, a deep mountain gorge in Co. Wicklow, over 30 miles from Dublin.

6 The United Arts Club in Dublin.

7 WBY's daughter Anne Butler Yeats, born 26 Feb 1919.

8 MG let rooms to Dorothy MacArdle.

343

1 P. William Purser, secretary to the Scottish Widows' Fund Life Assurance Society.

2 The family curse that no daughter of the Gonnes should ever find happiness in marriage was put on a Gonne (who had confiscated church land) by a priest. With the failure of her own, Kathleen's and May's marriages, and now Iseult's, MG felt she had cause to believe in it.

344

1 Ballinagoneen is a two-storeyed house in Glenmalure, Co. Wicklow, the last house in the Glen. It features in Synge's *The Shadow of the Glen* as Baravore, which is a neighbouring townland. MG purchased it in Oct 1919 with 15 acres and mountain grazing rights on 11,800 acres and sold it in 1928. It is now a youth hostel.

2 Cecil ffrench Salkeld (1901–1972) was an Indian-born artist who lived in Ireland from 1908 and studied art at Kassel in Germany. He painted the murals for Davy Byrne's pub, made famous by James Joyce's *Ulysses*. His mother, Blanaid (née Florence ffrench Mullen; 1880–1958), born in Chittagong (Bangladesh) of Irish parents, married an English member of the Indian Civil Service. Widowed at 28, she returned to Ireland with her two sons, and joined the second Abbey Theatre Company (as 'Nell Byrne') and Cumann na mBan. She wrote poetry and verse plays.

3 Janet Montgomery, of Benvarden, Co. Antrim, was a positive, capable woman, who, like her cousin Captain White, had moved from her Northern Unionist background to become a nationalist. For most of her life she farmed successfully in Co. Meath and was always very attached to her nephew's family.

345

1 Dr Bethel Solomons (1885–1965) was Dublin's leading gynaecologist at the time, master of the Rotunda, and vice-president of the British College of Obstetricians and Gynaecologists.

2 Christopher Friery, solicitor, coroner for the city of Dublin and election agent for Redmondite MPs for many years, acted for MG in her libel action against Colles in 1900 and was her solicitor in Ireland until his death, when his nephew, Christopher McGonagle, succeeded him.

346

1 The veronica is 'a veil or handkerchief, on which is impressed the true likeness of the adorable face of Our Lord and Saviour Jesus Christ, miraculously

imprinted, not produced by artificial colours but by the divine power of God the Son made man'. See *Veronica or the Holy Face*, trans. from the French (1870), 5. St Veronica offered her handkerchief to Jesus to wipe his face as he was carrying his cross to Calvary and he returned it to her 'having impressed on it his majestic and venerable image'. Cf. WBY, 'Veronica's Napkin' (*YP*, 353).

2 Stuart's mother Lily's second marriage on 4 July 1913 was to her cousin Henry Clements. An alcoholic, he had been a cowboy in Texas and Mexico. He left her – they had spent a good deal of their time together moving from one rented house to another – to live in the Grosvenor Hotel at Victoria Station for his last years, in company with a maid who came from Portrush, where George Stuart, Francis's uncle, lived. Francis disliked Henry Clements, who tried 'to make a man of him'.

3 Cushendall is one of the nine glens of Co. Antrim.

4 Lennox Robinson, who was in love with Iseult; WBY thought she should marry him. He married Dollie Travers-Smith, grand-daughter of Professor Edward Dowden.

348

1 Lady Ottoline Morrell (1873–1938), the daughter of Lieutenant-General Arthur Bentinck and a half-sister of the Duke of Portland, married Philip Morrell, a Liberal MP. Eccentric in appearance, she entertained many political and literary figures at Bedford Square and later at Garsington Manor, Oxfordshire. She appears in D. H. Lawrence's *Women in Love* and Aldous Huxley's *Chrome Yellow*. Garsington prompted WBY's 'Ancestral Houses', the first poem of 'Meditations in Time of Civil War' (*YP*, 308–9).

350

1 Oliver St John Gogarty removed WBY's tonsils in Dublin in Oct 1920.

2 Lennox Robinson.

3 See *Irish Independent*, 23 Aug 1920.

4 MG is referring to Mirebeau, which she and WBY visited with Everard Feilding in May 1914.

5 See WBY 8, note 1.

351

1 Seán had decided to study law and agriculture; he gave up the latter after

one year. He attended the 1920–1 session at University College, Dublin, but, preoccupied by politics and his arrest, in 1922 he ceased his attempts at study until the 1930s.

2 Constance Markiewicz, who gives a graphic account of this incident in a letter to her sister, Eva, on 10 Oct from Mountjoy Gaol (see Diana Norman, *A Terrible Beauty* (1987), 215). The police stopped the car because of a broken taillight; when no permit was produced and they discovered who was in the car, they phoned for the military. Constance Markiewicz was court-martialled for conspiracy in having formed the Fianna Éireann in 1910 and was given two years' imprisonment in Mountjoy. She was released when the truce was signed in July 1921. Seán and Maurice Bourgeois were released after two days.

3 A Dublin gaol.

352

1 L. Smith Gordon was chairman of the Standing Executive Committee of the Irish White Cross.

2 Martial law was in force.

3 The Black and Tans, recruited in England from demobbed soldiers to reinforce the police in Ireland, arrived in early 1920; they were paid ten shillings a day. They wore a mixture of army and police uniforms, khaki coats and black trousers, so earning their name, derived from a famous pack of foxhounds, the Scarteen Black and Tans. They in turn gave this name to the War of Independence.

355

1 The auxiliary police ('Auxies'), ex-army officers who started arriving in Ireland in the summer of 1920, were recruited in England, paid £1 a day, qualified for no pension, were not under military discipline and were not amenable to trial by civil courts.

2 Mrs Erskine Childers (née Mary Osgood), an American and an invalid, had been on the committee which organised the Howth gun-running in July 1914. Arthur Griffith had asked MG and Mrs Childers, who had worked on relief for the Belgians during the war, to organise aid for the widespread distress in the country. Her husband, Robert Erskine Childers DSO (1870–1922), was an English military historian and theoretician, whose best-known work is *The Riddle of the Sands* (1910). He and his

wife brought arms to Ireland from Germany in his yacht the *Asgard* in July 1914. He was Director of Publicity for the Revolutionary Government (1919-21) and Chief Secretary to the Irish Peace Delegation (1921). He was court-martialled and shot in the Civil War for carrying a gun.

3 The Lord Mayor (1916–23), Laurence O'Neill, convened an anti-conscription meeting on 18 April 1918, formed the White Cross Executive on 1 Feb 1921, and with the Archbishop of Dublin summoned a peace conference in April 1922. He organised women's peace delegations to opposing sides after the shelling of the Four Courts, in June 1922.

4 Mary Teresa Hayden, who had been a member of Inghínidhe, was a suffragist, a colleague of Pearse in the Gaelic League and Professor of Modern Irish History at University College, Dublin. This raid took place on 2 Nov, the day after the execution of a student there, Kevin Barry, and a few days after the funeral of the Lord Mayor of Cork, Terence Mac-Swiney, who had died on a hunger strike of 74 days in England on 25 Oct. These events preceded the worst month of the war.

5 Denis Joseph Coffey, former professor of Physiology at the Catholic University, was president of University College, Dublin, from 1908.

356

1 Dorothy MacArdle (1889–1958), an Irish author, teacher and historian, worked at propaganda during the War of Independence and also for the republican side in the Civil War. In the Second World War she devoted herself to helping refugee children. Her plays included *Atonement* (1918), *Anne Kavanagh* (1922) and *The Old Man* (1925). Her best-known work is *The Irish Republic* (1937; 1968), a history of the period 1916–23.

1921

357

1 Thora Pilcher, who married William Forrester in 1919.

358

1 Probably *Michael Robartes and the Dancer*, published by the Cuala Press in Feb 1921.

2 As the war intensified, the need for relief soon became apparent. Appeals to the Red Cross in Geneva and the British Red Cross had been unsuccessful. Members of the American Red Cross and others formed the American Committee for Relief in Ireland in Dec 1920 and raised $5 million. On 19 Jan 1921 Lord Mayor O'Neill sent an official invitation to MG to act on the executive committee being formed to administer aid. The White Cross was a strictly non-political, non-partisan organisation, with a large executive and management committee which formed various sub-committees. MG served on the publicity and Dublin relief committees, was involved with school meals for children in Dublin and Donegal, and aid for the disabled.

3 Born Edith Ellen (Nelly) Woodmass (*c.* 1868–1942), George's mother married William Gilbert Hyde Lees (*c.* 1865–1909). After his death she married Henry Tudor (Harry) Tucker (1866–1943), brother of Olivia Shakespear.

4 WBY's brother, the artist Jack B. Yeats, and his wife 'Cottie'.

5 Michael Dolan was an Abbey actor.

6 Desmond Fitzgerald (1888–1947), born in London, was one of the Imagist group of poets there. He joined the IRB in 1914, fought in the Post Office in 1916, was sentenced to life imprisonment but released in 1918 and became a Sinn Féin MP. As director of publicity for the Dáil Éireann, he edited the *Bulletin* (1919–21). Arrested in 1921, he then became a Free State Minister for External Affairs (1922-7), Minister for Defence (1927–32) and Senator (1938–43). His play *The Saints* was first staged at the Abbey Theatre on 2 Sept 1919.

7 Kilmainham Gaol, in Dublin near the Phoenix Park, is now a museum.

8 Patrick Harte was tortured in Brandon Military Barracks, Co. Cork, on 27 July 1920.

9 Barnett, on hearing that his friend Whelan had been condemned to be executed, went insane because he feared he had incriminated him under torture.

10 Richmond Lunatic Asylum in Dublin, otherwise known as Grangegorman.

11 Kevin Barry (1902–20), a university student, was caught while taking part in an ambush in Dublin on 20 Sept 1920 in which one soldier was killed and two fatally wounded. His arm was twisted while he was being interrogated in the North Dublin Union (not the Castle) and he wore it in a sling for three weeks. On 1 Nov, after court-martial, he was

hanged, in spite of many pleas for mercy. About 5000 gathered outside the gates of Mountjoy Prison to pray at the time of his execution, with a guard of soldiers and the guns of a double-turreted armoured car trained on them. Scores of his fellow students enrolled in the IRA as a result.

12 At the Oxford Union on 17 Feb 1921 WBY denounced British policy in Ireland, the terror created by the Black and Tans and the auxiliaries. His impassioned speech, saying he did not know which lay heaviest on his heart, the tragedy of Ireland or the tragedy of England, because of the 'horrible things done to ordinary law-abiding people by these maddened men', carried the motion that 'this house would welcome complete self-government in Ireland and condemns reprisals' by 219 votes to 129.

359

1 WBY's 'On a Political Prisoner', written in Jan 1919; it first appeared in *The Dial*, Nov 1920, then in *Michael Robartes and the Dancer* (1921).

2 Six republican prisoners were hanged two at a time on 14 March, a day of public mourning, with a crowd of 20,000 gathering on the streets around Mountjoy Gaol to pray. Whelan and Moran were convicted on unreliable evidence of the assassination of British officers on 21 Nov 1920, when Michael Collins's 'squad' had shot dead 14 British Secret Service agents – from which had flowed further reprisals, including 12 civilians shot at a football match.

360

1 Hamar, 1st Baron of Greenwood, was Under-Secretary for Home Affairs in 1919, Chief Secretary for Ireland in 1920, and defended the Black and Tans in Parliament. Lloyd George arranged the truce of July 1921 over his head. He signed the treaty in 1922 but then resigned.

2 *A Handbook of Rebels*. A Guide to Successful Defiance of the British Government, compiled by Thomas Johnson and published by the Irish Labour Party and Trade Union Congress Dublin (3rd ed.), 1913.

3 Dolores Veronica Stuart was born on 9 March 1921 at 75 St Stephen's Green.

4 The scraps consisted of a torn-off top section of a circular dated 3 March 1921

and two White Cross notices for meetings of the Foreign Collections Subcommittee and the Organisation Subcommittee.

361

MS Berg Collection, New York Public Library.

1 Lady Gregory's play was first produced in the Abbey Theatre on 17 March 1921.

2 Clements J. France was in Ireland from Jan to June 1922 representing the American Committee for Relief in Ireland. The delegation, having toured the country, returned at the end of March, reporting on the damage and the estimated need for help. The Society of Friends played a large part in both this committee and the White Cross.

362

1 Bettystown is a coastal village north of Dublin in Co. Meath where Stuart's mother, Mrs Clements, had rented a bungalow.

2 Charlotte Despard (née French; 1844–1939), a sister of Sir John French, later Earl of Ypres (1852–1925), Lord Lieutenant of Ireland (1918–21). She was a social reformer, advocate of women's rights and a pacifist. She met MG in London in 1917, moved permanently to Ireland in the summer of 1921, living with MG in 73 St Stephen's Green and Roebuck House, worked with the White Cross, was President of the Women's Prisoners' Defence League, supported the Workers' Party of Ireland and went to Russia at the age of 86 in 1929 with the Irish Friends of Russia. In 1933 she moved to Eccles Street, where she founded a Workers' College and housed the Friends of Soviet Russia, then left to live in Belfast in 1934.

363

1 The British Military headquarters in Ireland was stationed on the Curragh, a plain in Co. Kildare, and frequently used as an internment camp for political prisoners.

364

1 The truce was called in July 1921.

2 She kept her stockings on in anticipation of having to get up in the middle of the night if the house was raided.

3 Dolores Stuart died in St Ultan's Children's Hospital on 24 July 1921 and was

buried in Deansgrange Cemetery in Co. Dublin.

4 Lough Dan, Co. Wicklow.

365

1 Michael Butler Yeats was born on 22 Aug 1921 at Thame, Oxfordshire.

2 The visit was in connection with the White Cross School meals campaign. MG arranged for the feeding of 2500 children in Donegal.

1923

WBY 13

1 Joseph McGrath (1887–1966), a member of the IRB who fought in 1916, was elected Sinn Féin MP in 1918; he became Minister of Labour in the Irish Free State (1922), then Minister of Industry and Commerce (1922–4). He resigned in 1924, becoming adviser to Siemens Schuchart for the Shannon (Electricity) Scheme in 1925. In 1930 he founded the Irish Hospitals Sweepstake, and became wealthy.

2 The North Dublin Union (a poorhouse) was being used as a women's prison.

3 Richard Mulcahy (1886–1971), a post office clerk, joined the Irish Volunteers in 1913, fought in 1916 and was interned until 1917. He became IRA chief of staff and general officer commanding the army of the Free State Provisional Government (1922–3). With William Cosgrave and Kevin O'Higgins, he took charge of the Irish Free State government after Michael Collins's death. He was Defence Minister (1923–4), a senator (1943–4), led the Fine Gael Party (1944–59) and was Minister of Education (1948–51 and 1954–7).

1925

WBY 14

1 WBY was pleased with 'The Sorrow of Love' (*YP*, 75), first written in Oct 1891, described in *Early Poems and Stories* (1925) as one of several 'altogether new' poems produced by rewriting. See *The Variorum Edition of the Poems of W. B. Yeats*, ed. Peter Allt and Russell K. Alspach (1957), 119, for the different versions. The 'model' for the girl in the poem was MG.

1926

366

1 MG and Mrs Despard bought Roebuck House in Aug 1922. It was a large house which had extensive grounds, a walled garden and outbuildings which they intended to use to set up industries to assist those in need as a result of the war. They had already successfully operated White Cross workrooms, partly financed by Mrs Despard.

2 J. C. Dowdall (b. 1873) was involved in the creamery industry and industrial developments, particularly in Cork.

3 Mrs Hanna Sheehy Skeffington (1877–1946) was the daughter of Nationalist MP David Sheehy. She and her husband, Francis Sheehy Skeffington, founded the Irish Women's Franchise League in 1908. A close friend of MG, she helped with school feeding, was a militant suffragette and in the independence movement. Arrested in 1918, she was released from Holloway Prison after a short hunger strike. She was a member of the Sinn Féin executive and of Dublin Corporation, a judge in the Dáil courts, and worked with Lord Mayor O'Neill in his peace moves in 1922. She visited Russia in 1929 and founded the Women's Social and Progressive League. In 1943 she stood for Dáil as an Independent. She was refused compensation for her husband's death.

4 Ernest Blythe (1889–1975) was a member of the IRB in 1906, an organiser of the Irish Volunteers in 1914 and was imprisoned in 1916. He was Minister of Finance in the Irish Free State (1922–31) and managing director of the Abbey Theatre (1941–67), having given it state sponsorship when Minister of Finance.

1927

367

1 Josephine Pillon, the old Normandy woman who had accompanied the family to Ireland.

2 The Public Safety Act (1927), introduced after Kevin O'Higgins's death, gave the government power to declare unlawful any association aimed at the overthrow of the state, with severe penalties for membership of such an association, drastic measures of search, and provision for a special court with power to convict and sentence to death or life imprisonment for unlawful possession of firearms. Seán

MacBride, who had been out of the country at the time, was one of many arrested for O'Higgins's murder but was the first to be tried under this Act. An order was first sought for his detention for seven days on 16 Sept. He was held on suspicion and later charged. See 'Attorney General *v* MacBride' in *The Irish Constitution* by J.M. Kelly (Jurist Publishing Co., UCD, Dublin, 1980) for legal implications of this case. The evidence of Major Bryan Cooper, a senator and former Unionist who had travelled from Dublin on the same boat as Seán, eventually procured his release.

368

1 The industry that Mrs Despard had started in 1924 in the yard of the house was home-made jam, Roebuck Jam. It was failing in 1927 when Seán and his wife decided to take it over, and was sold to Donnelly's in 1932. Seán remained involved with the IRA until 1937, taking part in various attempts to form new political parties. He finally completed his legal studies and was called to the Bar in 1937, became a Senior Counsel in 1943, successfully formed a political party, Clann na Poblachta, in 1946, became Minister for External Affairs (1947–51), returned to the Bar in 1951 but was also active in international non-governmental organisations. He was a founder member of Amnesty International in 1961 and later its president, became Secretary-General of the International Commission of Jurists in 1963, UN Commissioner for Namibia (1973–9), and chairman of a Unesco commission on international communications which reported in 1980. He received the Nobel (1974) and Lenin (1977) peace prizes. He died in 1988.

2 Frank Bulfin, the youngest of ten brothers, had been an active member of the United Ireland League, a member of the IRB, and was arrested in 1918. He was elected to the Dáil (1918–27) and voted for the Treaty. He farmed in Co. Offaly.

3 Kevin O'Higgins (1892–1927), elected as Sinn Féin candidate while in prison in 1918, Vice-President and Minister of Justice in the Irish Free State, was assassinated on 10 July 1927 at Booterstown, Co. Dublin, on his way to mass. Believing in strong law and order measures, he defended the shooting of 77 republican prisoners as reprisals. His murder was thought to have been an act

of revenge. See WBY's letter about him to Olivia Shakespear, *L(W)*, 726–7.

4 Around this time there were up to 12,000 republicans in prison for varying periods. Over 400 detainees in Mountjoy Gaol went on mass hunger strike in October 1923, and prisoners in other camps followed suit, but it was called off after about 40 days when two men had died. Most of the detainees were released before Christmas.

5 Catalina (Kid) Bulfin (1900–76), the youngest daughter of William Bulfin, was born in the Argentine, where her father had emigrated in the early 1880s. He married Annie O'Rourke in 1891, eventually becoming owner-editor of the *Southern Cross*, an Irish Argentine paper, in which he espoused the cause of nationalism and the Gaelic League. His articles for Irish emigrants in the Argentine about his bicycle rides on holidays in Ireland were published in the *Southern Cross*, in the *United Irishman* (1902) and eventually in book form as *Rambles in Éireann* (1907). Around 1904 he brought his family home to the farm of Derrinlough outside Birr. In 1909 he made a tour of the USA with The O'Rahilly for Sinn Féin. He died early in 1910.

Like her brother and sister, Catalina became involved in nationalist affairs and worked with Austin Stack in the Department of Home Affairs. After the truce she worked with him in the Provisional Government's office of Home Affairs until the Civil War, when she carried dispatches for the Republicans. She was interned in the round-up of 1923 and later worked with Seán MacBride for the IRA. They were married on 26 Jan 1926. After they took over the management of Roebuck Jam in 1927, she kept the business going while Seán was on the run or in prison. Similarly, when the factory was sold in 1932 and an Irish Sweepstake agency was taken on, it was Catalina again who ran it, visiting the USA to secure her contacts in the late 1930s.

6 Brunswick Street in Dublin, where Patrick Pearse was born and lived, is now called Pearse Street. It runs from College Street to Grand Canal Quay. Seán was a member of B Company of the 3rd Battalion of the IRA which operated in this area.

WBY 15

1 William T. Cosgrave (1880–1966) was first president of Dáil Éireann (1922–32),

previously a Sinn Féin MP, then a member of Dáil Éireann from 1922 to 1944.
2 Gladstone's Home Rule Bill was defeated in 1886; his Second Home Rule Bill was passed by the Commons but rejected by the Lords in 1893.
3 See Warwick Gould, 'A Crowded Theatre: Yeats and Balzac', in *Yeats the European*, ed. Jeffares (1989), 69–90.

369
1 The Women's Prisoners' Defence League was founded after the Four Courts bombardment in 1922 'for the help, comfort and release of political prisoners' – a mild way of saying they were militant watchdogs for injustice and a considerable thorn in the side of the repressive Cosgrave government. Every Sunday morning they held meetings on the corner of O'Connell Street and what is now Cathal Brugha Street, then known as the 'ruins corner' because of the devastation from 1916. They organised placard marches, demonstrations and hunger strikes outside prisons. The WPDL remained active for nearly two decades.
2 Liam Mellows (1892–1922) joined the IRB in 1912 and was a founding member of the Irish Volunteers in 1913. Deported to England, he fought in 1916 and escaped to the USA, where he worked on *The Gaelic American*. He opposed the 1921 treaty, was a member of the garrison in the Four Courts, was arrested in Sept 1922 and executed on 8 Dec 1922.
3 John Redmond.

WBY 16
1 WBY's poem 'In Memory of Eva Gore-Booth and Con Markiewicz' (*YP*, 347) is set at Lissadell, Co. Sligo, where Yeats stayed in the winter of 1894–5. Eva Gore-Booth (1870–1926) wrote poetry and was committed to social work.
2 From WBY's poem 'Paudeen' (*YP*, 211).
3 MG was anti-Dreyfusard through the influence of Millevoye.

WBY 17
1 Plotinus (?205–70), one of the first Neoplatonic philosophers, was probably born in Rome in 244. Porphyry, his pupil, arranged his fifty-four groups in six groups of nine books, called the *Eneads*.
2 St Lidwina of Schiedam (1380–1453), later known as Lidwin or Liedwig, was a fasting saint devoted to healing others. WBY probably heard of her from Arthur

Symons; J. K. Huysmans, *Sainte Lydwine of Schiedam* (5th edn, 1901), was translated by Agnes Hastings and published in 1933. He may also have read of her in Claudel's writings. See WBY, *A*, 330–1.

WBY 18
1 See WBY's poem 'Demon and Beast', written in Nov 1918 (*YP*, 293). He probably got the idea from the *Lausiac History of Palladius*, trans. W. K. Lowther Clark in 1918 (Palladius was sent 'in Scotiam' (into Ireland) by Pope Celestine in AD 430). Yeats also learned about Egyptian monasticism from Flaubert's *La Tentation de Saint Antoine* (1874) as well as J. O. Hannay's *The Spirit and Origin of Christian Monasticism* (1903) and *The Wisdom of the Desert* (1904).
2 James Lynch Fitz-Stephen (or Fitz-Stephen Lynch) was reputedly a fifteenth-century Mayor of Galway who is said personally to have tried and executed a son who had stabbed a Spanish widow.
3 Johannes Eckhart (*c.* 1260–1327), Dominican provincial in Saxony, preached from 1312 at Strasbourg, Frankfurt and Cologne (where he was arraigned for heresy by the archbishop in 1325). He taught a mystic pantheism. After his death his writings were condemned by Pope John XXII.

372
1 In *The Spirit and Origin of Christian Monasticism* (1903) and *The Wisdom of the Desert* (1904) J. O. Hannay listed the Mareotic seas as one of the five regions where Egyptian monasticism flourished.
2 Either the Rt Hon. Sir Thomas O'Shaughnessy KC, a bencher of the King's Inn, Dublin, called to the Bar in 1870 and Recorder of Dublin (a minor judicial position now abolished), who lived at 64 Fitzwilliam Square, Dublin; or his son Sir Thomas Lopdell O'Shaughnessy, called to the Bar in 1904, who lived at 62 Dartmouth Square, Dublin.
3 Presumably John O'Byrne (d. 1954), a High Court judge, who was admitted to the Inner Bar in 1924 and lived at Ballyboden, Co. Dublin.
4 *Dublin Opinion* was a humorous magazine, largely of cartoons, started in 1922.

WBY 19

1 The Abbé Vachère at Mirebeau, whose oleograph, which apparently bled miraculously, was investigated in May 1914 by Everard Feilding, WBY and MG.

1928

WBY 21

1 WBY's poem 'Among School Children' (*YP*, 323) was written in June 1926 and included in *The Tower* (1928). WBY alludes to MG's youthful 'Ledaean body', contrasting it with 'her present image'.

373

1 WBY's *The Tower*, published Feb 1928.
2 Roebuck Shell Flowers was MG's industry which she started some time after moving to Roebuck, and which employed a few girls. She designed the flowers herself and made many of them. She records that she got the idea from seeing an ancient shell necklace from a pre-Christian tomb in the National Museum. The industry produced a great variety of floral arrangements and sold them to cinemas, hotels, at the Royal Dublin Society Shows and to private buyers. When she sold the little business in the mid-thirties she recovered her initial expenditure.

WBY 22

1 Moina MacGregor, widow of MacGregor Mathers.
2 From 1924 the Stuarts were living at Glencree, Co. Wicklow, and with Cecil Salkeld produced a literary magazine, *Tomorrow*. Around 1927 MG helped them to buy a converted 1798 barracks called Laragh Castle, near Glendalough. Iseult lived there for the rest of her life with her two children and her mother-in-law, Lily Clements, studying comparative religions, reading and writing, but never published anything. She died on 22 March 1954.

WBY 23

1 WBY's edition with Edwin Ellis of *The Works of William Blake, Poetic, Symbolic and Critical* (1893). WBY did inscribe

MG's copy and it was sold at Sotheby's.
2 The Yeatses looked for an apartment in Rapallo in Feb 1928; in Nov they took rooms in the Via Americhe 12–8 there; they disposed of this flat in the summer of 1934.
3 The Director of Ballet at the Abbey Theatre at that time was Ninette de Valois, stage name of Edris Stannis (b. 1898 in Co. Wicklow), who founded the Sadler's Wells Ballet School in 1931 and became artistic director of the company.

1929–1938

WBY 26

This letter describes a PEN club dinner (at which Lion Feuchtwanger was also a guest). Mrs Dawson Scott, in the chair, praising the work of centres in India, Cairo and Germany, regretted that Germany had had to be expelled from PEN (in 1933). See Marjorie Watts, *Mrs Sappho: a Life of C.A. Dawson Scott, Mother of International PEN* (1987), 191.

WBY 27

1 Jammet's was an exclusive French restaurant in Nassau Street, Dublin.

WBY 29

1 MG was writing her autobiography, *A Servant of the Queen*, published by Gollancz in 1938.
2 Helen Wills Moody, the tennis champion, called on WBY at Riversdale with Oliver St John Gogarty but the poet had cut himself shaving and she apparently did not meet him on that occasion. See Oliver St John Gogarty, *William Butler Yeats: A Memoir* (1963), 17.
3 Edith Shackleton Heald (1884/5–1976), 'the last of Yeats's loves', lived originally with her sister, later for thirty-five years with the artist Gluck (Hannah Gluckstein; 1895–1978) at the Chantry House, Steyning, Sussex.
4 Lady Gerald Wellesley was a minor English poet.
5 MG had put this letter, with WBY's letter after the death of William Sharp, in an envelope marked 'last letter of WBY'.

Bibliography

Alexander, Tania. *An Estonian Childhood*. Cape, 1987.

Boylan, Patricia. *All Cultivated People*. Colin Smythe, 1988.

Brennan, John. *The Years Flew By*. Gifford & Craven, 1974.

Burke, M. *John O'Leary: A Study in Irish Separatism*. Anvil Books, 1967.

Cardozo, Nancy. *Maud Gonne: Lucky Eyes and a High Heart*. Gollancz, 1978.

Clarke, Kathleen. *Revolutionary Woman: Kathleen Clarke 1878–1972*. O'Brien Press, 1991.

Cobban, Alfred. *A History of Modern France*. vol. 3: *1871–1962*. Penguin, 1965.

Davis, Richard. *Arthur Griffith and Non-Violent Sinn Fein*. Anvil, 1974.

Denson, A. *Letters from AE*. Abelard-Schuman, 1961.

Elborn, Geoffrey. *Francis Stuart: A Life*. Raven Arts Press, 1990.

Ellmann, Richard. *W. B. Yeats: The Man and the Masks*. 1948; Allen Lane, 1988.

Finneran, R. J., Harper, G. M., and Murphy, W. M. (eds). *Letters to W. B. Yeats*, 2 vols. Macmillan, 1977.

Foster R. F. *Modern Ireland 1600–1972*. Allen Lane, 1988.

Gonne MacBride, Maud. *A Servant of the Queen*. Gollancz, 1938.

Greaves, Desmond C. *The Life and Times of James Connolly*. Laurence & Wishart, 1961.

Haire, David N. 'In aid of the civil power, 1868–90' in *Ireland under the Union* eds. F. S. L. Lyons and R. A. J. Hawkins. Clarendon Press, 1980.

Harding, James. *The Astonishing Adventures of General Boulanger*. W.H. Allen, 1971.

Hogan, R. and Kilroy, J. *Lost Plays of the Irish Renaissance*. Proscenium Press, 1970.

Hone, Joseph. *W. B. Yeats 1865–1939*. Macmillan, 1942.

Hull, Eleanor. *Folklore of the British Isles*. Methuen, 1928.

Jeffares, A. N. *W. B. Yeats: Man and Poet*. Routledge & Kegan Paul, 1949.
> *W. B. Yeats: A New Biography*. Hutchinson, 1988.
> *Yeats's Poems* (ed.). Macmillan, 1989.

Kelly, John (ed). *The Collected Letters of W. B. Yeats 1865–1895*. Oxford University Press, 1986.

Lee, Emanuel. *To the Bitter End*. Viking, 1985. Penguin, 1986.

Lyons, F. S. L. *Ireland since the Famine*. Fontana/Collins, 1973.

Lyons, J. B. *The Enigma of Tom Kettle*. Glendale Press, 1983.

MacArdle, Dorothy. *The Irish Republic*. Gollancz, 1937.

MacEoin, Uinseann. *Survivors*. Argenta Publications, 1980.

MacLochlainn, Piaras F. *Last Words*. Kilmainham Jail Restoration Society, 1971.

Monick, S. *Shamrock and Springbok*. South African Irish Regimental Association, Johannesburg, 1989.

Moody, T. W. *Davitt and Irish Revolution 1846–82*. Clarendon Press, 1981.

Mulvihill, Margaret. *Charlotte Despard: A Biography*. Pandora, 1989.

Norman, Diana. *A Terrible Beauty*. Hodder & Stoughton, 1987.

O'Broin, Leon. *Fenian Fever: an Anglo American Dilemma*. Chatto and Windus, 1971.
> *Revolutionary Underground: The Story of the Irish Republican Brotherhood 1838–1924*. Gill and Macmillan, 1976.

O'Donnell, Elliot. *The Irish Abroad*. Pitman, 1915.

O'Donovan, Donal. *Kevin Barry and his Time*. Glendale, 1989.

O'Kelly, Michael J. *Newgrange Archaeology, Art and Legend*. Thames & Hudson, 1982.

O'Rahilly, Thomas F. *Early Irish History and Mythology*. Dublin Institute of Advanced Studies, 1946.

Reid, B. L. *The Man from New York*. Oxford University Press, 1968.

Shiel, M. and Roche, D. *A Forgotten Campaign*. Woodford Heritage Group, 1986.

Wade, Allan (ed). *The Letters of W. B. Yeats*. Rupert Hart-Davis, 1954.

Ward, Margaret. *Unmanageable Revolutionaries: Women and Irish Nationalism*. Brandon, 1983.
> *Maud Gonne: Ireland's Joan of Arc*. Pandora, 1990.

Yeats, W. B. *Autobiographies*. Macmillan, 1955.
> *Memoirs*, ed. Denis Donoghue. Macmillan, 1972.
> *Yeats's Poems*, ed. A. Norman Jeffares. Macmillan, 1989.

Young, Ella. *Flowering Dusk*. Longmans, Green, 1945.

Primary sources
MacBride Family papers, Stuart Family papers, Crime Branch Special papers (CBS), State Paper Office, Dublin, New York Public Library (Berg Collection), Public Record Office, London (WO 76/10–13 002894), NLI (*Visions Notebooks* N6895 P8886), Ethel Mannin (MS 17,875), O'Leary (MS 8001).

Newspapers and periodicals
Bean na hÉireann, Burke's Landed Gentry, Burke's Irish Landed Gentry, Dictionary of National Biography, Father Mathew Record, Hibernia, Review of Reviews, vols 5 & 6, *Shan Van Vocht, Sinn Fein, Connaught Tribune, Daily Nation, Freeman's Journal, Irish Independent, Irish Times, The Nation, The Western People, Thom's Directory, United Ireland, United Irishman.*

Index

Index